Marketing Management for Nonprofit Organizations

Marketing Management for Nonprofit Organizations

THIRD EDITION

Adrian Sargeant

OXFORD
UNIVERSITY PRESS

OXFORD

UNIVERSITY PRESS

Great Clarendon Street, Oxford OX2 6DP

Oxford University Press is a department of the University of Oxford.
It furthers the University's objective of excellence in research, scholarship,
and education by publishing worldwide in

Oxford New York

Auckland Cape Town Dar es Salaam Hong Kong Karachi
Kuala Lumpur Madrid Melbourne Mexico City Nairobi
New Delhi Shanghai Taipei Toronto

With offices in

Argentina Austria Brazil Chile Czech Republic France Greece
Guatemala Hungary Italy Japan Poland Portugal Singapore
South Korea Switzerland Thailand Turkey Ukraine Vietnam

Oxford is a registered trade mark of Oxford University Press
in the UK and in certain other countries

Published in the United States
by Oxford University Press Inc., New York

British Library Cataloguing in Publication Data
Data available

Library of Congress Cataloging in Publication Data
Data available

Typeset by Macmillan Publishing Solutions
Printed and bound in the United Kingdom
by CPI Antony Rowe,
Chippenham, Wiltshire

ISBN 978-0-19-923615-2

1 3 5 7 9 10 8 6 4 2

To my father Brian Francis Sargeant and my mother Gwendoline Doreen Sargeant. Your support, generosity and encouragement made this book possible.

■ PREFACE

Nonprofit marketing has finally come of age. Rising from its status as a relatively obscure variant in the early 1970s, it is now widely accepted that marketing has much to offer a variety of different categories of organization. This is a considerable feat of recognition for it was only a few years ago that one would have been severely chastised in many nonprofit circles for even daring to mention the 'M' word in public.

Perhaps part of the reason for marketing's increasing acceptance in the sector is due to the broadening and softening of its definition. Marketing is no longer defined as the provision of required goods and services at a profit. The focus has switched to the satisfaction of consumer wants and, more generally, to sensitively serving the needs of a particular society. Thus marketing has begun to lose something of its association with the relentless pursuit of profit and has evolved into a philosophical approach to the management of an organization that has just as much relevance for 'profit' and 'nonprofit' alike.

In recognition of this somewhat wider definition of marketing there are now a variety of texts on the market which address its specific application to one or more nonprofit subsectors. Broadly speaking, this literature can be divided into two categories—highly theoretical texts written for an academic audience and 'how to do it' books written by practitioners for the benefit of their peers. Both categories of approach have a valuable role to play, but the development of this dichotomy is perhaps unfortunate as both categories of author/audience could have much to offer one another. The approach taken in this text is therefore to combine the experience of practitioners working in each nonprofit subsector with the available academic research. As the reader will later appreciate, the amount of research in some areas of nonprofit marketing is often sadly lacking, but where it is available, it can prove a valuable aid to shaping the approach a particular organization might take to its market.

The text has been written primarily for use by undergraduate and postgraduate students, taking nonprofit marketing as an optional part of their studies. It has thus been structured to reflect the usual content of such course modules—namely, an introduction to marketing, the development of a marketing plan, and the complexities of marketing in a number of specific nonprofit contexts. It will, however, also be of interest to practitioners seeking to learn from the activities of marketers/researchers working in other parts of the nonprofit sector. A broad range of issues will be addressed and sufficient marketing concepts and frameworks introduced to allow the reader to approach the development of a marketing plan for their own organization with confidence.

The general approach adopted in this text has thus been to divide the subject into three sections. In the first of these sections the scale and scope of the nonprofit sector will be explored. We will endeavour to disentangle the complex web of terminology that is used to describe the sector and shed light on the mnemonics used to refer to different categories of organization. The ICNPO (International Classification of Nonprofit Organizations) will be introduced as a means of conceptualizing the great diversity of organizations that can be considered as nonprofit in nature. Clearly the exact categories of organizations that will be nonprofit in a given society will vary, depending on the historical development of that society, its relative degree of economic sophistication, the relative degree of state involvement, and the existence of appropriate infrastructure supports. Nevertheless the ICNPO constitutes an effective framework through which to analyse the work of nonprofits. In the first section of this text, therefore, marketing's relevance to a variety of these categories of nonprofit will be established and a number of the typically expressed reservations towards the concept explored.

While we are on the topic of reservations, I was criticized in the first edition of this text for using the word 'nonprofit' to define the audience and focus for my work. Many prefer the term 'not-for-profit' or 'not-for-gain', while others prefer to use a range of terminology defining different sectors by what they are, rather than by what they are not. My own perspective on this is that it would be desperately irritating to have to use a combination of different words to describe what is admittedly a very diverse sector. Clarification after clarification is not easy on the eye and from a pragmatic perspective in a global text such as this, it is undoubtedly easier to focus on one word, acknowledge its limitations, and move on. Of the available choices I admit a preference for 'nonprofit' because while this does define organizations by a negative I believe it can be a badge of considerable pride. Here we need not be slaves to the market. Nor do we need to ride roughshod over the needs of our fellow human beings in the pursuit of personal gain. Rather we are concerned with the general betterment of society and of facilitating groups of individuals of all races and creeds coming together to make that a reality. What is genuinely distinctive about this activity is that no one is concerned for their own financial betterment. It is the welfare of others, or the welfare of society that is at issue. Nonprofit therefore works well for me!

In the second section of the text, the implementation of marketing will be discussed at both philosophical and functional levels. With regard to the former, Chapter 2 will examine how a nonprofit might attain a market orientation, the benefits that this might bring, and the specific actions that might be required to bring this about. Chapters 3–7 will then move on to consider the subject of marketing planning and guide the reader through the necessary steps that will facilitate the development of a marketing plan for a given organization. Thus, the intention of this section of the text is to facilitate a discussion of how marketing should typically be managed in a nonprofit context. The reader will be introduced to a series of concepts and frameworks that have a general relevance to all nonprofit organizations.

In the third and final section of the text marketing's specific application to social ideas, fundraising, arts organizations, educational institutions, healthcare organizations, volunteer management, and the public sector will be explored. This third edition also contains a chapter on the application of marketing to the domain of social entrepreneurship. These have all been designed to build on the general framework for marketing planning provided earlier. The reader will be appraised of the key influences on the marketing function in each case and a number of the specific nuances of marketing in each particular nonprofit sub-sector. Whilst this section has been designed for the reader to 'dip in and out of', a number of the issues discussed in each chapter have relevance for all nonprofit organizations. These 'application' chapters have been carefully structured so as to minimize any overlap of coverage and the reader will hence find that each chapter deals with a different mix of nonprofit marketing issues such as direct/database marketing, the achievement of a marketing orientation, the management of service quality, and the development of a marketing communications campaign.

Of course the latter section of this text could be criticized on the grounds of scope. Whilst it is now almost universally accepted that fundraising, arts, and social marketing can now be legitimately regarded as nonprofit marketing activity, a number of readers may question the inclusion of chapters relating to healthcare, education, and the public sector. These latter chapters have been included because such activities are most definitely nonprofit in nature in a number of different countries. Even in the USA, where much healthcare marketing is for-profit in nature, for example, there remain a number of nonprofit hospitals that could stand to benefit from marketing at both conceptual and practical levels. Moreover in the UK, where perhaps a more hybrid system of healthcare is beginning to develop, the marketing of healthcare will benefit more from the concepts and frameworks introduced in this text than it would from a standard for-profit approach. This is simply because the healthcare environment exhibits many of the same characteristics as other categories of nonprofit—that is, there is a distinction between the markets for resource attraction and resource allocation, there is a need to achieve a balance between the satisfaction of individual customer requirements and the longer-term satisfaction of society as a whole—and there are also a greater number of different publics that each institution must address, even if no exchange (in the economic sense of the term) actually takes place between them and the institution concerned. Such complexities are characteristic of the majority of nonprofit marketing and the content of this text will hence be of particular relevance.

In this third edition the coverage of third-sector issues has been greatly expanded and the case studies accompanying each chapter rewritten or updated. In addition a website providing links to relevant sources of information, case studies, and advice has now been developed. The site also contains additional case studies, reading lists, and self-test questions. It is my intention to add to this resource over time to increase the value added by this book.

I hope it meets your needs.

Adrian Sargeant

■ ACKNOWLEDGEMENTS

The author gratefully acknowledges the assistance of Nathan Hand, Elaine Jay, Jen Shang, and Angie Stapleton in compiling the materials for this third edition. Thank you all, the new edition wouldn't have happened without you.

I am also very grateful to the many nonprofit organizations who took the time to supply materials for this text and the many individuals who agreed to be interviewed for the new Online Resource Centre or to write case studies and practitioner insights. Your experiences offer readers guidance on the practical applications of this text and will greatly assist students of the emerging discipline we now call nonprofit marketing.

Every effort has been made to trace and contact copyright holders but this has not been possible in every case. If notified, the publisher will undertake to rectify any errors or omissions at the earliest opportunity.

■ CONTENTS

PART ONE Introduction to Marketing

PART TWO Marketing Planning

PART THREE **Specific Applications**

LIST OF FIGURES

■ LIST OF TABLES

LIST OF TABLES

Introduction to Marketing

1 Scope, Challenges and Development of the Nonprofit Sector

OBJECTIVES

By the end of this chapter you should be able to:

1. distinguish between the public, private, and voluntary sectors;
2. define and describe the extent of the nonprofit sector;
3. understand the development of the nonprofit sector in both the UK and USA;
4. understand the contribution of the nonprofit and voluntary sectors to society;
5. describe a range of the current issues facing nonprofit and voluntary sector managers.

Introduction

A recent search on the Internet bookseller Amazon returned 29,149 textbooks on marketing. A further search on nonprofit marketing returned rather fewer examples—a mere 128, many of which appear to be out of print or available only through special order. In the 30 years since Kotler and Levy (1969) first mooted the possibility that the tools and techniques of marketing might have something to offer nonprofit organizations one might have expected interest in the topic to grow—yet relatively few scholars and practitioners have as yet given the subject serious consideration. While a number of universities now offer courses on non-profit marketing and two scholarly journals have emerged on the topic (*Journal of Nonprofit and Public Sector Marketing, International Journal of Nonprofit and Voluntary Sector Marketing*), our knowledge of this field remains very much in its infancy.

Of course one could argue that marketing need or societal issues requires identical skills and thought processes to the marketing of cars, perfume and other consumer products. The requirement to consider nonprofit marketing as a distinct discipline in its own right is thereby greatly diminished. But is it? Is it really possible to adopt commercial marketing practice to making a potential donor aware of a starving baby or encouraging a committed smoker to quit? Can one really promote brotherhood like soap?

In this text it will be argued that the answer to this question is no. Although many of the tools and techniques commonly used in commercial marketing practice are indeed equally applicable to the nonprofit realm, the ethos that drives their application can be radically different. Indeed the underlying marketing philosophy that should guide an organization's approach to its markets must be conceptualized and applied rather differently in relation to nonprofits—a theme we shall return to in detail in Chapter 2.

We are also at the point where we are able to adapt existing theory or develop our own about how nonprofit markets operate and the manner in which nonprofit resources should best be marshalled to deliver the maximum possible value to the various stakeholder and interest groups they serve. Many crass decisions have been taken by managers seeking to blindly apply marketing tools and concepts developed in a very different environment directly to the nonprofit sector. As we shall see in later chapters considerable adaptation may often be required.

In structuring this text I have sought to provide three distinct components. The first of these is concerned with introductions—an introduction to the nonprofit sector and an introduction to both the tools of marketing and to marketing philosophy itself. The second stage of the text addresses the marketing planning process and illustrates how marketing planning has equal relevance to the nonprofit context. A range of existing theoretical models will be adapted and extended and a variety of new theories introduced.

The final section of the text is designed to deal with sector-specific issues. As we shall shortly see, the nonprofit sector comprises a broad range of diverse organizations. The approach to arts marketing is different from the approach to healthcare marketing, which in turn is very different from fundraising. We will explore issues specific to each of these contexts and, in addition, education marketing, public sector marketing, social marketing, social entrepreneurship, and volunteer recruitment and retention.

We begin, however, with a discussion of what we mean by the term 'nonprofit', deal with definitional issues, and trace the development of the nonprofit sector in both the USA and the UK. We will conclude the chapter with an exploration of the key issues presently faced by the sector in both countries.

Defining the Nonprofit Sector

Given that it is our intention to examine the application of marketing to the nonprofit or not-for-profit (NFP) sector, it is important to begin by defining what we mean by this term. Over the years many authors have developed widely differing terminology for what is ostensibly the same cohort of organizations. Labels such as the third sector, independent sector, not-for-profit sector, nonprofit sector, charitable sector and voluntary sector are used with varying frequency in different countries. Unfortunately they are all too often used interchangeably and with rather different emphasis of meaning, making it impossible to be sure with any degree of certainty that any two writers are addressing the same facet of society. Salamon and Anheier (1997: 3) argue that this complexity develops because of the great range of organizations that are included in these umbrella headings 'ranging from tiny soup kitchens to symphony orchestras, from garden clubs to environmental groups'. Unfortunately the range of organizations embraced by each term also tends to vary, country by country.

Our first task in this text must therefore be to begin to navigate a way through this complexity. The logical starting place is the term 'third sector' which is now in common usage on both sides of the Atlantic and reflects the distinctive role the sector has in society. The notion of a third sector is illustrated in Figure 1.1. The third sector is distinguished by being somehow different from either government or the private sector. All three sectors are important facets of human society and all three have a role to play in the satisfaction of human need.

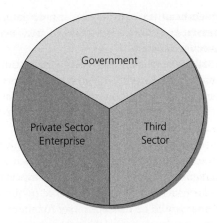

Figure 1.1 The role of nonprofits in society

The private sector or 'market' caters for the majority of human need, certainly in the developed world, matching the supply of producers with consumer demand for goods and services. This market ensures that people can obtain much of what they want and need from others at a reasonable price—or at least those with money are facilitated in doing so! Economists argue that the market works since suppliers are prevented from charging excessive prices by the knowledge that others will enter the market to cater for the need if they do so. Similarly the market ensures that a multitude of different needs are met, by ensuring that a reasonable profit will be available to suppliers in each case. There is no philanthropy at work here! The market works purely on the notion of self-interest. As Adam Smith (1776: 119) noted: 'It is not from the benevolence of the butcher, the brewer, or the baker that we expect our dinner, but from their regard to their own self-interest. We address ourselves, not to their humanity but to their self-love, and never talk to them of our own necessities but of their own advantages.'

There are instances, however, where this market mechanism fails and where governments may be compelled to intervene to ensure that certain minimum standards of consumption are met for all individuals in a given society. During and immediately after the Second World War many governments had to introduce food rationing to ensure that those on low incomes were not priced out of the market and starved as a consequence. Equally, the National Health Service established in the UK in the immediate post-war period had as its goal the provision of healthcare to all, irrespective of the ability to pay. The term 'public sector' is typically used to refer collectively to those institutions a society considers necessary for the basic well-being of its members. Adam Smith (1776: 122) defined the public sector as:

. . . those public institutions and those public works, which though they may be in the highest degree advantageous to a great society, are, however, of such a nature that the profit could never repay the expense to any individual, or small number of individuals; and which it, therefore, cannot be expected that any individual, or small number of individuals, should erect or maintain.

Such institutions are both founded and funded by the State, both with its own interests in mind (to prevent civil unrest and to facilitate re-election) and those of its citizens. The funds to provide these institutions and works are derived from taxation (either local or national) and the funding each will receive is a function of allocation, rather than the level of use per se. Thus in state-provided healthcare, it may be appropriate to allocate considerable funding to highly experimental and innovative forms of treatment that if successful will benefit only a very small number of people.

In the public sector, the State takes legal responsibility for institutions and the work they undertake. Indeed, as Chapman and Cowdell (1998: 2) note, 'it is one of the characteristics of public sector organizations that they are bounded by and operate within extensive legislation which creates an often creaking bureaucracy, much of which is concerned with the "proper" use of public monies.'

This notion of 'proper' use warrants elaboration. In a democracy, what may be deemed proper use will be subject to change. As various parties stand for election, they map out in their manifestos the role that government should play in all aspects of social life, but in particular in balancing the needs of society for the provision of public services, against the burden of the additional taxes that would be needed to pay for them. Whilst it would be ideal for government to meet every basic human need it is probably unrealistic to expect that wage earners in a given society would be willing to fund such comprehensive social provision through taxation and in practice a balance is therefore created with only the most widespread, popular, and/or fundamental needs being met in this way. Other facets of need are simply neglected.

It is within this neglected space, where neither government nor private sector enterprise is willing to engage, that the so-called third sector has a critical role to play. The third sector is distinctive since it comprises individuals or groups of individuals coming together to take 'voluntary' action. In other words the sector comprises people electing to help other people to resolve issues or concerns.

The essence of voluntary action is that it is not directed or controlled by the State and that in the main it is financed by private, in contradistinction to public, funds. It embodies the sense of responsibility of private persons towards the welfare of their fellows; it is the meeting by private enterprise of a public need. (Nathan 1952: 12)

It is the notion that the sector is not controlled by the State or by business that leads to the description of the sector in the USA as the 'independent sector'. Whilst organizations in this sector may indeed be free of direct control, the difficulty with this terminology is that in financial terms they can often be far from independent, drawing financial support from a plethora of government departments and/or private businesses. This has been a particular issue in the past 30 years as government has sought to withdraw progressively from many facets of social life leaving the third sector to shoulder the burden (albeit with support from often large government grants). This has particularly been the case in the USA. As Tempel and Mortimer (2001: vii) note:

Philanthropy and the nonprofit sector occupy a position in the American institutional landscape unlike that in any other developed country. Undertaking functions typically assigned to government in other countries and also accorded unparalleled tax advantages for so doing, these American institutions are thought to be central to furthering democracy and the search for social justice.

The fact that the sector occupies this third space means that the activities it undertakes can be quite unique. Third-sector or 'voluntary-sector' organizations often deal with local issues, politically unpopular issues, or with facets of life that attract little interest from politicians, all too often because few votes hang on the issue. Nevertheless these can be critical issues for a society to address and the need is none the less pressing simply because the state or private sector enterprise fails to take an interest.

The characteristic of voluntarism can give rise to what Lord Dahrendorf refers to as the 'creative chaos' of the voluntary sector. Most voluntary organizations are small and involve only a handful of people in trying to solve a particular problem. The individuals involved frequently believe passionately in the work they are undertaking and can apply the kind of constructive energy that can lead to highly innovative and creative solutions to social problems. It is important to realize, however, that the chaos that Dahrendorf refers to can also be a negative since there is a danger that organizations can proliferate and there can be considerable duplication of effort as a number of organizations quite independently seek to tackle an identical issue. There are neither the market nor the political pressures to achieve the merger of similar interests that would exist in either of the other two sectors.

The term 'civil society' has been used interchangeably with that of the voluntary sector by many authors. This too has been taken to refer to the formal and informal associations, organizations, and networks that are separate from, albeit deeply interactive with, the state and business sector. Authors such as Putnam (1993) argue that these organizations produce 'social capital' which he defines as the norms of trust and cooperation that permit societies to function. The voluntary sector thus plays a critical role in deepening the levels of trust that exist between individuals in a society. This, the author believes, is essential if a given country's economy is to expand and develop. In the absence of trust, trade will flounder.

The World Bank (2001) has highlighted what it regards as the other defining characteristics of the voluntary sector, outlining a number of key strengths and weaknesses of voluntary organizations. These include the following.

Strengths

- *Strong grassroots links.* Voluntary organizations comprise groups of individuals directly involved with the social issues or problems.

- *Field-based development expertise.* Many international organizations possess real expertise, gained over many years in dealing with the problems of the developing world and are thus better placed than government to deliver aid and ultimately development.

- *The ability to innovate and adapt.* Voluntary organizations are frequently, because of their small size and/or grassroots links, able to adapt and innovate faster than commercial organizations or government.

- *Participatory methodologies and tools.* Many organizations are democratic and inclusive, being driven by a mission rather than the pursuit of profit or votes. As such they are well placed to seek the views of minorities whose voices may not otherwise be heard.

- *Long-term commitment and emphasis on sustainability.* Since voluntary bodies are established to deal with specific issues they tend to do so until such issues are actually eradicated. Freed from the pressure of generating ever-greater profit or votes they do not pick and choose the issues they will address on the basis of how fruitful they might be for the organization.

- *Cost-effectiveness.* Many voluntary bodies are staffed by professional managers and many employ large numbers of staff. The overwhelming majority of voluntary organizations are, however, very small and may rely in no small measure on the time and resources of the volunteers or founders that hold them together. From a government's perspective they can thus be a very cost-effective way of making a difference to a social issue. This aside, voluntary organizations can also be 'cost-effective' because the individuals comprising them have a genuine and detailed understanding of the issue and how resources can best be applied to effecting change.

Weaknesses

- *Limited financial and management expertise.* The voluntary nature of these organizations often encourages the involvement of those with a great knowledge of, or passion for, the particular issue they are designed to address. They may thus have great 'subject' expertise, but lack financial or management expertise. This must frequently be bought in and/or takes time to develop.

- *Limited institutional capacity.* The small size of voluntary bodies may limit their ability to cope if the issue or cause suddenly becomes more pressing. Whilst international development charities are continually planning for the worst to happen and have well developed plans to cope for most eventualities, they are the exception rather than the norm.

- *Low levels of self-sustainability.* Whilst those individuals who found voluntary bodies may lack little by way of enthusiasm for the work they will undertake, these individuals may frequently lack the resources they need to achieve the mission of the organization. Funding must frequently be sought from government, companies, and individual donors, and in the absence of this the organization will fail.

- *Small-scale interventions.* Frequently the small size of these organizations can be a further drawback. The impact that individual organizations might have on a cause can be minimal.

- *Lack of understanding of the broader social or economic context.* Finally, the individuals that comprise voluntary organizations, as we have noted above, can be highly focused on the cause or issue itself. They can thus fail to grasp the 'bigger picture' and fail to see the wider role that they may play in bettering society were they to amend their approach or actions in some way. Some writers have referred to this as the 'blinkered' vision of many voluntary-sector bodies.

Of course in this text we are concerned with what Figure 1.1 refers to as the nonprofit or not-for-profit sector, rather than the voluntary sector, per se. Combining the public and voluntary sectors in this way makes intuitive sense since neither are concerned with profit and many nonprofit marketing tools and frameworks are applied in an identical way in each. Here, however, the similarity stops. The public sector is a highly distinctive and complex entity in its own right and the history of its development warrants separate elaboration. For this reason, although we use the generic term 'nonprofit' throughout, we shall focus on public-sector marketing issues, in particular, in a later and separate chapter.

In the meantime it is appropriate to settle on terminology that can comfortably embrace both voluntary-sector and public-sector organizations. The term 'nonprofit organization' will be used for this purpose, which we define as:

one that exists to provide for the general betterment of society, through the marshalling of appropriate resources and/or the provision of physical goods and services. Such organizations do not exist to provide for personal profit or gain and do not, as a result, distribute profits or surpluses to shareholders or members. They may, however, employ staff and engage in revenue-generating activities designed to assist them in fulfilling their mission.

This definition correlates strongly with the use of the term in the USA and comfortably embraces all the specific contexts of nonprofit marketing that will be considered in this text. It is important to recognize though that even this terminology is far from ideal. It still focuses attention on what the sector is not, rather then expressing anything positive about the distinctiveness of these organizations. As Young (1983) famously asks, 'if not for profit—for what?'

The Development of the UK Voluntary Sector

All of the great cultures of the world have proud traditions of individuals coming together to help others in their community. This is often enshrined in the doctrine of a particular religion, but it can arise purely as a consequence of historical tradition. The voluntary sector has also been shaped in no small measure by government, with particular pockets of activity being encouraged by the often-arbitrary award of 'tax exempt' or 'charitable status'. Over the years this has come to be defined somewhat differently from one country to another. In many countries, such as the UK, a charity is a distinctive legal form of organization that has a series of tax advantages enshrined in law. A charity is thus a particular type of voluntary organization.

One of the oldest charities in England is Weeks' charity, an organization originally set up in the fifteenth century to provide faggots (bundles of sticks) for burning heretics, an activity supported by the government of the day. The State has therefore long had a vested interest in controlling what should, or should not be considered charitable in nature. In Tudor times, those seeking to raise funds for the poor were well advised to stay within the law or risk fines, flogging, or worse. Even the donors themselves had to be mindful of this legislation, at one stage risking the punishment of having their ears forcibly pierced for giving to the unworthy.

Barbaric though this might sound, Tudor England was much concerned with public order and vagrancy, two concepts which governments of this time saw as inextricably linked. It was thus felt that giving should be strictly controlled to encourage the channelling of alms only to those who were referred to as the impotent poor (i.e. those prevented by their age, health, or other circumstances from earning their own living). The able-bodied poor were to be encouraged to take responsibility for the amelioration of their own condition. In short they should be compelled to find work or starve. Such a preoccupation would, it was felt, preclude the possibility of their finding time to pose a threat to the State. As a consequence all legitimate beggars were licensed and private persons were forbidden to give to anyone not in possession of such a document.

Aside from giving of this very individual and personal nature, there were many great 'general' causes that the public could support at this time. Indeed, many of these are very similar to those we are encouraged to support today. In probably the earliest reference to 'appropriate' charitable causes, William Langland's fourteenth-century work, the *Vision of Piers Plowman*, exalts rich and troubled merchants to gain full remission of their sins and thus a happy death by the fruitful use of their fortunes:

And therewith repair hospitals,

help sick people,

mend bad roads,

build up bridges that had been broken down,

help maidens to marry or to make them nuns,

find food for prisoners and poor people,

put scholars to school or to some other craft,

help religious orders and

ameliorate rents or taxes.

It was not until 1601, however, that English law officially recognized those causes that might be considered as charitable for the first time. The preamble to the Elizabethan Charitable

Uses Act of that year appears to have much in common with the fourteenth-century work alluded to above, delineating as it did the legitimate objects of charity:

Some for the Relief of aged, impotent and poore people, some for Maintenance of sicke and maymed Souldiers and Marriners, Schooles of Learninge, Free Schooles and Schollers in Universities, some for Repair or Bridges, Ports, Havens, Causewaies, Churches, Seabanks and Highwaies, some for Educacion and prefermente of Orphans, some for or towards Reliefe Stocke or Maintenance of Howses of Correccion, some for Mariages of poore Maides, some for Supportacion, Ayde and Help of younge tradesmen, Handicraftesmen and persons decayed, and others for releife or redemption of Prisoners or Captives, and for the aide or ease of any poore inhabitanta conceringe paymente of Fifteens, setting out of Souldiers and other Taxes.

The Act was significant, not only because it outlined these objects, but also because it acknowledged that trustees and officials of charitable institutions sometimes misused the assets under their care and hence created a means by which they would be made accountable to the public. The law empowered the Lord Chancellor to appoint Charity Commissioners whose responsibility it was to investigate abuses of these charitable uses and to thereby protect the interests of those that had chosen to endow charitable organizations. It perhaps bears testimony to the quality of work undertaken by these early charity legislators that this Elizabethan Act was only recently repealed.

Of course the law has been modified somewhat in the intervening centuries, most notably by a case in the late nineteenth century: the Income Tax Special Purposes Commission v Pemsel (1891) which clarified that charity in its legal sense should be viewed as comprising four principal divisions: trusts for the relief of poverty; trusts for the advancement of education; trusts for the advancement of religion; and trusts for other purposes beneficial to the community, not falling under any of the preceding heads.

Of course charities only comprise a very small proportion of voluntary-sector organizations—certainly today. In the UK alone there are estimated to be well over 500,000 voluntary organizations in existence of which only a small percentage are registered charities. The history of such voluntary organizations is a relatively recent one. Prior to the seventeenth century voluntary activity had largely been confined to charitable trusts and endowments and thus expressed the interests of particular individuals. As the very first joint stock companies emerged in the commercial sector, so too did collaborative philanthropy where groups of individuals got together to achieve social change. One of the most noteworthy developments here was the school movement with over 1400 voluntary schools being formed by 1729 catering for over 22,000 pupils (Davis-Smith 1995). Other great causes addressed in the eighteenth century included child welfare, moral reform, and discipline reflecting the need to boost the labouring population whilst minimizing the likelihood of civil unrest. Not all the voluntary organizations formed at this time were philanthropic. Debating societies like the Kit Kat Club and the Athenaeum were also created as were early equivalents of our modern Neighbourhood Watch schemes.

The real growth in the number and influence of voluntary-sector bodies took place in the nineteenth century. Between 1837 and 1880 there were 9154 new charities known to the Charity Commissioners and between 1880 and 1900 the number rose sharply to 22,607 (Williams 1989). This growth occurred as a consequence of the explosion of human need brought about by the population growth of the time and rapid industrialization and urbanization. Philanthropic organizations in this period were often formed by the middle classes and were frequently involved in campaigning to challenge the social injustices of the day. A few of these have survived to the present, evolving into modern-day charities. Dr Barnardo, for example, first began to establish orphanages and other services for children at this time. Causes such as the provision of social care, public health, and education all began to gain momentum as did some which we might mistakenly view as modern concerns, such as charities to support the arts and culture. Environmental causes were also championed, but at this time such organizations concerned themselves with issues such as preserving the common land and open spaces (Nathan 1952).

Working people also developed mutual groups for self-help and formed pressure groups to campaign on issues as diverse as factory legislation, sanitary improvements, slavery, and the observation of the Sabbath. Many friendly societies, trade unions, consumer co-operatives, and housing societies all originated in this period, epitomizing the notion of self-help that was later identified by the Royal Commission of 1871–4 as 'the spirit . . . by which that portion of the population which is most within the risk of pauperism endeavours to escape from it' (Beveridge 1948: 85–6).

In many ways, however, the social role of the voluntary sector was unchanged from that of the fourteenth century. The relationship between the State and the voluntary sector remained one of 'parallel' provision (Kendall and Knapp 1995). Just as their Tudor predecessors had done centuries before, the drafters of the Poor Laws of 1834 drew a firm distinction between the deserving and the undeserving poor. The State saw poverty among the able bodied as a moral failing and therefore intervened to control it, through the deterrent of the workhouse. By contrast philanthropic activity was deliberately directed at the deserving poor; the elderly or infirm and other individuals who through no fault of their own were unable to support themselves. Indeed, the nineteenth century saw the formation of the Society for Organising Charity and Repressing Mendicity (begging). This body was originally conceived as the umbrella organization for the philanthropic component of the nonprofit sector and it was ultimately to morph into our modern Local and National Councils for Voluntary Service.

Although the nineteenth century undoubtedly saw many great philanthropic achievements, historians now view most of the middle-class charity of the period as paternalistic, moralistic, and self-serving. As Kendall and Knapp (1995: 30) note: 'charity was an obligation on behalf of the better off, but it carried no rights of entitlement for the poor. As such it was part of the status quo and an instrument of oppression and injustice, irrespective of its moral underpinnings and good intentions.'

The early and mid twentieth century was marked by increasing collaboration between the voluntary sector and the State as society struggled to cope with the challenges created by two World Wars and the intervening Great Depression. With the founding of the Welfare State in the 1940s, the role of the sector was to change radically as the State began to enter and control facets of social provision like education, health, and social welfare. The traditional parallel approach to service delivery was no longer necessary, freeing the sector to switch to an approach based on 'extension', where it could supplement and complement the services provided by the State. It was also afforded a greater opportunity to develop its advocacy role and thus to act as a spokesperson for disadvantaged and marginalized groups.

As the broadened boundaries of the State became apparent, so too did its limitations. The latter half of the twentieth century was marred by problems of urban decay, child poverty, racial tension, and homelessness. The State was seemingly powerless to tackle these problems and was viewed by many as inefficient and unresponsive. Voluntary-sector bodies were therefore brought into partnership with the State, to work alongside government, often in a contractual relationship, to tackle these and other issues (Lewis 1993). The view of the voluntary sector as a partner has held sway with successive governments since Thatcher and led to greater regulatory control over the nonprofit agencies now responsible for the implementation of government policy. While some have welcomed the rise of a contract culture and improvements to the managerial professionalism of the sector, others have warned of the dangers of the sector losing its distinctiveness and traditional independence from government (Harris 1998). These are issues we shall return to later in this chapter.

The Nonprofit Sector in the United States

In the United States, the Elizabethan Charitable Uses Act was highly influential in shaping the development of the voluntary sector although the term 'charity' is not applied in the same way and does not define a distinct legal entity. In the USA the term has come to mean simply serving the poor and needy (Gurin and Van Til 1990). Historically the revolution of 1777 led to the creation of many nonprofits as the public was 'swept up in waves of civic enthusiasm and religious fervor' (Hammack 1998: 116) with many churches, clinics, schools, orphanages, libraries, colleges, and hospitals being built as a consequence. Indeed, the founding fathers had been careful in drafting the US constitution to make it difficult for their governments to levy taxes, take vigorous action, or grant wealth and power to a privileged few. In the absence of strong taxation, religion, education, healthcare, and social services had to be funded by alternative means. State legislators responded by making it easier to create nonprofit organizations and began shaping them to the needs of society in a variety of ways, notably excluding a number of them from property tax, which at the time was the most significant source of government revenue. States also granted 'appropriate' nonprofits land and began regulating their ability to create endowments.

It is important to note that this tradition of private philanthropy has continued and become what Marts (1966) regards as one of the most durable factors of American life. When Alexis de Tocqueville wrote in 1835 of his travels in America he was impressed by the willingness of the people to give freely of their own funds for social improvements (Probst 1962). He observed that when a community of citizens recognized a need for a church, school, or hospital, that they came together to form a committee, appoint leaders, and donate funds to support it.

Americans of all ages, all stations of life, and all types of dispositions are forever forming associations . . . In every case, at the head of any new undertaking, where in France you would find the government or in England some territorial magnate, in the United States you are sure to find an association (de Tocqueville 1969: 513).

Today the Internal Revenue Code permits 20 categories of organization to be exempt from federal income tax and the majority of those that are able to receive tax deductible contributions also fall into one specific category of the code: Section 501(c)(3). To qualify for this additional benefit organizations must fulfil three tests.

• They must operate to fulfil one of the following broad purposes: educational, religious, charitable, scientific, literary, testing for public safety, fostering certain national and international amateur sports competitions, or prevention of cruelty to children and animals.

• No substantial part of an organization's activity should be focused on attempts to influence government, either directly or indirectly through participation in political campaigns. A maximum of 20% of their annual expenditure can be applied to mission-related lobbying activity and they are barred from preparing or distributing campaign literature on behalf of political parties.

• These nonprofits must also demonstrate procedures to prohibit assets or income from being distributed to workers, managers, or the equivalent, except as fair compensation for service rendered. Organizations cannot be used for the personal benefit of founders, board members, staff, or associates.

It is interesting to note that religious groups are automatically granted exemption from taxation under this section of the tax code and are also exempt from the reporting requirements imposed on all other 501(c)(3)s. The reason for this liberal treatment can be traced back to the American constitution which specifically separated the Church and State. There are therefore severe limitations on government in regulating religious organizations even for the purposes of granting and supervising their tax exempt status. In recent times this has created something of an anomaly since US citizens are far more religiously active than the populations of other developed nations (Wuthnow 2002) and faith-based groups have recently moved much closer to the political agenda.

In 1998 there were a staggering 1.6 million nonprofit organizations in the United States or one nonprofit for very 150 Americans! The diversity of these organizations is shown in Figure 1.2.

It is important to recognize that the distinction drawn in the figure is very broad and one of 'tendency' (Anheier 2006), but it does illustrate the division in US law between public-serving organizations who receive more beneficial tax treatment (many hold 501(c)(3) status) and member-serving organizations. To European eyes it may appear odd that churches are considered public serving and political organizations are not, but this is a function of the complex history of the sector we referred to earlier. These faith-based organizations are a highly significant part of the sector and, if anything, their number is understated in the Figure. The data employed by Lester Salamon included only congregations recognized by their religious body. Informal groups and those formed by non-Christian faiths such as Islam, Hinduism, and Buddhism are therefore likely to be underestimated.

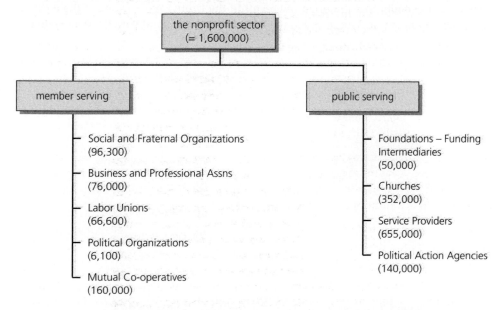

Figure 1.2 The nonprofit sector in the United States

Source: Salamon (1999: 22) © The Foundation Center. Used by permission of the Foundation Center, 79 Fifth Ave, New York, NY 10003, www.fdncenter.org

In terms of the economic significance of the US nonprofit sector, it accounts for 7.1% of employment (Weitzman et al. 2002), the majority of which (circa 75%) is in the service of the public benefit. Employment in the membership-based part of the sector accounts for a further 10% and employment in faith-based organizations only around 1%.

The sector primarily draws its income from a combination of three broad sources:

- private fees and charges—fees charged for services provided, membership dues, proceeds from sales, investment income;
- private giving—foundation grants, business or corporate donations, and individual giving;
- public-sector payments—grants, contracts, and transfers from government agencies and third-party payments.

While many people assume that private giving is the dominant source of income, it is actually the least important source, accounting for only around 12% of total revenue. A detailed breakdown is provided in Figure 1.3.

That said, Americans are very generous. In 2004, charitable giving reached a record $248.52 billion (Giving USA Foundation 2006). Although this total includes some giving in response to the 26 December tsunami in the Indian Ocean, these donations are actually a very small portion of the overall total, less than one-half of 1%. The annual Giving USA study reports giving from four key sources of contributions: individual (living) donors; bequests by deceased individuals; foundations; and corporations. All four sources of giving were estimated to have increased their contributions in 2004 by between 4 and 9%. Individual giving, the single largest source, rose by an estimated 4.1% in 2004 to reach $187.92 billion.

American giving has historically been targeted at organizations serving their community, but it is interesting to note that the sectors experiencing the most growth in giving in 2004 were environmental and animal welfare organizations. Giving here increased by 7%. All categories of cause experienced some growth except international affairs and human services.

There is little doubt that the nonprofit sector in the United States is one of the most vibrant, well supported, and successful in the world. As Steinberg and Powell (2006: 1) note:

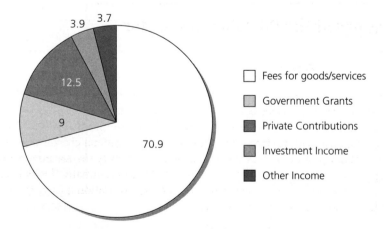

Figure 1.3 Sources of revenue for reporting public charities, 2004

Source: Urban Institute (2006) *The Nonprofit Sector in Brief: Facts and Figures from the Nonprofit Almanac,* The Urban Institute, Washington, DC.

Table 1.1 US civil society in comparative perspective

Factors encouraging civil society as associationalism in the United States	Factors discouraging civil society as associationalism elsewhere
Religious diversity with emphasis on local congregations rather than institutional hierarchy	Long history and legacy of dominant state religion with hierarchical institutional structures
Local elite do not rely on control of government for power; alternative spheres of influence exist	Weak local elites; few alternative power stratums
Concentrations of wealth and political power overlap but are neither identical nor dependent on each other	National political and economic elite networks overlap significantly
Ethnic, linguistic, and cultural heterogeneity as 'default value'	Ethnic, linguistic, and cultural homogeneity as 'default value'
Decentralized government, weak federal government with strong division of power at centre, and primacy of rule of law	Centralized government and state apparatus; limited capacity for local taxation and policymaking
Bridging capital, higher interpersonal trust	High bonding capital, lower interpersonal trust
'Diversity in unity' creates social innovation	Homogeneity and political control stifles innovation

Source: Anheier, H.K. (2006) *Nonprofit Organizations: Theory, Management, Policy,* London, Routledge. Reproduced with kind permission.

Nonprofit organizations are ubiquitous. Many people are born in a nonprofit hospital, attend a nonprofit university, send their children to a nonprofit day-care center, worship at a nonprofit religious institution, watch the performances of nonprofit symphonies and dance companies, visit their parents in a nonprofit nursing home and face the end of their life in a nonprofit hospice.

The reasons for the success of the sector in the USA are diffuse and a function of its unique history and character. Helmut Anheier, one of the leading scholars of nonprofit studies, has compared the factors encouraging civil society in the USA with the factors that have discouraged it elsewhere. Table 1.1 contains a summary of his analysis and indicates that a complex web of cultural, religious, and political factors, were and are at work.

Dimensions of the UK Voluntary Sector

Sector Facts and Figures

The UK too has a diverse and successful voluntary sector. Its scale is difficult to quantify exactly because of the definitional issues alluded to earlier. The National Council for Voluntary Organizations (NCVO), the body that now leads in the provision of sector data, has historically concentrated its efforts on trends among the 'general charities' (which excludes other forms of nonprofit as well as specific categories of charity such as housing associations and independent schools). This data therefore greatly underestimates the real value and significance of the sector. Nevertheless their data for 2005/6 (National Council For Voluntary Organizations 2008) shows that the sector:

- had an operating income of £31 billion;
- derived 38% of its income from statutory sources;
- had an operating expenditure of £29.1 billion;

- had net assets of £86.1 billion;
- had a paid workforce of at least 611,000;
- was concentrated in England. 78% of UK general charities were based in England.

The vast majority of the sector comprises very small organizations. Over half in 2005/6 had an annual income of less than £10,000. The very largest charities, however, have experienced considerable growth. The number with an income of over £1 million has more than doubled in a decade as a consequence of organic growth and the entry of new organizations holding significant assets from the outset.

NCVO's analysis illustrates that the sector's income is increasing each year, but that this appears to be due to the number of organizations entering the pool of general charities. For those already within the sector average income appears to have been broadly static since 2001/2. Only the very largest organizations reported significant growth, with the top 14 organizations (mainly household name charities) now accounting for 10% of the sector's income. The growth in their income can be attributed to greater success in raising funds from the public and from a growth in contract funding to provide services on behalf of the government.

Overall NCVO argues that the sector is coming ever more to resemble the private sector. A trend analysis shows that the sector is *earning* more of its income. In 2005/6, for the first time, NCVO recorded that more than half of general charities' income (50.3%) was earned. This compares with 43% in 2001/2 and 33% in 1994/5. Voluntary income has fallen in significance from 47% in 1994/5 to 41.6% in 2005/6. The balance (8%) is investment income, i.e. share dividends and interest on savings.

Turning to the sources of this income, the State now accounts for 34% of revenues and the majority of this is now awarded in the form of contracts (55%) rather than grants. This is a reflection of a long-term shift in government funding patterns away from the grants that dominated in the 1960s and 70s. A breakdown of sector sources of income is provided in Figure 1.4. The significance of government funding surprises many individuals new to the sector, as does the pitiful contribution made to our general charities by the private sector. Even though corporate social responsibility is increasingly practised by many business organizations, their relative contribution to sector income has actually fallen in recent years.

It is interesting to note that in 2008 the format of the Almanac produced by NCVO was changed to include for the first time a consideration of wider categories of organization that

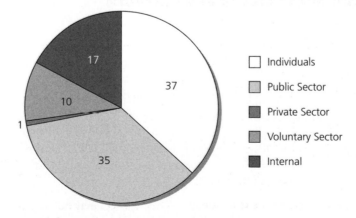

Figure 1.4 Sources of income for UK general charities, 2005/6

Source: Compiled by the author from data included in the Civil Society Almanac 2008 (NCVO 2008)

together comprise civil society. A focus on general charities is maintained to facilitate comparison with previous years, but for the first time we now have access to the performance of the broader sector.

Legal Structures

In the UK a nonprofit organization can adopt a variety of different legal forms. As we established earlier, the term 'charity' refers to a very specific subset of organizations which are granted exemption from income tax and to whom donations can be made tax effectively. In England, the Charities Act 2006 now defines a charity as a body or trust which exists for a charitable purpose, and exists for the public benefit. The notion of a test of public benefit is a new introduction to charity law and at the time of writing the Charity Commission is consulting to determine exactly how this will be defined and assessed. The Act also includes descriptions of the main purposes the law now considers charitable:

- the prevention or relief of poverty;
- the advancement of education;
- the advancement of religion;
- the advancement of health or the saving of lives;
- the advancement of citizenship or community development;
- the advancement of the arts, culture, heritage, or science;
- the advancement of amateur sport;
- the advancement of human rights, conflict resolution, or reconciliation or the promotion of religious or racial harmony or equality and diversity;
- the advancement of environmental protection or improvement;
- the relief of those in need by reason of youth, age, ill-health, disability, financial hardship, or other disadvantage;
- the advancement of animal welfare;
- the promotion of the efficiency of the armed forces of the Crown; or the efficiency of the police, fire and rescue services, or ambulance services; and
- any other purposes charitable in law.

This last provision might sound a little odd. To understand the reason for this 'bucket' clause, it is necessary to understand that the Act represents the first major attempt to overhaul charity law in over a century. It was therefore decided to include a provision that would ensure that everything that was presently charitable would still be included (Charity Commission 2006).

In law those responsible for the stewardship of a charity are known as trustees. They serve on the governing body of a charity and may be known as trustees, directors, board members, governors, or committee members. The exact title a particular organization chooses to give them is irrelevant. The principles and main duties are the same in all cases. These are illustrated in Figure 1.5.

What surprises many people new to the sector is that trustees may not be paid for their role. The 2006 Act ensures that voluntary trusteeship remains at the heart of charity. However, the Act does allow the trustees to pay an individual trustee for providing an additional service to the charity if they believe it is in the best interest of the organization. An example of this could be a trustee who is a plumber providing plumbing services to the charity as long as the trustees

Overall:
(1) Trustees have and must accept ultimate responsibility for directing the affairs of a charity, and ensuring that it is solvent, well-run, and delivering the charitable outcomes for which it has been set up.

Compliance—Trustees must:
(2) ensure that the charity complies with charity law, and with the requirements of the Charity Commission as regulator; in particular ensure that the charity prepares reports on what it has achieved and annual returns and accounts as required by law.
(3) ensure that the charity does not breach any of the requirements or rules set out in its governing document and that it remains true to the charitable purpose and objects set out there.
(4) comply with the requirements of other legislation and other regulators (if any) which govern the activities of the charity.
(5) act with integrity, and avoid any personal conflicts of interest or misuse of charity funds or assets.

Duty of prudence—Trustees must:
(6) ensure that the charity is and will remain solvent.
(7) use charitable funds and assets reasonably, and only in furtherance of the charity's objects.
(8) avoid undertaking activities that might place the charity's endowment, funds, assets, or reputation at undue risk.
(9) take special care when investing the funds of the charity, or borrowing funds for the charity to use.

Duty of care—Trustees must:
(10) use reasonable care and skill in their work as Trustees, using their personal skills and experience as needed to ensure that the charity is well-run and efficient.
(11) consider getting external professional advice on all matters where there may be material risk to the charity, or where the Trustees may be in breach of their duties.

Figure 1.5 Duties of trustees

Source: Charity Commission (2006) *The Essential Trustee: What You Need To Know* (CC3), Charity Commission, London.
© Crown Copyright. Reproduced with kind permission.

agree that it's in the charity's best interest, for example, because the trustee is charging a better price or in some way delivering a better service than the trustees could get elsewhere.

There are two main types of charity—unincorporated and incorporated. The exact legal position of trustees is slightly different in each.

• *Unincorporated charities*. These may be 'trusts' or 'associations'. Their governing document will usually be a trust deed or a constitution. These organizations do not have a legal 'personality' so unlike individuals they are unable to hold property or enter into contracts. In an unincorporated charity, the property of the charity is usually held by the trustees or their nominees.

• *Incorporated charities*. Most of these are charitable companies registered with Companies House as well as the Charity Commission. Here, the company is a legal entity in its own right, and the trustees are the directors of the company. It can therefore hold property and enter into contracts in the same way as an individual might. It can even be convicted of certain types of crime. Nonprofits which require corporate status typically form a company limited by guarantee, a legal form that originated in the Companies Act of 1862. A guarantee company does not have a share capital, but it has members who are guarantors instead of shareholders. These guarantors give an undertaking to contribute a nominal amount towards the winding-up of the company in the event of a shortfall upon cessation of business. It cannot distribute its profits to its members, and is therefore eligible to apply for charitable status if necessary. Common uses of guarantee companies include clubs, membership organisations, sports associations, and registered charities.

The Charities Act 2006 has made provision for a third organizational form, the Charitable Incorporated Organisation (CIO). At present, charities that want a corporate structure currently have to register as both a charity and a company, which means they have to meet the dual regulatory burdens of both the Charity Commission and Companies House. A CIO will have the advantages of a corporate structure (e.g. reduced personal liability for trustees) without the burden of dual regulation. Following a period of consultation it is possible that the first CIOs will appear in 2008.

There are other types of special incorporated charities which are not regulated by Companies House. Charities may be incorporated by Royal Charter (e.g. Toc H and the Royal Opera House) or formed by Statute (e.g. the National Trust).

For the sake of completeness there are two other significant forms of nonprofit organization that should be considered, namely Friendly Societies and Industrial Provident Societies. Friendly Societies have been around for centuries and were originally created as self-help organizations. They consist of a group of people coming together to contribute to a mutual fund, so that if they should ever fall on hard times they can apply to that fund for support. In previous centuries, the meetings of these societies were often held as a social gathering and it was typically at these events that individual subscriptions would be paid. Prior to the Welfare State they were often the only way a working person had of receiving help in times of ill health or old age. In centuries past, having no income normally meant a life of begging or living in the poorhouse, so the historical role of the Friendly Societies should not be underestimated. In the 1940s, following the creation of the Welfare State, membership of these societies fell, but today as the state progressively withdraws from welfare provision it is possible that there may be some resurgence in their popularity. At the time of writing there are approximately 200 Friendly Societies in the UK including one of the oldest, the Foresters Friendly Society (see Figure 1.6). Friendly societies must register with the Register of Friendly Societies under the Friendly Societies Act 1974 along with Building Societies, working men's clubs, and some of the older forms of cooperative organizations.

The Ancient Order of Foresters began in 1834, but its origins lie in a much older society called the Royal Foresters formed in the eighteenth century. Early meetings in Leeds were largely social affairs until the membership took the decision that they had a duty to assist their fellow men who 'fell into need as they walked through the forests of life' (Fisk 2006). In the nineteenth century this need typically arose when a breadwinner fell ill and could no longer earn his wages. Times were hard and sickness or death could often lead to whole families becoming destitute. Foresters was set up to relieve this need and it was accomplished by members paying a few pennies a week into a common fund from which grants could then be made to the needy. It is interesting to note that although once based solely in Leeds, the organization rapidly acquired new branches and after 1834 could be found in cities as geographically dispersed as Bristol and Southampton. A branch could even be found in Cornwall.

Today the Foresters Friendly Society is still owned by its thousands of members and therefore pays no profits to shareholders. It now offers a range of financial policies including Income Protection, Life Cover, and Savings Plans and operates from over 250 branches around the country. Unlike other financial services providers their branches are not to be found on the high street. They consist of groups of members who choose to meet socially on a regular basis to provide friendship and support to one another and on occasion to fundraise for charities. Participation in such events is not mandated, but many people still enjoy the interaction with people from their local community and like to get involved in the various events organized in their area.

Figure 1.6 The Foresters Friendly Society

Source: The Foresters Friendly Society (http://www.forestersfriendlysociety.co.uk)

Industrial and Provident Societies (IPS) are hybrids of limited companies and friendly societies. They fall into one of two categories:

- Cooperatives—which trade for the mutual benefit of their members; and
- Societies for the benefit of the community. These trade to benefit society and are granted charitable status by HM Revenue & Customs (HMRC) rather than by the Charity Commission (in England and Wales). Housing bodies and some recreational and social clubs adopt this structure.

Both types of IPS have a share capital, but these are not equity shares in the sense that their value will rise or fall according to the activities of the organization. The shares typically serve as a sign of membership and act as an entitlement to vote. Any profits or losses made by the organization are shared by members or ploughed into community benefit.

Classifying Nonprofit Organizations

As will already be apparent the voluntary sector is characterized by its diversity. Whilst this is certainly a key strength it is also an active hindrance to those looking to study the sector and evaluate the significance and scope of its economic contribution. To achieve this there needs to be an effective system of categorizing nonprofit organizations and a number of organizations and academic writers have attempted to get to grips with this issue. Hansmann (1980), for example, suggests that nonprofits should be distinguished according to their source of income and the way in which they are controlled.

Nonprofits that receive a substantial portion of their income from donations are termed 'donative' nonprofits, whilst those whose income derives primarily from the sale of goods and services are termed 'commercial' nonprofits. The RSPCA (Royal Society for the Prevention of Cruelty to Animals) is an example of the former, whilst an organization such as the Eden Project (a bio-diversity project in the UK) derives the majority of its income from the entrance fees it charges visitors to the site. Hansmann uses the term 'patron' to identify those individuals who supply the organization's funding. These may be donors, customers, or some combination of the same.

The notion of patron is important since it is this that is the key to the second of Hansmann's categorizing criteria—control. Those nonprofits in which ultimate control rests with the patrons are termed 'mutual', whilst those in which control is vested in a board of directors are termed entrepreneurial. Figure 1.7 illustrates the intersections between these criteria—donative mutual, donative entrepreneurial, commercial mutual, and commercial entrepreneurial.

Hansmann argues that this classification of nonprofits is helpful managerially since the category into which an organization might fall will impact on the nature of the strategies it might adopt and the difficulties it might encounter in implementation. He does however acknowledge that a number of organizations might simultaneously exhibit the characteristics of two or more groupings and that as a consequence the categories should not be regarded as mutually exclusive, merely as a guide.

Developing the theme of using ownership as the basis for classification, a number of organizations have begun to adopt a complex pattern of mnemonics to define often subtle differences in nonprofit categories. Texts may therefore be found which refer to NFPs, NGOs, NFGOs, and PVOs. Dig a little deeper and you may even find texts referring to subgroups

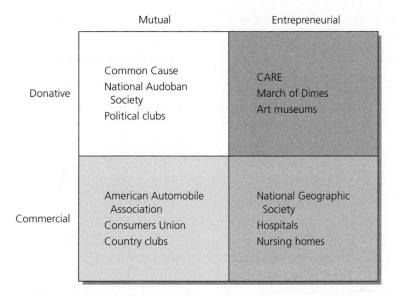

Figure 1.7 Hansmann's classification of nonprofits

Source: Hansmann (1980). Reprinted by permission of the Yale Law Journal Company and William S. Hein Company from *The Yale Law Journal,* Vol. 89, 835–901.

of organizations such as QUANGOs, BONGOs, GONGOs, FONGOs, and even PONGOs. Table 1.2 provides enlightenment.

There are also a number of more detailed classification systems in existence. In North America, for example, the National Taxonomy of Exempt Entities (NTEE) assigns a four-digit code to each distinct category of nonprofit, non-governmental organization in the USA. The first digit defines the purpose of the organization. The second and third digits define the major focus of the organization's programmes, whilst the fourth defines the nature of the primary beneficiary group.

A similar system has now been developed for the purposes of international comparison. The ICNPO (International Classification Of Non Profit Organisations) is illustrated in Figure 1.8.

Table 1.2 Common mnemonics

Mnemonic	Description
NFP	Not For Profit Organization
NFGO	Not For Gain Organization
PVO	Private Voluntary Organization
NGO	Non Governmental Organization
GONGO	Government Organized Non Governmental Organization
QUANGOs	Quasi Autonomous Non Governmental Organizations
BONGOs	Business Organized Non Governmental Organizations
FONGOs	Funder Organized Non Governmental Organizations
PONGOs	Political Non Governmental Organizations

Group 1: Culture and Recreation
Organizations and activities in general and specialized fields of culture and recreation

1 100 Culture
Media and Communications
Visual Arts, Architecture, Ceramic Art
Performing Arts
Historical, Literary and Humanistic Societies
Museums
Zoos and Aquaria

1 200 Recreation
Sports Clubs
Recreation and Social Clubs

1 300 Service Clubs

Group 2: Education and Research
Organizations and activities administering, providing, promoting, conducting, supporting, and serving education and research

2 100 Primary and Secondary Education
Elementary, Primary, and Secondary Education

2 200 Higher Education Fundraising Organizations
Higher Education

2 300 Other Education
Vocational/Technical Schools
Adult/Continuing Education

2 400 Research
Medical Research
Science and Technology
Social Sciences, Policy Studies

Group 3: Health
Organizations that engage in health-related activities, providing healthcare, both general and specialized services, administration of healthcare services, and health support services

3 100 Hospitals and Rehabilitation
Hospitals
Rehabilitation

3 200 Nursing Homes
Nursing Homes

3 300 Mental Health and Crisis Intervention
Psychiatric Hospitals
Mental Health Treatment
Crisis Intervention

3 400 Other Health Services
Public Health and Wellness Education
Health Treatment, Primarily Outpatient
Rehabilitative Medical Services
Emergency Medical Services

Group 4: Social Services
Organizations and institutions providing human and social services to a community or target population

4 100 Social Services
Child Welfare, Child Services, Day-care
Youth Services and Youth Welfare
Family Services
Services for the Handicapped
Services for the Elderly
Self Help and other Personal Social Services

4 200 Emergency and Relief
Disaster/Emergency Prevention and Control
Temporary Shelters
Refugee Assistance

4 300 Income Support and Maintenance
Income Support and Maintenance
Material Assistance

Group 5: Environment
Organizations promoting and providing services in environmental conservation, pollution control and prevention, environmental education and health, and animal protection

5 100 Environment
Pollution Abatement and Control
Natural Resources Conservation and Protection
Environmental Beautification and Open Spaces

5 200 Animals
Animal Protection and Welfare
Wildlife Preservation and Protection
Veterinary Services

Group 6: Development and Housing
Organizations promoting programmes and providing services to help improve communities and the economic and social well-being of society

6 100 Economic, Community, and Social Development
Community and Neighbourhood Organizations
Economic Development
Social Development

6 200 Housing
Housing Associations
Housing Assistance

6 300 Employment and Training
Job Training Programmes
Vocational Counselling and Guidance
Vocational Rehabilitation and Sheltered Workshops

Group 7: Law Advocacy and Politics
Organizations and groups that work to protect and promote civil rights, or advocate the social and political interests of general or specific constituencies, offer legal services, and promote public safety

7 100 Civic and Advocacy Organizations
Advocacy Organizations
Civil Rights Associations
Ethnic Associations
Civic Associations

7 200 Law and Legal Services
Legal Services

Crime Prevention and Public Safety
Rehabilitation of Offenders Victim Support
Consumer Protection Associations

7 300 Political Organizations

Group 8: Philanthropic Intermediaries and Volunteerism Promotion
Philanthropic organizations and organizations promoting charity or charitable activities

8 100 Philanthropic Intermediaries and Volunteerism Promotion
Grantmaking Foundations
Volunteerism Promotion and Support
Fundraising Organizations

Group 9: International Activities
Organizations promoting greater inter-cultural understanding between peoples of different countries and historical backgrounds and also those providing relief during emergencies and promoting development and welfare abroad

9 100 International Activities
Exchange/Friendship/Cultural Programmes
Development Assistance Associations
International Disaster and Relief Organizations

International Human Rights and Peace Organizations

Group 10: Religion
Organizations promoting religious beliefs and administering religious services and rituals; includes churches, mosques, synagogues, temples, shrines, seminaries, monasteries, and other similar institutions, in addition to related associations and auxiliaries of such organizations

10 100 Religious Congregations and Associations
Congregations
Associations of Congregations

Group 11: Business, Professional Associations, and Unions
Organizations promoting, regulating, and safeguarding business, professional, and labour interests

11 100 Business, Professional Associations, and Unions
Business Associations
Professional Labour Unions

Group 12: Not Elsewhere Classified
12 100 N.E.C.

Figure 1.8 The international classification of nonprofit organizations

Source: Salamon, L.M. and Anheier, H.K. *The International Classification of Nonprofit Organizations,* Johns Hopkins Institute for Policy Studies, Baltimore, MA.

Whilst the ICNPO system has enormous advantages in that we may now compare the performance of the nonprofit sector across international boundaries, it is not without some difficulty in its application. The reader will appreciate that the work of many nonprofits still cuts across the neatly defined categories listed in the Figure. A charity such as the International Red Cross, for example, is engaged in projects that could be classified under many of the headings provided. All such classification systems should thus be applied and interpreted with great care as a truly definitive classification of such organizations has yet to be developed.

Current Issues in the Nonprofit Sector

The nonprofit sector is undergoing a period of radical change. At the global level there has been an explosion in the number of nonprofit organizations over the past 30 years, almost certainly in response to rapidly changing environmental, social, and economic conditions. These conditions have recently included the impact of climatic changes, increasing national debt, the emergence of new diseases, the breakdown of some traditional political structures, and an ongoing succession of armed conflicts. Aside from this sheer growth there are a number of other key trends that warrant consideration. These include the following.

Blurring of Traditional Sector Boundaries

Historically, a key strength of the voluntary sector has been its independent nature. This independence is important because it can act to counterbalance an abusive and corrupt state, diffuse social and economic power, pluralize the political arena, and promote accountability and participatory governance, thus contributing toward the creation and maintenance of democracy (James and Caliguire 1996). To achieve this, however, it has to be capable of retaining its distinctive character and there are signs that this is proving increasingly difficult to achieve.

Earlier in this chapter we established two key trends in nonprofit income: a move towards greater government funding of the sector and a general trend towards fee income. Both have implications for the traditional distinction between the third sector and the public/private sector. Beginning with the former, government is the single biggest source of revenue for the US and UK voluntary sectors. The political discourse on both sides of the Atlantic is now emphasizing the partnership role that may be played by the sector with successive governments looking to the sector for help in tackling the most pressing social issues of the day. For there to be a genuine partnership, however, there must be a relative balance in power (Frumkin 1998) and this is far from the present reality. Government is typically immune to external pressure by virtue of its size and monopoly power while nonprofits, by contrast, have little power and their voices can frequently be stifled with the promise of funding. Indeed, this funding can lure them into activities they would not otherwise have undertaken, creating the real possibility that the sector may simply become an agent of the State (Wang 2006).

The State can control not only the activities undertaken, but the manner in which they are undertaken. As James (1993) notes, government regulations have historically followed government funding, turning the relationship from a partnership into a patron–client relationship where nonprofits are compelled to act in certain ways. Smith and Lipsky (1993: 10–11) argue that many radical organizations born in the 1960s were ultimately transformed into 'docile, homogenized, public supported social service bureaucracies—a process driven by years of dependence on government grants.'

More recently, Seddon (2006) has suggested that charities which derive more than 70% of their income from the State have reached a level of dependency that makes them more a part of the State than civil society. He argues that as a consequence they should lose their charitable status in order to preserve the integrity of the sector. He proposes that the law reflect three distinct categories of organization (see Table 1.3). Charities receiving less than 30% of their income from the state would still benefit from charitable status, while those receiving between 30% and 70% would be called state-funded charities, and would receive more modest benefits. Those receiving over 70% of their income from the state he regards as de facto state agencies and suggests that these nonprofits should be forced to choose either to reduce their dependency on statutory funding or lose their charitable status (pp. 145–6). The category of 'statutory agencies' that would thereby lose their charitable status would include some of the biggest and most famous charity brands: Barnardo's (78% state funded), NCH (88%), and Leonard Cheshire (88%).

While Seddon's arguments are persuasive, the removal of charitable status from many of our household-name charities would deter many in our society from democratically expressing their support for the work these organizations undertake. The fact that the government chooses to fund these organizations too does not negate the work they accomplish, nor does it negate the additional impact that might be achieved through voluntary contributions. Seddon also assumes a degree of homogeneity in provision, neglecting the fact that charities typically engage in a wide range of activities, only the most basic of which may qualify for

Table 1.3 Hypothetical breakdown of charities qualifying into new categories

Classification	Example charities
Independent charities (receiving less than 30 per cent of their income from the state)	NSPCC National Trust RNLI The Salvation Army
State-funded charities (receiving between 30 and 70 per cent of their income from the state)	Save the Children Oxfam Shelter British Red Cross
Statutory agencies (receiving 70 per cent or more of their income from the state)	Turning Point NCH The Shaftesbury Society National Family and Parenting Institute

Source: Seddon, N. (2006) *Who Cares?*, London, Civitas. Reproduced with kind permission.

government funding and support. It would create a serious anomaly for one gift to a children's charity to support a solvent abuse programme with no government funding to attract tax benefits, while a gift to another to support related work would not.

Turning to the second income trend we noted, many nonprofits now rely on fee income, charging for the services they deliver. Hard-nosed contractual negotiations and business deals now sit alongside the more traditional collecting tins and flag days. Nonprofits are no longer competing just with one another for funds; they are now competing with private companies (and other bodies) for the right to provide the services their mission suggests they should. If this trend continues the traditional distinction between nonprofit and for-profit will blur. To compete with for-profit providers, nonprofits will inevitably have to attract managers with commercial experience and to pay them salaries that may strike at the heart of the non-distribution constraint. Equally, with market forces increasingly in the ascendancy there is the very real danger that decisions will be taken for 'business' reasons (e.g. growing market share, income, or the profitability of a particular service) rather than because the impact on the beneficiary group will be optimal. In the current environment nonprofits are under increasing pressure to put aside the primacy of their missions and accountability to the communities they serve. If they succumb to such temptations there is a very real risk that they will begin to lose their distinctive identity (Boris 2001) leading to a crisis of trust in the voluntary sector as people begin to view all categories of organization as increasingly similar (Salamon 1999, Young 2002).

Growth of Capacity Building Initiatives

A further factor that may challenge the unique identity of the sector is the current enthusiasm of the State to engage in 'capacity building' as it seeks to persuade the voluntary sector to take an ever more active role in tackling social issues. As the then government minister Paul Boateng put it, in the introduction to a Treasury report:

As we begin the twenty-first century we [the UK government] look again to the voluntary and community sector to help us rekindle the spark of civic services that fires the building of strong civic communities; to reform the operation of public service and build a bridge between the needs of individuals living in those communities and the capacity of the state to improve their lives. (H.M. Treasury 2002)

This and other reports make it clear that the government is seeking to work with the voluntary sector to achieve four key goals:

- the social, economic, and physical regeneration of local neighbourhoods and communities;
- the building of social capital, social cohesion, and social inclusion;
- the reinvigoration of civic action and democratic participation; and
- improvement in the quality and quantity of public services.

In seeking to achieve these goals the government has become increasingly concerned with the efficiency and effectiveness of the sector (Kendall and Knapp 1995) and has sought ways to eliminate the 'barriers to the sector developing its full potential' and to enable nonprofits to deliver higher quality services (Strategy Unit, 2002: 29). To achieve this, the government regards capacity building initiatives as essential.

Cairns et al. (2005: 875) identify that the act of capacity building in a voluntary organization might include identifying and analysing management and organizational problems; taking action to solve management and organizational problems; developing action plans; developing vision or strategic plans; developing skills and capacities of individuals; gaining knowledge and information (individuals and/or the organization); training individuals or groups of individuals; education of individuals; consulting consumers/users; building organizational alliances; scanning the environment; securing resources; implementing organizational change; and expanding the range of services provided.

Clearly if governments are to concern themselves with facilitating these detailed actions there is a real danger that something of the unique character and historical independence of the sector may be lost (Harris 2001). There is increasing empirical support for this from the US where evidence tells us that organizations moving into the delivery of public services and therefore subject to greater meddling in their affairs will lose the ability to decide for themselves their mission, goals, priorities, and operating methods (Ferris 1993, Dahrendorf 2001).

Globalization

Many nonprofits are now truly global in scope. The number of international NGOs climbed from 13,000 in 1981 to 47,000 in 2001. According to Anheier (2006: 11):

Examples include Amnesty International with more than one million members, subscribers and regular donors in over 140 countries and territories. The Friends of the Earth Federation combines about 5000 local groups and one million members. The Coalition Against Child Soldiers has established partners and national coalitions engaged in advocacy, campaigns and public education in nearly 40 countries. Care International is an international NGO with over 10,000 professional staff. Its US headquarters alone has income of around $450 million.

The funding and dissemination of international aid is one notable global project as is the pattern of recent efforts to eradicate (in various ways) the Aids epidemic now sweeping the developing world. Organizations such as the World Bank and the International Monetary Fund have begun to impact on the strategy adopted by some nonprofits through their capacity to exert influence over the policies adopted by individual governments. Indeed, the number of formal links between nonprofits and international bodies like the World Bank have increased 46% between 1990 and 2000 (Glasius et al. 2002). Whilst some may welcome this activity, it is undeniable that moves towards globalization are gradually leading to the erosion of national traditions and cultures. There is also a danger that the uniquely tailored and innovative approach that characterizes so much of voluntary activity will be lost as people seek global solutions to what might better be regarded as national or even local issues.

It is important to note that it is not only the organization of nonprofit programmes that is experiencing pressure to globalize; the same may be said of the funding side of their operations. Large corporate donors, for example, may be global corporations in their own right and may require that the nonprofits they support offer a package of benefits in return in a number of the countries in which they operate. UNICEF, for example, has a number of large corporate donors who, in return for support, expect that the organization will work with them to provide recognition and benefits in each of the countries in which they operate.

Individual giving has been similarly impacted with the Internet creating a truly global market for the funding of nonprofits. It is now possible for individuals irrespective of their country of residence to identify and fund what they regard as worthy projects in countries all over the globe. Indeed, it is also possible for the provision of immediate feedback both to acknowledge the donor for the impact their gift will have and to seek other ways in which they could potentially engage with the cause (e.g. lobbying, campaigning, or fundraising).

Public Trust and Confidence

There has been increasing interest over the past ten years in the role of trust in the voluntary sector. Governments in both the UK and the USA believe that trust is essential if the levels of public support of the voluntary sector are to be maintained and developed. Prime Minister Blair indicated 'it is crucially important that public trust and confidence in the charitable and not-for-profit sector should be maintained and if possible increased' (Strategy Unit 2002: 6). Greater trust (the government feels) equates to greater giving and engagement in general with the voluntary sector. The maintenance of 'public goodwill' necessary to support both giving and volunteering activity is consistently tied directly to the presence of trust as the enduring and central relationship that sustains the sector as a whole (Strategy Unit 2002, Charity Commission 2001, 2002). Trust is also regarded as important in this context as it is trust that defines both the credibility and legitimacy of the sector and affords it a 'higher' moral tone than the private or public sector.

Regrettably the reason for the increasing interest of government in this issue has been the concern expressed in various national media about the activities of a number of nonprofit organizations. The press, in particular, has not been slow to criticize the sector for what it regards as inappropriate behaviour. Trust and confidence slipped, for example, after the events of 9/11 when nonprofits were seen as slow to respond and in 2003 alone the news media focused on improper payments, conflicts of interest, and the sacking of at least one controversial nonprofit CEO. Such events, it has been argued, serve to damage trust in the sector and giving/volunteering as a consequence.

Openness and Accountability

In a bid to bolster public trust, initiatives have been launched in both the UK and USA to improve the accountability of the nonprofit and voluntary sectors. The public, it has been argued, have a right to know how their donated monies have been applied, what has been achieved, and whether organizations spend too high a proportion of their income on fundraising and administration. In the past, information about the performance of voluntary organizations has been scant, with considerable scope for interpretation existing in the rules governing what must be reported and how this should be presented.

This has been allowed to occur because historically the accountancy profession has been more concerned with the measurement and control of for-profit enterprise. As Henke (1972:51) notes, 'the profession has never really faced up to the problem of trying to convey to the constituent groups of (nonprofit) organizations the data which would disclose the operational stewardship of the management of these entities'. This is partly due to the fact that there is seldom any real measure of operational efficiency for these organizations. Whilst in the for-profit sector, loss-making organizations are soon forced out of existence, in the case of nonprofits, an operating deficit could indicate to donors an organization worthy of additional support. Inefficient organizations can potentially survive as the donor has no way of distinguishing those that are efficiently meeting the needs of their recipient group(s) from those that expend needless sums of money on administration and management. In a bid to plug this gap a variety of bodies now stipulate 'acceptable' benchmarks of performance with the Council of Better Business Bureaus and the Philanthropic Advisory Service in the USA currently specifying a 35% limit, for example, on fundraising costs. Standards developed by the National Charities Bureau (NCB) specify that a minimum of 60% of annual expenses should be direct programmes whilst Hind (1995) recommends 70–90%. In all cases the recommendations appear somewhat arbitrary and little justification is offered.

In the US it is possible to access this kind of financial information on nonprofits through the public information website www.guidestar.org. The data hosted on the site comes from the IRS (Internal Revenue Service) Master File of tax exempt organizations. This comprises the annual returns nonprofits must make to the IRS on what is known as the Form 990. The data these contain is very limited and the categories of reporting are open to widespread abuse with many organizations thought to be actually lying on their returns (Tempel 2002). A large number of nonprofits (around 40%) show substantial sums of fundraised income, yet show absolutely no costs of fundraising. Such creative accounting does the sector no favours, suggesting it may have something to hide and attracting the interest of legislators as a consequence.

The Guidestar website now claims 20,000 visitors per day and the organization has supplemented the range of data available by posting other information, such as an organization's programmes, accomplishments, and goals. These are obtained directly from the nonprofit or compiled from the 990 as appropriate. A similar site has now been established for users in the UK at www.guidestar.org.uk which has opened up access to financial and other information on over 167,000 organizations. The site is populated with data made available by the Charity Commission who hold the annual accounts for every registered charity.

The UK has also seen two further initiatives aimed at bolstering accountability, making it clear to the public how the sector operates and dispelling a number of common myths. The educational website www.charityfacts.org was launched in 2004 and has as its goal the aim of educating the public about how much it costs to raise a pound and how this might vary by category of organization, the form of fundraising undertaken, and whether it is designed to recruit new donors or build relationships with existing ones. The site also provides important consumer advice on how to avoid receiving unwanted fundraising solicitations through media such as the mail or telephone.

In the second development, in 2005, the National Council for Voluntary Organizations and a number of the UK's leading charities formed the ImpACT (Improving Accountability, Clarity, and Transparency) coalition. Members of the ImpACT coalition have committed to increasing public understanding of charities' work and to communicate with clarity and openness by fulfilling a number of pledges, most notably:

- to be transparent about the fundraising process, how much is invested in raising money, and how this helps meet the needs of beneficiaries; and

- to collaborate in actively promoting sector-wide initiatives aimed at enhancing donor understanding that charities operate openly, honestly, and effectively.

Members of the coalition together with the Institute of Fundraising (the professional body for fundraisers in the UK) developed a Code of Practice for Accountability and Transparency in Fundraising which all of its members are now expected to abide by. The code can be viewed at www.institute-of-fundraising.org.uk.

Civic Disengagement

One of the biggest challenges the nonprofit sector will face in the coming decade is that of civic disengagement. In many Western countries the gap in income between the very wealthy in society and the very poor continues to grow. Whilst this is a serious issue in itself, for the nonprofit sector it creates a particular problem. It raises the need for programmes to support the poor yet reduces the number of individuals who might be prepared to undertake this work. Research tells us that participation in voluntary activity increases with education and income—so the widening disparity between the rich and the poor is becoming a real problem for societies to address (Guterbock and Fries 1997, Hodgkinson 1996).

Of particular concern is the level of engagement in voluntarism we are presently able to achieve amongst the young. Whilst the under 30s have always been the least engaged with the voluntary sector it appears that a smaller percentage elect to participate with every passing year. The young are increasingly hedonistic and less concerned with the welfare of the society in which they live (Yankelovich 1981, Verba et al. 1995, Pharoah and Tanner 1997, Boris 2001). Re-engaging with this important demographic will be an increasingly important goal of nonprofit strategy in the coming years.

■ SUMMARY

In this chapter I have introduced the terminology that will be used throughout this text. Whilst a number of different words have been used to describe what is ostensibly the same category of organization I prefer here to use the generic term 'nonprofit'. This is particularly appropriate given that it is our intention to focus on marketing in both the public and voluntary sectors. It is sufficiently broad in scope to embrace both these dimensions of society and has the further advantage that it is now in everyday usage, being preferred by most practitioners to the arguably more accurate terminology of 'not-for-profit'.

In this chapter we have focused largely on the development of the third or voluntary sectors and indicated the size and significance of each in modern society. We shall return to the development of the public sector in the final chapter of this text. In discussing the development of the voluntary sector in both the UK and the US I have also highlighted a number of schema that may be employed to categorize nonprofits and thus to define the focus of a particular activity. Finally we have discussed a number of key marketing-related issues that are currently impinging on the sector and/or are likely to over the coming years. In Chapter 2 we will move on from this broad consideration of sector issues to introduce the topic of marketing and in particular how the marketing philosophy could be adopted by a nonprofit organization.

■ DISCUSSION QUESTIONS

1. Explain, for a country of your choice, the role that the voluntary sector plays in society. How does this role differ from that of government or the private sector?

2. Why are there so many different terms employed to define what is ostensibly the same sector in society? Explain how these terms are applied in your own country. Does this differ from their application in the UK or the US? If so, why might this be?

3. What is meant by the term 'charity'? In the context of the UK what is the rationale for offering a distinctive legal charitable status?

4. What do you regard as the biggest challenges or issues that must be addressed by the nonprofit sector in your own country? How might these be addressed, both by the sector itself and by government?

■ REFERENCES

Anheier H.K. (2006) *Nonprofit Organizations: Theory, Management, Policy*, London, Routledge.

Beveridge W.H. (1948) *Voluntary Action: A Report on Methods of Social Advance*, London, Allen and Unwin.

Boris, E.T. (2001) 'The Nonprofit Sector in the 1990s' in Clotfelter C.T. and Ehrlich T. (2001) *Philanthropy and the Nonprofit Sector in a Changing America*, Indianapolis, Indiana University Press, 1–33.

Cairns B., Harris M. and Young P. (2005) 'Building the Capacity of the Voluntary Nonprofit Sector: Challenges of Theory and Practice', *International Journal of Public Administration*, Vol. 28, 869–885.

Chapman, D. and Cowdell, T. (1998) *New Public Sector Marketing*, London, Financial Times Publishing.

Charity Commission (2001) *Fundraising Through Partnerships With Companies*, Charity Commission Guidance Note, London, HMSO.

Charity Commission (2002) *Charities and Fundraising*, Charity Commission Guidance Note, London, HMSO.

Charity Commission (2006) *Charities Act 2006: A Guide to the Main Provisions*, http://www.charity-commission.gov.uk/spr/ca2006prov.asp accessed 20 February 2006.

Dahrendorf R. (2001) *Challenges to the Voluntary Sector*, Goodman Lecture. London, Charities Aid Foundation.

Davis-Smith, J. (1995) 'The Voluntary Tradition: Philanthropy and Self-Help in Britain 1500–1945', in Davis-Smith, J., Rochester, C. and Hedley, R. (1995) *An Introduction To The Voluntary Sector*, London, Routledge.

de Tocqueville, A. (1969) *Democracy in America*, New York, Doubleday.

Ferris, J.M. (1993) 'The Double Edged Sword of Social Service Contracting: Public Accountability Versus Nonprofit Autonomy', *Nonprofit Management and Leadership*, Vol. 3, No. 4, 363–76.

Fisk, A. (2006) 'History of the Society,' http://www.foresters.ws/about_us_history.htm accessed 20 February.

Frumkin, P. (1998) 'Rethinking Public-Nonprofit Relations: Toward A Neo-Institutional Theory of Public Management,' PONPO Working Paper, No. 248 (April) Yale University.

Giving USA Foundation (2006) *Giving USA*, Indianapolis, Giving USA Foundation.

Glasius, M., Kaldor, M., and Anheier, H.K. (2002) *Global Civil Society*, Oxford, Oxford University Press.

Gurin, M.G. and Van Til, J. (1990) 'Philanthropy in its Historical Context', in Jon van Til and Associates (eds), *Critical Issues in American Philanthropy*, San Francisco, Jossey Bass, 3–18.

Guterbock, T.M. and Fries, J.C. (1997) *Maintaining America's Social Fabric: The AARP Survey of Civic Involvement*, Report Prepared for the American Association of Retired Persons, Washington DC.

Hammack, D.C. (1998) *Making of The Nonprofit Sector in the United States*, Indianapolis, Indiana University Press.

Hansmann, H. (1980) 'The Role of the Nonprofit Enterprise', *Yale Law Review*, Vol. 89 (April), 835–899.

Harris, M. (1998) 'Instruments of Government? Voluntary Sector Boards in a Changing Public Policy Environment,' *Policy and Politics*, Vol. 26, No. 2, 177–88.

Harris, M. (2001) 'This Charity Business: Who Cares?' *Nonprofit Management and Leadership*, Vol. 12, No. 1, 95–109.

Henke, E.O. (1972) 'Performance Evaluation for Not-For-Profit Organizations', *Journal of Accountancy*, Vol. 133, No. 6: 51–5.

Hind, A. (1995) *The Governance and Management of Charities*, London, The Voluntary Sector Press.

Hodgkinson, V. (1996) *Volunteering and Giving Among Teenagers 12-17 Years of Age*, Washington, DC, Independent Sector.

H.M. Treasury (2002) *The Role of the Voluntary and Community Sector in Service Delivery: A Cross Cutting Review*. H.M. Treasury and Compact Working Group, London.

James, E. (1993) 'Why Do Different Countries Use A Different Public-Provate Mix in Education?' *Journal of Human Resources*, Vol. 28, No. 3, 571–92.

James, W. and Caliguire, D. (1996) 'Renewing Civil Society,' *Journal of Democracy*, Vol. 7, No. 1, 56–66.

Kendall, J. and Knapp, M.R.J. (1995) 'Boundaries, Definitions and Typologies: A Loose and Baggy Monster,' in Davis-Smith, J. (ed.) *An Introduction To The Voluntary Sector*, London, Routledge.

Kotler, P. and Levy, S.J. (1969) 'Broadening The Concept of Marketing,' *Journal of Marketing*, Vol. 33, No. 2, 10–15.

Lewis, J. (1993) 'Developing the Mixed Economy of Care: Emerging Issues for Voluntary Organizations,' *Journal of Social Policy*, Vol. 22, No. 2, 173–92.

Marts, A.C. (1966) *The Generosity of Americans: Its Source, Its Achievements*, Englewood Cliffs, Prentice Hall.

Nathan, L. (1952) *Report to the Committee on Law and Practice Relating to Charitable Trusts*, London: HMSO.

National Council for Voluntary Organizations (NCVO) (2008) *The UK Civil Society Almanac 2006*, London, NVCO.

Pharoah, C. and Tanner, S. (1997) Trends In Charitable Giving, *Fiscal Studies*. Vol. 18, No. 4, 427–43.

Probst, G.E. (1962) 'The Happy Republic: A Reader' in de Tocqueville, A. (ed.) *America*, New York: Harper and Brothers.

Putnam, R. (1993) *Making Democracy Work*, Princeton: Princeton University Press.

Rothschild, M.L. (1979) 'Marketing Education in Nonbusiness Situations or Why It's So Hard To Sell Brotherhood Like Soap,' *Journal of Marketing*, Vol. 43 (Spring), 1–20.

Salamon, L. (1999) *America's Nonprofit Sector: A Primer*, New York, Foundation Center.

Salamon, L.M. and Anheier, H.K. (1992) *In Search of the Non-Profit Sector II: The Problem of Classification*, Johns Hopkins Comparative Non-Profit Sector Project, Baltimore: Johns Hopkins Institute for Policy Studies.

Salamon, L.M. and Anheier, H.K. (1997) *Defining The Nonprofit Sector*, Manchester University Press.

Seddon, N. (2006) *Who Cares?*, London, Civitas.

Smith, A. (1776) *The Wealth of Nations*, Letchworth, Dent and Sons Ltd.

Smith, S.R. and Lipsky, M. (1993) *Nonprofits for Hire: The Welfare State in the Age of Contracting*, Cambridge MA, Harvard University Press.

Steinberg, R. and Powell, W.W. (2006) 'Introduction' in Powell, W.W. and Steinberg, R. (eds) *The Non-Profit Sector: A Research Handbook* (2nd Edition), New Haven, Yale University Press.

Strategy Unit (2002) *Private Action, Public Benefit: A Review of Charities and the Wider Not-For-Profit Sector*, Strategy Unit, HM Government Cabinet Office, September.

Tempel, E. (2002) 'Nonprofit Trends and Challenges', Presentation to the Charities Aid Foundation Conference – *A Lot of Give*, London, July.

Tempel, E.R. and Mortimer, D.H. (2001) Preface To Clotfelter, C.T. and Ehrlich, T. (2001) *Philanthropy and the Nonprofit Sector in a Changing America*, Indianapolis, Indiana University Press.

Urban Institute (2006) *The Nonprofit Sector in Brief: Facts and Figures from the Nonprofit Almanac*, Washington DC, Urban Institute.

Verba, S., Schlozman, K.L., and Brady, H.E. (1995) *Voice and Equality: Civic Voluntarism in American Politics*, Cambridge, MA, Harvard University Press.

Wang, S. (2006) 'Money and Autonomy: Patterns of Civil Society Finance and Their Implications,' *Studies in Comparative International Development*, Vol. 40, No. 4, 3–29.

Weitzman, M.S., Jalandoni, N.T., Lampkin, L.M., and Pollak, T.H. (2002) *The New Nonprofit Almanac and Desk Reference: The Essential Facts and Figures for Managers, Researchers and Volunteers* (1st edn), San Francisco, Jossey Bass.

Williams, I. (1989) *The Alms Trade: Charities, Past Present and Future*, London, Unwin Hyman Ltd.

World Bank (2001) 'Nongovernmental Organizations and Civil Society/Overview,' <http://wbln0018.worldbank.org/essd/essd.nsf/NGOs/home> accessed 8 June 2001.

Wuthnow, R. (2002) 'Bridging the Privileged and the Marginalized,' in Putnam, R. (ed.), *Democracies in Flux*, Oxford, Oxford University Press.

Yankelovich, D. (1981) *New Rule: Searching For Self Fulfilment In A World Turned Upside Down*, New York, Random House Inc.

Young, D.R. (1983) *If Not For Profit, For What? A Behavioural Theory of the Nonprofit Sector Based on Entrepreneurship*, Lexington, KY, Lexington Books.

Young, D.R. (2002) 'The Influence of Business on Nonprofit Organizations and the Complexity of Nonprofit Accountability: Looking Inside As Well As Outside,' *American Review of Public Administration*, Vol. 32 (March), 3–19.

2 Developing a Societal and Market Orientation

OBJECTIVES

By the end of this chapter you should be able to:

1. define the role of marketing as it applies to a nonprofit organization;
2. respond to typically encountered objections to marketing in the nonprofit context;
3. operationalize the marketing concept in a nonprofit organization;
4. distinguish between product, sales, market, and societal orientations;
5. understand the key requirements for achieving a societal orientation.

What Is Marketing?

Many definitions of marketing exist, and with each new textbook that is published another definition is added to the list. Resisting the temptation to add my own, it is useful to begin by examining in detail some of the best known and widely accepted. In the UK the most popular definition is that offered by the Chartered Institute of Marketing: 'Marketing is the management process responsible for identifying, anticipating and satisfying customer requirements profitably.'

Ignoring for a moment the unfortunate emphasis on profit, there are two very striking components to this definition, which are central to understanding marketing's role in any organization. In short, marketing is both a concept and a function. At a conceptual level, marketing represents a philosophy or approach to management that places the customer right at the centre of everything that an organization does. At a functional level it may be regarded as that part of the organization which gathers research, helps design new services, prices them, distributes them, and ultimately promotes them to the consumer. It is important, though, that a wider perspective on marketing be retained. In too many organizations, marketing is regarded only as this latter, somewhat narrow functional field of endeavour and the conceptual level is ignored altogether. Marketing should not be seen as the preserve of a few personnel in the marketing department, but rather as a global approach to an organization's operations that should be adopted by all, irrespective of their position in the organization.

The concept of 'process' is also an important one since the 'process' of marketing in a genuinely marketing-led organization should start by determining customer needs and using these to form the basis of the products or services that the organization will supply. Indeed, an understanding of customer requirements can offer an organization much more than the mere design of its market offering. Value can be created at every contact the customer has with an organization. If one understands what creates this value, it is possible to enhance the design of all an organization's systems with the simple goal of delivering the maximum possible value to the customer. The definition of marketing developed by Kotler and Fox (1985: 5) says far more about the mechanics of how this might be achieved:

Marketing is the analysis, planning, implementation and control of carefully formulated programs designed to bring about voluntary exchanges of values with target markets for the purpose of achieving organizational objectives. It relies heavily on designing the organization's offerings in terms of the target market's needs and desires and on using effective pricing, communication and distribution to inform, motivate and service the markets.

It is clear from both definitions that marketing is primarily concerned with identifying and satisfying the needs of an organization's customers and it is equally clear that the actual personnel responsible for fulfilling this role will not be exclusively those located in the marketing department. In the case of universities, for example, while the marketing department may well produce the prospectus and its associated advertising, the contact a student has with the admissions office, an academic in her selected department, the accommodation office, etc. will all be likely to have rather more impact on that student's ultimate decision about whether or not to study there. There is therefore a need for marketing to be embraced as a management philosophy which permeates all departments and all levels within an organization.

Regrettably, however, in some organizations the creation of a marketing department is simply a knee-jerk response to falling sales. The purpose of the marketing department in such organizations is not to ensure the satisfaction of the organization's customers, but rather to hard-sell failing products and services. It is no coincidence that many universities have now created marketing roles and even whole marketing departments as they find themselves competing for increasingly discriminating students. Rather than embrace the marketing concept and design new courses and services around the preferences of the market, many established organizations have simply looked to find better ways of selling their existing provision. This is not what good marketing is all about. These two contrasting views of marketing are illustrated in Figure 2.1.

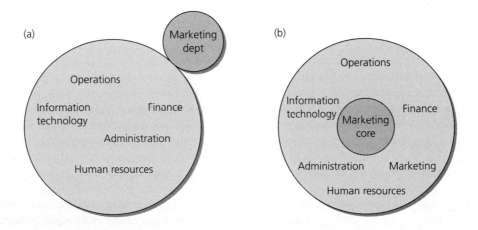

Figure 2.1 (a) Marketing as a 'bolt-on' discipline; (b) Marketing as a management philosophy

In the first figure (2.1a) marketing is regarded purely as a functional role that can be 'bolted on' to an organization, as and when circumstances require it. Nonprofits adopting this approach would tend to produce the services that the members of their board, often in isolation, decide are appropriate for the target group. Little or no effort would typically be made to ascertain the genuine needs of their users, and failing demand would usually be met with increasingly aggressive attempts to convince them of the desirability of the provision. The marketing function would therefore lack resources for activities other than promotion and would fail to have any real input to the strategic direction the organization might take. It is therefore with good reason that Professor Malcolm MacDonald, one of the UK's leading authorities on marketing, famously refers to such departments as the 'Corporate Zit'!

By contrast, an organization such as the one in Figure 2.1b would regard marketing as the guiding philosophy which drives the whole approach to the management of the nonprofit. Such organizations plan their service provision in close consultation with users and ensure that they are structured/designed so as to provide the maximum possible benefit and value. Moreover, each of the organization's systems are structured to enhance this value and every employee or volunteer is specifically encouraged to regard marketing as his/her responsibility. The marketing function would be expected to engage in a wide range of activities, including market research, new service development, pricing, etc., and would have representation at the most senior level in the organization concerned. The details of how a change in emphasis from that depicted in Figure 2.1a to that in Figure 2.1b might be achieved is a subject that we shall return to later in this chapter.

Certainly all organizations will want to consider and carefully manage the functional aspects of marketing in order to secure take-up of their service, but a focus solely on such activities will never actually involve the organization in genuine marketing. Indeed it is such narrow views of 'what marketing is' that have specifically contributed to earning the subject a bad name, particularly in some nonprofit quarters. Many arts organizations have until recently rejected the marketing concept because they saw it as being synonymous with selling, which by definition lowered the perceived quality of the service they were trying to provide. Indeed, when the author recently approached a senior member of staff in a neighbouring faculty to canvass views about arts marketing he was told quite categorically that the whole idea of marketing the arts was quite 'reprehensible'. While such one-word definitions of marketing have the merit of being easier to remember than those offered previously in this text, they represent a crass misunderstanding of what marketing is, and what it is trying to achieve. Genuine marketing both begins and ends with a thorough understanding of the needs of the 'customers' that a particular organization exists to serve. The concept therefore has a clear relevance to *all* types of organization, whether they are motivated by profit or not.

What Can Marketing Offer?

Having examined what marketing is, we are now in a position to explore the extent to which it can be of value to a nonprofit organization. There has been considerable debate over the years concerning whether the marketing concept can legitimately be applied to the management of such organizations.

In the late 1960s, Kotler and Levy (1969) were the first to open the debate on the relevance of the marketing concept to nonprofit organizations. In their view, marketing had the capacity to grow beyond its role as a narrow business activity and to take on a broader societal

Table 2.1 Nonprofits and key customer groups

Category of organization	Key customer groups
Charities	Volunteers
	Individual donors
	Corporate donors
	Charitable trusts
	Recipients of goods/services
Arts organizations	Visitors
	Audiences
	Corporate sponsors
	Arts funding bodies
Healthcare trusts	Patients
	Visitors/relatives of patients
	General practitioners
	Insurance companies
	Government funders
Education	Students
	Alumni
	Industry
	Research funders
	Local communities
	Local/national government

meaning. The authors defined marketing as 'sensitively serving and satisfying human need'. While this definition is somewhat broader than those introduced earlier, it does draw attention to what good marketing can achieve. It also has the merit of removing the emphasis on profit that was developed earlier in the CIM definition. Most nonprofits are, after all, by their definition less concerned with profit than they are with meeting some particular need in society. Marketing in this context is therefore concerned with facilitating an exchange process between an organization and its public, so that a societal need can be fulfilled. The question therefore remains—whose need? Dare we refer to customers? The term has already been used in this text and Kotler and Levy are in no doubt on this issue. The authors feel that all organizations have customers whether they choose to refer to them as such or not. A list of typical customers for a variety of nonprofit organizations is given in Table 2.1.

Viewing those groups in society that a nonprofit is designed to serve as customers is a very powerful notion because it forces those responsible for the marketing of such organizations to begin their planning processes by defining precisely the requirements of those customers. Think, for example, of those wonderfully boring museums we all encountered as children. Row after row of neat glass cases each displaying their sterile collection of antiquities. At least if you were physically fit you could drag yourself from one end of an exhibition to another, but what about those with some form of disability? Until comparatively recently few facilities were provided for the disabled and museums were therefore largely perceived as unwelcoming by such groups. Fortunately there has now been a sea change in the sector.

The new Indiana State Museum is a good example of a modern market-oriented museum. It contains a collection depicting the natural history of the State, alongside artefacts from the earliest settlements and more recent items from the nineteenth and twentieth centuries. In essence it tracks life in Indiana right through from pre-history to the present day. The mission of the museum is illustrated below and although education and preservation are still seen as central to its role, so to is providing value to the community and even entertainment. The museum takes the view that learning should be fun and displays have been created with that in mind. Children can touch fossil remains of early Indiana life and try their hand at some of the chores the later settlers would have had to accomplish. The focus is on interaction with careful consideration given to the environment visitors experience as they pass through each time period. Visitors are given a real 'feel' of each age.

What this example clearly illustrates is the difference between a product and a market orientation in the arts sector. At one extreme we have museums which view their collection as the primary or even sole reason for their existence. At the other end of the spectrum we can see museums that are so proud of their collection that they want to encourage as many people as they can to interact with it. Moreover, such museums want the visitor to be genuinely enthused about their collections and to go away believing that they have had an educational yet entertaining visit. In short, one form of museum is attempting to satisfy its customers while the other is not. Which of these should be regarded as performing the greatest service to society?

INDIANA STATE MUSEUM

Mission

The Indiana State Museum and Historic Sites preserves, interprets, and presents material evidence of Indiana's cultural and natural history in a context that encourages people to actively participate in discovering their world—as it was, as it is, and as it can be.

We will accomplish our mission by embracing these values:

- Learning—We promote the thoughtful discovery of new information through investigation, examination, exploration, and education—and we strive to nourish a creative learning environment for the public and for our own employees.

- Value—We are committed to providing excellent products and services that exceed people's expectations of quality, cost, and worthiness. This commitment to quality extends to all aspects of our programming, products, research, exhibits, and professional activities.

- Entertainment—We use our resources to engage people across generations in meaningful, memorable, and valuable fun.

- Community—We recognize that we exist as part of a larger community. We reach out to diverse audiences, and through collaboration with other organizations, we give and receive resources.

- Preservation—We hold in trust the legacy of Indiana's material culture and the evidence of its past so that people today and generations to come may better understand how they fit into the world.

- Authenticity—We present the true image of Indiana, foster clarity of understanding, and instill a sense of future possibilities. We offer people access to the real specimens, places, and artifacts that represent our past.

- Leadership—We strive for success in all our endeavors, and we strive to set standards that influence sister institutions and the citizens of Indiana.

continues

continued

a

b

c

Figure 2.2 Indiana State Museum interactive exhibits

Source: courtesy of Indiana State Museum and Historic Sites ©2008

There are many clues in this simple example to what marketing can offer a nonprofit. Specifically the following benefits are worthy of note:

• Marketing can improve the levels of customer satisfaction attained—in the simple example outlined above, the new layout and design of the Indiana State Museum has substantially improved levels of visitor satisfaction without compromising the integrity of the collection.

• Marketing can also assist in the attraction of resources to a nonprofit organization. Many nonprofits need to raise funds to support their work. Marketing tools and techniques can offer fundraisers substantial utility and afford them greater opportunities to fulfil an organization's mission.

• The adoption of a professional approach to marketing may help an organization to define its distinctive competencies. In other words, marketing can define what an organization can offer society that others cannot. This may be manifested in an ability to work with particular categories of people in society, or it may be manifested in the way in which such work is conducted. Whatever the case, if an organization can identify those areas where it can add value, over and above that which can be offered by 'competitors', it can refine those competencies and use them to enhance both fundraising and service delivery as a result.

• A professional approach to marketing also offers organizations a framework within which to work. A systematic approach to researching needs, setting objectives, planning to meet those objectives, and the instigation of formal control activities to ensure that they will actually be achieved should minimize the wastage of valuable marketing resources.

How Is Nonprofit Marketing Different?

Despite the obvious benefits that marketing can offer a nonprofit, there are a number of important differences between the application of marketing in a for-profit and a nonprofit context. Various authors have discussed these differences and there is considerable debate about whether the differences are as real as they might at first appear. Nevertheless, the following list developed by Lovelock and Weinberg (1990) may help to explain some of the complexities the marketing functions in a typical nonprofit may encounter.

Multiple Constituencies

In a for-profit context the marketing function is concerned with developing goods and services which will then be sold to customers. This, it is hoped, will generate revenue which can then be used to purchase the raw materials necessary to produce the next generation of goods and services, and so on. In short, there is only one constituency that needs to be addressed by the marketing function. In many charities, however, there are two constituencies, since the individuals who donate funds are rarely those who will actually be able to benefit from the services that the charity provides. In other words, there is a clear distinction between resource attraction and resource allocation.

From this simple description you can probably already see why the idea that multiple constituencies might be something unique to the nonprofit sector has been criticized by some writers. It has been argued, for example, that many business organizations draw income from a variety of sources, not necessarily just their primary customer group. Some may attract significant government funding or occasionally seek to raise funds from a new issue of shares. Thus marketers in business organizations can also find themselves dealing with multiple constituencies. It does seem safe to conclude however that the division between resource attraction and resource allocation is unlikely to be as clear-cut as it is in many nonprofit organizations.

Non-Financial Objectives

As Drucker (1990: 107) notes, 'performance is the ultimate test of any institution. Every nonprofit institution exists for the sake of performance in changing people and society. Yet, performance is also one of the truly difficult areas for the executive in the non-profit institution.'

Setting objectives which can then be used to monitor performance is a particular problem for nonprofit organizations because of the intangible nature of much of the service provided. It is also a problem because, as Drucker goes on to note, 'the results of a non-profit institution are always outside the organization, not inside'. Their results are therefore inherently more difficult to measure. This is not to suggest, however, that nonprofit organizations should not at least try to set targets, although the question then remains, to what should these relate?

It is fair to dispense with profit maximization theories in this sector. Most nonprofits are, by definition, little concerned with profit. They may, however, still be concerned with the concept of maximization, in the sense that they may have objectives that are concerned with input or output maximization. In the case of the latter, many nonprofits appear perpetually to find that demand always outstrips their capacity to supply. A charity for the homeless, Shelter, for example, would undoubtedly view its primary objective as being to help as many homeless people as possible. In the case of the former, some charities have as their goal resource attraction, on the basis that there will always be needs for them to meet. The charity Guide Dogs for the Blind is arguably one such organization as it has been criticized for generating substantial reserves in recent years. The charity would argue however that it is very necessary for them to continue fundraising as, some day, all the guide dogs they have already supplied will need replacing.

It is also clear that the subject matter of any objectives set will differ from the for-profit sector. Nonprofits cover a very wide range of human interests and behaviours and this is reflected in the broad diversity of objectives they possess. This author has encountered objectives written in terms of the numbers of people aided, an individual's quality of life, changes in public attitudes, and even mortality rates!

Services and Social Behaviours rather than Physical Goods

The majority of nonprofits produce services rather than physical goods. Indeed, many organizations do not even produce a service that one could clearly define. Some organizations exist simply to attempt to alter some form of social behaviour through either direct communication with the target group, or indirectly through the lobbying of government. Nevertheless, the distinction between services and products is an important one since many charities do market services and doing so is an inherently more complex process than the marketing of physical goods. As Zeithaml (1985) notes, there are four key differences which should be taken account of, namely:

1. *Intangibility.* When a customer purchases a physical item or service he/she can assess it by its appearance, taste, smell, etc. They can therefore 'confirm' their expectations about the properties of the product they are going to receive. With a service, however, the consumer has no way of verifying the claims of the producer until the service has actually been purchased.

2. *Inseparability.* Physical goods are produced and then purchased by the customer. With services, the process is the other way around. Services are sold first and then produced at the time of consumption by the customer. (In this sense production and consumption are said to be inseparable.) This means that producer and consumer have to interact to produce the service. Marketing a service therefore involves not only facilitating an exchange process, but also facilitating an often quite complex producer/consumer interaction.

3. *Heterogeneity.* Allied to the previous point, since production and consumption are inseparable there are few chances for a service supplier to carry out pre-inspection or quality control in the same way that one can with physical goods. Indeed monitoring and control processes are necessarily considerably more complex in the context of services.

4. *Perishability.* Services cannot be stored in the same way that one can store food or electrical items in a retail outlet. If a theatrical performance begins with a half-empty house, or there are last-minute cancellations of a physician's appointments, those services have been lost forever. Marketers, therefore, have a more complex balancing operation to perform to ensure that their services remain as optimally utilized as possible. These differences are summarized in Table 2.2.

Table 2.2 Services are different

Goods	Services	Resulting implications
Tangible	Intangible	Services cannot be inventoried
		Services cannot be patented
		Services cannot be readily displayed or communicated
Standardized	Heterogeneous	Service delivery and customer satisfaction depend on employee actions
		Service quality depends on many uncontrollable factors
		There is no sure knowledge that the service delivered matches what was planned and expected
Production separate from consumption	Simultaneous production and consumption	Customer participates in and affects the transaction
		Customers affect each other
		Decentralization may be essential
		Mass production is difficult
Non-perishable	Perishable	It is difficult to synchronize supply and demand with services
		Services cannot be returned or resold

Source: Zeithaml, V.A., Parasuraman, A. and Berry, L.L. (1985) 'Problems and Strategies in Service Marketing', 49 (2), 33–46. Reproduced with permission of the *Journal of Marketing* published by the American Marketing Association.

Where nonprofits are concerned with physical behaviours rather than services, additional complications arise. Attempting to influence social behaviours will never be a non-controversial task, no matter how much benefit may ultimately accrue to society as a result of such endeavours. Organizations such as ASH, the anti-smoking campaign, for example, continually face pressure from organizations with diametrically opposed views, such as nonprofits set up by smokers' rights activists. This is not competition in the way that one may define it in the for-profit context, but rather an attempt by one nonprofit to deride the work of another.

Public Scrutiny/Non-Market Pressures

Certain categories of organization within the nonprofit sector are open to intense levels of public scrutiny. The emergency services, local authorities, hospitals, and even universities are subject to regular public scrutiny. UK universities, for example, are subject to a comprehensive audit of the quality of their teaching and research every four years. In the healthcare sector, the government White Paper 'Working For Patients' introduced an independent body, the Audit Commission, into the UK healthcare framework. The Commission has responsibility for ensuring that the National Health Service continues to provide 'value for money'. Such public scrutiny simply does not occur on the same scale in a for-profit business context.

Nonprofits also have to contend with a variety of other non-market pressures. While no one would claim for a moment that it is easy for a business organization to be able to forecast demand for its products, demand for the services of a nonprofit can fall away to nothing or literally double overnight. The nature of Oxfam's work overseas with developing countries can change radically from year to year depending on political, economic, and climatic conditions. The very nature of their focus on the disadvantaged makes it almost impossible to know where future priorities might lie.

The instability of the environment in which many nonprofits operate thus contributes to the fact that such organizations often have less control over their own destiny than their counterparts in the for-profit sector. Marketers in nonprofits therefore have a much more complex role to perform.

Tension between Mission and Customer Satisfaction

The final key difference that may be encountered in the nonprofit sector relates to the nature of some nonprofit missions. Many such organizations are compelled by their mission to take a long-term view of their relationships with their target markets. Health and welfare groups in developing countries, for example, may be promoting the use of contraception in direct conflict with the established patterns of local belief and culture. Similarly many theatres and arts centres have a mission to explore a wide range of art forms, not just to provide those forms of entertainment that they know will be well patronized by their local community. There is therefore a tension between the satisfaction of current customer needs and the fulfilment of a particular organization's mission. Short-term customer satisfaction may often have to be sacrificed by nonprofits as they take a longer-term view of the benefit they can offer to society.

The idea that organizations should take this longer-term view of the welfare of their 'customer' groups is a notion that one would rarely encounter in the for-profit sector. Business organizations make their money by satisfying the immediate needs of their customers today, and need therefore to devote the maximum effort to the achievement of this goal. One of the key advantages of a strong nonprofit sector is that the division between resource attraction and resource allocation affords a greater opportunity for a longer-term perspective to be adopted. While the needs of the current customer group are important (and will be ignored completely at the organization's peril), nonprofits do have the luxury of being able to strike a balance between the short- and long-term needs of their key customer groups. Hence the role of marketing in this context genuinely becomes one of 'sensitively serving the needs of society'.

Typical Objections to Marketing

Despite the benefits that marketing can provide, there have been a number of objections raised over the years when writers have mooted the possibility of its application to the nonprofit sector. The most common of such objections, usually raised by managers working in the sector, are dealt with below.

'Marketing is not Necessary'

This objection stems from a belief that the nonprofit is doing worthwhile work and is therefore worthy of support for its own sake. In the UK this idea has been particularly prevalent in the education sector where established universities have traditionally not felt the need to market their services, as they have expected students to research the quality of various institutions and to seek them out to study a particular subject. The idea that academics are somehow intellectual monks to whom people will turn for an education because of the perceived quality of an institution is now hopelessly outdated. Students have a much wider choice of courses than they had even ten years ago and because of this can pick and choose the institutions at which they want to study. Given that a much larger percentage of young people are being encouraged to enter higher education, the profile of the student body has also changed. As a result, all but the Oxbridge or Ivy League universities are now finding themselves having to compete hard to attract the brightest students.

'Marketing Invades an Individual's Privacy'

Marketing is viewed by some as intrusive as it is seen as invading an individual's right to privacy. This criticism is perhaps a little more difficult to answer since at some point marketers will undoubtedly conduct research in an attempt to identify consumer needs. As Kotler and Clarke (1987: 22) point out, 'Market research in any consumer industry is invasive; market researchers may enter people's homes to ask about likes and dislikes, beliefs and attitudes, income and other personal characteristics. Moreover in (the nonprofit sector), the research is more likely to cover sensitive areas individuals would prefer not to reveal to strangers.'

Of course, if organizations are to get close to their market and understand what requirements customers might have, a certain amount of marketing research will always be necessary. This is particularly so in the context of the nonprofit sector since, as we have already seen, the concern is often with services and social behaviours which are by definition more difficult for an organization to monitor. However, if one considers that the ultimate aim of this research should be to benefit society as a whole, perhaps an occasional 'invasion of privacy' could be forgiven.

Of course, market research is simply one way in which an individual's privacy can be compromised. Many forms of promotion are judged to be unwelcome and invasive. Advertising, direct mail, telemarketing, etc. have all attracted a bad reputation at one point or another for entering someone's home with unwelcome messages about an equally unwanted product or service. This is not however a criticism of marketing per se, but rather a criticism of the way that marketing tools have been employed by particular organizations. Poorly planned and executed campaigns may often target individuals who have no interest in the service being promoted, and this gives the marketing profession a bad name. Neither does it make sense for nonprofits to engage in such activities as they waste valuable marketing resources. Instead organizations should look to refine their targeting and to develop a more focused campaign to promote their services only to those who would stand to benefit.

'Marketing Lowers Perceived Quality'

Until quite recently, it was unusual to find universities applying much effort and attention to the marketing of their undergraduate courses. All institutions had a prospectus and did some work with schools, but proactive marketing activity was rare. In his first academic role this author can vividly recall a meeting with a university admissions officer who felt aggrieved that the university was going to begin actively advertising its undergraduate courses. This, he felt, would lower the perceived quality of those courses in the minds of potential students. In his words, the university would appear 'desperate' to attract students.

However, the reader will by now appreciate that marketing is much more than mere advertising alone and this criticism is therefore based on a false premise. The idea that the attainment of a customer focus would somehow result in a drop in the quality of provision is frankly obtuse. There are, however, still a significant number of organizations that have failed to grasp the value of marketing as a concept and this objection is unfortunately still commonly encountered.

'Marketing is Immoral'

This objection also stems from a fundamental misunderstanding of the marketing concept. It is often raised because marketing is seen as manipulating consumers into purchasing goods and services that they don't really need. The origins of this objection are rooted in a failure to grasp the difference between marketing and sales. It is certainly true that a sales-oriented organization continually strives to persuade customers to buy as much of their product or service as possible. Such organizations are little concerned with the genuine needs of customers. Market-oriented organizations, on the other hand, have realized that such an emphasis is ultimately self-defeating. Instead they focus on supplying customers with the services they actually need and make it clear who their target groups actually are, in an attempt to avoid unnecessary purchases by those who would be better served by another organization. If this sounds a little trite, it is worth remembering that this is simply good business practice. Dissatisfied customers are estimated to discuss their experiences with an average of seven close friends, relatives, and colleagues. Making a sale at any cost can hence result in a significant amount of negative word-of-mouth 'advertising' and is ultimately self-defeating.

'Marketing will Stifle Innovation'

This criticism is a little more subtle. It is raised by those who argue that a marketing-oriented organization will attempt to serve studiously the needs of its target markets. It will concentrate harder on trying to exactly match its products/services with the profile of those demanded by its customers. In doing so, however, it will be unlikely to devote much time and effort to the development of radical new initiatives which could ultimately benefit society as a whole. Consumers do not generally enjoy change and are hence unlikely to suggest it to market researchers if asked.

Clearly there is a danger that marketing could force an organization unwittingly into a form of management myopia, but this pitfall is perhaps more relevant to a business organization where profit is the prime consideration. Since new product development is an inherently risky strategy, a business organization will tend to demand considerable evidence that an investment in a new product/service is likely to pay off. In the nonprofit context, however, one could legitimately argue that managers have considerably more latitude in terms of how they choose to fulfil an organization's mission, particularly where there is a separation of resource attraction and resource allocation. While one still has to be conscious that funders have their own agenda and would not wish to see a nonprofit engage in unnecessary risk, it is certainly true that some funders may actually encourage the organization they are supporting to be innovative. This is the case with much arts funding; indeed, evidence of the ability to innovate may well be one criterion to be awarded such funding in the first place.

In essence these are the typical objections that are raised to marketing in a nonprofit context. Those readers who are interested in learning more about specific objections raised in the context of healthcare or education are advised to consult Kotler and Clarke (1987) or Kotler and Fox (1985).

The Development of the Marketing Concept: Products, Sales, and Marketing Orientations

Marketing ideas and concepts are not new—the underlying concepts have been around for centuries. As long ago as 1776, Adam Smith, widely regarded as the father of modern economics, remarked that:

Consumption is the sole end and purpose of all production; and the interest of the producer ought to be attended to, only so far as it may be necessary for promoting that of the consumer. The maxim is so perfectly self-evident that it would be absurd to attempt to prove it. But in the mercantile system, the interest of the consumer is almost constantly sacrificed to that of the producer; and it seems to consider production, not consumption, as the ultimate end and object of all industry and commerce.

'Perfectly self evident' this concept may be, but in some quarters little appears to have changed over the past 230 years! Indeed it was not until comparatively recently that the idea of focusing on the needs and wants of consumers has come to the fore. Up to the beginning of the twentieth century much of British industry could be criticized for concentrating excessively on the economics of production. With an almost insatiable demand worldwide for the goods and services it could produce, there was little need to focus on consumer needs, as someone somewhere would undoubtedly want the product. It is therefore no surprise to find

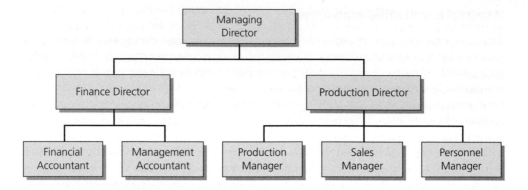

Figure 2.3 Structure of a typical sales production-oriented organization

that management theorists of the time were concerned with concepts such as efficiency and regarded management as a pure science which could be explored and developed in an attempt to find 'the one best way of doing things'. Organizations from around this time could therefore be regarded as being production-oriented. A typical structure for such an organization is given in Figure 2.3.

With the recession of the 1920s and 1930s, however, producers suddenly found themselves facing a considerable slump in demand. Being an efficient producer was no longer enough to guarantee survival. The efficient production of inventory which could not be sold was a sure route to disaster. In recognition of this, a change in emphasis evolved. The sales function within the organization began to take on a new significance. A typical organization structure for what might be termed a sales-oriented organization is shown in Figure 2.4.

Once again, organizations of the time were little concerned with the actual needs and wants of consumers. The focus was largely on how best to sell what the company could

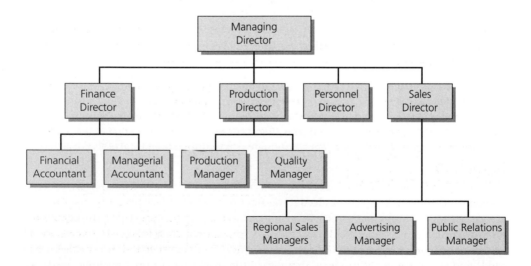

Figure 2.4 Structure of a typical sales-oriented organization

produce. It is worth noting in Figure 2.4 how the sales function has risen to a more dominant position and appears to embrace all forms of contact with the customer, including the provision of customer service. The division between sales and the advertising and PR function is also worthy of note, particularly as the latter function was perceived as being of far less significance. This is a division typical of the time and it reflects the dominant paradigm—the fervent desire to sell product to the customers.

It is interesting to note that while few genuinely production-oriented organizations remain in business today, there are a large number of sales-oriented organizations still in existence. Those organizations that have retained a sales orientation tend to be those that provide a product/service that will only ever have to be purchased once. It could therefore be argued that the concept of customer satisfaction is less important since the organization will not be looking to solicit a repurchase. Such a philosophy ignores the fact that consumers talk to one another, and organizations can very quickly obtain a poor reputation for customer service. If you would like some proof of this, compile your own list of organizations that you consider to be sales-oriented and ask a colleague to do likewise. My guess is that a comparison of both lists will reveal considerable similarity.

After the Second World War, the pattern of world trade was changed irrevocably. By the early 1950s, companies in the UK, for example, suddenly found themselves competing with organizations in America, Japan, and a revitalized Europe. Consumers were faced with a considerable choice of producer from whom to purchase. Moreover, the mushrooming of the mass media made consumers more generally aware of the range of purchase options open to them. Faced with this choice, consumers were finally able to exercise considerable power over producers and to elect to purchase only from those that they felt would adequately service their needs.

To be truly successful in these newly competitive markets, organizations needed to focus on customer needs and ensure that they met those needs better than any of the competition. Organizations therefore finally began to recognize the importance of developing a customer or market focus, and a new type of organization began to emerge. Figure 2.5 illustrates a structure typical of a market-oriented organization.

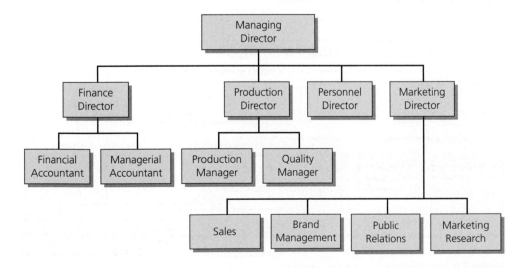

Figure 2.5 Structure of a typical marketing-oriented organization

This new type of organization placed a high emphasis on the collection of marketing research and its use to identify customer needs. This information would then be used to inform new product development, to develop appropriate pricing strategies, to make the product accessible to the market, and, finally, to promote the advantages that it could offer the consumer and reassure them that it could meet their needs. As a result, the sales function is no longer of such importance. Indeed, if the marketing is handled correctly there may be no need to 'sell' the product at all—it should 'sell' itself. It is interesting to note, therefore, that the sales function in this example has now been subordinated to marketing in recognition that selling is simply one component of an overall marketing mix.

Operationalizing the Marketing Concept

In the brief history of marketing described above, the term 'market orientation' was introduced. A market-oriented organization is in essence one that has embraced the marketing concept and successfully operationalized it. Kotler and Clarke (1987) define marketing orientation as follows: 'A marketing orientation holds that the main task of the organization is to determine the needs and wants of target markets and to satisfy them through the design, communication, pricing and delivery of appropriate and competitively viable products and services.'

While this definition makes it clear what market orientation is, it offers little insight into how it might be achieved. Kohli and Jaworski (1990) thus prefer to define it as 'The generation of appropriate market intelligence pertaining to current and future customer needs, and the relative abilities of competitive entities to satisfy these needs; the integration and dissemination of such intelligence across departments; and the coordinated design and execution of the organization's strategic response to market opportunities.'

Narver and Slater (1990) have usefully distilled the definition given above into three behavioural strands, namely customer orientation, competitor orientation, and interfunctional coordination, and argue that all three should be regarded as being of equal importance. These are illustrated in Figure 2.6.

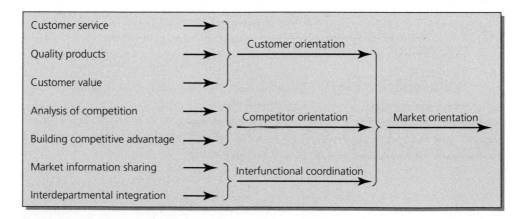

Figure 2.6 The components of market orientation

Source: adapted from Deng and Dart (1994).

Customer orientation involves the organization in achieving a sufficient understanding of its target markets to be able to create superior value for them. Since in a service environment the creation of value is often highly dependent on the quality of customer interactions with staff, the achievement of a market orientation thus involves the development of an appropriate set of cultural attitudes that should ultimately permeate the whole organization (Deshpande and Webster 1989).

The concept of a competitor orientation involves the organization in understanding the short-term strengths/weaknesses and long-term capabilities/strategies of both its current and future competitors. This is essential if the organization is to avoid being overtaken by competitive innovation (see, for example, Porter (1985)).

Interfunctional coordination refers to how the organization utilizes its internal resources in the creation of superior value for target consumers. It is important, for example, for opportunities for synergy to be exploited across traditional departmental boundaries and for customer and competitive intelligence to be shared constructively between all those who stand to benefit. Kohli and Jaworski (1990) expand on the concept of interfunctional coordination in a detailed study of a number of market-oriented organizations. The authors suggest that such organizations can be characterized as having:

- a close integration of the marketing function into the organizational structure and strategic planning process;
- a primary identification with the organization as a whole rather than individual departments;
- inter-departmental relations based on cooperation rather than rivalry.

It is important to recognize that the preceding discussion is of more than simply theoretical interest. A succession of studies have now demonstrated links between the extent to which an organization has successfully operationalized the marketing concept (i.e. its degree of market orientation) and its performance relative to others operating in the same sector. It is also important to note that while the majority of these have been conducted in the for-profit context, there is now an emerging body of literature that suggests it is equally well related to many facets of the performance of nonprofit organizations.

For this reason in the next section we shall examine each of Narver and Slater's behavioural strands in more detail, and suggest how each of these behaviours might be inculcated.

Achieving a Customer Focus

The achievement of a customer focus, particularly among recipient groups, has traditionally been harder for many nonprofits to accomplish because staff and even volunteers have historically failed to value them. While this sounds a little counter-intuitive given the ethos of many voluntary organizations, Bruce (1995) suggests that there are a number of reasons why this should be so, including the following.

Monopolistic Position
The position of many nonprofits in the market is one of a monopoly supplier. There can therefore be a danger that customers are so reliant on their services that such organizations may adopt a 'take it or leave it' attitude and fail to take the time to adapt their offerings to individual needs.

Demand far Exceeds Supply

Often even where competition does exist, the demand in many nonprofit markets for the services the organization can supply is so great that they can never hope to meet even a fraction of it. The temptation here for nonprofits is to tackle the most homogeneous categories of need, since these are usually easier to serve in volume with an undifferentiated service. There may be occasions, however, when such categories of need are not the most pressing and smaller groups of customers with more acute levels of need may find themselves ill-served by the standard services available.

Patronizing Attitude of 'Haves' to 'Have Nots'

There is a particular danger of this phenomenon in markets where the demand is high for the service provided. Service delivery staff may take the view that recipients are lucky to be among the 'chosen few' and should by implication feel only gratitude towards the supplying organization. The idea that recipients have the right to express any form of negative comment or criticism remains anathema to many.

Professional Training Encourages the View that 'I Know What's Best for You'

Many nonprofit service providers are highly trained professionals, who possess expert knowledge in their field. They may therefore feel that they have a complete understanding of the needs of the recipient and thereby not be sensitive to signs of differing individual need.

Motivation of Belief-Based Organizations

Nonprofits whose mission is to promote certain behaviours because of religious beliefs may fail to take a true account of the needs of their recipients. Service providers may strive to inculcate behaviour patterns that directly conflict with what the recipients perceive to be their needs. There is, of course, nothing inherently wrong with this approach, as it may cut to the heart of the reason for the nonprofit's existence, but even the most zealous of religiously oriented organizations may find their path somewhat easier if they begin by understanding current customer requirements. It is so much easier to plan a strategy if one understands where one is starting from.

Action-Oriented Approach

Historically one of the greatest strengths of the voluntary sector has been its ability to respond rapidly to changing patterns of need. Unconstrained by government bureaucracy or the profit needs of shareholders, voluntary organizations have been able to take immediate action, specifically tailored at a local level to alleviate the distress and/or suffering of those in need. While the speed of response may legitimately be regarded as a very real strength, there are also key difficulties that can be encountered with this approach. Principal among these is the fact that fundamental a priori customer research is not widespread throughout the sector. This in turn can create a situation where the solutions proposed by voluntary organizations are sub-optimal from a customer's perspective because their real needs have not been fully understood.

Bruce is clearly not optimistic about the ability of nonprofits to achieve a genuine customer focus among their beneficiary groups. In many cases there remain very real difficulties to be overcome. Nevertheless, the culture within the nonprofit sector is changing and it is fair to say that a great many organizations are now becoming increasingly focused on the task of satisfying their customers.

Developing a Competitor Orientation

The first step in developing a competitor orientation is once again research. Organizations with strong competitor orientations continually evaluate their positions in respect of each of their key competitors, in order to discover areas of strength and weakness and to find ways of strengthening their own competitive advantage (see for example Bennett (2003)). The only way that this can be achieved is through the creation of an effective competitor monitoring system, which generates benchmarking data in respect of each key aspect of competitor operations and alerts the organization to actual and potential competitive innovations. This benchmarking data allows a nonprofit organization to compare factors such as those listed below.

Its Own Portfolio of Provision Against Other Actual or Potential Providers
While an often insatiable demand for nonprofit services ensures that most adequately managed organizations will continue to have the capability to provide some form of service to their client groups, some organizations may be guilty of providing services which might be more effectively provided by others in the market. Nonprofits, perhaps more than any other category of organization (by virtue of their use of third-party funds), have a duty to ensure that they provide the most appropriate range of services to their recipient groups. They can only achieve this by monitoring competitive strengths and concentrating only on those areas where they have a comparative advantage. This may take the form of specialist expertise most closely suited to one form of need, or it may, for example, be the ease of access to one category of recipient group. A competitor orientation can hence optimize the use of resources across the sector as a whole and maximize the potential benefit to society as a result.

The Costs of Providing Goods and Services to Their Recipient Groups
The level of need that a nonprofit is able to cater for compared to other service providers will not only be of concern to management but also to potential funders. Most will want to ensure that their funding is directed to the organization that is likely to have the most impact on the target beneficiary group. It is thus no surprise to learn that most charitable trusts require quite detailed information about the category and level of need that will be serviced before their trustees will reach a decision in respect of whether an application for funding will be granted.

The Costs of Fundraising
All nonprofits that have to fundraise to conduct their primary activity should be concerned with the relative efficiency of each form of fundraising activity. They will want, for example, to ascertain from which sources major competitors derive their income and the fundraising techniques (such as direct mail, telemarketing, etc.) used to solicit it. A comparison of both the sources of funding utilized and the expenditures on each fundraising technique relative to income generated will aid management in targeting future scarce fundraising resources more effectively (see for example Sargeant et al. 2006).

The design of a competitive information system and the gathering of competitive and benchmarking data are but the first stages in developing a competitor orientation. Having gathered information about other providers in the market, or key competitors for funding, the next stage is to use it to the organization's own advantage. Profiling competitor strengths and weaknesses can allow an organization to see where its performance lags behind the competition, but it can also highlight areas where it either outperforms the competition, *or has the capacity to do so.* These areas are key, because they could represent a major source of competitive advantage that an organization has over its rivals. This can then form the basis of extremely powerful communications with all the categories of customer with whom the organization has contact. For example, if an organization by virtue of its extensive network of volunteers has the potential to be the lowest-cost provider in a given market, this fact needs to be communicated strongly to all potential funders who will undoubtedly be looking for the organization that can make the most effective use of their resources. Similarly, if an organization has the leading researchers working in a particular field on its payroll, this fact should be emphasized to both recipients and funders alike because it has the capacity clearly to identify the organization as a market leader and therefore position it as being the most worthy of support/patronage.

There are a number of bases that can be used to develop a competitive advantage. These include:

Low Cost
The key to the competitive advantage here is the fact that the organization can provide goods/services at a lower cost than their major competitors.

Service Quality/Content
Some organizations may elect to differentiate the standard of care they provide to donors and/or their recipient groups. They may strive to make the service in some way unique in areas that are important to their customers. To be truly sustainable, however, these distinctions in service quality/content should be difficult for competitors to emulate.

Access to Resources
As in the example quoted above, many nonprofits possess specialist expertise. This expertise in itself can serve to differentiate the organization from potential competitors in the minds of funders and recipients.

Access to Recipients
The channels used to deliver some services may be long and complex. Many charities dealing with developing countries, for example, have complex infrastructures which enable them to reach the most needy societies at comparatively short notice if disaster strikes. This flexibility of response can in itself form the basis of a competitive advantage, as speed may be of primary importance to funders and recipients alike.

Of course this list is not exhaustive but it does serve to illustrate one key point. If an organization is not clear about why it is distinctive, neither will its potential funders or the recipients of the goods and services provided. In the case of the former, this will lead to cash shortages as funds are diverted to other organizations that are perceived as being more deserving. In the case of the latter, those most in need of the support of the organization may be reluctant to come forward to seek the help that could be available, because they fail to understand what is unique about the provision and hence why it might match their need.

Enhancing Inter-Functional Coordination: Internal Marketing

Over the years much has been written about how enhancements could be made to the level of cooperation taking place between different departments within an organization. In recent years however a small body of literature has been building up which suggests that the key to achieving this enhancement might lie in applying the same marketing tools and concepts *within* an organization that have traditionally only been employed *outside* the organization, in its dealings with external customers. Not surprisingly, this paradigm has come to be known as 'internal marketing'.

The concept of internal marketing is based on one simple premise:

satisfied employees = satisfied customers

If one is able to recruit and maintain a motivated workforce and inculcate within them an understanding of the organization's mission and the needs and wants of its external customers, the argument runs that positive improvements in the quality of service provided by those employees to their customers should result. Moreover, if employees can be encouraged to view *other employees* in the service chain as their customers and treat them with the standards of care normally reserved for external customers, overall levels of morale should begin to rise as everyone within the organization begins to notice an improvement in the quality of service provided to them by other members of staff. The resultant 'customer'-driven culture, it is argued, should have a knock-on effect into dealings with external customers, who should also notice a difference in the quality of service provided.

The reader will doubtless be relieved to discover that there is now a sizeable body of evidence to suggest that this is indeed the case (see for example Berry 1987; Bowen and Schneider 1985; Grönroos 1981; Tansuhaj et al. 1988). The quality of employee interaction *is* strongly correlated with perceived (external) service quality. Indeed, the quality of the delivered service will be strongly correlated with the extent to which:

- employees feed back information to management in respect of customer requirements;
- management and staff pool their expertise to match service specifications to the needs of the target customer groups;
- staff are encouraged to deliver to the service standards set and, moreover, receive the support of their colleagues, where necessary, to do so;
- staff are kept regularly informed of the content of external communications and have the opportunity to feed back their views on the same to management.

Internal marketing activity can help facilitate each of these processes. So what exactly does the term 'internal marketing' mean? It has been variously described as 'viewing employees as internal customers, viewing jobs as internal products that satisfy the wants of these internal customers while addressing the objectives of the organization' (Berry 1981); 'a philosophy for managing the organization's human resources based on a marketing perspective' (George and Grönroos 1989); 'the spreading of the responsibility for all marketing activity across all functions of the organization and the proactive application of marketing principles to "selling the staff" on their role in providing customer satisfaction within a supportive organizational environment' (Gilmore and Carson 1995); and '(describing) the work done by the company to train and motivate its internal customers, namely its customer contact employees and supporting service personnel to work as a team to provide customer satisfaction' (Kotler and Keller 2006).

At the heart of these various definitions lie two basic principles. First, internal marketing is seen as a mechanism for spreading the responsibility for marketing across the whole organization, while the second key idea is that to achieve this effectively each employee should be encouraged to regard their successor in the service chain as an internal customer, not merely as a colleague.

Other authors such as George (1990) have chosen to focus on the two roles that internal marketing can perform in an organization. First, it may be viewed as a tool to help individuals understand the significance of their roles and to create an awareness of how these roles relate to others within the organization. The aim of this approach is to improve cross-functional coordination and cooperation. Second, it can help to promote, develop, and sustain the ethos of customer service for internal as well as external customers. Piercy and Morgan (1994: 5), meanwhile, propose a rather more elaborate set of internal marketing 'goals':

- gaining the support of key decision makers for organizational plans;
- changing the attitudes and behaviours of employees and managers who are working at key interfaces with customers and distributors;
- gaining commitment to making the marketing plan work;
- managing incremental changes in the culture from 'the way we always do things' to 'the way we need to do things to be successful'.

Internal marketing thus has a variety of benefits to offer a nonprofit organization. Of course, identifying goals and benefits is one thing—making them a reality quite another. To aid in this, there are a variety of techniques that could legitimately be regarded as components of internal marketing. Helpfully, Grönroos (1981) draws a distinction between what he sees as the strategic and tactical levels of internal marketing. While these levels should not be viewed as being carved in stone, because what are strategic issues for some will only be tactical concerns for others (and vice versa), it does constitute a useful framework within which to group the essential ideas. The next sections discuss Grönroos's idea.

Strategic Internal Marketing

Grönroos argues that each of the following dimensions of organizational management can be regarded as strategic internal marketing activity.

Adoption of Supportive Management Styles

If an internal marketing programme is to be developed and implemented, it must have the complete support and backing of senior management. Encouraging staff to view colleagues and volunteers as customers requires a major change in organizational thinking and without top-level support the change is unlikely to occur. Staff need to be given the necessary time to develop internal service standards and plan ways in which performance could be monitored against them. This will only occur if senior staff are seen to support the initiative.

Supportive Personnel Policies

One of the fundamental ideas underlying internal marketing is that individuals should be matched with the job(s) to which they are most suited. This requires careful recruitment, job, and career planning for all individuals within an organization. Many nonprofits have always put effort into attracting personnel with the right skills and attitudes for customer-facing roles, but perhaps rather less effort is typically applied to matching the right 'type' of person to the right job role internally, even if skill sets can be seen to match.

Customer Service Training

Critical to the achievement of a market orientation is customer service training. Staff need to understand the importance of both internal and external customers and how they should be treated. It is helpful if staff are developed from the outset with this form of training as they can then be involved in the setting of appropriate service standards and the monitoring thereof. In short, they should be allowed to 'own' the process and hence not fear the results that might accrue. One of the key mistakes made by many organizations initiating a customer focus for the first time is that the systems that should be used to monitor and enhance service standards are used only as a stick to beat staff with who are seen to be 'underperforming'. This is one way of guaranteeing considerable resistance to change.

Customer-Focused Planning Procedures

The author was introduced some years ago to a model known as the 'iceberg of ignorance'. Based on research, it posits the simple idea that the higher up an individual might be in their organizational heirarchy, the more 'ignorant' they are likely to be of the requirements of their customers. It's an interesting idea since taken to its logical conclusion it would suggest that to get on in this life, one should aspire to ignorance! Perhaps more constructively, however, the iceberg provides a very graphic illustration of a concept, an understanding of which still manages to elude many organizations. The idea is presented visually in Figure 2.7.

At the bottom of the iceberg are positioned the front line staff who, as a consequence of their job role, have a good understanding of the customer's requirements and problems. In the case of most service providers, these individuals are interacting with customers on a daily basis and if problems are encountered they will be the first to be aware of them. The higher up the iceberg you climb, the less in touch personnel become. A typical charity director will only be acquainted with around 1 per cent of the problems experienced by recipients of his/her goods/services. Even the lowest levels of managerial staff may get to learn of only 25 per cent of the problems/difficulties experienced by their customers.

It is therefore perverse that many organizations continue to plan the future of their organizations from the top down. In reality those who have the most responsibility for strategic planning often have the least understanding of the key issues at stake. For this reason, the

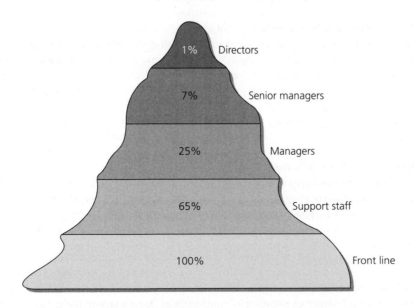

Figure 2.7 The iceberg of ignorance

adoption of an internal marketing perspective should facilitate the involvement of staff at all levels within an organization in the planning process. While it may be physically impossible (and probably not very desirable!) for all staff to be present when strategy is decided upon, there is absolutely no excuse for not seeking input and/or suggestions from those staff most frequently interacting with customers, as one of the first steps in the planning process.

Tactical Internal Marketing

Tactical internal marketing considerations include the following.

Training

While a commitment to customer service training should often be considered a strategic issue, as it will concern all individuals within an organization, there is also a case for investment in informal and ongoing training, the requirements of which will be specific to particular divisions or functions. Periodic training of volunteer fundraisers, for example, would fall under this general heading.

Encouragement of Informal and Interactive Communication

Staff from different functional areas within the organization should be encouraged to communicate with each other informally, as well as formally, in the course of performing their job role. Any form of communication that gets away from the traditional 'memo' would be desirable. Inter-disciplinary meetings, social events, and the informal monitoring of internal service levels should facilitate this goal. One voluntary sector organization recently built the factor 'delivery against internal service standards' into its criteria for the award of performance-related pay. This encouraged staff from all departments to develop informal links and communicate more effectively with each other, thereby maximizing the likelihood of improving overall performance in this key area.

Formal Internal Communications

Formal internal communications include newsletters, updates, intranets, briefing documents, etc. These serve a useful purpose in that they can convey developments to staff economically and explain often complex changes to the nature of service provision. The better of these communications also serve to promote a feeling of organizational identity rather than a series of departmental identities, which can often lead to internal conflict and competition.

Internal Market Research

A prerequisite to the attainment of internal customer satisfaction is understanding those elements of the service that are perceived as being most important and concentrating efforts accordingly. While this might sound a little obvious, many nonprofit organizations have been slow to recognize that volunteers in particular usually come to an organization with a series of expectations and requirements, which if not met (at least in part) will lead to the high attrition rates among volunteers currently experienced by many within the sector. Internal market research should therefore be regarded as essential.

Cross-Disciplinary Teams

This is a further technique that can be used to promote greater cooperation between departments. Teams are brought together of staff working in often quite disparate sections of the organization. These teams work together to solve quality and/or other organizational problems and report back their suggestions to management. Staff thereby have the opportunity to work with others and to understand a variety of different organizational perspectives.

Staff Secondments

Some organizations approach the problem of inter-functional coordination in a rather different way. They allow staff to experience what it might be like to work in another department with which they will ultimately have much contact, by seconding them there for a period of several weeks or months. This allows them to experience first-hand problems of internal service quality and to see these difficulties from the perspective of their internal customer.

Suggestion Schemes

The question of staff input to the strategic planning process has been dealt with above. In most organizations, however, the planning process (if it happens at all) will tend to happen only once, or at most twice, a year. In such circumstances a mechanism for communicating good ideas to senior managers quickly and efficiently may well be called for. Ideas are often collected centrally in a box, or a hotline is provided to staff so that they can speak directly to a senior executive. Staff suggestion schemes sometimes, but not always, reward the best of the ideas presented.

Once again this list is in no way exhaustive, but it should serve to provide an appreciation of the many techniques that can be used to promote inter-functional coordination and thereby enhance the overall level of market orientation attained.

Market versus Societal Orientation

As we noted above, a number of authors have studied the difference that achieving a market orientation can make to the performance of nonprofit organizations. The education sector appears to have attracted the most attention, and various authors have identified links between market orientation and the degree to which an institution can attract and retain students (see, for example, Caruana et al. 1998). Bennett (1998) has also explored the issue in the context of fundraising and identified a link between market orientation and fundraising performance in small/medium-sized UK charities.

It should be noted, however, that these and other studies begin from the fundamental assumption that it is appropriate to seek to achieve a market orientation in a nonprofit context. While I have elaborated on this in some depth there are a number of reasons why the notion of a nonprofit market orientation might be questioned.

First, the market orientation construct was an attempt to operationalize for-profit definitions of marketing that were developed in large commercial organizations in the mid-1960s. Very different definitions of marketing have been developed in the nonprofit context and attempting to operationalize Kotler and Levy's 'sensitively serving and satisfying human need', for example, is likely to have a very different outcome from operationalizing the definition of marketing provided by the Chartered Institute of Marketing.

Similarly, some of the terminology used in the for-profit context does not transfer well to the nonprofit arena. The very term 'market orientation' implies an orientation towards markets. Even though one could argue that nonprofits have a market for resource acquisition and a market for resource allocation, these are often not markets in the economic sense of the term. In fact, as Hansmann (1980) notes, nonprofits can often be seen as a response to a very particular form of market failure.

The second key argument for revising the terminology in this context is that the notion of 'market' implies that some form of exchange will take place between the supplier and the recipient of goods and services. There are a plethora of occasions when nonprofit organizations do exchange monetary value with the recipients of their goods or services (or even a warm feeling in return for donations), however there are also many occasions when the notion of exchange has little meaning. The recipients of international aid exchange nothing except their need and gratitude with their supplying organization.

The components of market orientation are also problematic in the nonprofit context. While a focus on customers is still important, in the nonprofit context (as was explained earlier) organizations are often less concerned with customer satisfaction per se than they are with the notion of longer-term benefit to society. It is thus necessary to broaden the focus on customers to address the needs of a wider range of stakeholders and perhaps even society as a whole.

Competition is also different in the nonprofit arena. Demand for nonprofit goods and services is often so insatiable that to regard other organizations as direct competitors would be ludicrous (Bruce 1995). Naturally there are occasions when competition is of significance—when, for example, organizations compete for funds—but it is often the case in relation to service delivery that potential collaboration between organizations is more of an issue than competition per se.

It has also been argued that to serve sensitively the needs of society, nonprofits must be responsive to such needs. While businesses too must be responsive, in the nonprofit context it is the rapidity of this response that defines many organizations. This is accomplished because there is no requirement to consider either the political consequences of action or the financial returns that might accrue to shareholders. Nonprofits have the necessary freedom, flexibility, and moral imperative to respond quickly to the dictates of social need and must ensure that they do so if the maximum benefit to society is to accrue (Jordan 1964; Dahrendorf 1997).

In recognition of these difficulties, Sargeant et al. (2002) propose the alternative framework of 'societal orientation' illustrated in Figure 2.8. The model is offered as an attempt to

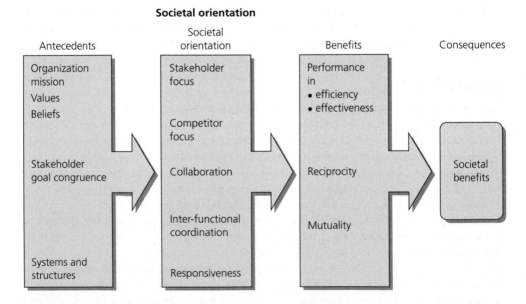

Figure 2.8 Model of societal orientation

Source: Sargeant et al. (2002), *Journal of Nonprofit and Public Sector Marketing,* Vol. 10, No. 2, 41–65.

operationalize the Kotler and Levy definition of marketing referred to earlier. In this case the authors have delineated the societal orientation construct itself and included what they regarded as the antecedents of a societal orientation and the benefits and consequences thereof.

Considering first the antecedents, the authors argue that nonprofits will only be able to achieve a societal orientation if they have a strong, clear mission that reflects the goals of the organization's key stakeholder groups. Similarly, these goals should be common (i.e. shared) across all the stakeholder groups and the nonprofit must have established appropriate systems and structures in place to ensure that they are in a position to be achieved.

In respect of benefits, the authors posit that societally oriented organizations will achieve significantly higher performance than those without such an orientation. In the nonprofit context, this means that nonprofits would be (a) more effective in achieving their mission and (b) make more efficient use of resources in doing so.

According to the authors, however, these should not be viewed as the only outcomes from the successful attainment of a societal orientation. An additional dimension derives from the division between resource acquisition and resource allocation; a defining characteristic for many nonprofit organizations. Those individuals who supply an organization's funding are not necessarily those who will derive the primary benefit therefrom. One of the primary outcomes from the attainment of a societal orientation can therefore be the bringing together of these two groups, resulting in a mutual exchange of values, ideas, and a sense of identity. The authors refer to this as reciprocity and mutuality.

Operationalizing Societal Orientation

Since both the market and societal orientation constructs share common dimensions we shall focus here on two critical differences, namely the need to focus on stakeholders rather than customers and the way in which organizations might assess the impact of a change in their orientation, in other words measures of nonprofit performance.

Stakeholder Analysis

The notion that organizations have stakeholders rather than merely customers is far from new. The concept of a 'stakeholder' has been traced to the Stanford research Institute and is almost half a century old. Freeman and Reed (1983) identify an internal document from the Institute dating back to 1963 that appears to be the earliest example of this usage. The document delineated customers, shareholders, employees, suppliers, lenders, and society and it is clear that these early writers were therefore employing quite a broad definition of the term.

Freeman (1984: 46) defines stakeholders as 'all of those groups and individuals that can affect, or are affected by, the accomplishment of organizational purpose'. The first task in operationalizing the societal orientation construct therefore lies in identifying relevant stakeholder groups and assessing their significance to the organization. The impact of different groups on the organization's ability to fulfil its mission will be very different as will the power that these various groups can exert over decision makers such as managers or trustees. It is therefore essential that nonprofits give careful consideration to an identification of relevant groups and their various needs and aspirations. From this the organization can move to an analysis of how focused it is on the needs of each group and the extent to which this

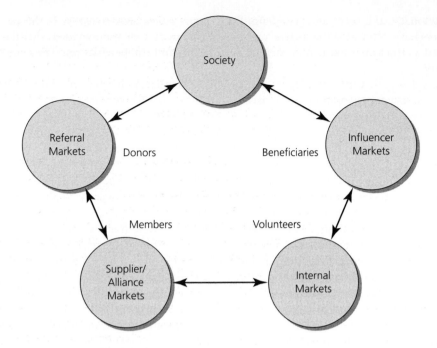

Figure 2.9 A stakeholder model

Source: adapted From Payne, A., Ballantyne, D. and Christopher, M. (2005) 'A Stakeholder Approach To Relationship Marketing Strategy: The Development and Use of the Six Markets Model,' *European Journal of Marketing,* 39(7/8): 855–871. Reproduced with kind permission.

should change in the future. Strategies can then be developed for making any changes that are felt to be necessary.

To assist in this process Payne et al. (2005) propose a simple framework that may be used to structure the identification of key stakeholders. Their original model delineated six market domains that included customer markets, referral markets, supplier and alliance markets, influence markets, recruitment markets, and internal markets. In Figure 2.9 we amend their approach to make it of more relevance to nonprofit organizations. We thus examine it in two halves, taking account of the broader range of stakeholders addressed by a typical nonprofit.

1. Customer Groups

   There are four primary categories of nonprofit 'customers' that will typically be of interest, namely:

   a. Donors: including individuals, businesses, trusts, foundations, local and national government. Each group may be further sub-divided into existing and potential supporters.

   b. Member markets: some organizations are supported by a membership base rather than donors per se and this can comprise individuals, businesses, or both. As with donors, both existing and potential member markets should be considered.

   c. Volunteer markets: again, it is necessary to segment this by looking specifically at both existing and potential volunteer markets. The needs of each group may be different and the extent to which an organization is recruitment or retention focused will be a key issue for management.

DEVELOPING A SOCIETAL AND MARKET ORIENTATION

    d. Beneficiary markets: each major category of beneficiary should also be identified, with a particular emphasis on those whose needs are most closely aligned with the mission of the nonprofit. Both current and future beneficiary groups should be considered.

2. Wider Stakeholders

There are also five wider categories of stakeholder that could potentially be of interest, namely:

    a. Society: the needs of the local community, sections of the community, or the wider society in which the organization operates should be delineated.

    b. Referral markets: these include both existing customers who recommend the non-profit to others and non-customer referrals which might come from related non-profit groups, local agencies, or the general public. It will be key for the nonprofit to look at each customer group and identify any pattern in where referrals come from in each case.

    c. Influencer markets: these might include other nonprofits with related (or opposing) missions, sector bodies, regulatory bodies, sector press and media, national press/media, and political/government agencies.

    d. Supplier and alliance markets: a nonprofit will also want to identify key suppliers to the organization and any groups or organizations that it collaborates with in the fulfil-ment of its mission. As previously it must examine needs and aspirations in each case.

    e. Internal markets: finally the nonprofit will want to identify groups within the organiza-tion whose needs should be considered. Payne et al. (2005) suggest that these could be segmented by function, job role, geography, and level of seniority. It may be relevant to look at both existing internal markets, and the stakeholders involved in their recruit-ment, such as executive search companies, employment agencies, and job centres.

These suggestions are obviously not exhaustive, but the advantage of the framework, like so many in marketing, is that it compels the manager to think in a structured way about the environment in which the organization is operating. The nine headings can be used to facil-itate a brainstorming exercise getting managers to focus on identifying relevant stakeholders in each category in turn.

Having identified them, the next step is to review the needs of each group and to assess the current and proposed level of emphasis on each. Not all stakeholders require the same degree of attention and managers need to prioritize and establish the appropriate mix of relation-ships needed for success (Gummesson, 1994).

To achieve this Payne et al. (2005) propose the use of a stakeholder network map. The map illustrates each of the major domains on a series of axes, enabling a group of managers within an organization to make an assessment of the current and desired levels of emphasis on each category. The authors suggest that this mapping can be achieved by using a jury of executive opinion. This recognizes that while individual perspectives may vary, there is frequently a strong degree of consensus within an organization. The scale of 1(low) and 10 (high) reflects the degree of emphasis placed on each market. In the example below (see Figure 2.10), a net-work map has been created with each of the two groups of stakeholders.

In this example it appears that the nonprofit has been too focused on the recruitment of new supporters, to the detriment of a focus on retention. It also seems clear that a greater focus on influencers is required in the future, as is more of a focus on internal markets and the society the nonprofit serves.

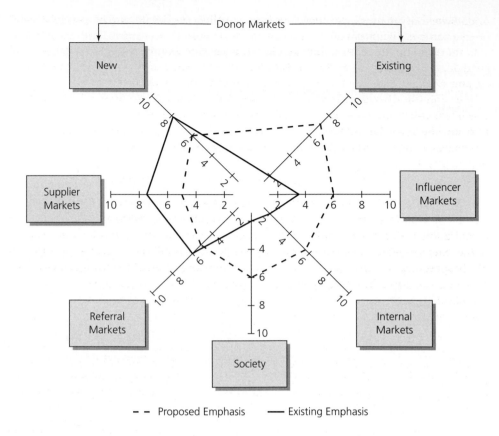

Figure 2.10 A case study

The key value that accrues from conducting an analysis of this kind is the organization develops a pattern of stakeholder focus that will facilitate the achievement of its mission and one that is also appropriate to the environment in which it is operating. As this environment will change over time it is essential that the analysis be repeated on a regular basis.

As a final step, the actions necessary for the organization to develop any change in emphasis that might be necessary can be outlined. The tools and techniques of relationship marketing may have much to offer in this context. This is a theme we will return to later in this text.

Assessing Nonprofit Performance

Academic interest in market orientation has arisen because of the need to somehow demonstrate marketing's worth. Studies of the link between market orientation and performance have thus proliferated with the overwhelming body of evidence now supporting the notion that market orientation matters, because it is either directly or indirectly related to performance. As we noted earlier, in the business context measures such as market share, profitability, sales growth, and customer satisfaction are frequently explored and related to market orientation. Its virtues have therefore been extolled on the basis that greater market orientation = greater profit.

In the nonprofit context our interest lies not in making a profit, but in achieving a social good defined by the mission. So in this sector, what measures of performance are appropriate and are these indeed linked to the degree of societal orientation attained?

In examining what measures may be appropriate it is helpful to draw a distinction between two critical dimensions of performance common across all sectors, namely effectiveness and efficiency. Effectiveness is the extent to which the organization may be said to be achieving its mission, while efficiency is the extent to which its resources are being applied in the optimal way.

In respect of effectiveness, three approaches to measurement are possible.

1. *Mission Directedness:* we have already noted in Chapter 1 that nonprofits define themselves not around financial returns, but rather around their mission. Any analysis of organizational effectiveness could therefore begin with an analysis of 'mission directedness' or the extent to which an organization may be said to be fulfilling its mission. While intuitively appealing, this approach is not without its difficulties, since for effectiveness to be assessed on this basis the measures of performance employed must be closely linked to an organization's mission. This isn't always as straightforward as it seems as the case study of the nature conservancy (see below) makes clear. Equally, how should a church measure its success? Its mission may require it to spread the word contained in the gospel, but what does this mean? Is it simply counting the number of attendees at church services, or is it somehow about the 'quality' of the faith or understanding of God's will they are able to generate? If it's the latter, how can this possibly be measured? In a unique study of the links between performance measures and missions Sheehan (1996) identified that very few nonprofits appeared to have developed appropriate performance measures.

2. *Achievement of Specific Objectives:* rather than measure mission directedness per se, some organizations have opted to assess the extent to which specific objectives have been met. In the church example we might therefore count attendees, frequent attendees, the number of new attendees, etc. We might also examine the age profile and the pattern of voluntary activities undertaken by church members. Again, while this is intuitive, it is an approach not without some difficulties in application. Perrow (1981) notes that in many cases a nonprofit's goals can be multiple, conflicting, and inconsistent, making it difficult to identify the most appropriate assessment measures. Those assessing effectiveness in this way therefore regard it as the balanced attainment of a variety of goals.

3. *Fit With Environment:* some writers advocate an approach which looks at the organization's impact on the key stakeholders we outlined earlier. Writers such as Connolly et al. (1980) and Padanyi and Gainer (2004) argue that measures of customer satisfaction should be used as measures of effectiveness. While this is inherently appealing from a marketing perspective, this approach too has its drawbacks. Notable here is the fact that some nonprofits exist to challenge behaviour or attitudes and are therefore not in the business of achieving client satisfaction per se. Others may have a multiplicity of different customer groups. It may be impossible to simultaneously satisfy the needs of them all.

Given the difficulties with each approach, it seems clear that to assess nonprofit effectiveness appropriately a variety of measures should be adopted (Herman 1990, Herman and Heimovics 1994).

THE NATURE CONSERVANCY

The Nature Conservancy is a leading conservation organization working around the world to protect ecologically important lands and waters. Since its creation in 1951 the Nature Conservancy has:

- protected more than 117 million acres of land and 5,000 miles of river around the world;
- operated more than 100 marine conservation projects in 21 countries and 22 US states;
- attracted about 1 million members and supporters;
- attracted more than 10,000 dedicated volunteers supporting on-the-ground conservation work;
- become the world's largest private conservation group.

In the year ending June 2006, the Conservancy attracted a staggering $517,879,431 in direct public support. Taken together, these various metrics paint an impressive picture of success, Despite this, in the early 1990s Sawhill and Williamson (2001) note that Conservancy managers began to realize that 'bucks and acres' were less than ideal measures of the organization's success in achieving its mission. Simply counting acres purchased or funds raised was not enough. They point out that since the Conservancy's goal was actually to preserve the diversity of life on earth, rather than either of these things, it had actually been 'falling short' every year of its existence. Extinction rates continued to be high.

> What particularly worried the Conservancy was the fact that species were declining even within its protected areas. For instance, several years after acquiring property around Schenob Brook, in Massachusetts, specifically to protect the remaining bog turtles, the population started to shrink. It turned out that activities outside the preserve were affecting the water on which the turtles depended. In response the Conservancy revisited its basic strategy. Instead of acquiring and protecting small parcels of land that harbour rare species—a Noah's Ark strategy—the organization began to work on preserving larger eco-systems (Sawhill and Williamson: 101).

The old 'acres protected' measure no longer made sense as there was no direct relationship between this and the quality of impact on conservation the organization was able to achieve. Equally, the 'bucks' measure had tended to push the Conservancy towards projects that appealed to donors. As an example, purchasing land near centres of population may have been a very attractive proposition for local donors, but it would not necessarily advance the Conservancy's mission.

As a consequence the organization developed a new family of performance measures, including capacity measures (e.g. fundraising revenue), activity measures (e.g. the number and nature of new projects launched), and the much more difficult impact measures. In respect of the latter, the Nature Conservancy now sets long-term goals for the abundance and geographic distribution of all biodiversity on Earth. These in turn are translated into nearer-term goals. Their current near-term goal is to conserve 'at least 10% of every major habitat type on Earth by 2015' (Nature Conservancy 2006, p7). The new capacity and activity measures had much in common with the old 'bucks and acres' approach, but the new focus on mission-related measures has had a profound effect on the strategy of the Conservancy.

Nonprofit efficiency is also very much an issue. As Drucker (1990) notes, the nonprofit organization has a duty towards its stakeholders to allocate its scarce resources to results, rather than to 'squander them on being righteous'. As we noted in the previous chapter, fundraising and administrative efficiency have generated the most interest of late, certainly in the popular press. Aside from fundraising and administration cost ratios, a number of authors have recommended calculating other measures such as percentage increases in certain categories of income or a 'collectiveness index' to measure the proportion of a nonprofit's total revenue raised by public contributions.

While all these measures of efficiency sound highly plausible, it should be noted that in practice it is very difficult to assess the relative performance of nonprofit organizations on any of these bases. To take an example, many sources of sector information now provide information about how much it costs an organization to raise one pound or the ratio of fundraising expenditure to total programme expenditure (FCE ratio) (Sargeant and Kaehler 1998).

The problem with these simplistic measures is that these ratios will vary:

1. By size of nonprofit, as there are real economies of scale in fundraising. This is the most significant driver of cost.

2. By category of nonprofit. In the UK it is a fact that it costs more to raise money for disability than it does for animal welfare or to end child abuse. Does this mean that a disability organization is less efficient than those in the other two sectors? Well technically yes, but the variation is well beyond the control of the individuals working there. It is due to the level of public interest and concern in the cause and says nothing about the quality of individual performance per se.

3. By the category of fundraising undertaken. Raising funds from corporates and grant-making bodies is considerably less expensive than raising funds from individuals, particularly through the medium of direct marketing. Unfortunately not every form of fundraising is open to every organization, so again these simplistic measures are problematic.

4. By the split between donor recruitment and donor development activity. Most nonprofits lose money on bringing donors into the organization for the first time. They generate significant returns when soliciting funds from their existing supporter base. Performance ratios will therefore be heavily impacted by the choice of where the fundraising effort will be directed in a given year.

5. By the income that is included in the calculation. As we will see in Chapter 9 legacies can be a highly significant source of income for a nonprofit and an arbitrary decision must therefore be made of whether to include income from legacies in these calculations or not. Since fundraising expenditure generates a significant number of legacies there is a strong argument for including it, but unfortunately this category of income is highly unpredictable. One large legacy can overnight transform an organization's fundraising team into the most efficient in the sector, yet would this really be a meaningful evaluation?

Nonprofit Performance and Societal Orientation

We posed the question earlier, 'is there a link between market/societal orientation and nonprofit performance?' As will now be clear this is not a simple question to answer, but the broad spectrum of evidence from the dozen or so studies that have addressed this issue is yes. There does appear to be a link between the degree of market/societal orientation and measures of performance such as fundraising efficiency, success in resource acquisition, peer reputation, and client satisfaction (e.g. Raju et al. 1995, Kumar et al. 1997, Voss and Voss, 2000, Vasquez et al. 2001, Padanyi and Gainer 2004). There remains a good deal of work to be done though on assessing the relationship between the orientation of an organization and the wider range of performance measures we discussed above.

That said, perhaps we shouldn't get too hung up on 'proving' the link between orientation and performance at all. It may sell academic papers to journal editors, but does it add much in terms of practical value? I would argue not. It must be remembered that nonprofits are an inherently moral proposition, focused on charitable purpose and/or community benefit (Lee 2007). It is this unique identity that should set them apart from other categories of organization and which justifies the sector's existence in the twenty-first century (Salamon 2003). There is therefore a sense in which nonprofits *ought* to achieve a societal orientation for its own sake, since it is the very nature of such a focus that sets the organizations in our sector apart. As Salamon (2003) argues:

More generally, nonprofit America must give broader and more concrete meaning to its claims to serve the public good by stressing the sector's commitments to reliability, trustworthiness, to quality, to equity, to community and to individual and community empowerment. These are powerful rationales in a society that values pluralism and freedom but wishes to balance them with a sense of solidarity and responsibility for others. But they must be more forcefully and concretely articulated and then be more fully interpreted and applied in the context of particular agencies and fields.

Although writing for an American audience, Salamon's fundamental argument that the sector needs to give greater thought to its identity has very real resonance across the Western world.

■ **CASE STUDY**

MARKETING ORIENTATION IN THE NONPROFIT CONTEXT: THE BRITISH LIBRARY

By Gary Warnaby, Senior Lecturer, University of Liverpool Management School and Jill Finney, Director of Strategic Marketing and Communications, The British Library.

INTRODUCTION

Libraries have traditionally existed to collect and organise information, make access to knowledge more democratic, and preserve the record of ideas for future generations. Now information is ubiquitous: 500 million webpages are just a keystroke away. Their content mutates constantly, and is subject to no structure. Google and other search engines have revolutionised the way people expect access to information'(British Library 2005: 3).

Libraries now exist in an increasingly dynamic environment. Battles (2003: 212) states that 'the library in the digital age is in a state of flux, which is indistinguishable from a state of crisis.' This environmental turbulence is acknowledged by the British Library—the national library of the UK—whose, Chief Executive Lynne Brindley (2004) writes: 'All libraries and information professionals face the challenge of keeping pace with the changing requirements of their users, in order to provide them with relevant, value adding services'. Facilitating this crucial task can be achieved via the adoption of a marketing orientation, and this case study outlines the efforts made by the British Library to become more market-oriented.

THE BRITISH LIBRARY

The British Library was created by Act of Parliament in 1972 through an amalgamation of existing institutions, including the library departments of the British Museum and the Patent

Office Library. The collection comprises 150 million items, including 13 million books, 7 million manuscripts (many of unique historical importance), 4.5 million maps, 56 million patents, 3.5 million sound recordings, 8 million stamps, and 58 million newspaper issues, serial parts, microfilms, and other formats. The British Library is a library of legal deposit, whereby it receives a copy of every publication produced in the UK and Ireland—around 600,000 new items each year. In 2003, the Legal Deposit Libraries Act extended this entitlement to electronic materials, including websites.

The main collections are housed at St Pancras in London, in the largest public building constructed in the UK in the twentieth century, opened in June 1998. The British Library also undertakes document supply and lending activities based in Boston Spa in Yorkshire, and also an increasingly important web presence (see www.bl.uk)—indeed, growth in the usage of the library's web resources averages 25 per cent a year. The most recent Annual Report gives an indication of the scale of operations—in 2005/6 there were nearly half a million visits to the reading rooms at St Pancras, over 5.8 million items supplied/consulted remotely and onsite, over 24.6 million searches of the Library's online catalogue, and over 865,000 visitors to the Library's onsite and virtual exhibitions (British Library 2006).

MARKETING ACTIVITY

Until 2001 the British Library had no coordinated marketing activity, with little uniformity in terms of how the organization was presented externally. Curators of subject collections developed their own communications activities, much of which could be regarded as product-oriented, aimed at subject specialists who already had a detailed knowledge of the area. A key task was persuading the curatorial staff that marketing per se was relevant in terms of more effectively raising awareness of their collections beyond the expert audiences to whom they had traditionally (and very successfully) appealed. This was in line with the organization's remit as a *national* library and its aim to make knowledge accessible to all those who wished to benefit from it.

An essential first step in widening awareness, participation, and usage—in other words, starting the process of becoming more market-oriented—was to develop a fuller understanding of the market. In 2001, following an extensive programme of research into user perceptions etc., five main 'broad audience communities' were identified, as follows.

- Researchers, including: teaching and research staff in higher and further education; postgraduates; high R&D industries; writers and scholars; individuals pursuing personal study; government researchers; and undergraduates researching projects.

- Business people, including: inventors and entrepreneurs; professional service firms; SMEs; science parks; and creative and media industries.

- The library network, including: libraries in further and higher education; UK legal deposit libraries; international research libraries; public and school libraries; corporate, professional, and government libraries; and national and regional archives and museums.

- Schools and young people, including: schools, sixth form, and further education colleges; teachers; and out-of-school groups and holiday schemes.

- The general public, including: local communities; lifelong learners; groups and societies; families; and UK and overseas tourists.

Source: Warnaby and Finney (2005)

For each of these communities, a Head of Marketing was appointed, reporting to the Director of Strategic Marketing and Communications. The British Library (2005: 4) has sought to meet the needs of these disparate groups by promoting 'ready access to the British Library's collection and information experts through a range of free and priced services which are becoming increasingly integrated'. These services include:

- Supporting research, including: online catalogue that resolves 15 million searches a year; reading rooms and document supply services that deliver 5 million items to researchers; imaging services—copying in digital and film formats; and reference and research consultancy and enquiry services.

- Supporting lifelong learning, including: permanent exhibition of the 'Treasures' of the British Library; temporary exhibitions throughout the St Pancras Building; workshops and tours; outreach projects; and an award-winning web space (www.bl.uk/learning).

- Professional services, including: collaboration with information professionals in the management of their collections; digitisation services; and metadata licensing.

- Public space, including: a culturally rich and exciting destination in the heart of King's Cross in London; concerts, performances, talks, and events; cafes and restaurants; and bookshop and retail services.

- Publishing, including: books, sound, and images; and licensing content to online and print publishers.

Indeed, meeting the needs of users has been explicitly articulated in the British Library's external marketing communications activity which, to ensure a consistency of approach, is themed around the concept of *Advancing Knowledge*. Thus, marketing communications activity aimed at each of these user communities incorporates case studies of how the British Library has helped organizations and individuals advance their own knowledge in order to achieve their business and/or personal aims and objectives, through enhanced individual development and effectiveness or improved business performance. Moreover, the introduction of a new logo and brand identity has also ensured consistency of approach. All the activities described above have increased public awareness of the British Library—research carried out by MORI in the summer of 2005 indicated that 75% of Britons knew about the British Library, a significant increase from under 50% five years previously (British Library 2006).

External communications are also targeted at 'resource generators' (Gwin 1990) such as central government and other funding stakeholders. Here, highlighting the efficiency and cost-effectiveness of the British Library is paramount. In order to do this, the organization has commissioned independent research to measure the economic impact of the British Library. This research concluded that for the public funding it received, the Library produced a benefit-cost ratio of 4.4:1—in other words, for every £1 of funding received £4.40 is generated for the UK economy. For the British Library, like other cultural institutions in receipt of public funding, this emphasis on cost-efficiency is ongoing—and *communicating* successes in reducing operating costs and increasing organizational efficiency is an important element of the marketing effort directed towards policymakers and related stakeholders.

STRATEGY DEVELOPMENT

An important aspect of a marketing orientation is responding to a changing marketplace, and the British Library—like all libraries—must respond to the changes brought about by the Internet, which have revolutionized the information storage and retrieval industry. As Howard (2004: 37) has stated: 'Today all libraries stand at a crossroads with forks leading to a future obscured by the fog of the new information technology'. The British Library has responded to the challenges of the 'digital age' in terms of 'redefining' the Library for the twenty-first century. The concept of a twenty-first century library has been articulated, which:

- plays a leading role in the changing world of research information;
- exists for everyone who wants to do research—for academic, personal, or commercial purposes;
- promotes ready access to the collection and expertise through an integrated range of services which are increasingly time and space independent;
- connects with the collections and expertise of others and works in partnership to fulfil users' needs (British Library 2005: 1).

The British Library has developed a new strategy for the period 2005–8 in recognition of this changing role, in which these four aspects above serve to achieve the mission of *Helping people advance knowledge to enrich lives*. Operationalizing this vision and mission is to be achieved through the following strategic priorities, which—in line with the market orientation perspective—are integrated and coordinated together.

Enrich the Users' Experience

We underpin UK research across all disciplines, providing a crucial range of services to businesses and individuals. We continue to broaden access to our collection and develop services that engage new audiences. We strive to make our services accessible to disabled people through the web, the provision of alternative formats, and around our physical sites. People increasingly need to use the same range of services offsite and onsite during different phases of their work, and we are integrating services to support their working methods. Making the Library easier to use adds value to the research process, saving time and enabling researchers to work more effectively and have confidence in their outputs.

Build the Digital Research Environment

We have the vision and the acknowledged expertise to play a leading role in defining and creating with others the UK's electronic research infrastructure. We've established the critical national and international partnerships we need, and are working to address the complex challenges inherent in actively managing digital information in the long term. Guaranteed access to digital material in the long term is vital to the successful future of UK research programmes. Digital resources also present new opportunities for people to undertake research for personal enrichment and self-development, and allow disabled people to engage with previously inaccessible sources.

Transform Search and Navigation

We're investing to open up access to the collection. We'll accelerate the modernisation and improvement of the ways in which users find what they need in our collection and in linked resources held by partner organizations. We'll enrich our catalogues and make incoming items available as quickly and efficiently as possible. We'll use new information retrieval technologies to enhance the search possibilities offered to our users, so they can trawl our online resources at the deepest level. Users will benefit from faster, targeted results, which are comprehensive in their breadth and depth.

Grow and Manage the National Collection

Our collection is a combination of traditional and digital materials. It's fundamental to the future of UK research, which in turn furthers the innovation and enterprise that drive the UK economy. We'll continue to collect to meet the needs of researchers, and will provide expert stewardship to ensure the nation's cultural and intellectual memory is sustained and accessible forever.

Develop our People

Our staff set a standard for excellence, and are dedicated and creative in the delivery of services. We're immensely proud of the record of achievement that colleagues have set in the 30 years since the British Library's foundation, and their commitment to meeting the challenges created by the new information environment. We aim to be an employer of choice, attracting and retaining talent; we strive to act as an exemplar in the library community in developing the skills and expertise of our staff.

Guarantee Financial Sustainability

The pace of delivery of our multi-faceted and challenging strategic agenda is dependent on securing the appropriate level of resources. We shall seek to increase the level of our Grant in Aid funding from Government. In addition, we are striving to supplement our public funding through fundraising and trading activities, and by maximising our efficiency to free up resources for our key priorities.

Source: British Library (2005)

Since the development of the strategy, operational activities have focused on these strategic priorities, and the marketing function has the potential to play a significant role in the achievement of all these priorities. What cannot be doubted, as the environment in which the British Library exists continues to be so dynamic, and possibly develops in as yet unanticipated ways, is that an effective marketing orientation will be a prerequisite for success.

A MARKETING ORIENTATION

The marketing concept proposes that corporate goals are achieved through meeting and exceeding customer needs better than the competition. Jobber (2007) identifies the following key components of a marketing orientation.

- *customer orientation:* the organization's activities are focused on providing customer satisfaction;
- *integrated effort:* all staff accepting responsibility for creating customer satisfaction;
- *goal achievement:* the belief that the organization's goals can be achieved through customer satisfaction.

The British Library has become more marketing oriented by researching its customer needs and positioning the organization in order to be able to satisfy these needs. Here it is important for the organization to be clear and consistent about how and what it communicates—the development of a new brand identity and marketing communications activities based around the theme of *Advancing Knowledge* is part of that process.

Obviously with any service organization, customer satisfaction is inevitably delivered via its staff, and keeping them informed of, and supportive towards, changes is crucial. Thus, the British Library has engaged in an extensive process of internal marketing to get staff 'on board'. The steps taken to increasingly integrate all the services provided by the organization is also part of this process.

Finally, focusing on the achievement of clear goals will highlight successes where they occur and will communicate progress made, not only to users, but also to wider (funding and other) stakeholders. The British Library's communication focus on demonstrating the contribution it makes to advancing the nation's knowledge, and the focus on the strategic priorities in measuring organizational performance, are elements of this.

Hopefully, the activities outlined above will ensure that the British Library remains successful into an increasingly dynamic future. As the Chief Executive (Brindley 2004) states:

The traditional roles of library and information professionals are still valid, but they must be reinterpreted in our changing environment. Understanding the needs of users is critical, and we must all develop new skills and competencies if we are to continue to meet these needs as they evolve.

Battles, M. (2003) *Library: An Unquiet History*. London, Vintage.

Brindley, L. (2004) 'Powering the world's knowledge,' *Research Information,* Jan/Feb. Available at www.bl.uk/about/articles/pdf/brindley1.pdf.

British Library (2005) *Redefining the Library: The British Library's Strategy 2005–2008.* Available at www.bl.uk/about/strategy.html.

British Library (2006) *British Library Annual Report Accounts 2005–06.* Available at www.bl.uk/about/annual/2005to2006/introduction.html.

Gwin, J. M. (1990) 'Constituent Analysis: A Paradigm for Marketing Effectiveness in the Not-For-Profit Organisation,' *European Journal of Marketing,* Vol. 24, No. 7, 43–48.

Howard, P. (2004) 'Spam and blog add to Library's load,' *The Times,* 8 October, p. 37.

Jobber, D. (2007) *Principles and Practice of Marketing* (5th edn), London, McGraw Hill.

Warnaby, G. and Finney, J, (2004) 'Developing a marketing orientation at the British Library,' *SCONUL Focus* Vol. 32, 42–44.

Warnaby, G. and Finney, J. (2005) 'Creating Customer Value in the Not-For-Profit Sector: A Case Study of the British Library,' *International Journal of Nonprofit and Voluntary Sector Marketing* Vol. 10 , 183–195.

■ SUMMARY

In this chapter we have introduced the topic of marketing and explained its relevance to nonprofit organizations. We have drawn a distinction between the functional aspects of marketing, which we shall deal with in subsequent chapters, and the philosophical aspects of marketing, namely the marketing concept itself. In relation to the latter we have explored how a nonprofit organization might seek to operationalize the marketing concept and to achieve what is known as a market orientation.

We stated that a market orientation might be thought of as having three dimensions, namely customer orientation, competitor orientation, and inter-functional coordination. A customer orientation involved developing an understanding of the dimensions of the service that were perceived as of greatest importance by customers, and engineering value in these key areas. The achievement of a competitor orientation was shown to deliver a number of strategic benefits to a nonprofit organization and involved the creation of an effective competitor monitoring system. This, it was argued, could provide valuable data against which to benchmark performance and suggest key areas to management that could be used as the basis for a sustainable competitive advantage. The issue of inter-functional coordination was also explored and the concept of internal marketing introduced as one route to the attainment thereof. A variety of both strategic and tactical applications were described.

We concluded the chapter by examining a competing view on how the marketing concept should be operationalized and explored some of the criticisms of nonprofit market orientation. The notion of societal orientation was discussed, and a variety of antecedents and consequences of adopting such an orientation suggested. It was argued that although the available evidence indicates that orientation does impact significantly on nonprofit performance, there is a real case for arguing that nonprofits should seek to achieve a societal orientation irrespective of the proof of that link. It was argued that developing such an emphasis is critical because it comprises part of the unique nonprofit identity.

Having now considered the philosophy of marketing in some detail, in Chapter 3 we will move on to examine the functional components of marketing and in particular the first steps in creating a typical marketing plan.

■ DISCUSSION QUESTIONS

1. Using examples from your own experience, list some nonprofit organizations that have a product, sales, or a market orientation. How do these differ?

2. What are the key benefits that marketing can offer a nonprofit organization?

3. What typical objections may be encountered in attempting to introduce marketing to a nonprofit organization for the first time? How might these be countered?

4. What is internal marketing? To what extent do you believe it is a valid context?

5. With reference to your own organization, or one with which you are familiar, describe how you might set about enhancing the level of market orientation it has attained.

6. How does market orientation differ from societal orientation? Which of these alternative perspectives do you find to be the most convincing? Why?

7. To what extent should nonprofits strive to attain a societal orientation? To what extent would you agree with Salamon about what makes the sector distinctive? Why?

■ REFERENCES

Bennett, R. (1998) 'Market Orientation among Small to Medium Sized UK Charitable Organizations: Implications For Fundraising Performance', *Journal of Nonprofit and Public Sector Marketing*, Vol. 6, No. 1, 31–45.

Bennett, R. (2003) 'Competitor Analysis Practices of British Charities', *Marketing Intelligence and Planning*, Vol. 21, No. 6, 335–45.

Berry, L.L. (1981) 'The Employee as Customer', *Journal of Retail Banking*, Vol. 3 (March), 33–40.

Berry, L.L. (1987) 'Service Marketing is Different', *Business*, Vol. 30, No. 2, 24–9.

Bowen, D.E. and Schneider, B. (1985) 'Boundary Spanning Role Employees and the Service Encounter: Some Guidelines for Management and Research', in Czepiel, J., Solomon, M. and Suprenant, C. (eds) *The Service Encounter*, Lexington, Lexington Books, 127–45.

Bruce, I. (1995) 'Do Not-For-Profits Value their Customers and their Needs?' *International Marketing Review*, Vol. 12, No. 4, 77–84.

Caruana, A., Ramaseshan, B. and Ewing, M.T. (1988) 'The Marketing Orientation—Performance Link: Some Evidence from the Public Sector and Universities', *Journal of Nonprofit and Public Sector Marketing*, Vol. 6, No. 1, 63–82.

Christopher M., Payne, A. and Ballantyne, D. (1991) *Relationship Marketing: Bringing Quality, Customer Service and Marketing Together*, Oxford, Butterworth Heinemann.

Connolly, T.E., Conlon, J. and Deutsch, S.J. (1980) 'Organisational Effectiveness: A Multiple Constituency Approach', *Academy of Management Review*, Vol. 5, 211–17.

Dahrendorf, R. (1997) Keynote Address to Charities Aid Foundation Conference, QEII Conference Centre, October, London.

Deng, S. and Dart, J. (1994) 'Measuring Market Orientation: A Multi-Factor, Multi-Item Approach', *Journal of Marketing Management*, Vol. 10, No. 8, 725–42.

Deshpande, R. and Webster, F.E. (1989) 'Organization Culture and Marketing: Defining The Research Agenda', *Journal of Marketing*, Vol. 53, No. 1, 3–15.

Drucker, P. (1990) *Managing The Non-profit Organization*, Oxford, Butterworth Heinemann.

Freeman, R.E. (1984) *Strategic Management: A Stakeholder Approach*, Boston MA, Pitman.

Freeman, R.E. and Reed, D.L. (1983) 'Stockholders and Stakeholders: A New Perspective on Corporate Governance', *California Management Review*, Vol. 25, No. 3, 88–106.

Gainer, B. and Padanyi, P. (2002) 'Applying The Marketing Concept To Cultural Organizations: An Empirical Study of the Relationship Between Market Orientation and Performance', *International Journal of Nonprofit and Voluntary Sector Marketing*, Vol. 7, No. 2, 182–93.

George, W. (1990) 'Internal Marketing and Organizational Behavior: A Partnership In Developing Customer Conscious Employees at Every Level', *Journal of Business Research*, Vol. 20, No. 1, 63–70.

George, W.R. and Grönroos, C. (1989) 'Developing Customer Conscious Employees at Every Level—Internal Marketing', in Congram, C.A. and Friedman, M.L. (eds) *Handbook of Services Marketing*, AMACOM.

Gilmore, J. and Carson, C. (1995) 'Managing and Marketing to Internal Customers', in Glynn, W.J. and Barnes, J.G. (eds) *Understanding Service Management*, Chichester, John Wiley and Sons.

Grönroos, C. (1981) 'Internal Marketing—An Integral Part of Marketing Theory', Proceedings, AMA Services Marketing Conference, 236–8.

Gummesson, E. (1994) 'Making Relationship Marketing Operational', *International Journal of Service Industry Management*, Vol. 5, No. 5, 5–20.

Hansmann, H.B. (1980) 'The Role of the Nonprofit Enterprise', *Yale Law Journal*, Vol. 89 (April), 835–98.

Herman, R.D. (1990) 'Methodological Issues in Studying The Effectiveness of Nongovernmental and Nonprofit Organizations', *Nonprofit and Voluntary Sector Quarterly*, Vol. 19, 293–307.

Herman, R.D. and Heimovics, R.S. (1994) 'A Cross National Study of a Method for Researching Nonprofit Organizational Effectiveness', *Voluntas*, Vol. 5, 86–100.

Jordan, W.K. (1964) *Philanthropy in England 1480–1660*, London, George Allen and Unwin.

Kohli, A.K. and Jaworski, B.J. (1990) 'Market Orientation: The Construct, Research Propositions and Managerial Implications', *Journal of Marketing*, Vol. 54 (April), 1–18.

Kotler, P. and Keller, K.L. (2006) *Marketing Management*, 12th edn, Englewood Cliffs, NJ, Prentice Hall.

Kotler, P. and Clarke, R.N. (1987) *Marketing for Health Care Organizations*, Englewood Cliffs, NJ, Prentice Hall.

Kotler, P. and Fox, K.F.A. (1985) *Strategic Marketing for Educational Institutions*, Englewood Cliffs, NJ, Prentice Hall.

Kotler, P. and Levy, S. (1969) 'Broadening the Concept of Marketing', *Journal of Marketing*, Vol. 33 (Jan.), 10–15.

Kumar, K., Subramanian, R. and Yaunger, C. (1997) 'Performance-Oriented: Toward A Successful Strategy', *Marketing Health Services*, Vol. 17, 10–20.

Lee, S. (2007) 'Fundraising Ethics.' A presentation to Sue Ryder Care, Thorpe Hall, Peterborough, March.

Lovelock, C.H. and Weinberg, C.B. (1990) *Public and Nonprofit Marketing*, 2nd edn, San Francisco, The Scientific Press.

Narver, J.C. and Slater, S.F. (1990) 'The Effect of a Market Orientation on Business Profitability', *Journal of Marketing*, Oct., 20–35.

Nature Conservancy (2006) *Conservation By Design: A Strategic Framework for Mission Success*, Arlington, VA, The Nature Conservancy.

Padanyi, P. and Gainer, B. (2004) 'Market Orientation in the Nonprofit Sector: Taking Multiple Constituencies into Consideration', *Journal of Marketing Theory and Practice*, (Spring): 43–57.

Payne, A., Ballantyne, D. and Christopher, M. (2005) 'A Stakeholder Approach To Relationship Marketing Strategy: The Development and Use of the Six Markets Model,' *European Journal of Marketing*, Vol. 39, (Nos. 7–8), 855–71.

Perrow, C. (1981) 'Disintegrating Social Sciences', *New York University Education Quarterly*, Vol. 12, No. 2, 2–9.

Piercy, N. and Morgan, N.A. (1994) 'The Marketing Planning Process: Behavioural Problems Compared to Analytical Techniques in Explaining Marketing Plan Credibility', *Journal of Business Research*, Vol. 29, No. 3, 167–78.

Porter, M. (1985) *Competitive Advantage*, New York, Free Press.

Raju, P.S., Lonial, S. and Gupta, Y.P. (1995) 'Market Orientation and Performance in the Hospital Industry', *Journal of Health Care Marketing*, Vol. 15, No. 4, 34–41.

Salamon, L. (2003) *The Resilient Sector: The State of Nonprofit America*, Brookings Institution Press, Washington DC.

Sargeant, A. and Kaehler, J. (1998) *Benchmarking Charity Costs*, West Malling, Charities Aid Foundation.

Sargeant, A., Foreman, S. and Liao, M. (2002) 'Operationalizing the Marketing Concept in the Nonprofit Sector', *Journal of Nonprofit and Public Sector Marketing*, Vol. 10, No. 2, 41–65.

Sargeant A, Jay, E. and Lee, S. (2006) 'Benchmarking Charity Performance: Returns From Direct Marketing In Fundraising,' *Journal of Nonprofit and Public Sector Marketing*, Vol. 16 (No. 1/2), 77–94.

Sawhill, J. and Williamson, D. (2001) 'Measuring What Matters In Nonprofits', *McKinsey Quarterly*, Vol. 2, 98–107.

Sheehan, R. (1996) 'Mission Accomplishment as Philanthropic Organization Effectiveness: Key Findings from the Excellence in Philanthropy Project', *Nonprofit and Voluntary Sector Quarterly*, Vol. 25, 110–123.

Smith, A. (1776) *The Wealth of Nations*, Letchworth, Dent and Sons Ltd.

Tansuhaj, P., Randall, D. and McCullough, J. (1988) 'A Service Marketing Management Model: Integrating Internal and External Marketing Functions', *Journal of Service Marketing*, 2, Winter, 31–8.

Vasquez, R., Alvarez, L.I. and Santos, M.L. (2001) 'Market Orientation and Social Services in Private Non-profit Organisations,' *European Journal of Marketing*, Vol. 36 (No. 9/10), 1022–1046.

Voss, G.B. and Voss, G. (2000) 'Strategic Orientation and Firm Performance in an Artistic Environment,' *Journal of Marketing*, Vol. 64, 67–83.

Zeithaml, V.A. (1985) 'How Consumer Evaluation Processes Differ between Goods and Services', *Journal of Marketing*, Fall, 186–90.

Zeithaml, V.A., Parasuraman, A. and Berry, L.L. (1985) 'Problems and Strategies in Service Marketing', Vol. 49, No. 2, 33–46.

PART TWO

Marketing Planning

<table>
<tr><td>**3**</td><td></td></tr>
</table>

Marketing Planning: The Operating Environment and Marketing Audit

---

OBJECTIVES

By the end of this chapter you should be able to:

1. outline a structure for a marketing plan;

2. explain the purpose of a marketing audit as the first part of the plan;

3. discuss the key information requirements of a marketing audit;

4. understand the categories of information gathered in the audit, why this data is important, and how it can be used in planning;

5. utilize key tools commonly employed in the audit process such as PEEST, SWOT, and portfolio analyses.

Introduction

In this chapter it is my intention to outline a process that may be employed by nonprofits in planning their marketing activities. While the format may differ slightly from one organization to another, at its core a marketing plan has three common dimensions:

1. *Where are we now*? A complete review of the organization's environment and the past performance of the marketing function. Only when the marketing department has a detailed understanding of the organization's current strategic position in relation to each of the audiences it serves can it hope to develop meaningful objectives for the future.

2. *Where do we want to be*? In this section of the plan the organization will map out what the marketing department is expected to achieve over the duration of the plan. Typically, there may be income generation targets as well as objectives for awareness, attitudes towards the organization, and the take-up of service provision.

3. *How are we going to get there*? This stage of the plan contains the strategy and tactics the organization will adopt to achieve its targets. The strategy, as we shall see in Chapter 5, specifies in general terms what the broad approach to marketing will be, while the tactics supply the minutiae of exactly how each form of marketing will be undertaken. In this chapter we will provide a generic framework for marketing planning and concentrate our attention on

the first of the above three components of a marketing plan. We will consider the information requirements of an organization when it commences the planning process, the sources that this information can be gathered from, and a range of analytical tools that can be used to help marketers interpret the data.

A Planning Framework

A simple marketing planning process is illustrated in Figure 3.1. It should be noted that there is no one right way in which to write a marketing plan and the style and format will hence vary considerably from one organization to another. There are almost as many different formats as there are authors of marketing texts! Nevertheless, the process outlined in Figure 3.1 includes the key ingredients of a typical marketing plan, namely an analysis of where the organization is at present, where it would wish to be in the future, and the detail of how it proposes to get there.

Many organizations find it helpful to begin the development of their marketing plan by restating their vision, mission, and organizational objectives. This helps to focus the minds of those responsible for marketing on the issues which are considered to be of paramount importance for the organization as a whole. It also assists them in delineating those aspects of the organization's role which warrant further investigation in the detailed marketing audit which follows. If an arts centre, for example, has the mission of supporting new forms of art and encouraging local talent, it will not only have to spend time and resources in identifying

```
Vision Statement
Mission Statement
Organizational Objectives
Marketing Audit
(a) PEEST Analysis
    • Political
    • Economic
    • Environmental
    • Socio-cultural
    • Technological
(b) Competitor Analysis
(c) Collaborative Analysis
(d) Stakeholder Analysis
(e) Analysis of own Organization

SWOT Analysis
Marketing Objectives
Key Marketing Strategies
Tactical Marketing Mix
    • Product/Service
    • Price
    • Place
    • Promotion
    • People
    • Process
    • Physical Evidence

Budget
Scheduling
Monitoring and Control
```

Figure 3.1 Marketing planning framework

these in the first place, it will also have to examine the nature of potential audiences for these new art forms as they emerge.

For a nonprofit a vision is typically an expression of the kind of society the organization would like to see. By contrast a mission defines the role that the organization will play in making that a reality. The vision of the National Society for the Prevention of Cruelty to Children (NSPCC) is thus 'a society where all children are loved, valued and able to fulfil their potential.' By contrast the NSPCC mission is 'to end cruelty to children.' I'm a particular fan of the eloquence of this mission. It is simple, brief, and powerful. It gives everyone connected with the organization a sense of purpose and makes a strong case for why the nonprofit would be worthy of support. Too many missions are couched in woolly, non-committal, or politically correct language which as a consequence could really be taken as the mission of many other organizations in the same sector. They contain nothing genuinely distinctive and convey nothing of the passion that the founders of the organization will presumably have felt at some stage in the organization's development.

In the ten years since the first edition of this text appeared, nonprofit mission statements have become commonplace. There are still some organizations that resist the terminology because it sounds too businesslike, but this is unimportant. Whether a nonprofit prefers to write a mission or use alternative terminology such as 'aims', 'purpose', or 'philosophy' is irrelevant. What matters is that the organization can summarize in a few words its *raison d'etre*. Potential supporters and clients should be able to see at a glance what the organization is trying to achieve.

A selection of 'missions' are given below.

In 1978, the World Wildlife Fund (WWF) decided that its 'purpose' was 'to raise the maximum funds possible from UK sources and to ensure that the funds are used wisely for the benefit of conservation of the natural environment and renewable natural resources with emphasis on endangered species and habitats'.

The Elizabeth Svendsen Trust For Children and Donkeys has as its stated 'aim' 'to bring enjoyment and pleasure into the lives of children with special needs and disabilities and the satisfaction that comes with the achievement of learning riding skills'.

The Horder Centre for Arthritis describes its 'philosophy' as follows:

The Horder Centre exists to improve the quality of life primarily to people stricken with arthritis. The mainsprings of our philosophy are:

- to provide professional help by all available methods for people suffering the pain and disabling effects of all forms of arthritis;
- to restore maximum independence and alleviate pain wherever possible;
- to remain at the forefront of the battle against arthritis as a Centre of Excellence.

The mission of Planned Parenthood is:

- to provide comprehensive reproductive and complementary healthcare services in settings which preserve and protect the essential privacy and rights of each individual;
- to advocate public policies which guarantee these rights and ensure access to such services;
- to provide educational programmes which enhance understanding of individual and societal implications of human sexuality;
- to promote research and the advancement of technology in reproductive healthcare and encourage understanding of their inherent bioethical, behavioural, and social implications.

The reader will appreciate that in all these examples there is a noticeable absence of figures. Mission statements should address what the organization wishes to achieve, but in such a way that the mission can be adopted consistently for a reasonable period of time. It should not be necessary to re-address the mission on an annual basis, since it should serve only to provide the most general of signposts.

The specific detail of what an organization seeks to accomplish within each planning period would normally form part of the content of the organizational objectives. Drucker (1955) isolated eight aspects of operations where organizational objectives could be developed and maintained. These have been modified slightly below to relate them more specifically to the context of nonprofit organizations:

- market standing
- innovation
- productivity
- financial and physical resources
- manager performance and development
- worker/volunteer performance and attitude
- societal needs to be served
- public responsibility.

Clearly, each of these areas has some relevance for marketers even if many of them do not specifically relate to the marketing function. It is important, however, to realize that these objectives are stated for the organization as a whole to work towards. Their achievement will require a coordination of effort across all divisions/departments within the organization. Managers with responsibility for finance, human resources, service delivery, etc. will all have a part to play in ensuring that the organization delivers what it says it is going to deliver. It is for this reason that it is common practice to restate such objectives at the beginning of a typical marketing plan. Marketers should then be able to isolate what they as individuals need to be able to achieve over the planning period to facilitate the achievement of these wider objectives. There would be little point, for example, in the marketing department raising vast sums of money for causes that are not perceived as congruent with the organization's goals, while failing to raise sufficient sums for those that are. A restatement of the corporate objectives can therefore serve as an important focus for the marketing plan which follows.

The Marketing Audit

The marketing planning process can be conceptualized as having three main components:

1. Where are we now?
2. Where do we want to be?
3. How will we get there?

The marketing audit specifically addresses the first of these issues. As such, it is arguably the most crucial stage of the whole planning process since without a thorough understanding of the organization's current position it will be impossible for planners to develop any kind of vision of what they wish to accomplish in the future. The marketing audit is essentially a

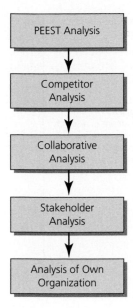

Figure 3.2 Marketing audit framework

detailed review of any factors likely to impinge on the organization, taking into account both those generated internally and those emanating from the external environment. The marketing audit is thus a systematic attempt to gather as much information as possible about the organization and its environment and, importantly, how these might both be expected to change and develop in the medium- and long-term future. A typical framework for a marketing audit is given in Figure 3.2.

PEEST Analysis

It is usual to begin the process by examining the wider or 'macro' environmental influences that might impact on an organization. Often these may be factors over which the organization itself has little control, but which will nevertheless affect the organization at some stage during the period of the plan. The framework utilized for this analysis is typically referred to as a PEEST analysis, and comprises the following elements:

- political
- economic
- environmental
- socio-cultural
- technological.

In each case the aim is to accumulate a list of all the pertinent factors and how these are expected to change over the planning period. It is best at this point in the process not to spend too much time deliberating about the impact that these factors might have on the nonprofit organization, but rather to note them, detail how they might change, and move on. The danger of precipitating a discussion at this stage, as the author has found to his cost, is that other clues as to the impact these PEEST factors might have will tend to emerge as the audit process

Political factors
Attitudes of government
Legal framework
Fiscal framework
Government contracts
Activities of pressure groups

Economic factors
Employment
GNP trends
Interest rates
Inflation
Business cycles

Environmental factors
Environment protection legislation
Levels of deterioration
Sustainable practices
Activities of major polluters
Location/development of major polluters

Technological factors
Government investment in research
Development of new materials
Sources of technology transfer
Manufacturing practices

Socio-cultural factors
Attitudes to recycling
Awareness of environmental decay
Consumer lifestyles
Demographic patterns
Content of school education
Major influences on consumer behaviour
Patterns of consumption

Figure 3.3 Sample PEEST analysis

progresses. It is therefore better to consider potential impacts en masse when the audit is complete. A sample PEEST analysis for a nonprofit concerned with raising public awareness of the impact of modern industrial practices on the quality of the environment is presented in Figure 3.3.

In researching these macro trends, the main challenge lies in the selection of accurate and pertinent information, and in the production of summaries succinctly setting out the main points for the reader. Data for PEEST analyses is gathered through secondary sources via desk research, i.e. information is found through existing publications rather than being sourced through the commissioning of new (or primary) research. In gathering information for a PEEST analysis one would look at practitioner and academic journals, books and reports, often via online information databases such as ProQuest available through libraries and academic institutions, or by searching the web more generally. Reports and publications published by trade bodies would also be utilized. Many nonprofits find that much of the necessary information for the production of PEEST analyses is already held internally in the form of publications and reports, or that staff have knowledge of where such information can be sourced internally or externally. The role of the 'auditor' is often therefore to interview staff, find out what information they have on file or can help with, and manage the gathering of that data. In this scenario the auditor would then seek to update the data where appropriate, and fill in any gaps through further research.

It is important to note that simply identifying the key factors is not enough, and it is vital that as much data as possible is gathered against each factor to ensure that decision makers are fully informed. For example, many nonprofits would identify 'increasing use of the Internet' as a key technological trend. Having identified this, the auditors would need to relate this factor to the context of the specific organization. They might hence collate information on new features and developments, and on best practice use of the Internet in raising awareness, fundraising, or providing nonprofit services. Likewise, a predicted fall in disposable income among members of the public might be identified as an important economic factor, but this would mean little if data on the impact of a fall in disposable income on, for example, fundraising or nonprofit performance was not included too. It needs to be clear why each factor is of relevance.

Analysis of Competitors

There are three categories of competitors who are worthy of investigation at this stage in the audit. They are:

1. *Competitors for resources.* Other nonprofit organizations which seek to attract resources from the same sources as the nonprofit in question.

2. *Competitors for provision of nonprofit services.* Nonprofits may also encounter competition from other organizations which seek to provide the same services. Increasingly this competition may come from for-profit organizations which may decide to compete, for example, for government service contracts.

3. *Organizations with competing missions.* Many nonprofits now exist whose primary goal is to persuade society to adopt new forms of purchasing, smoking, or sexual behaviours. Such nonprofits typically encounter opposition from other organizations which exist to further exactly the opposite forms of behaviour. In such circumstances these organizations should be regarded as competitors and be subject to an equally detailed level of analysis.

To be able to compete successfully in their chosen markets nonprofits need to have a sound understanding of the behaviours of organizations that might be regarded as competitors and attempt to determine what their future strategies might be. It is also helpful to understand something of the capabilities of each major player and to define clearly their individual strengths and weaknesses. The following checklist could therefore be used as the starting point for analysis, although it should be noted that the specific factors an organization will need to examine are likely to vary considerably from case to case:

- contact details of each competitor;
- size and geographic location(s);
- financial performance;
- resource capabilities;
- past strategies;
- tactical marketing mixes employed;
- key alliances formed.

When information has been gathered the auditor will need to present and summarize it in a suitable format. This might involve a comparative study, or an exercise plotting the position of competitors against various axes. One useful tool is to run an analysis of the apparent strengths and weaknesses of each competitor, and an assessment of how their activities might impact on the focal organization in the future.

Collaborative Review

Competition is a key strategic issue for many nonprofits, but collaboration is an equally important facet of their relationship with other organizations. Many agencies dealing with developing countries, for example, will share transportation channels to maximize the distribution and impact of aid, while minimizing cost. In addition to other similar organizations, nonprofits may be able to identify suitable opportunities for collaboration with both public and private sector bodies (Andreasen and Kotler 2003). It is also common for nonprofits to share lists of lower-value donors with other organizations, in the hope that every participant in the exchange will benefit from the sharing of these resources (Sargeant and Jay 2004).

Thus in conducting a fundraising audit it will be instructive to consider examples of where organizations have collaborated successfully in the past and the factors that led to that success. The nonprofit should look to see what it could learn from these collaborations and whether there might be any way in which it could work in partnership with others. If this is felt to be desirable, it will be useful to conduct background research into potential partners and to explore how such relationships might develop. An approach to one or more partners could then be included in the marketing strategy/tactics.

Stakeholder Analysis

The next stage of the audit involves conducting a thorough analysis of each of the stakeholder markets in which the nonprofit perceives itself and, importantly, is perceived by its stakeholders, as operating. As we noted in the previous chapter stakeholders are 'all those groups and individuals that can affect, or are affected by, the accomplishment of organizational purpose' (Freeman 1984). In conducting a marketing audit it is essential that an organization follow a similar process to that outlined in Chapter 2 and clearly identify each stakeholder of interest. It then needs to develop an understanding of the needs and behaviours of each group, so that they may be taken account of in the subsequent development of strategy. At a minimum the following information should prove useful:

- requirements/needs/wants of each group;
- basis (if any) for segmenting these groups;
- past buying/giving behaviours and the factors that influence this;
- attitudes to the nonprofit and its mission;
- media exposure;
- patterns of change in any of the above.

As the reader will appreciate gathering this information for every stakeholder group is a lengthy process. The investment will certainly be worthwhile if a strategic plan is being written for the organization as a whole. Taking account of the needs of each group, particularly those regarded as most significant, will be a key component of strategy formulation and thus rushing this process would be counterproductive.

More typically though, a marketing plan will be written for a specific purpose, or with a specific audience in mind. In these circumstances it is obviously not necessary to include an analysis of all stakeholder groups. Some will be irrelevant to the task at hand. The purpose of this stage of this audit is to identify *relevant* stakeholders and delineate their needs, attitudes, behaviours etc. Thus, if a marketing plan is being written to promote attendance at a local church, it may be necessary to consider only the needs of the existing congregation and the local community (from whom additional members may be drawn). A plan to raise funds for a new building may only need to focus on the needs of existing donors, potential donors, the local media/press, and, if appropriate, volunteers. If this were a for-profit text I would be talking here about gathering data about customers and their behaviour, but in the nonprofit context, as we have seen, there is typically a need to consider a broader range of audiences.

As with other sections of the audit, the author's task is simply to collate and summarize relevant data, with the goal of developing a detailed understanding of each target group and how it may be changing over time.

The Internal Environment

Having now summarized the key external influences on the organization it is possible to move on to consider an audit of the organization's own marketing activity. The aim here is to scrutinize past marketing performance and to appraise carefully what has worked well in the past and what has not. Current marketing activities, trends in performance, and the current structure and support systems that underpin marketing activity will all be considered. The following checklist is indicative of the categories of information that might typically be regarded as relevant, but it should not be regarded as exhaustive.

Resource Attraction Activities

- fundraising income (subdivided by source, e.g. individual, corporate, and trust donations);
- fundraising income (subdivided by method of fundraising employed, e.g. direct mail, telemarketing, etc.);
- income from contracts;
- sales (subdivided by channel) and margins achieved;
- attractiveness of service provision to potential funders;
- marketing procedures;
- marketing organization;
- marketing intelligence systems;
- marketing mix.

Resource Allocation Activities

- sales/service take-up rates (subdivided by location, market segment, and service category);
- market share analysis;
- cost-effectiveness of services being provided;
- marketing procedures;
- marketing organization;
- marketing intelligence systems;
- marketing mix.

Clearly, conducting a marketing audit can be a very time-consuming process and given that it is good practice to conduct an audit each year, it can place considerable demands on organizational resources. Nevertheless, the benefits that an audit can offer in terms of enhanced management decision making far outweigh the costs that might be incurred. If the auditing process is instituted on an annual basis, most of the necessary mechanisms for the gathering of data will have been put in place in the first year, and hence the costs in both time and effort should subsequently fall substantially.

Regrettably, however, many organizations continue to take the trouble to complete this exercise only when they are facing a crisis. Faced with decreased demand for their services, or a dramatic reduction in funding, organizations begin to panic and only then seek reasons for these occurrences. Had a systematic approach to environmental scanning been adopted, not only would they have been less likely to have been taken by surprise, but the development of suitable strategies to counter the problems might already be well under way.

Data for the internal audit is usually gathered through a mixture of desk research, meetings, and interviews with staff. Directors and senior staff will be able to provide information on past strategy, tactics, and performance, and will also provide the necessary data on financial performance, human resource strategy, and issues concerning governance, and the general direction of the organization. It is often necessary to interview non-marketing senior staff at this stage, such as the finance director and the CEO, to paint a full background picture of the nonprofit and to establish the positioning and importance of marketing within the organization.

As with the external audit, the internal data gathering should be an iterative process, with checks being performed throughout to ensure that full and accurate information is being gathered and expressed. The financial, structural, and performance information gathered can be used to provide benchmarking data for comparison against other organizations.

Analytical Tools

The audit of internal factors allows the auditor to capture a wealth of data on the performance of existing products or services. In essence, each product or service that the organization provides can be scrutinized to see whether it is worth continuing, what future performance might look like, and how it compares with other similar products or services being provided by other organizations. While it may be perfectly plausible to draw out a series of such conclusions from raw audit data, it may be preferable to use one of a number of analytical models which can assist the auditor in interpreting the mass of data accumulated. A number of the most commonly employed are outlined below.

Product/Service Life Cycle

One of the most fundamental concepts in marketing is the idea that a product or service will pass through several distinctive stages from the moment it is first introduced until it is finally withdrawn from the market. An understanding of these stages can greatly aid a marketer as the appropriate tactics for the successful management of the product/service will often vary greatly between each stage of its life cycle. From the perspective of the marketing audit, it can thus be a useful tool to assess whether the organization's existing marketing activity is appropriate given the product or service's position in its life cycle. Wilson et al. (1994: 274) summarize the implications of the life cycle concept thus:

- Services have a finite life.
- During this life they pass through a series of different stages, each of which poses different challenges to the seller.
- Virtually all elements of the organization's strategy/tactics need to change as the service moves from one stage to another.

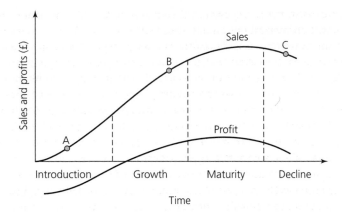

Figure 3.4 Product/service life cycle

- The profit potential of services varies considerably from one stage to another.
- The demands upon management and the appropriateness of managerial styles also vary from stage to stage.

This idea is illustrated in Figure 3.4.

During the introductory stage of the life cycle the service will take time to gain acceptance in the market and sales will hence be relatively low. At this stage the organization will be unlikely to have recouped its initial set-up and development costs and profitability remains negative. Over time, as the service begins to gain acceptability in the market, sales will experience a period of sustained growth and provision of the service should at this stage become profitable. With the passage of time, the level of sales will eventually begin to level off as the market becomes saturated, until ultimately the service becomes obsolete and sales begin to decline. At this stage the organization may wish to consider discontinuing the service, since with a lower volume of sales, the costs of provision may prove prohibitive.

The life cycle concept has been much criticized over the years but it is still useful to marketers in that it can help to define the form that the marketing mix might take at each stage. As an illustration of this point, consider the role of advertising in the marketing mix. At point (A) in Figure 3.4 the role of advertising would almost certainly be to inform the potential market that the service exists and the potential benefits that it might offer. Raising awareness would hence be a key objective at this stage. As the service moves to point (B) in the life cycle, however, the nature of the market has changed. If the new service has been particularly innovative it will be unlikely that competitors have stood idly around watching developments. Instead they will probably have entered the market with their own version of the service at this stage and the objectives of the advertising will thus need to change. A continual emphasis on raising awareness would be inappropriate since it would only serve to increase the overall level of demand in the market and thus benefit both the advertiser and its competition. Instead, a more useful objective might be to differentiate the service offered from those provided by the competition. The emphasis would change to identifying a clear positioning in the minds of target consumers. By the time that the service moves to point (C) in its life cycle, advertising support may be withdrawn altogether to reduce costs, or additional monies may be spent to 'prop up' ailing demand in the market.

While I have focused here solely on how the model can assist the planning of advertising, it is clear that equal utility could be offered to any other ingredient of the marketing mix. In most cases, pricing, distribution, and even the characteristics of the service itself will be modified as the life cycle progresses. Indeed, the model can also be used to help charities think about the nature of their provision. In such cases it is often helpful to move away from the concept of a service and to attempt to visualize the life cycle of a need. Bryce (1992), for example, makes the point that many nonprofits are addressing fairly specific needs within society. These may remain very stable from one generation to the next or they may change fairly rapidly. The need to deal with the design of a vaccine for polio has now been dispensed with, but the arrival of the AIDS virus poses a new threat. Disasters and emergencies create a more transient need, hence the likely life cycle of a need can have important planning implications, particularly when you consider that some needs are perceived by donors as being more immediate and worthwhile than others.

As with their counterparts in the for-profit sector, however, nonprofits normally have more than one service available at any one time and the life cycle concept has the significant drawback that it tends to focus management attention on each service individually without viewing the organization's portfolio as a coherent whole. A nonprofit organization may be viewed as a set of activities or projects to which new ones are intermittently added and from which older ones may be withdrawn. These activities and projects will make differential demands on, and contributions to, the organization as a whole. Hence some form of portfolio analysis might prove a useful tool in deciding how the service mix might be improved given the resource constraints that are valid at any one time.

Portfolio Analysis

While there are a variety of portfolio models that have been employed over the years, these have largely been developed in the business context and are thus difficult to apply to the context of nonprofit marketing. In particular, nonprofit marketers should studiously avoid any portfolio model which has as its base the concept of market share (e.g. the Boston Box), since this notion cannot be meaningfully applied to this context. This is the case for three reasons:

1. The sheer scale of the nonprofit sector and the fact that service and/or fundraising performance is usually reported in aggregate terms only means that it would be impossible to quantify meaningfully market share for most organizations.

2. Portfolio models employing market share assume that the performance of a product or service is related to market share (i.e. that there are economies of scale). This is simply not the case in many nonprofit contexts.

3. Finally, market share is employed in many portfolio models because it indicates the position of each competitor in a given market. Since many nonprofits do not compete, the use of such models is again problematic.

For these reasons the portfolio model shown in Figure 3.5 is to be preferred.

To utilize the model it is necessary to begin by examining in detail the components of the two axes, namely external attractiveness and internal appropriateness. If we consider first the question of external attractiveness, this relates to a particular organization's ability to attract resources. Not all an organization's services will be equally attractive to potential funders and while most charities would not exclude the provision of a service, simply because it was

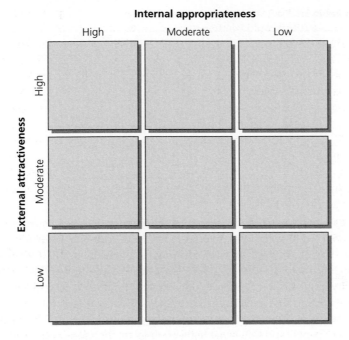

Figure 3.5 Nonprofit portfolio analysis

perceived by donors as unsavoury, few would argue that the ability to raise funds was not an issue. While the specific factors will undoubtedly vary from one organization to another, the degree of support donors are willing to give a particular activity is likely to depend on the level of general public concern, likely trends in public concern, the numbers of people aided, and the immediacy of impact on the beneficiary group. It is important to recognize that this list is not exhaustive and the beauty of this model is that organizations can utilize whatever factors they perceive as being relevant to their own environment and circumstances.

Turning now to the question of internal appropriateness, this relates to the extent to which the service 'fits' the profile of the organization providing it. In other words, is provision appropriate given the skills, expertise, and resources available within the organization? Relevant factors here might include the level of previous experience with the activity; the perceived importance of the activity; the extent to which the activity is compatible with the organization's mission; and the extent to which the organization has unique expertise to offer.

Once again, this list can be expected to vary from context to context and an organization should try to identify those factors which are most pertinent to its particular circumstances.

Having now defined the components of both internal appropriateness and external attractiveness, the reader will appreciate that not all the factors identified may be seen as having equal importance to a given organization. For this reason it is important to weight the factors according to their relative importance. This is illustrated in Table 3.1. The reader will note that the weights for the components of each axis should all add up to 1. In the example given, the numbers of people the organization can aid is seen as being a more important determinant of external attractiveness than how immediately the assistance can be provided. Donors to this organization do not appear to have any difficulty in taking a long-term view of the impact of their support.

Table 3.1 Calculation of external attractiveness

Vertical axis	Weight	Rating	Value
External attractiveness			
Level of public concern	0.2	5	1.0
Likely trends in public concern	0.3	3	0.9
Numbers of people aided	0.4	8	3.2
Immediacy of impact on beneficiary group	0.1	7	0.7
TOTAL	1.0		5.8

The next step is to take each activity in which the organization is engaged and give it a score from 1 (very poor) to 10 (excellent) in terms of how it measures up against each of the components listed. To make this process clear, a fictional example (let us call it Activity A) has been worked through in Tables 3.1 and 3.2. Considering first the question of how externally attractive this activity might be, it is clear that public support for it looks set to decline in the future and it is for this reason that a relatively low rating of 3 has been awarded against this factor. The activity does have the merit, however, of having an immediate and beneficial impact on a large number of people and somewhat higher ratings are therefore awarded for these factors. Multiplying the weights by the ratings assigned produces a value for each factor. Summing these values gives an overall score for (in this case) the external attractiveness axis of 5.8.

Similarly in the case of the internal attractiveness axis, each factor is assigned a weight. Each activity in which the organization is engaged is given a rating according to its performance in respect of each factor. Once again 1 = very poor and 10 = excellent. Returning to our analysis of Activity A, Table 3.2 makes it clear that the charity has only moderate experience to offer and does not view its provision as being particularly important (even though it would appear to come within the organization's mission). The charity does however have unique areas of expertise which it could offer to recipients. The result is an aggregate score of 5.3 on the internal appropriateness axis.

These figures can now be plotted on the matrix in Figure 3.6, where the position of Activity A has been clearly indicated. If it is conceptually useful, some organizations choose to progress the analysis one stage further and draw a circle around the plotted position, the diameter of which is directly proportional to the percentage of overall expenditure allocated to

Table 3.2 Calculation of internal appropriateness

Horizontal axis	Weight	Rating	Value
Internal appropriateness			
Level of previous experience	0.1	5	0.5
Perceived importance of the activity	0.2	2	0.4
Compatibility with mission	0.5	6	3.0
Possession of unique expertise	0.2	7	1.4
TOTAL	1.0		5.3

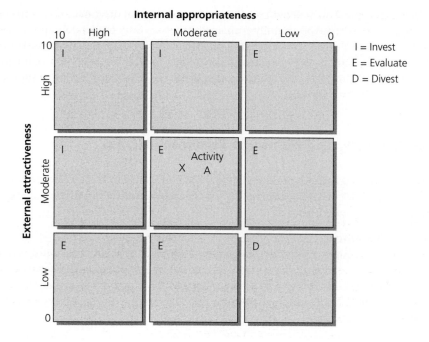

Figure 3.6 Utilizing the portfolio model

each activity. In this way managers can see at a glance how funds are allocated between each of the services in the portfolio. Of course, for this to happen, all the services that a particular organization provides would be plotted in this way and then an analysis undertaken of the health (and balance) of the portfolio as a whole. Depending on the location of each activity within the matrix, the organization can then either look to invest further in its development, divest the activity and use the resources elsewhere, or subject the activity to further evaluation if the position still remains unclear.

Activities falling in the top left-hand corner of the matrix are clearly those which are perceived as fulfilling an important need in society, and the attraction of funding is unproblematic. The organization also appears well placed to provide these services as it has the necessary expertise and/or experience in-house. The activities are also more likely to be seen as compatible with the organization's mission and are hence excellent candidates for continuing investment.

Activities falling in the bottom right-hand corner, however, are activities which could be causing an unnecessary drain on resources. They are not seen as being important by society and are not compatible with the organization's mission. Indeed, there may be other potential providers who could provide a much higher quality of service. Activities in this area of the matrix should then be scrutinized with a view to divestment. After all, if the activity is difficult to raise funds for, and the organization is not good at providing the service anyway, what could be the rationale for continuing? Of course, this is only a model and the activity would have to be scrutinized very carefully before a divestment decision was taken, but the analysis has at least yielded considerable insight into the potential for valuable resources to be conserved and perhaps put to other, more appropriate use.

This leaves the question of activities falling within the central diagonal, such as the one in our example. These should be carefully evaluated as they are only moderately appropriate for the organization to provide and they have only limited external attractiveness. It may be that there are very good strategic reasons for continuing to offer these services, or it may also be that they could comfortably be left to another better qualified organization to supply. Further analysis is clearly warranted.

Mission, Merit, and Money: A Portfolio Model

A more sophisticated three-dimensional model has been developed by Krug and Weinberg (2007). See Figure 3.7. In it, the authors suggest that the following dimensions are typically of interest in a nonprofit context.

Mission Contribution
Using the model requires a subjective judgement of the contribution of each programme or activity to the achievement of the mission. In reaching this assessment views can be sought from a variety of stakeholders and an 'average' perspective adopted. The average may reflect a genuine consensus, but could equally be a trade-off among widely divergent opinions about mission contribution.

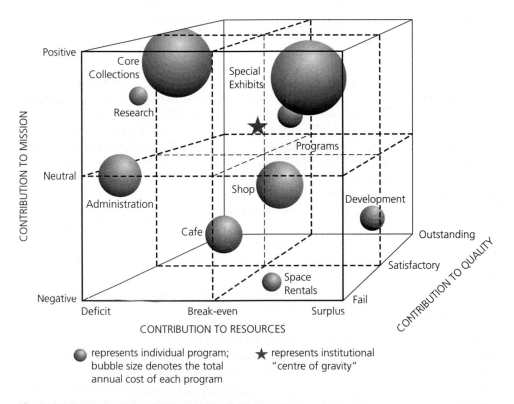

Figure 3.7 Example of three-dimensional portfolio analysis

Source: Krug, K. and Weinberg, C.B. (2007) 'Marketing Strategies and Portfolio Analyses', in Sargeant, A. and Wymer, W. (2007) *The Routledge Companion To Nonprofit Marketing,* London, Routledge. Reproduced with kind permission.

Contribution to Quality (or Performance)

An assessment must also be made of how well a programme is delivered. This should ideally combine both qualitative and quantitative measures depending on what criteria are relevant, what standards are applied, and what research instruments are used. For example, attendance or number of people served is a quantitative measure; assessment of what users or clients take from the experience is a qualitative one.

Resource Contribution

Finally a view must be taken on the contribution to resources made by a particular programme. This is usually decided on the basis of quantitative measures taken from financial tables, but it is important to note that these are often not organized in a format that allows for strategic judgements. Some manipulation of the data may be necessary for a programme's position on this axis to be plotted.

The authors advocate rating each programme on a scale ranging from -5 to $+5$ and plotting each programme in three-dimensional space accordingly. They also suggest that the size of the individual bubble (marking each programme) be adjusted to reflect the total annual cost of running each programme. The portfolio model can then be interpreted very much as the previous model was, with high-quality programmes, generating a surplus, and making a strong contribution to the mission, clear candidates for development. Those at the opposite end of each axis would be candidates for divestment, while those with a mix of different positions should be subject to further scrutiny. Some programmes making a deficit, for example, may be retained because they offer a strong contribution to the mission.

The Life Cycle Matrix

Finally, in examining the health of a nonprofit portfolio it is also possible to employ an adapted version of a matrix originally developed by consultants at Arthur D. Little Inc. (see Hofer and Schendel 1978). The matrix is illustrated in Figure 3.8. In this matrix the user plots competitive position against life cycle stages. The diameters of the circles around each activity are once again proportional to the revenue they generate. The goal of using this matrix, as with that detailed above, is to guide investment decisions in nonprofit services. In Figure 3.8, Activity A could be labelled a developing winner, Activity B a potential loser, Activity C an established winner, and Activity D a loser. The power of this matrix is that it illustrates graphically how the services are positioned in respect of various stages of evolution. This may be important in deciding when to create new services and divest those at the end of their life cycle lacking a clear rationale for their continuing existence.

The decision over where to place an activity on the competitive position axis depends on how that activity rates against a variety of factors. These typically include:

- how well the organization's strengths match the success factors in the particular market;
- the profitability associated with an activity;
- the extent to which the organization has the requisite marketing skills;
- the extent to which the organization has developed a reputation for delivering that activity; and
- the perceived costs/benefits to the user of engaging with the activity.

A combination of these factors determines how strongly positioned a particular product or service might be in its market. In employing the matrix, nonprofits can either take an

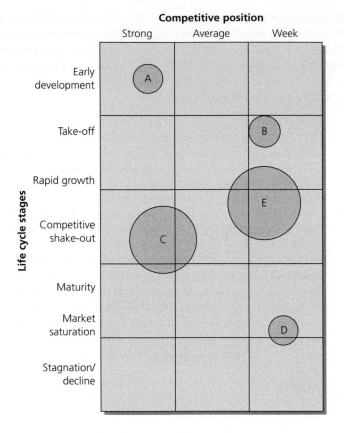

Figure 3.8 Life cycle matrix

Source: Hofer, C.W. and Schendel, D. (1978) *Strategy Formulation: Analytical Concepts,* The West Series in Business Policy and Planning, Belmont, CA, South Western.

entirely subjective view of the score on this axis, or they may construct a weighted axis just as with the previous matrix to impose a little more rigour on the analytical process.

In interpreting this matrix, it is possible to infer a number of conclusions in respect of how the performance of particular products/services might change over the duration of the plan. Similarly, the matrix can be used to guide investment decisions and in particular to highlight those products that should be divested. Those products/services towards the end of their life cycle where the organization does not have a strong competitive position are clear candidates for this.

Drawbacks of Portfolio Models

In electing to employ a portfolio model, it is essential that the user be aware of some of the disadvantages of such models.

Definition of a Programme/Activity
This sounds as though it should be relatively easy to accomplish. After all, most organizations know what they provide by way of services or programmes. While this is true, the difficulty in conducting a portfolio analysis is that sometimes these programmes are inter- related and it is

difficult to draw neat boundaries between one activity and another. When using the matrix in the context of fundraising further difficulties arise because there are fundraising products such as child 'adoption', but there are also fundraising media such as direct mail. Does it make sense to show both in one matrix and, if so, how does one deal with the overlap?

Innovation

The difficulty with some models is that they can understate the significance of an innovative new product. When such products first appear on a matrix, they are characterized by low profitability/revenues and a weak market position as they fight to get established. Thus a cursory glance at a portfolio model might suggest that such products are struggling and that divestment is warranted. This is clearly not the case and care is required in interpretation.

Divesting Unwanted Products

It should be recognized that while a number of products may be highlighted as candidates for divestment, this may frequently not be desirable. While it makes little financial sense to continue with a particular product, there may be a number of good human reasons why it should be continued. Perhaps volunteers have a long and proud tradition of managing the product and there are strong emotional attachments to its continuation. It may also be the case that some products gain the organization very welcome publicity that assists in the fulfilment of the mission, even though the performance of the activity itself is poor. Nonprofits thus need to subject the recommendations to emerge from a portfolio analysis to greater scrutiny before divestment decisions are taken.

The Desirability of Growth

Finally, most portfolio models assume that an organization is looking to achieve growth in usage or revenue and the prescriptions offered by such models may therefore not be appropriate to the circumstances facing every organization.

Swot Analysis

Clearly at this stage the output from the fundraising audit may be regarded as little more than a collection of data, and in this format it is of limited value for planning purposes. What is required is a form of analysis which allows the marketer to examine the opportunities and threats presented by the environment in a relatively structured way. It should be recognized here that opportunities and threats are seldom absolute. An opportunity may only be regarded as an opportunity, for example, if the organization has the necessary strengths to support its development. For this reason, it is usual to conduct a SWOT (Strengths, Weaknesses, Opportunities, and Threats) analysis on the data gathered during the audit. This is simply a matter of selecting key information from the audit, analysing its implications and presenting it under one of the four headings. The important word here is 'key'. It is important that some filtering of the data gathered at this stage is undertaken so that the analysis is ultimately limited to the factors of most relevance for the subsequent development of strategy. SWOT analysis addresses the following issues.

- What are the strengths of the organization? What is the organization good at? Is it at the forefront of particular developments? Does it have access to users/donors that are not reached by competitors? Does it have a strong database system/great support agencies/high local awareness?

- What are its weaknesses? In what ways do competitors typically outperform the organization? Are there weaknesses in terms of internal support or structures? Are there barriers to future development in some areas?

- What are the main opportunities facing the organization over the duration of the plan? Are there new ideas to test, new audiences to attract? Are new developments within the organization likely to present extra opportunities for either service provision or income generation?

- What are the major threats facing the organization? Is a major competitor likely to launch a new service or fundraising appeal? Will economic changes impact on certain core funders and leave them with less to give? Are planned changes to legislation likely to curtail service activity?

Good SWOT analyses have a number of distinctive characteristics.

- They are relatively concise summaries of the audit data and are typically no more than four or five pages of commentary focusing on key factors only.

- They recognize that strengths and weaknesses are differential in nature. This means that a strength is only a strength if the organization is better at this particular activity or dimension than its competitors. Similarly, weaknesses should be examined from the perspective of where the organization lags behind its competition.

- They are clear and easy to read. Quality suffers if items are over-abbreviated and the writer concentrates on micro rather than macro issues. As McDonald (1995: 406) notes, 'If a SWOT analysis is well done, someone else should be able to draft the objectives which logically flow from it. The SWOT should contain clear indicators as to the key determinants of success in the department.'

A separate SWOT should be completed for each segment of stakeholders critical to the organization's future. What may be perceived as a strength in relation to individual donors may well be a weakness when communicating with service users. Thus, the global SWOT analyses that are so frequently conducted by marketing departments can often tend towards the meaningless. For all but the smallest and simplest organizations, a series of highly focused SWOTs will be necessary.

■ SUMMARY

In this chapter we have examined the structure of a typical nonprofit marketing plan. While there are many such frameworks in existence, they all have the common core of 'Where are we now?', 'Where do we want to be?' and 'How will we get there?' The marketing audit comprises the first of these stages and it is therefore here that the marketer summarizes all the available data on the key factors that are likely to impinge on the organization over the duration of the plan and beyond. A framework for a marketing audit was provided and a series of information requirements delineated under each heading.

In the next chapter we will move on to look at how all this information might be gathered, at typical sources of nonprofit information, and at a variety of primary research methods. We will also examine how primary research data is typically presented.

■ DISCUSSION QUESTIONS

1. Why should a nonprofit organization consider developing a vision and mission statement? What advantages might this confer?

2. What is the purpose of a marketing audit? For an organization of your choice, develop a list of key information requirements utilizing the standard audit headings as a guide.

3. What is meant by the term 'stakeholders'? For an organization of your choice, identify who the key stakeholders might be and the demands they might place on the organization.

4. How might the portfolio models outlined in this text be amended to be suitable to the fundraising context?

5. Conduct a portfolio analysis for an organization of your choice. What conclusions do you draw? Which matrix did you find to be of most value? Why was this the case? How might you amend this model to make it even more relevant for use in your organization?

■ REFERENCES

Andreasen, A. and Kotler, P. (2003) *Strategic Marketing for Nonprofit Organizations*, Englewood Cliffs, NJ, Prentice Hall.

Bryce, H.J. (1992) *Financial and Strategic Management for Nonprofit Organizations*, Englewood Cliffs, NJ, Prentice Hall.

Drucker, P.F. (1955) *The Practice of Management*, London, Heinemann.

Freeman, R.E. (1984) *Strategic Management: A Stakeholder Approach*, Boston MA, Pitman.

Hofer, C.W. and Schendel, D. (1978) *Strategy Formulation: Analytical Concepts*, St Paul, MN, West Publishing.

Kotler, P. and Andreasen, A. (1991) *Strategic Marketing for Nonprofit Organizations*, Englewood Cliffs, NJ, Prentice Hall.

Krug, K. and Weinberg, C.B. (2007) 'Marketing Strategies and Portfolio Analyses', in Sargeant, A. and Wymer, W. (eds) *The Nonprofit Marketing Companion*, London, Routledge.

McDonald, M. (1995) *Marketing Plans: How To Prepare Them, How To Use Them*, London, Butterworth Heinemann.

Sargeant, A. and Jay, E. (2004) *Fundraising Management*, London, Routledge.

Wilson, R.M.S., Gilligan, C. and Pearson, D.J. (1994) *Strategic Marketing Management*, Oxford, Butterworth Heinemann.

4 Marketing Research

OBJECTIVES

By the end of this chapter you should be able to:

1. explain the relevance of research to marketing planning;
2. distinguish between primary and secondary research;
3. distinguish between qualitative and quantitative data;
4. utilize a wide range of secondary sources of data;
5. identify and employ relevant primary research methods;
6. present marketing research data.

Introduction

In Chapter 3 we explored a range of information needs typically encountered by a nonprofit in writing a strategic marketing plan. While this list seems extensive, it must be remembered that good information can be used to great effect in guiding the decisions and policies an organization might adopt, and is therefore invaluable.

Of course market research should not be seen as a substitute for good managerial decision making. The role of market research is not to usurp executive experience or judgement; rather, market research provides the basic data that managers can use to help *inform* the decision-making process. It thus reinforces good decision making rather than replacing it.

It is important to note that there is an element of risk associated with every management decision and that decision making in the absence of research data simply exposes an organization to unnecessary additional risk. In the nonprofit sector, this risk is all the more acute because of the agency role that nonprofits play in stewarding the resources supplied by donors. If, for example, a fundraising campaign goes badly wrong and loses money, it will effectively be wasting the resources donated by previous donors to the organization and will put the organization in breach of their trust. Similarly, if an organization designs a new service that fails to meet the key requirements of its beneficiary groups, a considerable amount of resources will be wasted and the organization's cause will be no further advanced.

There are thus a number of advantages to be gained by an organization in conducting thorough research in relation to each of the issues highlighted in Chapter 3. Given the plethora of information needs and the equal plethora of potential information sources, there is no shortage of data to be had about the marketing function or the environment in which it operates. Sadly, this is frequently irrelevant, incompatible with the specific information need, or excessive in terms of volume. Problems can also arise when managers fail to understand the nature of the information presented: then, even in the presence of high-quality data, the wrong decisions can be taken.

In this chapter we will navigate some of the pitfalls associated with conducting marketing research, outline a process that may be used to manage the activity, and explain the research tools and techniques available that might be employed to assist an organization capture data.

A Definition of Marketing Research

Before beginning with this process it is important to clarify exactly what we mean by marketing research. Over the years there has been considerable confusion between the terms 'marketing' and 'market research'. Although market research has tended to be used as a synonym for marketing research, there was originally a distinction drawn between these two terms by virtue of their scope. Market research was regarded as research into markets (e.g. in the case of fundraising; individual donors, corporate supporters, and foundations) whereas marketing research applies more broadly to every aspect of marketing. This would thus include researching the activities of competitors, trends in the external environment, the performance of an organization's own marketing activity, etc.

The American Marketing Association (AMA) (1961) defined marketing research as 'the systematic gathering, recording and analyzing of data about problems relating to the marketing of goods and services'.

More recently, Kotler (1967) preferred to emphasize the goals of marketing research and defined it as 'systematic problem analysis, model building and fact finding for the purposes of improved decision making and control in the marketing of goods and services'.

Thus marketing research is concerned with the disciplined collection and evaluation of data in order to help managers understand the needs of their target audiences more fully. It can be used to reduce risk in decision making and to control (to some extent) the risks surrounding each aspect of marketing.

While perspectives on the research process frequently differ from one organization to another, the approach adopted will always share a number of common features, as outlined in Figure 4.1.

The marketing research process is typically initiated by an organization realizing that it has a problem or issue to resolve. To operationalize this for the purposes of research it must first be expressed as a series of specific research objectives. These are then addressed through initial desk research of existing data. In some cases this may yield all the answers an organization needs, in which case an appropriate analysis of this material can result in the preparation of the requisite report for management. It is frequently the case, however, that not all of the information needs can be met in this way and that new or *primary* data may have to be collected and analysed for this purpose.

The sections below discuss each element of this process, beginning with the specification of the research problem.

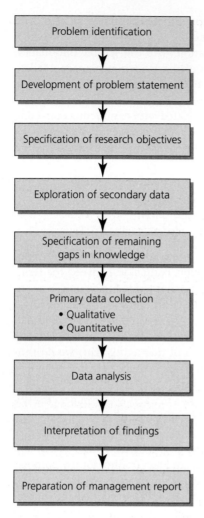

Figure 4.1 Marketing research process

Specifying the Research Problem and Research Objectives

The first stage of the research process involves a clear specification of the marketing problem on which the research is expected to focus. This is essential if the organization is to achieve a satisfactory outcome from the research process, particularly if external agencies are to be employed for the purposes of data collection.

Where it is intended that the organization will work with an agency, it is important that both management and the research team should work closely together in this crucial task of developing a problem statement. Unless the agency thoroughly understands the issues facing the client, it is quite possible that the research objectives designed to provide information to resolve these problems will be irrelevant or possibly even counterproductive.

Having defined the problem, it is then possible to design the research objectives. This requires the organization and/or agency to turn the problem into a series of information needs.

Thus, for example, if the problem facing the organization is a decrease in the demand for its service, the research objectives might be as follows:

- to profile existing and past users of the service;
- to identify user motives for utilizing the service;
- to identify user perceptions both of the service itself and of those provided by key competitors;
- to determine why previous users have terminated their use of the service;
- to determine why non-users are not trialling the service.

This list is by no means exhaustive and, depending on the circumstances facing a particular organization, the actual content of this list will vary considerably. The point is that the problem must be broken down into a series of research objectives that will address each of the likely causes for the decline, providing enough information for managers to take remedial action. Again, if an agency is to be employed for the purposes of data collection, it must also be involved in selecting research objectives since they may well have insight into the issues which could help shape these objectives, and also because they need to understand the rationale underlying each information need and how it pertains to the problem as a whole.

Secondary versus Primary Data

The next stage in the research process is to conduct desk research of existing information sources. Typically, many of the organization's information needs can be adequately and cheaply met by simply reading through the trade press, research reports, or specialist journals. Collectively, this is known as secondary data.

Secondary data is data that has already been collected for some purpose in the past. It has thus *not* been collected specifically to address the issues at hand. Such data can typically be found within the nonprofit organization in management/consultancy reports or an analysis of database records, but more frequently it will be found outside the organization in government publications, syndicated research, trade/professional reports, electronic databases, professional/academic journals, etc.

Secondary data is always the starting point in seeking to satisfy research objectives since it has the advantage of being cheap to collect and will typically be a fraction of the cost of the collection of new market research (surveys, focus groups, etc.). It does, however, have a number of distinct disadvantages, in that (a) it has been collected for another purpose that may not meet the exact information needs of the organization; (b) it is often out of date, having been collected a year or more prior to the current investigation; and (c) it can be of dubious quality and thus a careful consideration of the source and the methodology adopted will be necessary to ensure that the data offers appropriate validity and reliability.

Having exhausted the sources of secondary data, the organization may then return to the research objectives and determine those that have not been fully addressed with this extant data. Where information gaps remain, it will be necessary to commission primary research to supply the missing information. Primary research involves collecting new data specifically for the purpose of answering the questions posed by the current research objectives. This is typically an expensive exercise and will not be undertaken lightly by the commissioning organization. Primary research may be either qualitative or quantitative.

Qualitative Research

Nonprofit marketers are frequently concerned with issues such as how donors view the organization, what motivates them to support it, what they like and don't like about the communications they receive, etc. If the organization lacks an understanding of the factors likely to be at work in each case, it would be advised to begin by conducting what is known as *qualitative* research. This form of research is designed to provide such an insight and is a good way of gathering data about people's attitudes, feelings, and motives. It is impressionistic in style rather than conclusive, and it probes for data rather than counting responses. The most common qualitative research methods include focus groups (group discussions), detailed 'depth' interviews, and projective techniques.

Depth Interviews

The use of this technique involves the researcher in a free-flowing discussion with members of the group whose opinions are being sought. They are conducted on a one-to-one basis, so that there is no need for the interviewee to feel under any pressure to respond in a socially acceptable way, or to worry what other participants in the research process might think of their views. It is thus a very open and non-threatening research setting and interviewers are trained to put their subjects at ease. Such interviews can be either unstructured or semi-structured depending on the level of knowledge the researcher has about the factors likely to be of interest. Where detailed knowledge is lacking, the interviewer will find an unstructured approach of most value as this will facilitate a general discussion of the research question and allow the conversation to focus on whatever factors emerge.

Focus Groups/Group Discussions

This technique requires the researcher to assemble a group of six to ten respondents who agree to take part in (typically) a one- to two-hour discussion that addresses the research objective(s). This discussion may be held at the organization's premises or at a centrally located venue that is easy for the respondents to access. The researcher carefully facilitates a discussion of the topic and ensures that the views of each member of the group are elicited. He/she may also have to deal with 'difficult' personalities that attempt either to dominate the discussion, or fail to express a point of view. It is important that the views of every participant are considered equally and the process of facilitation is thus a highly skilled task. Focus group proceedings are typically either audio- or video-taped, so that they can subsequently be analysed by the research team. The biggest drawback of this technique is the cost, with a typical focus group costing between £800 and £1000 and between six and eight groups typically being necessary to address a given research task. Basing decisions on a smaller number of groups can be risky since focus group participants may prove to be highly unrepresentative of the donor/user (or other) population and thus the results will be misleading. The insights gained from focus groups can be of considerable value, but this is frequently gained at substantial cost.

Projective Techniques

The use of projective techniques has moved in and out of fashion over the past 50 years. They are said to generate considerable insight into feelings, beliefs, and attitudes that individuals find it difficult to articulate by other means. A number of techniques are in existence, where research subjects can express their views by 'projecting' those views onto objects, pictures, or third parties.

An organization interested in the perception of its brand might thus provide a group of eight to ten individuals with a set of cards and crayons and ask them to create an image that for them embodies the brand. This can also be achieved through the use of clay, where subjects create a physical representation of the brand in question. The shapes and pictures created will then be subject to expert analysis to identify the common themes to emerge.

A further common technique would involve asking subjects to create a personality for an organization or brand. Thus, 'If this organization were a well-known celebrity, who would it be?' The description and subsequent rationale can then form the basis for discussion.

Projective techniques have also been used in the context of cartoons, where research subjects are presented with a cartoon illustration of a social situation embodying the research objective(s). Blank dialogue boxes (or speech bubbles) are provided and the subject asked to supply appropriate speech. The technique works because subjects may find it easier to address some topics by projecting their own values and beliefs onto these cartoon characters thereby expressing views they would feel uncomfortable expressing in a traditional interview. Again, this speech can be subject to a content analysis at the end of the research process and common themes elicited.

A Caveat

It should be noted that qualitative techniques are rarely used in isolation. The samples are inadequate, the method of questioning inconsistent, and the means of interpretation subjective. Two or three people (or agencies) doing the same piece of qualitative research can often come up with very different results. This is simply because the use of eight to ten individuals in a focus group is rarely representative of the 'population' as a whole and the results will therefore always have a high degree of bias. To take a fundraising example, one might commission a series of focus groups to determine the reasons why donors support the organization. Such a group would likely generate an excellent list of reasons, but it could never tell you what proportion of the donor base might be motivated by each rationale for support. It is thus only half a story. The real strength of the technique lies in its ability to generate *hypotheses* about how the user population as a whole *might* feel or *might* behave. To be used to inform marketing strategy an organization might typically test these hypotheses with quantitative techniques and a larger, more representative sample of the target population.

Quantitative Research Techniques

Quantitative research typically involves the gathering of numerical information about the market or particular audience the researcher is concerned with. Unlike qualitative research the goal is to quantify the number of members of a particular group that hold certain views, donate in particular ways, are motivated by particular factors, etc. Quantitative research techniques include:

• *Personal interviews*. These may be conducted by a trained researcher in the home, an office, or a central location/street. Both qualitative and quantitative data could be gathered, although cost and time restraints frequently confine data collection to quantitative data. The interviewer follows a set script and simply poses a range of questions, noting down the replies he/she receives for subsequent analysis.

- *Telephone interviews.* Increasingly, marketing research is being conducted by phone. Researchers from the organization or agency ring a sample of individuals and again follow a set script, posing each question in turn. Modern technology now facilitates a process known as CATI (Computer Assisted Telephone Interviewing) where the questions appear on a screen in front of the interviewer and when each response is given it is typed into the database (or the appropriate box clicked on). Depending on the nature of the response the interviewer is then prompted by the system to ask the next appropriate question.

- *Postal questionnaires.* Here the contact with the research sample is impersonal. A series of questions are developed, printed onto a questionnaire and dispatched to members of the target audience whose opinion is sought. Often the response is incentivized in some way and facilitated through the inclusion of a reply paid or freepost envelope.

- *E-mail questionnaires.* The recent rise in computer ownership and access to the Internet has now made the acquisition of market research data much more affordable. In 1999 Sudman and Blair argued that electronic surveys will replace telephone surveys over the next 25 years as more and more individuals become comfortable with the medium. Surveys can easily be e-mailed to service users, donors, or other categories of supporter. Alternatively, if the questionnaire is lengthy, it is possible to post the questionnaire on an organization's website and then to e-mail respondents asking them to visit the site and complete it. Sudman and Blair (1999) recommend locating the questionnaire in a password-protected part of the site, so that responses from members of the sample do not become confused with those of other site users who decide to complete the questionnaire during their visit.

- *Fax questionnaires.* In the USA the fax is a medium now commonly employed for advertising and other forms of marketing solicitation. Its use is more common in the context of business-to-business (B2B) marketing, although home faxes are growing in number and significance. In some instances, if involved in research with corporate organizations it may thus be appropriate to consider employing a fax survey, which respondents may complete and fax back to the nonprofit. Such forms of research are unlikely to work in the UK, where unsolicited faxes are regarded as highly intrusive.

Taking a Sample

In undertaking quantitative research it may be possible to solicit the opinions of everyone in the whole group or *population* of interest. Under these circumstances the researcher is effectively conducting a *census* since everyone of interest can be contacted and asked for their views. More frequently, however, it is not practical to pose questions of everyone in a target population, by virtue of the sheer number of contacts involved, the costs of soliciting their views, or the difficulty of contacting them, perhaps because of their geographic spread. In such circumstances, researchers take a sample of the members of the population and calculate statistics about that sample, which allow them to make statements and estimates about the population as a whole, without the need to contact everyone.

There are four main methods for sampling of relevance to marketers: random sampling, systematic random sampling, stratified random sampling, and quota sampling. Random sampling is referred to as *probability sampling*, while quota sampling is referred to as *nonprobability sampling*. This difference matters because it impacts on the way we may interpret the results of the research undertaken.

Under random sampling each member of a population has an equal chance of being se-lected in the sample. Because of this it is possible to calculate a *level of confidence* and limit of accuracy from the results of such a sample. A level of confidence is a statement about how confident we can be about the results from the sample holding good across the population as a whole. At the 95 per cent level of confidence, for example, there is only a 5 per cent (or 1 in 20) chance that the sample results do not hold good for the whole population. Confi-dence levels can be set higher than this to offer greater accuracy, but this would add substan-tially to the cost since it would require the extraction of a larger sample.

It is important to note that probability samples are not necessarily more representative than non-probability samples. Indeed, the converse can often be true. The point is that prob-ability samples allow for the calculation of *sample error* or the extent to which errors in the results occur because a sample was used rather than asking the whole population for their views. You cannot do this with non-probability samples since no objective method is used in the first place to gather the sample.

We now consider each form of sampling in turn.

Random Sampling

To generate a random sample, as noted above, every member of the population must have an equal chance of selection. To take a random sample it is thus necessary to begin by defining or assembling a *sampling frame*. This is simply a complete list of all the individuals in the tar-get population. This may, for example, be a list of names on a database, a directory of organ-izations, or a list of contacts. Each name on this list would then be assigned a number and all the numbers entered into a hat. If a 10 per cent sample of individuals is required, 10 per cent of those numbers and associated names would then be drawn at random out of the hat.

Of course, modern technology now makes this process much less cumbersome and many modern software programs generate numbers at random which can be used to generate a random sample for the researcher. Indeed, in many cases the researcher will be oblivious to the process since it is necessary only to request this kind of sample from the database software.

Systematic Sampling

There are occasions, however, when a truly random sample is not practical, perhaps because the sampling frame is supplied in a list format and where the number of contacts on that list is large. Assigning numbers and then selecting numbers at random from the list would then be time-consuming and potentially costly. Under these circumstances it may be more practi-cal to take a *systematic random sample*. Suppose we wish to take a 10 per cent sample from a list of 1000 names. We could then proceed by selecting a random start point and thus select-ing at random a number between 1 and 10. Suppose we select the number 4. We would then work down through our list taking the 4th name, the 14th name, the 24th name, the 34th name, etc. until we had completed the list and extracted the 10 per cent of contacts required. This is a systematic random sample.

Stratified Random Sampling

To illustrate the need for this form of sampling let's consider the example of a local author-ity wishing to explore views on facilities that will be made available in a new community

Table 4.1 Stratified random sample

Age profile	% of population
Under 20	10
21–40	20
41–60	40
61–80	20
81+	10

sports complex. To investigate this issue, it has been proposed that a 10 per cent sample of the local population be sent a questionnaire to ascertain their views. Intuitively the marketing team feels that these reasons might vary by the age of the individual. Now suppose that the age profile of the local population is as depicted in Table 4.1.

By taking a purely random sample of 10 per cent of these individuals it is possible, however unlikely, that a sample could be generated where the individuals contacted are over 80. This could greatly bias the results, particularly in the context of a sports centre! Instead, researchers would better proceed by deciding in advance that of their sample 10 per cent will be under 20, 20 per cent will be aged 21–40, 40 per cent will be aged 41–60, 20 per cent will be aged 61–80, and 10 per cent will be aged 80+. In other words, the composition of the sample mirrors that of the population to ensure that each category or *strata* is properly represented.

Non-Probability Sampling

With non-probability sampling the chances of selection are not known therefore the ability to generalize about a population, based on the results of a sample, are much reduced. Kumar et al. (1999) argue that the results of non-probability sampling may contain biases and uncertainties that make them worse than no information at all. Not all writers are as pessimistic, however, and the decision of whether or not to use probability-based sampling will be a function of the degree of accuracy required, the likely costs of error, the population variability, and the type of information needed (Tull and Hawkins 1996).

Non-probability sampling does not require the use of a sampling frame and thus the project's costs might be reduced. The sample is chosen at the convenience of the researcher to fit the needs of the particular project. Samples can be created by convenience sampling (simply selecting individuals convenient to the research project), purposive sampling (where individuals are selected who are felt to be appropriate to the project objectives), or quota sampling.

In quota sampling, the researcher makes a clear effort to ensure that the sample he constructs mirrors the characteristics of the sample as a whole. Thus if a nonprofit were looking to assess the awareness of their organization/brand among members of the local population, the researchers could proceed by identifying the demographic profile of that population. They might do this by age and gender, for example. They would then create a quota such as that depicted in Table 4.2 to ensure that the balance of people whose opinions they solicit reflects that of the population as a whole.

It is important not to confuse quota sampling with stratified sampling. The major difference is that in the former the interviewer/researcher selects the individual respondent, while in the latter the selection process is carried out by random selection.

Table 4.2 Quota sample of 50 individuals

Characteristic	% of population	Quota sample
Male		
Aged under 30	10	5
Aged 31–60	10	5
Aged over 60	30	15
Female		
Aged under 30	20	10
Aged 31–60	10	5
Aged over 60	20	10
TOTAL	100	50

Sample Size

The question of how big a sample to use for research is not an easy one to answer as it depends on a number of factors. Much depends on the type of sample, the statistics that will be calculated, the homogeneity of the population, and the resources (time, people, and money) available. It is impossible in this chapter to cover all the pertinent factors, but it is worth noting that there are now a number of tables, calculator functions, and software programs that will prompt the user with the relevant questions and generate an appropriate sample size. There are also many websites hosted by research agencies that have sponsored online tools to help the inexperienced researcher. An often surprising point to consider when calculating the sample size is that it has little to do with the size of the population. The reason for this is quite straightforward. Rather than the size of the population being the key, it is the extent to which all the members of the population have the same value or response. If you had 20,000 people in a population who all responded in exactly the same way to an advertisement appeal to stop smoking, then obviously you would only need a sample of one of them to ascertain the behaviour of the others. Not a very likely scenario. Not everyone who sees the ad will smoke and individuals who do will respond in very different ways. Thus what affects the sample size that will be necessary is the variability of the population. Obviously the greater the variability, the larger will be the sample required to estimate aggregate behaviour with any precision.

Questionnaire Design

In designing a research questionnaire, there are a number of points to bear in mind.

Overall Length

People quickly get bored with completing surveys, particularly in face-to-face or telephone situations. In these circumstances the length of the questionnaire should be held to an absolute minimum with the questions posed tightly integrated with the overall research problem. Postal questionnaires can be longer since respondents may complete them at their leisure, but researchers employing questionnaires of over four pages will note a sharp drop-off rate in the achieved response rate.

Questions should be Clear and Unambiguous

Questions should be written in the language of the target audience. It should be remembered that while a marketer may be highly conversant with the language employed by the cause, members of the public may not understand much of the specialist terminology and even fewer of the mnemonics. These must be avoided or explained.

Each question should also be written and checked for clarity. The question should also avoid ambiguity and the notorious 'and' word. Consider the following example.

Please indicate the extent to which you agree with the following statement, employing the following scale:

1 = Strongly Disagree

2 = Disagree

3 = No Opinion

4 = Agree

5 = Strongly Agree

Donating money to this charity gives me a sense of real pride and I enjoy receiving the communications they send me.

1	2	3	4	5

If this question seems appropriate at first glance, consider how a donor might answer if donating to the organization gives them a sense of pride, but they hate the communications they receive. Each question in a questionnaire should address one dimension only.

Use Closed Questions Wherever Possible

It is important when designing a questionnaire to consider how the data will be analysed. Closed questions are much easier to analyse since they only allow respondents a range of options in respect of their response. The example below is thus a closed question.

Please indicate your age category:

[ ]   Under 20

[ ]   21–40

[ ]   41–60

[ ]   61–80

[ ]   81+

Open questions, by contrast, invite the respondent to offer an answer which then has to be coded into categories (or interpreted) post hoc by the researcher, e.g. 'Please tell us what you think of the communications you receive from us.' It is this latter dimension that makes the inclusion of open questions undesirable since they can substantially slow down the analysis undertaken and greatly increase the costs of analysis as a consequence. It should be noted, however, that the use of closed questions requires the researcher to have a firm grasp of the subject area in advance, since they must ensure that the options available to respondents are comprehensive. Where doubt remains, some researchers add a final category, namely 'other—please specify'.

Classifications should be Carefully Designed

Where closed questions are employed, researchers should take great care to design the categories appropriately. Each option should be discrete, unlike the example below where it is possible to tick two boxes if one is aged 20, 40, 60, or 80.

Please indicate your age category:

[ ]   20 and under

[ ]   20–40

[ ]   40–60

[ ]   60–80

[ ]   80+

Similarly, confusion can arise about the meaning of some categories. In the author's experience, asking a person's occupation can be a particular problem since in one instance an individual chose to describe his occupation as 'bank director' when in reality his role involved greeting customers at the door and directing them to the correct counter!

Avoid Leading Questions

Leading questions are those that direct the respondent to give a specific answer, thus, 'Did the recent financial scandal affect your giving?' is doomed to failure from the outset. Less obviously asking a donor whether they have read a particular magazine or communication may simply prompt them to say 'yes'. If a researcher is interested in recall of specific communications or the media exposure of a particular individual s/he will be advised to generate a list of communications and to ask the respondent which of them he/she can recall or has read, respectively. Respondents are then less likely to answer in an 'ego-defensive' manner.

Order Questions in a Logical Sequence

In designing a questionnaire it is also important to group together questions that pertain to a particular issue to avoid confusing the respondent as to what specifically is being asked. Similarly it is appropriate to seek to 'funnel' responses down from general questions about the issue as a whole down to the specifics of exactly what data is being sought. In other words, questionnaires should be constructed in a logical order that guides the respondent in an orderly manner through the topic.

Keep Personal Questions until the End

If it is necessary to ask any sensitive questions of respondents, perhaps their ethnic background, income level, religion, or attitudes to tough social issues, it is better to ask these at the end of the questionnaire rather than at the beginning. Asking these questions up front is likely to put off the respondent, as he/she is likely to assume that all of the questionnaire will probe for such personal data. Asking for this at the end of a questionnaire, when a respondent has already invested considerable time in the process, and when some form of relationship has been established, is far less likely to result in non-completion.

Pilot Test

It is absolutely essential that any questionnaire be piloted before rolling it out to a particular audience. While all the questions posed might seem entirely logical and appropriate to the researcher, there are inevitably a few that create confusion, fail to be understood, or attract answers that the research team were not expecting. A pilot test can be undertaken at low cost with a small percentage of the sample and any necessary changes can be made before the time and expense of the full survey rollout are incurred.

Scaling Techniques for Surveys

There are two important scaling techniques that are typically used by researchers in surveys: Likert scales and semantic differential scales. There are others, but these are the most commonly employed.

Likert Scales

A Likert scale is a list of statements with five (or sometimes seven) possible choices such as strongly agree, agree, neutral (or no opinion), disagree, and strongly disagree. The scale is used against a battery of questions that are given to respondents. The researcher is then able to measure the attitudes of respondents. Typically the items included in the battery will have been generated from prior qualitative research or secondary sources. An example battery of questions is provided below.

To what extent do you trust the Nature Conservancy to undertake each of the activities listed?

STATEMENT	Strongly disagree			Strongly agree	
Always to act in the best interest of the cause	1	2	3	4	5
To conduct their operations ethically	1	2	3	4	5
To use donated funds appropriately	1	2	3	4	5
Not to exploit their donors	1	2	3	4	5
To use fundraising techniques that are appropriate and sensitive	1	2	3	4	5

In presenting the results from questions designed in this format it is now common practice to present the mean and/or median scores calculated from all the respondents who answered each question. Thus the higher the average score, the greater the degree of agreement with each of the statements listed.

Semantic Differential Scales

These scales are designed to measure differences between words. As previously, qualitative work may have identified a series of constructs or ways in which people think about the organization and its services. An attitude battery consisting of bipolar constructs can then be developed. A five- or seven-point rating scale is frequently used. As an example, the name of

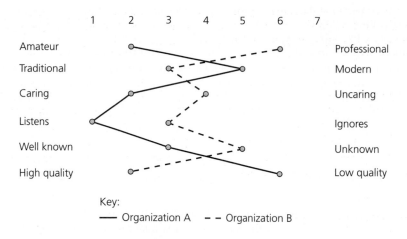

Figure 4.2 Profile of two nonprofits

a particular organization could appear at the top of a page on a questionnaire. Respondents could then be asked to rate this organization using each of the scales in the battery. Computed results could then allow the researcher to compile an attitude profile, perhaps comparing perceptions of their own organization with those of a key competitor.

In this example the bipolar constructs could include the following:

Amateur	Professional
Traditional	Modern
Caring	Uncaring
Listens	Ignores
Well known	Unknown
High quality	Low quality

The profile of two organizations could then be compared, as indicated in Figure 4.2.

Analysis of Qualitative Data

The process of data analysis differs greatly between qualitative and quantitative data. Qualitative data from interviews and focus groups is typically transcribed from recordings of the original research. The resultant text is then input into a software package such as NVIVO which allows the researcher to examine and code each aspect of the content.

The majority of qualitative software packages operate in a similar way and allow a researcher to highlight a line or lines of text that contain a particular idea. This idea is then assigned a code. Subsequent text containing similar ideas will also be assigned this particular code. In a typical analysis of focus group data there may be 100 or more codes that reflect different facets of the discussion and responses. Text can also be coded according to who is speaking and reflect gender, income, age, etc.

In writing up the results, researchers can then request that the software groups the text of the discussions by code—and thus the themes to emerge from each facet of the discussion can easily be written up and peppered with direct quotations from respondents to illustrate why a particular conclusion has been drawn. One might also explore, again using the codes, whether the views of participants varied by categories such as age, gender, income, etc.

An example of this form of analysis and how it is written up is provided below. In this example the researchers were interested to explore the factors that might lead individuals to offer a legacy (or bequest) to charity. A series of focus groups was conducted with individuals who had pledged a legacy gift, and a range of motives for support of this nature were identified. The researchers subsequently grouped these into one of two categories, namely organizational factors and individual factors. In the brief extract reproduced below, the researchers report their findings in respect of the organizational issues. Notice how each idea expressed in the interviews is expressed in turn, described, and, where appropriate, illustrated with a direct quotation. This is typical of the format of many qualitative research reports.

ORGANIZATIONAL FACTORS

Performance

The performance achieved by a particular organization was a key factor in determining whether a legacy gift would be offered. This was a theme that was addressed at many points through all the focus groups conducted. It appeared to be more of an issue than was the case in conventional giving because of the relative size of the gift that would be offered. As one participant noted, 'A legacy is a bigger decision. I thought long and hard about which charity to leave it to. I wanted to be sure they wouldn't squander it.' Others indicated that they had conducted a more thorough information search than had been the case for other types of giving they had engaged in. Again this occurred because of the likely size of the gift, but also because the individuals realized it would be the final contribution they would make to charity. 'I looked carefully at what they'd achieved and how they used their money. I had to be sure it would get to where it was needed. I had to be sure this gift would count.'

Professionalism

The quality of an organization's management was also very much an issue. Many participants felt that they needed to be sure that the organizations they were supporting in this way were well managed. As one participant noted, 'I'd never support organizations that were poorly managed—not with a legacy. I might send them a small donation if I really liked the cause, but not a legacy.' Many pledgers had sought information and advice from the charity before changing or making their will. This personal contact had caused many to form a view about the professionalism of the charity and in a number of cases deterred a donor from making a bequest. 'You can forgive a lot from charities. After all, they're focused on their work, aren't they? But there's a limit, you know. If I'm making such a major decision I expect them to behave professionally.'

Responsiveness

Participants stressed the uniquely personal nature of the legacy gift. For most it would be the single largest gift they would ever be able to offer a charity. There was thus a strong sense that this gift was in some way 'special' and that in offering it they were strengthening the bond between themselves and the organization. The financial and moral significance of the gift appeared to generate higher expectations of how the organization might deal with them in future. As one participant noted, 'It was a really

continues

continued

big thing for me. I'd had to discuss it with my family and go along to the solicitors. I think the least they can do in return is answer my letters and be prepared to call me if I have any queries or concerns.' Others indicated that the notion of responsiveness could also be a factor for them in deciding which charities to support with a legacy. 'I knew I couldn't support all eight of my favourites and I really wanted there to be a big gift, not lots of small ones. So I thought back about how I'd been treated and who seemed genuinely interested in me, who cared enough to send a personal letter and thank me properly.' Many respondents felt that a legacy was such a substantial gift that those who wanted recognition (perhaps a mention in a book of remembrance) should be afforded this.

Communications

Participants were generally satisfied with the quality of communications they received from the non-profits they support. They enjoyed being kept informed about how their gifts had been used and the issues/challenges facing those organizations. While they recognized this was true of all the organizations they supported, legacy pledgers were found to be particularly concerned with the quality of communications received from the organizations they had elected to support in this way. 'When I was giving just a few pounds a month I didn't really pay much attention to what they sent me. When I changed my will I guess I needed reassurance I'd made the right decision and I read everything they send me now.' Others indicated that communications were particularly important because they cared passionately about the cause. It was felt that anyone leaving a legacy to a charity by definition cared particularly about its work and that as a consequence they would be particularly interested to keep up to date with that work. As one participant noted, 'I don't read half of the charity solicitations I receive, but I lost my wife to cancer and (their work) really matters, you know—that's why I'll remember them in my will.' The quality of these communications was felt to be important, and pledgers were highly focused on being kept regularly up to date with information about what was being achieved.

Analysis of Quantitative Data

Software packages are also available to analyse quantitative data and these vary in terms of sophistication and cost. Among the most commonly employed are SNAP (which also aids in questionnaire design) and SPSS (Statistical Package for the Social Sciences). There are a range of statistics that may be calculated to assist the researcher in summarizing and interpreting the results they have achieved. Such analysis is beyond the scope of this text, but interested readers may wish to consult Hair et al. (2005).

The most common forms of summary used to represent this form of data include tables, bar charts, histograms, and simple numerical summaries such as the mean, median, and standard deviation.

Charts

Bar charts or frequency diagrams are probably the most common forms of graphical representation of statistical data. They consist of a series of bars, the height of which is either proportional to the frequency with which a particular outcome occurs, or to the probability that this outcome will occur.

A simple bar chart is presented in Figure 4.3. In this example, the seat utilization rate (i.e. the percentage of seats occupied) in each of the performances on offer at a local theatre

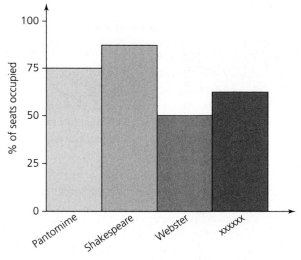

Figure 4.3 Bar chart of seat utilization rate

is presented for the period shown. While the same information could be presented in tabular form, the reader will appreciate the greater degree of impact that can be achieved with a graphic presentation. It is immediately obvious to the eye which of the performances has attracted the largest audience.

A second type of chart commonly employed for the presentation of data is the histogram (see Figure 4.4). In this case it is not only the height of the bars that is significant, but also the dimensions of the base. In this example the dolphin sanctuary has plotted the response rates that it has historically received to one of its most popular donor recruitment mailings. It seems clear that a common outcome for this particular mailing would be to achieve a response rate of circa 1–1.5 per cent.

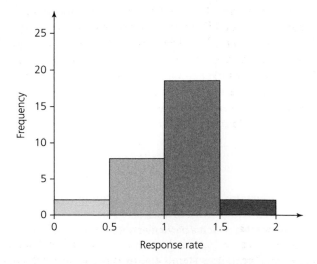

Figure 4.4 Histogram of mailing response rates

Descriptive Statistics

Mean

One of the most commonly encountered descriptive statistics is the mean, denoted by $\bar{x}$. It is also one of the simplest to calculate. You simply add up the results of a given set of measurements and then divide by the number of measurements. This is shown in mathematical notation below:

$$\bar{x} = \frac{\sum_{i=1}^{} xi}{n}$$

Median

A second commonly used descriptor is the median. This is simply the measurement that falls in the middle of a given set of observations or 'distribution'. There are many occasions when it is preferable to quote the median rather than the mean. The median is preferable where there are a number of outliers in the distribution that would bias the mean and thus give a misleading picture of the nature of the distribution. Suppose, for example, we were interested in reporting the 'average' salaries earned by service users. We take a small sample of the salaries earned for five individuals and obtain £20K, £22K, £23K, £24K, and £70K. In this case the median value would be £23K while the mean distorted by the outlier would be £31.8K. The median would thus be a more reasonable representation of this distribution than the mean.

Standard Deviation

Both the mean and the median give the researcher some idea of where the centre of a distribution is located. While this is clearly useful, information researchers are usually also interested to know how spread around this distribution might be. One possible way that this measure might be derived would be to take the difference between each measurement and the mean and then to calculate the average of this deviation. The problem with this approach, however, is that the deviations will be both positive and negative. Consider a distribution containing the measurements 1, 2, and 3. In this case the mean would be 2 and the deviation -1, 0, and $+1$. The mean deviation in this case would be zero and we would therefore be no further forward in attempting to find a measure of spread. The way around this difficulty is to calculate the deviations from the mean as previously and then to square these numbers (which removes any negative signs), add these squared numbers together, divide by the number of measurements, and then take the square root of the answer. In our previous example, the square deviations would be 1, 0, and 1 and their sum would be 2. If we then divide this by 3 to get the mean of the squared deviations and take the square root of the answer we obtain a result of circa 0.8. This somewhat wordy description is represented in mathematical notation below:

$$s = \sqrt{\frac{\sum_{i=1}^{}(x - \bar{x})^2}{n}}$$

Range

In cases where the median has been used to describe the 'average' point on a distribution, a good measure of spread to accompany this value is the range. The range is simply the highest value observed minus the lowest value. While this is a useful figure, it is helpful to recognize that this too can be strongly influenced by outliers. For this reason some researchers prefer to quote the inter-quartile range. This is simply the difference between two points. The lower of these corresponds to a point below which one-quarter of the observations lie (the lower quartile) and the second to the point above which one-quarter of the points lie (the upper quartile).

In the example provided below, we reproduce an extract from a quantitative research report. Here the researchers have chosen to present the data in tabular form and to cite many of the statistics listed above. The objective of this research was to compare the demographic profile and attitudes of individuals who have pledged a legacy (or bequest) to a nonprofit with members of the standard (i.e. non-pledger) supporter base. In this extract the researchers provide the details of their demographic comparison. It is interesting to note that alongside their comparison they have also performed a number of statistical tests to determine whether differences they note between pledgers and supporters are 'significant' differences, represented in the population as a whole, or not significant since they might well be due to sampling errors and the operation of random chance. Comparisons of this type are common in market research and the exact statistical tests that may be employed are a function of the categories of data being examined. This is beyond the scope of this text, but the illustration shows just how useful this additional form of analysis can be.

EXAMPLE

Profile of Respondents

Tables 4.3–4.8 present the details of the demographic profile of respondents. The results are presented for both legacy pledgers and supporters. The results in Table 4.3 illustrate the slight female bias present on many charity databases. There is no significant difference, however, in the balance of gender between the supporter and pledger groups.

The occupation of each group is depicted in Table 4.4. It may be noted that both the supporter and pledger groups have a high concentration of office/clerical and professional individuals, reflecting the bias towards socio-economic groups B and C1 in giving. The high concentration of teachers/lecturers is also noteworthy and again typical of the profile of many charitable databases. No significant differences between pledgers and supporters could be identified.

The income profile of respondents is reported in Table 4.5. In this case it can be seen that pledgers report a significantly lower annual income than supporters ($X^2 = 46.98$, significance level 0.000).

Significant differences between the two groups were also reported when examining the marital status of respondents. Pledgers are significantly more likely to be living alone, either because they are single or because they have been widowed (Table 4.6) (Goodman and Kuskal Tau value 0.061, significance level 0.000). This difference is also supported in Table 4.7 where it can be seen that pledgers are significantly less likely to have children ($x^2 = 107.55$, significance level 0.000).

Table 4.3 Gender of respondents

Gender	Supporter %	Pledger %
Male	40.2	35.1
Female	59.8	64.9

continues

continued

Table 4.4 Past/present occupation of respondents

Occupation	Supporter %	Pledger %
Director	5.4	4.2
Housewife/husband	8.5	6.4
Manager	6.9	7.8
Manual/factory	0.9	1.4
Office/clerical	12.6	16.9
Professional	27.0	23.7
Self-employed	6.6	8.0
Shop assistant	0.9	0.8
Skilled tradesman	2.1	2.0
Supervisor	0.7	1.6
Teacher/lecturer	17.0	18.1
Other	11.4	9.0

Table 4.5 Current income profile of respondents

Category	Supporter %	Pledger %
Up to £4,999	3.6	4.6
£5,000–£9,999	8.4	17.5
£10,000–£14,999	13.8	17.3
£15,000–£19,999	11.1	14.2
£20,000–£24,999	12.1	14.4
£25,000–£29,999	8.4	7.0
£30,000–£39,999	13.6	10.1
£40,000+	29.0	14.9

Table 4.6 Marital status

Status	Supporter %	Pledger %
Single	18.7	34.9
Married	55.1	33.3
Separated	0.3	1.8
Divorced	5.4	5.7
Living with partner	6.2	5.0
Widowed	14.3	19.4

continues

continued

Table 4.7 Presence of children

Children	Supporter %	Pledger %
No	31.1	61.3
Yes	68.9	38.7

Table 4.8 Demographic and behavioural characteristics

Variable	Supporter mean	Pledger mean	F	Sig
Age at which full-time education completed	20.9	19.0	1.27	0.26
Age	59.2	68.4	53.06	0.00
Amount given to charity each year	£600.64	£701.26	2.41	0.12

Table 4.8 presents the remaining demographic data captured in the survey and in addition presents the total amount donated by each group to the charity sector in the past year. As the results indicate, the mean age at which both pledgers and supporters completed their full-time education is very similar, suggesting that many individuals were educated to degree level. No significant difference between the two groups was reported. It can be seen that pledgers are significantly older than supporters, having a mean age of 68.4 years.

No differences could be discerned between the two groups in relation to the total amount given to charity each year, with supporters offering £601 per annum and pledgers £701. It should be noted that the distributions in each case were highly skewed and that as a consequence a better measure of the typical amount given per annum is the median. The median amount donated per annum by both supporters and pledgers was found to be £300.

■ **DISCUSSION QUESTIONS**

1. Distinguish, with examples, between qualitative and quantitative marketing research.

2. As the fundraising manager of a small children's charity looking to explore the motives for legacy giving, explain and justify a programme of marketing research you would propose to adopt to explore this issue.

3. In your role as the marketing director of a medium-sized arts charity you have been asked by your chief executive to prepare a marketing research plan to explore why audience numbers are in decline. Explain what primary and secondary research you would recommend the organization undertake.

4. As the marketing director of a local (government) council you have been asked to determine how satisfied local residents are with the refuse collection service and recycling facilities the organization provides. Suggest a programme of primary research that could be adopted to provide this information.

■ REFERENCES

AMA (American Marketing Association) (1961) *Report of the Definitions Committee*, Chicago, American Marketing Association.

Hair, J.F., Black, W.C., Babin, B. amd Anderson, R.E. (2005) *Multivariate Data Analysis*, 6th edn, Englewood Cliffs, NJ, Prentice Hall.

Kotler, P. (1967) *Marketing Management: Analysis, Planning and Control*, Englewood Cliffs, NJ, Prentice Hall.

Kumar, V., Aaker, D.A. and Day, C.S. (1999) *Essentials of Marketing Research*, New York, John Wiley & Sons.

Sudman, S. and Blair, E. (1999) *Sampling in the Twenty-First Century*, Greenvale, Academy of Marketing Sciences.

Tull, D.S. and Hawkins, D.I. (1996) *Marketing Research: Measurement and Method*, 6th edn, New York, Macmillan.

Marketing Objectives and Strategy

Introduction

Having now examined the first stage of the marketing plan (i.e., Where are we now?) and identified the research tools that may be used to supply this information, we are now in a position to address the second stage, i.e., Where do we want to be?

The marketing audit provides a concise summary of where the organization stands in relation to its environment and, as such, should provide a sound basis on which to decide what is going to be achievable over the duration of the plan. When this has been decided, the nonprofit is in a position to develop marketing objectives for the planning horizon in question. Once set, the nonprofit can then address how exactly these objectives are going to be met through its marketing strategies and tactics. In this chapter we will focus on marketing objectives and key marketing strategies. Tactics will be dealt with in Chapter 7.

Setting Marketing Objectives

The importance of setting objectives in a not-for-profit context has long been underrated. As Drucker (1990: 107) notes:

In a non-profit organisation there is no such [thing as a] bottom line. But there is also a temptation to downplay results. There is the temptation to say: 'We are serving a good cause. We are doing the Lord's work. Or we are doing something to make life a little better for people and that's a result in itself.' That is not enough. If a business wastes its resources on non-results, by and large it loses its own money. In a non-profit institution though, it's somebody else's money—the donor's money. Service organisations are accountable to donors, accountable for putting the money where the results are, and for performance. So, this is an area that needs special emphasis for non-profit executives. Good intentions only pave the way to Hell!

Objectives are an important part of the plan as they are the only mechanism by which its success can be measured. If a plan achieves its stated objectives we might reasonably conclude that it has been a success. Without them, one can only speculate as to the planner's original intent and the effectiveness of the activities undertaken have no benchmark against which to be assessed. Valuable resources could be being wasted, but the organization would have no mechanism for identifying that this was in fact the case. The style in which the objectives are written is also a significant issue.

Vague objectives, however emotionally appealing, are counter-productive to sensible planning and are usually the result of the human propensity for wishful thinking which often smacks more of cheerleading than serious marketing leadership. What this means is that while it is arguable whether directional terms such as decrease, optimise, minimise should be used as objectives, it seems logical that unless there is some measure, or yardstick, against which to measure a sense of locomotion towards achieving them, they do not serve any useful purpose. MacDonald (1984: 88)

To be managerially useful, good objectives should be:

• *Specific*. Objectives should be related to one particular aspect of marketing activity. Objectives which relate simultaneously to diverse aspects of marketing activity are difficult to assess since they may require the organization to use different techniques of measurement and to look across different planning horizons. Attempting to combine activities might therefore lead to confusion, or at best a lack of focus.

• *Measurable*. Words such as 'maximize' or 'increase' are not particularly helpful when it later becomes necessary to assess the effectiveness of marketing activity. To be useful, objectives should avoid these terms and be capable of measurement. They should hence specify quantifiable values whenever possible, e.g. 'to achieve a 20 per cent market share', or 'to produce a 5 per cent reduction in smoking nationwide'.

• *Achievable*. Marketing objectives should be derived from a thorough analysis of the content of the *marketing* audit and not creative thinking on the part of managers. Objectives which have no possibility of accomplishment will only serve to demoralize those responsible for their achievement and serve to deplete resources that could have had a greater potential impact elsewhere.

• *Relevant*. Marketing objectives should be consistent with the objectives of the organization as a whole. They should merely supply a greater level of detail—identifying specifically what the marketing function will have to achieve to move the nonprofit in the desired direction.

• *Timescaled*. Good objectives should clearly specify the duration over which they are to be achieved. Not only does this help to plan the strategies and tactics by which they will be accomplished, but it also assists in permitting the organization to set in place control procedures to ensure that the stated targets will indeed be met. Thus monthly 'sub-targets' for each form of fundraising could be set and corrective action initiated early in the duration of a plan, as soon as a variance is detected.

Thus good marketing objectives should be SMART!

Having now outlined the 'rules', it might be helpful to demonstrate what a typical non-profit marketing objective might look like. In the context of arts marketing, an objective for a theatre might take the form: 'To achieve a 20 per cent increase in student attendance at all performances between 15 October and 10 December 2009.'

In a fundraising context the objectives might read: 'To attract £200,000 in voluntary income from individual donors by the end of the calendar year' and 'To attract £50,000 of (cash) corporate support by the end of November 2009'.

Nonprofit Marketing Strategy

Having specified the objectives it is intended that the plan will achieve, it is then possible to address the means by which these will be accomplished. The overall approach to their attainment is termed 'marketing strategy'. Strategy deals with the major issues that will impact on the whole organization's approach to its markets (or subject). They differ from tactics since tactics supply the minutiae of exactly what will be done, when, and by whom. Thus it may be a strategy to continue to build the organization's brand through awareness-raising advertising, but the specifics of where the advertising will take place, how frequently it will appear, the nature of the copy or design, etc. will be left to the tactical component of the plan to follow.

What comprises the general approach to meeting an organization's objectives will clearly vary from one situation to another, and it is thus impossible to develop a definitive list of what might be regarded as strategic marketing issues. As a broad guide, however, the following issues are typical of those that need to be addressed:

- overall direction
- merger/collaborative strategy
- competitive strategy
- segmentation strategy
- positioning strategy
- branding strategy.

The order of this list is deliberate. It offers a logical flow of marketing ideas and each section to some extent will build on the previous. That said, after many years experience of writing marketing plans, this author has found that the order in which these should most helpfully be considered does vary by context and in most cases an element of iteration will be necessary. While these appear neat headings, the reality is that they are all closely inter-related facets of strategy and it will normally be necessary to revise the draft of some strategies as others parts of the plan begin to come together.

In the balance of this chapter we will consider each of these strategic issues in turn. Branding will be the focus of Chapter 6.

Overall Direction

There are four key strategic directions that an organization could follow if it wants to achieve growth. These are illustrated in Figure 5.1. All the options involve making decisions about the range of services that will be provided and the markets into which they will be delivered. Each strategic option will now be considered in turn.

Services

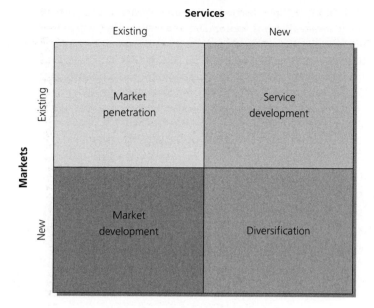

Figure 5.1 Ansoff's matrix

Source: adapted from Ansoff, H.I. (1968) *Corporate Strategy,* Penguin Books. Reproduced by kind permission of the author.

Market Penetration

This option involves the organization in attempting to gain a greater impact in its existing markets. The existing range of services continues to be marketed to the existing market segments and no changes are planned to either. There are many ways in which a nonprofit could look to penetrate the market, including finding some way to reduce the price charged for the service, enhancing promotional activity, improving distribution facilities, or more likely, maximizing output. Many charities, for example, face almost unlimited demand for the services they currently supply and could hence gain greater penetration simply by looking for ways to maximize the output from their own organization.

In cases where demand is less buoyant, however, or where the charity has a comparatively low level of awareness among its target audience, the organization may have to resort to intensifying its marketing activity to stimulate the additional demand it requires. If there are competitors in the market, this may prove to be no easy task, as additional 'sales' may have to be gained at their expense. This is perhaps less of a problem in an expanding market as there may be sufficient increases in demand per annum to allow all competing organizations to realize their growth objectives without having to compete directly with others in the sector. In static or declining markets, however, the reverse is true and additional sales will only be generated by stealing them from others competing within the same market.

Service Development

Service development will normally be an attractive option where the organization does not perceive sufficient opportunities for growth by continuing merely to deliver its existing services. The demand for service development may also be driven by demands from customers, as many local authorities have discovered in recent years. Faced with such a situation an organization may decide that it is appropriate to develop other services which the members of its existing markets may utilize. Indeed, for some organizations a continuing strategy of service development may be the sole reason for their existence. Those, for example, that provide care to patients suffering from terminal illness will continually seek to develop their services as levels of medical and technical knowledge are expanded.

It should be noted that service development is inherently more risky than market penetration since substantial investment is often required to develop new services and there is no guarantee that once developed they will be favoured by the organization's current customer groups.

Market Development

Market development involves the organization in continuing to provide its current range of services, but extending the range of markets into which they will be delivered. The nonprofit can hence elect to target additional market segments, to exploit new uses for the service, or both. A strategy of market development may be most appropriate where a given organization has distinctive expertise to offer. In such cases it may make more sense to target other segments rather than dilute the available expertise by attempting to broaden the range of services available.

A number of nonprofit organizations may be forced into a strategy of market development even in circumstances where they have yet to completely satisfy demand in their existing markets. The housing charity Shelter, for example, has found it necessary to support the homeless in an increasingly larger percentage of Britain's towns and cities, whereas only a few years ago it could have concentrated solely on a small number of these, secure in the knowledge that it was addressing the needs of the majority of individuals at risk.

Diversification

This is perhaps the most risky of all the four potential growth strategies. It involves the non-profit in beginning to deliver services of which it has no experience and supplying these to completely new groups of customers. The degree of risk the organization is subjecting itself to will depend on whether the diversification is related or unrelated. In the case of related diversification, the organization is continuing to operate within broadly the same sector but is attempting to do something new for the first time. The rush to create retail outlets for charities in the 1980s would have constituted related diversification for the organizations involved, since they had long experience of fundraising, but perhaps little, if any, of running a successful retail enterprise.

Unrelated diversification is perhaps less common since this would involve an organization in a radical departure from its existing services/markets. This may be necessary for some nonprofits who find that their *raison d'être* has ceased to exist as, for example, a cure is found for a disease, the relief of whose sufferers they exist to serve. Government legislation can also force organizations into unrelated diversification. Many of the oldest charity trusts in the UK were originally formed with the express purpose of maintaining bridges, highways, etc. Now that local authorities have statutory obligations to look after the transport networks within their boundaries, the objects of these trusts have changed over time to allow them to support other worthwhile causes, many of which, on the face of it, bear no resemblance whatsoever to the original reasons for the trust's creation. It should be noted, though, that for the sub-group of nonprofits—charities—unrelated diversification is a relatively rare strategy.

In many countries the reason for this is a legal one. Charities in the UK are obligated to pursue their 'objects', which are specified at the time of the charity's formation, and they require formal permission from the Charity Commission if these are to be extended or adapted in some way.

Are there other Strategic Directions?

For the sake of completeness it is worth noting that not every organization may wish to achieve growth. Ansoff's matrix as depicted in Figure 5.1 assumes that this is the case and ignores the other strategic options available, which include:

- *do nothing*—where the organization takes a conscious decision not to alter current strategy;
- *withdraw*—where the organization decides to sever its links with a particular service/market;
- *consolidate*—which involves the nonprofit in seeking strategies that will allow it to maintain its current market position. This should not be confused with the 'do nothing' option since the strategies necessary to support a current strategic position are unlikely to be identical to those that allowed an organization to create it in the first place.

Merger/Collaborative Strategy

The incidence of nonprofit merger activity in both the USA and the UK remains relatively low. Nonprofits are not subject to the same market pressures as business organizations and their founders often have such a passion for the cause that they are simply blinded to the activities of organizations undertaking related work. This is a great shame as there may be a variety of benefits that could accrue from either outright merger or some form of collaboration.

In their groundbreaking work, Singer and Yankey (1991) identify three potential motives for collaboration and merger: the lure of efficiency gains, the ability to build a monopoly position (based on a shared vision), and empire-building on the part of nonprofit managers. In their later study, Cowin and Moore (1996) confirmed these findings, and added the additional dimension that those mergers that had been enforced by funders (which can often be the case) appeared to be less successful than those undertaken willingly and based on a shared vision.

In his study of motives for merger in the nonprofit housing sector, Mullins (1998) identifies additional motives such as the potential to spread overheads, the achievement of scale economies, opportunities to increase the asset base/borrowing capacity, geographical and sectoral expansion, the elimination of competition, and responses to tax changes. Schmid (1995) further suggests that the need to control the operating environment and reduce uncertainty can be additional motives. Not surprisingly, in the nonprofit context, the needs of beneficiary groups can, in addition, precipitate merger or collaborative activity. Authors such as Singer and Yankey (1991) have noted the ability of a newly merged organization to increase the quality and range of services it provides to clients.

There is also evidence that organizations look to merge when a crisis threatens their future survival. In the UK the takeover of the children's charity Childline by the National Society for the Prevention of Cruelty to Children (NSPCC) was only prompted when the former organization faced a shortfall in income (Anon 2005). The service provision of both organizations was highly complementary, so there was a good strategic fit between them, but the final impetus was undoubtedly the crisis facing Childline. As Singer and Yankey (1991: 361) note, mergers are 'often depicted as a last resort for survival in the face of intense competition for resources' (see also Golensky 1999).

The role of funders in precipitating merger or collaborative activity is also receiving increasing attention and there is now considerable anecdotal evidence of the direct or indirect role that funders can have in precipitating a merger or collaborative decision. Cowin and Moore (1996) have provided empirical evidence that pressure from funders is a key factor in 38 per cent of all mergers (both planned and actual). Funders are quoted as wanting value for money, wanting evidence that their money makes a real difference, and wanting their funds to be professionally and honestly accounted for. Many funders (especially the better informed trusts and foundations) therefore encourage collaboration and joint working, and are critical of what they regard as needless duplication (Hiland 2003).

In respect of the direct influence of funders, the rationalization of HIV/AIDS charities has been described as a forced development; the result of improvements in drug therapy and treatment, and pressure from health service funders for more cost-effective services. The merger in the UK undertaken in 1999 between Parentline and the National Stepfamilies Association was also, reportedly, undertaken because of pressure from a corporate funder (British Telecom). Even in the nonprofit housing sector, where traditionally a considerable degree of autonomy has existed, the 'best value' agenda of the government is putting increasing pressure on organizations to rationalize and cut costs by stripping out duplicate layers of management.

Funders may also impact indirectly on a decision to merge. A recent opinion poll in the UK conducted by MORI concluded that over 82 per cent of the British public believe that there are too many charities (Wethered 1999). Similarly more recent work undertaken in the commercial sector concludes that 75 per cent of businesses believe that charities should merge if conducting similar work. Mather (2000) notes that the opinion of donors and potential donors is now often cited as a reason that charities should consider merger as an option:

There is a danger that the patience and support of funders and the general public is growing thinner as the number of charities and their calls for help escalate. There is a real need to show that the sector is behaving responsibly for charitable causes and beneficiaries and not for the vested interests of paid and unpaid charity workers (2000: 12).

Although full-blown mergers are rare, other forms of nonprofit collaboration are common with partnerships frequently being forged between a mixture of different organizational types. Lagarde et al. (2007: 40) suggest that:

NGOs may partner with other NGOs because partnerships can lead to greater political influence, they have complementary skills, they may have mutual goals, such as joint fund raising, and their partnerships may lead to more effective outcomes.

NGOs may initiate partnerships with governments because they have complementary goals, for example to obtain financial and other resources and/or to influence policy.

Governments may initiate partnerships with NGOs because they have complementary goals, but also to encourage NGOs to provide services or technical assistance and conduct research— in other words to have NGOs do what governments cannot or do not want to do.

NGOs may initiate partnerships with businesses to obtain financial and other resources for specific projects, to access the businesses' distribution channels and audiences, and, in some instances, to influence more directly rather than confront business practices.

Businesses may consider partnerships with NGOs for public relations or marketing reasons, to access their technical assistance or comply with government regulation, avoid greater government regulation, or promote their products and services.

In reviewing their marketing objectives, it is therefore important that nonprofits identify appropriate partners with whom they might collaborate, either in respect of income generation or, more likely, service delivery. It may be that a number of partnerships may be developed across a range of different services, and at the strategic level of the marketing plan it will be important to outline who these partners might be and how ongoing relationships may be inculcated. As these relationships develop it will thereafter be important to specify how each partnership will operate and the relative strengths of each partner that it is intended to utilize.

Competitive Strategy

There may also be instances where a nonprofit finds itself faced with competition. This may take the form of competition for funds, or it might be competition to provide specific services to a beneficiary group. Here, just as in the commercial sector, the organization needs to decide on what basis it will compete. Authors such as Porter (1980) have argued that organizations may either compete on the basis of being the lowest cost provider, or on the basis of being differentiated in some way. The mistake organizations make, at least according to Porter, is in being unclear as to what the basis for competition will actually be and thus creating a strategic fudge lying somewhere between these two options. Porter argues that successful strategy is predicated on the selection of one of these alternatives.

Choosing to compete on the basis of cost is only a viable strategy where economies of scale or other cost advantages are genuinely achievable (or have already been achieved) by the nonprofit in question. It must also be difficult, or ideally impossible, for a competitor to match this performance. Assuming this is the case, a cost leadership strategy will flourish where:

- price competition is especially vigorous;
- the product or service is essentially standardized and readily available from a range of suppliers (which encourages buyers to select on the basis of price);
- there are few ways to differentiate the service;
- buyers incur low switching costs in changing from one supplier to another, thus giving them the flexibility to switch readily to lower priced sellers having equally good products/services; and
- buyers are large and have significant power to bargain down prices.

It is interesting to note that a number of charities are now beginning to compete for donations on the basis of cost leadership. Some charities now advertise the fact that 'all donated monies will be employed directly on the cause' or 'no donated monies will be spent on management overheads'. Others specify the exact percentage of the gift that will be applied to the cause and use this as the primary basis for competing with other similar organizations. Putting aside the legitimacy of such claims (administration never comes entirely for free!, see Figure 5.2) it is interesting that such strategies appear to be on the increase and that many of the criteria listed above now appear to be met in the fundraising context.

SOMETHING FOR NOTHING?

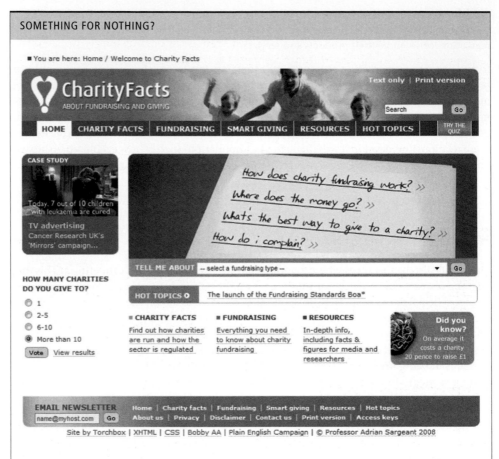

Figure 5.2 Charityfacts website
Source: www.charityfacts.org ©2008

The public information website www.charityfacts.org is highly critical of nonprofits that claim to have zero costs of fundraising or no administration costs. The authors of the site argue that such claims are highly misleading, give rise to unrealistic public expectations about what is achievable, and ultimately damage the public trust. While in seeking funds, some nonprofits may claim that 'every penny goes to the cause' this is often because another, perhaps institutional donor, has already covered the administrative costs of running the organization, or buying the media time. Such claims create the illusion of a highly efficient organization (and are often deliberately selected to do just that) whereas the reality can be very different.

Alternatively some organizations will make this claim because they are raising funds for other organizations and are thus a grant-making body. It is therefore no surprise that they have little by way of administrative overheads. They don't have to manage programmes themselves, they merely raise funds for others. The trick here is that the organizations they give money to will certainly have administration costs, but since these are incurred by another organization further down the funding chain, the claim of the fundraising nonprofit is technically legitimate. An open and honest approach? I suspect not.

Differentiation strategies become an attractive competitive approach whenever buyers' needs and preferences are too diverse to be fully satisfied by a standardized product/service. To succeed with a differentiation strategy, an organization has to study buyers' needs and behaviour carefully to understand what they regard as being important, what they think has particular value, and what they are willing to pay for.

Differentiation can be achieved by:

- *Physical differentiation of the market entity.* The design of the product/service may be enhanced in some way to distinguish it from the competition.

- *Psychological differentiation of the market entity.* The imagery associated with the product/service may be formulated to be in some way unique.

- *Differences in purchasing environment.* The outlets through which the product/service is marketed or delivered may offer features which differentiate it from the competition.

- *Difference by virtue of physical distribution capability.* Thus customers may find that the products/services are delivered more efficiently or on a more timely basis than would be available from another supplier.

- *Difference in after-purchase assurance of satisfaction in use.* After-sales service can also be used for the purposes of differentiation, perhaps through the provision of a higher-quality service than that offered by competitors. This may be of particular relevance to fundraisers who could seek to reassure donors that their monies have been used to good effect.

Segmentation Strategy

Having decided on overall direction and the basis for competition it will be important to define the customers or users whose needs will be addressed in the marketing plan. This process is known as market segmentation, which Kotler (1991: 66) defines as 'the task of breaking the total market (which is typically too large to serve) into segments that share common properties'. In a similar vein, Simpson (1994: 564) defines it as 'the process of dividing up a market into two or more parts, each having unique needs and then developing products and related marketing programmes to meet the needs of one or more of these segments'.

A number of different methods may be used to segment the market. Green (1977) suggested that these methods could be categorized as being either *a priori* or *post hoc*. An *a priori* approach is based on the notion that the marketer decides in advance of any research which basis for segmentation he/she intends to use. Typically this might involve categorizing customers according to their demographic and/or psychographic characteristics. The marketer would then carry out research to identify the attractiveness of each segment and make a decision on the basis of the results as to which segment or segments to pursue. *Post hoc* segmentation involves the marketer in carrying out an amount of initial research into the marketplace. This research might highlight attributes, attitudes, or benefits which relate to particular groups of customers—information which may then be used to decide how best to divide the market. In practice, whether *a priori* or *post hoc* segmentation is undertaken will depend on the relative degree of experience a marketer has within a given market. In cases where the marketer is close to the market and has considerable experience of it an *a priori* approach may best suit the company's needs. Alternatively, where the marketer has little knowledge, a *post hoc* method of segmentation may be most appropriate.

Criteria for Segmenting Consumer Markets

Over the years a plethora of different variables have been used as the basis for market segmentation. Fortunately the majority of these can now be grouped as follows:

- demographic
- geographic and geodemographic
- behavioural
- psychographic.

Each of these classes of variables will now be considered in turn.

Demographic Variables

It may be possible to segment a market on the basis of variables such as age, gender, socio-economic group, family size, family life cycle, income, religion, race, nationality, occupation, or education. These are collectively known as *demographic variables*. This method of market segmentation is particularly popular in consumer markets since consumer wants, needs, and preferences are often highly correlated with these characteristics. The other reason for the popularity of demographic segmentation is a historical one. Such data have been collected over a great many years and hence much is known about the consumer behaviour of each target group. It is possible to purchase, for example, data relating to the media exposure of each demographic category. A selection are therefore considered below:

Age

Age has frequently been used as the basis for segmentation since purchasing patterns are clearly related to an individual's age. One interesting reason for this observation may have been revealed by a study carried out by Philips and Sternthal (1977) who concluded that age differences result in changes to the sources of information a particular individual will use. Age was also shown to affect the ability to learn and the susceptibility to social influence. Clearly these are all factors which could influence purchasing behaviour and all three have a relevance to the nonprofit sector.

Gender

Kotler and Keller (2006) note that an individual's gender has proved to be a good indicator of a propensity to buy a particular product or brand. In particular he cites cosmetics, clothing, magazines, and toiletries. Gender has proved to be a useful criterion in the nonprofit sector too, as it seems that charity donors are more likely to be female. Females have also been shown to respond differently to different forms of appeal. In seeking to raise funds for cancer research, for example, one major nonprofit identified, through testing a variety of messages, that females responded best to case studies of successful treatments for the disease, while males responded best to specific sets of scientific data (e.g. research results). Much social marketing may also have to be designed on the basis of a segmented approach by gender. Attitudes, for example, to safe sex, abortion, and healthcare screening have all been found to vary significantly by gender, and communications messages must be tailored to reflect this.

MIT SLOAN SCHOOL OF MANAGEMENT

In an effort to appeal to a declining number of prospective female students, leaders at Massachusetts Institute of Technology's MIT Sloan School of Management adopted a new approach. Throwing aside traditional marketing tactics used by business schools nationwide, MIT Sloan decided to answer the questions women typically have concerning their education.

Working together with consulting firm Sametz Blackstone Associates, MIT Sloan brought together 20 of its current female students to find out what issues they were facing and what inspired them to pursue their education at MIT. They created an inspiring 12-page pamphlet entitled *Six Stories from the Women of MIT Sloan*. Each page featured a black-and-white photograph of a current student, her biography, and a short paragraph detailing what MIT Sloan has offered her, as a student as well as a woman. MIT Sloan distributed the pamphlet to women who directly requested information as well as through unsolicited mass mailings and recruitment fairs.

To bring the print piece to life, MIT Sloan uploaded a website specifically for its current and prospective female students. The site hosts pictures of women and their families, profiles of female staff, students, and alumni, and additional resources and links that cater to women's needs. The site also designates MIT Sloan as 'a place where everyone is heard, and where some of the strongest voices and most interesting ideas belong to women.'

These tactics have proved successful, increasing female enrolment from 26 per cent during the 2004/5 academic year to 32 per cent in 2006/7.

Family Life Cycle

Segmentation conducted on this basis is based on the premise that demand for goods/services will vary depending on the stage that customers have reached in terms of the development of their family. Segmentation can hence be based on whether individuals are single, married, married with children, etc. The idea is certainly not new. Rowntree first suggested it at the beginning of the twentieth century. However, the model now in most common usage is that first presented by Wells and Gubar (1966), and illustrated in Figure 5.3.

As a composite model (made up of age, number of years married, ages of children, and working status), the concept of the family life cycle has proved to be more useful than simple segmentation based on age alone. It is however not without its critics since it is based on the conventional nuclear family. When one views the current pattern of family life in many countries, this model is clearly no longer completely valid. The model, for example, takes no account of the high divorce rate and subsequent increase in one-person households and has a somewhat outdated view of women. Women are now able to work a larger proportion of their lives and are able to continue working even during the early years of their children's lives. Despite the criticisms, however, the model is still in wide usage and has been proven to be a good indicator of a propensity to purchase certain categories of services (see, for example, Dominguez and Page (1984)).

In recent years a new version of the family life cycle has emerged which also takes account of an individual's aspirations and behaviour patterns as they progress through the phases of the life cycle model. Four main stages of the life cycle are defined and these are then subdivided by income and occupation. The resultant model, known as sagacity, is shown in Figure 5.4.

Stages in the family life cycle	Buying patterns
1. Bachelor stage: young single people living at home	Few financial commitments—recreation and fashion oriented
2. Newly married couples: young, no children	High purchase rate of consumer durables—buy white goods, cars, furniture
3. Full nest 1: youngest child under six	House buying is at a peak. Liquid assets are low—buy medicines, toys, baby food, white goods
4. Full nest 2: youngest child six or over	Financial position is improving—buy a wider variety of foods, bicycles, pianos
5. Full nest 3: older married couples with dependent children	Financial position is improving still further. Some children now have jobs and wives are working. Increasing purchase of desirables—buy furniture and luxury goods
6. Empty nest 1: older married couples, no children at home, head of household still in workforce	Home ownership is at a peak—savings have increased and financial position improved. Interested in travel, recreation, and self-education. Not interested in new products—buy luxuries and home improvements
7. Empty nest 2: older married, no children living at home, head of household retired	Substantial reduction in income. Buy medical products and applications that aid health, sleep, and digestion
8. Solitary survivor in the workforce	Income still high but may sell home
9. Solitary survivor, retired	Same medical and product needs as group 7. Substantial cut in income. Need for attention and security

Figure 5.3 The family life cycle

Source: Wilson, R.M.S., Gilligan, C. and Pearson, D.J. (2004) *Strategic Marketing Management,* Oxford, Butterworth Heinemann. © Elsevier 2008. Reproduced with kind permission.

This model improves on the earlier family life cycle since an individual's needs will clearly be related not only to his/her position in their life cycle but also to their occupation and relative income level. The definition of a typical segment would hence involve all three variables and on the basis of these one would then be in a position to identify the purchasing patterns of the individuals concerned.

Income/Occupation

Income is also a useful base for segmentation and, despite difficulties in identifying a true picture of income for a particular group of consumers (i.e. taking account of the black economy and traditional reluctance to disclose such data), has been shown to be a good indicator of a propensity to purchase certain categories of products or services, or even to give to certain categories of cause.

A more common method of segmentation, however, is to be found by combining income and occupation into a single model. Since its conception in the UK, the NRS (National Readership Survey) has classified readers of press/magazines into one of six categories according to social grade. Buyers of magazine/press advertising space may then use this data to select media that provide a high concentration of readers belonging to one or more of their target groups. The NRS classification is shown in Table 5.1.

It should be noted, however, that the system is now almost 50 years old and therefore based on a time when society was considerably more stable than it is at present. Social strata no longer exist in the way that they once did. Educational opportunities are now spread

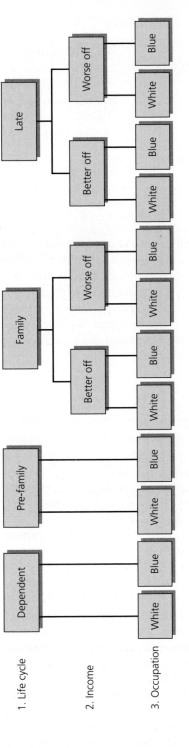

Figure 5.4 The sagacity model

Source: IPSOS-RSL © 2008. Reproduced with kind permission.

Table 5.1 Socio-economic groupings

Social grade	Example occupation
A	Senior professional/managerial
B	Middle professional/managerial
C1	Supervisory management—clerical
C2	Skilled manual labour—e.g. electrician
D	Unskilled manual—e.g. labourer
E	Unemployed, students, etc.

through all societal levels and many women are now providing a primary or second income for their households, making it difficult to identify a 'head of household' on whose profession a categorization could be based. The system is further flawed because it takes no account of customer lifestyles, needs, or aspirations—in short, it says nothing about consumers as people. All of these characteristics clearly have the capacity to influence one's choice of product or service and since the social grading system was based on the fundamental premise that people's propensity to purchase certain categories of products would depend primarily on their level of income, it now appears quite dated and in practice is used only in tandem with other bases for segmentation.

Geographic Segmentation

It has been argued that in terms of historic development, segmentation on the grounds of geographic location was the first to develop. Until quite recently, transportation systems would have limited the access that organizations had to more distant geographical markets. They therefore had little choice but to set up their businesses in close proximity to a key concentration of potential buyers. Given that many nonprofits are set up with the objective of supplying services to a particular geographic community this may be a very effective (and necessary!) method of segmenting the potential market for a wide variety of such organizations. However, segmentation on the basis of geography represents a very broadbrush approach to segmentation and can supply little in the way of fine detail, particularly when one is investigating consumer markets. By contrast, 'geo-demographics' offers considerably more insight.

Geo-Demographics

The study of geo-demographics arose from work carried out by Webber in 1973. He was originally interested in studying urban deprivation in Liverpool, and classified neighbourhoods using techniques of cluster analysis to produce a system containing 25 separate neighbourhood types. Each exhibited different mixes of problems and required a different type of social policy. Each neighbourhood was also defined in terms of its population, housing, and socio-economic characteristics. With the collaboration of the Census Office, he was later able to extend this analysis and derive 38 separate neighbourhood types with which he was able to classify the UK as a whole.

The next significant development came when Baker (1982) of the British Market Research Bureau was able to identify that Webber's system had considerable potential for controlling the activities of the TGI (Target Group Index). He was able to identify that certain neighbourhood groups displayed a particular type of purchasing pattern. In short, similar neighbourhoods tended to buy similar types of products. The techniques of geo-demographics have recently been refined and a variety of commercial systems are now in existence. In the UK the best-known of these is undoubtedly a system produced by CACI called ACORN (A Classification Of Residential Neighbourhoods). The full classification system is shown in Table 5.2.

Table 5.2 The ACORN classification system

Wealthy Achievers	Wealthy Executives	01 - Affluent mature professionals, large houses
		02 - Affluent working families with mortgages
		03 - Villages with wealthy commuters
		04 - Well-off managers, larger houses
	Affluent Greys	05 - Older affluent professionals
		06 - Farming communities
		07 - Old people, detached houses
		08 - Mature couples, smaller detached houses
	Flourishing Families	09 - Larger families, prosperous suburbs
		10 - Well-off working families with mortgages
		11 - Well-off managers, detached houses
		12 - Large families & houses in rural areas
Urban Prosperity	Prosperous Professionals	13 - Well-off professionals, larger houses and converted flats
		14 - Older professionals in detached houses and apartments
		15 - Affluent urban professionals, flats
		16 - Prosperous young professionals, flats
	Educated Urbanites	17 - Young educated workers, flats
		18 - Multi-ethnic young, converted flats
		19 - Suburban privately renting professionals
		20 - Student flats and cosmopolitan sharers
	Aspiring Singles	21 - Singles & sharers, multi-ethnic areas
		22 - Low income singles, small rented flats
		23 - Student terraces
Comfortably Off	Starting Out	24 - Young couples, flats and terraces
		25 - White collar singles/sharers, terraces
		26 - Younger white-collar couples with mortgages
		27 - Middle income, home-owning areas
	Secure Families	28 - Working families with mortgages
		29 - Mature families in suburban semis
		30 - Established home-owning workers
		31 - Home-owning Asian family areas
	Settled Suburbia	32 - Retired home owners
		33 - Middle income, older couples
		34 - Lower income people, semis
	Prudent Pensioners	35 - Elderly singles, purpose-built flats
		36 - Older people, flats

Table 5.2 (Continued)

Moderate Means	Asian Communities	37 - Crowded Asian terraces
		38 - Low income Asian families
	Post Industrial	39 - Skilled older family terraces
	Families	40 - Young family workers
		41 - Skilled workers, semis and terraces
	Blue Collar Roots	42 - Home-owning, terraces
		43 - Older rented terraces
Hard Pressed	Struggling Families	44 - Low income larger families, semis
		45 - Older people, low income, small semis
		46 - Low income, routine jobs, unemployment
		47 - Low-rise terraced estates of poorly-off workers
		48 - Low incomes, high unemployment, single parents
		49 - Large families, many children, poorly educated
	Burdened Singles	50 - Council flats, single elderly people
		51 - Council terraces, unemployment, many singles
		52 - Council flats, single parents, unemployment
	High Rise Hardship	53 - Old people in high-rise flats
		54 - Singles & single parents, high-rise estates
	Inner City Adversity	55 - Multi-ethnic purpose-built estates
		56 - Multi-ethnic, crowded flats

Source: CACI Limited (2008). ACORN and CACI are registered trademarks of CACI Ltd.

Users of the ACORN system can take an individual's postcode and identify the type of housing that that individual lives in, approximately what income they have, whether they are house owners or tenants and approximately what stage they have reached in their family life cycle. They can also identify details of those product categories most likely to be of interest to the individual in question. This is a powerful marketing tool since an organization can request that its database be profiled and if certain ACORN categories are found to predominate, the information can then be employed to good effect by targeting other households which have a similar profile. This would ensure that only individuals who are more likely to have an interest in (or need for) an organization's services will be selected for contact. The ACORN system can hence help save valuable marketing resources, particularly when one considers that the subsequent purchase of lists of prospects is relatively inexpensive.

It should be noted that a number of other companies are now offering geo-demographic systems on a commercial basis. These systems include MOSAIC and PINPOINT.

Behavioural Segmentation

Kotler (1991: 272) defines behavioural segmentation as dividing buyers 'on the basis of their knowledge, attitude, use, or response to a product'. He goes on to say that 'many marketers believe that behavioural variables are the best starting point for constructing market segments'. There are many bases for segmentation under this general category, among them benefit segmentation, brand loyalty, and user status.

Benefit Segmentation

Almost certainly the best-known writer concerning benefit segmentation was Haley (1968). His research related to the toothpaste market and he identified four benefit segments: seeking economy, protection, cosmetic, and taste benefits. In Haley's view, the benefits identified in each case are the primary reason for the existence of true market segments. Interestingly, his analysis showed that each benefit group was associated with distinct sets of demographic, behavioural, and psychographic characteristics. For example, the category seeking decay prevention were found to have large families, use consequently large amounts of toothpaste, and be conservative in nature. All this information is clearly valuable to toothpaste manufacturers, who can use it to buy space in media channels which reach the target group cost effectively and, more importantly, design promotional straplines (or unique selling propositions) that will appeal to the target market. A single product or brand may even be dedicated specifically to the needs of that target audience.

The concept of benefit segmentation has also been explored in the nonprofit sector. Cermak et al. (1994), for example, have attempted to derive a benefit segmentation of potential donors. Their study was based however not on the behaviour of members of the 'donor market' but rather on an analysis of the reasons why decision makers in charitable trusts choose to make donations to a particular cause. The authors identified four distinct benefit segments, namely:

1. *affiliators*—donors who benefit through social affiliation and the opportunity to exercise humanitarian impulses;
2. *pragmatists*—donors who are primarily motivated by the tax advantages that might accrue from a donation;
3. *dynasts*—donors who give because there is a family tradition of giving;
4. *repayers*—donors who seem to give because of a need to reciprocate—perhaps because someone close to them has benefited from the cause.

An understanding of the key benefits sought by such donors could hence be of immense value to fundraisers in facilitating the design of appropriate marketing communications.

Benefit segmentation has also been used to great effect in the health sector. Historically, healthcare professionals (and governments!) have tended to segment the population by looking only at the providers whose services are being utilized by the public at any given point in time. They have therefore looked at the market for nursing care, hospital care, home-based care, and care provided at the offices of a general practitioner. As Lynn et al. (2007: 158) note, 'the results are dehumanizing and produce discontinous wasteful and unreliable care'. The authors argue that each person's needs are somewhat different, requiring a different package of benefits for optimal health. They therefore propose the segmentation system illustrated in Table 5.3. This approach, they argue more accurately reflects the likely priorities and needs of large segments of the population and therefore leads to the provision of more efficient and reliable health care, supporting the improvement of health across the entire population. Although the authors don't use the term, what they are in essence arguing for is a societal orientation. After all, 'it is the voices of patients and family members who face (particular) circumstances that should determine their health and clinical priorities' (p205). The old approach was based on providers, not on the needs of the market.

Brand Loyalty Status

The second technique encompassed by behavioural segmentation is that of brand loyalty status. This is an attempt to segment consumers on the basis of their purchase/usage patterns. Wilson et al. (1994) identify the following four segments.

Table 5.3 Characterizing population segments by health priorities

Population Characteristics	Priority Concerns for This Population	Major Components of Health Care	IOM/AHRQ/EACCT Goals for Health Care
1. Healthy	Longevity, by preventing accidents, illness, and progression of early stages of disease	Physicians' offices, health clinics, occupational health, and health information available to the public	Staying healthy
2. Maternal and infant health	Healthy babies, low maternal risk, control of fertility	Prenatal services, delivery and perinatal care, fertility control and enhancement	Staying healthy
3. Acutely ill, with likely return to health	Return to healthy state with minimal suffering and disruption	Emergency services, hospitals, physicians' offices, medications, or short-term rehabilitative services	Getting well
4. Chronic conditions, with generally 'normal' function	Longevity, limiting disease progression, accommodating environment, caregiver support	Self-management, physicians' offices, hospitalizations, and ER visits	Living with illness or disability
5. Significant but relatively stable disability, including mental disability	Autonomy, rehabilitation, limiting progression, accommodating environment, caregiver support	Home-based services, environmental adaptation, rehabilitation and institutional services	Living with illness or disability
6. Dying with short decline	Comfort, dignity, life closure, caregiver support, planning ahead	At-home services, hospice and personal care services	Coping with illness at the end of life
7. Limited reserve and serious exacerbations	Avoiding exacerbations, maintaining function, and specific advance planning	Self-care support, at-home services, 24/7 on-call access to medical guidance and home-based care	Coping with illness at the end of life
8. Long course of decline from dementia and/or frailty	Support for caregivers, maintaining function, skin integrity, mobility, and specific advance planning	Home-based services, mobility and care devices, family caregiver training and support and nursing facilities	Coping with illness at the end of life

Source: Lynn, J., Straube, B.M., Bell, K.M., Jencks, S.F. and Kambic, R.T. (2007) 'Using Population Segmentation To Provide Better Health Care For All', *The Millbank Quarterly,* 85(2): 185–208. Reproduced by kind permission of Blackwell Publishing.

1. *Hard-core loyals*—consumers who buy one brand all the time. Hence a buying pattern of AAAAA may be used to represent the consistent purchasing pattern of brand A.

2. *Soft-core loyals*—consumers who buy from a limited set of brands on a regular basis. Their purchasing pattern may be represented by AABABB.

3. *Shifting loyals*—consumers who switch loyalty on a regular basis. Their purchasing pattern may be represented by AABBCC.

4. *Switchers*—consumers who show no loyalty to any one brand. This group may be considered especially susceptible to special offers or be attracted by variety. Their purchasing pattern may be represented by ABBCACB.

If one is considering the use of loyalty as the criterion for segmentation one should also consider the difficulties that might be encountered in its measurement. What appear to be brand-loyal purchase patterns might in reality reflect habit, indifference, a low price, or the non-availability of other brands. There is therefore a need to probe what lies behind the purchase patterns observed. Even when various degrees of loyalty in the marketplace have been identified, it is not always a straightforward exercise to take advantage of this information. While one can clearly identify one's own 'hard-core loyals' etc. it may not be easy to identify those of other organizations. The utility of the concept will hence depend on the extent to which each segment also exhibits a unique set of demographic or lifestyle characteristics. Knowledge of these details may lead to the development of a strategy designed to influence traditional patterns of loyalty, specifically targeted at those groups of consumers most likely to respond. Soft-core loyals purchasing competing services may, for example, be a particularly worthwhile segment to address.

User Status

A further popular method for segmenting the market is to utilize data relating to product/service usage rate. Customers may be classified according to whether they are heavy, medium, or light users of the product and treated accordingly. This method may be particularly useful since it is often a relatively small percentage of the market that accounts for a large percentage of consumption. Twedt (1964) argued that in many markets 20 per cent of the customers account for 80 per cent of the consumption. Thus there would be considerable utility in profiling those consumers who exhibit high usage rates. Not only can existing heavy users then be treated with an appropriate level of care, but other individuals in society who have a similar profile can be targeted in an attempt to get them to sample the organization's services. This method does however have the drawback that not all heavy consumers are usually available to the same provider because they are seeking a different set of benefits. For example, regular theatre attenders may be subdivided by a preference for different categories of performance.

Lifestyle Segmentation

Lifestyle or psychographic segmentation is an attempt to move away from earlier views of people expressed mainly in behavioural, demographic, and socio-economic terms. In this case, individuals are grouped in terms of their hobbies/interests, feelings, aspirations, attitudes, media exposure etc. This represents one of the most powerful criteria which can be used for market segmentation since a mass of lifestyle data now exists in respect of the readership of a whole variety of different publications, making it possible to target individuals on this basis very cost-effectively.

Kotler (1991: 171) defines lifestyle as a 'person's pattern of living in the world as expressed in the person's activities, interests and opinions. Lifestyle (therefore) portrays the whole individual interacting with his/her environment.' It is therefore distinct from 'personality'. Personality variables describe the pattern of psychological characteristics that an individual might possess but say nothing of that individual's hobbies, interests, opinions, or activities. Lifestyle data can supply these missing variables.

A number of early lifestyle classification systems can be found in the marketing literature; among them Wells (1975: 201) who questioned some 4000 male respondents and using the technique of factor analysis was able to derive the simple classification system shown in Table 5.4. Aside from their attitudes, Wells was able to define the media and product usage of each group, greatly adding to the value of his analysis. His analysis suggests target segments, the promotional messages that can be used with each, and the media that could be utilized to convey these messages cost effectively. Group 4, for example, may well be deemed an appropriate target for arts marketers promoting a series of live classical music concerts. If so,

Table 5.4 Wells's psychographic classification system

Group 1. The Quiet Family Man—8% of total males

He is a self-sufficient man who wants to be left alone and is basically shy. Tends to be as little involved with community life as possible. His life revolves around the family, simple work, and television viewing, has a marked fantasy life. As a shopper he is practical, less drawn to consumer goods and pleasures than other men. Low education and economic status, he tends to be older then average.

Group 2. The Traditionalist—16% of all males

The man who feels secure, has self-esteem, follows conventional rules. He is proper and respectable, regards himself as altruistic and interested in the welfare of others. As a shopper he is conservative, likes popular brands and well-known manufacturers. Low education and low or middle socio-economic status. The oldest age group.

Group 3. The Discontented Man—13% of all males

He is a man who is likely to be dissatisfied with his work. He feels passed by life, dreams of better jobs, more money, and more security. He tends to be distrusting and socially aloof. As a buyer he is risk conscious. Lowest education and lowest socio-economic group, mostly older than average.

Group 4. The Ethical Highbrow—14% of all males

This is a very concerned man, sensitive to people's needs. Basically a puritan, content with family life, friends, and work, interest in culture, religion, and social reform. As a consumer he is interested in quality, which may at times justify greater expenditure.

Group 5. The Pleasure Oriented Man—9% of all males

He tends to emphasize his masculinity and rejects whatever appears to be soft or feminine. He views himself as a leader among men. Self-centred, dislikes his work. Seeks immediate gratification for his needs. He is an impulsive buyer, likely to buy products with a masculine image. Low education, lower socio-economic class, middle aged or younger.

Group 6. The Achiever—11% of all males

This is likely to be a hard-working man, dedicated to success and all that it implies, social prestige, power, and money. Is in favour of diversity, is adventurous about leisure time pursuits. Is stylish, likes good food, music, etc. As a consumer he is status conscious, a thoughtful and discriminating buyer. Good education, high socio-economic group, young.

Group 7. The He Man—19% of all males

He is gregarious, likes action, seeks an exciting and dramatic life. Thinks of himself as capable and dominant. Tends to be more of a bachelor than a family man, even after marriage. Products he buys and brands preferred are likely to have self-expressive value, especially a man-of-action dimension. Well educated, mainly middle socio-economic status, the youngest of the male groups.

Group 8. The Sophisticated Man—10% of all males

He is likely to be intellectual, concerned about social issues, admires men with artistic and intellectual achievements. Socially cosmopolitan, broad interests. Wants to be dominant and a leader. As a consumer he is attracted to the unique and fashionable. Best educated and highest status of all groups, younger than average.

Source: reprinted with permission from the *Journal of Marketing Research,* published by the American Marketing Association, Wells, W.D. (1975) Vol. 12, No. 2, 196–213.

price may be less of an issue for this group and rather than trying to compete with other arts events on this basis, marketers may instead try to emphasize the quality of their events and price them to reflect this.

Of course, this is an early example and in the modern era many large advertising agencies now have their own lifestyle classification systems to assist in campaign planning. There are also a number of commercially available systems. One of the most popular on psychographic measurements is SRI Consulting Business Intelligence's VALS™ framework. VALS classifies all US adults into eight primary groups based on personality traits and key demographics.

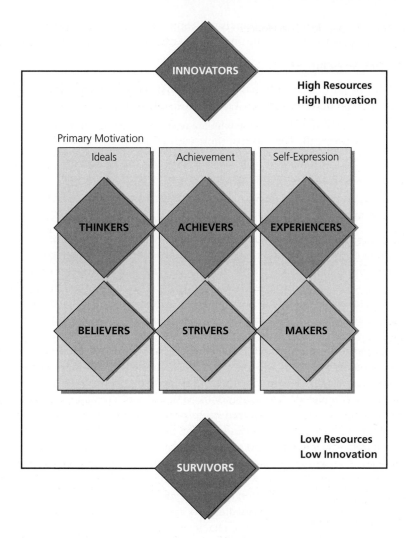

Figure 5.5 The VALS™ network

Source: SRI Consulting Business Intelligence © 2008. Reproduced with kind permission.

It is kept well up-to-date with more than 80,000 additional surveys being distributed each year. (Kotler and Keller 2006). The system is depicted in Figure 5.5.

The four groups with highest resources are:

- *Innovators:* successful, sophisticated, active, take-charge people with high self-esteem. Purchases often reflect cultivated tastes for relatively upscale niche-oriented products and services;

- *Thinkers:* mature, satisfied, and reflective people who are motivated by ideals and value order, knowledge, and responsibility. Favour durability, functionality, and value in products;

- *Achievers:* successful goal-oriented people who focus on career and family. Favour premium products that demonstrate success to their peers;

- *Experiencers:* young, enthusiastic, impulsive people who seek variety and excitement. Spend a high proportion of income on fashion, entertainment, and socialising.

The lower resource groups are:

- *Believers:* conservative, conventional, and traditional people with concrete beliefs. They favour familiar products and are loyal to established brands;
- *Strivers:* trendy and fun-loving people who are resource constrained. Favour stylish products that emulate the purchases of those with greater material wealth;
- *Makers:* practical, down to earth, self-sufficient people who like to work with their hands. Favour American-made products with a practical or functional purpose;
- *Survivors:* elderly, passive people who are concerned about change. Loyal to their favourite brands.

Helpfully, it is possible to purchase lists of individuals who can be categorized as belonging to one or either of these segments, so targeting can now be greatly enhanced.

There are many other systems available commercially, most of which work on a similar principle although the variables tested in each case are slightly different. It would therefore be advantageous prior to utilizing one of these systems to have carried out some initial market research to identify specifically which lifestyle variables are significant in a given market. Other commercially available systems include Young and Rubicam's 4Cs and Taylor Nelson's Monitor.

Many suppliers of lifestyle data offer a service that can be immensely valuable in donor or new customer acquisition. They will analyse an organization's database and match it against individuals whose details they hold on file. These may be people who have completed a lifestyle survey or completed lifestyle questions on the back of a product warranty card. Both are common methods for these organizations to gather details in respect of members of the public. If a high number of matches can be found between the two databases, the lifestyle agency can supply valuable information about the lifestyles of the individuals on the nonprofit's database. In essence they can help the organization to 'fill in the blanks' and understand much more about the kind of individuals that support (or patronize) the organization. This can greatly assist with the creation of appropriate promotional messages and the selection of appropriate communications media. Most agencies are also able to supply names and addresses of individuals who match the characteristics of existing donors/customers. Purchasing such lists is usually very cost effective. At the time of writing, this service is relatively inexpensive, costing typically only around £80–£150 per thousand names and addresses, depending on the degree of refinement (i.e. number of criteria) required. It should be noted, however, that for smaller nonprofits, even this cost may be prohibitive as most lifestyle agencies have a minimum order quantity of between 5000 and 10,000 names.

Criteria for Segmentation of Industrial Markets

Many nonprofits will be concerned not only with individuals in society but also with corporates, particularly those that have the potential to act as sponsors, partners, or donors. Indeed the support of corporate donors remains an important source of income for the voluntary sector. As a result it is worth briefly examining the criteria that can be used as the basis for segmentation in industrial markets.

Wind and Cordozo (1974) suggest that business segmentation should be considered in two stages. The first stage involves defining the segments in terms of industry demographics, size, industrial sector, SIC (Standard Industrial Classification) code, and product usage. The

Table 5.5 Criteria for segmentation of industrial markets

Demographic

Industry type—Which industries that buy the product should be focused on?

Company size—What size companies should be focused on?

Location—What geographical areas should we focus on?

Operating variables

Technology—What customer technologies should we focus on?

User status (i.e. heavy, medium, light)—Which type of user should we concentrate on?

Customer capabilities—Should customers having many or few needs be concentrated on?

Purchasing approaches

Buying criteria—Should customers be targeted that are looking for price, quality, or service, etc.?

Buying policies—Should customers requiring leasing facilities, for example, be targeted?

Current relationships—Should the company focus only on those customers with whom a relationship already exists?

Situational factors

Urgency—Should customers requiring immediate delivery be targeted?

Size of order—Should customers requiring large or small orders be targeted?

Applications—Should customers requiring only a certain application of the product be targeted?

Personal characteristics

Loyalty—Should only companies exhibiting high degrees of loyalty to their suppliers be targeted?

Attitudes to risk—Should risk-taking or risk-avoiding customers be targeted?

Buyer–seller similarity—Should companies with similar characteristics to the seller be targeted?

Source: developed from Bonoma, T.V. and Shapiro, B.P. (1983) *Segmenting the Industrial Market,* Lexington, Lexington Books.

second stage they advocate is to define the segments in terms of the behavioural characteristics of their decision-making units or buying centres. The result is a hybrid segmentation system that reflects not only the type of business, but also the manner in which it operates. To help illustrate the variety of criteria that are available it is worth briefly reviewing the work of Bonoma and Shapiro (1983) who developed one of the most comprehensive reviews of industrial segmentation currently available. The criteria that the authors identify are given in Table 5.5.

The authors originally suggested that these criteria are arranged in descending levels of importance. In the specific context of the nonprofit sector, however, many of the criteria towards the bottom of the list can actually offer considerably more utility than those towards the top. As an example, charities will look particularly to solicit support from corporate organizations that have a track record of loyalty to their suppliers. It takes time to establish relationships and a charity can invest considerable amounts of time and money securing appropriate corporate partnerships. They clearly have a vested interest in ensuring that, once established, these relationships prove to be as enduring as possible and to a certain extent this can be researched up-front.

Similarly the purchasing approaches adopted might also form the basis for appropriate market segmentation. Those organizations that are looking for a genuine degree of commercial gain to accrue from their involvement with a nonprofit organization should be approached rather differently from those that are likely to view their association purely as a philanthropic activity.

Since criteria such as company size and location will clearly determine the likelihood and amounts of funding to be supplied, it would seem that charities should give the greatest consideration to a mix of demographic, purchasing approach, and personal characteristic variables when designing an appropriate commercial segmentation system.

Criteria for Evaluating the Viability of Market Segments

The reader will by now appreciate the diversity of variables that could potentially be used as the basis for market segmentation. While there are many potential segments that an organization could look to pursue, it is likely that only a few of them will actually be worth engaging. The difficulty facing marketers is just how to evaluate the possibilities.

In practice, there are seven criteria that can be used to evaluate the potential offered by each segment proposed. Only if the analysis is favourable in each case should the segment be pursued. The segment must be:

1. *Measurable.* The market should be easily measurable and information should therefore either exist or be obtainable cost-effectively about the segment and its characteristics.

2. *Accessible.* It should be possible to design a distinct marketing mix to target the segment cost-effectively. One would therefore need to look, for example, at appropriate channels of distribution and media opportunities which could be used to target customers cost-effectively with the minimum of wastage.

3. *Substantial.* It should be cost-effective to market to the segment. Clearly the segment should be large enough in terms of sales volume (or small with sufficiently high margins) to warrant separate exploitation.

4. *Stable.* The segment's behaviour should be relatively stable over time to ensure that its future development may be predicted with a degree of accuracy for planning purposes.

5. *Appropriate.* It should be appropriate to exploit a particular segment given the organization's mission resources, objectives, etc.

6. *Unique.* The segment should be unique in terms of its response (to marketing activity) so that it can be distinguished from other segments.

7. *Sustainable.* Sustainability is an issue that is rapidly gaining in importance. It refers to the extent to which particular categories of customer can be sustained by the organization. The National Trust, for example, would hope to attract only conscientious walkers to their coastal paths; those that will treat the countryside with respect, stick to the signposted paths, take home their litter, etc. Not every segment of society will thus be sustainable, and marketing activity must hence be carefully targeted.

Point six warrants further elaboration. A segment may meet all of the other criteria but may behave identically to other segments in terms of its response to different types and timing of strategy. If this is the case, Kotler and Andreasen (1991: 170) identify that 'although it may be conceptually useful to develop separate segments in this way, managerially it is not useful'. As an example, if two segments of attenders at arts events both enjoy the same category of performance, both expect the same level of service at the venue, and both exhibit the same sensitivity to price, it is not managerially useful to continue to regard them as unique, even if they differ in demographic or lifestyle terms, since the organization will treat both

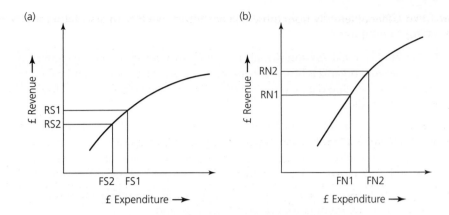

Figure 5.6 Hypothetical responses of two markets to fundraising activities

Source: Kotler, P. and Andreasen, A. (1991) *Strategic Marketing for Nonprofit Organizations,* 5th edn, 1996. Adapted by permission of Prentice Hall Inc. Upper Saddle River, NJ.

these segments of customers alike. Differential treatment is only appropriate where there is some form of differential response.

As a further example, Figures 5.6a and b show the allocation of a fundraising budget between two geographically separate markets, North and South. It can be seen from the slope of the two graphs that the North is more fundraising elastic (i.e. more sensitive to fundraising expenditure) than the South.

The points FS1 and FN1 represent equal fundraising expenditures in the two markets. This allocation strategy yields total response results of (RS1 + RN1). However, if the expenditure is shifted around between the two regions and £2000 is moved from the South to the North, then the total amount raised will rise (RS2 + RN2) even though total expenditures are unchanged. Clearly, fundraisers should continue shifting their fundraising budget to the North until such time as the incremental gain in one market just equals the incremental loss in the other. One would normally take advantage of any differential responsiveness until there is no variation in total responsiveness given any small changes that might be instigated. It should also be remembered that in this simple example the only variable under consideration is fundraising expenditure. In reality, segments may exhibit differential responsiveness to a wide range of differing criteria and these data can be utilized to great effect in marketing planning. Clearly, if no differential responsiveness is exhibited one might question the value of segmenting the market on that basis since no managerial advantages accrue.

Positioning

Once the organization has decided appropriate targets for the marketing plan to address, it will be necessary to develop a strategy that will shape the image that the nonprofit wishes to project in the minds of those targets. This is in essence what marketers refer to as positioning and it may be defined as the act of defining in the minds of the target market what a particular organization's services can offer (or stand for) in relation to the others on the market.

For Chew (2006) a number of key developments have elevated the strategic relevance of positioning for nonprofits:

1. The impact of external environmental changes on increasing competitive intensity among nonprofit organizations, and between these organisations and their counter- parts in the private and public sector for the right to provide services that their missions suggest they should.

2. Increasing competition for funding, making the achievement of long-term financial sta- bility much harder (Frumkin and Kim 2001). In the charity sector, for example, although the largest organizations continue to be able to grow their voluntary income, many smaller and medium-sized organizations have recently witnessed a decline in real terms.

3. Labour and skill resources have the capacity to play a greater role in the positional advantage of nonprofit organizations (NCVO 2004); and

4. Pressures on charitable organizations to differentiate their offerings has resulted in a proliferation of promotional activities in the media that are often targeted to the same audiences.

All these factors make it essential that the organization understands how its various cus- tomer groups perceive it in relation to the other 'suppliers' in the market, otherwise its com- munications messages will fail to stand out from the crowd and illustrate why a particular service is worthwhile and/or desirable. For example, imagine that a university (let's call it Bloomsville) wanted to identify how it was perceived by prospective undergraduate students. It understands that students are attracted to it for a number of reasons, and decides to inves- tigate how it is positioned in relation to other institutions in respect of just two of these—its academic reputation and the quality of life it offers to its students. The process would begin by some exploratory research to determine how the university and each of its competitors was rated on these two dimensions. A perceptual map could then be developed such as the one in Figure 5.7.

Bloomsville administrators could then see at a glance how their university was perceived in relation to others. It seems quite clear from the figure, for example, that although the qual- ity of life offered by the university is perceived as being quite reasonable, the university has a relatively poor academic reputation. This may be a reputation that is entirely deserved and felt by the management to be a reasonable perception, in which case no further action might

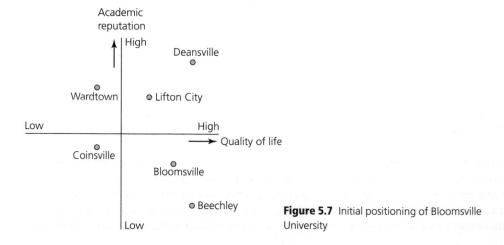

Figure 5.7 Initial positioning of Bloomsville University

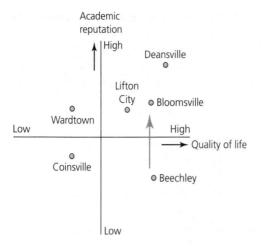

Figure 5.8 Final positioning of Bloomsville University

be necessary. If, however, Bloomsville academic research is actually well respected in the academic community and/or the university has recently figured well in the latest Research Assessment Exercise (RAE), management might take the view that this perception is unacceptable and initiate action to improve it. A communication plan could thus be implemented which would highlight recent Bloomsville research success in an attempt to shift its relative positioning, in the manner indicated in Figure 5.8. Further research would then be necessary to track the implementation of the communications plan, to ensure that it was having the desired effect in the market.

EXAMPLE

In 2003 St Luke's Medical Center in Milwaukee ran an advertising campaign implying that a general hospital with a full roster of specialists was safer for patients who might suffer complications during surgery. The campaign included print advertisements in local newspapers and a series of 60-second TV commercials aimed at countering competition from two newly opened specialized heart facilities in the metropolitan area. The commercials clearly define the positioning of the institution, suggesting that competitors cannot provide the kind of comprehensive service available in a full-service hospital. The commercials featured appearances from several specialists at the hospital, including an emergency physician who tells the camera, 'Many patients that come to St Luke's with symptoms of heart attacks are not having a heart attack at all. These patients' lives depend on our ability to treat more than heart problems.'

The examples cited in this section have focused on the positioning of whole organizations. While positioning can and does operate at this level, Hooley et al. (2003) make the point that it can also be a relevant strategic consideration at lower levels, such as specific products/ services or specific brands. Each of these may have its own positioning strategy. The organizational level is a distinct form, but of critical importance since it provides direction for positioning at these lower levels of marketing planning (Fill 2002).

We have also majored in this section on the points of difference between organizations and the desirability of achieving a degree of distinctiveness in the minds of the target audience. Again, while this is certainly the case, consideration must also be given to what

Keller et al. (2002) refer to as 'points of parity'. These are associations that may be shared with competitors. They are associations that consumers may view as essential to a legitimate and credible offering within a certain product or service category. In other words they represent necessary, but not necessarily sufficient, conditions for consumer choice. Thus a nonprofit providing care services for the elderly may position itself as caring and sympathetic, knowing that these attributes are shared with other providers, but equally knowing that prospective clients would not consider availing themselves of a service provided by an organization that did not have these characteristics.

Keller et al. (2002) argue that any selected points of parity should be relevant to the needs of the target audience and be genuinely believable. If they lack these characteristics any attempt to position on this basis is likely to be ineffective.

SUMMARY

In this chapter we explored how organizations can develop marketing objectives to identify exactly what will be achieved over the duration of a plan. We have argued that to be truly effective, such objectives should be SMART. We then focused on how these objectives might be achieved, drawing a distinction between strategy (i.e. the overall approach to the achievement of the objectives) and tactics (the minutiae of exactly what actions will be taken, when, and by whom). It is important to recognize that in the case of very small nonprofits, this division is unlikely to be so clear-cut and as a consequence, while a consideration of all these issues will remain important, tactics may be considered alongside strategy.

It is impossible to be definitive about the issues that will be strategic for a particular nonprofit to address, but I have suggested five layers of strategy that might typically be considered: overall direction, competitive/collaborative strategy, market segmentation, positioning, and branding. This list should not be regarded as exhaustive, merely indicative of the headings that might be considered. In this chapter we have dealt with the majority of these topics. We will explore branding in Chapter 6.

DISCUSSION QUESTIONS

1. Explain the relationship between corporate objectives and marketing objectives.
2. Under what circumstances should a nonprofit consider merger or collaboration as a strategic alternative?
3. What factors might a nonprofit organization take into account when deciding on an appropriate partner for a strategic collaboration?
4. How might a charity such as the RNLI (Royal National Lifeboat Institution) proceed to segment the market for potential donors to its organization? What issues would it need to consider?
5. With reference to your own organization, or one with which you are familiar, identify the basis that is currently used for market segmentation among potential funders and/or users of the nonprofit products/services. How might this be improved/refined?
6. Selecting a nonprofit sector you are personally familiar with, identify the criteria that are typically used for the purposes of positioning. Produce a series of perceptual maps that illustrate how each organization in this sector is presently positioned against these criteria. What conclusions might you draw from this analysis?

■ **CASE STUDY**

LIFESTYLE SEGMENTATION: A PERSPECTIVE FROM NEW ZEALAND

In 2001, Sarah Todd and Rob Lawson conducted an analysis of the 'New Zealand Towards 2000' database containing lifestyle and attitudinal data on 3773 New Zealanders. This work is of interest to nonprofit marketers because included in their original survey had been questions about frequency of visits to art galleries and museums. Using clustering techniques the authors were therefore able to derive the lifestyle segments depicted in Table 5.6. More detailed descriptions are given below.

Active 'family values' people: are characterized by values and activities which revolve around tradition, specifically the church, family, and community. They hold traditional social, moral, and religious principles. They spend a lot of time with their children in family outings and are low consumers of radio and television. Their family size is typically larger with three to four children living at home. Most are well educated and come from middle income households with one income earner.

Table 5.6 Lifestyle cluster profiles

Active 'family values' people	Family and community focus
	Traditional principles
	Positive outlook
Conservative quiet lifers	Homebodies
	Conservative views
	Reflective and nostalgic
Educated liberals	Socially concerned
	Progressive and egalitarian
	Enjoy variety and diversity
Accepting mid-lifers	Observe rather than partake
	Accepting of status quo
	Content
Success-driven extroverts	Self-oriented
	Value free enterprise
	Actively ambitious
Pragmatic strugglers	Family survival focus
	Politically conservative
	Determined
Social strivers	Outer-directed
	Conformist
	Feel life is a struggle

Source: Todd, S. and Lawson, R. (2001) 'Lifestyle Segmentation and Museum/Gallery Visiting Behaviour', *International Journal of Nonprofit and Voluntary Sector Marketing,* Vol. 6, No. 3, 269–277. Reproduced with kind permission.

Conservative quiet lifers: are typically older, retired, and may be widowed. They live a passive and solitary existence, have little debt, and have low education and income levels. They enjoy watching the television, listening to the radio and attending church.

Educated liberals: sophisticated adults concerned with social issues and open to change. They are highly educated, on above average income, and prefer city life to that of the country-side. They thrive on richness and diversity and are heavy readers of books and magazines. They consume the least television and two-thirds have no children.

Accepting mid-lifers: these individuals are generally accepting of life and have no strong po-litical and social views. They are largely content with their own company and represented in all age categories—although with a slight bias towards the 30–44 age bracket. The majority are married, both individuals work, and there is typically at least one dependent child at home. They have average incomes and education.

Success-driven extroverts: are ambitious and need to feel in control of their lives. They pos-sess abundant resources and possessions and are motivated by success. They have a strong urge to impress and pay careful attention to their image. They enjoy life in the big city and enjoy sports and other entertainments. One in five are self- employed and they are typically aged be-tween 20 and 39. They are well educated, married, and have either no dependents or one to two children living at home.

Pragmatic strugglers: who enjoy simple, natural living. Their interests revolve around the home and they enjoy television and radio. They are typically under 35 and more likely to be fe-male. Although almost two-thirds have at least one dependent child living at home the major-ity are unmarried. They have lower incomes and education.

Social strivers: experience a conflict between their ambitions and the circumstances they find themselves in. Their outlook is generally pessimistic and they are concerned with the opinions and approval of others. They are cautious and identify with traditional codes such as religion, family, and the community. They watch a lot of television, listen to the radio, and read maga-zines. They can be found in all age groups, although with a bias towards over 45. They have low incomes and have a low education.

Table 5.7 shows the frequency each category of individual typically attend an art gallery or museum.

Table 5.7 Visiting behaviour by lifestyle segment

Segments	Never %	Yearly %	Monthly %	Weekly %
Active 'family values' people	34.7	59.0	5.0	1.3
Conservative quiet lifers	55.1	41.4	2.5	1.0
Educated liberals	11.8	66.7	18.3	3.1
Accepting mid-lifers	55.9	41.1	2.7	0.3
Success-driven extroverts	32.7	60.4	5.6	1.3
Pragmatic strugglers	48.2	45.4	4.7	1.7
Social strivers	49.1	43.9	4.7	2.2

Source: Todd, S. and Lawson, R. (2001) 'Lifestyle Segmentation and Museum/Gallery Visiting Behaviour', International Journal of Nonprofit and Voluntary Sector Marketing, Vol. 6, No. 3, 269–277. Reproduced with kind permission.

QUESTIONS

1. Given your knowledge of the various segments, who do you think museums should focus on in a drive to boost attendance? What messages might work best with your chosen segments?

2. If your brief were to increase participation in the museum among non-attenders, which group or groups would you target? Why? What communication messages might work best in each case?

Case compiled from Todd, S. and Lawson, R. (2001) 'Lifestyle Segmentation and Museum/Gallery Visiting Behaviour', *International Journal of Nonprofit and Voluntary Sector Marketing*, 6(3): 269–277. Details reproduced with kind permission.

■ **REFERENCES**

Anon (2005) 'NSPCC Rescues Struggling Childline', *Marketing Week*, 24 November, p5.

Ansoff, H.I. (1968) *Corporate Strategy*, Penguin Books.

Baker, K. (1982) quoted in Clark, E. (1982) 'Acorn finds new Friends', *Marketing*, 16 December, 13.

Bonoma, T.V. and Shapiro, B.P. (1983) *Segmenting The Industrial Market*, Lexington, Lexington Books.

Boyd, H.W. and Levy, S.J. (1967) *Promotion: A Behavioural View*, Englewood Cliffs, NJ, Prentice Hall.

Brown, J.D. (1992) 'Benefit Segmentation of the Fitness Market', *Health Marketing Quarterly*, Vol. 9, No. 3, 19–28.

Cermak, D.S.P., File, K.M. and Prince, R.A. (1994) 'A Benefit Segmentation of the Major Donor Market', *Journal of Business Research*, Vol. 29, No. 2, 121–30.

Chew, C. (2006) 'Positioning and Its Strategic Relevance: Emerging Themes From The Experiences of British Charitable Organizations', *Public Management Review*, Vol. 8, No. 2, 333–50.

Chisnall, P. (1992) *Marketing Research*, Maidenhead, McGraw-Hill.

Cowin, K. and Moore, G. (1996) 'Critical Success Factors for Merger in the UK Voluntary Sector', *Voluntas*, Vol. 7, No. 1, 66–86.

Dominguez, L.V. and Page, A. (1984) 'Formulating a Strategic Portfolio of Profitable Retail Segments for Commercial Banks', *Journal of Economics and Business*, Vol. 36, No. 3, 43–57.

Drucker, P. (1990) *Managing The Non-profit Organization*, Oxford, Butterworth Heinemann.

Fill, C. (2002) *Marketing Communications: Context, Strategies and Application* (3rd edn), Prentice Hall, Harlow.

Frumkin, P. and Kim, M.T. (2001) 'Strategic Positioning and the Financing of Nonprofit Organizations: Is Efficiency Rewarded in the Marketplace', *Public Administration Review*, Vol. 61, No. 3, 266–75.

Golensky, M. (1999) 'Merger as a Strategic Response to Government Contracting Pressures: A Case Study', *Nonprofit Management and Leadership*, Vol. 10, No. 2, 137–52.

Green, P.E. (1977) 'A New Approach to Market Segmentation', *Business Horizons*, Vol. 20, No. 1, 61–73.

Haley, A.T. (1968) 'Benefit Segmentation: A Decision-oriented Research Tool', *Journal of Marketing*, Vol. 32, No. 3, 30–5.

Hiland, M.L. (2003) 'Nonprofit Mergers', *Consulting To Management*, Vol. 14, No. 4, 11–14, 60.

Hooley, G., Saunders, J.A. and Piercy, N.F. (2003) *Marketing Strategy and Competitive Positioning*, 3rd edn, Prentice Hall, Harlow.

Keller, K.L., Stenthal, B. and Tybout, A. (2002) 'Three Questions You Need To Ask About Your Brand', *Harvard Business Review*, Vol. 80 (Sept), 80–89.

Kotler, P. (1991) *Marketing Management: Analysis, Planning, Implementation and Control*, 8th edn, Englewood Cliffs, NJ, Prentice Hall.

Kotler, P. and Andreasen, A. (1991) *Strategic Marketing for Nonprofit Organizations*, Englewood Cliffs, NJ, Prentice Hall.

Kotler, P. and Keller, K.L. (2006) *Marketing Management*, 12th edn, Prentice Hall, Englewood Cliffs.

Lagarde, F., Doner, L., Donovan, R.J., Charney, S. and Grieser, M. (2007) 'Partnerships From The Downstream Perspective: The Role Strategic Alliances Play In Implementing Social Marketing Programmes', *Social Marketing Quarterly*, Vol. 11, No. 3, 38–45.

Lansing, J.B. and Kish, L. (1957) 'Family Life Cycle as an Independent Variable', *American Sociological Review*, Vol. 22, No. 5, 512–19.

Levy, D.R. (1992) 'Segment your Markets', *Association Management*, Vol. 44, No. 8, 111–15.

Lynn, J., Straube, B.M., Bell, K.M., Jencks, S.F. and Kambic, R.T. (2007) 'Using Population Segmentation To Provide Better Health Care For All', *The Millbank Quarterly*, Vol. 85, No. 2, 185–208.

MacDonald, M.H.B. (1984) *Marketing Plans: How To Prepare Them, How To Use Them*, London, Heinemann.

Mather, B. (2000) *Merging Interests*, London, The Baring Foundation.

McCurry, P. (1999) 'Society Finance', *The Guardian*, 27 October, 45.

Mullins, D.W. (1998) Managing Ambiguity: Merger Activity in the Non-Profit Housing Sector, *International Journal of Non-Profit and Voluntary Sector Marketing*, Vol. 414, 349–64.

NCVO (2004) *Voluntary Sector Strategic Analysis*, London, NCVO Publications.

Nicosia, F. and Wind, Y. (1977) 'Behavioural Models of Organizational Buying Processes', in Nicosia, F. and Wind, Y. (eds) *Behavioral Models of Market Analysis: Foundations for Marketing Action*, Hinsdale, IL, Dryden Press, 96–120.

Philips, L.W. and Sternthal, B. (1977) 'Age Differences in Information Processing: A Perspective on the Aged Consumer', *Journal of Marketing Research*, Vol. 14, No. 4, 444–57.

Porter, M.E. (1980) *Competitive Strategy: Techniques for Analysing Industries and Competitors*, New York, Free Press.

Rubinger, M. (1987) 'Psychographics help Health Care Marketers Find and Serve New Market Segments', *Marketing News*, Vol. 21, No. 9, 4–5.

Schmid, H. (1995) 'Merging Nonprofit Organisations: Analysis of a Case Study', *Nonprofit Management and Leadership*, Vol. 5, 377–91.

Simpson, J.A. (1994) 'Market Segmentation for Appraisal Firms', *Appraisal Journal*, Vol. 60, No. 4, 564–7.

Singer, M. and Yankey, J. (1991) 'Organizational Metamorphosis: A Study of Eighteen Nonprofit Mergers, Acquisitions and Consolidations', *Nonprofit Management and Leadership*, Vol. 1, No. 4, 357–69.

Stanton, W.J. (1978) *Fundamentals of Marketing*, 5th edn, New York, McGraw-Hill.

Twedt, D.W. (1964) 'How Important to Marketing Strategy is the Heavy User?' *Journal of Marketing*, Vol. 28, No. 1, 301–35.

Wells, W.D. (1975) 'Psychographics: A Critical Review', *Journal of Marketing Research*, Vol. 12, No. 2, 196–213.

Wells, W.D. and Gubar, G. (1966) 'Lifecycle Concept in Marketing Research', *Journal of Marketing Research*, Vol. 3, No. 4, 355–63.

Wethered, J. (1999) 'Public say there are too many charities', *Third Sector*, 20 October, 7.

Wilson, R.M.S., Gilligan, C. and Pearson, D.J. (1994) *Strategic Marketing Management*, Oxford, Butterworth Heinemann.

Wind, Y. and Cordozo, R. (1974) 'Industrial Market Segmentation', *Industrial Marketing Management*, Vol. 3, No. 1, 153–65.

Young, S. (1971) 'Psychographics Research and Marketing Relevancy', in King, C.W. and Tigert, D.J. (eds) *Attitude Research Reaches New Heights*, Chicago, American Marketing Association, 220–2.

Branding

OBJECTIVES

By the end of this chapter you should be able to:

1. define branding and describe a number of models of 'brand';
2. describe why an organization might elect to develop brands;
3. explain the various approaches to brand management an organization may adopt;
4. develop a brand strategy for a nonprofit organization.

Introduction

In the previous chapter we concluded by examining positioning strategy—in other words, how an organization communicates why it is in some way distinctive from other providers in the market. In this chapter, it is my intention to focus on a closely related topic: brand strategy. Both positioning and branding are closely intertwined, since as we shall see, if a nonprofit develops a brand for the organization as a whole (e.g. the United Way, or the NSPCC—National Society for the Prevention of Cruelty to Children) a positioning statement is one way in which this overall brand can be expressed. As we shall also see, however, brand strategy can have many more facets than mere positioning. In order to deal with this complexity we will focus exclusively on brand strategy in this chapter.

This separate consideration is also warranted because the topic of branding has recently generated significantly more interest in nonprofit circles. It is increasingly recognized that organizational brands, in particular, can convey significant advantages in terms of a nonprofit's ability to fundraise, campaign, and even deliver mission-related goals through service provision, education, and lobbying.

It is interesting to reflect on how times have changed. Branding was until recently regarded as something of a 'dirty' word by nonprofit managers afraid of being seen to grasp at some of the most 'disreputable' elements of for-profit marketing practice. There was a fear that in giving active consideration to branding, nonprofit organizations would somehow lose a sense of what made them distinctive (Ritchie and Swami 1998).

In reality, nothing could be further from the truth; attempts to manage an organization's brand should actually enhance the character of the nonprofit, emphasizing its strengths and achievements alongside its modus operandi. Saxton (1995) suggests that the practice of branding in this context should differ from commercial approaches in so far as it should both draw on, and project, the beliefs and values of a nonprofit's various stakeholders. This leads to what Hankinson (2000) regards as the greater complexity associated with managing charity brands. She argues that charity brands require a different approach that distinguishes between the 'functional attributes of the brands—their causes—and the symbolic values of the brand—their beliefs' (Hankinson 2001: 233). She cites the example of the RSPCA whose cause is preventing cruelty to animals, while its values are 'caring', 'responsible', 'authoritative', and 'effective'. Both dimensions pervade its communications.

In this chapter we examine the concept of 'brand' and explore what it can offer a nonprofit. We will also discuss a number of models of brand and discuss the implications for brand strategy and the development of integrated communications.

What Is a Brand?

The American Marketing Association (AMA) defines a brand as follows: 'A brand is a name, term, sign, symbol, or design, or a combination of them, intended to identify the goods or services of one seller or group of sellers and to differentiate them from those of competitors.'

In the nonprofit context, a brand is thus a device to allow members of the public to recognize a particular nonprofit that may take the form of a name, trademark, or logo. Legislation in Northern Europe and North America provides protection to the owners of these devices that ensures that no other organization can impinge on their intellectual property. Brands may not be borrowed or copied without permission. This degree of protection is important since brands are in essence a promise to the public that an organization possesses certain features, or will behave in certain ways. Aaker (1997) argues that in fact brands can convey up to six distinct levels of meaning to a consumer:

1. *Attributes.* Brands can suggest certain attributes the organization might possess. These attributes may include the size of the nonprofit, the scope of its activities, the nature of the work undertaken, etc. In short, the brand can act as a vehicle for summarizing what the organization does and how it does it. While there is much more to a brand than a mere logo, these can play a critical role in a brand strategy, in suggesting the characteristics a nonprofit organization might possess. Figure 6.1 depicts four distinctive brand logos. The UNICEF brand (United Nations Children's Fund) makes clear both the nature of the organization's work and the truly global nature of its coverage. The US nonprofit, Mothers Against Drunk Driving (MADD), is similarly expressive, indicating both the nature of the organization's work and making a statement about those who do choose to drink and drive. Arts organizations too are making increasing use of brands to convey the nature of what they do, London's Science Museum offering a particularly inventive example. Finally, even the public sector has recognized the utility of branding, as the e-Plymouth logo clearly demonstrates. The brand logo designed by the city council immediately conveys the maritime history of the city.

2. *Benefits.* Brands also offer a series of functional and emotional benefits. From a donor's perspective, when they elect to associate themselves with a particular brand by offering their support they are buying a distinct set of functional benefits either for themselves, or more likely the beneficiary group. Donors to the US nonprofit Planned Parenthood, for example, know that when they support that organization the monies will be used for the purposes of

© 2008. Plymouth City Council
Reproduced with kind permission

© 2008 MADD. Reproduced with
kind permission

unicef

© 2004 UNICEF. Reproduced
with kind permission

© 2008 The Science Museum
Reproduced with kind permission

Figure 6.1 Nonprofit brand logos

education, but also to campaign for a woman's 'right to choose'. By electing to support a branded organization, donors are able to circumvent the usual search for information (about what the organization stands for and what it does) that would have to take place if they were approached by an organization that they were not already familiar with. A well-developed brand can provide this sense of familiarity.

Benefits can also accrue to the donor and these again could be functional in nature. Some donors may be motivated to give because of the status their association with the organization will confer. They may also wish to attract the rewards on offer through a donor recognition programme. However, donors may also gain emotional benefits from their association with a brand. Wearing the logo or symbol of a nonprofit organization might confer an identity to the donor, just as in the commercial world wearing a brand such as Nike conveys an identity to the young people who sport its shoes. Of course in the nonprofit context this process may be a little more thoughtful and can often involve a desire to express a sense of solidarity with the cause. A powerful UK example of this would be the Royal British Legion's Poppy Appeal, where many millions of small gifts are solicited in return for the token of a poppy that may then be worn in public from the time of purchase until Remembrance Sunday when the nation acknowledges the sacrifice of its armed forces. It is interesting to note how many public figures elect to wear their poppy in the run-up to the commemoration, and that over 33 million poppies are produced in total.

The concept of functional and emotional benefits can also apply in many other non-fundraising contexts. Arts organizations, for example, can use their brands to remind individuals of the enjoyment they experienced when they attended a particular event or exhibition. Branded merchandise is often the most frequently purchased of items in the retail outlets associated with these organizations and they serve as pleasurable reminders of the experience each time a coffee mug is used or a T-shirt worn, etc.

Increasingly, healthcare providers are also recognizing the utility of brands to provide reassurance to patients, potential patients, and their relatives that the service provided will be professional and that they can be trusted to do all they can to bring about a satisfactory outcome. Brands might convey a particular specialism of the organization or say something of the caring nature of the staff that comprise it.

3. *Values.* The brand can also convey something of the organization's values, not only what it stands for, but also the way in which it will approach key issues related to the cause.

A nonprofit for example may have the values 'bold, authoritative, and challenging', while another might be 'helpful, sympathetic, and caring'. The values of an organization will often be derived from the passion of the founders of the organization, from religious associations, or from the nature of the work undertaken. What is actually happening here is that the values of the various stakeholders to the organization are being projected into how the organization communicates with the outside world.

4. *Culture.* In the nonprofit context this element is tough to differentiate from values. In the commercial sector an individual brand may have distinctive values, but it will also communicate something of the corporate culture of the parent organization (i.e. the way it does business). For nonprofits, the culture of the organization will be driven in large measure by the values of the various stakeholder groups. A nonprofit organization is often a melting pot of such values, which in turn drive the organization's behaviour. Greenpeace's culture, for example, has historically been very confrontational as the nonprofit seeks to put pressure on commercial organizations it sees as damaging the environment. On 14 June 2003, Greenpeace volunteers from the Forest Crime Unit visited 24 Travis Perkins stores across the UK. At the Dalston store in East London, a crew of eight people from the unit cordoned off what they claimed to be illegally logged Indonesian timber. They found 19 crates of Barito Pacific ply in one section and branded it a 'forest crime scene'. The volunteers then hung a banner which read 'Stop Rainforest Destruction'.

5. *Personality.* Nonprofit brands can also convey a distinctive personality and there are often personal characteristics that can accrue to the image of an organization. This may occur because of the activities of a particularly flamboyant founder whose own personality becomes indelibly stamped on the organization's brand, but equally it can simply develop over time as the public come to view the nonprofit more as a personality than an organization. The charity Comic Relief is an excellent example of this.

6. *User.* Many brands also convey a sense of the nature of the user. Charity brands can suggest the kind of individual who will either donate to the cause, benefit from the work it undertakes, or some combination of the two. Age Concern, for example, has built a brand that is regarded as responding to the needs of the elderly, tackling the issues that are of concern to this group, and attracting funding both from this age category, but also from caregivers (carers) in the preceding generation, who will be facing these issues themselves in ten or twenty years' time. Similarly the charity ENABLE uses its brand to good effect. It is the largest membership organization in Scotland for people with learning disabilities and family caregivers. It was formed in 1954 by a small group of parents because many families with a child with learning disabilities felt alone and isolated. They wanted better services for their sons and daughters and better support for parents. The brand they have now built over the years conveys a strong sense of what the group is really looking for from supporters. The message is not one of sympathy or pity, but rather that the organization seeks to empower its beneficiaries to make a real change in their lives. The brand conveys to donors that this is what they are 'buying' by making a donation.

Of course, there is more to branding than the mere selection of an appropriate name. All the communications the organization creates, both in character and style, should reinforce the brand image the nonprofit is trying to project. The focus should thus be not only on what is said, but how it is said, and this should pervade all the communications channels employed. Thus all direct mail, press, TV, radio, Internet, and outdoor advertising should reflect the brand, but so too should the manner in which the organization responds to telephone enquiries, interacts with all its beneficiary groups, and even presents required statutory data such as annual accounts.

The complexity of branding is illustrated in Figure 6.3. As the figure makes clear, a non-profit's purpose or mission is the starting point for the development of a branding strategy.

■ CASE STUDY

SUSAN G KOMEN FOR THE CURE

Nancy G. Brinker promised her dying sister, Susan G. Komen, that she would do everything in her power to end breast cancer forever.

In 1982, that promise became the Susan G. Komen Breast Cancer Foundation and launched the global breast cancer movement. Today, Susan G. Komen for the Cure® is the world's largest grassroots network of breast cancer survivors and activists fighting to save lives, empower people, ensure quality care for all, and energize science to find the cures. It has 122 US affiliates representing some 18,000 communities and three affiliates outside the US. Thanks to events like the Komen Race for the Cure, the organization has invested $1 billion to fulfil its promise, becoming the largest source of nonprofit funds dedicated to the fight against breast cancer in the world.

In 2007, the organization rebranded to enable the nonprofit to connect with a larger, younger, and more diverse constituency. Their research told them that the word 'Foundation' was limiting and that many individuals felt more connected to the Race for the Cure than the nonprofit itself.

After much consultation and testing, which involved the affiliates extensively (in interviews, focus groups, concept testing etc.) the organization decided on a new approach. This was launched internally to affiliates, staff, partners, and key constituents well before the public unveiling of the newly defined brand. The internal launch not only exposed the new identity, it also kicked off training to help affiliates with the new philosophy and how best to use the brand. The process was positioned carefully, not as 'going from a bad to a good' situation, but as one moving the nonprofit from 'good to great'. Learning about the brand was also positioned as being fun, to keep the team's spirits up and generate a genuine sense of excitement.

Following the launch, affiliates who had been trained on the new brand were sent back as 'brand ambassadors' with information and DVDs as well as modified version of the training presentation delivered at headquarters. The aim was to pass information back through to all relevant stakeholders.

As the organization's website notes:

Simply put, it's our anniversary. We're 25 this year, and we're shifting into another gear. With renewed urgency and inspiration. With an energized commitment to finally, once and for all, finish what we started.

Figure 6.2 Susan G. Komen for the Cure brand

Source: Susan G. Komen for the Cure © 2008. Reproduced with kind permission.

Our new name and logo symbolize who we are and what we stand for. "Susan G. Komen" reminds us of Nancy G. Brinker's promise to her sister Susan to do everything in her power to spare other women and men the agony of breast cancer. "For the Cure" reaffirms our vision of a world without the disease. The name conveys the original promise quickly and simply . . . Susan G. Komen = the Cure.

As Susan G. Komen for the Cure, we'll continue to be the world's largest, boldest and most progressive grassroots network of survivors and activists, the only organization fighting to cure breast cancer at every stage. To date, we've invested $2 billion in research, education and health services. And because so many millions of people are counting on us to fulfill our promise, we will invest an additional $1 billion over the next decade to do just that.

Copyright material reproduced with kind permission. Susan G. Komen for the Cure® © Copyright 2008.

The organization can be found online at www.komen.org

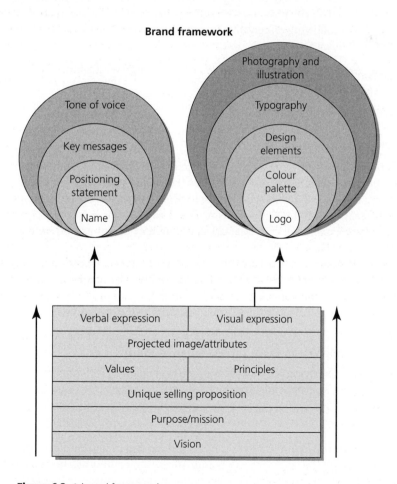

Figure 6.3 A brand framework

Source: © NSPCC 2008. Reproduced with kind permission.

The reason for the nonprofit's existence will be likely to drive what is distinctive about the nature of the organization's work and why therefore it might deserve our attention. There is little point in developing a brand that follows a 'me-too' strategy merely emulating the activities and values of another organization. Indeed, in the nonprofit context, one would have to question the rationale for the existence of such an organization. If an alternative is already undertaking identical work in an identical way, there would seem little point in a duplicate being developed.

Fortunately, most nonprofits do make a genuine contribution to society and may lay claim to some aspect of their work, or the way it is conducted, that is genuinely distinctive. It is important in developing a brand strategy that this is recognized from the outset. What makes an organization distinctive may be a function of its values (as discussed above), the actions it will take, or the manner in which these actions will be undertaken (i.e. the organization's principles). Indeed, it may well be some combination of these three. The values and principles espoused by the NSPCC, for example, are illustrated in Figure 6.4.

Having delineated the values, actions, and principles that define the organization, it is then possible to construct the brand image or attributes that the organization wishes to convey. When the WWF went through a rebranding exercise they determined that the brand should convey the following dimensions that, in their case, they elected to classify as functional, comparative, and emotional.

- *Functional*: 'We influence attitudes and behaviour through education, fieldwork, advocacy, and partnerships.'

- *Comparative*: 'We bring practical experience, knowledge and credibility to build towards long-term solutions, locally and globally.'

- *Emotional*: 'Improving the quality of life on earth.'

The next step in developing a brand strategy is to decide on how these attributes will be expressed to the target stakeholder groups, both verbally and non-verbally. If an organizational brand is being developed, it will be important to begin by deciding on an appropriate name. The previous example of MADD (Mothers Against Drunk Driving) is a particularly effective case study of how a name can convey a variety of different meanings and simultaneously be an effective aid to recall.

Verbal expression can also be accomplished through an effective positioning statement. As we discussed in Chapter 5, this will map out how exactly the organization is different from its competitors and/or the stance on a social issue that the organization will take. The organization will also wish to consider the key messages that will be conveyed. These may be:

- *campaign related*—encouraging specific behaviours on the part of the target audience (e.g. recycling, stopping smoking, preventing child abuse, etc.);

- *funding related*—specifying why the work of the organization is important, why it warrants support, and stressing how the funds will be used;

- *education related*—deepening stakeholder understanding of some aspect of the organization's work.

Finally, the tone of voice that the nonprofit chooses to use in its communications will also convey dimensions of the organization's brand. All written communications have the potential to influence how an organization is regarded and it is all too easy for an organization that wishes to be seen as 'confident' to be perceived as 'arrogant' or 'smug' through a poor choice of language. It is important to note that all communications an organization sends out have

Courage
Trust
Respect
Protect

We also uphold the values of the UN Convention on the Rights of the Child:
The Convention on the Rights of the Child consists of 54 articles. A 'child' is defined as every human being below the age of 18. The key principles of the Convention are: That all rights apply to all children without exception or discrimination of any kind (article 2): that the best interests of the child must be a primary consideration in all actions concerning children (article 3); that States have an obligation to ensure as much as possible every child's survival and development (article 6); and that children's views must be taken into account in all matters affecting them (article 12). The key provisions covered by the Convention can be summarised within four broad categories.

Survival rights, from the child's right to life through the most basic needs, including food, shelter, and access to health care. *Development rights,* or all those things that children require in order to reach their fullest potential, from education and play to freedom of thought, conscience and religion.

Protection rights, requiring that children be safeguarded against all forms of abuse, neglect and exploitation
Participation rights, including the right to free expression, which allow children to take an active role in their communities and nations.

The UN Convention on the Rights of the Child
- UNICEF-February 2000

NSPCC Principles

1. We will pursue our objectives with courage. We are ready to challenge and lead change for children through our service provision, campaigning, public and professional education, fundraising and communications.

2. We are open and transparent with all those who seek our assistance, fellow professionals, employees, volunteers, the media and the public.

3. We will not compromise the principle that everyone, every individual, every organisation, every community, has responsibility for the care and protection of children, to safeguard them and take action to end abuse. Every child should have someone to turn to.

4. We challenge inequalities for children and young people. In all our activities, including our employment practice, we seek to demonstrate respect, inclusion and appreciation for the value of diversity including ethnicity, nationality, gender, belief, ability, sexuality, age or status.

5. We strive to be a learning organisation. Our collective knowledge, understanding and information must be shared, and this is enabled by the most effective use of information systems infrastructure. We learn from people, research, external changes and experience, and use this to inform our future programme of work.

6. We seek to support and fulfil the potential of the children and young people with whom we work, and that of employees and volunteers. We listen to their views with respect and respond to them, giving due weight to what we are told.

7. We recognise our employees as our most important resource. We will treat them with fairness and respect, involve them in decisions affecting their own jobs, help them fulfil their potential and support them in their own efforts to help children.

8. We seek to co-operate and forge partnerships with others to share learning and ensure safeguarding support is accessible to all children. Most abuse of children is avoidable but we cannot end it on our own.

9. We will work in partnership with donors to achieve our objectives.

10. We will use our independence, our experience and our partnerships with many organisations and individuals to influence changes in the law to the benefit of children.

11. We will be open and honest in all our communication. We will use all channels of communication ethically, with a sense of responsibility and with respect for the children on whose behalf we are speaking out.

12. We work directly in England, Wales, Northern Ireland and the Channel Islands. We collaborate closely with child protection charities in Scotland and Ireland and nongovernmental organisations for children in Europe.

13. We are accountable to all our stakeholders, including those who use our services, partners, donors and other funders, employees, volunteers, those who campaign on our behalf, those who publicly support us and the wide public.

14. Everything we do must contribute towards ending cruelty to children and have a clear and assessable objective. There must be evidence of effectiveness and a balance between long- and short-term impact and commitment to continuous improvement.

15. We will be effective and efficient in raising and allocating our resources, communicating with others and secure sustainability.

Figure 6.4 NSPCC values and principles

Source: © NSPCC 2008. Reproduced with kind permission.

Figure 6.5 Evolution of WWF brand logo
Source: © 2008 WWF. Reproduced with kind permission.

the potential to influence this dimension, not just those that are deliberately created by the marketing and/or fundraising departments. All external (and ideally internal) communications must reflect the organization's brand.

The visual expression of the brand in communications is similarly important. The most obvious facet of visual expression is an organization's logo, which as we noted earlier should be designed in such a way as to convey as much meaning as possible to the target group. It is interesting to note how much time and effort is applied to the design of a logo. Once decided upon, organizations tend to retain their logo for a considerable period of time. This reflects the obvious investment of resources that has been made in the design and subsequent promotion of the logo, but it also reflects the need for continuity. Where a symbol or image has been successfully linked to a brand, or where it successfully evokes it, change can seriously impede an organization's ability to communicate, as individuals become confused as to whether they are still being addressed by the same organization or not. When the National Canine Defence League became the Dogs Trust in 2003 the organization was careful to maintain some continuity in identity so as not to confuse its various stakeholders. While the name changed, the logo was only slightly modified and the espoused organizational values continued unaltered. Thus, if change should be necessary the favoured strategy for many organizations is simply to update their logo, and for the design to evolve with the passage of time, reflecting subtle changes in the organization or its approach. The WWF logo in Figure 6.5 provides a good example of how this evolution can take place.

Colours can also convey meaning, even at a subconscious level. Some colours are rich and welcoming, while others are stark and cold. Organizations thus expend equal amounts of energy on deciding what colour palette will be right, both for the logo, and also for all the brand-building communications the organization will produce. Figure 6.6 contains a selection of brand-building ads designed by UK charities. The WWF example uses subtle tones of blue and green to convey the medical nature of the ad, while the NSPCC uses the pink of a child's wallpaper to evoke a sense of innocence in this 'still' from a television campaign. Clearly other design elements, such as the content and layout, have a critical role to play, as does the choice of photography and even typography (e.g. Times New Roman, Arial, etc.).

Why Brand?

It is important to recognize that the issue of whether to brand or not may not be something that a nonprofit organization has much control over. Even where the management do not believe the development of a brand strategy will be worthwhile, there may still be instances

WHO CARES IF THEY CUT DOWN A FEW TREES?

Four of five children with leukaemia are saved by the rosy parlwinkle from the Madagascan rainforest. In fact plants create a quarter of all prescribed medicines. Yet more and more life-saving plants are becoming extinct as we destroy the rain forest. Who knows what potential cures for cancer, AIDS or heart disease are being lost forever? To find out what you can do to help WWF protect our forests, wild life and children call 01483-426333 or visit www.wwf.org.uk/whocares

TAKING ACTION FOR A LIVING PLANET

WWF

© 2008 WWF and Science Photo Library. All Rights Reserved.

Barry Stark
Died: Age 2 years

Barnado's

When Barry was repeatedly beaten from the age of two, a large part of him died. His hope and ability to love died. His future died. 38 years later, he put a shotgun in his mouth and died for real. What a waste.

At Barnardo's we want to save children like Barry from a living death. We combat the effects of domestic violence on children through counselling and help give them back their future and life. This takes time. That's why Barnardo's works over the long term, helping over 50 000 children a year with nowhere else to turn.

Soon, you'll read a story, in this paper, about someone just like Barry. 'How sad', you'll say. There are thousands of future Barrys and they don't want your sympathy, they need your help.

© 2008 Barnado's. Reproduced with kind permission.

NSPCC

© 2008 NSPCC. Reproduced with kind permission.

Figure 6.6 Examples of brand-building advertisements

where the organization develops a brand 'by default'. Members of the public may come to ascribe differing attitudes and behaviours to the organization with the passage of time and may use the name or title of the organization to group these associations. The organization may thus develop a brand in the absence of a conscious generation of strategy. For many organizations the choice of whether to brand or not is illusory—instead it becomes a question of whether it will be proactively managed or not.

Where a genuine choice does exist, organizations may find that developing a brand strategy conveys a number of benefits.

• *Differentiation*. As we established earlier, a brand can communicate what is distinctive about the range of activities undertaken, or the manner in which these are approached. This is important since it can convey to service users what they might expect to receive from the organization and allow them to 'self-select' whether they wish to use the organization's services or not. On the income generation side it can also aid recognition of the organization and ensure that it does not become confused with others in the minds of the public. Extant fundraising research has shown that organizations with similar brand names, values, or personalities can quickly become confused to the point where a regular payment is offered to one organization, while the donor believes they are supporting another (Sargeant and Jay 2003).

EXAMPLE

In 2003 the University of Ottawa conducted awareness research among high school students in Ontario and Quebec. It discovered that only one in 20 was 'very familiar' with the institution. In response, the university recently launched a major branding campaign repositioning itself as 'Canada's University', a national, bilingual institution offering unique opportunities. At the core of the campaign was a promise that the university was determined to 'live' its brand. In this case living the brand entailed a considerable investment in a wide range of student services specifically designed to meet the needs of current and future students. As an example, the university purchased a 16-storey hotel with the intention of increasing both the quantity and quality of its first-year accommodation.

• *Enhanced performance*. Effective brands encourage the take-up of nonprofit goods and services. Brands that are effectively and consistently communicated over time begin to engender trust, which encourages individuals who might not otherwise have used the service to turn to the organization. Extant research also tells us that organizations that develop brands are more successful at fundraising than those that do not. Frumkin and Kim (2001) found that nonprofit organizations that spent more money on marketing themselves and branding their organization to the general public did better at raising contributed income. Regardless of the field that nonprofit organizations serve in, positioning around mission and using this to drive the brand positively influenced the flow of contributions.

• *Reputation insurance*. Branding can also offer a form of reputation insurance to a nonprofit. Having built up a consistent image over time that becomes trusted and increasingly well understood by donors and other stakeholders, short-term crises can be survived (Fogel 2007). The Aramony scandal rocked the United Way in the USA when the chief executive was accused of wasting donated funds by building up expenses such as unnecessary flights on Concorde. This had a dramatic impact on donations in the short term; however, the reputation of the organization was such that in the medium term the organization was able to regain its share of gifts and relative position in the market. Thus while one would hope that scandals as acrimonious as the Aramony affair would be relatively rare, nonprofits will inevitably find that on occasion they will make mistakes. A strong brand makes it considerably more likely that such mistakes will be forgiven or even overlooked.

• *Enhanced loyalty.* As we discussed earlier, individuals choosing to associate with a particular brand may derive functional or emotional benefits from so doing. In the nonprofit context this frequently accrues from the pleasure of associating with a particular campaign or cause. In such cases, the personality of the brand can actually add value or deepen the emotional benefits that the supporter derives. Polonsky and Macdonald (2000) thus argue that organizations with an established brand can leverage this to build donor loyalty and protect themselves from competitive pressures.

• *Additional partnerships.* Successful branding can open up opportunities to offer the brand to appropriate third parties, as is the case with cause-related marketing (see Chapter 9). Research has consistently shown that both commercial entities and nonprofit organizations can benefit from a brand alliance (Dickinson and Barker 2007). In the USA a number of large charities have even introduced their own branded products, earning substantial sums of revenue as a consequence. The Children's Television Workshop has been highly successful in its licensing arrangements for some 1600 *Sesame Street* products, ranging from a Big Bird battery-operated toothbrush to a Cookie Monster bulldozer, to 30 companies, including J.C. Penney and Hasbro (Meyers 1985).

There are thus a number of benefits that can accrue from the development of a brand strategy. These primarily arise for one of two reasons. First, brands are an aid to learning. If branding has been used as a tool to educate members of the public over time there is then no need for a marketer to begin from a 'zero base' in communicating with them. There will be a baseline of understanding about the work the organization undertakes and its values in the minds of potential supporters. This makes the marketing task a lot easier, as brand communications drip-feed information to the market over an extended period of time. In effect brands serve as a 'hook' in memory on which subsequently received messages can be hung.

Second, brands also serve to reduce risk for individuals looking to have contact with the organization. This is particularly the case where individuals might be having contact with a particular category of organization or service for the first time. In such circumstances individuals look to reduce the risk to them in selecting an appropriate 'supplier'. If they are already familiar with a particular brand name they will be significantly more likely to trust this particular supplier than those of which they have no knowledge or awareness. In the context of fundraising this also holds true. Brands provide assurance that an organization is worthy of trust and that funds donated will be used in a manner consistent with standards that have been established over time (Ritchie and Swami 1998).

Branding—A Caveat

Despite the numerous advantages that branding conveys, a number of authors have criticized the manner in which nonprofit organizations have embraced commercial branding ideas and approaches. The first and most pervasive criticism is typically raised by members of the press, who feel that charities, in particular, can spend excessive sums building their organization's brand to the detriment of service provision. After all, they argue, the advertising budget could easily be spent on service provision. While this argument is a little facile, it is certainly an issue that charities need to be sensitive to and be prepared to counter, should the need arise.

More significantly, Spruill (2001) argues that branding can create barriers that prevent nonprofits from creating collaborative partnerships with each other for either service delivery or fundraising. Managers are understandably reticent about diluting their brand and are thus unwilling to develop partnerships as a consequence. Spruill also argues that branding can develop a spirit of 'unhealthy competition' for visibility, prompting others to undertake similar expenditure, none of which will directly help beneficiaries. There can also be a sense that the voice of smaller causes is buried under the noise created by high-profile 'names'. Meyers (1985) notes that such concerns prompted Planned Parenthood to drop the idea of licensing condoms, which could have earned about $300,000 a year in royalties.

Brand Strategy

Having discussed the concept of branding and how it can be of relevance to nonprofits, we will now move on to consider how a brand strategy is developed.

Brand Relationships

Thus far in the text we have implicitly assumed that it is only the nonprofit as a whole that will be branded. This need not be the case. While the nonprofit's name may constitute one level of branding, it is quite possible that distinct fundraising products could be branded, or even discrete components of the service the organization provides to beneficiaries. A number of approaches are thus possible.

• *Corporate umbrella brand.* Here the organization itself is branded. There are numerous examples of this, as it is by far the most common nonprofit practice. The United Way, Red Cross, UNICEF, and the World Wildlife Fund (WWF) all have strong and in some cases international corporate brands. Examples of advertisements utilizing corporate branding are depicted in Figure 6.6.

• *Family brand.* Nonprofits may elect to have separate brands for their fundraising and service provision products. Schemes such as Adopt A Dog or Sponsor a Granny have been branded by their respective nonprofits as distinctive fundraising vehicles. These may well be subdivided to send a different message to distinct donor segments. Similarly, there may be branded components of service provision such as Talking Books or Lifeline, which could in turn have sub-brands for specific categories of service user.

• *Individual branding.* Finally, an organization can simply elect to brand aspects of its service provision or fundraising with separate and entirely unrelated brands. Such a strategy may be appropriate where the donor or service user population is diverse and/or where service provision is complex, with many different components. In such circumstances it is unlikely that a family or umbrella brand could be coherently developed and thus it would be more practical to simply brand each product.

In taking such decisions, it is important to bear in mind that there can be risks in relying too heavily on one brand. While we have noted that a strong brand can help mitigate the risk of unfavourable publicity should something go wrong, weaker brands may not weather the storm and any ill-performance or dissatisfaction can directly reflect on the organization. When an organization develops multiple brands this risk is mitigated since if public trust in one is damaged there are one or more opportunities to regain this through the work of the other brands in the portfolio. By developing multiple brands and a leadership in multiple target markets, the organization increases its chances of survival (Andreasen and Kotler 2003).

Differentiation

Whatever approach is ultimately adopted, each brand must be carefully differentiated from those of the competition. To achieve this, an organization must undertake a detailed analysis of the other provision in the market and identify in particular those organizations with similar names, brands, values, activities, and stakeholder groups. For each brand, the organization should look at how it compares with the nature of other provision and what, if anything, is distinctive about it.

In seeking to achieve this, organizations frequently employ a model such as that depicted in Figure 6.7. There are notable similarities between this and Aaker's six categories of meaning discussed earlier. It is simply a further way of conceptualizing a brand and thus seeking to identify components that either are, or could be, genuinely distinctive. It also draws a helpful distinction between the rational components of a brand, where perhaps the donor is consciously aware of the rationale for their support, and the emotional aspects of a brand, which may impact at a more subconscious level. It comprises:

- *Brand essence.* This is the core of what the brand will stand for.

- *Source of authority and support.* The brand may be differentiated on the basis of the quality of the organization's authority (i.e. those whose views are expressed). A number of the

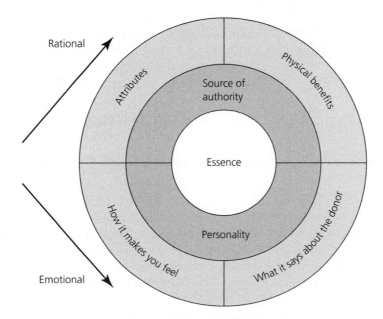

Figure 6.7 A model of brand

large cancer research charities, for example, can draw on the authority of the medical staff and researchers they represent.

- *Attributes*.
- *Physical benefits*. These are the benefits to the donor or service user.
- *Personality*. These are the human attributes of the brand.
- *How it makes the individual feel*. Does the brand offer any emotional benefits to the donor or service user as a reward for their support?
- *What it says about the individual*. Does the brand convey an identity to the donor or service user by virtue of their support?

Brands may be differentiated by one or more of these components. The strongest brands tend to be those that can offer a strong sense of differentiation on all seven components, but on a practical level this is often very difficult to achieve.

Brand Partnerships

The majority of the largest nonprofit organizations in both the USA and UK have developed strong brands, either by a conscious evolution of strategy, or by default where, whether the organization likes it or not, a brand has evolved by virtue of the organization's presence in a given market. Other brands have been built through collaboration with for-profit commercial organizations. There are numerous examples of small nonprofits that have been helped to become household names by virtue of their association with a large corporate partner. American Express, in particular, has been very helpful to a number of fledgling nonprofits.

Equally, many nonprofits will elect to develop brand partnerships with corporates in return for a fee or some form of cause-related marketing agreement. In such circumstances the nonprofit brand is very much a partner in the agreement and may have more to offer the corporate by way of meaning and values than could ever be offered in return. Whether an agreement is worth entering into will be a function of the following advantages and disadvantages.

Advantages

- The relationship can generate considerable income for little financial or human cost on the part of the nonprofit.
- The positive brand images of the for-profit can be transferred, at least in part, to the nonprofit.

Disadvantages

- A nonprofit organization will probably have little say in how the branding process will evolve, since the branding strategies will typically be developed by the commercial partner to ensure that their specific objectives are met.
- There are very real risks that the image of the nonprofit could be damaged if the commercial partner is later found to be behaving inappropriately in some aspect of its operations. This can be particularly damaging where these activities are at odds with the mission of the nonprofit.

Voluntary Sector Brand Values

Before leaving the topic of brand management it is worth focusing for a moment on the voluntary sector context and discussing how the management of charity brands, in particular, might differ from the management of brands in other contexts. Recent research (Smith et al. 2006, Sargeant and Ford 2006, Sargeant et al. 2008) has suggested that the management of brand values might be more complex.

Authors such as de Chernatony (1999) have argued that organizations should aim for clarity in presenting their values and how these might be distinctive from other players in a particular market. In the voluntary sector context, this process is complicated by the fact that being value(s)-based is one of the features that distinguishes charitable organizations from those in the public or private sectors (Aiken 2001). Indeed, there are felt to be key voluntary sector values that drive the distinctive way in which such organizations manage and organize themselves (Batsleer et al. 1991, Stride 2006).

There may thus be organizational brand values that accrue by virtue of an organization's voluntary or charitable status. The very fact that organizations have elected to take this form imbues them, from the public's perspective, with a discrete set of values that are a function of their charity nature. Malloy and Agarwal (2001) argue that the dominant climate in the voluntary sector is based on a caring or feminine model, but there may well be other values common to all, such as trustworthiness or voluntarism.

In fact recent research by Sargeant et al. (2008) and Sargeant et al. (2008) shows that a large part of the personality of a brand *is* shared with other nonprofits (see Figure 6.8). There are a wealth of benevolent characteristics such as being fair, honest, ethical, and trustworthy that the public imbue organizations with because they are charitable. In their initial focus groups, comments such as 'well, it's a charity so it must be caring, mustn't it?' and 'compassionate—

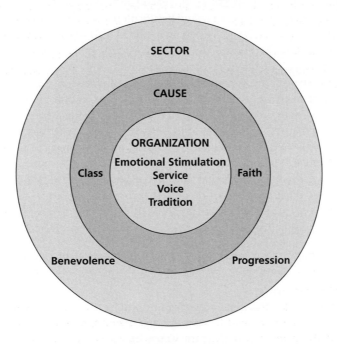

Figure 6.8 Structure of nonprofit brands

goes without saying' were typical. Nonprofits didn't need to earn these characteristics, rather individuals started from the assumption that they applied until evidence appeared to the contrary. Similarly participants saw nonprofits as agents of change and imbued organizations with traits that reflected the nature of this progressive engagement with society. Characteristics such as transforming, pioneering, responsive, and engaging were viewed by participants as being charitable traits. Out of the 61 personality characteristics identified in the exploratory research over half were later found, in a large-scale survey of 4500 donors, to be shared with the sector as a whole.

They also identified a causal dimension to personality. Faith-based organizations were identified by participants as having a personality distinctive from the balance of the sector. Traits such as spiritual, devout, holy, and religious, for example, were applied to church and parachurch organizations. Catholic, Methodist, Jewish, and Muslim charities were all viewed as having distinctive identities that reflected the nature of each faith and the emphasis on the various behaviours and ideas expressed in that faith. The Mission Aviation Fellowship, for example, strives to provide aid to developing countries, investing in projects such as sanitation and the provision of fresh water, while simultaneously raising awareness of the gospel in the communities in which they work. Donors are therefore supporting both practical and spiritual aid when they offer a donation. The Christian values the organization embodies can therefore differentiate the organization from many other international relief agencies such as Oxfam or the Red Cross, but not from other faith-based agencies such as Christian Aid or in the US Samaritan's Purse. They distinguish the sector, not the organization.

They also found evidence that some causes were perceived as being 'upper class', 'intellectual', or 'sophisticated'. Education- and arts-based charities were frequently referred to in these terms and regarded as 'elite'. For some these traits were terms of derision, while for others they were viewed as desirable personality traits that would actively draw in donors and foster engagement with the organization. Thus many museums, galleries, opera houses, concert halls, colleges, and universities may find it difficult to carve out a unique identity on the basis of class-based attributes. Donors will tend to imbue such organizations with these characteristics on the basis of their connection with a particular cause, rather through an understanding of identity built up through communication.

Delineating the shared aspects of brand matters because the shared and unique aspects of personality impact on giving in different ways. A belief that nonprofits are progressive and benevolent is a necessary pre-requisite to an individual becoming a donor in the first place. An understanding that an organization is faith-based may be a necessary pre-requisite for a follower of that faith to consider including it in what marketers refer to as their 'consideration set' (i.e the range of brands they will consider supporting). This research indicates that they have no impact at all on the actual amounts people will give, or the levels of loyalty a charity might gain. What does impact on both these aspects of a donor–nonprofit relationship are those facets of personality that are genuinely distinctive. Projecting a unique or differentiated brand personality makes it more likely that donors will give at a higher level and give for extended periods of time.

Nonprofit brand personalities can currently be differentiated in one of four ways:

1. Emotional Stimulation

Traits such as exciting, heroic, innovative, inspiring all have the capacity to evoke an emotional response in the donor and to drive giving as a consequence. The Royal National Lifeboat Institution has been patrolling the waters off the coast of Great Britain since 1824. It responds to emergency calls and has saved the lives of many sailors in distress. The organization's brand projects the courage and rugged heroism of the lifeboat crews, and these values are reflected in many of the images used in campaign materials (see Figure 6.9). Research has taught the RNLI that donors most strongly identify with these characteristics and therefore respond better to communications that reinforce them. Although many lifeboat coxes are now female and few of their male counterparts actually sport beards, the

He'll face 10m waves, blizzards, force 9 gales and sub-zero temperatures

All we ask of you is £20

- -

To: The Chief Executive, RNLI, FREEPOST BH173, West Quay Road, Poole, Dorset BH15 1XF.

I wish to support the RNLI with: ☐ £20

☐ Another amount £ ....

I wish to give my support by: ☐ Cheque Please make payable to the Royal National Lifeboat Institution

OR   ☐ Mastercard   ☐ Visa   ☐ Maestro

Credit card number/Maestro number   Maestro only

☐☐☐☐ ☐☐☐☐ ☐☐☐☐ ☐☐☐☐

☐☐/☐☐   ☐☐/☐☐ ☐☐

Start date   Expiry date   Maestro issue no.

PLEASE TURN OVER AND COMPLETE THE OTHER SIDE

Lifeboats

Charity registered in England, Scotland and the Republic of Ireland.

Figure 6.9 RNLI donor recruitment insert

Source: © 2008 Royal National Lifeboat Institution. Reproduced with kind permission.

depicted ad remains a most effective recruitment device because it best reflects the perceived personality of the organization and creates a 'focus' for donations. Interestingly, this ad was developed some years ago by an elderly volunteer living about as far from the sea as it is possible to get. It very powerfully reflected her view of the brand, and the response it engenders has yet to be beaten by any of the RNLI's commercial agencies.

2. Voice

Brands can also be differentiated on the basis of their media presence or the tone of 'voice' adopted. Some nonprofits are viewed as distinctive because they are ambitious, authoritative, or bold. The National Society for the Prevention of Cruelty To Children, for example, regards itself as challenging, courageous, protecting, and respectful. Its communications as a consequence do not shy away from difficult issues. It sets out to challenge, while having the sensitivity not to distress the very audience it is determined to help. The charity is therefore careful to avoid overtly shocking depictions of abuse that may upset some audiences and instead uses powerful imagery that leads the reader inexorably to the conclusion that abuse is about to take place. Few charities are willing to be as challenging in their media imagery. The green full-stop logo is now one of the most widely recognized brand symbols in the UK as donors, potential donors, and members of the wider UK public are encouraged to play a part in putting an end to child cruelty—'full stop'.

3. Service

The style and/or philosophy behind service provision can be an effective route to differentiation. Human service charities, in particular, might carve out a unique identity on the basis of characteristics such as whether they are seen as inclusive, approachable, dedicated, or compassionate in the way in which they deal with their beneficiaries or service users. The RSPCA (Royal Society for the Prevention of Cruelty to Animals), for example, is the oldest established animal welfare charity in the UK. Figure 6.10 depicts a still from the close of a DRTV (Direct Response Television) advertisement looking to recruit individuals into a low-value regular monthly gift of £3. The ad focuses on the distinctive nature of the organization's services, namely the provision of animal welfare inspectors who have similar powers to the UK police to investigate and prosecute instances of animal cruelty or neglect. In the current advertisement a kitten is shown being rescued by an inspector from the bin in which it has been abandoned and left to die by its former owner. The ad was designed both to raise funds and communicate the organization's brand personality, namely being authoritative, compassionate, effective, and responsible.

4. Tradition

Some nonprofits are seen by donors as traditional. Giving is regarded by donors as a duty, or the personality of the brand is tied to a particular event or season, when giving is specifically encouraged. In the US who can deny the power of the Salvation Army kettles positioned outside shops and shopping malls during the holidays? In the UK the Royal British Legion sells poppies in advance of Remembrance Sunday in recognition of those who have lost their lives in the service of their country. So powerful has the symbol become that no politician, newscaster, or person of influence in the media will be seen without wearing one in the run-up to the event.

It is important to stress that there may be other avenues open to nonprofits to use as the basis for differentiation that were not tested in this study. The key lesson, however, is that it appears to be the distinctive facets of personality that drive behaviour. Nonprofits therefore need to clarify what these may be and prioritize effort accordingly.

Figure 6.10 RSPCA donor recruitment advertisement
Source: © 2008 Royal Society for the Prevention of Cruelty to Animals.

Integrated Communications

While we have stressed on numerous occasions throughout this chapter the need for all communications to reflect the nature of the brand, we have not yet focused on the increasingly important topic of integrated communications; in other words, ensuring that all the communications an organization generates represent a coherent whole. This is particularly important where a nonprofit has elected to brand the organization. In such cases all the forms of communication the nonprofit generates should reflect the organization's overall brand. Too many nonprofits assume that they are dealing with discrete groups of stakeholders who will not have access to other communications that the organization might generate for other stakeholder groups, thus they do not see the need to be consistent from one form of communication to another. To be successful, however, the whole organization has to 'live the brand' and to reflect its various dimensions in every form of communication that leaves the organization.

Achieving consistency in approach is not easy, but there are a variety of steps that a nonprofit might take to ensure effective integration. These include:

• *Stakeholder consultation and buy-in.* In seeking to generate an organizational brand it is important that all the major stakeholder groups are consulted in respect of the form that this might take, the messages it would seek to communicate, and the values it would seek to espouse. Failure to consult widely and integrate stakeholder input will typically result in an inability on the part of the organization to secure the buy-in of all those who have a stake in the organization (Hankinson and Lomax 2006). This matters since, once created, it will be the individuals in these groups who will ultimately shape how the brand is perceived through their communications and dealings with others. Unless they actively support the initiative it is likely either to fail or be distorted to reflect the miscellany of different values and messages that disparate groups feel are most appropriate (Brown 2007).

• *The generation of a brand book.* This document provides all the detail of what the brand is, what it stands for, and how it will be communicated; in effect all of the components we discussed earlier (see Figure 6.3). Brand books provide detail in respect of the design of the logo and where, when, and how it must be used. It also outlines in detail how the organization should convey its core values and how an appropriate style of communication may be fostered. It also provides information on where individual members of staff can turn to for advice if they are unsure how to implement any aspect of the guidelines.

• *Training for contact staff or volunteers.* As has been noted on many occasions throughout this chapter, all forms of communication can influence how the brand will be perceived. It is therefore essential that an organization develops and implements an appropriate programme of training for all those who will have contact with external stakeholder groups such as donors, volunteers, service users, the news media, etc. All such staff should ensure that they know how to operationalize the guidelines contained in the brand book in the context of their own role. This may require training in the style to be adopted in formal communications, or training in answering the phone, writing letters, press releases, etc.

• *Cross-functional briefings and meetings.* In many nonprofits, responsibility for external communications is split between the fundraising, campaigning, service provision, and corporate communications (e.g. branding) departments. Frequently each may have developed its own micro-marketing function, with considerable expertise having been amassed in relation to the task in question. The key barrier to ensuring effective integration is thus the extent to which each of these respective functions communicates (or not) with the others. There is therefore a need to establish regular contact between these groups of individuals to ensure that the approach adopted in one aspect of the organization's communications is consistent with that adopted in another. Regular team meetings and briefings are essential to achieve this.

• *Map a year in the life of . . .* The final lesson from professional practice is that it can be advantageous to nominate one individual who will 'pose' as a member of each key stakeholder group, signing on to the relevant stream of communications such individuals receive. This is undertaken anonymously so that no one else within the organization is aware that this is happening. These individuals then keep a record of all the communications they receive from the organization. The reason for this is straightforward. Many brands are designed to build and develop relationships with stakeholders by adding to the emotional and functional value we discussed earlier. One department may feel it has created communications that do a pretty good job of this, carefully building up the recipient's knowledge and level of engagement over time. In most modern organizations, however, 'house lists' of particular stakeholder groups are often accessed by other parts of the organization. Members of the public, for example, who have agreed to participate in e-mail campaigns to lobby for social change may also be approached for donations. They may also receive a copy of the trading catalogue and be invited to buy nonprofit merchandise. In some circumstances they could also be approached to become service users or volunteers to aid the cause. In short, many different departments will have access to individuals who originally joined the organization to campaign. Thus, while the campaign department may have a perfectly cogent strategy for relationship development, this can quickly lapse into the absurd when different and perhaps conflicting communications are received from other parts of the organization. While to a certain extent the team briefings referred to above may minimize the potential for conflict, it can be a very useful exercise to have an individual track what is actually received and for the team to reflect thereafter on whether a year in the life of a particular stakeholder is as the organization would wish it to be. If not, changes can be made.

■ SUMMARY

In this chapter, we have focused exclusively on the subject of branding. As we have seen, the process of branding a nonprofit organization bears many similarities to the process of developing an umbrella brand in the corporate sector. Many of the issues involved and indeed many of the models of brand developed in that context are of equal relevance to nonprofits.

However, it also seems clear that the branding of nonprofits may be inherently more complex. The need to reflect the needs and aspirations of a variety of stakeholder groups means that organizations, unlike their commercial counterparts, cannot simply take decisions that are optimal for a particular objective (e.g. increased market share or sales). Nonprofit brands communicate something of the values of different stakeholder groups and in the case of charities may even be shaped by the values of the sector as a whole, or of particular categories of cause.

To assist in managing a brand I have introduced a number of frameworks that can be used to plan both the content of a brand and also its embodiment in every contact that an organization has with external stakeholder groups. As we have seen, this includes a consideration of both verbal and non-verbal forms of communication and employing each to express one or more values associated with the brand. Managing these issues properly is important, since successful branding can lead to enhanced income generation and enhanced performance in the delivery of the mission. In short, branding can enhance many aspects of nonprofit performance while at the same time adding value for a multitude of different stakeholder groups: a genuine win-win situation for all.

■ DISCUSSION QUESTIONS

1.   In your role as the communications director of a large environmental protection charity, you have been asked by your board of trustees to explain why it is necessary for the organization to allocate funds to brand-building communications. Prepare a brief presentation to the board outlining the benefits to the organization of continuing to develop its brand.

2.   What are brand values? Why might projecting the right values be of particular concern to a nonprofit organization, and what additional complexities might exist in managing brand values in this context?

3.   Is the development of an organizational brand always appropriate? Are there any circumstances under which it might not be appropriate to develop such a brand?

4.   As the director of communications of a children's charity you have been approached by a large multinational organization which has indicated that it would be interested in partnering with your brand in return for a substantial initial donation and a small donation from each subsequent sale of jointly branded merchandise. What might be the advantages and disadvantages of

entering into such a relationship? What questions would you ask of the potential corporate partner before proceeding with this deal?

5. What is meant by the term 'integrated communication'? Why is this an important issue, and how can a nonprofit organization ensure that its communications are effectively integrated?

■ REFERENCES

Aaker, J.L. (1997) 'Dimensions of Brand Personality', *Journal of Marketing Research*, August, 347–56.

Aiken, M. (2001) *Keeping Close to Your Values: Lessons from a Study Examining how Voluntary and Co-operative Organisations Reproduce their Organisational Values*, Milton Keynes, Open University.

Andreasen, A.R. and Kotler, P. (2003) *Strategic Marketing For Nonprofit Organisations*, 6th edn, Englewood Cliffs, NJ, Prentice Hall.

Batsleer, J., Cornforth, C. and Paton, R. (1991) *Issues in Voluntary and Non-profit Management*, Wokingham, Addison Wesley.

Brown, E.L. (2007) 'Are You Following the 4Cs of Branding?' *Nonprofit World,* Vol. 25, No. 3, 11–13.

de Chernatony, L. (1999) 'Brand Management through Narrowing the Gap between Brand Identity and Brand Reputation', *Journal of Marketing Management*, Vol. 15, 157–79.

Dickinson, S. and Barker, A. (2007) 'Evaluations of Branding Alliances Between Non-Profit and Commercial Brand Partners', *International Journal of Nonprofit and Voluntary Sector Marketing*, 12(1), 75–89.

Fogel, E. (2007) 'Invest in the Future By Branding The Organization', *Marketing News*, Vol. 41, No. 11, 13–14.

Frumkin, P. and Kim, M.T. (2001) 'Strategic Positioning and the Financing of Nonprofit Organizations: Is Efficiency Rewarded in the Contributions Marketplace?', *Public Administration Review*, Vol. 61 (May/June), 266–75.

Hankinson, P. (2000) 'Brand Orientation in Charity Organizations: Qualitative Research into Key Charity Sectors', *International Journal of Nonprofit and Voluntary Sector Marketing*, Vol. 5, 207–19.

Hankinson, P. (2001) 'Brand Orientation in the Charity Sector: A Framework for Discussion and Research', *International Journal of Nonprofit and Voluntary Sector Marketing*, Vol. 6, No. 3, 231–42.

Hankinson, P. amd Lomax, W. (2006) 'The Effects of Re-branding Large UK Charities On Staff Knowledge, Attitudes and Behaviour', *International Journal of Nonprofit and Voluntary Sector Marketing*, Vol. 11, No. 3, 193–207.

Malloy, D. C. and Agarwal, J. (2001) 'Ethical Climate in Nonprofit Organizations: Propositions and Implications', *Nonprofit Management and Leadership*, Vol. 12, No. 1, 39–54.

Meyers, W. (1985) 'The Nonprofits Drop The "Non"', *The New York Times*, 24 November, 14.

Polonsky, M.J. and Macdonald, E.K. (2000) 'Exploring the Link Between Cause-related Marketing and Brand Building', *International Journal of Nonprofit and Voluntary Sector Marketing*, Vol. 5, No. 1, 46–57.

Ritchie, R.J.B. and Swami, S. (1998) 'A Brand New World', *International Journal of Nonprofit and Voluntary Sector Marketing*, Vol. 4, 26–42.

Sargeant, A. and Ford, J.B. (2006) 'The Power of Brands', *Stanford Social Innovation Review*, Winter, 41–7.

Sargeant, A., Hudson, J. and West, D.C. (2008) 'Conceptualising Brand Values in the Charity Sector: The Relationship Between Sector, Cause and Organisation', *Service Industries Journal*, forthcoming.

Sargeant, A., and Jay, E. (2003) *An Empirical Investigation of Attrition Amongst Face-To-Face Recruits*, Cullompton, Sargeant Associates Ltd.

Saxton, J. (1995) 'A Strong Charity Brand comes from Strong Beliefs and Values', *Journal of Brand Management*, Vol. 2, No. 4, 211–20.

Smith, A.C.T., Graetz, B.R. and Westerbeek, H.M. (2006) 'Brand Personality in a Membership-Based Organisation', *International Journal of Nonprofit and Voluntary Sector Marketing*, Vol. 11, No. 3, 251–66.

Spruill, V. (2001) 'Build Brand Identity for Causes, not Groups', *Chronicle of Philanthropy*, Vol. 13 (June), 45.

Stride, H. (2006) 'An Investigation Into The Values Dimensions of Branding: Implications for the Charity Sector', *International Journal of Nonprofit and Voluntary Sector Marketing*, Vol. 11, No. 2, 115–24.

7 Marketing Programmes and Services: The Operational Mix

OBJECTIVES

By the end of this chapter you should be able to:

1. develop a marketing mix for a nonprofit product or service;
2. discuss other approaches to grouping tactical marketing activities;
3. write a marketing plan for a nonprofit product or service;
4. suggest how the quality of a nonprofit service might be measured and evaluated;
5. explain how a consideration of ethics might impact on nonprofit plans and activities.

Introduction

This is the final chapter of the text that will deal with marketing planning issues. In previous chapters we examined the first two stages of a marketing plan (i.e. 'Where are we now?' and 'Where do we want to be?'). We also addressed the strategic aspects of 'How will we get there?', focusing on overall direction, segmentation, positioning, competitive/collaborative strategy, and branding. In this chapter, we will examine the tactical marketing mix and a range of issues that nonprofits typically have to address in specifying exactly how their objectives will be achieved.

To structure the discussion, the chapter has been divided using the headings of a typical marketing mix. Since most nonprofits produce services rather than products, a service marketing perspective has been adopted. It is important to recognize, however, that many of the ideas expressed have equal relevance to both product and service contexts. It is also important to recognize that while a 'mix' can be a good way to group ideas, it is far from being a new idea. The notion of a marketing mix has been around for almost 50 years and has been criticized by many authors as too constricting or formulaic. The key to writing a successful marketing plan undoubtedly lies in applying a little common sense and grouping tactical plans in a way that makes sense for the organization in question. This frequently reflects the structure of the marketing department itself so that it is relatively easy to delineate individual responsibilities for implementation.

What follows is thus a standard structure that will work in most cases, albeit with some modification. The two key instances where it will probably not be appropriate are in Internet marketing (particularly where this is the primary route to market) and where the organization serves only a small number of high-value clients where it should instead look to manage specific aspects of its relationships with each client (see, for example, Payne et al. 1999). An appropriate e-marketing mix will be outlined later in this chapter.

Products/Services

The Components of Products and Services

The starting point for examining this component of the marketing mix lies in determining the requirements of the target market. What needs do the target segments have and how can they best be satisfied? Armed with this knowledge, marketers can then ensure that the products and services their organization provides are appropriately tailored to the needs of each of their customer or stakeholder groups.

The marketing literature presents a variety of frameworks for the analysis of the components of a product/service and these provide a useful guide for examining and defining the market entity that the organization is looking to provide. Kotler, for example, distinguishes between the core, tangible, and augmented aspects of a service while Levitt focuses on a service's generic, expected, and augmented components. In each case, the analysis is based on the idea that any service can be seen as offering a basic set of features from the point of view of the consumer. Beyond this, services are augmented by a variety of additional features that associate it with a particular supplier, differentiate it from competing services, and make it in some way distinctive.

Kotler's perspective is presented in Figure 7.1. Adopting this model in the nonprofit sector aids the marketer in clarifying the components of the service that they are offering to both recipients of goods and services and also to those that elect to fund such activities. The 'core' service from the perspective of the donor, for example, is arguably the knowledge that one has contributed to a worthwhile cause. In the case of healthcare, the core product is the diagnosis and programme of treatment prescribed.

At this point, however, the service is only being defined in terms of the generic available in the market. One would hope for example that two or more competent physicians would reach the same conclusion in respect of a patient's ailment. Similarly most charities are capable of providing a 'feelgood' factor to one degree or another. In short, it is unlikely that the

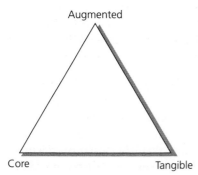

Figure 7.1 Components of a product

core service will vary much from one organization to another. It may be thought of as being simply the minimum necessary to satisfy the needs of the customer.

The tangible component of the service is of particular importance since recent research indicates that consumers are more likely to purchase and re-purchase a service if they can take away something tangible from the experience. Enhancing the tangible nature of the service can also serve to reduce risk from the perspective of the purchaser (see for example George and Berry 1981 and Palmer 1994) and act as a useful reminder of their experience that can assist in word-of-mouth advertising among friends and colleagues. In the fundraising context the tangible part of the service would therefore include the 'thank you' tokens that are typically received for making a donation in the street. While rewarding a donor for his generosity, such tokens also serve the ancillary purpose of providing protection against further requests for donations.

In the healthcare context the concept of tangibility would more usefully relate to the quality of the environment provided for patients. Many hospitals and private clinics now give considerable thought to the physical design and layout of those areas where patients and their loved ones are likely to spend time. As obvious as this may sound, there is now a considerable body of research to suggest that in the absence of other evaluative criteria, patients will tend to rely on these tangible cues to judge the quality of the service they receive.

The reader will therefore appreciate that giving consideration to the tangible components of their service may be one way in which a nonprofit could look to differentiate its service from that supplied by potential competitors. Given that the core service is widely available, however, it is unlikely that simply adjusting the tangible components will in itself be enough to create and sustain an advantage over the competition. The augmented part of the service is the real key to this issue. While the consumer is paying for a certain core experience and will doubtless be happy if she receives it, the augmented component goes beyond what the consumer was expecting. It may be thought of as value added which can be used to draw a distinction in the minds of consumers between the service provided by one organization and that provided by another. Returning to our earlier examples for a moment, there may be many ways in which both organizations could augment their service. Donors could receive personalized mailings, individual attention from staff, invitations to visit a particular project to see how their money has been used, a commemorative plaque, etc. In the healthcare context the service could be augmented by the quality of information provided to relatives, allowing greater time for a patient–physician dialogue, access to support groups, personal follow-ups by hospital staff when the patient has returned home, etc. Augmenting the service in any of the ways described would be costly, but the rewards in terms of enhanced customer satisfaction and hence loyalty to the organization could well be worth the initial investment.

Together these three components form the basis of the market offering. Each component should be considered in isolation and as a part of the complete service offering. This latter point is of particular significance since all three aspects of the service have the capability to communicate a message to target customer groups.

Service Quality

Of course the components of a service will not be the only issue a nonprofit will have to address. Marketers in this context will also want to ensure that an appropriate level of quality is maintained for the service, across all the stakeholder groups that will have contact with it. There are a number of reasons why this is an important consideration. First, nonprofit marketers will want to ensure that the quality of service reflects the values and mission of the organization (which often regard the satisfaction of stakeholder needs as being paramount). They will also be aware of the dramatic impact that the quality of the service can have on their ability to attract new service users and to retain them. This latter point is an issue we shall return to later in this chapter.

In its simplest form, service quality is a product of the effort that every member of the organization invests in satisfying customers. More specifically, service quality has been defined as 'the delivery of excellent or superior service relative to customer expectations' (Zeithaml and Bitner 1996) and 'Quality is behaviour—an attitude—that says you will never settle for anything less than the best in service for your stakeholders, whether they are customers, the community, your stockholders or the colleagues with whom you work every day' (Harvey 1995).

At the heart of these and other definitions of quality lies the suggestion that perceived quality is what the consumer sees and is the result of a comparison between expectations of service quality and the actual service received. To illustrate this, suppose that potential applicants to a particular university are promised in the prospectus the latest laboratory facilities, excellent tuition, access to a wide range of sports, and catering covering a broad spectrum of different traditions and tastes. When the students actually arrive on campus they discover that the catering is somewhat limited and mediocre, only outdoor sports are offered, and both the teaching and laboratory facilities are a little old-fashioned. The inevitable result is a great deal of student dissatisfaction. If, on the other hand, the university had painted a more modest picture of what would be provided, those students who did elect to study there would find their expectations met (or exceeded) and would undoubtedly be satisfied with their experience. This is an example of what Churchill and Suprenant (1982) regard as the 'disconfirmation paradigm' in action. While this is a concept that has recently received criticism in the literature, largely because there is no real evidence that the comparative process actually takes place, it does represent a useful starting point in our analysis.

Accepting for a moment that the disconfirmation paradigm is an appropriate way to model customer perceptions of delivered service quality, a number of interesting implications begin to emerge. Peters (1987) argues that on this basis organizations should look to 'under-promise' and 'over-deliver'. In this way customer expectations will be low, their perceptions of delivered service quality high, and as a consequence their satisfaction will also be high. The problem with this argument is that expectations are learnt from experience, so this process will only work once. As soon as consumers perceive a high standard of service, they will come to expect it on subsequent occasions and could potentially be dissatisfied if their expectations are not fulfilled. As a result, this author contends that by far the safest way of ensuring customer satisfaction is simply to deliver consistently to one's service promises. The second interesting consequence of the disconfirmation paradigm is that it leaves organizations looking to identify the criteria against which consumers build expectations. As Levitt (1981: 100) explains, this is not easy: 'The most important thing to know about intangible products is that the customers usually don't know what they're getting until they don't get it. Only then do they become aware of what they bargained for; only on dissatisfaction do they dwell'.

Even where those factors important to overall satisfaction can be adequately identified, organizations still have the task of setting objective measures of quality and ensuring that they deliver against the targets that they set. Indeed, this is not an easy task, since while the quality of physical goods can be measured satisfactorily by monitoring variables such as durability or the number of physical defects (Crosby 1979), in the case of services there is an almost total absence of objective methods of assessment.

Some consolation can be drawn, however, since it is not only the service providers who have difficulty in assessing the quality of their services. Consumers can have equal difficulties in formulating their own individual assessments. While the disconfirmation model looks quite neat in theory, in practice consumers can make quality assessments on the most superficial of cues. To explain why this might be, it is worth looking at the work of Nelson (1974) who drew a useful distinction between two categories of consumer goods, namely:

- *those high in search qualities*—which consumers can evaluate prior to making a purchase (e.g. size, colour, feel, smell);

- *those high in experience qualities*—where the attributes can be discerned only during use, and hence (in most cases) only after purchase (e.g. taste, wearability, etc.).

For our purposes, however, Darby and Karni (1973) helpfully add a third category:

- *Credence qualities*. These are characteristics which are difficult to evaluate, even after consumption. Many nonprofits offer services which are high on credence qualities, e.g. a heart operation or a charity donation.

The existence of these three qualities can best be conceptualized on a continuum. As can be seen from Figure 7.2, different products/services have varying degrees of credence qualities. It will be inherently more difficult to assess the quality of a service that contains a high degree of credence qualities. Consumers may find it all but impossible to evaluate their experience. Nevertheless, marketers should not lose heart, since evidence suggests that in such cases consumers use a variety of surrogate variables to evaluate such services. In the case, for example, of a bypass operation consumers are unlikely to have the technical knowledge to appraise the skills of the surgeon—they might hence appraise service quality on the basis of the perceived professionalism of staff, the level of technology employed, the decor of their ward/building, etc. This is a simple but important concept to grasp as these criteria could

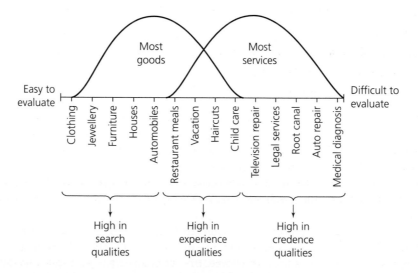

Figure 7.2 Continuum of evaluation for different types of products

Source: Zeithaml et al., *Services Marketing,* New York, McGraw Hill. Reproduced with the kind permission of McGraw Hill.

quite easily be radically different from those that the hospital itself might use to evaluate the quality of the same operation (e.g. survival rates, number of medical complications, technical proficiency, use of resources, etc.). Nonprofits must monitor service quality not only against their own internal criteria but also in terms of those that are likely to be used by their customers. In the case of services that are high on credence qualities, these dimensions can usually only be identified through research.

The Measurement of Service Quality

Given the difficulties alluded to above, the reader could be forgiven for believing that the measurement of service quality is an almost impossible task. A variety of methods of measurement have been advocated, but there is still considerable disagreement in the literature in respect of the best method to use.

Øvretveit (1992: 23) argues in favour of a market-focused approach. As he puts it: 'The question is not the general "What do customers think about our service?" but the more specific "Which features of our service are the most important to potential, current, and past customers in relation to the actions which the service wishes to influence, and how does the service compare to the alternatives on these features?"'

It is therefore too simplistic merely to ask customers what they think about each dimension of the service. Each group of customers will have its own priorities in terms of those elements of the service that it perceives to be most important. Measuring every service component may therefore not be necessary and, where deficiencies are encountered, additional resources may be required only in those areas which will have the greatest impact on customer satisfaction.

It therefore seems clear that an organization looking to monitor service quality should

1. identify its key customer groups or segments;
2. identify the key components of the service;
3. assess the relative importance of each component for each customer segment;
4. set performance targets for each key component;
5. measure actual service performance against each target;
6. prioritize necessary improvements;
7. allocate investment accordingly.

Following such a procedure should ensure that where deviations are detected against the desired targets, scarce resources can be targeted at only those aspects of the service that are perceived as of greatest importance. Of course, these factors will not be static over time and the process described above should be iterative.

While many of the steps appear quite straightforward, step (5) is somewhat problematic as in practice it is not an easy task to measure service quality. Three broad approaches are possible.

Counting Complaints

The simplest approach is to count the number of complaints that relate to each service provided, or each specific component thereof. This is clearly an unsatisfactory method of monitoring service quality as a relatively low proportion of customers will actually take the trouble to complain. Most will simply rate the service as poor and look for alternative suppliers.

Rating Service Attributes

A rather more sophisticated method of measuring service quality consists of deriving a list of service attributes and asking customers to rate their perceptions of each attribute, typically on a five- or seven-point scale.

In a study of student satisfaction with higher education institutions, Stewart (1992) utilized a series of attitudinal statements with a Likert scale for responses ranging from 'strongly agree' to 'strongly disagree'. The statements selected probed customer perceptions of each element of the traditional marketing mix, including:

- *product*—the variety of curriculum, course scheduling, student evaluations of faculty, opportunities for personal growth via professional and leadership activities, academic advising, student interaction with faculty and administrators, library holdings, and cultural, athletic, and social opportunities;

- *price*—tuition expenses—finance packages available;

- *place*—environmental issues—campus attractiveness and safety, availability of lounge facilities, study areas, and parking spaces; health and library service offerings; procedures for selecting dormitory and room-mate assignments; adequacy of meals/other catering;

- *promotion*—accuracy of promotional material—prospectus, departmental literature. Do students know where to go for advice, are they informed of extra-curricular activities on campus? Availability of information in respect of changes in curriculum procedures and requirements.

Importantly, the author also advocated the gathering of data relating to the perceived importance of each element. For each of the components of the HE service, it is hence possible to plot the position of a given university's performance in a matrix such as that in Figure 7.3.

Service components falling within the top right-hand segment are those that are both very important to customers and those areas where the university performs well. The level of service should clearly be maintained in these areas. Service components falling within the bottom right-hand quadrant are those where the university performs well, but are considered to be areas of little importance by customers. It is possible here that the institution may be engaged in 'overkill', spending too much resources on dimensions of the service that really

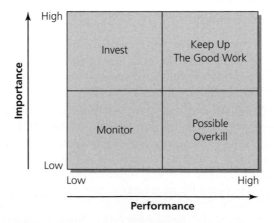

Figure 7.3 Importance/perception quadrants

don't matter to its clients. It should hence give consideration to whether these resources should be directed elsewhere.

In the case of service components falling within the top left-hand quadrant, the prescription would be to invest in improvement. They are perceived to be of considerable importance by customers, but the actual performance is rated poorly. Service components falling within the bottom left-hand area can also be seen to be underperforming, but in their case this appears not to matter because they are also perceived to be of little importance. The prescription here would be to monitor these components over time. In the dynamic environment in which many nonprofits operate, customer tastes and preferences are subject to change and a number of these dimensions could therefore become important over time.

The SERVQUAL Method

Perhaps the most famous of the techniques of service quality measurement is that proposed by Parasuraman et al. (1988). The authors posited the existence of four key service gaps (five if the aggregate gap is included). These gaps are together responsible for the difference between expected and perceived service quality.

- *Gap 1*. Not knowing what customers expect—the difference between consumer needs and management's perceptions of those needs.

- *Gap 2*. Not selecting the right service design—the difference between management perceptions of customer needs and the service standards set.

- *Gap 3*. Not delivering to service standards—the difference between service specifications and actual service delivery.

- *Gap 4*. Not matching performance to promises—the difference between the service promises made in external communications and the actual service delivered.

Parasuraman et al. (1988) evolved this concept of 'gaps' into a quantitative technique for measuring service quality known as SERVQUAL. This is based upon a generic 22-item questionnaire designed to cover the broad dimensions of service quality. The model has received widespread support in the literature, although it has been refined and adapted to make it suitable for application in a number of different sectors (see Babakus and Boller 1992). The SERVQUAL instrument is illustrated in Figure 7.4.

The idea behind the questionnaire is that

$$Q = P - E$$

where

    Q = the perceived quality of each item
    P = the performance achieved in each item
    E = the customer's expectations of performance in each item.

To measure the quality of each service dimension one therefore subtracts the expectations score from the performance score for each item. A high positive result would hence indicate a high perceived standard of service, while a high negative score would indicate a low perceived standard of service. In testing the responses received to this instrument, the authors determined that service quality can best be viewed as having five underlying dimensions, namely:

- *tangibles*—physical facilities, equipment, and appearance of personnel;

- *reliability*—ability to perform the promised service dependably and accurately;

- *responsiveness*—willingness to help customers and provide prompt service;

Directions: This survey deals with your opinions of—services. Please show the extent to which you think firms offering—services should possess the features described by each statement. Do this by picking one of the seven numbers next to each statement. If you strongly agree that these firms should possess a feature, circle the number 7. If you strongly disagree that these firms should possess a feature, circle 1. If your feelings are not strong, circle one of the numbers in the middle. There are no right or wrong answers—all we are interested in is a number that best shows your expectations about firms offering—services.

		Strongly disagree						Strongly agree
E1	They should have up-to-date equipment	1	2	3	4	5	6	7
E2	Their physical facilities should be visually appealing	1	2	3	4	5	6	7
E3	Their employees should be well dressed and appear neat	1	2	3	4	5	6	7
E4	The appearance of the physical facilities of these firms should be in keeping with the type of services provided	1	2	3	4	5	6	7
E5	When these firms promise to do something by a certain time, they should do so	1	2	3	4	5	6	7
E6	When customers have problems, these firms should be sympathetic and reassuring	1	2	3	4	5	6	7
E7	These firms should be dependable	1	2	3	4	5	6	7
E8	They should provide their services at the time they promise to do so	1	2	3	4	5	6	7
E9	They should keep their records accurately	1	2	3	4	5	6	7
E10	They shouldn't be expected to tell customers exactly when services will be performed (-)	1	2	3	4	5	6	7
E11	It is not realistic for customers to expect prompt service from employees of these firms (-)	1	2	3	4	5	6	7
E12	Their employees don't always have to be willing to help customers (-)	1	2	3	4	5	6	7
E13	It is okay if they are too busy to respond to customer requests promptly (-)	1	2	3	4	5	6	7
E14	Customers should be able to trust employees of these firms	1	2	3	4	5	6	7
E15	Customers should be able to feel safe in their transactions with these firm's employees	1	2	3	4	5	6	7
E16	Their employees should be polite	1	2	3	4	5	6	7
E17	Their employees should get adequate support from these firms to do their jobs well	1	2	3	4	5	6	7
E18	These firms should not be expected to give customers personal attention (-)	1	2	3	4	5	6	7
E19	Employees of these firms cannot be expected to give customers personal attention (-)	1	2	3	4	5	6	7
E20	It is unrealistic to expect employees to know what the needs of their customers are (-)	1	2	3	4	5	6	7
E21	It is unrealistic to expect these firms to have their customers' best interests at heart (-)	1	2	3	4	5	6	7
E22	They shouldn't be expected to have operating hours convenient to all their customers (-)	1	2	3	4	5	6	7

Figure 7.4 SERVQUAL

Source: Parasuraman, A., Zeithaml, V.A. and Berry, L.L. (1988) 'SERVQUAL: A Multiple Item Scale for Measuring Consumer Perceptions of Service Quality', *Journal of Retailing*, Vol. 64, No. 1, 12–40. © 2008 New York University. Reproduced with kind permission.

- *assurance*—knowledge and courtesy of employees and their ability to inspire trust and confidence;

- *empathy*—caring, individualized attention the firm provides its customers.

Hence a number of the statements in the questionnaire can be viewed as addressing the issue of reliability, while others together address the issues of responsiveness, etc. As a result, the scale has a number of applications within a service environment. These include:

- *Tracking service trends.* SERVQUAL can be used over time to plot changes in customers' perceptions of key service components (i.e. responses to individual questions).

- *Analysing each service dimension.* Average 'difference' scores can be calculated for each of the five dimensions referred to above. The possibility also exists to average each of these to arrive at an overall measure of service quality which could then be tracked over time.

- *Identifying the relative importance of each service dimension.* A statistical technique known as regression can be used to isolate which of the five dimensions are felt by customers to be of the greatest importance. Resource allocation can then be planned accordingly.

- *Determining whether specific groups of customers exist that prioritize differently the dimensions of service quality.* If this is the case, each group can be profiled to determine its demographic and/or lifestyle characteristics.

- *Tracking and comparing the service provided across different outlets and/or channels of distribution.*

- *Benchmarking against competitors.* A separate series of 'perceptions' questions could be included in the instrument for each key competitor and the resultant information used for benchmarking purposes.

SERVQUAL has been found to be very effective in a variety of different contexts including healthcare, charity service provision, and even in evaluating the service provided by the arts. As the reader will appreciate, however, it is a very generic instrument and a degree of tailoring will be necessary to maximize the utility it can offer. Thankfully, the literature is replete with adapted versions of the SERVQUAL scale, including work in the donations context (Sargeant and Jay 2004), the nonprofit service delivery context (Shiu et al. 1997), and the public sector context (McFadyen et al. 2001 and Marshall and Smith 2000). Details of a number of these scales are provided on the website that accompanies this volume.

Customer Value

We have so far in this chapter talked about customer perceptions of service quality and identified three ways in which this might be measured. The reader will recall that the latter two methods allow the researcher to identify those attributes of the service from which the customer derives the most value and it is this latter concept that we will focus on here.

Service organizations, whether they are profit-making or not, are unlikely to provide a service which has only one ingredient. When an arts customer buys a ticket for a museum, for example, the opportunity to view the exhibits is not the only component of the service purchased. Factors such as the ability to be able to interact with the displays, to understand something of the history of the items, and to be able to have an occasional dialogue with staff might also be significant components of the experience. Identifying which of the dimensions are of most importance is crucial, since it allows management to invest in those areas where customers derive the most value from their visit and cut costs in those areas

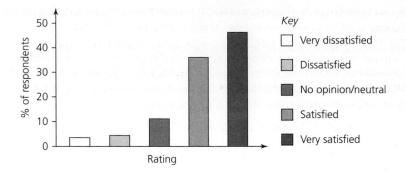

Figure 7.5 Customer satisfaction with an art gallery exhibition

which are not perceived to be of particular importance. This very simple idea has recently taken on a whole new significance because of the work of Jones and Sasser (1995). Consider the graph in Figure 7.5.

The figure illustrates the satisfaction ratings recently obtained from a survey of customers to a one-off exhibition at an art gallery. Now ask yourself the following questions.

Putting yourself in the position of the manager of that gallery for a moment, would you be happy with these figures?

The conventional wisdom has always been that you should be. After all, some 82 per cent of your customers are either satisfied or very satisfied. Consider an additional question.

Which category of customers should we be most concerned with?

Again the conventional wisdom has always been that we should work to improve the ratings that we are currently receiving from customers rating their satisfaction with the service as a one, two, or three. Clearly they are not satisfied with the service and we need to improve what we offer these groups of customers.

If you were then told that the customers who rate their satisfaction as a 5 are six times more likely to purchase from you again than the customers who rate their satisfaction only as a 4, would your opinion change?

In a study which embraced a variety of different sectors, Jones and Sasser concluded that this was a pattern of loyalty common to all the sectors studied. In the example quoted, even if *all* the customers who rated their satisfaction as a 5 repurchase, only 17 per cent of those who rated it as a 4 will do so. This revelation helps to focus the mind on the group of customers who should clearly be regarded as most important. If an organization can improve on the percentage of customers who rate their satisfaction as a 5, it can substantially improve on the levels of loyalty that will be exhibited as a result.

Before moving on, it is worth noting that the factor of six quoted above is not static across all industries and sectors; it will clearly depend on the availability of substitute services and the nature of the competition. For many nonprofit organizations, which provide unique services, the factor is likely to be considerably lower, but even if it should prove to be as low as two or three, a significant difference will still exist between the loyalty patterns exhibited by the customers who consider themselves satisfied and those who consider themselves very satisfied. It is interesting to note that recent research has explored this issue in the context of fundraising and concluded that donors who perceive themselves as very satisfied with the quality of service provided by the fundraising department are significantly more likely to remain loyal than those that perceive themselves as merely satisfied. The multiple isn't as high as the factor of six referred to above, but very satisfied donors are twice as likely to remain loyal as donors who are simply satisfied (Sargeant 2001).

The reason for elaborating on this research is a simple one. The key to moving customers from a 4 to a 5 is customer value. If you think back to some of your own experiences with service organizations and in particular those that you might have been asked to evaluate, you can probably very quickly recall why you failed to award a 5 yourself to a particular organization. The organization almost certainly met your basic requirements, but did not excel in one area that was of particular importance to you. As a result, organizations need to be particularly alert to those aspects of their service offering that customers perceive to be most important and ensure that they 'engineer in' value in these key areas. If loyalty is to be preserved and/or enhanced, customers must be made to feel that they have received an exceptional service.

Price

The second of the ingredients of the marketing mix concerns issues connected with price. In a not-for-profit context, price can take on many guises and could take the form of entrance fees, tuition fees, service charges, donations, contributions, etc. In many organizations, particularly those with a good or service to sell, the pricing decisions may be almost identical to those taken in the for-profit sector. For other organizations, however, the 'price' charged to the beneficiaries may well be kept to an absolute minimum and indeed may even be set at zero. Such practices definitely do not have parallels in the for-profit sector, unless they are an integral part of a coordinated attempt to gain market share at any cost—witness for example the newspaper price wars that took place in the UK in the mid-1990s.

Price versus Cost

To begin a discussion of price in the nonprofit context it is useful to start with an understanding of costs. All transactions with an organization, be it in relation to the sale of physical goods, or the handing over of a £20 donation, have costs associated with them. These costs essentially break down into one of three distinct types (Rados 1981). In other words:

$$\text{Total costs} = \text{OOP costs} + \text{opportunity costs} + \text{AO costs}$$

where

$$\text{OOP costs} = \text{out of pocket costs}$$

and

$$\text{AO} = \text{all other costs}$$

To aid us in a discussion of these three different types of cost, we will consider the example of a charity donor who intends to attend a gala event in support of her local hospice. She understands that at the end of this event she will be asked to give around £50 to support the cause and this is what most organizations would consider to be the cost to her of her continuing support. They would be wrong! To get to the gala, our donor would incur some form of travelling expense, either on public transport or in her own car. She may also have to pay a babysitter and use the telephone to put off any other appointments which she might have had planned. All these may be viewed as OOP expenses.

Our donor will also incur opportunity costs by attending the gala. Put simply, opportunity costs are the value of an opportunity passed up or forgone. She may have had the opportunity of attending the theatre, going to a friend's birthday party, enjoying a candlelit dinner for two, or earning an extra few hours overtime at the office. While in only the latter example is she actually out of pocket, a value could equally well be placed on the enjoyment she would gain from any of the other three alternatives. Since she has decided to forgo these in favour of attending the charity gala, the value of the next most attractive alternative can be viewed as the opportunity cost of attending.

Of course, there may be other costs associated with the evening. She may arrive a little late to find that no car parking places remain and she may have to spend time walking from one nearby. If it is a wet evening, this may be more than just a slight inconvenience. When she actually gets to the gala, the seating may be uncomfortable, she may find the staff unwelcoming, and the best of the food could already have been eaten. What a night! This final category of costs we call AO costs and, when added to the opportunity costs and out-of-pocket costs, we can derive the total cost of the evening to our valiant donor.

It is important to recognize that total costs can often amount to significantly more than the actual price paid, because it is the perception of total price that is the important factor. While easily able to afford the £50 donation, the donor in this instance may well fail to attend similar events in the future as the sum of all the other costs could have persuaded her that the evening was too expensive. Charities, and indeed all nonprofits, need to be sensitive to these issues. There would be little point, for example, in setting the price for theatre tickets without considering variables such as the attractiveness of the performance (affecting the value of the opportunity cost), or the costs to the audience of physically getting to the venue. In the case of the latter, if there are theatres more conveniently located, audiences will not have to incur the same level of transportation cost and may take this into consideration when they decide which of their local theatres to attend. This is an important concept to grasp, since in manipulating price a nonprofit can often be more creative than merely tinkering with whatever charge it happens to make for the goods and services it provides. Staying with our theatre example, negotiation with third parties might result in free car parking, special late night transport (to get people home after the performance), or a discount at a local restaurant to enable the theatre to market the evening as a package and thereby impact on opportunity costs.

Setting the Price

There are a variety of ways in which an organization can go about setting price, namely:

- *cost plus*—identifying what it costs to provide the service and adding on a profit margin if appropriate;
- *what they can afford*—setting the price to match the organization's expectations of what the recipient group can afford to pay;
- *penetration pricing*—setting a price far enough below economic value with the deliberate intention of attracting a large base of customers. The organization generates a healthy return over the duration of the customer relationships that ensue;

- *skimming*—setting a price with deliberately high margins in the knowledge that some buyers will purchase because of the perceived prestige or exclusivity a high price offers. Some arts events or charity galas may be priced on this basis;
- *competitor matching*—identifying what competitors are demanding for their products/ services and setting your own price accordingly;
- *pricing to achieve organizational objectives*—using price as a tool to affect the overall levels of demand for the service in the market. The higher the total cost (see above) to the market, the less demand for the service there is likely to be. Nonprofits can therefore use price to achieve their objectives in terms of the penetration a given service provision will have.

Price Discrimination

The methods of price setting outlined above all make the assumption that all the organization's customers will pay a set price. This is not necessarily the case. Often nonprofits will have quite different categories of customers with widely ranging abilities to pay. Arts organizations, for example, will undoubtedly want to cultivate their student audience as they will ultimately form 'the audience of tomorrow' but they recognize, too, that this segment of the market is more susceptible to price than say a professional couple in their fifties. The answer is to price discriminate between these two segments and to charge a different price to each segment of the market. Price discrimination is a widespread practice among nonprofits and there are a variety of bases on which such discrimination can be based:

- *By market segment*. As in the example above, the organization charges different segments of customers different prices for the service provided. Hence museums might offer discount packages to students, OAPs, family groups, schools, etc.
- *By place*. Theatre tickets are usually sold according to the desirability of their location. Customers will therefore pay very different prices for the same performance depending on where they elect to sit—the stalls, the dress circle, or up in the gods.
- *By time*. Discrimination by time could take many forms. Performance prices could vary at different times of the day; entrance fees could vary by season to encourage off-peak demand; last-minute discounts could be offered on unsold theatre tickets to fill the auditorium, etc.
- *By service category*. Often an organization will elect to offer several grades of service, many of which could be perceived as exclusive—the first night of a show for example, or a celebrity opening. Although the additional costs associated with the creation of such an exclusive event will clearly need to be taken into consideration when pricing, organizations often charge well in excess of what it actually costs them to provide these 'add-ons'. Certain categories of customers are often prepared to pay for the prestige of being able to take advantage of this exclusivity.

Steinberg and Weisbrod (2005) argue that price discrimination can be used as a tool to play three key roles. It can be used to determine:

1. how much revenue the organization generates;
2. which individuals will have access to the organization's services;
3. the distribution of consumer surpluses among those consumers (i.e. the difference between the price each group of consumers are willing to pay and the actual price charged).

PRICING IN THE MUSEUM CONTEXT

Rentschler et al. (2007) argue that four approaches are possible. These are depicted graphically in Figure 7.6.

The Access strategy is adopted by museums who believe that their social mission is paramount. They therefore keep fees to a minimum, if they are even charged at all. There is now evidence that this does succeed in promoting access (Anderson 1998), particularly among lower income segments (Wiggins 2003), but there can be a danger that a low price can send a signal to the market that the exhibition is of low quality (Kotler and Scheff 1997, Bebko 2000).

The Integrity strategy is a hybrid approach that attempts to promote access while at the same time boosting income. Museums following this approach may employ price discrimination to maximize revenue from segments that can afford to pay and through the use of techniques such as step discounts (where the more one visits, the cheaper the admission becomes) or product bundling (where additional features are included in the admission such as car parking or a free refreshment) (Nagle and Hogan 2005).

The Utilitarian approach may be appropriate where price is not a primary factor in deciding to visit an exhibition. A number of museums and galleries keep the entrance fees low, but will charge a significant sum to their visitors to attend a special exhibition or event. They know that the name or the brand of the exhibition will be strong enough for price to be less of a barrier.

Finally, Rentschler et al. (2007) argue that the Idealist strategy is adopted by curators who see their primary purpose as the care of the artefacts in their collection. They regard their function as one of

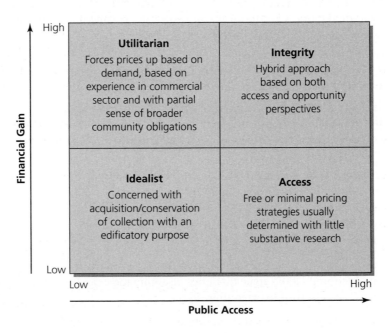

Figure 7.6 Approaches to museum pricing

Source: Rentschler, R., Hede, A. and White, T.R. (2007) 'Museum Pricing: Challenges to Theory Development and Practice', *International Journal of Nonprofit and Voluntary Sector Marketing*, Vol. 12, No. 2, 163–173. Reproduced with kind permission.

continues

continued

preserving our intellectual heritage and the traditions of society. They are therefore relatively uncon-
cerned with either maximizing visitor numbers or the income accruing to the museum.

It is interesting to note that through their empirical work Rentschler et al. (2007) determine that most
museum marketers cluster in the Access and Idealist quadrants with little attention paid to the Utilitarian or Integrity approaches.

Place

The 'place' element of the marketing mix is concerned with issues such as the degree of accessibility required to a service, how the service will be distributed to clients, the level of control required over any intermediaries that might be used, and the geographical coverage for
the service that is desired. While the place element of the marketing mix has a clear relevance
for organizations of all kinds, whether profit-making or not, there are additional complexities to be encountered in the nonprofit sector. Each of these will now be considered.

Service Accessibility

Service accessibility refers to the degree to which the customers of a particular organization
should have easy access to the service being provided. Because of the inseparable nature
of services, there are often few choices for nonprofit organizations but to site themselves as
close as possible to the target market. The difficulty for some nonprofits, however, is that they
have two (or more) such targets. They must site themselves appropriately for both resource
providers and resource consumers and often have to make trade-offs between the two.

In the case of resource providers, location is important for the following reasons:

• Many nonprofits rely on the services of volunteers and must clearly have regard for
  where such individuals might typically live. It is much easier to attract volunteers if they
  do not have far to travel from their home.

• Location can greatly facilitate fundraising. If a charity can be seen to have a local
  presence, it will be easier to raise funds from both individual and corporate donors (see
  Sargeant and Stephenson 1997).

• Location also needs to be considered in respect of the accessibility that will be offered to
  donors to make a donation. Many charities thus adopt a fairly intensive pattern of
  distribution, attempting to make their collection boxes available in as many different
  locations as possible.

In terms of resource consumers, location is important for the following reasons:

• Nonprofits need to consider how accessible their services will be to members of their
  target market. Where the service is aimed at persons with some form of disability any
  service will clearly need to be provided as close to their home as possible. For many
  visually impaired persons, for example, the requirement to use public transport to access
  a day centre provision would deter many from attending.

• There is an intrinsic link between the physical locations selected and the coverage that
  might be gained of the target market. Organizations must thus consider the geographical
  spread of their recipient base and select those areas with the highest concentrations of need.

Channel/Route to Market

For many nonprofit organizations, obtaining an appropriate route to market can be problematic. For-profit organizations have the 'luxury' of a plethora of channels of distribution that could be appropriate. These might include wholesalers, retailers, agents, distributors, franchises, etc. A typical manufacturer will have to determine which particular channels are likely to suit its needs best and then seek to develop relationships with these to encourage intermediaries to stock and perhaps promote its product(s). The key difference in the for-profit sector is that manufacturers generally have a series of 'carrots' which they can use to motivate intermediaries to stock, such as variable commission rates, bulk discounts, merchandising assistance, dealer competitions, and so on. For most nonprofit organizations, these options do not exist. Many services for the elderly, for example, are distributed primarily through the auspices of social service or housing departments. Social workers receive no commission for passing on contacts to nonprofit organizations and do so simply because of the regard they have for their clients.

The additional complexity of managing nonprofit channels of distribution is well illustrated by the following case study.

■ **CASE STUDY**

NON-MAINTAINED SPECIAL SCHOOLS

Within the current legislative framework there are a number of schools within England and Wales which provide a specialist education for children with a variety of disabilities. Local education authorities (LEAs) currently have a duty to provide the best possible education for children, irrespective of their level of disability. This encourages local authorities to create provision within their area for children with common disabilities, such as learning disabilities. In the case of children with a less common disability it is possible that an LEA will be unable to find appropriate provision within one of its own schools. Under such circumstances the LEA may decide to send a child to a non-maintained special school, perhaps located outside their area. These organizations are charitable in status and rely for their funding on the fees paid by LEAs.

Under the terms of the 1981 Education Act, LEAs are under an obligation to integrate as many children as possible into mainstream schools, a move which, while it would clearly be in most children's interest, is certainly one which saves the LEA the expense of financing a number of special education places. Moreover, under the Act LEAs have a duty to take into account the wishes of parents in respect of a child's education. Thus if a decision in respect of a particular child is borderline, the wishes of the parent should influence the LEA to make the choice that the parents desire. In cases where the LEA and parents fail to reach agreement an appeals procedure may be instigated.

These extremely complex arrangements leave many non-maintained special schools with something of a marketing dilemma. Such organizations often have no alternative but to rely on the goodwill of intermediaries to pass on details of the services that they can provide. Advisory teachers employed by LEAs are the key source of information for parents, as are social workers and medical specialists, none of whom receive any remuneration from the non-maintained sector. Indeed one could argue that the one key intermediary, the LEA, has a vested interest in persuading parents to send children to a mainstream school as it could then

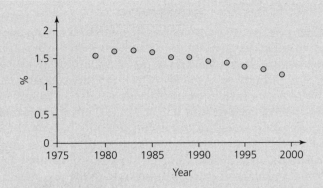

Figure 7.7 Percentage of pupil population placed in special schools

avoid the substantially higher fees payable to the specialist sector. While there is no evidence that this actually occurs in practice, the potential for a conflict of interest is clear. Figure 7.7 illustrates the percentage of the school population that has been receiving a special education, year on year since 1979.

To compound this dramatic drop in numbers it is almost impossible for special schools to gain direct access to parents of potential students. Mailing lists of individuals with a particular disability simply do not exist and neither would it be desirable to create them. This makes it difficult for such organizations to communicate to parents the very real benefits that their schools can sometimes offer over a mainstream education.

Faced with these difficulties, non-maintained special schools must therefore learn to deal with an extremely complex pattern of distribution, the majority of which they can exert no control over.

Customer Perceptions of the Channel

In its simplest form this might involve decisions about the decor of the premises (relatively simple surroundings may suggest to potential donors that donations are not being wasted on spurious decorations). More usually it may involve a consideration of the image that the channel might hold in the minds of potential customers. A decision may be taken, for example, not to use the technique of outbound telemarketing in a fundraising mix, since in the minds of many people it is still associated with the 'hard sell' techniques of the mid-1980s and therefore as an unacceptable intrusion.

Those nonprofits that are involved in fundraising activities may instead make use of a range of distribution channels, including direct marketing, agents, volunteers, and (if collecting boxes are utilized) possibly a range of different retail outlets. Interestingly, Horne and Moss (1995) determined that collection box yields vary significantly between different categories of retail outlets and they should hence be selected with care. The retail types associated with the highest yields are (in descending order) takeaways, cafes, bars, newsagents, supermarkets, and ironmongers. Soft furnishing, sports and clothes shops were found to be the outlets with the smallest yields.

The Emergence of Electronic Channels

The Internet has opened up a whole new range of opportunities for nonprofits not only to communicate with their market, but also to deliver their services to their clients. Most non-profits now boast websites where enquirers can download information about the organization, its services, staff, facilities, etc. A number offer much higher degrees of interactivity. A number of universities, for example, are embracing the Internet as a means of delivering their programmes. Live conferences with staff and indeed whole educational programmes can now be delivered online. Such developments not only increase the number of fee-paying students that might be attracted to an institution, but because of the inherently convenient mode of delivery, many mature learners who would not have the time to return to a traditional classroom environment are being encouraged to return to their studies.

The domain of philanthropy has been similarly impacted, particularly since the terrorist attacks of 9/11 when, in the two months immediately following the disaster, more than 1.3 million contributors donated over $128 million online. Hart (2007) talks of an 'e-philanthropy' revolution where new technologies are increasingly embraced by nonprofits seeking to build relationships with a wide range of stakeholders.

For Hart, e-philanthropy techniques fall into six categories:

1. communication/education and stewardship;

2. online donations and membership;

3. event registrations and management;

4. prospect research (i.e. the process of seeking new supporters);

5. volunteer recruitment and management;

6. relationship building and advocacy.

The full range of developments is too rich to embrace in a summary chapter such as this. The use of the electronic media is a subject that will be returned to in more detail in Chapter 10.

Promotion

The promotional element of the mix is responsible for the communication of the marketing offer to the target group. Promotion is 'the process of presenting an integrated set of stimuli to a market with the intent of evoking a set of responses within that market set and setting up channels to receive, interpret and act upon messages from the market for the purposes of modifying present company messages and identifying new communication opportunities' (Delozier 1976).

It can be used for a variety of purposes within the marketing mix, typically:

• to inform potential customers of the existence and benefits of the service;

• to persuade potential customers that the benefits offered are genuine and will adequately meet their requirements;

• to remind members of the target group that the service exists and of the key benefits that it can offer;

• to differentiate the service in the minds of potential customers from the others currently on the market, i.e. to define clearly the positioning of the service.

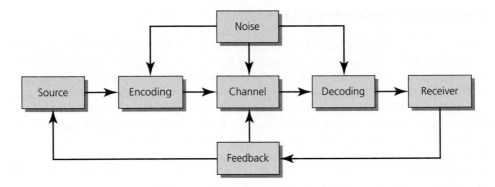

Figure 7.8 A simple model of communication

Before moving on to examine the elements of the communication mix and how they can be utilized to achieve the purposes outlined above, it will be instructive to begin by a short analysis of the communication process. Figure 7.8 illustrates a simple model of communication.

The source of the communication message is simply the organization that intends to communicate with its market. To enable it to do so, it must decide on the message that it wishes to convey, i.e what does it want to convey about itself, and what action (if any) would it like members of the target group to take on receipt of the message. In a social marketing context, this might involve the organization in trying to get across the danger of unprotected sex exposing people to the risk of AIDS. The message might be a simple one—'unprotected sex puts you at risk of AIDS'. However, the reader will appreciate that simply transmitting this message to the target market is unlikely to be successful. To begin with, people react in different ways to fear appeals such as this and many might screen out the message as a result. Others might not perceive the message as being relevant to them because they do not perceive their lifestyle as putting them at risk. It is normal therefore for communications messages to be encoded.

Encoding involves the source in deciding what the communications will actually contain to get across their message to consumers. In essence this is the creative treatment applied to the message to ensure that when it arrives at the receiver he decodes it as being of relevance to him and acts on it. This may be done by using ordinary-looking people in the advertising, conveying the selfishness of putting those you love at risk, explaining that AIDS can affect all sections of society, etc. Of course, there is no guarantee that when the message is received it will be decoded in the manner in which the source had originally intended. There are a variety of factors which can interfere with a communications message, and these are typically referred to as *noise*.

Noise acts to distort the message or to prevent its reception by the receiver. It can thus take many forms including:

- a lack of attention on the part of the receiver;
- heavy promotional spending by other competing organizations;
- selection of inappropriate media;
- poor creative treatment, resulting in ambiguous messages;
- poor perception of source—if it is not regarded as credible the message may be ignored;
- environmental distractions—the message may be received under conditions that make it impossible for the recipient to concentrate.

It is thus important for an organization to try to minimize the effects of noise by selecting the most appropriate communication channels available to reach its target market. It can also help reduce noise by giving adequate thought to the encoding process and making sure that the promotional budget allows it to gain an appropriate 'share of the voice'. Clearly this is not an easy process to manage and it is essential to ensure that there are mechanisms in place to gather adequate feedback from the target market. If messages are either not being received or are being decoded and wrongly interpreted, it will be essential for the source organization to take immediate corrective action. Indeed, it would be usual to test all forms of marketing communications prior to exposing them to the market, although even this is no guarantee of success. There is hence a need for ongoing monitoring of marketing communications.

It is clear from the model in Figure 7.8 that the promotional element of the marketing mix involves the establishment of a dialogue with customers, the quality of which can vary considerably depending on the nature of the communication channel selected and the degree to which noise has the capacity to interfere with message reception. Of course, this model is very general and does not address issues which relate to the use of specific promotional tools. These are essentially advertising, sales promotion, public relations, and direct marketing, collectively referred to as the communications mix. We will now give a brief consideration to each of these elements in turn.

Advertising

Kotler (1994: 627) defines advertising as 'any paid form of non-personal presentation and promotion of ideas, goods or services by an identified sponsor'. Advertising can be placed in a variety of media, including websites, television, radio, cinema, newspapers, magazines/ trade press, and outdoor (poster and transport advertising). With an ever-increasing number of promotional media becoming available, it is becoming more difficult to identify those which offer the most appropriate use of promotional resources. Essentially one is looking to find the medium which can reach the largest number of members of the target market at the lowest price. Thus the measure of 'CPT' (Cost Per Thousand) is used by many organizations to compare the use of various media. CPT is calculated as you would expect. If a full-page advertisement in a national newspaper circulated to three million readers is £9000, the cost per thousand is £3. This figure can then be used to compare the various media options available. It is a very simple measure and it is necessary to be very clear about the profile of the media audience. If the profile does not exactly match your requirements (and it rarely does), you may be underestimating the CPT figure since you could be communicating with a large number of people who are not in your target market.

Media can also be selected on the basis of how many competitors use the medium, since if a large number of competitors are present the returns accruing to each advertiser are likely to be less than they would be in a publication where it is possible to enjoy a wider 'share of the voice'. It may also be important for many nonprofits to consider the environment of the medium. Does the medium offer an environment that is appropriate for the message being conveyed? There would be little point, for example, in placing an advert for a modern art exhibition in a publication whose editorial was generally critical of such art forms. Similarly, the term 'environment' can be applied to the environment in which the message is received. Some media demand a lot of concentration of readers, such as specialist trade journals, making it possible to provide much more detailed information about the product/service in advertisements. Television advertising, on the other hand, offers little opportunity in this regard since it commands little attention. Indeed many people leave the room, perhaps to make a coffee, when commercial breaks begin.

Sales Promotion

The term 'sales promotion' in the nonprofit sector refers to any immediate stimulation to buy (or to give a donation) that might be provided at or near the point of sale.

The purpose of sales promotion is to prompt the customer to engage in a transaction with the nonprofit. It is thus more immediate in its effects and hence favoured in times of budgetary constraint since an immediate return on the investment can be demonstrated. The same, regrettably, cannot be said of advertising, whose effects are considerably less tangible and certainly longer-term. Sales promotion activity includes the provision of free gifts, discounts, premiums, leaflets, contests, display material, or demonstrations. The key to the selection of successful sales promotion activities lies in selecting something which reflects the needs and wants of the customer group and offers them something which they will find to be of value. This may be as simple as an introductory discount on a service to tempt customers into sampling, or it may be something more elaborate. In the fundraising context, for example, the simple poppy which indicates a donation to the British Legion has a very powerful and emotive appeal. It offers a potential donor the opportunity to associate with a nation's grief and thanksgiving, and this promotion is so powerful most people in the public eye ensure that they wear their poppies for at least a week before Remembrance Sunday. The donor in this case is receiving a very real, if intangible, benefit. Other organizations allow donors to 'sample' their product and as a result guide dogs and even air ambulances can each have their part to play in a promotion. (The Cornish Air Ambulance Service recently charged donors for an opportunity to look inside the ambulance.) If the donor is able to share in a unique experience and is made to feel involved in the charity, fundraising will be greatly enhanced. It should also be noted that sales promotions can have a more mundane role to fulfil in that they allow volunteers to have something to sell and ensure (in the case of flags, pins, and stickers) that the donor is protected from further requests to give.

Public Relations

Public relations is often confused with publicity, crisis management, lobbying, etc. In fact, PR can embrace all these elements, but it should also be regarded as a somewhat wider function within an organization. One of the most frequently used definitions of PR is as follows: 'Public relations is the management function that evaluates the attitudes of important publics, identifies the policies and procedures of an individual or an organization with the public interest, and executes a programme of action to earn understanding and acceptance by these publics' (*Public Relations News*, 27 October 1947).

It is hence concerned with the development of each of the organization's publics and might typically involve an organization in proceeding through the stages outlined in Figure 7.9.

The process begins with an analysis of the current perceptions of each of an organization's publics. Those perceptions are then assessed to see how desirable they might be from the organization's perspective and, where weaknesses/ambiguities are identified, a programme of PR can be developed to address them. The process Kotler and Fox (1985) advocate also makes it clear that it is important for an organization to plan for potential crises, however unlikely

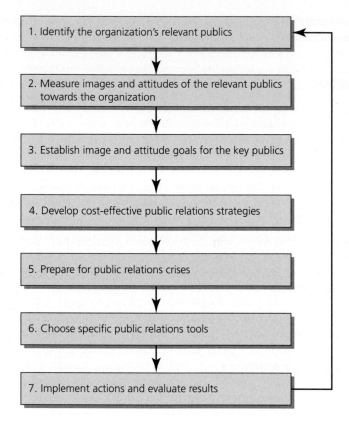

Figure 7.9 The public relations strategic planning process

Source: Kotler and Fox (1985) *Strategic Marketing for Educational Institutions.*
Adapted by permission of Prentice Hall Inc., Upper Saddle River, NJ.

these may be. If an organization has plans to deal with all potential contingencies, should the unthinkable happen it will be well placed to implement a cogent response.

A variety of PR tools may be utilized to develop the desired perceptions among its target publics. These include:

- *Production of written material.* This might include leaflets, flyers, magazines, annual reports, and volunteer newsletters.

- *Organizational identity media.* Most nonprofits today have some form of corporate identity which features prominently in the organization's stationery, brochures, signs, and business cards. These are what might be referred to as organizational identity media and it is essential that through the careful use of design, logos, etc., that all these media conform to a standard format and convey a consistent message to the publics targeted.

- *Publicity.* The PR department can often identify newsworthy activities within the organization and seek to promote these in the media. The problem with such 'free advertising' is that there is no guarantee the media will elect to cover it. Unlike advertising which must be sent to the media and paid for, publicity must be sent to the media and prayed for!

• *Provision of expert speakers.* Many nonprofits have unique expertise or act as the mouthpiece for a particular section of society. In such circumstances it is important that all the key media understand that this expertise exists, so that should an occasion arise where an expert comment is called for, they know exactly who to approach. For this reason, many universities now produce a publication called 'Who can Speak on What', or something similar, which can be distributed to regional and national media, in the hope they will use it to source subject specialists for expert comment.

• *Telephone helplines.* Many nonprofits which provide a service to members of the public are already providing very successful telephone helplines which provide help and guidance to those in need. Many of the medical charities, for example, provide a 24-hour helpline which sufferers and/or their relatives can ring for reassurance and guidance. Given that it now costs very little to provide a toll-free or freephone number many nonprofits are now prepared to cover the costs of this activity themselves as part of a coordinated PR strategy.

Nonprofits generally have very complex audiences to whom they must communicate their message. This audience may be made up of current and potential sponsors, the media, the business and local community, their own volunteers, and the recipients on whose behalf they are working. Given this complexity it is not surprising that PR takes such a prominent place in the marketing mixes of many nonprofit organizations. Unfortunately, PR has a much less obvious price tag than media advertising and its results are perhaps even more difficult to assess. It remains an important tool for many organizations however, primarily because of the impact it can have on the market. Messages carried through third parties are perceived by the public as having greater credibility than messages conveyed in advertising where the organization may have a tendency to portray itself in an overly positive light.

Direct Marketing

Currently a major growth area in marketing, direct marketing is increasing in importance for a great many organizations. Traditionally charities have been perceived as being particularly strong in this field, with their creative use of the marketing database putting them very much at the forefront of developments. Direct marketing can take many forms, the most common of which are briefly described below:

• *Direct mail.* With the increasing sophistication of database technology it is now possible to refine the contact strategies that nonprofits have with a wide range of customers. A theatre, for example, can look back over the purchase histories of its clients and write to those who it knows from past experience will be interested in certain categories of performance. Similarly, charities can use their knowledge of the database to treat high-value donors differently from low-value donors and target direct mailshots at the time of year that specific segments of donors find most acceptable. Indeed, nonprofits that make wise use of their database are moving away from a broadbrush approach to market segmentation and are beginning to develop almost one-to-one dialogues with their customers.

Most modern databases also allow a nonprofit to profile its customer base. While the data so gained can be used to help develop existing customers, it can also be used to good effect to target other potential customers in society who match the profile of existing customers. With a proliferation of consumer and industrial lists now available, nonprofits can target prospective customers in a way that could only be dreamed of a mere 20 years ago. This is a subject that will be returned to in more depth in Chapter 9.

• *Telemarketing.* While it is still comparatively rare for a nonprofit to attempt telemarketing activity in-house, unless it is on a very small scale, there are now a number of specialist agencies who offer telemarketing expertise to the nonprofit sector. It can be used for either inbound or outbound activity. Inbound activity remains the most common, whereby a freephone or toll-free number is provided for clients and/or donors to contact the organization free of charge. The number is frequently quoted in all other forms of marketing communication and the telemarketing service provided free of charge to make the exchange process more accessible to clients. Outbound telemarketing is still rather less common, although growing in popularity. At a recent general election, for example, the Conservative party made every effort to contact all the voters of a marginal seat in Cornwall by telephone to ensure that they were able to get their message across to potential waiverers.

• *E-marketing.* We have already mentioned the increasing use of the Internet in our discussion of 'place'. While it can be an effective vehicle for service delivery it can also be a very effective communications medium. For this reason some organizations will place their consideration of e-marketing in the 'place' element of the mix, while others will consider the relevant issues under 'promotion'. As with so many of the frameworks we use in marketing it really doesn't matter where this material is presented as long as it is presented in a cogent and easy-to-operationalize fashion.

Where organizations are involved with marketing predominantly in an Internet environment it may be worth developing a separate e-marketing mix. One possible suggestion for the form this might take is presented in Figure 7.10. A plan may be developed for each distinctive facet of the mix to ensure that a high-impact experience is created for visitors to a given site.

Of course, e-marketing is not restricted to the use of the Internet alone. Many organizations now make use of SMS or MMS (Short Message Service and Multimedia Message Service) messaging to communicate with either service users, members, campaigners, or donors. Individuals can receive text messages which alert them to the need to take action, or bring them up to date with the activities of the nonprofit. From a fundraising perspective, some nonprofits have set up arrangements with mobile operators where texting a certain number in reply to a message will result in a donation to their organization. Such techniques can be

---

Entertainment—the way in which the site is designed to be imaginative, fun, and/or entertaining to use.

Informativeness—the extent to which the site informs and/or provides a helpful resource for those interested in a particular issue.

Organization—the extent to which the site is easy to use and convenient to search for information, services, etc.

Aesthetic design—the extent to which the use of colour, graphics, and creative design is appropriate on the site.

Processing speed—the extent to which it is easy and quick to download pertinent materials and/or functionality. The number of steps it takes to make a purchase, order a service, or take action on a particular issue.

Security—the extent to which the site is secure and embues users with confidence in respect of how their personal data will be used.

Fulfilment—the detail of how actions taken online will be operationalized thereafter. For example, the accurate processing of the payment, despatch of an order, and communication thereafter. To achieve this satisfactorily, there needs to be an appropriate degree of linkage between the wbsite and other IT systems that will be responsible for delivering the promises made by the site.

Figure 7.10 E-marketing mix

particularly effective at engaging with younger audiences who tend to be more comfortable with the latest technology.

We have also seen in recent years the testing of web TV. While many countries, the UK included, now have a form of interactive television where viewers can make purchases or order services using their TV remotes, this is only the beginning of the revolution in traditional broadcasting. A number of US cities have piloted web TV which moves beyond the fairly simplistic operation of interactive television to offer a genuine merger between web-based technology and traditional broadcasting. Users of web TV are able to view television channels in the usual way, but may also switch from a TV programme to its associated website, engage in chat, make a purchase, and surf to related sites or sources of information before returning to the broadcast in question. From a nonprofit's perspective, such developments offer significant opportunities to interact with a variety of stakeholder groups. Their website, for example, might be featured on a television programme dealing with issues related to the cause or mission. Viewers can then leave the programme to visit the website, download information, make contact with service provision, sign up to a campaign, or even offer a donation.

• *Door-to-door.* Door-to-door canvassing and/or selling remains a popular way of fundraising for many, particularly 'local' charities. It can also be a very effective means of raising awareness of the activities of an organization, or canvassing to reach prospective volunteers.

• *Personal selling.* While this is perhaps less common in the nonprofit sector, there may be a number of organizations who find it desirable to maintain a direct salesforce which can negotiate on a one-to-one basis with prospective clients and/or funders. This is likely to be more appropriate where an organization has a small number of high-value clients or where the clients are narrowly concentrated in a small geographical area. In such circumstances the increased overhead of employing a sales team may be justified in terms of the quality of the contact/service that will be provided.

People

To an organization providing a service to clients, the people element of the marketing mix is arguably the most important. After all, it may reasonably be argued that the people ARE the organization, whether they are paid employees or unpaid volunteers. Interestingly the latter category of staff are more prevalent than many people believe. Lynn and Davis-Smith (1992), for example, found that almost half of the adults in the UK will engage in some form of voluntary activity over the course of a typical year. Indeed Bruce and Raymer (1992) found that, on average, for every paid employee retained, the larger charities utilize the services of 8.5 volunteers.

Ensuring that all staff, whatever their status, deliver a service of the highest quality is a key issue for all nonprofits. The inseparability of services makes it impossible to distinguish between service production and service delivery and it is the people of the organization who are therefore responsible for both. In this section of the marketing plan, the nonprofit must therefore give consideration to the people skills that it will need to provide its service and, indeed, to deliver every component of the marketing plan. This can then be matched against the profile of the existing human resource and appropriate gaps identified. The organization can then ensure that those 'gaps' are represented in the recruitment programme and that the appropriate person specifications are in place. On some occasions it may be possible to plug these gaps by the recruitment of full-time or part-time staff. On others it may be more appropriate to look to the recruitment of suitably qualified volunteers. Hind (1995) suggests that before recruiting paid staff, a process which results in a considerable drain on organizational resource, the organization should ensure that their recruitment is absolutely necessary. To determine this, he suggests that paid staff are necessary only under the following circumstances:

- when specialist expertise is required on an ongoing basis;
- when continuous attention is needed to tasks which must be performed in accordance with the organization's timetable and in compliance with its formal procedures and standards;
- when roles exist requiring the management of other staff or large groups of volunteers.

Of course, if the attraction of volunteers is the preferred option it is useful to understand something of an individual's typical motivations for volunteering. If the tasks for which volunteers are sought cannot be fulfilled by volunteers, an organization may be left with little choice but to pay for staff. Fenton et al. (1993) found that the following three categories of volunteer motivation are most common.

- *Demonstrative motivations*. Individuals who volunteer for this reason are essentially seeking some form of ego reward. They donate their time because they believe that some form of social recognition will follow.
- *Social motivations*. Researchers found that this was the most common form of motivation and involves individuals volunteering because they see it as an active form of giving to support charity. It is seen as an opportunity to socialize with other volunteers and to feel collectively that they are doing good.
- *Instrumental motivation*. Less commonly expressed than the other two, individuals who volunteer for this reason are doing so simply because they feel the need to help others. They feel they have a duty to help others less fortunate than themselves.

It is, of course, usually much easier to develop and retain existing staff/volunteers than it is to attain new ones. The second focus of this section of the plan is hence to identify the steps that need to be taken to retain existing personnel. By far the easiest way of achieving this is to survey those who decide to leave and, having discovered the reasons for dissatisfaction, implement any changes that may be necessary to ensure that problems are corrected. One can also ensure that an ongoing dialogue is maintained with existing staff so that they do not feel compelled to leave in the first place! In the case of volunteers, it would also be advisable to ensure that the organization responds to the various categories of motivation identified above and understands what the volunteers actually want to get out of their relationship with the organization. Retention strategies can then be developed, taking account of these needs.

Process

When marketers talk of process, they are talking about the process that a particular client group must go through to purchase and enjoy the service being provided. Clearly, for a service organization, every aspect of the encounter that a customer has with staff will be important. Each stage of the service will be evaluated by customers and many will have a substantial impact on the overall level of satisfaction experienced. The question is, however, which elements

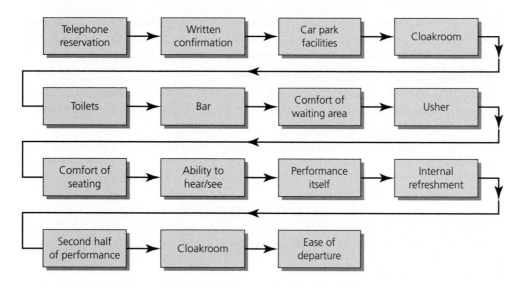

Figure 7.11 Flow chart of a visit to the theatre

of the process are deemed by the customer to be most important? To answer this, it is often useful to draw a flow chart of the various components of the service that the customer experiences. An example is shown in Figure 7.11.

Although this is a gross simplification of the process that one might go through in purchasing and enjoying an evening at the theatre, it does at least serve to illustrate that the process consists of a number of specific encounters with the organization. Each of these may of course be broken down into a number of sub-encounters. Take, for example, the telephone reservation process; there are a number of components to this including the length of time you wait to have your call answered, the efficiency and friendliness of the operator, and the accuracy with which he performs his role. For the moment, however, we will stick with the general process depicted in Figure 7.11. The reader will appreciate that not every aspect of the service will be equally important. The provision of a cloakroom, clean toilets, and the existence of a bar may be relatively unimportant for the segment of customers addressed. If research is conducted which identifies those aspects of the service that the customer places most importance on, the organization can invest in those areas, ensure that they are of the highest quality, and hence enhance overall customer satisfaction. Conversely, in those areas that are considered unimportant, the organization can look to minimize costs and perhaps even remove that aspect of the service altogether, utilizing the resource saved in other areas that are perceived as being important. The idea of engineering customer value in this way was first suggested by Porter (1985) who referred to the concept discussed above as the *value chain*. In his view it represents an essential tool for organizations to use in appraising their service process with a view to enhancing it.

Physical Evidence

The final ingredient of the service marketing mix is physical evidence. Since the service product is largely intangible, it is important for the organization to focus on those tangible cues that do exist and to ensure that they convey appropriate messages to the consumer about the quality of the service she is purchasing. As has already been identified above, in the absence of a physical product consumers will use tangible cues to make their judgements in respect of service quality. In a typical organization these cues may include the following.

- *Premises*. Thought will obviously be given in the healthcare context, for example, to the physical design of waiting areas. They should generally be clean, comfortable, and informative, in the sense that reading materials may be left for patients informing them of various aspects of the services that are available.

- *Facilities*. The appearance of the facilities on offer is also important. In selecting a school, for example, parents are unlikely to rely totally on the reputation that a school has in a given area. They are also likely to inspect the facilities it has to offer for themselves and may ask to see the sports/library and IT provisions.

- *Dress*. The presentation of the staff can help reinforce the corporate image that the organization is looking to project. Smart, attractively presented staff can infer quality, in the absence of other cues, and may reassure potential customers of the professionalism offered by a particular organization.

- *Reports*. The written communications of the organization may also be regarded as tangible cues. The annual report, the 'sales' brochure, will all be used to evaluate the service. In selecting a course of study at a university, for example, unless a visit to the site is planned, prospective students may have little more to build their perception of quality on than the presentation and contents of the prospectus.

Summary of the Tactical Marketing Mix

We have now examined each of the ingredients of a typical service marketing mix. In developing a marketing plan, an organization will need to give careful consideration to each of these seven elements, while at the same time being careful not to fall into the trap of viewing each ingredient in isolation. The mix should be viewed as a collective whole and opportunities for synergy will only be exploited if it is regarded as such. Each ingredient of the mix should consistently reinforce the 'message' being conveyed by the others. To ensure that the plan represents a coherent whole, the author should ensure that the organization's approach to each of the seven Ps is presented in the plan in a clear and easy-to-read format. It should then become obvious whether flaws or ambiguities are present, and corrective action can be taken.

Ethics—An Additional Component of the Mix?

Before moving away from the concept of the mix to examine the remaining elements of a typical marketing plan, it is worth noting that a number of authors have suggested that an explicit consideration of ethics is warranted as a dimension of the marketing mix. The rationale here is that one of the distinguishing characteristics for many nonprofit organizations is the ethical nature of their operations. Since they do not have to seek to maximize profit they can (and perhaps should) take decisions that seek to maximize the benefit that accrues to society as a whole. In other words they are freed up to 'do the right thing' or take 'the right decision'. Of course it is then necessary to decide what exactly the 'right' decision might be.

The study of ethics involves determining right from wrong. Such decisions will be driven by an individual's own beliefs and values, those of the organization, and those of the wider society in which they live. In Judaeo-Christian society, for example, these values may be derived from respect and compassion for the individual and a wider concern for the impact of one's actions on others. Ethics operate at a different level from the laws of a particular society since laws frequently provide for minimum standards of behaviour. They deal with the worst excesses of a society and with aspects of that society that are of wider interest and concern. They also reflect the prevailing view of the government, which one hopes in a democracy would in turn reflect the views of the majority of the members of that society.

Ethics by contrast operate at a 'higher' level. While a particular action may not be illegal, it may nevertheless be regarded by a given individual as wrong because it indirectly harms others, or is not in the best interests of the organization that employs them. It is this grey area beyond the realms of the law that is the domain of ethical judgements and where the fundraising profession has invested considerable time and effort to determine what does and does not constitute appropriate behaviour.

My own perspective on the role of ethics in nonprofit marketing is that it should not be considered as a distinct element of the marketing mix. Rather, it should be regarded as something that pervades the mix as a whole (i.e. each of the elements described above). Organizations need to decide what constitutes appropriate behaviour and delineate what

---

AFP MEMBERS ASPIRE TO

- Practise their profession with integrity, honesty, truthfulness, and adherence to the absolute obligation to safeguard the public trust.
- Act according to the highest standards and visions of their organization, profession, and conscience.
- Put philanthropic mission above personal gain.
- Inspire others through their own sense of dedication and high purpose.
- Improve their professional knowledge and skills, so that their performance will better serve others.
- Demonstrate concern for the interests and well-being of individuals affected by their actions.
- Value the privacy, freedom of choice, and interests of all those affected by their actions.
- Foster cultural diversity and pluralistic values, and treat all people with dignity and respect.
- Affirm, through personal giving, a commitment to philanthropy and its role in society.
- Adhere to the spirit as well as the letter of all applicable laws and regulations.
- Advocate, within their own organizations, adherence to all applicable laws and regulations.
- Avoid even the appearance of any criminal offence or professional misconduct.
- Bring credit to the fundraising profession by their public demeanour.
- Encourage colleagues to embrace and practise these ethical principles and standards of professional practice.
- Be aware of the codes of ethics promulgated by other professional organizations that serve philanthropy.

Source: Association of Fundraising Professionals.

they are and are not prepared to do. Many nonprofits now enshrine this in an ethical policy which explicitly deals with the ethical issues likely to be encountered by staff. The document specifies both the general principles that will be applied and how staff should deal with specific examples. Many nonprofits also encourage their staff to join the relevant professional association and to adopt the code of ethics that their particular profession feels is appropriate. The ethical code developed by the Association of Fundraising Professionals is reproduced on the previous page.

Any readers interested in a further exploration of the topic are advised to consult Anderson (1996) for a consideration of ethics in fundraising, Malaro (1994) for ethics in arts management, and the Humanitarian Studies Unit (2001) for ethics in aid and development. The ethical literature in relation to healthcare and education is perhaps the best developed (see, for example, Weber 2001 and Nash 2002).

Budget

Having detailed the steps that are necessary to achieve the marketing objectives, the writer of the plan should then be in a position to cost the various proposals and to derive an overall marketing budget for the planning period. Of course, in reality, life is just not that neat. Cost will undoubtedly have been in the minds of marketing planners even before they commenced the marketing audit. At the very least the development of a suitable budget is likely to have been an iterative process, with proposals being re-evaluated in the light of budgetary constraint.

There are a variety of ways of determining the marketing budget. The ideal would clearly be to specify the strategy and tactics that are felt necessary to achieve the marketing objectives, and then to cost these to arrive at an overall budget. This is usually referred to as the 'task method' of setting a marketing budget. In reality, this method is seldom employed since financial pressures from senior management, the budgeting/accounting practices of the organization, and uncertainty about resource attraction all hamper the derivation of an appropriate budget. In practice, therefore, budgets tend to be set by the following methods:

- *Percentage of last year's sales/donations.* There is a danger with this method that if the organization has been suffering from a poor performance of late, reducing the marketing budget in line with sales/donations could actually serve to worsen the situation. Clearly, when sales or donations fall there is a strong case for enhancing, not reducing, the marketing budget.

- *Percentage of budgeted year's sales/donations.*

- *Competitor matching.* The amounts spent on marketing by the competition are estimated, and the resource allocation is matched.

- *What can be afforded.* Perhaps the least rational of all the methods of budget calculation, this method involves the senior management of the organization deciding what they believe they can afford to allocate to the marketing function in a particular year. Little or no reference is made to the marketing objectives, nor to the activities of competitors.

Irrespective of the method used, it is usual to specify how the eventual budget has been allocated and to include such a specification in the marketing plan itself. It would also be normal for an allowance to be made for contingencies in the event that monitoring by the organization suggests that the objectives will not be met. Sufficient resources should then exist for some form of corrective action to be taken.

Activity	Jan.	Feb.	Mar.	Apr.	May	June	July	Aug.	Sept.	Oct.	Nov.	Dec.
Direct mail		x	x							x	x	
Press advertising	x			x			x			x		x
Display advertising (Posters)											x	x
Telemarketing		x			x			x			x	x

Figure 7.12 Schedule of a fundraising campaign

Scheduling

The reader will appreciate that a large number of tactics will have been specified in the main body of the plan. To ensure that these tactics are executed in a coordinated fashion over the duration of the plan, it is usual to present a schedule which clearly specifies when each activity will take place. This often takes the form of a Gantt chart (an example for a fundraising campaign is given in Figure 7.12). If the responsibilities for various marketing activities are split between different departments/sections of the organization, the schedule will act as an important coordination mechanism. Indeed, if responsibilities are split in this way it is usual to add an addition to the plan specifying the individual postholder who will have responsibility for the implementation of each component of the plan.

Monitoring and Control

As soon as the plan has been implemented, marketing management will then take responsibility for monitoring the progress of the organization towards the goal specified. Managers will also need to concern themselves with the costs that have been incurred at each stage of implementation and monitor these against the budget. Thus control mechanisms need to be put into place to monitor (a) the actual sales/donations achieved against the budget; (b) the actual costs incurred against those budgeted; (c) the performance of individual services against budget; and (d) the overall strategic direction that the organization is taking—i.e. will the overall corporate objectives be achieved in a manner commensurate with the organization's mission?

If variances are detected in any of these areas, corrective action can then be initiated, if necessary by utilizing the resource allocated for contingency.

■ **DISCUSSION QUESTIONS**

1. Distinguish, with examples, between marketing strategies and tactics.
2. What would you describe as the key components of the fundraising product?

3. With reference to your own organization (or one with which you are familiar) identify the key costs that will be experienced by both your donors and the recipients of your goods or services. What are the implications of these costs for your pricing decisions?

4. What channels of distribution might typically be used by:

    - a modern art museum?

    - a charity working in developing countries which is looking to solicit funds?

    - a library service for elderly persons with a visual impairment?

5. In what ways might the communications mix utilized by a university development office (i.e the fundraising office within the university) differ from that adopted by a charity concerned with raising funds for cancer research?

6. 'Promotion is not the only element of the marketing mix that can communicate with customers. All seven elements of the service mix have the capacity to communicate with the customer.' Discuss.

7. What role should ethics play in the development of a nonprofit marketing mix? Why are ethics considered particularly important in the context of nonprofit management?

■ REFERENCES

Anderson, A. (1996) *Ethics for Fundraisers*, Indianapolis, IN, Indiana University Press.

Anderson, R.G.W. (1998) 'Is Charging Economic?', *Journal of Cultural Economics*, Vol. 22 (2–3), 179–187.

Babakus, E. and Boller, G.W. (1992) 'An Empirical Assessment of the SERVQUAL Scale', *Journal of Business Research*, Vol. 24, 253–68.

Bebko, C.P. (2000) 'Service Intangibility and Its Impact on Consumer Expectations of Service Quality', *Journal of Services Marketing*, Vol. 14, No. 1, 9–26.

Bruce, I. and Raymer, A. (1992) *Managing and Staffing Britain's Largest Charities*, VOLPROF, Centre for Voluntary Sector and Not-For-Profit Management, City University Business School, London.

Churchill, G.A. and Suprenant, C. (1982) 'An Investigation into the Determinants of Customer Satisfaction', *Journal of Marketing Research*, Vol. 19, 491–504.

Crosby, J. (1979) *Quality is Free*, New York, McGraw-Hill.

Darby, M.R. and Karni, E. (1973) 'Free Competition and the Optimal Amount of Fraud', *Journal of Law and Economics*, Vol. 16 (April), 67–86.

Delozier, M. (1976) *The Marketing Communication Process*, Maidenhead, McGraw-Hill.

Fenton, N., Golding, P. and Radley, A. (1993) 'Thinking about Charity: Report of a Pilot Study into Public Attitudes to Charities and Volunteering', in *Researching the Voluntary Sector*, West Malling, Charities Aid Foundation.

George, W.R. and Berry, L.L. (1981) 'Guidelines for the Advertising of Services', *Business Horizons*, Vol. 24, July/August, 52–6.

Hart, T. (2007) 'e-philanthropy: leveraging technology to benefit charities and donors', in Sargeant, A. and Wymer, W. (eds) *The Routledge Companion to Nonprofit Marketing*, London, Routledge.

Harvey, T. (1995) 'Service Quality: The Culprit and the Cure', *Bank Marketing*, June, 24–8.

Hind, A. (1995) *The Governance and Management of Charities*, Barnet, Voluntary Sector Press.

Horne, S. and Moss, M. (1995) 'The Management of Collecting Boxes: Analysis of Performance and Site Location', *Journal of Nonprofit and Public Sector Marketing*, Vol. 3, No. 2, 47–62.

Humanitarian Studies Unit (2001) *Reflections on Humanitarian Action: Principles, Ethics and Contradictions*, Pluto Press.

Jones, T.O. and Sasser, W.E. (1995) 'Why Satisfied Customers Defect', *Harvard Business Review*, Nov/Dec, 88–99.

Kotler, P. (1994) *Marketing Management: Analysis, Planning, Implementation and Control*, Englewood Cliffs, NJ, Prentice Hall.

Kotler, P. and Fox, K. (1985) *Strategic Marketing for Educational Institutions*, Englewood Cliffs, NJ, Prentice Hall.

Kotler, P. and Scheff, J. (1997) *Standing Room Only: Strategies for Marketing The Performing Arts*, Boston, MA, Harvard Business School Press.

Levitt, T. (1981) 'Marketing Intangible Products and Product Intangibles', *Harvard Business Review*, Vol. 50 (Sept.–Oct.), 41–52.

Lynn, P. and Davis-Smith, J. (1992) *The 1991 National Survey of Voluntary Activity in the UK*, Berkhamstead, Volunteer Centre UK.

Malaro, M.C. (1994) *Museum Governance: Mission, Ethics, Policy*, Englewood Cliffs, NJ, Prentice Hall.

Marshall, K.P. and Smith, J.R. (2000) 'SERVPERV Utility for Predicting Neighbourhood Shopping Behavior', *Journal of Nonprofit and Public Sector Marketing*, Vol. 7, No. 4, 45–57.

McFadyen, K., Harrison, J.L., Kelly, S.J. and Scott, D. (2001) 'Measuring Service Quality in a Corporatised Public Sector Environment', *Journal of Nonprofit and Public Sector Marketing*, Vol. 9, No. 3, 35–51.

Nagle, T.T. and Hogan, J. (2005) *The Strategy and Tactics of Pricing: A Guide to Growing More Profitably* (4th edn), Englewood Cliffs, Prentice Hall.

Nash, R.J. (2002) *Real World Ethics: Frameworks for Educators and Human Service Professionals*, Boston, MA, Teachers College Press.

Nelson, P. (1974) 'Advertising as Information', *Journal of Political Economy*, Vol. 81 (Jul/Aug), 729–54.

Øvretveit, J. (1992) *Health Service Quality*, Oxford, Blackwell Scientific Press.

Palmer, A. (1994) *Principles of Service Marketing*, Maidenhead, McGraw-Hill.

Parasuraman, A., Zeithaml, V.A. and Berry, L.L. (1988) 'SERVQUAL: A Multiple Item Scale for Measuring Consumer Perceptions of Service Quality', *Journal of Retailing*, Vol. 64, No. 1, 12–40.

Payne, A., Christopher, M., Clark, M. and Peck, H. (1999) *Relationship Marketing For Competitive Advantage*, Oxford, Butterworth Heinemann.

Peters, T.J. (1987) *Thriving On Chaos: Handbook for a Management Revolution*, New York, Harper Collins.

Porter, M.E. (1985) *Competitive Advantage: Creating and Sustaining Superior Performance*, New York, Free Press.

Rados, D.L. (1981) *Marketing For Non-Profit Organizations*, Dover, MA, Auburn House.

Rentschler, R., Hede, A. and White, T.R. (2007) 'Museum Pricing: Challenges To Theory Development and Practice', *International Journal of Nonprofit and Voluntary Sector Marketing*, Vol. 12, No. 2, 163–73.

Sargeant, A. (2001) 'Relationship Fundraising: How to Keep Donors Loyal', *Nonprofit Management and Leadership*, Vol. 12, No. 2, 177–92.

Sargeant, A. and Jay, E. (2004) *Fundraising Management*, London, Routledge.

Sargeant, A. and Stephenson, H. (1997) 'Corporate Giving—Targeting the Likely Donor', *Journal of Nonprofit and Voluntary Sector Marketing*, Vol. 2, No. 1, 64–79.

Shiu, E., Vaughan, L. and Donnelly, M. (1997) 'Service Quality: new horizons beyond SERVQUAL: an investigation of the portability of SERVQUAL into the voluntary and local government sectors', *Journal of Nonprofit and Voluntary Sector Marketing*, Vol. 2, No. 4, 324–31.

Steinberg, R. and Weisbrod, B.A. (2005) 'Nonprofits with Distributional Objectives: Price Discrimination and Corner Solutions', *Journal of Public Economics*, Vol. 89, 2205–30.

Stewart, K.L. (1992) 'Applying a Marketing Orientation to a Higher Education Setting', *Journal of Professional Services Marketing*, Vol. 7, No. 2, 117–24.

Weber, L. (2001) *Business Ethics in Healthcare: Beyond Compliance*, Indianapolis, IN, Indiana University Press.

Wiggins, J. (2003) 'Motivation, Ability and Opportunity To Participate: A Reconceptualisation of the RAND Model of Audience Development', Paper Presented to the 7th International Conference in Arts and Cultural Management, Milan, 29 June–2 July.

Zeithaml, V.A. and Bitner, M.J. (1996) *Services Marketing*, New York, McGraw-Hill.

PART THREE

Specific Applications

8 | Social Marketing: The Marketing of Ideas

OBJECTIVES

By the end of this chapter you should be able to:

1. define social marketing;
2. distinguish between social marketing, education, and social communication;
3. understand the contribution of market research techniques to the field of social behaviour;
4. design a social marketing campaign.

Introduction

In Chapter 7 we concluded our work on the development of a marketing plan for products and services. We developed a generic framework and explored how a wide variety of non-profits might use this to market to an equally wide variety of different stakeholder groups. In this chapter, the last on marketing planning, we move away from a consideration of products and services and consider instead the marketing of ideas. We will explore the history of what has come to be known as 'social marketing', the social marketing mix, and some of the key findings from research studies conducted in this domain. We will then focus particularly on the role of communications.

What Is Social Marketing?

Social marketing first emerged as a distinct concept in the early 1970s when Kotler and Zaltman (1971: 5) recognized that marketing tools and techniques typically applied to products and services could be applied equally well to the marketing of ideas. The authors define social marketing as 'the design, implementation, and control of programmes calculated to influence the acceptability of social ideas and involving considerations of product planning, pricing, communication, distribution, and marketing research.'

The wording of this definition is quite precise. The authors have deliberately avoided any reference to education or the facilitation of a change of attitudes or values. This is because social marketing is concerned with neither of these processes. The ultimate goal of any form of marketing is to influence behaviour. This may be to influence a particular individual to purchase an organization's product/service, or it may be to influence an individual to start recycling a proportion of his household waste. In either case, a concrete and voluntary change in behaviour has resulted. Marketing and the variant social marketing are therefore conceptually different from the process of education, where the ultimate goal is knowledge, not necessarily a change in behaviour. Similarly, marketing should be viewed as distinct from a process designed merely to elicit a change in the law. Individuals or organizations concerned with this process may essentially be regarded as lobbyists, since once again behavioural changes are not directly involved.

It is important to note that more recently Rothschild (1999) has argued that education, changes in law/regulation, and marketing can all be regarded as tools for achieving behaviour change. Thus a government wishing to effect a change might seek to make use of all three processes in achieving its goals. In the context of charity giving, for example, governments could see to encourage individual giving by:

- Changing the legal/regulatory environment to minimize the opportunity for fraud and thereby enhance public trust and confidence in giving.

- Educating the public (and notably schoolchildren) about the work of nonprofits and dealing with common misconceptions about giving, or how donated funds will be expended. The public, for example, believe that it costs charities around 40p to raise £1, which is around twice the figure than is actually the case.

- Promoting key forms of giving such as legacies/bequests; altering the price of giving through tax concessions and encouraging specific giving 'channels' such as payroll giving, or giving through the Internet by text message.

In this sense, while education and legislative changes do not equate to social marketing per se, they can certainly form part of an integrated campaign to bring about behavioural change.

To understand a key difference between marketing and social marketing, it is also necessary to examine the question of objectives. In the generic marketing discussed so far, some form of benefit has usually accrued to the marketing organization as the result of its marketing activity, e.g increased patronage, enhanced levels of voluntary donation, etc. Thus, even if the objective of the organization is not to make a profit and the work of the organization is philanthropic, some form of 'benefit' will nevertheless accrue to the marketing organization. In social marketing this is not the case. The marketing activity is aimed at society, with the aim of inducing a change in the behaviour of that society for the good of all (MacFadyen et al. 2001). French and Blair-Stevens (2005: 31), for example, define social marketing as 'the systematic application of marketing concepts and techniques to achieve specific behavioural goals relevant to the public good.'

Of course the word 'good' is a relative term. What is considered an action advancing society is basically in the eye of the beholder. Could the Taliban, for example, utilize social marketing in a bid to keep girls and young women out of schools? Andreasen (1993) is clear on this point and argues that anyone can use social marketing including, to use his example, organizations such as the Ku Klux Klan.

We need to be clear that social marketers are 'hired guns' (excuse the metaphor). That is, give us a behavior you want influenced and we have some very good ways of making it happen. The decision about which behaviors 'ought' to be influenced is not ours to make. Clients, or even societies or governments – make those judgements (Andreasen 2006).

In this view the tools of social marketing hold no inherent value position and social marketers are not bound to be doers of good so much as users of a tool kit (Dann 2006). For the current author, however, social marketers do have a duty to ensure that their actions are focused on enhancing the society they serve. Just as commercial marketers are under a moral obligation not to 'sell' products they know will not meet the needs of their customers, so too must social marketers avoid practices that will harm their society. It is up to the individual to form their own view on where these boundaries may lie, but not to consider the issue is fundamentally at odds with the concept of societal orientation we discussed in Chapter 2. As in the commercial parallel, there is a very real difference between social selling and social marketing.

Fox and Kotler (1980) draw a further distinction between what they term 'social communication' and 'social marketing'. They view the former as a paradigm of thought which majors on the use of mass media advertising, public relations, and personal selling. The aim of social communication is simply to take advantage of all possible opportunities to communicate a message to a target group. The social marketing paradigm, however, adds five more dimensions which are typically missing from a purely social communication approach. These are as follows.

Marketing Research

The social marketer only begins work on a campaign after the target market has been thoroughly researched. The size of the overall market, its needs/wants, attitudes, behavioural patterns, and the likely costs and benefits of addressing individual market segments will be carefully evaluated. Appropriate campaigns can thereafter be designed for those segments it is felt most appropriate to address.

The power of effective marketing research cannot be understated. It can greatly improve the relevance and ultimate impact on behaviour of a social marketing campaign. It was recently identified, for example, that prostitutes in Tijuana, Mexico, had little fear that they might die of AIDS. Traditional social communications messages extolling the virtues of safe sex were therefore largely ineffectual with the members of this important target group. Research, however, identified that the prostitutes were very much afraid of leaving their children without mothers. The emphasis of the resulting social marketing campaign was hence switched from 'I want to live' to 'I want to protect my child'.

Product Development

Assume, for example, that the purpose of a campaign is to influence consumers to adopt a recycling behaviour. The social communicator will tend to see the problem as a need to exhort people to change their behaviour. The social marketer, on the other hand, will also seek to promote the necessary means to more easily facilitate this change. The campaign would highlight the technology that is available to assist in recycling and offer practical opportunities for the behavioural change to be adopted at minimal cost. In short, the 'product' being promoted is not just a need to change behaviour, but also the means by which it is possible to do so.

Two decades ago, international health experts recognized that simply telling people about birth control was unlikely to have any significant impact on behaviour. Their early attempts were hindered by misconceptions about contraceptives, such as they would make women ill or children sick, the expense, or unfavourable religious beliefs. A social marketing approach was then adopted by many organizations which took account of these difficulties and segmented the market according to the sets of perceptions that were held. The emphasis was changed from mere mass communication to the creation of support frameworks which were tailored to the needs of each market segment.

   A further example from social marketing folklore is the story of a project developed at Johns Hopkins University in partnership with USAID and a number of Mexican agencies. The aim was to encourage Latin teenagers to become more sexually responsible, something which had hitherto proved difficult to achieve by mere mass communication alone. The team therefore sought a route which might appeal to teenagers that would not be perceived as a 'lecture' on the subject. Moreover, the team wished to ensure that as high a percentage as possible of teenagers had access to appropriate advice. The solution was to create two pop songs, 'Stop' and 'When We Are Together', performed by Tatianna and Johnny, which contained lyrics that made it clear that sex does not have to be part of a loving relationship. The two songs were a great success and when teenagers purchased the record, the sleeve opened out into a poster which contained information about where to obtain birth control information.

The Use of Incentives

Social marketing can involve the use of incentives to encourage the desired behaviour change. Thus some campaigns in South America or in developing countries have offered small gifts to those who agree to use a particular service. Similarly, price incentives have been offered to encourage take-up rates among the poorest groups in a given society. The use of such 'sales promotion' activities can pay rich dividends in a good social marketing campaign (see Sihombing 1994 or Schellstede 1986).

EXAMPLE

Health agencies in Tanzania have employed a voucher system to encourage poorer segments of society to protect themselves against malaria. Since the early 1990s, insecticide-treated nets have become a key strategy for controlling the disease. Health agencies have attempted to subsidize the price of nets through a voucher system that makes the nets affordable and helps establish a commercial market in their provision. The vouchers were targeted particularly at families with young children and/or pregnant women. When the scheme was initially introduced the voucher redemption rate was very high (97 per cent) but within two years this fell away considerably. The team responsible for the compaign concluded that vouchers were a feasible system for targeted subsidies, although considerable effort was required to achieve high levels of awareness and uptake. They also concluded that within a poor society vouchers may not necessarily ensure health equity unless they cover a high proportion of the total cost, since some cash is needed when using a voucher as part-payment. Poorer women among the target group are, as a consequence, less likely to take up the offer.

Facilitation

The social marketer is concerned not only with the communication of a message; she must also attempt to make the adoption of a behavioural change relatively easy to achieve. Thus community recycling initiatives which galvanize the whole community into action (and where individuals can draw support from each other) may be more effective than a simple advertising campaign alone. Similarly, if individuals are to be encouraged to adopt safer sexual practices, access to appropriate advice and contraception must be convenient and freely available. In Uganda, contraceptives were almost impossible to sell in conventional retail stores. Social marketers therefore created booths in traditional markets and sold contraceptives at prices acceptable to the target market.

Marketing Upstream

The final difference that is typically cited is the ability of social marketing to target individuals, but also to move 'upstream' to focus on professionals, organizations, and policy makers (Lefebvre 1996, Andreasen and Kotler 2003). Thus a nonprofit concerned with solvent abuse might seek to influence those at risk, but it might also attempt to target teachers, doctors, and other professionals so that they might be able to recognize the signs of abuse and take appropriate steps to aid the individual concerned. They might also seek to alter the marketing of products that could potentially be abused, perhaps by persuading manufacturers to voluntarily limit their availability, or by making their product less attractive for this purpose. Policy makers might also be the target of social marketing, in an attempt to enhance the services available to individual addicts and to shape any relevant legislation.

Social Marketing Domains

Social marketing has been used to good effect to tackle many social issues worldwide (Andreasen 2003). Indeed, it has recently become fashionable for many governments to adopt a social marketing perspective as they seek to bring about societal change. In the UK, for example, the potential was recognized in the White Paper on Public Health, which talked of the 'power' of social marketing (Department of Health 2004). A new National Social Marketing Strategy Centre has also been created, led by the National Consumer Council and the Department of Health to help realize the potential of social marketing to influence the public good. A National Social Marketing Strategy for Health in England is currently being developed and similar initiatives may be found in the USA, Canada, New Zealand, and Australia.

The domain of social marketing is increasingly broad. Social marketing campaigns have tackled issues such as:

- drink driving (e.g. Braus 1995);
- problem gambling (e.g. Byrne et al. 2005);
- obesity/healthy eating (e.g. Hastings et al. 2003);
- carbon-emitting behaviours (e.g. Marcell et al. 2004);
- 'de-marketing' the use of the car (e.g. Wright and Egan 2000);
- management of pest control (e.g. Binney et al. 2003);
- recycling/energy conservation (e.g. McKenzie-Mohr 1994);
- encouraging composting (e.g. McDermott et al. 2004);
- tobacco/drug/alcohol abuse (e.g. Gordon et al. 2006);
- disaster management and preparedness (Guion et al. 2007).

Table 8.1 A categorization of social behaviours

Behaviour	Low involvement	High involvement
One-time behaviour		
Individual	Donating money to a charity	Donating blood
Group	Election of a local council	Creation of a Neighbourhood Watch scheme
Continuing behaviour		
Individual	Not smoking in elevators	Stopping smoking or drug intake
	Recycling newspapers	Recycling all household waste
Group	Driving within the speed limit	Supporting a woman's right to abortion

Source: Kotler, P. and Andreasen, A. (1996) *Strategic Marketing For Nonprofit Organisations,* 5th edn. Reproduced by kind permission of Prentice Hall.

The reader will appreciate that many of these are difficult issues and the behaviours concerned may be firmly entrenched. Marketing may therefore offer no magic solution. Even with the most finely tuned social marketing campaign, the targeted behaviours may prove difficult, if not impossible, to change. According to Kotler and Andreasen (1991) there are three major dimensions which determine just how difficult it may be to achieve such a change:

- whether the behaviour is high or low involvement;
- whether the behaviour is a one-off (or one-time) or continuing;
- whether the behaviour is exhibited by individuals or groups.

Examples of each of the eight categories of social marketing produced by these dimensions are given in Table 8.1.

High Involvement versus Low Involvement

The more 'involved' with a purchase decision a consumer is, the more thought they are likely to give to alternative solutions and the costs and benefits associated with each. It is thus important for marketers to recognize whether a decision is high or low involvement as this will impact on the amount of factual information provided. Sadly there is no consensus on what constitutes 'involvement'. See, for example, Kapferer and Laurent (1985) or Ratchford (1987). Most researchers would agree though that consumers will be more 'involved' in a situation if they perceive it as having immediate and personal relevance to themselves. Moreover, if the situation is perceived as having a high degree of risk associated with it, the level of involvement will also be enhanced. The choice of a method of birth control, for example, would for most constitute a high-involvement decision since it is of immediate personal relevance and the social and financial risks of an unwanted pregnancy are very real.

Low-involvement decisions on the other hand are typically of little importance to the consumer as the outcome of the decision will not have a major impact on their lifestyle. Such decisions involve little thought, do not involve a detailed search for information in respect of the alternatives, and carry few penalties if the wrong decision is taken. Thus, in the social context, low-involvement behaviours may be easier to change than those requiring high involvement. If a particular behaviour pattern is not deemed significant and changing it would expose the individual to little social risk, it will be easier for the marketer to encourage a change to take place. Persuading car drivers to switch to non-alcoholic lager might thus be somewhat easier than persuading them to switch to soft drinks, since they can still be seen to enjoy a pint with their friends at a party. They can hence offset any social pressure that they might feel to join in and have a drink.

Interestingly, there are a variety of products and services which are capable of evoking high levels of involvement purely on the basis of the emotional appeals that are associated with them. Tobacco is one such product, and understanding the reasons why this is so might significantly aid social marketers in a bid to reduce deaths from heart disease and lung cancer. Hirschman and Holbrook (1982) found, for example, that many smokers imagined themselves as 'Marlboro Men' and felt that their habit (and brand) was a statement of both their masculinity and their desire to imagine themselves as idealized cowboys. The weakening of this association might thus be one issue for social marketers to address.

One-Time versus Continuing Behaviour

One-time behaviour changes are usually easier to instigate than longer-term adjustments. They require the target merely to understand the communication message and to take action on that basis. Of course, the easier it can be for the target audience to take the desired action, the more likely it is that they will actually take it. Communicating the benefits of a change in behaviour is therefore not enough in itself; thought must also be given to how easy an individual will find it to act on the information presented. Thus immunization programmes in developing countries will visit individual rural communities, rather than expecting people to travel to major towns and cities for treatment. In this way, as large a percentage of the population as possible can be affected. Similarly political parties of all persuasions will usually offer free rides to the polling station for the elderly or infirm to ensure that they turn out to vote—it is hoped, in the manner desired!

Persuading individuals to change their behaviour patterns permanently is a little more problematic. Over time, behaviour can become habitualized, in the sense that it happens without any thought on the part of the individual. Moreover, justification for the behaviour can become firmly entrenched in an individual's value systems. People have to be convinced of the need for them to change and the benefits that might accrue as a result. They also have to be convinced that these benefits will be substantive enough to warrant the effort necessary to instigate the change in behaviour. In the case of low-involvement decisions, this may only involve an occasional reminder of the need to behave in a particular way. High-involvement, continuing behaviours are the most difficult to change. In many cases these may prove impossible to alter without resorting to legislative change to provide a final backdrop of enforcement.

Individual versus Group

Group behaviour is inherently more difficult to change than the behaviour of particular individuals. The complex dynamic of relationships that exist within a societal group act to reinforce and legitimize the attitudes and values of the members of that group. Acceptance of any form of change can be interpreted as disloyalty to the collective identity of the group and individuals brave enough to deviate from the norm may have a number of social penalties imposed on them as a result.

To address changes in group behaviours, it is important to recognize the distinction between opinion leaders, opinion formers, and opinion followers. Communication strategies that acknowledge the significance of the opinion leaders and formers are far more likely to effect the desired change in behaviour.

Opinion Leaders

Opinion leaders are those individuals that have the ability to influence behaviour because of their perceived status within their social group. Reynolds and Darden (1971) identified that these individuals tend to be more gregarious and self-confident than non-leaders and, importantly from a marketing perspective, also tend to have a greater exposure to the mass media. Clearly if group behaviours are to be modified, it is the opinion leaders within those groups who must be targeted in particular with the communications message. Given that they tend to read more publications than others in society, are among the first to return promotional coupons, and have a propensity to take and enjoy risks, they are not impossible to identify.

Opinion Formers

Unlike opinion leaders, opinion formers exert influence over group behaviour because of their actual authority, education, or status. In essence, opinion formers may be looked to for advice because of the formal expertise that they have in a particular area. Thus government ministers, community group leaders, newspaper editors, etc. can all be viewed as opinion formers. Once again, since this group has a great capacity to be able to influence others, it will form an important target group in any social marketing campaign. Fortunately opinion formers are easier to identify than opinion leaders since, by virtue of their position, they normally seek to be seen as having an important impact on the attitudes and behaviours of others. Targeting them is therefore not problematic.

Opinion Followers

The majority of members of society can be categorized as opinion followers. They are unlikely to set a new trend in behaviour themselves unless such a behaviour change has previously been legitimized and endorsed by their societal group. They look for advice in respect of appropriate behaviours, both from opinion formers and opinion leaders.

Researching Social Behaviours

The research of social issues is undoubtedly one of the most difficult facets of marketing that nonprofit practitioners have to deal with. Many traditional primary research techniques are difficult, or even downright inappropriate, to apply in this field. People are understandably reluctant to talk about sensitive personal matters and when one considers that a high proportion of postal questionnaires asking respondents about the relatively innocuous topic of personal income will often be returned with the relevant section incomplete, something of the difficulty researchers face in this sensitive area becomes readily apparent. Various forms of questionnaire, including telephone/postal, will be particularly difficult to apply in this context, making the collection of quantitative data problematic.

For this reason, much social research is qualitative in nature and as a consequence conducted with smaller numbers of subjects, although often in considerably more depth. Of the techniques that are most helpful in accumulating this category of data, personal interviews and focus groups are probably the most commonly utilized (Weinreich 1999).

Interviews

Personal interviews with subjects from a particular societal group can play a pivotal role in a social marketing research project. Although they are relatively costly to administer, the researcher is able to take her time with the research and to establish a rapport with each subject before more intimate and personal details are probed later in their discussion. The researcher can also benefit from being able to observe the body language of the subject and hence be sensitive to those aspects which he finds it particularly difficult to talk about.

As we said in Chapter 3, interviews can be either fully structured, semi-structured, or conducted in a free format closely resembling an everyday conversation. In the first, the researcher has a prescriptive list of the questions that will be posed and has decided in advance the order in which they will be delivered. The interviewer has little or no authority to adjust the wording of the questions in each case, making it easier to compare the findings of the interviews undertaken, but potentially stifling a debate of any interesting issues that might emerge. For this reason, a semi-structured approach is more common since although the researcher must follow a prescribed pattern for the interview, there is more scope for her to tailor the conversation to follow up on matters of particular interest.

At the other end of the scale, a free format interview is one in which the researcher has only an idea of the subjects that will be covered, and the interview is conducted as far as possible as a natural conversation. These naturalistic 'conversations' are normally tape-recorded so that the researcher is free to concentrate on the development of the interaction between him and the subject. This technique is commonly used in social marketing research since the subject can more easily be put at their ease and approached with questions that reflect the natural order of the conversation taking place.

Focus Groups

Focus groups, by contrast, involve the researcher assembling a 'panel' of between six and eight members of the subject group. A trained facilitator then explores with this group the issues under research. The discussion is usually unstructured, in the sense that the researcher has a clear idea of the ground that must be covered, but is happy for the group to emphasize those aspects of the discussion that they find particularly exciting or of relevance to them. Once again it would be normal practice to either audio- or video-tape the proceedings so that the facilitator is free to concentrate on the development of the discussion and ensure that each individual has the opportunity to contribute.

As with personal interviews, focus groups can be used to investigate difficult social issues and the key findings can be developed from a careful analysis of the tape of the discussion after it has taken place. Focus groups often yield valuable insight into the underlying motivations for particular categories of behaviour, and as participants begin to recognize that they are not alone in holding a particular view, open and honest discussions often emerge.

A good example of the use of focus groups to inform social marketing practice is reported in the case study below. In this case, the agency employed to design a campaign aimed at encouraging younger females to adopt safer sexual practices decided to use focus groups as the vehicle for discovering why it was that many such individuals were still failing to take adequate birth control precautions. Many of the focus group participants indicated that they would sometimes take a gamble by not using birth control and, especially when younger, did not use any form of contraception at all. The following statements represent a selection of direct quotes from focus group participants, giving some clue as to why this might be the case.

Figure 8.1 Specimen poster from 'Don't Kid Yourself' campaign

Luckily, I haven't gotten pregnant, but yeah, it's certainly been a gamble, you know, and if I'm in a situation where nothing's available, you know, just those situations you can get into I know it's stupid but, you know, at the time that's not as real as the moment is.

I was so immature that it was like almost a game to me, to say, 'Oh, no, it won't matter this time,' you know. Or 'Don't worry about it' or 'I can't get pregnant.' I know so many girls that say, 'Oh, I can't get pregnant. I think I must be one of those women that can never get pregnant.' I thought that until I got pregnant.

When I first started having sex and stuff, I honestly believed that I could not get pregnant.

The quotes given above were used by the creative agency to directly inform the development of the poster in Figure 8.1. As the reader will appreciate, it was designed specifically to get across the vital statistic that 80 per cent of young women who do not use birth control become pregnant within a year. In short, it was designed to counter the thought that 'it can't happen to me'. The preliminary artwork for the poster was itself subsequently the subject of a focus group discussion to ensure that it was likely to be successful in imparting the required message to the target group. In this latter case, members of the group were asked to interpret the message contained in the poster.

Their responses were:

Your odds of getting pregnant are pretty good.

Start using birth control. You're not always lucky.

This one's really easy to understand. It's concrete and believable.

It's eye-catching. If I saw this somewhere I'd stop and look at it.

The full details of the campaign and its development are given in the case study below.

■ CASE STUDY

THE 'DON'T KID YOURSELF' CAMPAIGN

The 'Don't Kid Yourself' campaign is the result of a collaboration among the Title X Family Planning grantees in Public Health Service Region VIII—Colorado, Montana, North Dakota, South Dakota, Utah, and Wyoming. The grantees pooled their funds in order to create a social marketing campaign to reduce unintended pregnancies in the region. They selected Weinreich Communications, a social marketing firm in Washington, DC, to plan, develop, and implement the programme. Every element of the 'Don't Kid Yourself' campaign was developed based upon social marketing research conducted by Weinreich Communications. An initial set of five focus groups were conducted in Butte and Salt Lake City with members of the target audience—low-income women aged 18 to 24. These focus groups provided insight into how they thought about birth control and pregnancy, as well as how best to reach them with campaign messages. Based on the results of the initial research, draft materials and campaign ideas were developed and tested in six additional focus groups before being finalized. In addition, eight individual interviews were conducted with target audience members to be used as a source of soundbites for the radio spots. The campaign was then pilot-tested in Butte and Salt Lake City.

In Salt Lake City, the number of phone calls to Planned Parenthood's clinics increased by 72 per cent during the two months the pilot campaign was implemented. In Butte, the number of people listing the Butte Family Planning clinic as a place they would go for answers about sexual health or birth control issues nearly doubled after the campaign.

The campaign included the following elements.

RADIO ADVERTISEMENTS (TEN 30-SECOND SPOTS)

Most of the radio ads used actual voices of members of the target audience to model attitudes, change misconceptions, and spark thoughts and conversations about the topic. Radio was selected as a key element of the campaign for several reasons. First, in the focus groups, nearly all participants said that they listened to the radio regularly. Second, radio allows the campaign to reach a very specific audience; it is possible to target precisely women aged 18 to 24 and reach a large percentage of that population. Third, because radio is ever-present in many people's lives, the target audience may hear messages when they are in a situation in which they should use birth control—the radio spot may thus serve as a reminder and make it more likely that they use it. Fourth, the spots may play when friends or partners are together and promote conversations about birth control issues. Finally, the older people who are more likely to be offended by the ads are less likely to be listening to the same stations as the 18- to 24-year-olds.

POSTERS (FOUR DESIGNS)

A set of four posters was developed to get the campaign message out through community organizations, including clinics, schools, businesses, government agencies, recreational facilities, and local 'hangouts'. The tagline on all the posters and visual materials, 'Don't Kid Yourself', came from a focus group participant who was summing up the point of the poster visuals. Although she didn't realize it at the time, these words provide a clever double entendre for this campaign. This idea of 'kidding oneself' came up often in the focus groups, with many young women saying that they often had unprotected intercourse because they thought that pregnancy couldn't happen to them or that they would be safe 'just this once'. The bright neon colours, rough drawings, and text typeface of the posters were designed to draw attention from the 18- to 24-year-old age group and younger.

NEWSPAPER ADS (FOUR DESIGNS)

Four newspaper ads were designed in several different sizes. The focus group research showed that many of the women read particular types of newspapers or sections of the paper. Newspaper ads were felt to be helpful in reaching those who respond better to visual information, or who do not hear the radio ads. They also provided the phone number and campaign messages in a form that could be cut out and kept until someone is ready to call.

DRINK COASTERS

Bright pink drink coasters with campaign messages were designed for distribution to bars and clubs. The focus group participants said that bars, clubs, and coffee houses were good places to reach women aged 18 to 24. These venues were particularly appropriate, since potential sexual partners or groups of friends might be drinking together and could use the coaster as a method of initiating conversations about birth control.

BROCHURES (TWO TOPICS)

Two three-colour brochures were developed, based on the needs identified by focus group participants. One brochure presented birth control options, while the other assisted in talking to a sexual partner about birth control. They provided in-depth information and skills-building content at an appropriate reading level, using the target audience's language. The brochures also served as a proxy for those who would not come into the clinic to speak with a counsellor. They were placed in locations frequented by the target audience, including schools, grocery stores, bars and clubs, public libraries, and doctors' offices.

The Social Marketing Mix

The reader will appreciate that since in a social marketing context we are no longer concerned with physical products or even services, the traditional marketing mix introduced in Chapter 7 is more difficult to apply. While this is so, it is possible to extend and adapt the marketing mix to generate a greater relevance to the marketing of ideas (Kotler and Roberto 2001). Since marketers seem to prefer to talk about 'P's, a six-P framework for use by those working in the social arena is proposed below.

Product

The product in this context is the idea that the marketer wishes to get across to stimulate a change in behaviour. Unlike traditional marketing, which advocates the development of the product carefully designed to mirror customer preferences, the social marketer strives to engineer a change that (in their opinion) would be good for society as a whole. The element of persuasion is therefore important since the behaviour change must be marketed on the basis of the benefits that could accrue either directly or indirectly as a result. The product might hence be a change in sexual behaviour, a change in recycling behaviour, or the stimulation of demand for health programmes to counter social problems such as drug or solvent abuse.

Price

The price may be regarded as the monetary costs associated with adopting a change in behaviour. Attendance on a health programme may require the individual to fund some of the treatments that might be suggested. More usually, however, the important costs of a change in behaviour will be social. Individuals may suffer embarrassment or even ridicule within their social group for responding to a social marketing campaign. One can even place a cost on the fear that individuals might have of attending a health programme such as an annual mammogram. Some women may simply feel that they could not deal with the stress of having a lump discovered and may take the conscious decision that it is better not to know.

Cost is also an issue in the realm of recycling; Shrum et al. (1994) conclude, after a review of the literature, that cost viewed in terms of inconvenience acts as a very powerful motivator to avoid recycling. Identifying all the potential costs is therefore important, as the social marketing campaign can take account of these and make every attempt to minimize them as far as possible.

A final point on price that experience has taught social marketers is that it is often better to make some form of charge for any products that they might be involved in distributing (Kotler et al. 2002). Simply giving away items runs the risk that little value will be placed on them. It is often better to sell items cheaply to encourage a perception of value among members of the target segment. Indeed, doing so may also help engage the support of the local infrastructure, which will be necessary if the programme is to have any form of long-term impact. It is therefore not unusual, for example, for a small charge to be made for contraception, even in some of the world's poorest societies.

Place

'Place' refers to the location at which any service component of the social marketing campaign will be delivered. In the case of many birth-control programmes, for example, access to the programme must be straightforward and provided at a location geographically close to the target market. Place can also refer to the channels of information that are used to reach the target market. Information on the dangers of HIV, for example, might be conveyed to the target market by distributing leaflets via schools, colleges, universities, general practitioners, family planning clinics, etc.

Promotion

Social marketers will make use of most of the promotional tools described in Chapter 4. Many campaigns utilize advertising, public relations, sales promotion, and direct marketing to communicate with their target audience. The mechanics of exactly how this might be achieved and the stages involved in developing a typical communications plan are outlined later in this chapter.

Partnerships

It has already been suggested that certain categories of behaviour are not easy to influence. Many nonprofits may simply be too small to make much of an impact on their own.

They may lack the necessary resources in terms of both staff time and monetary backing. As a consequence, many nonprofits involved in social marketing look for potential partnerships with other organizations with similar goals. This may involve working closely with a wide variety of different organizations in both the private and public sectors. Clearly social marketers will need to identify and liaise with potential allies for a particular campaign to ensure that the overall approach to society is as coordinated as possible.

Policy

The difficulties of influencing continuing behaviours have already been alluded to above. In many cases the only method of achieving the desired outcome may be to compel individuals/ groups to institute the change in behaviour required. Ultimately, it may become necessary for governments to ban all forms of tobacco advertising to reduce sales. Simply trying to persuade individuals to give up smoking of their own volition may work up to a point, but there will always be a few 'die-hard' smokers who simply will never have either the necessary willpower or desire to give up their habit. For these reasons, marketers also have to be aware of the social policies that influence behaviour and attempt to influence those who have the power to instigate legislative change.

Thus, it is possible to utilize an adapted marketing mix in a social marketing context. The familiar concepts of product, price, place, and promotion all have a role to play in the creation of an effective social marketing campaign, even where the provision of no physical products or services is involved.

The Behavioural Ecological Model

In our discussion of the social marketing mix we have tended to focus our discussion at the level of the individuals whose behaviour it is intended to influence, developing a mix that is likely to be effective in that context. More recent thinking in social marketing suggests that this may not be the optimal approach. Rather than focus effort solely at the individual level, it may be more effectual to develop interventions that take account of the wider environment in which that individual may be living. This thinking forms the basis of the behavioural ecological model depicted in Table 8.2. In this example social marketing effort is being applied to tackling the problem of childhood obesity.

At the individual level the focus of effort is directly on the individual and the close social group that surrounds him/her. A mix of education and activities designed to stimulate parental involvement in the issue are suggested. At the local level the focus widens to include schools or other neighbourhood groups that have the capacity to influence behaviour. Suggestions here include encouraging exercise, by opening up access to facilities that would make this accessible and fun.

At the community level, attention is given to a specific societal group or geographical area. A target community might also take the form of a particular faith or racial group; any group in fact with its own power and/or authority structure. Thus, for example, any campaign to end the suffering caused by forced marriage would have to take account of and address the needs of the faith community in which this was taking place. In the healthy eating example, the community in question can be defined as the UK population since obesity is a problem affecting most sections of our society. Recommendations at the community level therefore

Table 8.2 Behavioural ecological model

Level	Strategies
Individual level	Education programmes focusing on health may lead parents to purchase more healthy foods and make them more readily available in the home
	Programmes to overcome constraints imposed on parents in order to promote a healthy lifestyle (e.g. the time parents have available to prepare healthy meals and to create opportunities for the family to be active)
	Encourage positive beliefs and attitudes toward physical activity
	Increase levels of parental nutritional knowledge
	Stimulate parents to encourage their children to exercise
	Encourage parents to interpret advertising messages for their children
Local level	Encourage schools to increase availability of physical education and to increase children's knowledge about how to be physically active
	Advocate for increased access to school facilities on weekends and holidays
	Initiatives to include healthier food and 'walking bus' programmes
	Eliminate unhealthy food sponsorship supply arrangements with schools
	Institute stricter standards for school food sales
Community	Advocate for development of additional youth recreational facilities
	Increase availability of healthy foods
	Increase funding for education and social marketing
	Reduce visibility and restrict supply of high fat/sugar products
	Require warnings on high fat foods and high sugar drinks
	Restrictions on advertising during children's TV programmes
Social structure	Change attitudes to childhood inactivity to make it socially unacceptable
	Greater focus on healthy role models and behaviours in media
	Greater restraint on marketing activities to children
	Encourage fast food chains to provide more diverse and lower fat menus

Source: Dresler-Hawke, E. and Veer, E. (2006) 'Making Healthy Eating Messages More Effective: Combining Integrated Marketing Communication With The Behaviour Ecological Model', *International Journal of Consumer Studies,* Vol. 30, No. 4, 318–326.

include interventions to subsidize healthy foods and encourage manufacturers to place health warnings on high fat foods.

Finally, it may be possible to plan interventions designed to alter the culture of society as a whole and to manipulate the whole social ecology to bring about change. Only when childhood obesity and lack of exercise become socially unacceptable will the problem ever be fully brought under control. Getting to this point will involve a sea-change in the way that 'fast food' and unhealthy lifestyles are portrayed in our media and the level of 'abuse' by manufacturers and advertisers that society is willing to tolerate.

The social marketing mix has relevance for each level in the model and marketers need to ensure that their approach across these different levels is fully integrated. As the UK government has recently found to its cost, interventions targeted at one level in isolation can be doomed to failure from the outset. With one in ten young people between the ages of 2 and 10 now regarded as obese, the government responded to pressure from the celebrity chef Jamie Oliver and the national media to improve the nutritional quality of school meals. As a consequence of this intervention, 400,000 fewer children at the time of writing are now taking school meals than was the case before the changes were implemented. The proportion of secondary school children, in particular, eating these meals has fallen from a third to a quarter, as children desert their schools for the unhealthy options available in nearby fast-food outlets. Some mothers have even responded to the changes by setting up pressure groups to lobby against the changes and selling fast-food snacks to children outside school gates.

Designing a Communications Campaign

Since previous chapters of this text have already examined the use of the marketing mix in different nonprofit contexts, the remainder of this chapter will focus on the development of a social marketing communications campaign and examine in detail the stages involved in its creation.

Seven steps are normally followed in designing a communications campaign. These are listed below:

1. specification of the target audience
2. communications objectives
3. specification of promotional message
4. media selection
5. schedule
6. budget
7. monitoring/control.

Each of these will now be examined in turn.

Specification of the Target Audience

Chapter 3 highlighted a variety of criteria that could be used to define the target audience. They may be specified in terms of their geographic, demographic, geo-demographic, behavioural, or lifestyle characteristics. However, in a social marketing context it would be also usual to specify in detail the behaviours within each segment and the current pattern thereof. With only finite resources available, social marketers will usually have to select only those segments that they perceive as being of particular importance. If a variety of segments are to be addressed, the behaviours of each should be identified so that planners can be clear about the point from which the behaviour change will be started. Such a specification will aid in setting campaign objectives and will be essential if the overall effectiveness of the campaign is to be assessed.

Communications Objectives

Communications objectives, like any other form of objective, should be specific, measurable, achievable, relevant, and timescaled. They are written to address various aspects of the campaign, so that the resulting communications strategy is focused on achieving the goals of the initiating organization. Colley (1961) developed a model for setting communications objectives entitled DAGMAR (Defining Advertising Goals for Measured Advertising Results). Although Colley's ideas were originally developed to assist in the assessment of advertising effectiveness, the model he developed can be applied to all forms of social marketing promotion. Colley believed that the process of communications was essentially hierarchical in nature and hence, for our purposes, if an idea is to be effectively communicated consumers should be moved through the following five stages:

Unawareness—Awareness—Comprehension—Conviction—Action

Before a social idea can gain acceptance, the target audience must be appraised of the concept and made to realize that alternative behaviours exist. Communities in developing countries thus need to be made aware that birth control methods exist and that pregnancy can be avoided. Similarly in the marketing of oral rehydration therapy, mothers in parts of Asia need to be made aware that diarrhoeal disease need not necessarily be fatal, given the proper (and rudimentary) treatment.

Simply making an audience aware of alternative behaviours is unlikely to be enough in itself to encourage a change, however. The social marketer must strive to ensure that the target audience actually understands the benefits that a change in behaviour could bring. Taboos or fallacies about the use of birth control methods must hence be overcome. Similarly, information about the success and simplicity of oral rehydration tablets in treating diarrhoeal disease must also be conveyed.

Having achieved a certain level of understanding in the target market, it is then necessary to generate a sense of conviction. Smokers, for example, may be aware of the dangers of their habit and understand the relationship between it and fatal diseases such as heart disease and cancer, but they may lack the necessary conviction to quit. Establishing conviction in such a high-involvement decision is not an easy task, though, and a variety of carefully targeted messages may be necessary to secure it.

The final stage of Colley's model can be viewed as the ultimate goal: securing a change in behaviour. Communications messages could be used to guide their recipients through the steps necessary to effect a change in behaviour. A freephone number could be provided to give individually tailored advice to callers about health or welfare issues, for example.

Colley held the view that communications objectives could be written to reflect any of the five important stages of the model. One could hence write objectives in terms of the number of people who are aware that alternative behaviours are available/acceptable (awareness), the number of people who understand why a behavioural change might be necessary (comprehension), the number of people who express an intention to change in the future (conviction), and finally the number of people who actually implement a change in their behaviour (action). Social communication objectives typically address all four of these areas.

Specifying the Promotional Message

There are a number of considerations which must be addressed in the design of appropriate promotional messages. These include the level of involvement a particular behaviour invokes, the content of the message, and the manner in which it will be conveyed. Each of these issues will now be explored in turn.

Level of Involvement

Fill (1995) argues that the effectiveness of a message from a receiver's perspective depends on two factors. The first is the amount and quality of information communicated, while the second is the overall judgement made about the manner in which it is presented. There is therefore a need to strike a balance between an individual's need for information and their need to

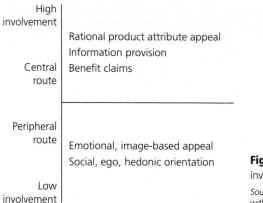

Figure 8.2 High-involvement versus low-involvement decisions

Source: Fill, C. (1995) *Marketing Communications.* Reproduced with the kind permission of Prentice Hall.

enjoy the consumption thereof. However, different styles of message may be appropriate depending on the nature of the behaviour that it is intended to influence. As Figure 8.2 makes clear, decisions that are high-involvement in nature require that the individual is presented with detailed information about the options available and the benefits thereof. This is because such decisions will require the individual to use his cognitive functions and the decision-making processes are hence relatively (although not exclusively) rational in nature. What is termed a central route to persuasion is adopted, consisting of strong, well-documented, and supported arguments in favour of the idea being raised. After the scare over risks associated with the MMR vaccine in the UK, for example, numerous agencies were involved in a large-scale campaign to convince the public that the vaccine was safe. The Department of Health, the British Medical Association, and others all united to convey the key message that the overwhelming body of evidence was clear on this issue; the MMR was safe. Care was also taken to advise parents of the risk that would otherwise be posed by diseases such as measles and that they might be putting other children at risk by not having their own child vaccinated. These key messages were conveyed through the national media and supplemented by the provision of information online and through a plethora of different healthcare providers.

Low-involvement decisions, on the other hand, require less thought from the individual and messages will hence be more effective if they concentrate on imagery. The aim here is to engender an emotional response which reflects an individual's ego or self-image, and marketers follow the peripheral route to persuasion through an emphasis on non-content message ingredients such as music, lighting, scenery, or the use of celebrity endorsements. The advertising that preceded the compulsory use of seatbelts in the UK focused on the use of powerful imagery which illustrated the pain and suffering that could be caused to family members by a failure to comply with the new regulations. Celebrity endorsement was also offered by Jimmy Savile who coined the catchy advertising strapline 'Clunk click every trip'.

Content of the Message

There are a number of issues relating to message content that social marketers must consider, including the following.

One- and Two-Sided Messages

Some promotional messages contain only one side of the argument. They convey only the positive impacts of the change in behaviour required, while ignoring any drawbacks completely.

Other messages may be termed two-sided in that they present a more balanced view to the audience, showing both the advantages and disadvantages of a given behaviour change. In general, research would seem to indicate that one-sided messages are more effective where the recipient group already has a favourable view of the behaviour change, or where their level of education is low. Conversely the use of two-sided messages is preferred where the recipients are either highly educated or hold a very negative view of the behaviour change presented.

Drawing Conclusions

Marketers must also decide whether the message they intend to convey will draw a firm conclusion about the need for a change in behaviour, or whether the message will be left open and the individual encouraged to draw her own conclusions. There is no easy way in which to choose between these two options but a variety of factors have been found to impact on the most appropriate form of message to use (Hovland and Mandell 1952). Specifically, the desirability of drawing a conclusion for the audience has been found to depend on the following factors:

1. *The level of education of the message recipients.* The higher the level of education possessed by the audience, the more likely it is that they will prefer to draw their own conclusions. There is a danger that members of a highly educated group will feel patronized by an approach which claims to know what is right for them. Those with lower levels of education, however, may be incapable of drawing the correct conclusion from the data presented for themselves and may require it to be drawn for them.

2. *Level of complexity.* If the idea being marketed is technically complex or multifaceted, it may be less easy for the recipient to see the end to which they are being led. Guidance may hence have to be more specific where complexity is encountered. Similarly, completely new ideas may need a greater degree of explanation and conclusion-drawing than those that have been around for some time.

3. *When action is required.* In the case of marketing the oral rehydration tablets mentioned earlier, the action required of the recipient is often immediate. Any delay in decision making may substantially reduce the chances of saving a child's life. Promotional messages in such circumstances must therefore be forceful and the results of inaction spelt out very clearly. If, on the other hand, the timescale for action is somewhat longer, the necessity for immediate action is diminished and the need for firm conclusion-drawing is less pronounced.

4. *Level of involvement.* As one would expect, high-involvement decisions are best approached by giving individuals the appropriate facts to make their decision alone. Any attempt to 'force' a change in behaviour on individuals in these circumstances is likely to be counterproductive. Indeed, recipients may actively resent such messages (see Sawyer and Howard 1991).

Framing the Presentation

In presenting any new social ideas to a potential audience, there will always be a variety of arguments that could be used to attempt to persuade. Of course, not all of these messages will have an equal impact on the target group; some will be seen as weak arguments, while others will not be as easy to counter. The issue for marketers then becomes the order in which these messages should be presented. Should a promotional message begin with the stronger points or the weaker ones?

Once again we must return to the question of the level of involvement that the audience has with the idea. If the audience has a low level of involvement it may be necessary to begin with a strong message to generate attention. It is also true that if the audience holds a strongly opposing view, a weak argument at the beginning of the message will only serve to raise counter-arguments in the minds of recipients, and the remainder of the message may be filtered out as a result. Of course, the converse of these points is also true. Messages which begin with weaker points and build up to the strongest arguments at the end tend to be more appropriate where the position adopted is not controversial, or where the issue evokes a strong but positive sense of involvement.

Social marketers must also decide whether to use positively framed messages (i.e. messages which refer primarily to the benefits of the desired change in behaviour) or negatively framed messages (which draw attention to the drawbacks of not implementing the change in behaviour). So, for example, a campaign directed at persuading people to stop smoking will need to decide whether the campaign will be positively framed and feature the details of how much better people will feel if they stop, or whether it should focus on the health implications of not giving up (negatively framed messages). Maheswaran and Meyers-Levy (1990) conclude that positively framed messages are more appropriate in situations where the individual does not have to process information (low involvement) and negatively framed messages more appropriate where a detailed level of information processing is required (high-involvement decisions).

The Nature of the Appeal

There are a variety of ways in which a social idea can be communicated in a promotional message. If individuals are highly educated, or where the decision is a high-involvement decision, we have already seen that a factual appeal may be the most appropriate to use. However, where the target audience is less well educated, or where the appeal is addressing low-involvement behaviours, the social marketer may find that an emotional appeal is more effective. Indeed, even where an appeal is largely factual there may still be scope for the social marketer to design campaigns which make an indirect use of fear, humour, or sexual imagery. The advantages and disadvantages of each of these approaches will now be considered in turn.

1. *Fear appeals.* Fear is an emotion often evoked to good effect by social marketers. This may be an immediate fear, such as the fear of contracting a particular disease, or it may be more longer-term in nature and reflect a concern for issues that will have a greater impact on future generations (e.g. some recycling behaviours). Fear may also be categorized according to whether it is a health-related fear or a fear of social disapproval, resulting from taking (or not taking) a particular form of action. Social marketers may utilize a variety of messages from each category.

Many researchers working in the field of fear in advertising have found that there is a linear relationship between the arousal of fear in advertising and its power to impact on attitudes and behaviour. In other words the greater the fear induced, the greater will be the persuasion (Witte and Allen 2000). That said, the position is actually quite complex. The degree to which individuals believe that they have the power to affect the behaviour change acts to moderate the impact of fear. Thus if smokers believe that they don't have the necessary willpower to quit, the efficacy of the ad will be greatly reduced (Girandola 2000, Ruiter et al. 2001). Fear ads therefore work best where the coping response is feasible and within the consumer's perceived ability (Blumberg 2000).

Other evidence suggests that shock ads can be effective immediately, but after numerous screenings can simply stop working (Fry 1996). Too much repetition can lead to habituation as has proved to be the case with the new health warnings on cigarette packs. Devlin et al. (2002) show that smokers have now become very adept at screening them out.

It is also interesting to note that a decision by a social marketer to opt for a fear-based campaign has been shown to have consequences for the messages that can be used successfully in the future. In some circumstances consumers can become conditioned to expect a fear-based message and will reject non-fear-based alternatives (Eadie and Stead 1998). Stead and Eadie (2000), for example, show that smokers now expect that ads designed to make them stop smoking will contain pictures of blackened lungs and clogged arteries, while drivers expect that drink-drive campaigns will show the carnage that can result from an accident while under the influence. Other, perhaps empathy-based alternatives, can be rejected by the target audience.

2. *Appeals based on humour.* Numerous studies over the years have addressed whether humour can enhance the effectiveness of a promotional campaign. Helpfully, Weinberger and Gulas (1992) present a review of the relevant literature which concludes that:

- humour attracts attention;
- humour does not harm comprehension (indeed, in some cases it can aid it);
- humour is no more effective at increasing persuasion than other promotional messages;
- humour enhances 'liking'; individuals are more likely to develop a favourable impression of advertising that utilizes humour;
- humour that is relevant to the product is superior to humour unrelated to the product;
- audience characteristics (gender, ethnicity, age) affect the response to humorous appeals;
- the nature of the product affects the appropriateness of a humorous treatment;
- humour is more effective with existing products than with new products;
- humour is more effective with low-involvement decisions than those with a high involvement.

EXAMPLE

In 2004 the UK's National Blood Service commissioned a national campaign to encourage young people to give blood. It explained the urgent and ongoing need for 2.5 million donations a year to meet hospital demand in England and Wales. The campaign was ongoing throughout the year and aimed to encourage 200,000 youngsters who had just reached their seventeenth birthdays to get into the habit of donating. Direct mail was the chosen medium, and the creative tapped into the desire of young adults to be treated as 'grown-ups', using a powerful ransom-style note. An offbeat envelope proclaimed 'We Want Your Blood'.

---

3. *Sexual appeals.* The very nature of many social marketing campaigns ensures that a percentage of marketers working in this area have will have to address the level of sexual messages/imagery that will be contained in the messages they have to convey. The use of sex in advertising can take many forms, such as nudity, double entendre, or perhaps more subtle devices such as that depicted in Figure 8.3. The extent to which blatantly sexual imagery will be appropriate will vary from society to society and from year to year. In the mid-1980s, for

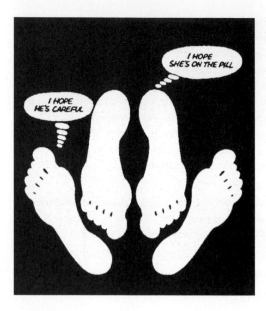

Figure 8.3 Health Education Council advertising
Source: Health Education Council.

example, visual sexual imagery was commonplace in many forms of advertising. By the end of the decade, advertisers had reverted to the use of more romantic imagery in response to an increased awareness of the threat of AIDS.

The key advantage of an appeal based on sex is simply that it is unrivalled in terms of its power to attract attention. Studies have shown that advertising with a sexual appeal is capable of arousing the immediate attention of both men and women. Regrettably, however, attention does not necessarily equate with interest in the product or idea being marketed. Social marketers may therefore find that they attract immediate interest among the target group, but ultimately the group fails to learn anything about the ideas the marketer is attempting to communicate. Nudity in particular has been found to impact negatively on the ability to communicate a message.

If used, sexual imagery must therefore be used with care. Research suggests that the key seems to lie in:

- using the sexual content largely as a device to attract attention;
- using the sexual component only where it is necessary to display a product function— or the expression of an idea;
- using sex symbolically rather than overtly—sexual imagery tends to be more effective than overt portrayals of sex. Nudity is also less effective in advertising than the use of sexual symbolism.

4. *Cartoons/animation.* Animation techniques have begun to rise in popularity in recent years. Although campaigns featuring animated characters have tended to address a younger audience, characters can also be created that allow the communication of hard-hitting messages that would otherwise be too distressing to show in the mass media. In March 2002, for example, the National Society for the Prevention of Cruelty to Children launched a campaign featuring a cartoon boy. It used 'Tom and Jerry' imagery to show a cartoon child 'bouncing back' from several attacks by his father (see Figure 8.4). After the final act of abuse the character becomes a real child lying motionless on the floor. The aim was to encourage more action to help the hidden victims of child cruelty.

Figure 8.4 NSPCC cartoon boy

Source: © NSPCC 2008. Reproduced with kind permission.

Media Selection

There are a variety of different media which can be utilized in a social marketing campaign, each with their own advantages and disadvantages. These include the following.

Television

If the campaign is to be directed at broad target groups within society, the cost of reaching each individual within that market will be comparatively low if television is selected as an appropriate medium. Television also lends a certain status to a campaign, in that organizations which advertise on television are generally perceived as being more reliable and trustworthy than those that don't. Thus the credibility of a social idea may be greatly enhanced by even an occasional airing on television. Of course, given that a typical television commercial is only a few seconds long, it may be necessary to repeat the message on several occasions to ensure that the idea has been effectively communicated. This in turn increases the absolute level of cost associated with the campaign and when one adds in the costs of producing the commercial in the first place, the overall cost can often be prohibitive.

In 2003 Elections Ontario ran a campaign with the ultimate goal of encouraging voter turnout at the forthcoming elections. The campaign centred around a series of TV commercials. In 'Restaurant' a 20-something couple inquiring tentatively about the menu are interrupted by a brazen young man at a neighbouring table. 'A cheeseburger for this young lady,' he instructs the server. 'On a Pita. And he'll have nothing.' 'Great, thank you,' murmurs the server, who bustles off as the couple exchange sheepish glances. In 'Hair Salon' a woman's meek request for a trim is overruled by a smirking boor in the waiting area who orders the stylist to go 'short, short and spiked, with some tiger-striped highlights'. Each spot is tagged coyly, 'When you don't vote, you let others speak for you'. The ads generated 250,000 calls to the organization's call centre and its website generated 47 million hits, representing 650,000 unique visitors. The campaign succeeded in adding about 600,000 names to the voters' register.

Print

Print media represent a very flexible communication opportunity for the marketer. Advertisements of all shapes and sizes can be presented utilizing a wide range of colours and effects. Adverts can be targeted specifically at those newspapers or magazines known to have a high readership among the target audience and, because of the enhanced segmentation this provides, messages can be tailored to suit the environment of the publication in which they are housed. Print also offers opportunities for inserts (which are incidentally six times more likely to be read than advertising carried on the pages of a magazine) and cut-out coupons, which can be completed to obtain further information, etc.

The weaknesses of press advertising relate to the fact that increases in circulations have tended to lag somewhat behind increases in advertising rates, gradually making print financially a less attractive option. The other major difficulty with press advertising is that readers of the publication will not necessarily read ads. Readers can, and do, select those advertisements which they feel they want to read. Magazines have the further weakness that it is often necessary to book space months in advance of the intended publication date. Given that at this stage the details of the promotional campaign are unlikely to have been finalized, this can create significant problems.

Radio

Expenditure on radio advertising has been cyclical over the past 15 years. It recovered from a dip in the mid-1980s to level off at approximately £160 million per annum in the UK in 1990. More recently the sector has experienced another rise in its fortunes and expenditures are currently closer to £200 million. Radio advertising is thus clearly becoming an increasingly attractive option for many organizations. Largely this is because it is possible to identify specific audiences tuning in to various stations at various times of the day. Radio campaigns are relatively cheap to produce and comparatively easy to modify, should this become necessary. Radio also has the advantage that it can often fire the imagination of the recipient, and effects can be achieved which would be unthinkable on television.

On the downside, radio advertising obviously lacks any form of visual stimulus which can be helpful in gaining attention. The other difficulty is that listening can often be a background activity and the level of attention advertising receives can, as a consequence, below. Radio is a useful medium, however, for reinforcing other forms of promotional activity, because sound triggers can be used to aid recall of, for example, a television commercial.

Outdoor

All forms of posters and signs are usually referred to as outdoor media. Outdoor media traditionally receive less attention than other types of media, and overall expenditure is a very small percentage of promotional spend in general. The amount of information that can be conveyed on a poster is relatively limited, and for this reason many poster campaigns elect to focus on the creative use of imagery. As with radio, poster campaigns can be very effective at reinforcing messages conveyed by other media and very large numbers of people have the opportunity to see (OTS) promotional messages conveyed in this way. Poster sites are sold on the basis of the number of 'sheets' that make up the display panel and these vary in size from 1 to 86 sheets (see Figure 8.5). Similarly a purchase is typically made of a package of sites, rather than a series of one-offs.

Posters can be much more effectively targeted than many people believe. The introduction of the OSCAR (Outdoor Site Classification and Audience Research) system in the UK enables

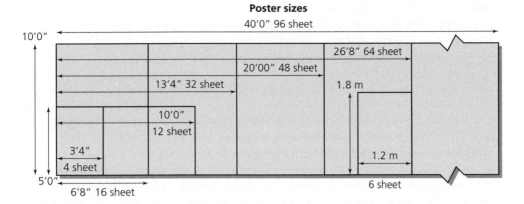

Figure 8.5 Poster advertising sheet specification

Source: © 2004 The Media Pocket Book, World Advertising Research Center, www.warc.com

advertisers to select those sites likely to be most effective at reaching their target audience. Locations can be selected on the basis of key demographic variables and targeting greatly enhanced as a result.

The key disadvantages of outdoor advertising are the long lead times. Many sites are booked up months or even years in advance, particularly if the site is one of the increasing number of three-dimensional displays, which tend to command a greater degree of attention. There are, of course, many other, often very creative, forms of outdoor advertising. One can book advertising space on the sides of most forms of transport, hire balloons, airships, or even, as the Devon Wildlife Trust did, create a six-foot replica of a dodo and 'release' it into the wild!

Electronic

There has been a proliferation in the availability of other electronic media over the past 20 years. Aside from the fragmentation of the television industry and the growth in Web TV, advertising space can also now be bought on Internet sites and text messages sent to a variety of different users in a range of specific locations or contexts.

EXAMPLE

The UK's National Health Service (NHS) recently sought commercial sponsorship for a text message reminder service. The initiative was designed to save the NHS over £400 million through missed appointments with doctors and specialists each year. The NHS initially worked in partnership with milk drink brand Yakult and five other commercial organizations. The NHS Trusts who piloted the scheme encouraged out-patients to register their mobile phone numbers to take part in the service. Thirty NHS Trusts, representing 20 per cent of the NHS, adopted the service in its first year.

Schedule

To ensure that all the communications activities undertaken are fully integrated, it would be usual to specify the exact timings of each on a Gantt chart (see Chapter 7) which can then be utilized by those responsible for the campaign to ensure that not only does each activity commence on the prescribed date, but that opportunities for synergy are fully exploited. Thus, for example, if it is intended to run a brief television campaign, outdoor and radio advertising can be implemented as a follow-up in subsequent months to ensure that enhanced levels of awareness of the social idea are maintained cost-effectively for as long as possible in the minds of the target market.

It is also important to note that the original objectives for the campaign can impact on the schedule that it is intended to follow. Campaigns which are ground-breaking and designed to raise awareness of a totally new concept may thus require promotional effort to be concentrated in a major initial burst, to expose as many members of the target audience to the social ideas as early as possible. This can then be supported with periodic reminders at various points throughout the year. If, on the other hand, the campaign is designed merely to extend and develop an idea already established in the minds of the targets, the need for an expensive initial burst is likely to be greatly reduced. In such circumstances it is rather more likely that the promotional budget will be evenly allocated across the whole duration of the campaign, allowing a gradual infusion of learning to take place.

EXAMPLE

The Like Minds campaign in New Zealand was designed to improve the public's understanding and acceptance of mental illness and to counter negative stereotypes of people suffering with such a condition. Initial research identified that European, Maori, and Pacific Island views on mental health differed. A segmented approach to the campaign was therefore deemed necessary to reflect the attitudes of each key audience. The campaign was run in the native language of each community and featured personalities well known to each audience. The communications did however contain a common strapline, namely, 'One in five New Zealanders will be affected by mental illness. How much they suffer depends on you.' The campaign was timed to coincide with the launch of *A Beautiful Mind*—a film portraying Professor John Nash's struggle with schizophrenia. Post-campaign research showed a significant increase in agreement that 'People who've had a mental illness can still lead a normal life' (increased 7 per cent to 87 per cent); and 'I am feeling more accepting of people with mental illness' (up 5 per cent to 80 per cent).

Budget

As in the case of the marketing plan referred to in Chapter 7, it would be usual in a communications plan to specify the overall budget and the manner in which it will be allocated across the various activities to be undertaken. Variances between proposed and actual expenditure can then be easily monitored and, where necessary, corrective action initiated.

Evaluation and Control

There are four types of evaluation which would typically be undertaken in a social marketing context. These are:

1. *Formative evaluation.* This form of evaluation is undertaken to pre-test the materials that will be used during the campaign. This would typically include the copy, design, and layout of any advertising, together with an assessment of the effectiveness of any sales promotion techniques that it is intended to use.

2. *Process evaluation.* The process of implementation will also be subject to review. Each stage of the communication plan will be evaluated to ensure that the campaign objectives will be achieved and that appropriate messages have been received and understood by members of the target market.

3. *Outcome evaluation.* This typically consists of a detailed analysis of whether or not the desired change in behaviour has been facilitated. Of course, there are many variables that could be examined for the purpose of outcome evaluation. These include:

- the number and form of requests for information;
- the source of requests for information—the profile of respondents;
- the awareness, recall, and acceptance of the campaign messages; changes in attitude may also be measured;
- the extent to which the target market has been exposed to the message—the coverage achieved by the campaign;
- the nature and extent of behavioural change achieved within the target segment.

4. *Impact evaluation.* It may be impossible to measure the impact of a social marketing campaign in the short term. The campaign could be concerned with changing societal behaviours, which would only impact on society in the longer term. Thus, while one would obviously be concerned with the immediate impact on behaviour achieved by a campaign, it may also be necessary to track those behaviours over time to ensure that they are sustained. Some social marketers may even attempt to evaluate the benefits that have accrued to society as a result of the behavioural changes achieved. It is worth noting that such forms of evaluation are seldom used for communication programmes alone because the costs of conducting this form of research are formidable.

Control procedures are usually set up to monitor each stage of the campaign. The overall objectives would usually be broken down to derive a set of targets for each month (or aspect) of the campaign to achieve. Any deviance from these interim targets would be recorded and, if significant variations have occurred, corrective action may be implemented to ensure that the campaign objectives are met in full. Typically around five to ten per cent of the communications budget would be set aside to allow for such contingencies.

■ **CASE STUDY**

PROMOTING THE IUD IN NEPAL

By Sheena Leek, Birmingham Business School, University of Birmingham, and Sally Kidsley, Ella Gordon Unit, Portsmouth

INTRODUCTION

The Nepalese government and other non-governmental organizations (NGOs) including Sunaulo Parivar Nepal (Marie Stopes International (MSI) partner) and the Family Planning Association of Nepal (FPAN) wanted to create a sustainable family planning campaign. In order to achieve this they tested a multimedia campaign entailing posters, an infomercial, and female community health volunteers (FCHV) to promote the use of the intra-uterine device (IUD).

THE OBJECTIVES OF PROMOTING USE OF THE IUD IN NEPAL

In Nepal contraception is only used by 39.3% of the whole reproductive population. The most common method of contraception is sterilization, used by 21.3% of the reproductive population. Female sterilization is more common (15.0%) than male sterilization (6.3%). Depo-provera—a three-monthly injection—is the second most common method of contraception, used by 24.0% of women who use contraception (Ministry of Health Nepal 2002).

The government and other NGOs wanted to increase the use of contraception but wished this to be achieved in a sustainable manner as funding from international donors to NGOs such as MSI is decreasing. Depo-provera is one of the least cost-effective methods of contraception as it requires relatively expensive injections every three months. By contrast, although the costs of sterilization are high, it is permanent and over a person's reproductive lifespan it becomes cost-effective. However, sterilization has two major disadvantages: it is a major operation for women which entails a degree of risk and it is a permanent form of contraception that the patient may regret, i.e. they may want children after the operation.

The IUD is a cost-effective method of contraception which is why the Nepalese government and NGOs are promoting it. Insertion of the IUD is a less costly procedure than sterilization but it may need to be replaced three times over a woman's reproductive lifespan so the overall cost of the IUD is roughly equivalent to sterilization. Nevertheless, the IUD is beneficial to the user in that it does not involve the risks of a surgical procedure and it is reversible.

THE PROMOTIONAL CAMPAIGN

The promotional campaign developed to promote the IUD aimed to increase uptake of IUD among Nepalese women. The level of awareness was low with only 56.5% of people being aware of the IUD, in comparison to over 90% of the population being aware of sterilization, the pill, injections, and condoms (Demographic Health and Surveys 2004). The promotional campaign was intended to provide accurate information emphasizing the benefits of the IUD. It would also dispel myths that discourage use of the IUD, including the belief that the IUD can make women weak and dizzy, leave the uterus and pierce the heart, cause cancer, and spear the man's penis during sexual intercourse.

Nepal is a patriarchal society, therefore a husband and his parents' opinions are of paramount importance when making a decision. If they believe any myths surrounding the use of the IUD they may apply pressure not to use it. The promotional campaign therefore aimed to educate not just the women of reproductive age but also men (Parker Lessig and Whan Park 2001).

To assess the initial campaign and inform future strategy, data was collected from all ten of the MSI clinics. There were three test clinics—one in each area where the promotional campaign was executed. As multimedia campaigns have been found to reinforce one another and facilitate learning, the promotional campaign consisted of three communication methods: a poster campaign, a radio infomercial, and FCHV (Keller 2001, Kliatchko 2005).

Posters. The posters were in colour and had a close-up of a Nepalese woman's face. On the poster were positive messages about the IUD which were: one-time use for 12 years, no need for operation, reliable, easily removed, no hormonal effects, no need to remember daily pills or three-monthly injections. It also contained information about where the IUD could be obtained in the respondents' area. Five thousand posters were divided equally amongst the test areas and placed indefinitely in areas such as village centres and bazaars.

Radio infomercial. This was a 60-second sketch highlighting the positive aspects of the IUD. The issues mentioned were the same as those highlighted by the poster. It was also used to dispel the myths surrounding the use of the IUD. This was broadcast daily on a national radio station, Radio Nepal, at 5.00pm for three months, April–June 2002. Five o'clock was deemed an appropriate time as it was thought that the target audience would be at home and able to attend to the message.

Female community health volunteers. These are local women employed by the family planning and reproductive health clinics. The FCHV were unfamiliar with the IUD so they were given an intensive two-day course; this ensured they were equipped with the correct knowledge which they could then impart to potential users. One female volunteer worked in each of the three areas. They worked independently, talking to women in their own village and neighbouring villages.

On entering one of the test clinics to be fitted with an IUD the women were asked what referral method brought them to the clinic.

EVALUATION OF THE CAMPAIGN AND THE LESSONS LEARNED

The promotional campaign did increase the number of women taking up the IUD (see Figure 8.6). However, the effect of the campaign was short-lived with IUD uptake declining rapidly at the end of the promotional campaign. These results suggest that the campaign needs to be continued for a longer period of time in order to make the contraceptive service sustainable.

The FCHV was found to be the most common method of referral (see Table 8.3) for a number of reasons. She is perceived as being a family planning expert and therefore a reliable and trustworthy source of information. The FCHV can convey the information about the IUD to the women in their own language, in a clear, comprehensible manner and simultaneously dispel any myths. Being local, the FCHV may be trusted more than an outsider. The FCHV have an advantage over the radio infomercial and posters as they enable two-way communication; the women are able to ask the FCHV questions to clarify any concerns they may have. Health

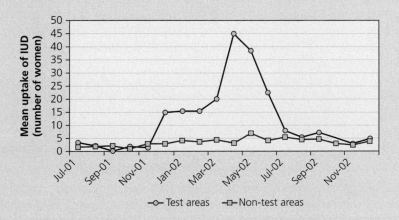

Figure 8.6 Mean uptake of the IUD in the test and non-test areas

Table 8.3 Methods of referral stated by women taking up the IUD

Method of referral	Overall % (n)
FCHV	48.2% (160)
Radio	21.4% (71)
Poster	2.1% (7)
Family or friends	9.9% (33)
Health professionals	16.6% (55)
Other	1.8% (6)

professionals have similar advantages to the FCHV but the women may be less likely to come into contact with them as they are likely to be infrequent visitors to clinics.

The radio infomercial was a popular referral method as it had a broad reach and overcame any literacy problems, unlike the poster. It conveyed a greater amount of information than the poster and attempted to dispel the myths. It was vital that the appropriate broadcast time was identified so that the infomercial was broadcast at a time when the target audience, i.e. women and men of a reproductive age, would be listening to the radio.

Posters were the least effective method of communication which could be due to a number of reasons. Literacy levels in Nepal are relatively low with only 62.7% of men and 27.6% of women aged 15 and over being able to read and write (www.cia.gov/ciapublications/factbook/fields/2103.html 2005). Posters therefore are not reaching a large proportion of the population. Information on the IUD may be conveyed to women through their husbands who are more likely to be able to read it. Posters may also be an uncommon method of referral due to the literate women not receiving enough exposure to them. The posters may also not have conveyed enough information to convince women to use the IUD.

Family and friends are quite an important source of referral. After being exposed to the promotional campaign, family and friends will have obtained knowledge about the benefits of the IUD and may recommend its uptake. The fact that Nepal is a patriarchal society, combined with the fact the men are more literate, means they may play an important role in conveying contraceptive information, so it is important that they are convinced of the benefits of the IUD so they encourage their wives to use it.

Post-campaign IUD uptake was higher in the test areas than the non-test areas. Women may absorb the information and use it at a later date when they decide to change their method of contraception. Word of mouth may also be occurring; both women and men who have had a positive experience using the IUD will pass this information on to family and friends who will use it when considering their contraceptive options. Word of mouth is an important method of referral as it is perceived to be credible and reliable (Edgett and Parkinson 1993).

CONCLUSIONS

The multimedia campaign succeeded in increasing uptake of the IUD but it clearly needs to be sustained in order to further increase uptake of the IUD. Although the FCHVs were the most popular method of referral, it cannot be said that the infomercial and posters did not have an effect. A multimedia approach is essential for ensuring the message is reaching the target audience and reinforcing the message (Babalola et al. 2001). Word-of-mouth communication has also been found to have a significant impact on people's response to an advertising campaign and may continue to influence the uptake of the IUD once it has finished.

REFERENCES

Babalola, S., Vondrasek, C., Brown, J. and Traore, R. (2001) 'The Impact of a Regional Family Planning Service Promotion Initiative in Sub-Saharan Africa: Evidence from Cameroon', *International Family Planning Perspectives,* Vol. 27, No. 2, 186–193, 216.

Demographic and Health Surveys (2004) www.measuredhs.com

Edgett, S. and Parkinson, S. (1993) 'Marketing for Service Industries—A Review', *The Service Industries Journal,* Vol. 13, No. 3, 19–39.

Keller, K.L. (2001) 'Mastering the Marketing Communications Mix: Micro and Macro Perspectives on Integrated Marketing Communication Programs', *Journal of Marketing Management,* Vol. 17, No. 7/8, 819–847.

Kliatchko, J. (2005) 'Towards a New Definition of Integrated Marketing Communications (IMC)', *International Journal of Advertising,* Vol. 24, No. 1, 7–34.

Ministry of Health [Nepal], New ERA and ORC Macro. (2002) *Nepal Demographic and Health Survey 2001,* Family Health Division, Ministry of Health; New ERA and ORC Macro, Calverton, Maryland, USA.

Parker Lessig, V. and Whan Park, C. (2001) 'Promotional Perspectives of Reference Group Influence: Advertising Implications', *Journal of Advertising,* Vol. 7, No. 2, 41–47.

QUESTIONS

1. In your role as a consultant to MSI and FPAN design a follow-up campaign to continue to promote the use of the IUD.

2. What methods of campaign evaluation would you recommend these organizations employ?

3. How would you characterize the campaign described in the case study? Is this a social marketing campaign, or is it one of the alternatives described in this chapter? Justify your answer.

■ SUMMARY

In this chapter we have defined social marketing as the marketing of ideas with the specific intent of influencing social behaviours. It is this latter dimension which distinguishes the concept from mere education or lobbying activities. The relevance of social marketing to various social domains was established, including efforts to alter forms of sexual, smoking, drug/alcohol abuse, pollution, and recycling behaviours. In each case social marketers have no concrete product or service which they can 'sell' to a target market—they have only an idea which, if accepted by the selected segments, could impact favourably on the whole of society. Of course, one's perception of what would be a favourable outcome will differ from individual to individual and there are thus strong ethical dimensions to any social marketing campaign.

A number of factors were introduced that have been found to affect the extent to which it is possible to influence behaviour, namely whether the behaviour is high or low involvement, whether the behaviour is one-off or continuing, and whether the behaviour is exhibited by groups or individuals. Continuing behaviours exhibited by groups were introduced as being the most difficult to alter, largely because group dynamics serve to legitimize and support antisocial behaviours which may otherwise be discarded.

This chapter introduced the concept of a social marketing mix which could assist in changing these behaviours, adding two additional 'Ps' to the traditional 'four-P' mix, namely partnerships and policy. These additional elements together allow the social marketer to recognize the desirability for many organizations of forging links with others in order to exert greater influence over their target market. They also acknowledge what is often a final necessity—convincing governments to instigate legislative change, when less forceful attempts at persuasion have failed.

The chapter concluded with a review of the contents of a typical communications plan and the key considerations which must be borne in mind by a social marketer as each stage is developed. A surprising amount of research has been conducted into issues such as the suitability of various forms of emotional appeals, message order effects, and the manner in which information is presented. Only by taking account of such research can social marketers ensure that they benefit from knowledge gained through past failures and ensure that their particular campaign is as effective and efficient as possible.

■ DISCUSSION QUESTIONS

1. To what extent does the element of persuasion inherent in a social marketing campaign conflict with the marketing philosophy of satisfying customer requirements?

2. Distinguish social marketing from the processes of social communication, education, and lobbying.

3. What primary data would you advise a social marketing organization to gather in an attempt to inform the design of a campaign intended to reduce levels of teenage smoking? How might this data be gathered?

4. You are a consultant employed by the communications manager of Waste Concern, an organization whose primary aim is to encourage households to recycle as much of their domestic waste as possible. How could this organization proceed to segment the 'market' for its communications? For each segment you identify, design appropriate communications messages and specify the media that you would recommend the organization to utilize to deliver them.

5. Design a marketing communications plan for your own social marketing organization, or one with which you are familiar.

■ REFERENCES

Andreasen, A.R. (1993) Presidential Address: 'A Social Marketing Research Agenda For Consumer Behavior Researchers' in *Advances in Consumer Research*, Vol. 20, ed. Rothschild, M. and McAlister, L., Association for Consumer Research, Provo UT.

Andreasen, A.R. (2003) 'The Life Trajectory of Social Marketing: Some Implications', *Marketing Theory*, Vol. 3, No. 3, 293–303.

Andreasen, A.R. (2006) 'Issues and Social Marketing' E-mail note sent to soc-mktg@listproc. georgetown.edu (a list for social marketers) on 03/17/06.

Andreasen, A. and Kotler, P. (2003) *Strategic Marketing for Nonprofit Organizations* (6th edn), Prentice Hall, Upper Saddle River, NJ.

Binney, W., Hall, J. and Shaw, M. (2003) 'A Further Development in Social Marketing: Application of the MOA Framework and Behavioural Implications', *Marketing Theory,* Vol. 3, No. 3, 387–403.

Blumberg, S.J. (2000) 'Guarding Against Threatening HIV Prevention Messages: An Information Processing Model', *Health Education and Behavior*, Vol. 27, 780–95.

Braus, P. (1995) 'Selling Good Behavior', *American Demographics*, Nov, 60–4.

Byrne, A., Dickson, L., Derevensky, J., Gupta, R. and Lussier, I. (2005) 'An Examination of Social Marketing Campaigns for the Prevention of Youth Problem Gambling', *Journal of Health Communication,* Vol. 10, 681–700.

Colley, R. (1961) *Defining Advertising Goals for Measured Advertising Results*, New York, Association of National Advertisers.

Dann, S. (2006) 'Reaffirming the Neutrality of the Social Marketing Tool Kit: Social Marketing as a Hammer, and Social Marketers as Hired Guns', *Social Marketing Quarterly*, Vol. 8, No. 1, 54–60.

Department of Health (2004) *Choosing Health: Making Healthier Choices Easier*, Public Health White Paper, Series No. Cm 6374, The Stationery Office, London.

Devlin, E., Eadie, D., Hastings, G. and Anderson, S. (2002) *Labelling of Tobacco Products in Europe: Results from the UK.* Report prepared for the European Commission, Cancer Research UK Centre for Tobacco Control Research, University of Strathclyde, Glasgow, Scotland.

Dresler-Hawke, E. and Veer, E. (2006) 'Making Healthy Eating Messages More Effective: Combining Integrated Marketing Communication With The Behaviour Ecological Model', *International Journal of Consumer Studies*, Vol. 30, No. 4, 318–26.

Eadie, D.R. and Stead, M. (1998) 'Developing the Foolsspeed 40" Commercial – Main Findings', Centre for Social Marketing, Strathclyde University, Glasgow.

Fill, C. (1995) *Marketing Communications*, Hemel Hempstead, Prentice Hall.

Fox, K.A. and Kotler, P. (1980) 'The Marketing of Social Causes: The First 10 Years', *Journal of Marketing*, Vol. 44, No. 3, 24–33.

French, J. and Blair-Stevens, C. (2005) *Social Marketing: A Pocket Guide*, London: National Consumer Council.

Fry, T.R. (1996) 'Advertising Wearout in the Transport Accident Commission Road Safety Campaigns', *Accident Analysis and Prevention*, Vol. 28, 123–29.

Girandola, F. (2000) 'Fear and Persuasion: Review and Re-Review of the Literature (1953–1998)', *Annee Psychologique*, Vol. 100, No. 2, 333–76.

Gordon, R., McDermott, L., Stead, M. and Angus, K. (2006) 'The Effectiveness of Social Marketing Interventions for Health Improvement: What's The Evidence?', *Public Health*, Vol. 120, No. 12, 1133–39.

Guion, D.T., Scammon, D.L. and Borders, A.L. (2007) 'Weathering the Storm: A Social Marketing Perspective on Disaster Preparedness and Response with Lessons from Hurricane Katrina', *Journal of Public Policy and Marketing*, Vol. 26, No. 1, 20–32.

Hastings, G., Stead, M., McDermott, L. (2003) *Review of Research on the Effects of Food Promotion to Children,* London: Food Standards Agency, Online. Available at http://www.food.gov.uk/ news/pressreleases/foodtochildren.

Hirschman, E.C. and Holbrook, M.B. (1982) 'Hedonic Consumption: Emerging Concepts, Methods and Propositions', *Journal of Marketing*, Vol. 46, 92–101.

Hovland, C.I. and Mandell, W. (1952) 'An Empirical Comparison of Conclusion Drawing by the Communicator and the Audience', *Journal of Abnormal and Social Psychology*, Vol. 47 (July), 581–8.

Kapferer, J.N. and Laurent, G. (1985) 'Consumer Involvement Profiles: A New Practical Approach To Consumer Involvement', *Journal of Advertising Research*, Vol. 25, No. 6, 48–56.

Keller, K.L. (2001) 'Mastering the Marketing Communications Mix: Micro and Macro Perspectives on Integrated Marketing Communication Programs', *Journal of Marketing Management*, Vol. 17, No. 7/8, 819–847.

Kotler, P. and Andreasen, A. (1991) *Strategic Marketing Management For Nonprofit Organizations*, Englewood Cliffs, NJ, Prentice Hall.

Kotler, P. and Roberto, E.L. (2001) *Social Marketing: How To Create, Win and Dominate Markets*, New York, Free Press.

Kotler, P. and Zaltman, G. (1971) 'Social Marketing: An Approach to Planned Social Change', *Journal of Marketing*, Vol. 35, No. 2, 3–12.

Kotler, P., Roberto, E.L. and Lee, N. (2002) *Social Marketing: Improving The Quality of Life*, Sage Publications.

Lefebvre, R.C. (1996) '25 Years of Social Marketing: Looking Back to the Future', *Social Marketing Quarterly*, Special Issue: 51–8.

MacFadyen, L., Hastings, G.B. and MacKintosh, A.M. (2001) 'Cross Sectional Study of Young People's Awareness of and Involvement With Tobacco Marketing', *British Medical Journal*, 322 (3 March): 513–17.

Maheswaran, D. and Meyers-Levy, J. (1990) 'The Influences of Message Framing and Issue Involvement', *Journal of Marketing Research*, Vol. 27 (Aug), 361–7.

Marcell, K., Agyeman, J. and Rapport, A. (2004) 'Cooling the Campus', *International Journal of Sustainability in Higher Education*, Vol. 5, No. 2, 169–89.

McDermott, L., Eadie, D., Peattie, K., Peattie, S., Hastings, G. and Anderson, S. (2004) 'Domestic Composting: Challenges and Opportunities for Social Marketing', *Academy of Marketing Conference*, Gloucester, UK.

McKenzie-Mohr, D. (1994) 'Social Marketing for Sustainability: The Case for Residential Energy Conservation', *Futures*, March, 224–33.

Ratchford, B. (1987) 'New Insights about the FCB Grid', *Journal of Advertising Research*, Aug/Sept, 24–38.

Reynolds, F.D. and Darden, W.R. (1971) 'Mutually Adaptable Effects of Interpersonal Communication', *Journal of Marketing Research*, Vol. 8 (Nov.), 449–54.

Rothschild, M. (1999) 'Carrots, Sticks and Promises: A Conceptual Framework for the Management of Public Health and Social Issue Behaviors', *Journal of Marketing*, Vol. 63, No. 4, 24–37.

Ruiter, R.A.C., Abraham, C. and Kok, G. (2001) 'Scary Warnings and Rational Precautions: A Review of the Psychology of Fear Appeals', *Psychology and Health*, Vol. 16, 613–30.

Sawyer, A.G. and Howard, D.J. (1991) 'Effects of Omitting Conclusions in Advertisements to Involved and Uninvolved Audiences', *Journal of Marketing Research*, Vol. 28 (Nov), 464–74.

Schellstede, W. (1986) 'Social Marketing of Contraceptives', *Draper Fund Report*, December, 21–6.

Shrum, L.J., Lowrey, T.M. and McCarty, J.A. (1994) 'Recycling as a Marketing Problem: A Framework for Strategy Development', *Psychology and Marketing*, Vol. 11, No. 4, 393–416.

Sihombing, B. (1994) *Overview of the Indonesian Family Planning Movement: The Blue Circle and Gold Circle Social Marketing Policies*, Jakarta, National Family Planning Coordinating Board.

Stead, M. and Eadie, D.R. (2000) 'Developing the Foolsspeed Phase 2 Commercial – Main Findings', Centre for Social Marketing, Strathclyde University, Glasgow.

Weinberger, M.G. and Gulas, C.S. (1992) 'The Impact of Humor in Advertising', *Journal of Advertising*, Vol. 21, No. 4, 35–59.

Weinreich, N.K. (1999) *Hands on Social Marketing: A Step by Step Guide*, Thousand Oaks, CA, Sage.

Witte, K. and Allen, M. (2000) 'A Meta Analysis of Fear Appeals: Implications for Effective Public Health Campaigns', *Heath Education and Behavior*, Vol. 27, 591–615.

Wright, C. and Egan, J. (2000) 'De-marketing the Car', *Transport Policy*, Vol. 7, No. 4, 287–94.

9 Fundraising

OBJECTIVES

By the end of this chapter you should be able to:

1. develop, plan, and implement a plan for individual donor recruitment;
2. develop, plan, and implement a plan for individual donor development;
3. develop, plan, and implement corporate fundraising activity;
4. develop, plan, and implement grant fundraising activity.

Introduction

The fundamental components of the marketing plan introduced in Chapter 3, namely the marketing audit, marketing objectives, strategies, and tactics, are all of equal relevance to the task of planning the activities that will be undertaken to raise funds for an organization. There is still a need for a comprehensive audit and the thoughtful derivation of fundraising objectives in the light of the information obtained.

Fundraisers will also wish to consider the overall strategies they wish to pursue to raise the level of funds indicated in the objectives. This will undoubtedly involve apportioning effort between the various types of funder and, within these groups, the specific segments that will be addressed. The positioning of the organization within each segment will also warrant consideration at the strategic stage of the plan since it will be important to define clearly the values and imagery that the organization wishes to convey. It should also be made clear how these might differ from those of potential competitors for funds.

At a tactical level, the fine detail of exactly how the objectives will be achieved is provided. Typically this will be structured using headings that reflect each target audience (e.g. individuals, corporates, or grant-making bodies). A separate tactical mix will then be delineated for each of these targets. To complicate matters a little, it is normal for a nonprofit to draw a distinction between donor recruitment and donor development activity. In the case of the former, the aim of the marketing is to attract new donors into the organization for the first time, while in the case of the latter the aim is to retain and develop these donors over time. The structure proposed for a fundraising plan is summarized in Figure 9.1.

Since many of these issues have already been explored in preceding chapters, it is intended here to concentrate solely on the tactical aspects of fundraising, looking in particular at three

Fundraising audit
SWOT analysis
Fundraising objectives
Fundraising strategies
Fundraising tactics
(a) *Individual giving*
    (i) Donor recruitment activity
        Tactical marketing mix
    (ii) Donor development activity
        Tactical marketing mix
(b) *Corporate giving*
    Tactical marketing mix
(c) *Trust/foundation giving*
    Tactical marketing mix
Budget
Schedule
Monitoring and control

Figure 9.1 Structure of a fundraising plan

target audiences: individuals, corporates, and grant-making organizations such as trusts and foundations. We begin, however, by considering a concept of key strategic importance in fundraising, namely the case for support.

Case for Support

In fundraising a key strategic consideration is the case for support. This is the formal expression of the cause and why it warrants support. It has to be well articulated and capable of being thoroughly understood by all a nonprofit's donors. It typically communicates:

- mission and values
- importance and urgency
- specific objectives
- history and credibility
- what would happen if the organization failed
- how the donor can help.

As Ted Bayley notes, the case for fundraising 'should aim high, provide perspective, arouse a sense of history and continuity, convey a feeling of importance, relevance, and urgency, and have whatever stuff is needed to warm the heart and stir the mind' (Bayley 1987: 22).

The case for support for the Open University is depicted on the next page.

Typically organizations write an organizational case for support and then tailor this to match the needs of specific segments of funders, specific campaigns, or even individual donors if major gifts are being solicited. These tailored versions of the case are known as case statements. Many major gift fundraisers write a separate case statement for every one of their contacts. At the very least an organization is likely to have a separate statement for individuals, corporates, and grant makers (Seiler 2001).

The Open University (OU) is an extraordinary university with an extraordinary history. It changed the face of British education and led the way in the world for open and distance learning. To date it has over two million alumni and now has a student population of over two hundred thousand.

The OU is recognised for its abilities and achievements in many areas. Our research is at the leading-edge in a range of disciplines ranging from art and design to planetary science. We are immensely proud of being recently awarded the highest mark in the UK in the National Student Survey of students' university experience, scoring 4.5 out of a possible 5.

We believe in the power of higher education to promote economic development, transform society and improve the quality of life for all citizens.

We also believe that unless lifelong learning is made available to more of the world's population, the human and economic benefits of rapid communications and global markets will remain limited to the few.

Our vision is to provide high-quality university education to all who wish to realise their ambitions and fulfil their potential. We have the experience, the expertise and the will to do it. Now, we need your support.

Fundraising from Individual Donors

Nonprofits engage in a variety of forms of marketing to raise funds from individual donors. The major categories are:

1. *Direct marketing:* employing media such as the Internet, direct mail, or direct dialogue fundraising (where individuals are asked for a donation on the High Street or at an event).

2. *Community fundraising:* a blanket term for fundraising, as the name suggests, that takes place in a local community. It may include local events, street collections, jumble sales, tea/coffee mornings, schools fundraising, and house-to-house collection of cash.

3. *Fundraising events:* many nonprofits run annual events, or a rolling programme of event activities to promote the cause. They can be as diverse as formal dinners, galas, fun-runs, and sponsored events.

4. *Payroll giving:* some nonprofits use specialist agencies or their own volunteers to recruit employees to give through their payroll in the workplace. It has been shown to be an effective way of approaching individuals who would not typically respond to other forms of fundraising. The operation of the scheme is depicted in Figure 9.2.

5. *Major gift fundraising:* it is increasingly common for nonprofits to solicit funds from wealthy individuals with the capacity to support the organization at a high level. While the definition of what constitutes a major gift varies considerably from one nonprofit to another, solicitation is generally undertaken on a one-to-one basis, with either the fundraiser, or more usually a senior member of staff or trustee making the solicitation. Major gifts are cultivated over extended periods of time and successful organizations take great care in developing and retaining these relationships.

6. *Legacy fundraising:* legacies (i.e. gifts offered in a last will and testament) are a significant source of income for many nonprofits and offer a significant opportunity for future growth. While over 80% of us will give in our lifetime to a favoured cause, fewer than 10% of us currently offer a donation in our will (Farthing 2007).

OPERATION OF PAYROLL GIVING IN THE UK

Once an employee has notified the employer of his/her intention to donate through payroll, the employer then makes the deduction and passes the donation to an 'agency charity' (which must be approved by the Inland Revenue). The agency charity collects the donation and passes it to the recipient nonprofit. In return for a 5% commission these agency charities typically assist an employer in creating a scheme, encourage internal promotion of the scheme, and provide information and statistics in respect of how the scheme is progressing. The agency system is also helpful as it makes it possible for employees to give to any charity of their choice. The cost for employers to provide this service directly would be prohibitive.

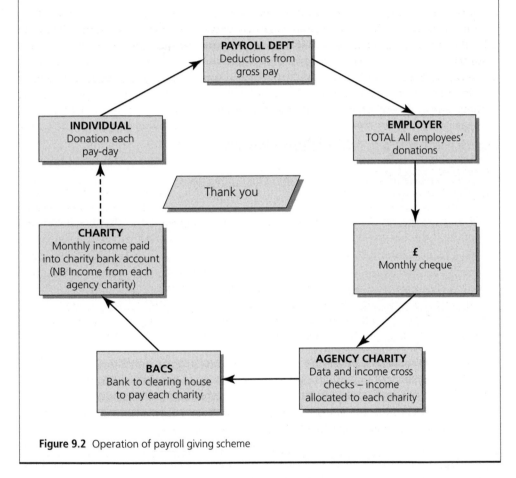

Figure 9.2 Operation of payroll giving scheme

In the course of one brief chapter it would be impossible to do justice to the full range of fundraising activities and techniques. Instead we focus on donor relationships and look first at the primary recruitment methods employed by nonprofits, before moving on to consider how to develop these relationships over time.

Donor Recruitment

It is widely accepted in fundraising, as in commercial marketing activity, that it costs five times as much to conduct business with a new customer than an existing one. Whilst fundraisers can expect to generate a return on investment (ROI) of up to 5:1 from a campaign targeting existing (warm) donors, acquisition campaigns are more likely to require an invest-ment, or at the very best achieve break even, than to generate a positive return.

New donor acquisition efforts usually cost 75 to 150 percent of what they raise. The reality is that this has been the practice for decades. Many of the most prestigious and successful charities have developed very efficient multimillion-dollar appeals and major donor programs with donors orig-inally acquired at 100 percent fund-raising costs (Center on Philanthropy 1999).

In terms of the balance of fundraising resource, it makes sense to target the majority of the resources available at those donors that will generate the highest levels of profitability. Typi-cally, therefore, donor retention and development activity will account for 70–80 per cent of a fundraising budget. However, there will always be a need to recruit new donors to every organization. Even if relationships are excellent and levels of satisfaction high, some donors will terminate their relationship as interests and financial circumstances change, or they die or move away. Donor recruitment also provides an opportunity to refresh a database, as in-dividuals often give most generously and demonstrate most enthusiasm for a cause during the 'honeymoon' period of their relationship with a nonprofit.

Recruitment Objectives

In donor recruitment the most common simple target set by fundraising managers is the re-cruitment of X new donors for Y cost, with overall levels of expenditure and investment set in accordance with a requirement to grow or to maintain the total size of the organization's individual donor database.

More valuable and thoughtful objectives and targets involve the consideration of the qual-ity as well as the quantity of the donors to be gained, and are further broken down by seg-ment and activity. Many organizations now recognize the long-term value of recruitment directly onto a regular gift, so additional objectives may involve the percentage of regular versus one-off givers to be acquired. This distinction between regular and cash givers is important, particularly in the UK where each group may be defined as follows:

- one-off or cash givers—individuals who do not commit to a regular gift, but who will typically respond to one or more direct mail appeals in a given year, by sending through a cheque;

- regular or committed givers—who sign up from the outset to give a regular monthly (or yearly) donation, direct from their bank account or credit card.

The economics of dealing with each group are quite different and separate objectives should therefore be derived.

It is also essential that the objectives set for donor recruitment are tied in to those set for the subsequent development of the donors. Many organizations make the mistake of view-ing acquisition and development as separate entities, working to separate, unrelated, and sometimes opposing targets. Over time this can cause huge problems if the donors recruited are found subsequently to be unprofitable or problematic: they may be unresponsive, exhibit high attrition rates, or require a different programme of communication from the rest of the database in order to continue giving. For example, many UK nonprofits have had great success in recent years in recruiting new donors with requests for a small regular monthly gift. These recruits tend to be much younger than the 'traditional' donor and to have very different lifestyles. Whilst this can be seen as a success for the recruitment manager, these donors often prove difficult to retain and develop subsequently as they do not respond to direct mail, and prefer communication through alternative routes such as email and text messaging—media which many nonprofits have not yet fully developed. The recruitment of younger donors is also likely in the longer term to work against the efforts of fundraisers promoting legacy giving. It is thus essential that recruitment and development targets are complementary and that planning for both is undertaken as a holistic exercise.

Donor Segmentation

Having delineated recruitment objectives, the next stage is to determine which potential donors (or prospects) will be targeted. As we noted in Chapter 5 there are two approaches, the appropriateness of which will be determined by the extent to which an organization has prior knowledge of its markets. An a priori approach is based on the notion that fundraisers decide in advance of any research which categories of individual (perhaps by demographics or lifestyle) they intend to target. The fundraiser would then carry out market research to determine the attractiveness of each segment and make a decision on the basis of the results as to which target audience to pursue. Post hoc segmentation by contrast involves the fundraiser in carrying out an amount of initial research into the market. The research might highlight attributes, attitudes, or benefits that relate to particular groups of donors. This information can often be obtained by profiling discrete groups of donors on the database (e.g. cash givers or regular givers). If a certain type of individual emerges as 'typical' this information can be used to refine the criteria for list selection and other similar individuals can be targeted.

Donor Profiling

To inform the choice of segments to be targeted, those organizations who already hold a database of donors have a distinct advantage. Such organizations can profile their existing database to identify whether specific types of people seem to be:

- giving higher sums;
- giving in certain ways;
- responding to different media;
- responding to certain types of message.

This profile can then be used in the selection of prospects—in other words list and media selection can be undertaken to ensure that individuals who match the profile of the required category of givers are targeted with appropriate recruitment messages. At its best, profiling can serve to bring audiences to life by painting pictures of their main differentiating characteristics thereby suggesting fundraising messages they are likely to find appealing.

In some instances this simple replication of the current donor profile may not be desirable, in which case the same techniques can be used instead to define a picture of alternative target audiences. If one of the objectives of a recruitment campaign is, for example, to recruit younger regular givers to supplement a database comprised of older cash donors, a supplemental profile of the new target audience will have to be generated. Equally, higher value donors or those who have pledged a legacy may be profiled as a separate group if it is feasible to conduct a recruitment campaign to enlist high-value givers, perhaps through the promotion of a high-value 'product' such as a child sponsorship package.

Donor Targeting

Having developed a detailed prospect profile, the information can be used to tailor the nature of the communication to be received and to make decisions on the channel or channels through which it will most effectively be communicated. A picture of the individuals a nonprofit is attempting to reach, even in outline or aggregate form, is an enormous advantage in designing recruitment materials, in deciding where such individuals are most likely to be reached, and what media and approach they are most likely to respond to. Targeting is the single most important consideration in recruitment campaigns. No matter how strong the creative treatment, if it does not reach the right people the campaign will fail. It is generally accepted in nonprofit as in commercial direct marketing that the list is six times more important than the creative in the success of any campaign.

In seeking to recruit new donors as cost-effectively as possible it makes sense to start by gathering prospect data from within the organization rather than embarking on the purchase of cold lists or other broadscale media immediately. Whilst it may prove difficult to obtain the names of service users, enquirers, campaigners etc. from within an organization these are almost always the most worthwhile source of new donors. Lapsed donors, volunteers, and traders (catalogue buyers) should likewise be tested. These lists will be free (or low cost if the data needs to be captured) and the individuals appearing on them will almost certainly be more sympathetic to the needs of the organization, and therefore more responsive to a recruitment message, than individuals who may not have had any prior contact with or knowledge of the nonprofit and its work. In planning a recruitment campaign, those prospects likely to be recruited at the lowest cost should be targeted first. Once the 'warmest' prospects have been identified the remainder of the budget can be allocated to 'colder' media. The idea is depicted graphically in Figure 9.3.

An outline picture of the prospects being targeted will be of huge interest and utility to those designing recruitment materials. Information on the demographics and lifestyle of target audiences can be used to guide creative outputs generally (what sort of message is the

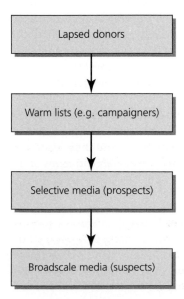

Figure 9.3 Sources of recruitment

audience most likely to respond to? What 'triggers' and cultural references are appropriate to the age/social group?) and practically—if an older audience is to be reached the typeface should be larger.

Media Selection and Planning

Once 'internal' warm lists of prospective donors have been assembled, the selection of external 'cold' media can begin. Media selection and planning is potentially one of the most complex areas of any tactical recruitment plan.

Even if the profiling process has been undertaken for the first time, or profiles have been revised or refreshed, part of this process will involve the review of past experience and results. Nonprofits that are undertaking recruitment campaigns over time amass volumes of data on the response rates and profitability of certain recruitment routes, on response to a range of creative approaches and messages, and on the subsequent behaviour and lifetime value of the donors recruited. All this past history should be part of the planning process, though it is also important to rethink and review recruitment approaches regularly and to remain aware of new opportunities. In the nonprofit sector peer networks can also be used to gather generic information on the likely performance of new routes and media and to compare notes on the pitfalls associated with new recruitment ventures. In the commercial world such information sharing would be impossible under commercial confidentiality. Specialist agencies and consultants can also provide valuable insights into the likely performance of certain media and creative routes.

The most commonly used recruitment media are discussed below.

Direct Mail

Cold mail remains the most common means of donor recruitment even though it has become far less cost-effective in recent years. Those charities using cold lists to recruit new donors would typically get back only half of what they choose to invest. They would only make money on the second and subsequent gifts. Achieving break-even in donor recruitment activity is rare.

Thousands of mailing lists can be provided to facilitate donor recruitment, so navigating the range of alternatives can be problematic if an organization has no past experience on which to draw. List buying is an area where the services of a specialist advisor (list broker) are therefore essential. If you provide a list broker with the profile of the prospect audience, he/she will provide recommendations and advice on the lists which best meet those requirements. Lists can be rented for once only use, for repeat use, or can be purchased outright (which is a much more expensive option).

Lists fall broadly into the categories of geodemographic and lifestyle and an amount of profiling will usually be required to refine the criteria that are eventually used in list selection. Lifestyle list providers will run a profile against their own base to find those names on their file that most closely resemble the target group. Lists vary considerably in terms of the level of sophistication that can be offered.

List Swaps (or 'Reciprocals')

The nonprofit sector is unusual in that organizations often exchange the names of supporters for use in recruitment campaigns (again, exchanging customer names with competitors would be unheard of in the commercial world). These lists of known current givers are much more responsive than 'cold' lists, and are supplied free of charge by nonprofits or at a nominal cost by agency intermediaries. They thus recruit new donors very cost-efficiently.

However, there are a number of negative points associated with this practice. Few nonprofits monitor the subsequent giving patterns of donors whose details are supplied to competitor nonprofits through list swaps. Research has shown that the response rate to development mailings can drop by 10–20 per cent amongst donors whose names have been included in reciprocal deals (Sargeant 2001). List swaps, though ostensibly an effective tool for recruitment managers, can in the longer term prove to be damaging. One of the most common complaints amongst donors is that they tend to be 'deluged' with nonprofit direct mail appeals once they have given to one nonprofit. In countries such as the UK with strict data protection legislation in place, names can only be exchanged if donors have had the opportunity to opt out of name exchanges. Many charities use the Reciprocate system, by Occam. In its latest version it allows a high degree of flexibility over the names swapped. For example, women only can now be selected and names can be selected by recency of gift. Clients can select 0–6 months, 7–12 months, 13–18 months, and 19–24 months onwards. The database now comprises over 28 million supporters managed on behalf of 110 charity clients.

Unaddressed Mail

Mail can also be delivered unaddressed. These mailings are targeted by postcode/zipcode, and are distributed through a number of suppliers, either through the mainstream postal service so that the packs arrive with the normal mail, or through specialist delivery companies. The response rates to unaddressed mail are considerably lower than those generated through personalized direct mail as the targeting is less sophisticated and the mailings less personal. However, the costs of distribution are also much lower as there is no list cost and there is no data processing or personalization involved. Unaddressed mail can reach individuals whose names do not appear on mailing lists and therefore may comprise a fresher audience.

Successful unaddressed mailings tend to be amended versions of a 'winning' cold mail pack. Some restrictions apply in terms of the delivery of bulky items or unusual sizes, so the creative options for this media tend to be slightly restricted in comparison with cold mail. Delivery can be arranged as either 'solus' or as a 'shared' delivery.

As the mailing piece does not carry personal details in this case, many nonprofits find that up to 20% of responses to unaddressed recruitment mailings are anonymous.

Press and Magazine Advertising

Press and magazine advertising is an expensive recruitment route, and press adverts tend only to be cost-effective if the nonprofit is recruiting donors onto a high value or regular gift, if the advert is soliciting funds against a high-profile emergency event, or if the newspaper or magazine is carrying a great deal of supporting editorial coverage of the event or cause.

Nonprofit recruitment adverts tend to look very formulaic. This is partly because the cost of advertising space is prohibitive and nonprofits therefore buy the cheapest standard ad. sizes, and buy at the last minute to keep the costs down. Years of experience of press advertising have taught practitioners how best to use design and copy to maximize response. Headlines, coupons, and response telephone numbers tend therefore to be of a certain size and prominence, with copy and images arranged in a certain way to ensure readability and impact within a small space and where the production values tend to be low. Best practice suggests that nonprofits should provide the donor with both the problem and the solution within the copy of the ad.

As with all direct response recruitment, off the page advertising should be run over time as a series of tests; of copy and creative, of ad. size, of media title, of placement of the ad. within the publication, day of the week, and so on.

Inserts

Some organizations use inserts into press and magazine titles in the recruitment of new donors. Like press advertising, there a number of standard design and copy guidelines that should be followed in the preparation of the inserts themselves. Again, the key point is to attract the eye, and as inserts can fall out of the publication, both sides of the insert should be arresting and attractive. Inserts can be successful, especially in specialist publications where the reader profile is a suitable match against the prospect profile. They typically achieve a response rate of six times that which would be generated by off the page advertising, but regrettably are substantially more costly. As with all direct marketing media they should thus be tested to ascertain the return on investment that will ultimately accrue.

When arranging inserts it is important to ensure that no nonprofit competitors are placing inserts in the same publication on the same day, and to check the number of inserts that will be carried at any one time. As with cold lists, publications get 'tired' quickly, and may need to be 'rested' before another insertion is placed. It is possible to test a small number of inserts on a random basis initially before rolling out to the full run of any publication. Some publications can also offer segmentation by geographical area, or by subscribers versus newsstand copies.

Direct Dialogue and Door-to-Door

In Europe a large proportion of donors are now recruited via direct dialogue or face-to-face fundraising. The initial impetus for this new development was the imposition of strict data protection legislation that made cold mail recruitment more difficult. In this form of recruitment trained recruiters stand in the street or in private sites such as shopping malls. Recruiters are clearly identified as representing a nonprofit as they wear a brightly coloured tabard featuring the nonprofit logo. They approach passers-by and encourage them to sign up to support the nonprofit through regular giving. Whilst this approach has proved unpopular with some sections of the media in the UK, where it is now an important source of new donors, it is currently one of the most cost-effective recruitment routes on offer to UK fundraisers. Face-to-face recruits tend not to have given to any nonprofit before, and to be much younger (80 per cent being under 30 years of age) than the 'typical' UK charity donor. It is impossible to undertake a great deal of targeting by this method as sites only work effectively if a high 'foot traffic' of passers-by is evident.

New donors are also solicited by trained recruiters going door to door in selected neighbourhoods, asking householders to consider signing up to support a nonprofit with a regular gift. This activity is targeted by zipcode/postcode. In door-to-door fundraising (which again is used mainly in the UK and Europe, but is also now working successfully in Canada) several nonprofits may be represented in a 'basket' approach. Prospective donors are offered the opportunity to give to one of a selection of nonprofits.

Direct Response Television (DRTV)

Direct response television advertising is an expensive media to enter, but can prove an effective means of donor recruitment. The cost of airtime has lessened considerably in recent years, whilst the number of channels available, and the number of niche specialist channels, have increased enormously, allowing nonprofits to begin to target specific audiences through television.

However, production costs and the costs of telephone fulfilment still mean that DRTV is complex to manage, and tends to be used most successfully only by high-profile nonprofits with a 'mass' appeal message. The most successful uses of the DRTV have tended to be organizations asking for a low-value committed (regular) gift. It is also interesting to note in the UK that those charities asking for a direct debit which can be completed over the telephone, when the respondent calls, have tended to generate much higher returns than those that elect to send the user a standing order form through the post which must then be returned to the organization. The difference here is the number of stages that are required to complete the transaction and if this can be limited to one, the return on investment will be substantially higher.

In the US, some charities are able to take advantage of public service broadcasting slots and may thus acquire free airtime from the media owner. This can have a dramatic effect on the economics of DRTV and make it cost-effective for even smaller local nonprofits to utilize the medium.

The Internet

As a fundraising medium, the use of the Internet is still in its infancy, but recent growth has been rapid. The aftermath of the terrorist attacks on New York on 9/11 gave rise to unprecedented online giving. It is estimated that in the two months following the disaster, more than 1.3 million contributors donated over $128 million online. As Hart (2007: 197) notes:

Contributors were aided by several for-profit websites that quickly linked their online credit card processing systems to create an opportunity for millions of their visitors to make a contribution. The prior relationship online customers already had with the for-profit websites provided both the comfort level and mechanism donors needed to create an unprecedented outpouring of online giving. The online movement was massive; the American Red Cross reported that for the first time in its history online, donations had outnumbered those given via their 800 number, by a three-to-one margin.

Since then fundraising in the US, one of the few countries for which data is available, exceeded $4.5 billion in 2005. The ePhilanthropy Foundation, one of the leading sources of information for this category of giving, estimates that over $9.0 billion was given globally in the same year (http://ephilanthropy.org).

In the UK research by Saxton (2007) indicates that nonprofits are increasingly creative in the range of tools that they use online to solicit funds. As the data in Figure 9.4 makes clear, almost 50% of nonprofit sites now offer a facility to make a credit card donation and 40% offer a facility to make a regular gift.

Research by Sargeant and Jay (2003) indicates, however, that levels of online giving are still relatively low in the UK with a typical site attracting fewer than 100 donations per annum. More positively, the level of the average gift compares very favourably with other fundraising media, with a typical donation being worth around £26. Sargeant et al. (2007) demonstrate that successful fundraising sites:

- make it easy to give by offering a link to make a donation on every page;
- make it clear how donations and an individual's personal data will be used;
- take care to educate the donor about the cause, both in the course of the initial solicitation, but also in ongoing (ideally e-mail) communications. The key here is that fundraisers have to actively plan the 'journey' that they will take their supporters on, not just ask repeatedly for money;
- offer numerous opportunities for the individual to interact with the organization, perhaps by signing up for news, being able to ask for information, taking part in events, completing short online quizzes etc.;
- empower the donor to feel that they have made a genuine difference to the cause.

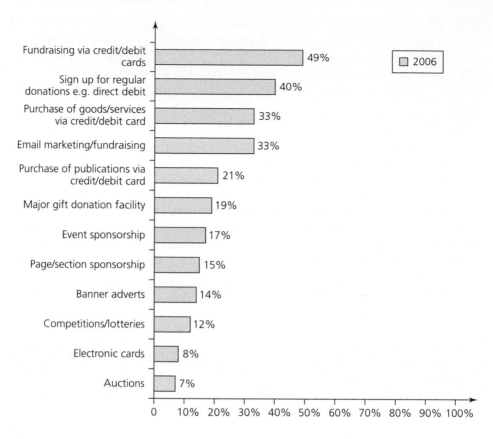

Figure 9.4 Nonprofit website functionality

Source: Saxton, J. (2007) *The Virtual Promise,* nfpSynergy, London. © 2008. Reproduced with kind permission.

It is interesting to note that the strength of the case for support online seems unrelated to the fundraising performance of a site, either in terms of the level of the average gift, or the number of new donors attracted. Sargeant et al. (2007) argue that this is because individuals visiting a nonprofit site are by definition already aware of the significance of the cause or issue. They would not otherwise have chosen to visit the site. Thus, rather than a strong case for support per se, a much more pressing concern should be making it easy for an individual to give at the point they are motivated to do so. Asking on every page must therefore be a priority.

Text Messaging

Text messaging is also being used to great effect in fundraising. There are two options here.

The first option is that nonprofits can take inbound donations by having individuals text them at a certain number. The network provider pays the nonprofit an agreed fee for every message sent. At the time of writing, the Institute of Fundraising is negotiating with the communications industry in an attempt to persuade them to lower their fees and allow a greater percentage of the cost of the text to be offered as a donation. At present it is not unusual for less than half of the cost of the text to make it through to the nonprofit. This is unacceptable. The mutually beneficial arrangement between Unicef and Orange discussed below is highly unusual.

Orange has supported UNICEF over several emergency appeals by enabling their customers to donate via text message. Most recently Orange raised £130,000 for UNICEF's South Asia Earthquake Children's Appeal. By simply texting 'DONATE' to a special shortcode, Orange customers were able to give £2.50 to the appeal. The donation was added to customers' phone bills, or deducted from their credit, with Orange passing the full amount charged for each text message to UNICEF. No VAT or operator contributions were deducted. Orange also sent a text message to nearly 4 million customers inviting them to make a text donation.

This fundraising method was exceptionally effective following the tsunami in December 2004. Orange set up the text donation mechanism quickly and also texted 4 million of their customers inviting them to donate. Again Orange generously agreed that the full amount would come to UNICEF, with no VAT or operator deductions. Orange also held collections in all of their office sites and 250 stores across the UK. In recognition of their efforts for the tsunami appeal Orange were shortlisted in the New Media Campaign category at the 2005 Third Sector Excellence Awards. Over £200,000 was raised for the appeal.

Orange set up a similar texting donation mechanism during the Children of Iraq emergency appeal, which was also a great success.

The second option is to use the media in tandem with others, such as outdoor. Some nonprofits have run poster campaigns or distributed leaflets (as the RNLI did recently on a number of beaches) encouraging individuals to text them to make a donation. Once received a text reply is generated asking when would be a convenient time for the organization to contact them. Outbound telemarketing is then employed to sign up the donor to a regular gift by direct debit.

Integrated Recruitment Campaigns

It is now generally accepted that acquisition campaigns that use several media within the same time period, carrying a common message, and which combine awareness development with fundraising objectives, are more successful than single media campaigns. By integrating a message across different media streams a nonprofit can build the momentum of a campaign. The promotion of the appeal or programme through public relations and communications work will likewise raise the profile of the campaign in the eyes of the public. Individuals who come across multiple messages are more likely to respond positively when given an opportunity to give.

Some media routes tend not to be successful when used alone, but can provide uplift when used in conjunction with other routes. The most effective integration employs each route or discipline to carry out the functions it does best, whilst pursuing a common communications objective—ensuring that each element reinforces the others without compromising its own effectiveness. Direct response radio advertising, for example, rarely delivers new donors profitably despite the relatively low costs of production and airtime. However, if radio ads are run at the same time as doordrops or direct mail the response rates to the mailpacks will increase.

Integrated multimedia campaigns, where the aim is to coordinate different channels in a cohesive and seamless way, can be extremely complex to schedule, manage, and track, especially as awareness and direct response targets differ fundamentally and have to be measured very differently.

The Case for Making a First Donation

In designing a case statement and producing the materials required for recruitment both the target audiences and the position and brand of the nonprofit organization have to be considered. There can be a tendency in recruitment creative to 'oversell' in order to boost recruitment. In the longer term this can lead to high rates of donor attrition and to donor dissatisfaction.

Recruitment creative needs to be powerful in order to be seen and heard by the target audience—the strongest and most engaging message the organization has. Recruitment communications have by necessity to focus on and illustrate a limited part of the work of the organization, but that aspect should be representative, sustainable, and should fit absolutely with the image and mission the organization wishes to project. For instance, it may be tempting for an art gallery or museum to tempt potential donors with a forthcoming blockbuster exhibition or exhibit and the benefits they receive should they become a donor rather than focusing their recruitment message on the depth and strength of the permanent collection; and organizations working in developing countries find that they will attract a different (and often less committed) donor if they emphasize short-term emergency disaster relief efforts as opposed to longer-term sustainable development projects.

Premiums, Benefits, and Fundraising Products

Many nonprofits, especially in the US, use premium offers in recruitment campaigns. These may be 'front end' such as name stickers, stamps, and notecards or 'back end' offers which can range from coffee mugs and certificates to plaques. Many UK and US fundraisers likewise use 'involvement devices' (such as pens or photographs) to increase response rates to cold mail.

Whilst such devices in many cases guarantee an uplift in recruitment response rates, the longer-term impact of their use should be considered carefully. In many cases the donors recruited through these routes are not of the highest quality, and may prove expensive to retain if they require the provision of premiums as a constant feature of the relationship. Any involvement device or premium gift must also fit with the image, mission, and message of the organization, or damage will be done to the brand over time.

Some nonprofits utilize benefit-led packages or donor products in the search for new fundraising supporters, such as membership schemes or sponsorship offers. Again, the costs of the maintenance of such schemes have to be monitored with great care, with thought given to how such relationships are to be maintained and grown over time.

Fulfilment

The 'back end' fulfilment of a recruitment campaign is a further key feature of donor acquisition work. The way that response to the campaign will be handled and followed up is often treated as something of an afterthought, but the treatment of new donors is hugely important in terms of building the image of the organization and beginning the relationship with the new recruit.

At base, fulfilment planning should ensure that systems and materials are in place to thank all new donors quickly, to deal with complaints and enquiries arising from the campaign, and to bank the cash donations and set up regular giving arrangements quickly and accurately. In many instances a great deal of time and thought is put into profiling, media selection, targeting, and creative work on a campaign that then fails because the thought process was not carried through to the next stage. There are many case studies in existence of DRTV campaigns where the TV ad is hugely successful and generates a huge volume of calls, which

- Number of new donors
- Average donation
- % response
- Cost per response
- % conversion (if 2 or more stage process)

- Cost per donor
- £ revenue per donor
- £ profit per donor
- £ lifetime value per donor
- % return on investment
- Lifetime return on investment

Figure 9.5 Campaign evaluation criteria

cannot be handled by the telephone agency. Donors receiving an engaged tone or a holding message do not hold on or call back and the new recruits are lost.

Relationships can be made or broken with new donors during the initial or 'honeymoon' stage of the relationship with a nonprofit, so the timing, accuracy, and tone of the first 'thank you' or 'welcome' communication is extremely important. Fulfilment is a highly specialized operation and in many cases it is most cost-effective to outsource fulfilment to an external supplier rather than to attempt to handle responses in-house. Where fulfilment is out-sourced, careful and detailed briefing is essential, alongside the testing of systems and com-munications between the chosen supplier and the nonprofit.

Reporting and Evaluation

In documenting and reporting on recruitment campaigns each media necessitates slightly different controls and requirements. Each media route should be evaluated against, as well as in conjunction with, the other media employed. Some key performance measures used across a range of media are presented in Figure 9.5. These calculations should be performed across the campaign as a whole, and by each segment, media, and creative treatment.

In reporting the success of any given segment or media route there are some standard pitfalls to avoid. One is the effect of extreme data or outliers—an exceptional result that can radically distort the true picture and mislead the readings of results. Outliers can occur by chance because of the extreme behaviour of one or two recruits, especially those giving very high-value initial gifts. Likewise, there is a danger in relying on average measurements—often the measurement of the median (or middle) value is more reliable, though more com-plex to calculate.

The costs of fulfilment should also be included and set against the income generated. It may not be possible to allocate such costs in detail to specific media or segments, but it is essential that they are allocated at least at the top level of the campaign.

A detailed assessment of the performance of any campaign is essential in building data over time and guiding future recruitment strategy and tactics. At this stage the results should be shared with those responsible for donor development to ensure that the whole process is managed holistically and that donor development and upgrade communications are appro-priate for the newly recruited donors and likely to maintain and maximize their support over the full duration of their relationship with the nonprofit organization.

Individual Donor Development

The initial 'macro' stages of strategic planning for donor development (such as the audit and the development of overall fundraising objectives) will be identical to that for acquisition activity. Donor development objectives can be written in terms of the desired returns from each appeal, but ideally there should also be a focus on measures of retention and donor lifetime value (see below).

Development planning usually involves the testing and adoption of a broad programme or annual plan of regular donor communications, which is then broken down by segment. Within this overall picture individual campaigns will be planned and targeted to achieve maximum effect. Some campaigns will be driven by clear income targets, whilst others will be designed as retention vehicles, and thus are not likely to be judged solely in terms of campaign profitability.

Discussions of donor development tend to be based on the belief that once supporters have been recruited, they can be cultivated over time and their contribution to the organization can be grown. Thus a new recruit who gives a small cash gift to an emergency appeal can be 'moved up' the scale of support to become a major giver or a legator. The development process also involves the 'cross selling' of other philanthropic 'products', so the one-off cash donor might also be introduced to retail trading goods, prize draws, membership or adoption schemes, or to volunteering or advocacy roles within the organization as a means of increasing the depth and profitability of the relationship with the donor for the nonprofit.

This process is often referred to visually as a 'ladder' or 'pyramid', as in Figures 9.6 and 9.7. The 'loyalty ladder' was originated in principle by Considine and Raphel (1987). The 'pyramid' model for donor development processes is intuitively attractive as it corresponds to the 'pyramid of giving', i.e. the observation that many small gifts are made, and fewer large gifts—so 80–90% of the value of donations tends to come from just 10–20% of the supporter base.

These models have been criticized in recent years as over-simplistic and static. Both assume a single route into a charity, the response to a first appeal at the base of the ladder or pyramid. In reality first donations can be a major gift, and major givers can 'descend' over time (if the relationship with them is not managed well) to lower-value levels of support. Large legacy gifts are often received by UK charities from individuals who have never

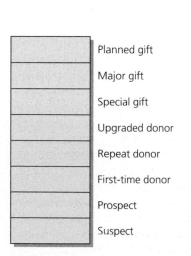

Figure 9.6 The development ladder

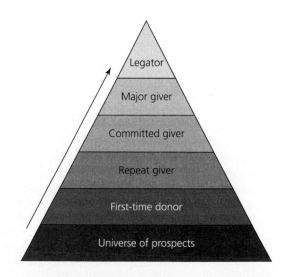

Figure 9.7 The UK donor pyramid

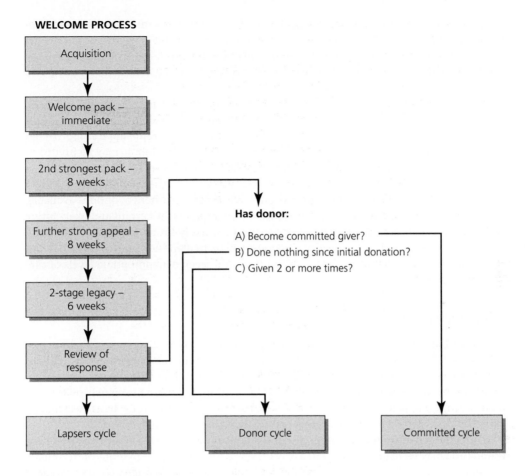

WELCOME PROCESS

Figure 9.8 RSPCA donor mailing cycle

Source: © 2008 Elaine Jay. Reproduced with kind permission.

appeared on the charity's supporter database. Donor development planners must bear in mind that models are merely general guidelines, and that the reality is often more dynamic and less predictable than the theory would suggest.

Nonprofits commonly refer to their core donor development 'programme' or 'cycle'. This is the regular pattern of communications and events for donors that form the central development process for that organization. The cycle may be very simple, based around a single annual fund drive or a membership renewal system, or it can be a complex system of timed communications. An example is provided in Figure 9.8.

Many organizations treat a newly acquired donor differently during the first period of their support. It can be very difficult to persuade cash donors to give for a second time. It is therefore essential that the first stages of acknowledgement, welcome, and re-solicitation are handled well, and that the first communications a new supporter receives are a logical development of the recruitment communication (in terms of both content and tone) that elicited their first gift. Special 'welcome' packages are often used, designed to thank the new donor, to introduce them to the organization, and to renew or deepen their interest. Some organizations then continue to treat new donors as a separate segment for a certain time period, targeting them with a special series of communications (usually by mail or phone) designed to foster interest and loyalty and to educate the donor about the organization and the ways in which they can become involved. After this set period the donor will be integrated into the main supporter base.

Donor development communications range from appeals for repeat support (by mail, phone, or email), updates, and newsletter communications providing feedback and background information, through to events invitations and higher-value appeal approaches which might involve video (CD) mailings and face-to-face visits. Donors may be invited to become members of clubs or schemes, to give regular gifts to the general fund, or to sponsor an area of work or a beneficiary. Campaigning organizations might ask donors to take personal action through lobbying or protest activity. With such a plethora of options available, it is essential that fundraisers are equipped with information on the current and likely future value of individual donors, and with guidance on their likely future responses and behaviour. In the absence of this knowledge all donors will be treated the same, so some will not reach their full potential profitability whilst others will receive inappropriate levels of care and investment.

Relationship Fundraising

Fundraising practice has undergone rapid change since the early 1980s and the dominant paradigm has shifted away from transactions to relationships. At the core of relationship fundraising is the development and maintenance of long-term relationships with donors, rather than simply a series of discrete transactions. Such a change in emphasis more accurately reflects real market behaviour, where few donation decisions are taken on a 'once only' basis. Real market behaviour consists of a series of exchanges rather than purely one-off transactions.

Whilst the move from a transaction to a relationship approach to donor development fundraising may seem little more than a play on words, the differences in terms of the impact on strategy and performance are profound. In a transaction-based approach, development activity is driven by the need to maximize the returns generated by each individual campaign (except perhaps where a campaign has been jointly designed to achieve other goals such as awareness, participation, or education). Strategy is based on achieving the highest possible return on investment (ROI) when the costs and revenues of a campaign are calculated.

Fundraisers following such a strategy tend to offer donors little choice. They can't afford to—to do so would merely add to the cost. Little segmentation takes place and donors typically receive a standard pack. The emphasis of the content is usually on the immediacy of each appeal and donors are exalted to give 'now' because of the urgency of a given situation. They may then be approached in a few weeks or months time with a further seemingly urgent issue the charity feels they should support. The donor thus receives a series of very similar communications each designed with an eye to achieving the maximum possible ROI.

A relationship approach by contrast recognizes that it is not essential to break even on every communication with a donor. The relationship approach recognizes that if treated with respect donors will want to give again, and fundraisers are therefore content to live with somewhat lower rates of return in the early stages. They recognize that they will achieve a respectable ROI over the full duration of the relationship. At the heart of this approach is the concept of 'lifetime value' (LTV). Once fundraisers understand how much a given donor might be worth to the organization over time, they can tailor the offering to that donor according to the individual's needs/requirements, and yet still ensure an adequate lifetime ROI.

Table 9.1 Comparison of transactional and relational approaches

Differences	Transaction-based fundraising	Relationship fundraising
Focus	Soliciting single donations	Donor retention
Key measures	Immediate ROI, amount of donation, response rate	Lifetime value
Orientation	Urgency of cause	Donor relationship
Time scale	Short	Long
Customer service	Little emphasis	Major emphasis

These differences between the transaction and relational approaches to fundraising are summarized in Table 9.1.

Relationship fundraising may therefore be defined as 'an approach to the management of the process of donor exchange based on the long-term value that can accrue to both parties.' From a donor's perspective, this style of approach addresses how an organization:

1. finds you;

2. gets to know you;

3. keeps in touch with you;

4. tries to ensure that you get what you want from them in every aspect of their dealings with you; and

5. checks that you are getting what they promised you.

Naturally, as Stone et al. (1996: 676) point out, this depends on the effort being worthwhile to the organization concerned. This is clearly of paramount importance as donors themselves expect that the maximum possible percentage of their donation will be applied directly to the cause (Harvey and McCrohan 1988).

Burnett (1992: 48) was the first to recognize the need for what he termed 'relationship fundraising', which he defined as 'an approach to the marketing of a cause which centres not around raising money but on developing to its full potential the unique and special relationship that exists between a charity and its supporter.'

Burnett championed a move towards dealing with donors individually, recognizing each donor as unique in terms of their giving history, their motivation for giving, and the overall standard of care that they expect to receive from the charities they support. The entire relationship with a donor, he argued, should be viewed holistically and fundraising decisions taken in the light of the perceived value of the overall relationship.

Relationship fundraising is characterized by donor choice. Recognizing the benefit of future income streams, fundraisers are not afraid to invest in their donors and to allow them greater flexibility over the content, nature, and frequency of the communications they receive. As Burnett notes, this makes people feel important and thereby fulfils a basic human need. Whilst the initial costs of implementing such a strategy are undoubtedly higher, the benefits in terms of enhanced patterns of donor loyalty—and therefore future revenue streams—far outweigh this investment.

Fundraising departments operating relationship fundraising therefore make every effort to segment their donor base and to develop a uniquely tailored service and importantly 'quality of service' for each of the segments they identify. At the core of this approach is the concept of lifetime value. It is this that drives the nature of the contact strategy and the dimensions of the relationship.

Lifetime Value (LTV)

Bitran and Mondschein (1997: 109) define lifetime value as 'the total net contribution that a customer generates during his/her lifetime on a house-list.' It is therefore a measure of the total net worth to an organization of its relationship with a particular donor. To calculate it one has to estimate the costs and revenues that will be associated with managing the communication with that donor during each year of his/her relationship. If, for example, the relationship extends over a period of four years, one can subtract the costs of servicing the relationship with that donor from the revenue so generated. In essence the contribution each year to the organization's overheads and charitable appeals can be calculated. Of course there is a certain amount of crystal-ball gazing involved since it becomes increasingly more difficult to predict costs and revenues the further one looks into the future. To take account of this uncertainty and to reflect the fact that a $20 donation in four years time will be worth in real terms much less than it would today, it is also important to discount the value of the future revenue streams that will be generated. After all, instead of investing the money in donor acquisition activity the charity could simply elect to place the money concerned in an interest-bearing account. Unless the return from the fundraising activity can be expected to match, or hopefully exceed, what could be generated by an interest-bearing account, it will clearly not be worthwhile. If this analysis is conducted right across the database a key advantage accrues. Charities can employ an LTV analysis to increase their overall profitability by getting rid of donors who will never be profitable and concentrating resources on recruiting and retaining those that will (see also Lindahl and Winship 1992).

There are two key decisions to be taken in this examination of donor value. Firstly non-profits must choose between the uses of historic or projected future value. Secondly they must elect to calculate value on either an individual basis or, more usually, on a segment-by-segment basis, examining specific groups of donors on the database.

The majority of voluntary organizations continue to equate lifetime value with 'total historic value' and thus to calculate lifetime value by conducting a simple historic analysis of their database. The question fundraisers are asking, by conducting their analysis in this way, is simply 'how much has this particular individual, or segment, been worth to my organization in the past?' However, lifetime value can and should be used as a projective measure, offering information in respect of how much a given donor or segment will likely be worth in the future.

Recency/Frequency/Value Analysis (RFV)

An alternative to lifetime value analysis that is often available on database systems is Recency, Frequency, Value (sometime referred to as RFM—Recency, Frequency, and Monetary amount). Data on recency (i.e. the time since the last gift was given), frequency (i.e. the number of gifts that have been given), and value (i.e. the value of the gifts given) is calculated and used in segmentation or in the selection of data for a particular campaign. RFV data is often used in the generation of scores against each donor, assuming that:

- higher-value donors are more attractive than lower-value donors;

- donors who give frequently are statistically more likely to respond to a communication than those who don't;
- donors who have given to you in the last six months are more likely to give than those who have not given for the past two years.

RFV scoring can reflect the differences in individual donor behaviour and give the fundraiser considerable insight into who to target in a particular campaign.

Many charities use RFV scoring in conjunction with other forms of targeting in the selection of donors for development communications. Other targeting criteria might include donor communication preferences and ratings based on the sort of campaign approaches the donor has responded to, or rejected, in the past.

RFV can be used effectively in identifying those donors likely to lapse, and in patterns of lapsing. 'Pre-lapse' campaigns can be generated for those donors who have not given recently or where frequency and value patterns have been interrupted.

Segmenting for Growth

'You need to keep in mind that there are really many kinds of donors inside your donor base. This diversity is important to remember because in each case there are logical things to ask for and logical ways to make the request' (Squires 1994: 37).

As we have discussed above, effective segmentation is an essential part of successful donor development activity. Using the tools of LTV or RFV analysis donors can be streamed into groups according to current or predicted value levels and communication programmes designed and implemented accordingly. In database selections for particular campaigns, data may also be used on past response to similar appeal themes, or past patterns of communication preference. In the following section we run through some of the main definitions and development programmes that are commonly used in donor segmentation.

Major Givers

Most US charities, and an increasing number in the UK, deal with potential and actual major donors through a discrete programme of personal contact, stewardship, and events. This is often carried out by specially nominated staff, or by a separate department or division within the development function.

Ongoing RFV or LTV analysis will obviously identify donors who have already made a major gift, or where a number of high-value gifts have been made, indicating a propensity and ability to give at a higher level. These donors can then be flagged as such and provided with a personal level of stewardship and recognition. They can also be profiled to provide guidance for prospecting. The main donor base should also be 'trawled' for major donor prospects on a regular basis.

The cultivation, retention, and development of major givers is a very different process to that utilized in the development of the bulk of the donor base. Much of the contact is on a personal, face-to-face basis. It is therefore unlikely that there will be a great deal of overlap in terms of the communications that are used for major givers and for the rest of the supporter base. Occasionally event invitations, feedback vehicles, and special appeals may be sent to major donors and lower-level donors, but even in these cases it is likely that the major givers will receive an enhanced version of the standard package, or will receive a more highly personalized version of the communication.

Legacy/Bequest Pledgers

The gift of a legacy is generally seen as the peak of the giving pyramid in donor development in the UK, the theory being that a donor moves from initial low-value single gifts, through to repeat or committed gifts, on to gifts of an increased size, and, once committed to the aims of the charity and happy with the relationship, may pledge to leave that charity a gift in their will. Legacy fundraisers therefore target committed donors from the base who have an established relationship with the charity. They may also target by age if the data is available, as individuals tend not to make a will or to consider what their legacy gifts might be until they reach a certain lifestage.

The promotion of legacies in the UK has traditionally been by way of direct mail to known supporters. Donors are sent a personally addressed mail package that introduces the idea of legacy giving, explains the importance of legacies to the organization, talks about the importance of will making for the donor and provides information on how to go about leaving a legacy to the charity. The donor is then typically asked to send a response card or form to the charity to provide feedback on whether they have already made a legacy provision in favour of the organization, or will now do so. Within this outline, charities take many different creative approaches to asking for a legacy. An example is shown in Figure 9.9. If a donor indicates that they have left a legacy to the charity, or plan to include one in their will, they will be flagged on the charity database as a legacy pledger, and treated as a special group in terms of future communications, receiving, for example, special newsletters and Christmas cards.

Figure 9.9 RNIB legacy solicitation © 2008. Reproduced with kind permission.

In recent years, the tone of voice used in legacy communications to donors has changed greatly in response to research and feedback which has demonstrated that, whilst giving after death is of course a sensitive subject, donors are prepared in the main to take a rational and businesslike approach to the idea of will making, and think it entirely appropriate that a charity they support should approach them about this form of giving (Sargeant 2002). As such the language used in legacy communications now mirrors the usual tone and style of the charity in question rather than, as had been the case formerly, tending to employ legalistic and flowery terminology. As legacies are such valuable gifts, legacy communications are often highly produced, with costly additional items such as will advice booklets and videos utilized.

The main barriers to will making (and therefore to the making of a legacy to charity) in the UK have been found to be the cost of making a will and the perceived complexity involved (Sargeant 2002). Some charities have sought to combat these by offering free or reduced-price will schemes in conjunction with solicitors.

The promotion of legacies also tends to involve donor recognition schemes, which is an otherwise rare feature in UK fundraising practice. Incentive gifts such as pens, pins, or prints are often offered in recognition of a legacy pledge, and on receipt of a legacy gift many charities offer the opportunity for the donor to be recognized through an entry in a Book of Remembrance, or, for larger gifts, a plaque, the planting of a tree or flower, or indeed the naming of a room or a building in the case of substantial legacies or 'in memoriam' gifts.

Whilst direct mail is still the core of most legacy promotion strategies, an increasing number of UK charities are now also undertaking legacy fundraising through face-to-face solicitation. This is undertaken in much the same way as major gift solicitation in the US, with legacy fundraisers or fundraising volunteers approaching donors in their own homes. This approach, whilst costly in terms of staff/volunteer time, enables charities to engage donors on a very personal level and facilitates a dialogue during which many of the traditional barriers and concerns surrounding legacy giving can be addressed with sensitivity. Trained face-to-face legacy fundraisers also arrange group presentations to prospective legacy donors.

High-Value Donors

Many charities utilize a segment of 'high-value' donors. These are donors who have given at above average levels, but where they have not given a major gift (nonprofits use various definitions of the amount that qualifies as a major or high-value gift and these differ from one organization to the next. As an example, a major gift might be defined as £10,000, and a high-value gift as £250–9,999). High-value donors may be researched to see whether they are likely to become major donors in the future. They are valuable to the organization, and should receive an appropriate programme of communications.

High-value donors should be approached via appeals addressing areas in which they have demonstrated an interest, invitations to events, courtesy and feedback mailings. Mailing packages will tend to be of a higher production value than the 'standard', and may carry additional items. All communications should be highly personalized and should reference the previous giving history of the donor and recognize the value of their contribution.

Committed Giving

Donor development in the UK is largely based around the conversion of the maximum number of donors to committed giving through automated bank payments. As we discussed in the previous chapter, UK donors are often recruited directly on to a low-value monthly giving proposition. Where donors are introduced to the organization through a cash gift, they will be asked to change their giving method as early in the relationship as possible.

Monthly giving is increasingly being introduced in the US (where the banking systems are less friendly to automated payments) as 'monthly sustainer' or pledge programmes (McKinnon 1999), and is already prevalent in Canada.

UK charities have found that committed givers have a much higher LTV than one-off or cash givers. Maintaining relationships with regular givers is cost-effective, as the charity does not need to send out a new communication in order to obtain a gift each time. Donors who have committed to a regular payment tend not to cancel the arrangement, and so appear more loyal than cash donors (though this may be due as much to inertia as to a strong commitment). Monthly giving attracts a younger cohort of givers, and is also popular amongst those people who like to organize their giving and dislike receiving a high volume of repeat gift requests.

The development of committed givers is most effectively done via requests to increase the level of the monthly gift (upgrades). Regular givers will, however, on occasion also give additional cash donations (especially if the appeal request is in response to an emergency or a one-off opportunity for the charity, for example a once-only chance for a heritage group to purchase a historical building and preserve it for posterity). UK charity experience indicates that requests to increase the regular gift level are often more effectively delivered by phone than mail, as the donor base tends to be younger and the extra gift can be negotiated more flexibly in a conversation than on paper.

Much of the attraction for donors of a regular gift commitment is that this type of giving is cost-effective for nonprofits to administer, ensuring that the bulk of the donation can be directed towards programmes, and in the fact that the donor need not 'be bombarded' with further fundraising appeals. Communication programmes for committed givers should therefore feature feedback and recognition vehicles, courtesy communications, an upgrade approach (perhaps once a year or every two years), and an occasional cash appeal if and when the theme appears appropriate. As with legacy pledgers, it is likely that committed givers will have a wide range of communication preferences, which should be respected wherever possible.

Whilst committed givers tend to provide a very healthy ROI over the duration of their relationship with the charity, care should be taken in promoting the committed giving product to certain audiences. High-value givers and major givers are obviously not good prospects for low-value monthly giving, as they would be of greater worth to the charity over time through gifts of occasional cash support. Committed giving programmes do tend to 'level' the base, which can mean that patterns and giving behaviours are harder to identify.

Low-Value Donors

One of the main advantages of LTV analysis is that low-value donors can be identified and a programme developed to ensure that the nonprofit is not investing more in this cohort than is warranted by the level of income expected over time. Individuals who regularly give in small amounts can easily become a segment delivering a negative ROI. However, whereas in a commercial setting these 'customers' might be ignored or divested, in the nonprofit scenario this is never advisable, as there is a great deal of anecdotal evidence to suggest that sizeable legacy bequests can come from donors who have given little during their lifetime.

Efforts should therefore be made to maintain a relationship and to retain low-value donors if this is possible, whilst also obtaining a positive ROI. Low-value donors might therefore receive a restricted number of appeal and update communications each year, and will also be approached to convert their giving to a regular commitment in order to reduce administration and retention costs.

Low-value donors can also be used in reciprocal mailings (list swaps). As the least valuable donor segment, it may be considered worthwhile to use these donors (where data protection legislation permits) in exchanges with other nonprofits in order to minimize recruitment costs. However, as we discussed in the last chapter, reciprocal mailings are inherently risky ventures and should be utilized only with care.

Lapsed Donors

Investment in lapsed donor reactivation is usually worthwhile, especially when the returns are compared with the costs of recruiting a new donor from a commercial list. However, as with low-value donors, it is easy to invest too much in this group. When a lapsed donor is reactivated their subsequent giving history should be tracked carefully. In many instances reactivated donors lapse again, and the investment of the nonprofit in keeping that donor on board is therefore not recouped.

GiftAid

In many countries donations to certain types of nonprofit are tax deductible. In the UK all donations to registered charities attract a tax incentive for all individuals who pay the requisite amount of tax. The GiftAid scheme was created in the Chancellor's budget statement of March 2000. It allows registered charities to reclaim the tax that would have been paid by donors on the income they gift to charity. In the case of lower-rate taxpayers, the charity may claim back the lower-rate tax that would have been paid on the gift, and in the case of higher-rate taxpayers the donor may also claim the balance between the higher and lower rates of tax paid on the gift.

As an example, a donation of £100 would cost a lower-rate taxpayer £100, but be worth £128.21 to their chosen charity who claim back the additional £28.21 from the exchequer. If the individual were a higher-rate taxpayer they would also be able to claim a personal tax deduction of £23.08, reducing the cost of their £100 gift to a mere £76.92. The charity would still claim the £28.21 in the usual way.

For charities to be able to make these claims they require taxpayers to make a formal declaration that they have paid enough tax to cover the amount the charity will reclaim. These GiftAid declarations may be offered in writing by ticking a box on a donation form, electronically by clicking a box on a website donation form, or made verbally, typically during a telemarketing call. A key development task for charities is therefore to ensure that all donors who qualify to use the GiftAid scheme submit such a declaration.

Corporate Fundraising

In the UK the total value of community involvement on the part of the Charities Aid Foundation's Top 500 corporate donors was just over £1 billion in 2004/5 (CAF 2006). While this figure may sound impressive, it represents only 0.8% of pre-tax profit for these organizations. To add further perspective it is estimated that around one-third of this total value was supplied in gifts in kind and it is small when compared with the total given by individuals. Individual giving stood at £8.2 billion in the same year.

While the aggregate value of corporate support represents a significant amount of income to the sector the percentage of corporate organizations that offer their support remains relatively small and the value of particular relationships can often be low and can be reduced further by the 'strings' attached to particular gifts by a corporate. Thus corporate fundraising should not be regarded as a panacea for all cash-starved nonprofits. Rather it is a highly complex form of relationship fundraising that will not suit either the needs or capabilities of every organization. The potential to truly make money from this market must be carefully evaluated and a strategy for entry developed only where there is a clear rationale for doing so.

In this section we will examine why corporate support is offered, the forms that it might take, and explore some of the pitfalls of engaging in this form of fundraising.

Why Do Corporates Give?

At the turn of the nineteenth century corporate philanthropy was little more than an extension of individual philanthropy. The large corporate organizations of the day supported the causes that their Chairman or Chief Executive believed were important—certainly within the UK. It is important to recognize however that before 1950 in the US corporate giving was legally restricted to nonprofits that were in some way connected to the activities of the business. It was thus not uncommon for philanthropy to be targeted at local communities that served to attract and thereafter foster the general welfare of the workforce. It is interesting to note that post-1950, when the American courts ruled that it was possible to give to any nonprofit organization, corporate funding of the arts and education increased significantly.

However, the role of the Chief Executive should not be underestimated in the US and even in the early part of the twentieth century these individuals were still able to indulge their particular interests, either directly through corporate giving, or indirectly through the personal wealth that had been accumulated through the business. High-profile individuals such as Andrew Carnegie and John D. Rockefeller endowed institutions seemingly at random but in keeping with their own individual preferences and tastes. Indeed, up until the early 1980s corporate giving still owed much to the interests and concerns of chief executives who usually made the final decision in respect of the organizations they wished to support. Under this paradigm corporate giving could be viewed as a genuinely 'philanthropic' activity where the primary objective was for the business to give something back to the society in which it operated.

An alternative approach to corporate support first began to emerge in the late 1960s and early 1970s with a number of organizations beginning to look for benefits to accrue from their charitable giving. This 'opportunity'-based paradigm regarded a liaison with a nonprofit as a means of attaining key business objectives. As Dienhart (1998: 67) notes, 'a firm charitably invests when it believes donations will increase the ability to produce products in the future or field consumer benefits in the future.'

Writers such as Mescon and Tilson (1987) or Wokutch and Spencer (1987) identified a shift towards what they call 'dual agenda' giving whereby organizations will be predisposed to giving to charities that have a good strategic fit with their own strategic objectives. As an example Hallmark (a greeting card manufacturer) chooses to support fine arts and design programmes in the hope that a supply of both employees and customers will be generated as a result. Similarly Yankey (1996) cites the example of Chanel which, when it wanted to launch an exlusive new fragrance to wealthy 'elite' consumers, sponsored the opening night dinner and fashion show connected with a performance at the Metropolitan Opera. The Met received $1.2 million in donations and Chanel was able to gain the exposure it required for its product.

In dual agenda giving the benefits sought by a business from its relationship with a non-profit have been felt to include: increased sales; brand differentiation; enhanced brand image; improved employee recruitment, morale, and retention; demonstration of shared values with target market, enhanced government relations, broadened customer base, and the ability to reach new customer segments (see for example Andreasen 1996, Sagawa 2001, Wymer and Samu 2003). Authors such as Shell (1989) and Amato and Amato (2007) have, in addition, emphasized the benefits of giving in relation to strengthening ties to the local community and offering companies an opportunity to express corporate values in the public arena.

Putting aside the philanthropic and opportunity-based paradigms Himmelstein (1997) argues that in some communities where philanthropy thrives out of proportion to per capita income (e.g. Minneaapolis/St Paul), there are further reasons why corporate philanthropy is stimulated. He argues that corporate leaders with strong links to the philanthropic community effectively set the agenda/tone for their peers and encourage others to give by example. Galaskiewicz (1985) has shown that the more ties a given CEO has to these leaders the more their particular corporation will give away. It is interesting to note that so pervasive is this culture of giving in these communities that for a manager to succeed in business and to become a powerful figure in the business life of that community s/he must publicly demonstrate their generosity and have a proven track record as a philanthropist.

Other work conducted by Useem (1991) reinforces the view that norms are enormously important. Where organizations collaborate on other business matters it would appear that they begin to develop very similar patterns of corporate giving. Whilst it may not be possible for a business to share all the aspects of the corporate strategy it is adopting, those aspects that pertain to giving are not regarded as sensitive and are significantly more likely to be shared and perhaps copied by others. It is also interesting to note that Useem identified that the more 'professional' an organization's approach to managing giving, the more likely its pattern of support was to resemble that of the corporate sector as a whole. He argues that where managers have a strong tie to their professional community, they share their experiences of philanthropy through that community and thereby establish norms of support.

Forms of Business Support

Whatever the initial motive for engaging with a nonprofit there are a variety of different forms of corporate support that could be solicited. A selection of the most common are listed below.

Cash Donations

This remains the most common form of corporate support of nonprofits and in many countries is popular since there are corporation tax benefits that can accrue as a consequence of the gift.

Donations of Stocks/Shares

In some countries corporates can also elect to give stocks and shares to a nonprofit of their choice. Again, this is typically tax efficient since the gift accrues a tax deduction to the value of those shares at the time of donation.

Publicity

Nonprofits can gain from the association with a business since that business may promote its link to the cause and thereby heighten public awareness of the organization. The relationship in the early 1980s, for example, between American Express and a little-known charity 'Share Our Strength' served to greatly increase the standing of this organization (Himmelstein 1997). This enhanced awareness has been shown to lead to greater success in attracting public donations, members, volunteers, advocacy support, and community understanding of the goals of the nonprofit (Wagner and Thompson 1994, Hall 2006).

Gifts of Products/Services (also Known as Gifts-in-Kind)

Frequently the goods or services produced by a corporate can be of value to the beneficiaries of a charity. The donation of food at or near its sell-by or'expiry date to soup kitchens is one such example. The donation of computer equipment to schools and colleges is also common, and gifts of office equipment, furniture, computer supplies, or even photocopying facilities have been reported. In both the US and the UK there are now specialist charities that encourage corporates to provide gifts of this type and act as a clearing house for organizations which wish to find appropriate recipients (Elischer 2002). Such gifts can also be tax-effective in some countries with the current value of those goods (i.e. not their full sale value) typically being tax-deductible. Finally it is important to recognize the PR value to some companies of this form of gift. If a clothing company disposes of 500 coats with slight imperfections at the local dump whilst inner-city children are freezing in the cold it could very well end up facing a major public relations challenge. Such gifts can therefore benefit both parties.

Staff Time

Some corporates will agree to second staff to a nonprofit where specific expertise is being sought. This may be management expertise or perhaps technical expertise that would assist in improving the service provision to beneficiaries. Other corporates are willing to release staff who can act as volunteers to work with the nonprofit in whatever way desired (Smith 1994). Indeed some companies have even created their own volunteer departments complete with their own budget and staff. Yankey (1996: 15) notes that the most successful employee volunteer programmes have several elements in common: 'Employees drive the effort, and those doing the volunteering are allowed to select the causes they support. Also, successful programs are vigorously supported by the company with volunteers being featured in the corporate newsletter and being recognized in other ways by management.'

Sponsorship

Corporates are often willing to sponsor a particular aspect of a nonprofit's service provision in return for an acknowledgement, or perhaps placement of the organization's name or logo. Organizations may also sponsor events or gala dinners which offer brand enhancement to the corporate whilst at the same time facilitating fundraising for the nonprofit from those present (Mescon and Tilson 1987).

Fundraising from Staff

A number of corporates are prepared to open up access to their workforce. Rather than give as an organization some businesses will allow a fundraising team to solicit donations from their staff, perhaps through a simple monetary collection or by facilitating payroll giving. These are topics we will return to in detail below.

CHECK OUT FOR CHILDREN

Check Out for Children is the global fundraising partnership between UNICEF and Starwood Hotels and Resorts. Since its launch in November 1995, the programme has raised over US$18 million, helping UNICEF to save the lives of thousands of children across the world. In 2005, UNICEF and Starwood Hotels proudly celebrated the tenth anniversary of Check Out for Children.

Check Out for Children gives every guest at Starwood Hotels the opportunity to support UNICEF's work through the addition of US$1 (or its equivalent in foreign currency) to their bill. Materials produced by UNICEF, containing information about the programme are presented to guests at various points during their stay in a Starwood hotel. Any guest not wishing to donate merely informs reception accordingly. Guests wishing to make a larger donation are invited to contact any member of the front-office staff.

One million children have been immunized against the six major childhood diseases as a result of Starwood guest donations raised by Check Out for Children. The partnership underwent a rebranding in 2008, with individual Starwood brands in Europe, Asia, and the Middle East now supporting different areas of UNICEF's work, namely water and sanitation and the global campaign on children and AIDS, including programme activities for orphans and vulnerable children, as well as related to HIV prevention and the prevention of mother-to-child-transmission (PMTCT). Starwood in Asia continues to support immunization for the time being.

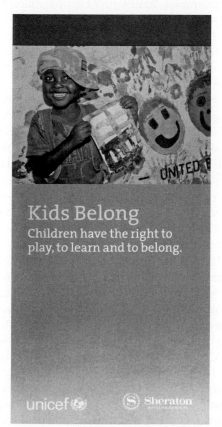

Figure 9.10 UNICEF Check Out for Children
Source: © 2008 UNICEF.

Fundraising from Customers

Finally, some corporates make it possible for nonprofits to fundraise from their customers. This may be either direct or indirect. In the case of the former nonprofits can solicit funds directly from customers—perhaps collecting money on a business's premises or placing a collection box in a retail outlet. In the case of the latter the arrangement is more complex and would involve either collecting a donation from the customer when they pay their bill, or making a donation on the customer's behalf when a purchase of a product/service has been made. This final category of arrangement is known as cause-related marketing and we will consider this in further detail below.

Cause-Related Marketing

McDonald's in the US was the first organization to develop cause-related marketing, linking the purchase of their products to the Ronald McDonald house charities. It was not until 1981 however when the term was coined by American Express which introduced the phrase 'cause-related marketing' or CRM to define a new form of corporate 'giving'. Under CRM the link with a nonprofit is used to assist the business in increasing sales of its product. Its motivation is thus not philanthropic since such arrangements often make considerably more money for the corporate partner than they do for the nonprofit. As the Senior Vice President of American Express noted in 1984, 'if your primary goal is to make money for a worthy cause, stay away from it. Its not meant to be philanthropy. Its objective is to make money for your business' (Josephson 1984).

Varadarajan and Menon (1988: 60) define cause-related marketing as 'a process of formulating and implementing marketing activities that are characterized by an offer from the firm to contribute a specified amount to a designated cause when customers engage in revenue providing exchanges that satisfy organizational and individual objectives'.

The exact form that the relationship takes varies considerably, but classically what this means in practice is that in return for utilizing the nonprofit's brand name on a particular product (or service) the business will make a donation to the nonprofit every time a purchase is made. From its humble beginnings in 1974 work conducted by the PMA/Gable Group in 2000 identified that 85% of US corporations and 65% of nonprofit organizations in the US now report participation in some form of cause-related marketing scheme (see also Basil 2002). In the UK participation rates are similar with CRM experiencing 52% growth between 2000 and 2001 (Corporate Citizen 2002). This rapid growth appears to have been driven by a recognition that consumers generally favour organizations which have demonstrable links to good causes (Wymer and Sargeant 2006).

Large-scale surveys in both the UK and the US have consistently shown that if key factors such as price and quality are equivalent, consumers are willing to break a previous tie with a product in favour of an alternative identified with supporting a particular cause (Cone Inc 2007). In the UK Mintel (2003) reports that consumers feel that companies supporting causes are more trustworthy and innovative than other companies. The study also reports that 79% of consumers are positively influenced in their buying decisions by CRM programmes. It is interesting to note that this seems particularly true of female customers. Authors such as Ross et al. (1991) have consistently shown that females are more favourably disposed to pro-social appeals and hence more receptive to CRM appeals. Women also develop more favourable attitudes towards both the cause and the sponsoring company (see also Kropp et al. 1999). On balance the evidence thus suggests that there may be very real advantages for a business in developing a CRM scheme, particularly where a substantial proportion of their customer base is female.

SWEET CHARITY

The Sweet Partnership has been associated with ChildLine since 1999. To date (May 2006) over £1,100,000 has been raised for ChildLine from the sale of packets of sweets, from attractive point-of-sale merchandizing boxes situated at thousands of companies throughout the lower half of the United Kingdom. The Sweet Partnership have a large number of dedicated staff and franchise holders who roam the country refilling the boxes with people's favourites such as wine gums, chocolates, and mini eggs. With over 30 different products to choose from there is a sweet for every person!

The Sweet Partnership business is about a lot of people at their place of work enjoying a quality packet of sweets and contributing funds to ChildLine every time a packet is purchased.

Figure 9.11 Sweet Partnership logo

Source: Logo reproduced by kind permission of the Sweet Partnership.

Figure 9.12 ChildLine logo

Source: Logo reproduced by kind permission of ChildLine.

Before leaving the topic of CRM it is important to note that such schemes are not without their critics. Writers such as Gurin (1987) have argued that CRM can deflect corporate attention away form genuine philanthropy and mislead consumers. He has also argued that CRM tends to generate funds for those causes which are the least likely to require such funding and thus acts to concentrate corporate support in the hands of just a few organizations.

Work by Webb and Mohr (1998) has further identified that some segments of individual consumers are highly sceptical of CRM activities and writers such as Kingston (2007) and Melillo (2006) regard CRM as little more than a shallow sales ploy that will leave consumers largely unimpressed. More recent empirical work suggests that how consumers will feel about a particular scheme is likely to be a function of the degree of benefit that accrues to the nonprofit. Where only paltry sums are donated relative to the value of the product/service consumers are significantly more likely to react negatively to the scheme. There is thus a strong case for both partners to a CRM initiative to sit down together to work out a mutually beneficial arrangement. There is nothing to be gained on the part of the business by being seen to exploit the nonprofit partner.

Where CRM schemes do work well they can raise significant sums. Johnson and Johnson, for example, raised $1.5 million in 1987 for Shelter Aid (a charity which runs shelters for battered women) and the link between Share Our Strength and Evian resulted in 20% more sales of the 1-litre bottles of water produced by the company and $30,000 per annum for the charity (Shore 2001).

Employee Fundraising

As we noted above, corporates can sometimes open up access to their workforce for other forms of fundraising. In such cases there are a variety of activities that may typically be organized to solicit funds from members of the workforce. Each of these may be established either as a stand-alone programme or as part of an integrated pattern of corporate support where the organization too will participate in giving, perhaps through a variety of the methods alluded to above.

Employee fundraising can either be initiated by a corporate opening up access for a nonprofit to its workforce, or it may be initiated by individual members of the workforce who put pressure on the employer to support the philanthropic activity that they are already engaged in. Both forms are common and there are a variety of activities that come under this general heading.

Events

The employer may donate time or space for the hosting of a charity event that members of staff may participate in. This may be a social gathering or dinner, but it may equally be an 'activity' such as a sponsored walk, golf, tennis, swimming, or challenge event. Whilst it is the employees themselves who fundraise, it is often the case that an employer will donate funds too, perhaps matching the funds generated by the employees.

Workplace Collections

Often where particular members of staff have a link or commitment to a particular cause they will raise funds simply by collecting cash donations from their peers. Typically, permission would be sought from the employer for this to happen on work premises and/or the employer's time.

Sales of Merchandise

Some corporates will permit members of staff to distribute the trading catalogues of nonprofits they are involved with and for purchased goods to be held on the premises for collection by members of staff who have made a purchase.

Group Activities

A further common form of employee fundraising involves the nonprofit in making a presentation to groups of staff who have expressed an interest in the cause. The goal here is to explain to members of staff how they can get involved with the work of the organization or in fundraising for it and to suggest activities that these groups of individuals may engage in. Such presentations are usually made on the company's premises and/or on company time.

Charity of the Year

The final category of activity is really only an amalgam of those noted above. Some businesses will focus attention in a given year on one specific cause or organization. Usually the corporate will offer a donation of cash, time, or gifts in kind and take steps to encourage the employees to conduct additional fundraising of their own. The result is an overall commitment on the part of everyone within the organization to provide meaningful support to one particular nonprofit. Indeed, several large corporations now have 'charity of the year' schemes and since the value of support can in aggregate be very substantial, the competition amongst nonprofits to achieve this status is intense.

Importance of Measuring Outcomes

When a relationship is initiated it is important to determine from the outset how that relationship will be assessed and measured by both parties. This not only serves to reduce the capacity for conflict later, but it can actually serve as an aid to the retention of corporate support. A very high number of businesses do not assess the relationships they have with nonprofits even though these relationships may be entered into for clear business reasons. Whilst this might be good for benefiting nonprofits in the short term, since they are freed from stringent evaluation, there is a danger that support will be abandoned in times of economic downturn, since no clear business case will ever have been established and any expenditure thus rendered impossible to justify. Steckel and Simmons (1992) suggest that businesses should use the following criteria to assess their relationships with nonprofits.

- impact on sales;
- target market results;
- retailer and distributor activity and response;
- scope and timing of publicity;
- employee involvement and attitudes;
- managerial support and attitudes;
- public reaction to partnership choice;
- revenue and expense results;
- the quality of the working relationships with partners.

Nonprofits should also assess the quality of any relationship from their perspective and consider factors such as the value of monetary and other support received, the exposure and media coverage generated, the public response to the partnership, and the increased public awareness of the cause.

The literature on the financial outcomes of business–nonprofit relationships is sparse. Work by Sargeant and Kaehler (1998) and the Center for Interfirm Comparisons (2001) suggest that for the nonprofit, an association with a corporate can be a highly lucrative venture. Sargeant and Kaehler (1998), for example, report that the mean revenue generated per £1 of fundraising expenditure in this area was found to be £6.62, noting a correlation between the size of a nonprofit and the rate of return it was able to generate. This was felt to reflect the fact that many large corporate donors wished to associate themselves with a top charity brand. The study by the Center for Interfirm Comparison (2001), based on a much smaller sample, reported a somewhat lower rate of return from this activity at only £4.67 per £1 invested.

The Pitfalls of Corporate Partnerships

It is important to note that many potentially valuable relationships fail as the result of unrealistic expectations, inappropriate implementation of marketing tactics, or a flawed partnership or programme (Barnes and Fitzgibbons 1992, Madden et al. 2006). They can also fail because businesses can be perceived by the public to be exploitative. As was noted earlier, relationships that are perceived as being exploitative can actually have a harmful effect on a business's sales. There is also risk inherent in the planned longevity of a relationship. If a nonprofit decides to pull out early as a consequence of some unfavourable action on the part of the corporate partner, the resultant publicity could disproportionately damage the reputation of the organization.

Of course the risk accruing to a relationship can also affect the nonprofit partner. Whilst the for-profit's brand may benefit from the values imbued, the nonprofit's brand may suffer disproportionately if negative publicity accrues to a partner (Andreasen 1996, Donlon 1998). A nonprofit can be viewed as being guilty by association and even accused by other nonprofits of 'selling out' (Charter 1994) if it associates with the 'wrong' organizations.

Nonprofits can also be accused of turning away from their core values, or somehow becoming more commercial in the minds of supporters (Caesar 1986). Indeed there can be a danger that traditional supporters may elect to offer their support elsewhere when they learn of the corporate support. They may either not agree that monies from a particular corporate should have been accepted, or they could decide in the light of the additional sums being donated that their own support is no longer needed (Andreasen 1996, Caesar 1986). A further risk for the nonprofit is the potential for wasted resources. If the alliance doesn't work out, the nonprofit may have committed scarce resources and staff to the alliance that could have been used in other areas. Some corporate partners may seek to place restrictions on nonprofits which may limit their ability to criticize their partner should the need arise. This is of particular relevance in respect of alliances between environmental protection nonprofits and the corporate sector (Andreasen 1996, Himmelstein et al. 1996).

Corporate Social Responsibility

Corporate Social Responsibility (CSR) programmes are becoming increasingly popular elements of corporate marketing strategies and philanthropy has an obvious role to play as a component of these initiatives. In this section we therefore outline the development and influence of this agenda before exploring its implications for nonprofit marketing and fundraising practice. CSR practices are certainly experiencing rapid growth, driven in part by a recognition that CSR is good for business, as firms with an active programme tend to outperform those that don't. Research has consistently shown that consumer purchase intent is positively related to perceptions of a company's ethical behaviour (Creyer and Ross 1997) and consumers seem generally more interested in doing business with companies that are socially and environmentally responsible (Ellen et al. 2000, Sen and Bhattarcharya 2001).

What Is CSR?

The World Business Council For Sustainable Development defines CSR as 'the continuing commitment by business to behave ethically and contribute to economic development while improving the quality of life of the workforce and their families as well as of the local community and society at large' (http://www.wbcsd.org. Accessed 14 June 2007).

McWilliams and Siegel (2001: 117) similarly define CSR activities as 'actions that appear to further some social good, beyond the interests of the firm and that required by law'.

It is important to note that CSR definitions are plentiful but vary greatly in scope. While the preceding definitions suggest that in implementing CSR, companies should go in some way beyond the requirements of the law and/or common industry practice and attempt to deliberately influence the welfare of a community, other writers suggest a much more limited approach. Carroll (1991: 40) for example argues that socially responsible firms 'should (only) strive to make a profit, obey the law, be ethical and be a good corporate citizen'.

There is no requirement in this final definition for firms to undertake developmental activities. This difference in perspective is more than mere semantics and should be a source of great practical concern since corporations can accrue a good deal of negative publicity for acting well within the law and local ethical norms, but contravening someone's else's sense of social justice. The Nike Corporation was famously embroiled in a scandal when it was discovered that it was paying workers in a Southeast Asian plant wages which were locally appropriate, but on a global scale quite low. The company found itself in difficulties as it was paying other workers elsewhere at a higher rate (Martin 2003). Was the company wrong to have acted in this way? Unfortunately there are more questions than answers in this domain.

Accounting for CSR

For practical purposes the corporate social responsibility agenda centres on three components:

1. the basic values, policies, and practices of a company's owned and operated business at home and abroad;
2. the management of environmental and social issues within the value chain by business partners, from raw material production to product disposal;
3. the voluntary contributions made by a company to community development around the world.

These are in broadly descending order of importance. The day-to-day practice of running a business has a much more profound impact on society than any contributions it might offer voluntarily to nonprofits. Companies create wealth, jobs, skills, and technology and are capable of transferring this around the world, enhancing and perhaps even saving lives as they do so.

In creating this wealth they face many management choices: how to source and manage labour, how to manage customer relations and product safety, how to manage any impact on the environment, how to promote the health of the industry in which they are operating, etc. More profoundly, business also has the opportunity through its decisions to impact on smaller organizations that may supply it with its raw materials. Through a tightening of trading and procurement practices, good corporate citizens can have a real impact on how their partners run their local businesses. It is now not uncommon for suppliers to be asked about their labour practices, their record on environmental issues, etc.

Driving CSR is the notion that companies should account for their actions. Businesses are obviously directly accountable to their owners, but CSR suggests that they should also be accountable to a wider group of stakeholders. Recent years have therefore seen a trend toward companies reporting on their relations with employees, customers, investors, business partners, and governments, as well as their wider society and community. The breadth of CSR reporting is depicted in Fig 9.13. The figure makes it clear that charitable gifts and community investment are but the tip of the 'responsibility' iceberg.

Dealing with the measurement of this complex network of impacts has become an industry in itself. Numerous tracking studies of performance have emerged such as the State of Corporate Citizenship in the USA (an annual report highlighting trends and corporate attitudes to CSR); Covalence's Ethical Ranking (a reputation index of the largest market capitalizations in the Dow Jones Index based on their contributions to human development); and the Business Week/Climate Group's Climate Change Rankings (ranking multinational companies by their total reduction in greenhouse gases).

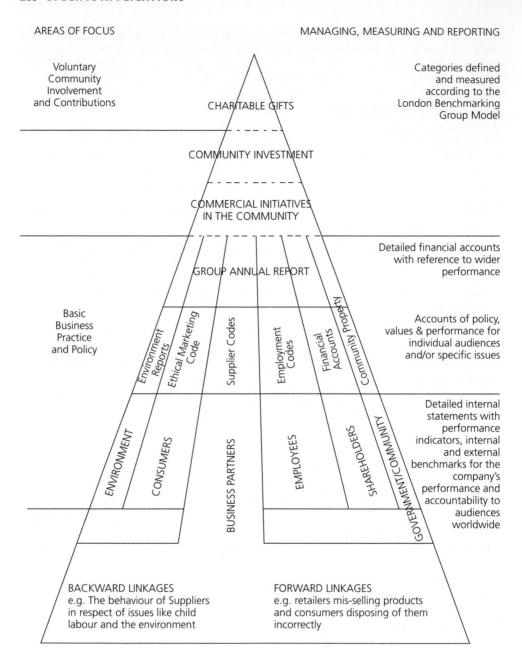

AREAS OF FOCUS

MANAGING, MEASURING AND REPORTING

Voluntary Community Involvement and Contributions

CHARITABLE GIFTS

Categories defined and measured according to the London Benchmarking Group Model

COMMUNITY INVESTMENT

COMMERCIAL INITIATIVES IN THE COMMUNITY

GROUP ANNUAL REPORT

Detailed financial accounts with reference to wider performance

Basic Business Practice and Policy

Environment Reports

Ethical Marketing Code

Supplier Codes

Employment Codes

Financial Accounts

Community Property

Accounts of policy, values & performance for individual audiences and/or specific issues

ENVIRONMENT

CONSUMERS

BUSINESS PARTNERS

EMPLOYEES

SHAREHOLDERS

GOVERNMENT/COMMUNITY

Detailed internal statements with performance indicators, internal and external benchmarks for the company's performance and accountability to audiences worldwide

BACKWARD LINKAGES
e.g. The behaviour of Suppliers in respect of issues like child labour and the environment

FORWARD LINKAGES
e.g. retailers mis-selling products and consumers disposing of them incorrectly

Figure 9.13 CSR reporting

Source: Corporate Citizenship © 2008. Reproduced with kind permission.

As Blowfield (2007: 685) notes:

Fifty-two percent of the 250 largest public companies in the world issued CSR reports in 2005, and 68% of these contained economic as well as social and environmental information. Often these reports use guidelines and standards such as the Global Reporting Initiative Sustainability Reporting

Guidelines, the UN Global Compact, The International Labour Organisation's core labour standards and other agreements which, while not binding on business are often used in defining CSR performance.'

Why Adopt CSR Practices?

Of course many organizations still choose to ignore the notion of CSR or pay only lip service to its strictures. In a recent review of the CSR literature Campbell (2007) identifies sets of circumstances under which firms would be more and less likely to engage in CSR activities.
Firms will be less likely to behave in a socially responsible manner when:

- They experience relatively weak financial performance and thus lack the 'spare resources' to act responsibly.

- There is either too much or too little competition. Monopolistic suppliers have little incentive to innovate in this way, while under conditions of excessive competition, profit margins are squeezed, putting pressure on procurement practices and limiting resources that might be invested in the community. The immediate needs of shareholders are likely to predominate.

- Strong and well-enforced state regulations are lacking. An absence of a base level of regulation not only makes it easier for firms to act irresponsibly, it also sends a clear normative message that these issues are of little concern to the society in which the business is operating.

- A well-organized system of self-regulation is lacking. Self-regulation too has a role to play as it establishes industry norms, making it easier to benchmark performance and highlight the practices of those cutting corners for profit.

Firms will be more likely to behave in a socially responsible manner when:

- Private, independent organizations, including NGOs, social movement organizations, institutional investors, and/or the press monitor their behaviour and if necessary mobilize to change it.

- They act in an environment where there are normative calls for such behaviour and these are institutionalized in some way, for example through business school curricula and other educational opportunities.

- They belong to trade associations that promote socially responsible behaviour among the membership base.

- They are engaged in sustained institutionalized dialogue with unions, employees, community groups and other stakeholders.

CSR and Nonprofit Relationships

The impact of the CSR agenda clearly has implications for nonprofits that extend well beyond fundraising. Nonprofits are uniquely placed to develop mutually beneficial partnerships with business, transferring knowledge about the impact of business policies on local communities and the environment and helping shape new practices more appropriate to local conditions and long-term sustainability. The CSR agenda offers significant opportunities for nonprofits to find new ways of achieving their mission working with business, rather than campaigning against it. It is now relatively easy to identify businesses with a desire to behave responsibly and equally unproblematic to identify those who might need help to move in that direction. Approaches can be tailored accordingly.

From a purely fundraising perspective, CSR can manifest in many of the forms of business support discussed in the previous section. Enhanced levels of reporting make it much easier to identify, a priori, companies that may be interested in assisting a particular cause, or working in a particular way. New data sources and the increased transparency of those working to a CSR agenda make segmentation, targeting, and solicitation much easier.

CSR also offers fundraisers an opportunity to follow the business agenda, through websites such as http://www.corporate-citizenship.co.uk or the London Benchmarking Group at http://www.lbg-online.net/ and to reflect on ways in which the package of benefits they might offer to business could be managed to make them more appealing to potential supporters. Such sites also offer food for thought in respect of the metrics that might be used to measure the success of any nonprofit relationships and again the opportunities to amend an approach are obvious.

Grant Fundraising

There are numerous bodies that can provide grant support to nonprofit. They might include local and national government (or their agencies) and charitable trusts or foundations. A charitable trust or foundation is a body set up privately to make grants for charitable purposes. There are about 10,000 charitable trusts and foundations in the UK and they give in the region of £2 billion in grants each year, which makes them as important an income source as local authorities or central government departments. Data suggests that grant-making trusts are responsible for supplying roughly 13% of an 'average' UK charity's income. In the UK, grant-making trusts and foundations are regulated under the same laws as other charities, being required to register with the Charity Commission in England and Wales (the law is slightly different in Scotland and Northern Ireland) and to publish an annual report and accounts giving information about their grants. They are thus required to be transparent, though as independent bodies they are not publicly accountable. UK grant-making trusts have been classified (Clay 1999) into the following groups:

- *Institutional*—set up with a number of trustees. Institutional trusts tend to make grants according to detailed procedures, have established criteria and guidelines on which to base their decision making, and employ professional staff.

- *Private*—set up by a single individual who takes most of the grant-making decisions alone or after discussion with a spouse.

- *Family*—often set up by one individual, often in memory of an earlier family member or as a result of a discretionary form of will, with trustees who are related or at least closely connected to each other. Decisions tend to be taken collectively but informally.

- *Corporate*—these are trusts where the income of the trust is dependent upon the profits of a company or group of companies. Decisions tend to be made by committees and ratified by directors of the company. These trusts now increasingly take account of the views and interests of employees.

Giving Patterns and Preferences of Trusts and Foundations

Most trusts and foundations derive their income from an endowment: a capital sum given by a wealthy individual, family, or company. The endowment may take the form of cash, stocks, shares, or land. It provides a tax-exempt income that funds grant giving. Some trusts derive income from other sources, such as gifts from a company's current profits, or from a regular public appeal (e.g. Comic Relief or Children in Need).

Overall, trust and foundation giving levels are closely tied to the performance of the stock market as most assets are held in the form of stocks and shares. In the late 1990s the market rose quickly and foundation giving rose alongside. With market drops in recent years, trust and foundation grant-making has been sustained by the formation of new trusts and foundations (both individual and corporate), by continued payments against multi-year commitments, and by some large gifts of assets to existing foundations. In future years it is thought that the trusts and foundations marketplace will continue to grow as an increasingly popular method of giving for individuals with significant personal wealth.

Trusts and foundation giving decisions reflect individual and often idiosyncratic preferences and styles. These will depend on the history of the trust, on its stated policies and priorities, and also on the personalities and preferences of individual trustees at any given time. Many trusts are set up to give grants for 'general charitable purposes', whilst others have narrowly defined objects, and most fall somewhere in between. Trustees have to bear the origin and ethos of the trust in mind when allocating grants, but are also duty-bound not to ignore external changes in social, economic, and political conditions. Where trusts date from previous centuries their objects sometimes have to be reinterpreted by trustees to reflect present-day circumstances. All trusts and foundations are different, and they range from those where a single trustee makes giving decisions on an informal basis to those with a professional secretariat and formal application, selection, and decision making processes and materials in place. Within the terms of their trust, trustees can be creative, unorthodox, and independent in the decisions that they reach on the awarding of grants.

In the UK there is little data available on patterns of trust giving by charitable cause. Generally, trusts and foundations like to fund areas that do not attract government funding. According to the Association of Charitable Foundations, key preferences include:

- new methods of tackling problems;
- disadvantaged and minority groups which have inadequate access to services;
- responses to new or recently discovered needs and problems;
- work which is hard to finance through conventional fundraising;
- one-off purchases or projects;
- short- and medium-term work which is likely to bring a long-term benefit and/or to attract long-term funding from elsewhere.

Twenty-five per cent of grant expenditure in the UK is made by a very few large scientific and academic research-oriented trusts, which hold 44% of the assets of the trust sector (CAF 2003). These trusts make an important contribution to activity in their areas of interest.

Raising Funds from Trusts and Foundations

As discussed above, trusts and foundations cover a huge range; from the small informal personal trust, operating on a voluntary basis from a home address, through to the large,

Strengths	Weaknesses
• Availability of information. Online resources are multiplying and it is easy to obtain information • Many trusts will fund over a three-year period, providing stability and the potential for planning • Trusts exist to give money away! • Trusts will often fund areas which are not attractive to other categories of funder • Applying to trusts is relatively easy and straightforward	• Lack of in-depth information on giving patterns • Lack of feedback, especially in the case of smaller trusts • Tend to only fund short-term projects and not to fund overheads • Difficult to build relationships • High levels of competition for funding

Figure 9.14 Strengths and weaknesses of grantmaking trusts and foundations

professionally run concern. The first category of trust seldom has the capacity to communicate with applicants and is unlikely to acknowledge applications or reply to organizations that have been unsuccessful. In some cases the information available on the previous giving history and founding objects of such trusts is scant. Larger trusts and foundations by contrast are likely to have a professional staff, a range of printed information materials and a website (some US foundations now encourage online applications), and will issue formal application forms or guidelines, deadline dates for submissions, requirements for supporting information, and full details of previous grants given.

In seeking to raise funds from trusts and foundations each trust should therefore be approached as a unique organization. As with the other forms of fundraising discussed in this book, there are essential stages that can be followed in the preparation and submission of any funding request to a grant-making trust or foundation, of whatever size and level of professionalism. Figure 9.14 outlines some of the strengths and weaknesses of trusts and foundations as a fundraising source.

Trust/Foundation Research

Directories and databases of grant-making trusts and foundations are available, and are increasingly kept updated with information. In both the UK and the US this data is now available online. The Directory of Social Change in the UK and the Foundation Center in the US provide the core services in this area. A sample entry from the DSC online directory is provided as Figure 9.15.

Whilst such entries provide the basic information required to make an application, more can often be gleaned from the Internet, or through enquiries to previous grant recipients. Trustees can also be researched as individuals as in major gift prospecting to ascertain whether any links between the individual and the charity requesting funding can be made or any further information about the interests of individual trustees can be gathered.

Most trusts and foundations are hugely over-subscribed with applications. It is therefore essential that approaches are only directed at those grant givers with a clear mandate to support the area of charitable activity the nonprofit organization is engaged in. Application guidelines should always be respected as trusts and foundations receive a high level of

The Leche Trust

84 Cicada Road
London
SW18 2NZ

Contact:	Mrs Louisa Lawson
Position:	Secretary
Phone:	020 8870 6233
Fax:	020 8870 6233
Email:	info@lechetrust.org
Web:	http://www.lechetrust.org
	(Opens in a new window)

Close this window

[Save]   [Print page]

Registered Charity Number: 225659

Last update: 10/04/2008

Grant total
Grant total   £ 174,000

Areas of work
Preservation and restoration of Georgian art, music and architecture.

Trustees
Mrs Primrose Amander, Chair, Dr Ian Bristow; Mrs Felicity Guinness; Simon Jervis; Lady Greenstock; Martin Williams; Simon Wethered.

Beneficial area
UK.

Information available
Accounts were on file at the Charity Commission.

General information
The trust was founded and endowed by the late Mr Angus Acworth in 1950. It supports the following categories:

1. 'the promotion of amity and good relations between Britain and third world countries by financing visits to such countries by teachers or other appropriate persons, or providing financial assistance to students from overseas especially those in financial hardship during the last six months of their postgraduate doctorate study in the UK or those engaged in activities consistent with the charitable objects of the trust;
2. 'assistance to academic, educational or other organisations concerned with music, drama, dance and the arts;
3. 'the preservation of buildings and their contents and the repair and conservation of church furniture (including such items as monuments, but excluding structural repairs to the church fabric); preference is to be given to buildings and objects of the Georgian period;
4. 'assistance to conservation in all its aspects, including in particular museums and encouraging good practice in the art of conservation by supporting investigative and diagnostic reports;
5. 'the support of charitable bodies or organisations associated with the preservation of the nation's countryside, towns, villages and historic landscapes.'

In 2005/06 the trust had assets of £6.7 million and an income of £234,000. Grants approved to organisations and individuals totalling £201,000, broken down as follows:

Historic buildings—11 grants totalling £49,000. These included: Strawberry Hill—Twickenham (£10,000); the Royal Institution of Great Britain—London (£7,000); the Merchant's House—Marlborough (£5,000); Medway Historical Ordnance—Chatham (£3,000); Sulgrave Manor—Oxfordshire (£2,000); and the Hospital of the Blessed Trinity—Guildford (£1,500).

Churches—13 grants totalling £32,000. These included: the 1805 Club and St Mary Magdalene Church, East Ham (£5,000 each); Holy Trinity Church—Badgeworth, (£4,000); St Mary and St Nicolas Church—Spalding (£3,000); Church of St Peter and St Paul—Rock (£2,500); St John on Bethnal Green—London (£2,000); St Nicolas Church—Grainsby (£1,500); St Peter's Church—Cheverell (£1,000); and Westminster Abbey Library (£790).

Figure 9.15 Sample entry for the DSC online directory

Source: © 2008 Directory of Social Change, Directory of Grantmaking Trusts. Reproduced with kind permission.

Education (institutions and museums)—7 grants totalling £24,000. These included: Frome Museum—Somerset (£5,000); Royal Cornwall Museum—Truro (£4,000); Ashmolean Museum—Oxford (£2,500); the Royal Scots Dragoon Guards Museum—Edinburgh (£2,000); and the Company of Watermen and Lightermen—London (£860).

Arts—25 grants totalling £69,000. These included: National Opera Studio—London (£7,500); Duchy Opera (£7,000); Rambert Dance Company (£4,000); Live Music Now (£3,600); Henri Oguike Dance Company (£3,500); English National Opera, the Motion Arts Group and the Parkhouse Award (£3,000 each); Aesta Musica (£2,700); Lake District Summer Music and Opus Anglicanum Trust (£2,500 each); Academy of Ancient Music, English Chamber Orchestra, London New Wind Festival and Opera North—Leeds (£2,000 each); Tunbridge Wells International Young Concerts Competition (£1,500); and Royal Orchestral Society (£1,000).

Overseas students—grants totalling £14,000. The trustees gave 14 hardship grants to overseas students who are in the last six months of their PhD courses. The students came from 11 different countries. The average grant was just under £1,000.

Education (individuals)—6 grants totalling £13,000. These were made in the form of bursaries, including those to Courtauld Institute of Art, London Contemporary Dance School and London Film Academy.

- -

Exclusions
No grants are made for: religious bodies; overseas missions; schools and school buildings; social welfare; animals; medicine; expeditions; or British students other than music students.

- -

Applications
In writing to the secretary. Trustees meet three times a year, in February, June and October, applications need to be received the month before.

Close this window

Figure 9.15 (continued)

misdirected applications and will screen out any that are not presented in the required way, clearly fall outside their area of interest, or where deadlines have not been adhered to. Research is also essential on the level and type of grant that tends to be given to ensure that any application made is for a suitable gift amount. Many trusts stipulate that grants will not be given for certain types of cost such as staff or overheads and, again, given the level of competition for trust funding, there is little point in ignoring such guidance.

The Application or Proposal

Some trusts and foundations require an initial outline letter of enquiry to be sent for consideration prior to a full application. If this is the case, the letter should be very concise, providing initial information about the nonprofit, the project, and the way a grant would be used. If this is seen to fall within their guidelines and current priorities clearance will be given for a full application to be submitted.

Some trusts require the completion of a standard application form, while others encourage more individual applications. In the case of the latter, these should be kept as concise as possible. Those trusts and foundations that issue application forms often severely restrict the word length as all trustees are required to read and consider a high number of applications.

The application should include a short opening paragraph on the fundraising organization, its history, mission, and objectives. This should be followed by more specific information relating to the nature and size of the need to be addressed, a more detailed description of the project or part of the organization for which funds are being sought, and an indication of the impact a grant would have. Innovative or unique features of the proposal that may set it apart from others should be clearly featured.

The full cost of the project should be stated, and an itemized budget presented. A realistic timescale should be included, plus information on what other fundraising is being undertaken to resource the project, including the names of other foundations being approached, or from whom funding has already been secured. If the project is long term, information should be provided on how the work is likely to be sustained after the grant income is exhausted. Every application should include an outline of how the success of the work will be judged and monitored.

In terms of presentation, applications to trusts should be personalized and professional, attractively presented but not produced to such high standards that profligate spending on fundraising might be suggested. Where photographs are included they should be carefully chosen and limited in number. Clarity and simplicity is key.

If specific forms of supporting information is requested in trust application guidelines (such as supporting letters from beneficiary groups or letters of reference from partnership agencies) these, and nothing extra, should be submitted. Where no specific guidance is given, trusts and foundations should always be provided with evidence of the legal standing of the nonprofit, its governance structures, senior trustees and personnel, and of its current financial situation. The latest annual report and accounts of the nonprofit usually serves these purposes.

In some cases, often with larger trusts and foundations, a visit will be arranged by an assessor as part of the decision making process. If this is the case, the trust representative is usually there to assess the need for the project and the extent to which the applicants have found a good and workable solution. They may also be looking for reassurance that the applicants are able to deliver what they promise. This is the chance for the nonprofit to bring the project to life, so the assessor should meet individuals who know about the project and are passionate about it. If the application is for a capital project it may be necessary for the potential funder to request technical plans, equipment specifications, and specialist assessments to ensure that they understand what is intended and that the project is viable and well planned.

When UK trusts were asked to rank the criteria they used to evaluate applications, the data in Table 9.2 was obtained.

Internal Procedures and Tools

To fundraise successfully from trusts and foundations a nonprofit needs to have certain internal procedures in place. It is essential that programmes and support requirements can be costed and packaged into discrete units, and that budgetary procedures enable support services and overhead costs to be allocated to these units. Trusts and foundations will only consider covering these essential costs if they are presented to them as part of a fundable unit or project.

Procedures must also be in place to facilitate financial management and accountability of grant funds received. Grant funders differ widely in the sort of feedback and reporting they require, but all nonprofits applying for such funding must be able to offer transparency in grant allocation and to ensure that where restrictions are imposed these are honoured.

Tailored database applications relating to trust and foundation fundraising are available. These enable fundraisers to record details of trusts approached, their basic grant criteria, the

Table 9.2 Criteria used by trusts in evaluating applications

Factor	Mean ranking
Strategic fit with trust's mission	1
Figures requested realistic	3
Amount requested within acceptable parameters	4
Evidence of applicant's own efforts to raise funds	4
Past experience of applicant	5
Amount of benefit to accrue to society	5
Evidence of support from other trusts	6

Source: Sargeant and Pole 1998. © *International Journal of Nonprofit and Voluntary Sector Marketing.* Reproduced with kind permission.

size of grants given, and application requirements and deadlines. All correspondence between the nonprofit and the grant-making trust can be recorded, alongside grants given and reporting required.

Whether a database or a less sophisticated system is in place for recording trust approaches and relationships, the trusts and foundations marketplace should be segmented and targeted for best effect, with larger trusts prioritized over smaller ones, and those with remits closely matching the nonprofit organization prioritized over those with wider or less closely matching objects.

Building Relationships with Trusts and Foundations

Once a grant has been obtained, a letter of thanks should be dispatched immediately, and any requirements for reporting, recognition, anonymity, or feedback clarified. These should be diarized and adhered to strictly. Where no specific guidance is issued, reports on progress should be submitted every six months.

Designing a suitable 'stewardship' or relationship-building process for trust and foundation funders can be problematic, as they range widely in the way that they are structured, and in terms of what they deem suitable in terms of levels of communication from grant recipients. In most cases trustees and trust administrators will not wish to be added to general mailing lists or given subscriptions to magazines or newsletters, as this would add to the deluge of mail and information they receive. They may, however, respond positively to invitations to events, and often request that new annual reports and accounts should be sent to them.

In each case the best rule for the fundraiser is to treat every instance as a separate and unique relationship. Table 9.3 reports on what feedback is preferred by UK trusts (Sargeant and Pole 1998).

It is also interesting to note that whilst 26.9% of trusts welcomed invitations to visit the project, only 11.5% of trusts when probed further said they would actually attend, with over 48% saying that they would appreciate being asked but would be unlikely to attend.

Once a grant has been given a nonprofit can consider that a relationship of some sort exists, and that prospects for further support are positive if the nonprofit proves responsible,

Table 9.3 Additional feedback preferred by trusts

Additional feedback welcomed	% of respondents indicating
Financial information about how the grant was used	51.1
Invitations to visit the project	26.9
Requirements for likely future funding	26.7
Number of eventual beneficiaries	24.4
Nature/profile of eventual benefactors	22.2
Problems encountered with the project	20.0

Source: Sargeant and Pole 1998. © *International Journal of Nonprofit and Voluntary Sector Marketing.*
Reproduced with kind permission.

communicative, and respectful of the trust funder. Research should be a continuous process, and should build a comprehensive picture of the requirements and preferences of all the trusts and foundations that fund an organization. This ongoing research should include the tracing of any personal links between trustees of charitable trusts and individuals involved in the beneficiary charity, as any such personal links can be invaluable in fostering the relationship and enabling more direct and individual approaches to be made. However, it should also be noted that many trusts and foundations deliberately maintain an impersonal and strictly businesslike approach and discourage unnecessary 'familiarity'.

The Grant Cycle

Grant-making trusts and foundations differ greatly in relation to how often they will accept applications from an individual charity, and how long they will take to consider and make a decision on any application.

Figure 9.16 represents this as a cycle taking place over a one-year period. Many trusts will not consider submissions from a charity that has been given a grant more than once a year, though in special cases additional funding may be given before this date if a good relationship has been built and the charity can build a sufficiently urgent and impressive case for support. In the case of some larger trusts and foundations a three-year period is stipulated as a mandatory 'gap' between grants. Some trusts prefer to allocate the bulk of their funds each year to an established cohort of charities they have selected for ongoing support, whilst others will adhere to a policy that a proportion of all gifts given each year should go to new recipients. The fundraiser must be responsible for researching the grant cycle in the case of each trust or foundation to ensure that applications adhere to the correct timings.

Why Applications Fail

Research undertaken amongst UK trusts (Sargeant and Pole 1998) provides useful information on why applications for trust funding fail. Table 9.4 provides data on key mistakes made by applicants.

Respondents in the research project were also asked what areas required most additional research by fundraisers. Table 9.5 records the findings.

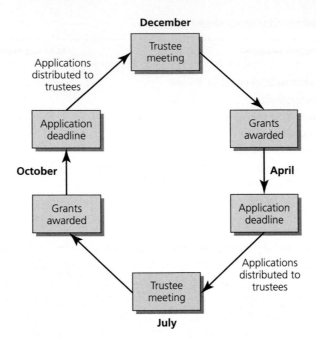

Figure 9.16 The grant cycle

Table 9.4 Reasons for declining grant applications

Additional feedback welcomed	% of respondents identifying
Applicant did not read requirements	55.3
Applicant sent large amounts of unnecessary information	23.4
Application poorly presented	19.2
Applicant did not state how funds would be used	14.9
Applicant did not read instructions for making an application	14.9
Applicant did not send a copy of their accounts	14.9
Applicant did not make it clear they were a charity	12.8
The application was impersonal and mass produced	12.8
No stamped addressed envelope was enclosed	10.6
Applicant was 'over friendly' in postal or telephone communications	8.5
Applicant sent insufficient information for a decision to be made	8.5
Applicant did not state the amount of funding that was sought	6.4
Application was too 'plush'	6.4
Other	8.6

Source: Sargeant and Pole 1998. © *International Journal of Nonprofit and Voluntary Sector Marketing.*
Reproduced with kind permission.

Table 9.5 Additional research suggested by trusts

Additional research	% of respondents
Nature of causes supported	58.9
Past record of giving	30.6
Interests of trustees	14.6
Submission dates	14.3

Source: Sargeant and Pole 1998. © *International Journal of Nonprofit and Voluntary Sector Marketing.* Reproduced with kind permission.

■ SUMMARY

In this chapter we have examined three key areas of fundraising activity: fundraising from individuals, corporate organizations, and grantmaking trusts/foundations. In the case of the former a distinction was drawn between donor recruitment and donor development activity. It has been argued that while it would be rare for donor recruitment campaigns to break even, a careful profiling of existing donors to an organization can greatly enhance the response rates likely to be obtained. Moreover, if charity records permit, even greater utility can be gained by profiling only those individuals with a propensity to donate higher sums, and using this as the template from which to design the donor recruitment activity.

In the case of donor development, it has been argued here that charities should differentiate the standard of care, and hence the approach that is used to develop donors based on the worth of each individual to the organization. In particular, fundraising strategy should recognize the importance of keeping high-value donors loyal to the organization and to achieve this the design of an appropriate donor recognition programme may be warranted.

Corporate fundraising was also examined and two key paradigms of corporate giving were described, with the responsibility-oriented paradigm being shown to predominate. It was noted however that organizations that give because they view their involvement with a charity as an 'opportunity' tend to give more on average than those with a more philanthropic perspective. The chapter also considered each of the major forms of corporate giving and the benefits and pitfalls of establishing a range of corporate partnerships.

The chapter concluded with an analysis of trust fundraising. A structure for planning trust fundraising was introduced, and the practicalities of fundraising from this target group were discussed.

There are thus many different categories of donor that a charity can elect to target. The appropriate balance for fundraisers to achieve among these three groups will undoubtedly depend on the size of the charity and the nature of its cause. Some categories of cause are inherently more appealing to individual donors, while others have an appeal that is perhaps more suited to the cultivation of corporate donors or charitable trusts. Whatever the balance that is most appropriate in a particular instance, there can be no substitute for a formal planned approach to the fundraising activity to be conducted.

■ DISCUSSION QUESTIONS

1. With reference to an organization of your choice, identify the key environmental influences currently acting on the fundraising function.

2. Why is it important for fundraisers to segment the donor market? What criteria might be employed for this purpose?

3. What do you understand by the term 'donor recognition programme'? Develop and outline such a programme for an organization with which you are familiar.

4. Many charities are now treating 'major' donors rather differently from those who give only small amounts to their organization. Are there any circumstances under which such a strategy would not be appropriate?

5. In your role as the fundraising director of a major charity, what advice would you offer to a junior colleague who is about to commence fundraising from grantmaking trusts for the first time?

▨ REFERENCES

Amato, L. and Amato, C. (2007) 'The Effects of Firm Size and Industry on Corporate Giving', *Journal of Business Ethics*, Vol. 72, No. 3, 229–241.

Andreasen, Alan R. (1996) 'Profits for Nonprofits: Find a Corporate Partner', *Harvard Business Review*, Vol. 74 (Nov/Dec), 47–59.

Barnes, N.G. and Fitzgibbons, D.A. (1992) 'Strategic Marketing for Charitable Organizations', *Health Marketing Quarterly*, Vol. 9, No. 3/4, 103–114.

Basil, D.Z. (2002) 'Cause-Related Marketing and Consumer Attitudes: The Effects of Balance and Fit on Cognitive Processing', Ph.D. dissertation, University of Colorado.

Bayley, T.D. (1987) *The Fund Raiser's Guide To Successful Campaigns*, New York, McGraw Hill.

Bitran, G. and Mondschein, S. (1997) 'A Comparative Analysis Of Decision Making Procedures in the Catalog Sales Industry', *European Management Journal*, Vol. 15, No. 2, 105–16.

Blowfield, M. (2007) 'Reasons To Be Cheerful? What We Know About CSR's Impact', *Third World Quarterly*, Vol. 28, No. 4, 683–95.

Burnett, K. (1992) *Relationship Fundraising*, London, White Lion Press.

Caesar, P. (1986) 'Cause-Related Marketing: The New Face of Corporate Philanthropy', *Business and Society Review*, Vol. 59 (Fall), 15–19.

CAF (2003) *Dimensions of the Voluntary Sector,* West Malling, Charities Aid Foundation.

CAF (2006) *Charity Trends 2006*, West Malling, Charities Aid Foundation.

Campbell, J.L. (2007) 'Why Would Corporations Behave in Socially Responsible Ways? An Institutional Theory of Corporate Social Responsibility', *Academy of Management Review*, Vol. 32, No. 3, 946–67.

Carroll, A. (1991) 'The Pyramid of Corporate Social Responsibility: Toward the Moral Management of Organizational Stakeholders', *Business Horizons*, Vol. 34, 39–48.

Center on Philanthropy (1999) *Principles and Techniques of Fund-Raising*, Indianapolis, Indiana University.

Centre for Interfirm Comparisons (2001) *Fundratios 2000/2001*, Winchester, Hants., Centre for Interfirm Comparisons.

Charter, M. (1994) *Greener Marketing*, Sheffield, UK, Greenleaf Publishing.

Clay, A. (ed.) (1999) *Trust Fundraising*, West Malling, Charities Aid Foundation.

Cone Inc. (2007) *Our Research*. Available online 15 June 2007 at http://www.coneinc.com/Pages/research.html

Considine, R. and Raphel, M. (1987) *The Great Brain Robbery*, Golconda, IL., Rosebud Books.

Corporate Citizen (2002) 'Major Charities' Corporate Income', *Professional Fundraising*, January, 14–18.

Creyer, E.H. and Ross, W.T. (1997) 'The Influence of Firm Behavior on Purchase Intention: Do Consumers Really Care About Business Ethics?', *Journal of Consumer Marketing*, Vol. 14, No. 6, 421–32.

Dienhart, J. (1998) 'Charitable Investments: A Strategy For Improving The Business Environment', *Journal of Business Ethics*, Vol. 7 (No. 1–2), 63–71.

Donlon, J.P. (1998) 'Zen and the art of cause-related marketing', *Chief Executive*, Vol. 138 (October), 51–7.

Elischer, T. (2002) *Corporate Fundraising*, London, Directory Of Social Change.

Ellen, P.S., Mohr, L.A. and Webb, D.J. (2000) 'Charitable Programs and the Retailer: Do They Mix?', *Journal of Retailing*, Vol. 76, No. 3, 393–406.

Farthing, P. (ed.) (2007) *Legacies: Last Chance to Change the World*. Melrand, France, The White Lion Press.

Galaskiewicz, J. (1985) *Social Organization of an Urban Grants Economy: A Study of Business Philanthropy and Nonprofit Organizations*, Orlando, FL, Academic Press.

Gurin, M.G. (1987) 'Cause Related Marketing in Question', *Advertising*, (27 July), 16.

Hall, M.R. (2006) 'Corporate Philanthropy and Corporate Community Relations: Measuring Relationship-Building Results', *Journal of Public Relations Research*, Vol. 18, No. 1, 1–21.

Hart, T. (2007) 'E-Philanthropy: Leveraging Technology To Benefit Charities and Donors', in Sargeant, A. and Wymer, W. (eds) *The Nonprofit Marketing Companion*, London, Routledge, 196–208.

Harvey, J.W. and McCrohan, K.F. (1988) 'Fund-raising Costs—Societal Implications for Philanthropies and Their Supporters', *Business and Society*, Vol. 27 (Spring), 15–22.

Himmelstein, J.L. (1996) 'Corporate Philanthropy and Business Power', in Burlingame, D.F. and Young, D.R (eds) *Corporate Philanthropy at the Crossroads*, Indianapolis, Indiana University Press, 144–157.

Himmelstein, J.L. (1997) *Looking Good and Doing Good: Corporate Philanthropy and Corporate Power*, Indianapolis, Indiana University Press.

Josephson, N. (1984) 'AmEx Raises Corporate Giving To Market Art', *Advertising Age*, 23 January, 10.

Kingston, A. (2007) 'The Trouble With Buying For A Cause' *Maclean's*, 26 March, Vol. 120, No. 11, 40–1.

Kropp, F., Holden, S.J.S. and Lavack, A.M. (1999) 'Cause Related Marketing and Values In Australia', *Journal of Nonprofit and Voluntary Sector Marketing*, Vol. 4, No. 1, 69–80.

Lindahl, W.E. and Winship, C. (1992) 'Predictive Models for Annual Fundraising and Major Gift Fundraising', *Nonprofit Management and Leadership*, Vol. 3, No. 1, 43–64.

Madden, K., Scaife, W. and Crissman, K. (2006) 'How and Why Small to Medium Size Enterprises (SMEs) Engage With Their Communities: An Australian Study', *International Journal of Nonprofit and Voluntary Sector Marketing*, Vol. 11, No. 1, 49–60.

Martin, R.L. (2003) 'The Virtue Matrix: Calculating The Return on Corporate Responsibility', In *Harvard Business Review on Corporate Social Responsibility*, Boston, Harvard Business School Press, 83–104.

McKinnon, H. (1999) *Hidden Gold*, Chicago, Bonus Books Inc.

McWilliams, A. and Siegel, D. (2001) 'Corporate Social Responsibility: A Theory of the Firm Perspective', *Academy of Management Review*, Vol. 26, 117–27.

Melillo, W. (2006) 'The Greed For Goodwill', *Adweek*, Vol. 47, No. 11, 14–18.

Mescon, T.S. and Tilson, D.J. (1987) 'Corporate Philanthropy: A Strategic Approach to the Bottom Line', *California Management Review*, Vol. 29, Winter, 49–61.

Mintel (2003) *Cause-related Marketing*, London, Mintel International Group Ltd.

Ross, J. K., Stutts, M.A. and Patterson, L. (1991) 'Tactical Considerations for the Effective Use of Cause-Related Marketing', *The Journal of Applied Business Research*, Vol. 7, No. 2, 58–65.

Sagawa, S. (2001) 'New Value Partnerships: The Lessons of Denny's/Save the Children Partnership for Building High-Yielding Cross-Sector Alliances', *International Journal of Nonprofit and Voluntary Sector Marketing*, Vol. 6, No. 3, 199–214.

Sagawa, S. and Segal, E. (2000) *Common Interest, Common Good: Creating Value Through Business and Social Sector Partnerships*, Boston: Harvard Business School Press.

Sargeant, A. (2001) 'What Drives Donor Loyalty?', Association of Fundraising Professionals' Annual Conference, March, San Diego, California.

Sargeant, A. (2002) 'Legacy Marketing: Just What Is The Potential?', Charities Aid Foundation Conference, London, November.

Sargeant, A. and Jay, E. (2003) 'The Fundraising Performance of Charity Websites: A US/UK Comparison', *Interactive Marketing*, Vol. 4, No. 4, 330–42.

Sargeant, A., Jay, E. and West, D.C. (2007) 'The Relational Determinants of Nonprofit Website Fundraising Effectiveness: An Exploratory Study' (forthcoming in *Nonprofit Management and Leadership*).

Sargeant, A. and Kaehler, J. (1998) *Benchmarking Charity Costs*, West Malling, Charities Aid Foundation.

Sargeant, A.. and Pole, K. (1998) 'Trust Fundraising—Learning to Say Thank you', *Journal of Nonprofit and Voluntary Sector Marketing*, Vol. 3, No. 2, 122–35.

Saxton, J. (2007) *The Virtual Promise*, London, nfpSynergy.

Seiler, T. (2001) *Developing Your Case For Support*, San Francisco, Jossey Bass.

Sen, S. and Bhattacharya, C.B. (2001) 'Does Doing Good Always Lead To Doing Better? Consumer Reactions To Corporate Social Responsibility', *Journal of Marketing Research*, Vol. 38, 225–43.

Shell, A. (1989) 'Cause Related Marketing: Big Risks, Big Potential', *Public Relations Journal*, Vol. 45, No. 7, 8, 13.

Shore, B. (2001) 'Companies and Communities Sharing A Message', *New Century Philanthropy*, Vol. 11, No. 2, 3.

Smith, C. (1994) 'The New Corporate Philanthropy', *Harvard Business Review,* Vol. 72 (May–June), 105–16.

Squires, C. (1994) 'Picking the right gift to ask for: Donor renewal and upgrading', *Fund Raising Management*, Vol. 25, No. 5, 37.

Steckel, R. and Simmons, R. (1992) *Doing Well By Doing Good,* New York, Dutton Adult.

Stone, M., Woodcock, N. and Wilson, M. (1996) 'Managing The Change From Marketing Planning To Customer Relationship Management', *Long Range Planning*, Vol. 29, No. 5, 675–83.

Useem, M. (1991) 'Organizational and Managerial Factors In The Shaping of Corporate Social and Political Action', *Research in Corporate Social Performance and Policy*, Vol. 12, 63–97.

Varadarajan, P.R. and Menon, A. (1988) 'Cause-Related Marketing: A Coalignment of Marketing Strategy and Corporate Philanthropy', *Journal of Marketing*, Vol. 52 (July), 58–74.

Wagner, L. and Thompson, R.L. (1994) 'Cause-Related Marketing', *Nonprofit World*, Vol. 12, No. 6, 9–13.

Webb, D.J. and Mohr, L.A. (1998) 'A Typology of Consumer Responses to Cause-Related Marketing: From Skeptics to Socially Concerned', *Journal of Public Policy and Marketing*, Vol. 17, No. 2, 226–38.

Wokutch, R.E. and Spencer, B.A. (1987) 'Corporate Saints and Sinners', *California Management Review*, Vol. 29, Winter, 72.

Wymer, W.W. Jr. and Samu, S. (2003) 'Dimensions of Business and Nonprofit Collaborative Relationships', *Journal of Nonprofit and Public Sector Marketing*, Vol. 11, No. 1, 3–22.

Wymer, W.W. and Sargeant, A. (2006) 'Insights from a Review of the Literature on Cause Marketing', *International Review on Public and Nonprofit Marketing*, Vol. 3, No. 1, 9–21.

Yankey, J.A. (1996) 'Corporate Support of Nonprofit Oragnizations' in Burlingame, D.F. and Young, D.R. (eds) *Corporate Philanthropy at the Crossroads*, Indianapolis, Indiana University Press, 7–22.

10 Arts Marketing

OBJECTIVES

By the end of this chapter you should be able to:

1. describe the nature of the arts 'product';
2. understand the contribution that marketing can make to the development of the arts;
3. segment arts audiences and non-attenders and design marketing strategies appropriate for each;
4. develop an online promotional campaign;
5. understand how data mining techniques and customer relationship management (CRM) tools can be employed with a box office database to facilitate the achievement of arts marketing objectives;
6. describe the arts funding framework and appreciate the role of marketing in securing funding from statutory and corporate sources.

Introduction

It is the purpose of this chapter to explore many of the key issues currently impacting on the marketing of the arts. Rather than go back over material covered elsewhere in this text it is intended to deal here with a number of specifics that taken together will complement the coverage of other chapters. To this end, the chapter is divided into five major sections. In the first, we examine the nature of the artistic product and the relevance of marketing to this domain. We deal with many of the common objections to marketing a provide a new perspective on the role it might play. In the second we will examine what we know from research about arts audiences and the wider issue of audience development. In the third we move on to consider how new audiences might be recruited by using new digital media and the Internet. Coverage of traditional communications media has already been provided in Chapters 7 and 8. Here we focus on topics such as online advertising, online PR, and search engine optimization. The chapter will then conclude with a brief consideration of audience development/retention and finally marketing's application to the attraction of arts funding. In particular its relevance to securing both statutory funding and corporate sponsorship will be examined.

Defining the Arts

It is important to begin this section by defining what we understand by the term 'arts'. For the purposes of this text, the definition first provided by the US Congress (and later adopted by the Arts Council in the UK) will be employed, namely:

The term 'the arts' includes, but is not limited to, music (instrumental and vocal), dance, drama, folk art, creative writing, architecture and allied fields, painting, sculpture, photography, graphic and craft arts, industrial design, costume and fashion design, motion pictures, television, radio, tape and sound recording, the arts related to the presentation, performance, execution and exhibition of such major art forms, and the study and application of the arts to the human environment (ACGB 1993).

Thus the term 'arts marketing' can be considered as embracing a wide variety of human endeavours, many of which are nonprofit-making in nature. While the focus of this text is quite clearly nonprofit, many of the ideas that will be presented here will be equally applicable to all arts organizations, whether they are profit-making or not. Indeed, whatever the goals of a particular organization, managed wisely they are all capable of making a substantial contribution to the health of the society in which they operate. The arts form an integral part of the fabric of the world in which we live. They help define the origin of societies across the globe and they legitimize and give meaning to a whole range of intellectual and individual feelings and ideas. They therefore offer opportunities for expression and personal fulfilment in a way unrivalled by any other facet of society.

In looking to market the arts, one therefore has to be sensitive to the nature of the 'product' in a way that is unparalleled in the realm of most consumer goods and services. In no other context does one have to be so sensitive to the need to preserve the essence of what is being marketed, even if from a commercial standpoint the restrictions that this imposes might potentially be a recipe for 'failure'. Many arts organizations continue to provide access to material that is likely to appeal to only a very small segment of society. Indeed, still others may support new and emerging art forms for which an audience has yet to develop. They undertake these endeavours because they strongly believe in the merit of what they are doing and the contribution it will make to society in the longer term.

The Artistic Product

One perspective on the nature of the artistic 'product' is depicted in Figure 10.1. At one extreme of the scale, the arts are viewed very much as one might view a traditional product. From this perspective art is reduced to a set of features and thus, for example, marketing focuses on promoting a collection of paintings of a certain type, style, from a certain period of history, or by a certain artist. The emphasis here is on the details that define the art and customers are seen as attending an exhibition because they appreciate these for their own sake; they want to see work by Impressionists, they want to see a collection of Egyptian antiquities.

At the other end of the scale the emphasis is placed, not on the art itself, but on the experience that results from engagement with it. Rather than devouring functional attributes,

Product   Experience

Supply focus   Consumption focus   **Figure 10.1** The product–experience continuum

from this perspective consumers derive their value from the consumption of a total experience. So-called 'experiential marketing' is now commonplace in the heritage sector (Schmitt 2000) with organizations such as the Robin Hood Experience (Nottingham) and the Beamish Open Air Museum succeeding in increasing visitor numbers even in the face of adverse economic conditions. For Leighton (2007) the key to their success has lain in providing visitors with a diverse range of stimuli including the use of multimedia displays, drama, and live performance. All these serve to enhance the experience.

■ CASE STUDY

BEAMISH OPEN AIR MUSEUM

Beamish is a world-class open air museum. It tells the story of the people of the North East of England at two important points of their history—1825 and 1913. In 1825 the region was rural and thinly populated. The industrial revolution, especially the coming of the railways, accelerated change and by 1913 the region's heavy industries were at their peak.

Beamish is not a traditional museum. It is a collection of houses, shops, and other buildings that visitors can experience as they would have been in the nineteenth and early twentieth centuries. Many of the buildings have been 'deconstructed' from elsewhere in the region and rebuilt there. A few—the Drift Mine, Home Farm, and Pockerley Manor—were there already. All are filled with objects, furniture, and machinery that would have been in use at the time and these are in plain view, rather than being presented in glass cases, so as to recreate the atmosphere of the age and allow the visitor to develop a strong sense of what life must have been like (see Figure 10.2).

Figure 10.2 Beamish Open Air Museum
Source: © 2008 Beamish Open Air Museum.

Botti (2000) prefers to conceptualize the arts 'product' as a combination of four consumer benefits, namely: functional, symbolic, social, and emotional. They are described in detail below.

Functional or Cultural Benefits

As we have already noted above, many consumers may derive value from the characteristics of the artistic product itself and attend an exhibition because they want to learn more about the art on display, the life of the artist, their technical skills etc. In the case of the performing arts, they may attend because they wish to view a particular interpretation, or deepen their understanding of the category of performance. Audiences may also derive value from the 'bundle' of services that comprise the exhibition or performance. As an example, Figure 10.3 illustrates the process an arts audience will progress through as they enjoy a night at the theatre. Value for the customer can be engineered in any of the areas indicated in the figure and the performance itself is only part of the overall package. Marketers need to understand where their audience derives the most value and enhance the quality of service provided in those areas (Butcher et al. 2002, Hume et al. 2006).

Symbolic Benefits

Other arts patrons may derive value from being able to demonstrate their social position and/or some aspect of their personality through their attendance (Swanson and Davis 2006). This is a perspective shared by Bourdieu (1984) who identifies three zones of taste which have parallels in educational level and social class. These are 'legitimate taste' (taste for high art and art rich in educational capital), common among sections of the upper classes, 'middlebrow taste', and 'popular taste', popular among the working classes. For Bourdieu (1984: 6) art and cultural consumption plays an important function in legitimizing social differences, since people 'distinguish themselves by the distinction they make between the beautiful and the ugly'. From this perspective, some individuals may attend a classical music concert because they perceive themselves as upper class, or perhaps aspire to this status.

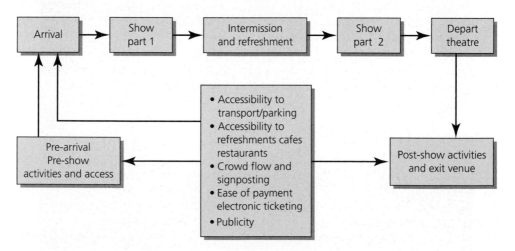

Figure 10.3 Value chain for a theatre

Source: Hume, M., Sullivan-Mort, G., Liesch, P.W. and Hume, W. (2006) 'Understanding Service Experience in Non-Profit Performing Arts: Implications for Operations and Service Management', *Journal of Operations Management* 24 (4) 304–324. Reproduced with kind permission of Elsevier.

Social Benefits

Equally, others may attend that same classical music concert because it offers an opportunity to socialize with friends, chat at the bar during the interval, and meet other like-minded people. Arts events offer many opportunities to identify and interact with others who by definition share a common interest. Kotler and Scheff (1997) acknowledge that art can satisfy a need for social contact, since it provides material to discuss with others. This is of more than passing interest, because if arts marketers determine that their customers do derive social benefits from their association with the organization, this motive can be reflected both in the design of the overall product and specifically highlighted in promotional material.

Emotional Benefits

Authors such as Boorsma (2006: 79) argue that arts consumption may be explained in part by the 'pleasure, hedonistic fulfillment, emotional arousal and sensory stimulation experienced by the consumer'; in other words the emotions they experience when enjoying a performance or exhibition. Boorsma argues that individuals gain utility from two types of hedonistic experiences, namely those that they find stimulating, entertaining, and exciting, and those that they find comfortable, familiar, and relaxing. The former is driven by a motive to seek out novelty and stimulation, while the latter is driven by a desire to escape from, or relieve stress (Colbert et al. 2001). As previously, an understanding of this motive can greatly aid the marketer in designing an appropriate marketing mix.

Boorsma (2006) also adds a fifth category of benefit to Botti's (2000) original list.

Artistic Benefits

Boorsma's argument here is that the customer is rarely a passive consumer of art and that they actually play a role in completing the art form they are viewing. As the author notes, 'arts consumers play a central role as co-producers in the final stage of the art process by giving meaning to the artifact by means of the imaginative powers – independently of existing concepts and external interests. As such, the art consumer completes the work of art' (p85). From this perspective arts marketing should help consumers to complete the artistic product by furnishing them the communications skills, knowledge, and attitudes that they might need to gain the most from the experience. In a wider sense arts marketers must therefore give consideration to those audience segments most suited to completing a particular work of art.

Balance in Arts Marketing

It should by now be clear that arts marketing is a much more complex animal than would be the case in many other sectors. It isn't, for example, merely a matter of putting on and promoting the exhibitions that will attract the largest audiences and/or maximizing the revenue to the organization. In the arts sector there are a number of 'balances' that must be struck between the view of the arts that suggests that they have inherent worth and are worth preserving even at a loss and the view that suggests that the arts, like many other human activities, should be forced to 'pay their own way' and that a consideration of likely audiences should therefore be paramount. This idea of balance needs to be examined in relation to performances, portrayal, and audience.

Balance in Performance

Examining first the question of the art forms or performances that should be made available to society, it seems clear that there is an inherent conflict here between the marketing concept on the one hand and the whole ethos of the arts on the other. Should arts organizations start with a thorough analysis of what their potential audiences are likely to want and then build into their programmes a mix of all the art forms desired, or should they steadfastly continue to produce art forms that they believe would be good for the society they serve, irrespective of the level of demand that will be forthcoming? Mokwa et al. (1980: 6) hold to the former view:

Most might deny that the arts have lived too long in a world comprised of faith, hope, and charity—the quicksand of the arts. Faith—that the arts have values, Hope—that someone will recognize the values and come to view them, Charity—that someone will pay for them (and) absorb the deficits. The faith is valid and must be kept, but the hope is of a blind nature and the charity is not forthcoming as it is needed.

Searles (1980: 610), however, supports the latter view:

If the audience were to decide, our arts world would become narrower and narrower and increasingly sterile. All of us need to be pulled, pushed, or even thrown into new artistic experiences. This part of life—the content and makeup of the US arts world—is simply too important to be entrusted to the non-artist.

Caust (2003: 58) warns that a businesslike approach 'will lead to the production of safe, consumer-oriented arts products which, in the end, may not be what the audience either wants or needs.' This is a view similar to that of Colbert (2003) who quite bluntly argues that the artistic product does *not* exist to fulfil a market need and that the goal of arts marketers should be to seek customers who are attracted to it.

Without the creative freedom to explore new art forms, creative teams will be incapable of enriching the society in which they work, yet without the income that the more popular art forms are capable of generating, individual arts organizations may simply fail to survive. There is clearly, therefore, a need to reconcile these two extremes of opinion and to strike some form of balance between the preferences of audiences on the one hand and the needs of those producing the arts on the other. To quote Diggle (1984: 23): 'The whole art of programming for an arts organization is based on a sensitive appreciation of who the market is, what it wants now *and what it may be persuaded to want in the future* and the relating of those perceptions to what the organization is capable of delivering.'

It would be foolish for any arts organization, no matter how pure its ideals, to completely neglect the current needs of potential audiences. Given the current funding constraints facing the sector, it is simply not realistic to design a comprehensive arts programme without recognizing the need to achieve a balance between those activities that are likely to generate a surplus and those that are likely to make a loss. Only by satisfying current audience desires can an arts organization achieve an adequate revenue stream to support the equally worthwhile fringe activities for which large audiences simply do not exist. Moreover, if audiences can be encouraged to attend a venue to view a more 'popular' art form, it may be possible to persuade a number of them to return to sample other, perhaps more challenging, forms of art. The adoption of such a strategy therefore guarantees that the organization will have sufficient revenue to support less popular art forms and that as wide an audience as possible can be encouraged to view them. The facilitation of this process is the real contribution that marketing can make to the sector.

Of course, marketing still has to fight for the right to make this contribution, and there are often healthy debates in many organizations between the artistic and marketing directors, each of whom approaches the design of the next portfolio from a radically different perspective. As Keith Cooper, the first director of public affairs and marketing at the Royal Opera House, put it:

Art and commerce have not been happy bedfellows. If we were to be completely commercial I might have to say to the opera director: 'We can only do the popular productions, we can't do the modern works because they don't sell so many seats.' Of course I don't say that because it doesn't get me anywhere (Ford 1993).

Despite the difficulties, there are many examples of organizations that have successfully achieved this balance in performance. The Kooemba Jdarra Theatre Company is one such organization, where marketing has successfully integrated the needs of customers with the needs of its contemporary performers.

■ CASE STUDY

KOOEMBA JDARRA THEATRE COMPANY

By Vera Ding: reproduced by kind permission of the author.

Based in Brisbane, Australia, the Kooemba Jdarra Theatre Company is dedicated to developing and producing contemporary performances that present the stories of Aboriginal and Torres Strait Islander Queenslanders (Figure 10.4). Since its incorporation in 1993, the company has maintained a strong commitment to professionalism and excellence in the arts.

Figure 10.4 A Kooemba Jdarra Theatre Company production
Source: © Kooemba Jdarra Theatre Company 2008. Reproduced with kind permission.

Kooemba Jdarra is recognized by its peers as the major developer and producer of contemporary indigenous Australian texts and has enjoyed many successes in the areas of community workshops held throughout the state; community festivals and celebrations; the development and production of over 22 new indigenous texts and inter-, intra-state, and international tours of its work.

Although enjoying a strong, consistent, artistic record, Kooemba Jdarra had reached a plateau in the development of new audiences for its product. In 2001 Kooemba's strategic planning incorporated a strong marketing focus in order to address this lack of growth. A permanent marketing position was created and an integrated marketing and communications approach was adopted for all of Kooemba's activities, including the development of new products.

Many arts organizations would avidly resist the concept of audience needs dictating the development of products. However, Kooemba, whose cultural roots are firmly embedded in more than 60,000 years of history, embraced the possibilities that a marketing approach could contribute to the creativity, vibrancy, and maintenance of indigenous Australian culture. At the same time the company remained committed to ensuring a strong focus on artistic and cultural integrity within this marketing approach.

Examples of recent productions developed for specific market segments include *Piccaninni Dreaming and Yarnin' Up*. *Piccaninni Dreaming* was specifically developed to deliver a culturally appropriate performance for the primary school education market, while *Yarnin' Up* was developed as a product suitable for touring to regional and remote indigenous communities throughout Western Australia, the Northern Territory, and Queensland.

To augment its marketing approach for the development of product, Kooemba Jdarra stringently undertook a variety of market research strategies to engage with audiences in order to assess the success of its productions. Focus groups, direct mail surveys, telephone surveys, and exit surveys have been employed to ascertain both the number of audience members engaged in viewing Kooemba's performances, and the level of success of that engagement. A useful by-product of this research has been the collection of valuable data on Kooemba, which supports the company's activities in the areas of lobbying and advocacy.

Kooemba's strong cultural responsibility for the incorporation of community participation and a history of valuing community opinion diverts the focus of the company from one of individual artistic vision to one of collective community vision. This collective vision, coupled with a culture unencumbered by embedded Western theatre protocols, provides freedom for Kooemba to develop a new form of creativity within its management. It is perhaps this freedom that allows marketing to be perceived as a valuable tool in the development of cultural product, rather than being perceived as a dangerous step into the world of commercialization. The irony is that one of the most contemporary Western business approaches is being embraced by, and successfully serving the needs of, one of the world's oldest cultures.

Balance in Portrayal

Aside from the need to achieve a balance in terms of the art forms supported, there is often a need to decide on the extent to which an organization is prepared to 'exploit' art for commercial purposes. Just how far should our arts bodies go, for example, in popularizing artistic work to make it more accessible? Many museums, for example, have altered the way in which they present their exhibits in a bid to open up their artefacts to a wider audience. As a consequence, many larger museums now offer displays that have much in common with theme parks. There are interactive displays, videos, special effects, and a whole new range of promotional merchandise, including children's toys and cheap replicas of historic artefacts. While no one can deny that this has had the desired effect in terms of encouraging larger numbers of the public to view, there are legitimate concerns that in presenting art in this way, one is actually degrading it. Consumers have simply been encouraged to collect momentary experiences without any real reflection, and to move hurriedly from one 'fix' of culture to another. As Strehler (1990: 211) comments: 'Reducing the presentation of an artistic work to instantaneous, consumable entertainment is consistent with the undeniable needs of the consumers, but misses the primary cultural purpose of revealing its deeper causes.'

In short, something of the original experience that the artist intended is lost in the drive to popularization. It is for individual arts organizations to decide how far they are willing to permit this to happen and to reach some form of balance.

Balance in Audience

The third 'balance' is arguably the most difficult to achieve. As will shortly be demonstrated, the mission of many arts organizations requires them to expand the potential audience for their offerings with almost missionary zeal. Indeed, many of the traditional sources of funding for arts activities require that a substantial amount of development work be undertaken to ensure that 'non-standard' audiences are encouraged to attend. Historically this has proven to be problematic, as certain groups within society appear to be openly hostile to much arts-related activity. In an attempt to change attitudes, organizations have had to commit valuable marketing resource to the cause and as a result have perhaps neglected their existing core audience. Mokwa et al. (1980: 10) phrase this more eloquently, narrating a story of a ship lost at sea for weeks:

. . . its crew dying of thirst because of no fresh water. Finally, sighting another vessel, the thirsty captain signalled: 'Water, water . . . dying of thirst!' The other ship signalled back: 'Cast down your bucket where you are.' Thinking he was misunderstood, the first captain repeated: 'Water, water . . . send us water!' 'Cast down your bucket where you are,' came the response again. The same messages were repeated again before the first captain thought to cast down his bucket. It came up full of fresh drinkable water. Although adrift on the ocean, the ship was in a sea of fresh water forming the nearly shoreless mouth of the Amazon River.

The moral of the tale, according to the authors, is that arts administrators tend to continue to look elsewhere for their help, rather than exploiting the potential close to home. Arts organizations need to strike a balance between prospecting for new audiences and looking after and cultivating their existing ones. If properly developed, this latter segment can generate much revenue that can in turn be redirected to the task of encouraging other, more reticent, segments of society to attend as well.

The Arts Audience

There has been relatively little academic research conducted to date on the analysis and segmentation of arts audiences. Much of the data that is available is unpublished, of dubious quality, or highly focused on a small group of broad demographic variables. This is to be regretted, since an understanding of the type of person who attends specific types of arts events, and their motivations for so doing, will allow an organization to develop a targeted marketing plan that will reach the prospective audience cost-effectively and with the message that they will find most persuasive (Reiss 1994). As the reader will appreciate from previous chapters, arts organizations also need to be clear that it should be possible to segment both the market for non-attenders (who may require specific types of recruitment activity) and the market for existing attenders (who may require specific forms of development).

Segmenting Arts Attenders

A recent study of arts audiences in the UK by Neill and Orme (2006) profiled individuals who booked for a wide variety of different art forms, looking at those who booked at least an hour before a performance (advance bookers) and those who booked in the hour immediately before the performance (walk-up bookers). The authors also examined non-bookers (who bought a seat when they arrived) but these individuals were found to be very similar in profile to the advance booker. Their findings are illustrated in Table 10.1.

The results are typical of previous audience research in that they show that individuals attending arts events are more likely to be drawn from mosaic categories A, C, and E. Although category A makes up less than 10% of UK households, it provides over 24% of the advance bookers to arts events. It is worth noting that advance bookers are a particularly significant category of arts attendee since they tend to buy 37% more tickets in any single transaction than walk-ups and pay an average of one-third more for each ticket.

Of course this is an aggregate study of arts audiences and there will be differences between the profiles of individuals who attend different kinds of performances and events. Individual organizations will need to conduct their own research to profile their typical audience and, where appropriate, the typical audience for specific forms of art. This gives the marketer an understanding of the type of person they are addressing and a sense of the communications

Table 10.1 Booker type by mosaic group

Base 16,992	Advance bookers %	Walk-up bookers %	Mosaic base %
A: Symbols of success	24.2	20.5	9.62
B: Happy families	7.8	6.2	10.76
C: Suburban comfort	17.0	14.5	15.10
D: Ties of community	9.1	9.7	16.04
E: Urban intelligence	19.4	24.1	7.19
F: Welfare borderline	4.7	8.9	6.43
G: Municipal dependency	1.6	1.4	6.71
H: Blue collar enterprise	4.3	4.1	11.01
I: Twilight subsistence	1.2	1.2	3.88
J: Grey perspectives	4.9	4.6	7.88
K: Rural isolation	5.7	5.0	5.39

Source: Neill and Orme (2006) © Reproduced with kind permission. Original study commissioned by the Arts Councils of England, Wales, Scotland, and Northern Ireland. Full report may be downloaded from www.audience.co.uk.

mix that might be most appropriate. A useful supplement to this kind of data is behavioural information (i.e. information about how specific categories of attender behave) and as an example of how this can be used, Semenik and Young (1979) studied the potential to segment arts audiences utilizing data gathered from patrons of two large opera companies. The authors concluded that three distinct segments of attender existed:

1. *Season ticket subscribers* (73.8 per cent of the sample): individuals who rely for their information about performances on direct mailings from the opera companies themselves. Members of this segment tend to be older, from higher socio-economic groups, and have a higher degree of education than the other two segments. Season ticket subscribers attend the opera because they view themselves as fans.

2. *Infrequent attenders* (11.6 per cent of the sample): individuals who rely for information about performances on word-of-mouth recommendation from friends and acquaintances. They do not regard themselves as 'fans' in the same way as season ticket subscribers, and will attend only if a big-name star is performing.

3. *Non-subscribing frequent attenders* (14.6 per cent of the sample): these individuals also rely on word-of-mouth recommendations for information. This group also regards itself as being a general fan of the opera, but is younger and less well educated than the season ticket subscriber segment.

These findings are important in so far as they suggest that an arts organization could draw a distinction between each category and apply a mix of attraction and retention activities to each. This idea is illustrated in Figure 10.5.

Subscribers are clearly committed to attendance at a particular venue. They are likely to have the most frequent pattern of attendance and be worth a significant sum of money to an arts organization over the duration of their relationship with it. The loss of even a small percentage of the members of this segment per annum will therefore result in a significant drop in revenue. It is therefore important that considerable effort is expended in keeping this segment loyal. As they are already enthusiastic about the arts 'product', they do not need to be 're-convinced' of its merits. Instead the focus with this group should be in establishing and building a meaningful relationship that builds loyalty and keeps retention rates high.

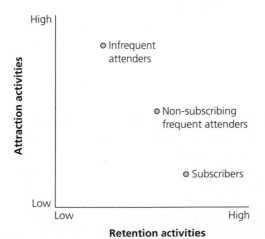

Figure 10.5 A classification of arts consumers

Non-subscribing frequent attenders are somewhat more problematic. Evidence suggests that this segment will attend a very wide variety of different categories of event and it may be difficult to build loyalty in the face of competition from other venues perceived as of equal value. A mix of attraction and retention activities might hence be more appropriate.

Infrequent attenders are likely to have to be convinced of the 'need' to attend specific events and the focus with this category will hence lie in attraction. They will therefore need to be informed of the merits of a particular performance, why it represents an opportunity, and the status of the 'star' who is performing. Efforts to develop this group further are likely to be futile since they will tend only to attend performances that are perceived as in some way unique. It is interesting to note that many arts managers would disagree with this assessment, arguing that infrequent attenders could be developed over time and eventually become subscribers. There is no evidence, however, that this is the case. Ryans and Weinberg (1978) in a five-year study of theatre audiences attempted to verify their hypothesis that an entry pattern to subscriptions existed. The researchers felt that subscribers would begin as single ticket buyers, progress to the purchase of several tickets in a season, and then ultimately become a season ticket holder. They found, quite surprisingly, that there was a high incidence of sudden subscribers (those who subscribed without attending previously) and were hence forced to conclude that their perception of an entry pattern to the arts was invalid.

Additional studies that have examined attendance patterns at other forms of arts events have derived similar findings to those given above. Importantly, Kaali-Nagy and Garrison (1972) were among the first to recognize that the Pareto principle can be applied equally well to arts audiences and, in their study of the Los Angeles Music Center, found that 10 per cent of patrons accounted for nearly 45 per cent of the attendance pattern of their sample. The authors thus concluded that a relatively small number of people constituted the core of the Center's audience. Importantly these findings have been replicated at other venues and indeed in other countries (see for example Sargeant 1997).

Businesses will be familiar with the Pareto rule and will ensure that they expend considerable effort on those customers who generate the majority of their income. Many arts organizations have yet to grasp this principle. If there are certain segments of society that may be deemed regular attenders of arts events, these segments must be the focus of considerable effort. They are by their very nature the easiest to encourage to attend and may hence be readily developed over time. As long ago as 1980 Dawson (p7) identified what he saw as a paradox in arts management, namely that of 'the missionary effort (taking place) to develop arts audiences from those marginally interested and the near exclusion of effort to develop the fullest possible response from that segment of society most likely to support the arts.' Regrettably, little has changed since then.

Non-Attenders

Mention has already been made of the need for many arts organizations to broaden their appeal through societal groups that would not normally consider attending an arts event. Indeed the ability to attract non-traditional audiences may be a requirement for the attraction of some categories of funding. Identifying and categorizing non-users can therefore be of equal utility to an arts organization, since different forms of non-user may prove susceptible to different forms of approach in an attempt to persuade them to sample the arts for the first time. Diggle (1984) makes a particularly strong argument for this approach in recognition of the fact that many arts organizations have a mission to develop audiences across as wide a spectrum of society as possible. He concludes that there are three segments of non-attenders:

1. *The intenders*. These individuals have a positive perception of the arts and plan to go to a venue or performance at some stage in the future, but for various reasons never quite seem to get around to it. Clearly, an organization wishing to develop this group may need to find some way to incentivize them, perhaps through the creative use of sales promotion-type techniques.

2. *The indifferent*. This group has no strong opinions about the arts and has no great motivation to set about attending. They are an interesting group, however, because they tend not to have negative perceptions of the arts and may be suitable candidates for development if positive attitudes can be encouraged.

3. *The hostile*. From an arts marketer's perspective this segment will hardly be worth pursuing at all. They have clear and firmly established negative attitudes towards the arts and will tend to dislike most art forms altogether. Clearly, if an arts organization is to make an effective use of its marketing resource there will be little point in focusing specifically on this segment.

Of course, there may be some merit in attempting to address all of the segments that Diggle identifies, but the approach will be radically different in each case. In the case of the intenders, the barrier to achieving attendance is relatively small. Members of this segment need either to be given some incentive to attend, or it needs to be made easier for them to do so.

In the 'indifferent' category, the marketing task is clearly one of changing attitudes. An interesting piece of research by Cooper and Tower (1994: 306) suggested that many who are indifferent to the arts may not attend because:

- they lack confidence in their ability to enjoy the arts, possibly because of a lack of education or any form of background in the subject;
- of social pressure from peer groups acting to dissuade individuals from sampling the arts;
- there is a feeling that the arts are only for the upper classes;
- of the positive alternative of television, which has achieved the status of myth and 'meta medium' and which comprises many consumers' social and intellectual universe.

If a more positive attitude towards the arts could be cultivated, there is a high probability that in future the members of this group could be persuaded to attend. Members of this segment will, however, need considerable encouragement and the process of persuasion may require a substantial investment in both human and financial resources. There are a number of development strategies that could be adopted with this group.

Investment in Education

Links could be forged with schools and colleges to encourage young people to sample (and even participate in) the arts. School parties could be encouraged to visit arts organizations and interact with staff in workshops/seminars, etc. Staff could provide guest 'lectures' in schools which support the national curriculum and in the case of some larger organizations, educational material could even be produced to help young people to appreciate the art form in question. One art gallery in the USA produced a series of Impressionist kits consisting of slides of 12 paintings, biographies of the artists, texts on the movement, and suggested questions for discussion.

Exposure to the arts in this way can be non-threatening and may serve to demystify the arts for a new generation of young people. Indeed if an interest can be cultivated, a proportion of them may even persuade friends and relatives to sample an art form for the first time.

Facility Enhancement

A second option concerns altering the nature of the art facility itself. While this is not a move to be taken lightly, some arts organizations, particularly those with display material, can optimize the use thereof to attract new audiences. Ricklefs (1975: 169) cites the example of Washington's National Gallery, which started a separate exhibition department with a full-time architect with this very thought in mind. The aim was to enhance for the public the enjoyment of the artworks on display and by so doing to make them accessible to a wider proportion of society. As an example, to provide the rustic background for a show of Alaskan native art, the gallery acquired weathered boards from a man who made his living tearing down old barns. Stone statues were placed on deer hides and the lights were arranged to simulate the Arctic sunlight. '"In the old days (they) just hung things on the wall," said one impressed viewer.'

Of course there is a need not to alienate traditional audiences by being seen to cheapen the arts through the use of gimmicks, but in the example quoted above, the reader will note that the gallery had gone to great lengths to ensure that the ambience supporting their works was as authentic as possible. In short the changes introduced served to enhance the experience for both new and existing customers.

Portfolio Enhancement

It may also be possible to encourage new audiences to attend a given venue by extending the range of art forms that are supported. Most categories of art contain forms that are perceived as more accessible by the general public. If these are from time to time included in the portfolio, new customers might be attracted who might otherwise not have attended. Moreover if they enjoy their experience they may be persuaded to sample other art forms that would hitherto have lacked appeal. In the case of museums, travelling exhibitions could for example be booked. Often these are of great public interest and while they might represent something of a financial gamble, because of the expense of the hire, can yield great benefits in terms of both the revenue generated and the wider spectrum of the public attracted to view. Once again, if only a small percentage of these individuals are persuaded to return to sample another (perhaps local) exhibition in the future, the recruitment strategy will have been effective.

There are therefore a variety of strategies that could be adopted to attract the indifferents to attend the arts, although none of those suggested is without some form of financial risk. Individual organizations will therefore need to determine the extent to which they are prepared to focus on recruitment activity and decide on the allocation of budgets accordingly.

The remaining category of non-attender, the hostile, is almost certainly the only category that will not be worth some form of recruitment expenditure. This group has absolutely no interest in the arts and is openly hostile towards any attempts to encourage them to attend. Many in this category may view the arts as inappropriate for their social grouping, a waste of public funds, or worse! Targeting this segment is hence likely to be a waste of valuable marketing resource which, as has been shown above, could be gainfully employed elsewhere.

■ **CASE STUDY**

BROADENING AUDIENCE PARTICIPATION AT THE HORNIMAN MUSEUM

Victorian tea trader Frederick John Horniman began collecting specimens and artefacts from around the world in the 1860s. Horniman's mission was to bring the world to Forest Hill in South London, and he opened part of his family house to the public so they could view the riches he had collected. As the collections increased they outgrew his home and in 1898 Horniman commissioned Charles Harrison Townsend to design a new museum (Figure 10.6).

The museum opened in 1901 and was dedicated with the surrounding land as a free gift to the people of London by Frederick Horniman forever for their recreation, instruction, and enjoyment. The original collections comprised natural history specimens, cultural artefacts, and musical instruments. Over the last 100 years the museum has added significantly to the original bequest, with Horniman's original collections comprising only 10 per cent of current

Figure 10.6 A view of the Horniman Museum

ethnography and musical instrument holdings. The museum now holds in total some 350,000 objects and related items. The collections have been recognized as being of national importance, with the anthropology and music collections having Designated status.

Further buildings were added to the original during the course of the last century, notably in 1911 when a new building was donated by Frederick's son Emslie. In 1999 the museum demolished some of the later additions and embarked on a centenary development to create a new extension and several associated spaces. This new development opened on 14 June 2002, doubling the public space of the museum.

The museum was constituted a charitable trust in 1989 and is run by a board of trustees. It has an annual turnover of around £4 million, and is largely funded by the government through the Department of Culture, Media, and Sport. As such, the museum's agenda is set by the government to a great extent both in terms of its educational objectives (where the museum caters for the requirements of the schools syllabus) and in terms of the visitors it sets out to attract.

The Department of Culture, Media, and Sport (DCMS) currently requires the museums it funds to market themselves in such a way that they attract the widest audience—but especially to bring in people who don't tend normally to visit museums. In the case of long-established museums like the Horniman, over the years there has been something of a shift in audiences, away from the people whom museums were designed to serve—often the 'working classes' that museum founders wished to inspire and educate. Today the 'traditional' museum visitor tends to be predominantly white and 'ABC1'—i.e. from the better-educated higher-income social groups. The DCMS would like to see more museum visitors from 'C2DE' socio-economic groups and from ethnic minority groups. The current DCMS targets represent the most recent attempt to address this issue.

At first glance, this would seem to be a tough requirement for museum marketers generally, and perhaps especially for those at the Horniman—founded at the height of the British Empire, situated in what was in 1901 a wealthy London suburb of villas and gardens, and housing an idiosyncratic personal collection of exotic curiosities from 'strange' lands; very much an exploration of 'otherness' from the perspective of white Victorians.

However, Horniman staff have found that their museum is in fact in a unique position to fulfil the DCMS agenda. Forest Hill is now part of Lewisham, one of the most culturally mixed boroughs of London and one with a fairly high level of social deprivation. Much of the Horniman's collection is relevant to this multicultural local population; as Marcus Pugh, the Horniman's Head of Development and Marketing, says, 'We are blessed with a collection that actually reflects the communities we now serve.' The depth and variety of the Horniman's anthropology collection in particular enables the museum to fulfil a key role in promoting cultural understanding and integration.

A number of routes have been employed to ensure that diverse 'new' audiences are attracted to the museum and to encourage repeat visitors from within the local community. The museum is free to enter (this was one of Horniman's original requirements) and the recent extension of the museum was designed in part to increase the 'recreational' appeal of the site in addition to its 'educational' function. The museum site comprises the exhibition halls and extensive landscaped gardens. One feature of the new formation of the building is that the gardens have been directly linked to the museum. Previously the museum entrance was off the main road—to access the gardens required a walk to a separate entrance. The two facilities have even, at various times, been administered by different bodies! The new arrangement brings the visitor through to the museum entrance from the gardens and a cross-fertilization is already in evidence, with gardens visitors also visiting the museum, and museum visitors (who tend to have more of a learning agenda) discovering the gardens. Marketing staff are now developing this further by promoting the integration of the museum collection and the gardens, for instance linking the environment section of the museum to practical observations that can be made outside.

One of the main features of the new development was the building of a new space in which to house major temporary exhibitions. This was designed primarily to get more of the collection on view but also to bring large-scale touring exhibitions to the museum. In marketing terms, it allows staff more opportunities and facilitates the attraction of new audiences as it means the museum can offer a new angle on a regular basis and provide something original and different to see. These temporary exhibitions can be used to access new audiences and segments of the community that would not necessarily be attracted by the permanent Horniman 'product'. An exhibition on Caribbean and Amazonian culture is currently planned, and will include a celebration of Caribbean heritage through an active programme of community involvement.

The temporary exhibitions, which will play a high-profile part in the museum's offering in the years to come, should also encourage repeat visits. Local people often visit on a generational cycle, with individuals who were introduced to the Horniman through a school visit returning with their own children, and then again with their grandchildren. Such developments are likely to prompt these visitors back more regularly in future years.

The temporary exhibition hall (and the other facilities introduced as a result of the new development) will also allow Horniman staff to involve local companies with the museum for the first time. The new exhibition gallery has a real synergy with commercial sponsorship; it is flexible, exhibitions can be tailored to incorporate sponsors' needs to an extent, and the exhibitions will be high profile. Museum staff now have a more complete package of products to offer corporate donors and can offer entertainment facilities and space for corporate events.

The Horniman attracts around 260,000 visitors each year. The museum undertakes an annual audience survey of approximately 400 individuals. This has revealed that the mix of visitors the museum attracts reflects closely the mix of the community the Horniman serves. Situated in the heart of one of the most diverse communities in London, this is not a statistic many other urban museums in the UK can boast. This, combined with dramatically increasing visitor numbers (an increase of 100 per cent since the Horniman's relaunch), it is hoped will encourage the DCMS and other funders that they are supporting a thriving museum which is continually evolving to serve its growing and changing audiences.

Developing Audiences Online

As we have previously examined the use of traditional media for audience recruitment, in this section we will focus deliberately on digital media and in particular examine how new audiences may be attracted to arts organizations online. In this environment arts organizations have six additional communication tools at their disposal. These are depicted in

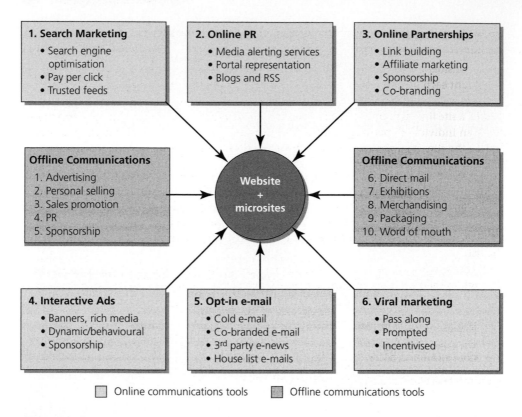

1. Search Marketing
- Search engine optimisation
- Pay per click
- Trusted feeds

2. Online PR
- Media alerting services
- Portal representation
- Blogs and RSS

3. Online Partnerships
- Link building
- Affiliate marketing
- Sponsorship
- Co-branding

Offline Communications
1. Advertising
2. Personal selling
3. Sales promotion
4. PR
5. Sponsorship

Website + microsites

Offline Communications
6. Direct mail
7. Exhibitions
8. Merchandising
9. Packaging
10. Word of mouth

4. Interactive Ads
- Banners, rich media
- Dynamic/behavioural
- Sponsorship

5. Opt-in e-mail
- Cold e-mail
- Co-branded e-mail
- 3rd party e-news
- House list e-mails

6. Viral marketing
- Pass along
- Prompted
- Incentivised

☐ Online communications tools   ▨ Offline communications tools

Figure 10.7 E-marketing mix

Source: Smith, D. and Chaffey, D. (2005) *E-marketing Excellence: At The Heart of E-Business,* 2nd edn, Oxford, Butterworth Heinemann. © Elsevier 2008. Reproduced with kind permission.

Figure 10.7. Although our focus in this chapter is on the arts, the reader will appreciate that the tools presented below will offer equal utility to all categories of nonprofit.

Search Engine Marketing

Search engines such as Google, Ask and Altavista allow users to search for materials online by typing in keywords or phrases. A list of the matching web content is then provided by the engine. The task for the arts marketer is to ensure that their organization's website nears the top of the list when relevant searches are conducted. Two approaches are possible here, since many search engines generate both natural search listings and paid for or 'pay-per-click' listings.

In respect of the former, natural or organic listings emerge 'naturally' from the results of the search the user has conducted. Results are listed in order of the relevance of the match between the content of the web page and the keyword or phrase typed in. They appear on the left in Google, Yahoo, and MSN Search. To improve their position in these listings marketers must engage in search engine optimization to take account of the way in which search engines typically collate their listings. In particular marketers need to:

1. Match the key words on the organization's website with the words most likely to be used by potential customers searching for the work the organization does. Particular attention

should be given to the frequency these words appear in the site (keyword density) and the title tags given to each page.

2. Consider the links that drive traffic into each page. In deciding on its rankings, Google will count each inward link to a site as a 'vote'. Sites with lots of inbound links will therefore perform well. Equally, some algorithms take into account the quality of those links so, for example, a site linked to by the British Museum is likely to get a better ranking than one linked to by an individual's personal website. The presumption would be that if high-quality sites link to the site, then the content must be reliable and worthwhile.

Pay-per-click listings, by contrast, function rather like traditional advertising. To get a high listing here it is necessary to be willing to pay a higher fee than one's competitors. The highest bidder for a particular keyword or phrase will usually be listed at the top of the page, although the Google algorithm does factor in the number of click-throughs that a given ad is able to achieve. Those with a higher click-through rate will tend to appear near the top of the list.

Of course with pay-per-click, as the name suggests, the marketer must pay for each click-through to their site from the search engine. It is therefore not just a matter of achieving the highest rate of click-through possible. A good deal of money can be wasted driving traffic to the site that has absolutely no interest in the products or services on offer. The key to successful pay-per-click advertising lies in writing the best possible copy for the text box that will appear in the listing so that users can judge the relevance for themselves and only genuinely good prospects will follow the link. Marketers using pay-per-click also have to consider the appropriate amounts to bid for each listing and manage their budgets accordingly.

Online Public Relations

Smith and Chaffey (2005) argue that there are four core activities of online PR.

Link Building

The goal of online PR is to maximize the number of favourable mentions of the brand, organization, its website, and/or performances on third-party websites. Third-party endorsements are as useful in the online environment as they are in the offline. Such mentions are also useful because they often contain links back to the organization's website and thus aid in search engine optimization. A useful way of identifying who is currently linking to your organization is to visit the Google website and in the search box enter 'link: www.(your domain name)'. A list of the websites linking in to that site will be generated.

Communicating with Journalists Online

E-mail and websites can be used to pass on information to journalists who might be interested in featuring the work of the organization in an upcoming article or comment. Some organizations go so far as to establish dedicated press rooms on their site where an archive of press releases and other information is provided that journalists may use. It is also possible to submit genuinely newsworthy material to the media through news feeds such as www.prweb.com or www.prnewswire.com.

Blogs and RSS

Web logs or 'blogs' are an increasingly popular way of publishing news and event listings online. Many arts organizations have now established blogs to demonstrate the credibility of the organization and engage with their audiences, e.g. http://www.artinliverpool.com/blog/. As an aside, readers with a particular interest in interactive marketing will find the digital marketing guru Dave Chaffey's blog worth following. It can be found at www.davechaffey.com.

Really Simple Syndication (RSS) allows users to sign up for regular news on topics of interest. Blogs, video, and news of any type is sent directly to an individual's computer where it is read by specialist reader software such as FeedDemon. News feeds also allow the user to see when new website content has been added and to view all the latest headlines and video in one place, as soon as its published, without having to visit the original website. Since users can specify the kinds of information they are specifically interested in, marketing in this way can be highly effective.

Online Reputation Management

There are two types of reputational management of interest. In the first the organization takes a proactive approach to seeding positive content about itself on popular sites. As an example, YouTube's 2007/2008 Clinton Global Initiative commitment enables nonprofit organizations that register for the program to receive a free nonprofit-specific YouTube channel where they can upload footage of their work, public service announcements, calls to action, and more. The channel also allows them to collect donations with no processing costs using the newly launched Google Checkout for Non-Profits. YouTube's global platform thus enables nonprofits to deliver their message, showcase their impact and needs, and encourage supporters to take action.

The Boston Pops Orchestra has recently attempted to attract a newer, younger audience with a couple of programmatic changes and an *American Idol*-like contest included on the YouTube site. For the 2007 season, the Pops made a splash by featuring singer-songwriter Ben Folds as part of the orchestra's opening performance, drawing an audience packed with young listeners. Soon after, the Pops launched POPSearch 2007, a competition in which contestants uploaded videos of themselves performing to YouTube. The winner won the once-in-a-lifetime opportunity to perform with the Pops during their 4 July concert, and was featured as a guest artist during its summer tour. It is interesting to note that the Pops also promoted the opportunity on the highly popular social networking website Myspace (http://www.myspace.com/popsearch).

The second facet of online reputation management concerns managing unfavourable coverage and responding where appropriate to criticism. A key facet of online PR is therefore monitoring how an organization is being covered by third-party websites. Services such as Googlealert (www.googlealert.com) and Google alerts (www.google.com/alerts) can be used to alert you to when any new pages are published that include mention of your organization. As an aside, these tools can also be a valuable way of checking on the online promotions undertaken by competitors or similar organizations in other parts of the country. They may well have good ideas that can be borrowed or adapted for your own use.

Online Partnerships

Online partnerships may take one of four forms.

Links

The significance of developing a good network of links has already been highlighted and nonprofits should exploit potential partnerships where they can encouraging reciprocal links (i.e. where two-way links are agreed between each site). The specialist site Linking

Matters (www.linkingmatters.com) provides considerable guidance on how best to maximize this opportunity.

Affiliate Marketing

It may be appropriate for some organizations to consider establishing a network of affiliates who earn a commission for the sales or leads that they generate. Amazon.com for example has an active network of affiliates who earn a commission on the purchases made by every visitor they direct to the Amazon website. A commission-based system lowers the risk for the organization as it only need pay for results, but on the downside affiliates can ultimately become competitors for search engine optimization and pay-per-click advertising, thereby pushing up the costs. The nonprofit also loses some control over how the brand is presented and if the affiliate is involved in a wide range of activities there may even be reputational risk involved in operating in this way.

Online Sponsorship

Online sponsorship involves a sponsoring organization linking its name with that of the nonprofit for the purpose of strengthening its brand. It is more than the provision of a simple banner or other form of advertising and typically takes the form of a genuine involvement with what the nonprofit is trying to achieve online, perhaps by sponsoring specific forms of content, or engagement with specific stakeholder groups. Nonprofits in the UK seeking to publicize their sponsorship opportunities may wish to consider placing a listing in the UK sponsorship database at http://www.uksponsorship.com/.

Co-Branding

Co-branding takes online sponsorship one stage further. It is an opportunity for partnership rather than mere sponsorship, so the difference is one of degree. In co-branding, both partners work to leverage the client base of the other. An arts organization might therefore work with a corporate partner to co-brand a password-protected part of its website for season ticket subscribers. The corporate partner has exposure to the most loyal customers of the arts organization, while the arts organization gains an additional facility it might not otherwise be able to afford.

Another might achieve the co-branding of a particular season or production and ensure that the sponsor's name is clearly associated with this on the nonprofit's website and that the arts brand in turn is showcased on the site of its corporate partner. In the case of the latter, detailed information about the work, the musicians, the performance itself etc. would be embedded in the corporate site. In all these examples each partner is seeking access to the client base of the other to promote its own products/service and is doing so by offering them some additional value, typically relevant information or enhanced functionality.

Interactive Advertising

The term 'interactive advertising' refers to all advertising through the web, e-mail, wireless technologies, and interactive television. Internet advertising commonly takes the form of banner ads, skyscrapers, and underlay/overlays.

Banner ads are the most common and can appear in several different locations on a webpage. Skyscrapers are also common and these vary, as their name suggests, by the nature of their shape. They tend to be long and skinny and run along one side of the page. Webpages can be viewed in many different resolutions (typically set by the user in their browser) and the selected resolution refers to the dots or pixels per inch (dpi or ppi). The term 'resolution' can also refer to how many pixels are set to fit horizontally (across) and vertically (down) a monitor. Essentially, 800×600 and 1024×768 are currently the most common resolutions, and the normal width of a skyscraper ad is 120 pixels. Some people prefer a slightly wider building, however, or perhaps one that expands when a mouse passes over it.

The term 'overlay' is also quite intuitive and refers to an ad that is served over the page being viewed by the user. The video-sharing website YouTube has many clips featuring discussions of how overlays can be used to good effect and the range of effects that can be achieved using different technologies. A search on 'overlay ads' on www.youtube.com will bring up these materials. Underlays, by contrast, are ads that appear under the page being viewed and which therefore become visible only when the relevant browser window is closed.

Each time an ad is served an ad impression is created. The number of ad impressions is thus a key metric in this environment, although many users may view the same ad on a number of occasions, so the advertising reach is also key. This refers to the number of unique individuals who view the advertisement.

The three most common ways online ads are purchased are CPM, CPA, and CPC.

CPM (cost per impression) is where advertisers pay for exposure of their ad to a particular audience. CPM costs are the cost to serve a thousand impressions. The use of the M in the acronym is a little confusing, but it refers to the Roman numeral for one thousand.

CPC (cost per click) or PPC (pay-per-click). In this scenario advertisers pay each time a user clicks on their listing and is directed to their website. They do not pay for the listing itself and pay only when the listing is clicked on. As discussed earlier, under the pay-per-click system, advertisers bid for the right to be listed under a series of target-rich words that direct relevant traffic to their website. They only pay when someone clicks on that listing.

CPA (cost per action or cost per acquisition). With this method payment is made on the basis of performance. It is typical of the remuneration method employed for affiliates. Here, the publisher carries all the risk of running the ad and the advertiser pays only for those consumers who actually complete a desired action, usually a purchase. CPL (cost per lead) is also common with publishers being remunerated when users complete a registration form or 'sign-up' to something that is core to the nonprofit's mission. For the sake of completeness, CPO (cost per order) may also be encountered where, as the name suggests, a fee is payable every time an order is placed.

CPC (cost per conversion). This is simply the cost of acquiring a customer and is typically calculated by dividing the total cost of a campaign by the number of conversions. What constitutes a 'conversion' will vary depending on the purpose of the campaign. It might be a sale, but it may also be taking action or registering an interest in some aspect of the nonprofit's work.

Nonprofits seeking to evaluate between the various advertising alternatives open to them will typically need the following information:

- the CPM or cost per thousand ad servings;
- the click-through rate (the percentage of ad servings that result in an individual clicking the ad);
- the conversion rate (the percentage of customers clicking through that will make a purchase or take the desired action).

Consider the following fictitious example for an ad on Yahoo.

CPM = $1.50

Click-through rate = 0.1%

Conversion rate = 2%

What will it cost to generate one impression?

This is simply the CPM rate ÷ 1000

So $1.50 ÷1000 = $0.0015

How many impressions will it take to generate one click?

This is simply 100 ÷ click-through rate

So 100 ÷ 0.1 = 1000

How much will one click cost?

This is calculated as:

Cost per impression × how many impressions to generate one click

So $0.0015 × 1000 = $1.50

How many clicks are needed to generate a sale?

This is calculated as:

100 ÷ conversion rate

So 100 ÷ 2 = 50

How much will one sale cost?

This is calculated as:

The number of clicks needed to generate a sale × the cost of each click

So $1.50 × 50 = $75

With experience, as ads with different publishers are trialled nonprofits can use these calculations to compare between the various advertising options open to them and optimize their online communications mix. They may for example develop a table comparing the costs of generating a sale by advertising on each of the major search engines and allocate their budget accordingly.

Opt-In E-Mail

Opt-in e-mail is critical to the successful development of online relationships. In the arts context it can be used to build awareness of the performances available, to provide additional 'behind the scenes' information, or to sell seats for the performances themselves. The key to success lies in the 'opt-in' and in many countries this is now a legal requirement. When users visit a site and have the opportunity to sign up for e-mail newsletters or alerts, they should specifically tick a check box to indicate their consent. Ideally they should also be able to specify the frequency and content of the information they will receive.

Most opt-in e-mail is 'warm' in the sense that a visitor to a site or customer has explicitly signed up to receive communications from the organization. Such house list campaigns can be very effective and organizations should think through carefully the pattern of communications each segment of individuals will receive. Over time the efficacy of the timing and content of this can be evaluated and changes made to strategy accordingly.

'Cold' e-mail is often conducted too, perhaps where an organization rents a list from a provider such as Experian (www.prospectlocator.com) which consists of the contact details of individuals who have given permission to be approached by specific categories of organization. Given the hostility that many people feel towards unsolicited e-mail it is important when renting lists to include a statement of origin indicating how the communication was initiated to differentiate it from spam.

In the arts context, it may also be appropriate to consider the use of co-branded e-mail and work jointly with other arts organizations or corporate partners, designing communications that will be of interest to their customers and jointly communicating with shared lists. Although this is technically still cold e-mail, because a relationship already exists with one of the partners it is likely to generate a higher response.

Viral Marketing

Viral marketing or 'word of mouse' uses the power of the web for rapid and personal communication. It is a mechanism whereby an organization's customers (or other stakeholder groups) are encouraged to pass along a message to their friends and associates promoting the organization. This message may be a video clip, cartoon, political message, or news item. It could be sent as a link, a Flash e-mail. a JPEG, or a text message over the Web or SMS networks. Whatever its form, the key to successful viral marketing is that the content should be compelling enough for people to want to pass it along.

Kirby (2003) argues that three components should be considered in a viral campaign:

1. the viral agent—creative material, message, or offer and how it is spread (text, image, video);
2. seeding—identifying websites, blogs, or people to send your e-mail to, to start the virus spreading;
3. tracking—to monitor the effect, to assess the return on the cost of developing the agent and seeding.

Smith and Chaffey (2005) identify five categories of viral e-mail:

Pass Along E-Mail

In this case the e-mail itself is the only mechanism involved in spreading the message. The viral message may be contained in an attachment or it may perhaps contain a link to a video clip or game. The aim here is to ask recipients to pass the message along to their friends and acquaintances.

Web Facilitated Viral (E-Mail Prompt)

The e-mail contains a button labelled 'e-mail a friend' or 'tell someone else about our work.' When users click through they open a form which requests the address to which the e-mail should be forwarded and there is also (typically) an opportunity to send an accompanying message to the friend.

Web Facilitated Viral (Web Prompt)

In this case a webpage on an organization's site will be set up to contain the link 'tell a friend'. In the arts context this may, for example, appear on a page promoting a new season or special event. Users can be given the opportunity to spread the word to family and friends they know will be interested.

Incentivised Viral

Here the contact details are not freely given. Instead the organization encourages an individual to part with the contact information by offering some form of incentive, perhaps entry into a draw the prize for which, in the arts context, might be a season ticket. Each time a set of details are passed on a new entry can be made in the draw. Such incentives can be offered on the organization's webpage or through an e-mail communication. Please note, however, that before undertaking a campaign of this nature it will be important to consider the privacy rules that apply in your home country. Since the recipient has not given their consent to be contacted it can be illegal in some jurisdictions.

Web-Link Viral

This final category refers to links that are seeded in newsletters, articles, discussion group listings, or blogs. These may be communications the organization itself has initiated or they may be seeded in third-party communications. The key here will be to use online PR to get as much coverage for the viral agent as possible.

Customer Retention and Development

In the preceding discussion of digital marketing we have focused our attention largely on the issue of customer recruitment or to use the industry term 'acquisition'. Once recruited an arts organization will be able to store basic information about the individual in its box office database. At a minimum this will include contact details, payment method, recruitment source (i.e. the media that bought them in), their communication and data protection preferences, and basic FRAC data concerning their buying behaviour. FRAC stands for frequency of purchase, recency of purchase, amount of purchase, and category (e.g. what categories of performance have been purchased). The data can then be used for a variety of purposes including building customer loyalty; cross-selling; up-selling; and effective targeting.

Building Customer Loyalty

Box office data can be used to add value to a client's experience with an arts organization. Frequent attenders can be rewarded for their loyalty by offering them concessions, invitations to special events, and even loyalty points which can be exchanged for either merchandise or seats at subsequent performances. It may come as a surprise to learn that even the Royal Opera House now operates such a scheme. Of course, the creation of consumer rewards must be handled with care—it would hardly be appropriate for example to offer a scheme entitled Aria Miles, or in the case of a ballet company, Pirouette Points. Loyal customers to these art forms are entitled to be rewarded for their loyalty, but in a manner that is wholly appropriate for the art form in question. Often the safest way of achieving this is through the provision of points which can be redeemed for additional tickets or free seat upgrades. Indeed given that few performances will completely sell out, a loyalty scheme can often operate at minimal cost.

Cross-Selling

Cross-selling can take two different forms in arts marketing. The first might involve the marketer in encouraging customers for one category of event to attend and view another. Thus ballet customers could be informed of upcoming classical music concerts in an attempt to broaden their attendance pattern. More usually though, cross-selling may involve developing a link with a second organization and the sharing of names/addresses so that customers are informed of appropriate events taking place at other venues in the area. While this might on the face of it sound like commercial suicide, a review by DiMaggio et al. (1978) of 270 audience studies confirmed that high-value patrons of one art form are also likely to be high-value patrons of another. The sensitive sharing of names and addresses can therefore work to the benefit of both organizations.

Up-Selling

Up-selling involves the marketer in trying to develop the arts customer to a higher level of value. In other words, an attempt could be made to persuade customers to take higher-value seats, or to attend on a more frequent basis. The McCarter Theater in Princetown, New Jersey, installed a client/server system that facilitated an increase in subscription sales by 20 per cent. As the curtain rises on each performance, the system allows sales and marketing staff to begin work generating a list of all ticket holders. Current subscription holders are separated from those who do not currently have a subscription and the latter category are targeted for a marketing campaign the following day. Clearly, if the audience have enjoyed the evening's performance, they will be more likely to accept a subscription package while the enjoyment is still fresh in their minds.

Effective Targeting

When an organization recognizes the buying behaviour of its clients, it can utilize this knowledge in targeting specific campaigns at those it knows will be most likely to respond. Offers and information pertinent to performances of ballet can therefore be targeted only at those customers who enjoy this art form. Similarly advanced information in respect of the annual pantomime can be targeted at those individuals known either to have small children, or to have attended such categories of performance in the past.

In addition, the comments made in respect of profiling in the previous chapter are equally pertinent here. Attenders at specific categories of events can be profiled and the data used to inform the purchase of lists of other individuals who might also be predisposed to attending such categories of event.

Data Mining

The establishment of a marketing database can open up remarkable insight for marketers into the nature of the customers they are interacting with and key facets of their behaviour.

In other words, the database can be a key learning tool and organizations can 'mine' customer data for new and actionable information.

The term 'data mining' refers to 'the extraction of previously unknown yet comprehensible and actionable information from large repositories of data, used to make crucial (marketing) decisions and support their implementation, including formulating tactical and strategic marketing initiatives and measuring their success' (Edelstein 1999: 15).

As this definition makes clear, data mining techniques are usually applied in the context of a large amount of data, typically stored in what is known as a data warehouse. A data warehouse is simply a system kept separate from the operational systems of an organization, and is available solely for the task of being interrogated for information. Many commercial organizations now establish warehouses of data and then apply a range of statistical tools (such as cluster analysis) to try and find relationships between the variables stored on the database that would simply not be detectable by other means. Some organizations may also seek to supplement this data with other profiling information about customers and also input this into their analysis.

In the context of arts marketing, data mining could therefore answer questions such as:

- What are the lifestyle interests of my customers?
- What is the profile of my high-value customers?
- Do certain types of people attend certain types of performance?
- Are there segments of people on the database who are responsive to certain forms of communication?
- What is the best way to develop customer value across the database?

To discern this information it is necessary to have a large database at your disposal and for a copy of this to be available offline so that the necessary manipulation of data can take place. Organizations employing data mining also need to have a fair amount of historic data about the behaviour of their customers and this data must be clean (i.e. contain few errors or omissions).

In the context of the arts and wider nonprofit sector, there are relatively few large databases that are big enough to support data mining in the commercial sense, but many organizations can, and do, mine their databases for the answers to particular questions to inform their marketing strategy.

Customer Relationship Management

Customer relationship management, or CRM as it is now widely known in marketing textbooks, is a collective term for methodologies, technologies, and e-commerce capabilities used to manage customer relationships (Foss and Stone 2001). In the context of arts marketing it is therefore about how one establishes and builds an appropriate relationship with all the customers who patronize the organization. CRM tools can help to identify customer relationships that will never be profitable, usually because over time it costs more to communicate with these individuals than they ever contribute in revenue. It can also help develop the value of all the customers who *will* be profitable to deal with.

The detail of CRM methodologies is beyond the scope of this text, but good CRM involves thinking through the marketing process as the customer experiences it and thus designing appropriate systems to deal with enquiries, to welcome new customers, to get to know those customers, to develop those customers, to manage any problems they might have and, if the relationship fails, to try to win back customers who have stopped purchasing from the organization.

CRM thus moves beyond the simple management of the customer database we alluded to above; it is more about thinking through the systems and processes that are in place to manage customer relationships. Organizations embracing CRM also need to consider the fit of the people they employ with customer needs and to reflect on the technology that will be necessary to support their decision making and any marketing plans they might develop. CRM effectively integrates all these ingredients.

Attracting Funding

The Arts Funding Framework

The funding framework for the arts in the UK is complex. Arts funders include central government, national assemblies, local authorities, the lottery, and private bursaries. Arts organizations will typically generate income through a number of streams: earned income, government subsidy, private donations, and business sponsorship.

In operating this 'mixed economy' in arts funding, the UK occupies the middle ground between heavy dependence on the State—as in European countries such as France and Germany—and almost entire reliance on private investment, as in the USA. The reason for the UK government's interest in the sector has morphed in recent years. The arts are now seen as an important vehicle for facilitating social change. Arts organizations are now expected to do more than merely carry out their roles as arts producers or a part of the cultural industries. They are being positioned as experts who are able to produce and deliver programmes for social inclusion, community empowerment, and lifelong learning. As agents for social regeneration and creative educators, they are required to contribute directly towards the fulfilment of a wide range of social objectives in return for public subsidy.

It is therefore no surprise that increasing the number of people taking part in arts activities is now embedded in Government policy. Targets have been agreed between the Department of Culture, Media, and Sport (the department which funds the Arts Council) for the period 2005–8 and the Treasury in the form of Public Service Agreements (PSAs). PSA 3, for example, required an increase in the take-up of cultural and sporting activities by people aged 16 and above from priority groups by 2008. This was to be measured by a number of indicators including:

- increasing the number who participate in arts activity at least twice a year by 2%;
- increasing the number who attend arts events at least twice a year by 3%;
- increasing the number accessing museums and gallery collections by 2%;
- increasing the number visiting designated historic environment sites by 3%.

The Arts Councils

The Arts Councils of England, Scotland, Northern Ireland, and Wales are entrusted with the power to hand out money provided by government and the National Lottery to arts bodies and institutions. Since 1999 the assemblies in Wales and Northern Ireland and the parliament in Scotland have taken on the role of giving the arts councils each a block grant, which they can then distribute to the arts in respective countries as they see fit. Individual funding decisions are thus taken at 'arm's length' from the government, which in theory enables them to be free to operate without government interference.

The Arts Councils' objectives are:

- to develop and improve the knowledge, understanding, and practice of the arts;
- to increase the accessibility of the arts to the public throughout Britain;
- to advise and cooperate with departments of government, local authorities, and other bodies.

The criteria for funding encourages applicants to give consideration to many of the 'balances' alluded to earlier. Arts organizations are expected to recognize the need to make a contribution to the cultural traditions of the region in which they operate. To do so will involve a careful identification of the nature of the existing local provision and an analysis of any gaps that would contribute to the range of experiences available. These gaps can then be compared with the resources available in-house to identify any opportunities that might exist for development.

Aside from the need to demonstrate a contribution to the cultural health of a region, potential applicants must also demonstrate the quality of their management and in particular the quality of their marketing management. They must be able to show that they have the capability to communicate effectively with target audiences and attract (and involve) reasonable numbers of customers given the nature of the performances/attractions provided. Marketing can therefore no longer be viewed as a peripheral activity. It must permeate the core of an organization's thinking and, moreover, be shown to have done so.

Local Authorities

Local authorities are the second largest supporter of the arts in the UK. They play a central role in supporting the arts regionally, not only through direct funding of arts organizations and events, but also through the provision and management of arts venues and the promotion of arts events. Local authority funding of the arts is discretionary; they are able to support the arts but it is not an official requirement. All local authorities operate differently, with their own structures, policies, grant criteria, and schemes.

Commercial Sponsorship

No chapter on arts marketing would be complete without a brief discussion of arts sponsorship, which remains for many organizations an important source of income. Sponsorship involves a company in exchanging (usually cash) support for a series of benefits which the arts organization, by virtue of the nature of its portfolio, or the profile of the audience it expects to attract, is able to provide.

From the corporate perspective, sponsorship can offer a number of benefits, many of which are so attractive in nature that a sizeable proportion of a marketing budget may be parted with to acquire them. The following benefits are the most common and form the basis of most solicitations initiated by arts organizations. Sponsorship can be used very effectively:

- to build up awareness of a corporate name or brand;
- to add value to that name or brand by demonstrating good citizenship;

- to generate favourable publicity for the sponsor;
- to romance important customers/distributors/staff through the provision of executive entertainment.

This latter point is worthy of elaboration, since some organizations look to their sponsorship as a means of being able to offer hospitality to important clients. As a condition of its support, the corporate sponsor insists on access to reserved seating, a special performance, or other such benefit. It can then offer free seats to selected individuals. Not only can this be an effective and non-threatening way of securing new business, it can also help reward staff, distributors, or intermediaries for their efforts over the preceding months. Corporate sponsorship was instrumental, for example, in allowing the management of an exhibition centre to meet the costs of hiring a touring exhibition of Chinese dinosaurs. The key condition of the support was that the sponsor would be able to host a dinner for its key personnel and clients in the building and that the evening would include an opportunity to view the dinosaur exhibition privately. Indeed the dinner was scheduled so that these individuals were actually the first to view what proved to be an enormously popular exhibition.

More commonly, however, the business places greater emphasis on the generation of favourable publicity, since if this is timed correctly, and occurs in media likely to be viewed by the target audience, a direct impact on sales can often be measured. Any arts organization looking to secure sponsorship for the first time would therefore be well advised to seek organizations that have some synergy either with the nature of their productions or the target audience they are attempting to serve. This should not be the end of the search, however. In the author's experience it is also well worth consulting information sources such as market reports, trade and quality press, and the Internet, since useful intelligence can often result. Companies often support arts organizations that, on the face of it, would seem difficult to justify. AT&T, for example, has a history of supporting arts organizations which seemingly would be able to offer little in return. The company supported the Almeida (a small 300-seat venue in North London) in staging an obscure Russian satire by Sergeyevich Griboyedov. When one understands, however, that AT&T takes credit for producing the first transistor, the first laser, and the first commercial satellite, one begins to understand that the company is not afraid to take risks and this is reflected in the pattern of sponsorship it chooses to provide. The company likes to take risks with its sponsorship monies and to support performances that might otherwise not be seen. Nor is AT&T alone in its somewhat unorthodox pattern of sponsorship, making it essential for arts organizations serious about seeking sponsorship to look beyond the most 'obvious' lists of prospects to approach.

Before leaving the question of sponsorship, however, it is important to sound a word of caution. While arts organizations will doubtless be grateful for any offer of support they receive, there are wider considerations than the mere receipt of money. The culture and/or history of an organization may make it inappropriate for gifts to be accepted from certain categories of corporate organization. Those involved in dubious environmental practices, or organizations with less than reputable connections to developing countries, are particular candidates for avoidance, although altogether more subtle reasons will often be found to exist. As with other forms of corporate fundraising, there is therefore no substitute for the careful research into potential sponsors prior to the initial contact. This can conserve valuable marketing resources and avoid considerable embarrassment if the decision must be taken to withdraw at a later stage.

■ SUMMARY

In this chapter we have examined the relevance of marketing to the arts sector. It was argued that although many of the tools and techniques of marketing are of direct relevance, there is a need to adapt the fundamental marketing concept to accommodate the need for arts organizations to take a longer-term view of the needs of the society in which they are located. It was further suggested that this modification to the marketing concept could best be articulated as a need to achieve a series of balances: the balance of performances in a portfolio, the balance in portrayal of the arts, and the balance in terms of audiences attracted.

The chapter then examined the issue of audience recruitment and in particular through an extended digital communications mix. The use of search engine marketing, online PR, online partnerships, opt-in email, interactive advertising, and viral marketing was discussed and a number of suggestions offered in respect of best practice.

The development and use of a box office database was also introduced and suggestions were offered in respect of both the most appropriate information to hold and how this might best be used for the purposes of building customer loyalty, cross-selling, up-selling, and the targeting of individuals who might be most likely to respond to particular campaigns.

The final part of the chapter examined marketing's application to the attraction of funding. The criteria for Arts Council funding were noted and the significance of marketing in allowing an organization to satisfy these was noted. The chapter concluded with a discussion of the role of corporate sponsorship and the benefits that could accrue to both the sponsor and the sponsored.

■ DISCUSSION QUESTIONS

1. Why has the arts sector been slow to recognize the significance of marketing, both as a guiding philosophy and as a functional area of management?

2. How might an understanding of the audience motivations for attending an arts event inform the development of an appropriate marketing mix? Illustrate your answer with examples.

3. You have been asked to give a talk to the Arts Marketing Association about the importance of segmenting a box-office database. What would be the key dimensions that such a talk would need to address?

4. With reference to your own arts organization, or one with which you are familiar, suggest appropriate fields of data that marketing management should look to create in the design of its customer records.

5. How might a gallery improve its natural search engine listing for critical key word searches?

6. Identify three examples of successful viral marketing online. What characteristics do these campaigns have in common (if any)? Why do you believe they were successful?

7. Sign up to receive an e-mail newsletter from two or three arts organizations. How would you rate the communications you receive? Explain your view.

8. Access the website YouTube. Do a search for 'charity' video clips. Select three that you like. How effective are these clips at getting you to think through the work of the organization? Do they appear to be part of an integrated digital communications mix (hint—check out the organization's website too)? Might the approach adopted be improved in any way? Explain your view.

■ **REFERENCES**

Arts Council of Great Britain (1993) *A Creative Future: The Way Forward for the Arts: Crafts and Media in England*, London, HMSO.

Boorsma, M. (2006) 'A Strategic Logic for Arts Marketing: Integrating Customer Value and Artistic Objectives', *International Journal of Cultural Policy*, Vol. 12, No. 1, 73–92.

Botti, S. (2000) 'What Is The Role for Marketing in the Arts? An Analysis of Arts Consumption and Artistic Value', *International Journal of Arts Management*, Vol. 2, No. 3, 16–27.

Bourdieu, P. (1984) *Distinction: A Social Critique of the Judgement of Taste*, London, Routledge.

Butcher, K., Sparks, B. and O'Callaghan, F. (2002) 'Effect of Social Influence in Repurchase Intention', *Journal of Services Marketing*, Vol. 16, No. 6, 503–15.

Caust, J. (2003) 'Putting the "art" back Into Arts Policy Making: How Arts Policy Has Been "Captured" by the Economists and Marketers', *International Journal of Cultural Policy,* Vol. 9, No. 1, 51–63.

Colbert, F. (2003) 'Entrepreneurship and Leadership in Marketing The Arts', *International Journal of Arts Management*, Vol. 6, No. 1, 30–9.

Colbert, F., Nantel, J., Bilodeau, S. and Rich, J.D. (2001) *Marketing Culture and the Arts*, Montreal, HEC.

Cooper, G.A. and Tower, R. (1994) 'Inside the Consumer Mind: Consumer Attitudes to the Arts', *Journal of the Market Research Society*, Vol. 34, No. 4, 299–311.

Dawson, W.M. (1980) 'The Arts and Marketing' in Mokwa, M.P., Prieve, E.A. and Dawson, W.M. (1980) *Marketing the Arts*, New York, Praeger Press.

Diggle, K. (1984) *Arts Marketing*, London, Rhinegold Publishing.

DiMaggio, P., Useem, M. and Brown, P. (1978) *Audience Studies of the Performing Arts and Museums: A Critical Review*, Washington DC, National Endowment for the Arts.

Edelstein, H.A. (1999) *Introduction to Data Mining and Knowledge Discovery*, Chicago, Two Crows Corporation.

Ford, C. (1993) 'Tuning up for Promotion', *Incentive Today*, Sept., 14–16.

Foss, B. and Stone, M. (2001) *Successful Customer Relationship Marketing: New Thinking, New Strategies, New Tools For Getting Closer To Your Customers*, London, Kogan Page.

Hume, M., Mort, G.S., Liesch, P.W. and Winzar, H. (2006) 'Understanding Service Experience in Non-Profit Performing Arts: Implications For Operations and Service Management', *Journal of Operations Management*, Vol. 24, 304–24.

Kaali-Nagy, C. and Garrison, L.C. (1972) 'Profiles of Users and Non-Users of the Los Angeles Music Center', *California Management Review*, Vol. 15, Winter, 133–43.

Kirby, J. (2003) 'Online Viral Marketing: Next Big Thing or Yesterday's Fling?' *New Media Knowledge*, March 2003. http://nmk.co.uk/knowledge_network/kn_item?ItemID=4884&ThreadID=46

Kotler, P. and Scheff, J. (1997) *Standing Room Only: Strategies for Marketing the Performing Arts*, Boston MA., Harvard Business School Press.

Leighton, D. (2007) 'Step Back in Time and Live the Legend: Experiential Marketing and the Heritage Sector', *International Journal of Nonprofit and Voluntary Sector Marketing*, Vol. 12, No. 2, 117–25.

Mokwa, M.P., Prieve, E.A. and Dawson, W.M. (1980) *Marketing the Arts*, New York, Praeger Press.

Neill, T. and Orme, E. (2006) *Walk Ups, Advance Bookers and Non Bookers*, London, Cultural Intelligence. Available for download at http://www.audience.co.uk.

Reiss, A.H. (1994) 'The Arts Look Ahead', *Fundraising Management*, Vol. 25, No. 1, 27–31.

Ricklefs, R. (1975) 'Museums Merchandise more Shows and Wares to Broaden Patronage', *Wall Street Journal*, Vol. XCIII, No. 32, 14 Aug.

Ryans, A. and Weinberg, C. (1978) 'Consumer Dynamics in Nonprofit Organisations', *Journal of Consumer Research*, Vol. 5, 89–95.

Sargeant, A. (1997) 'Marketing the Arts—A Classification of UK Theatre Audiences', *Journal of Non Profit and Public Sector Marketing*, Vol. 5, No. 1, 45–62.

Schmitt, B. (2000) 'Marketers Seeking Sense In Sensibility. Forget The Features, How Do Consumers Experience Your Product? That's Central To The Idea of Experiential Marketing', *Financial Times*, 24 October, 12.

Searles, P.D. (1980) 'Marketing Principles in the Arts', in Mokwa, M.P., Prieve, E.A. and Dawson, W.M. (1980) *Marketing the Arts*, New York, Praeger Press.

Semenik, R.J. and Young, C.E. (1979) 'Market Segmentation in Arts Organisations', *Proceedings of the 1979 American Marketing Association Conference*, 474–8.

Smith, D. and Chaffey, D. (2005) *E-Marketing Excellence: At The Heart of E-Business*, 2nd edn, Oxford, Butterworth Heinemann.

Strehler, G. (1990) 'The Marketing Oriented Diffusion of Art and Culture: Potential Risks and Benefits', *Marketing and Research Today*, Nov., 209–12.

Swanson, S.R. and Davis, J.C. (2006) 'Arts Patronage: A Social Identity Perspective', *Journal of Marketing Theory and Practice*, Vol. 14, No. 2, 125–38.

11 Education

Introduction

It is proposed to begin this chapter by introducing some of the major changes that have taken place in British education over the past 30 years. While such an introduction could be criticized on the grounds of being geocentric, an understanding of the environment in which educational establishments now operate provides an essential background against which to assess the immediate benefits that might accrue from addressing issues such as the attainment of a marketing orientation and, particularly, a focus on students as customers. Indeed, while the specific nature of the pattern of education provision will vary considerably from country to country, many of the same forces for change are in evidence. It is thus hoped that the subsequent discussion in this chapter will be equally relevant for all educational institutions, irrespective of the country in which they are based. This chapter will therefore examine what might be viewed as the generic difficulties experienced by educational establishments in achieving a market orientation, and define the needs of the key publics on which a focus must be developed. The chapter will also examine the decision-making process as it applies to two key publics: prospective students and their parents. It will conclude with an overview of the unique nature of the educational product and discuss some of the difficulties that are likely to be encountered in the design of an appropriate educational marketing mix.

Recent Changes in the UK Education Framework

Primary/Secondary Education

In the UK, the Education Act of 1988 unleashed the power of market forces on the management of schools for the first time. Prior to the introduction of the Act the pattern of primary and secondary education could perhaps best be described as a series of small markets each dominated by a monopoly player. Since implementation however, this position has altered, and in some regions quite dramatically. In essence, the Act has shifted power away from the schools and the staff working in those schools towards pupils and parents. Key changes implemented by the Act included:

1. The creation of Grant Maintained Schools (GMS). Primary and secondary schools could, under this provision, remove themselves fully from their respective Local Education Authorities and instead opt to be fully funded by central government.

2. Similarly, the Local Management of Schools (LMS) was introduced. This part of the Act allowed all schools to be taken out of the direct financial control of local authorities. Financial control would be handed to the headteacher and governors of a school.

3. A National Curriculum (NC) was introduced.

4. 'Key Stages' (KS) were introduced in schools. At each key stage a number of educational objectives were to be achieved.

    *   Key Stage 1: Years 1 to 2 (5–7 years old)

    *   Key Stage 2: Years 3 to 6 (7–11 years old)

    *   Key Stage 3: Years 7 to 9 (11–14 years old)

    *   Key Stage 4: Years 10 to 11 (14–16 years old). GCSE (General Certificate of Secondary Education) examinations are typically sat at the end of key stage 4.

    *   Key Stage 5 (or Sixth Form): Years 12 to 13 (16–18 years old). A (Advanced) level examinations are typically sat at the end of key stage 5.

5. League tables, publishing the examination results of schools, were introduced.

6. An element of choice was introduced, where parents could specify which school was their preferred choice.

Parents now have the ability to select the school they feel is right for their child and, provided that the necessary place exists and that the child in question meets any entrance requirements, their wishes are usually respected. Of course, in practice there are real constraints which reduce the level of parental choice. In many cases, the number of local schools might be very small, making it difficult to exercise genuine choice. Alternatively parents may not have the resources necessary to transport their child to a school more distant from their home. The Act has, however, had a dramatic effect in many parts of the country and school rolls have genuinely begun to reflect the local pattern of parental choice, favouring 'good' schools over those which are felt to perform less well. Since the system of government funding is now based on a simple formula which reflects the numbers of children enrolled, a failure to recruit can starve a school of resources for IT, library, and sports facilities. Under these circumstances a greater percentage of the school's income will be absorbed by fixed costs, such as the maintenance of school buildings or staff salaries, which must be paid irrespective of the number of pupils enrolled. Competition is thus a real issue for many organizations and marketing has a crucial role to play in encouraging parents and pupils to view a particular school in a favourable light.

In an age where there is considerable public interest in levels of school discipline and when a school's reputation can often hang on this issue alone, effective communication with local communities takes on a new significance. Relationships need to be built with all stakeholder groups in the locality to ensure that strong positive images of the role of a particular school and its pupils are developed over time. Moreover, a good public image, while it will doubtless aid in the attraction of students, will also help to attract and retain new staff. It is no secret that many UK schools now find it difficult to attract suitably qualified professionals because of their poor reputation. This may have been generated by the attainment of low academic standards, by a lack of resources, by poor management, or by a perceived threat of violence by pupils. In many cases the perception may be an accurate one and therefore difficult to counter, whereas in others the reputation might be entirely unjustified and marketing may thus have a role to play in correcting any erroneous elements.

In recent years the publication of league tables of school performance and the publication of regular Ofsted (Office for Standards in Education) reports have had a key role to play in providing additional guidance to parents about which school(s) they might select for their child. Not only is data in respect of performance at each key stage now available, but so too is a range of other indicators, including the 'improvements' that schools are able to show in their pupils' educational attainment. This measure compares educational attainment at the point of recruitment with changes in subsequent years of the child's education. An example of the data provided is supplied in Figure 11.1 where the performance of a school at Key Stage 4/5 is reported. The data shows that the performance of this school has slipped recently. The trend data indicates that it used to outperform the national average at GCSE level. A poor set of results is also reported at A level both in relation to other schools in the local authority area and the national average.

Parents may read Ofsted reports published on every state school in England at least every three years. When assessing a school, inspectors consider evidence from a range of sources including:

- the school's self-evaluation (the school's assessment of its own performance);
- performance data;
- pupils' work;
- lesson observations;
- input from parents;
- discussions with pupils and staff.

The inspection report includes an overall assessment of the school's effectiveness, along with specific judgements on:

- achievement and standards;
- pupils' personal development and well-being;
- the quality of teaching and learning;
- curriculum provision;

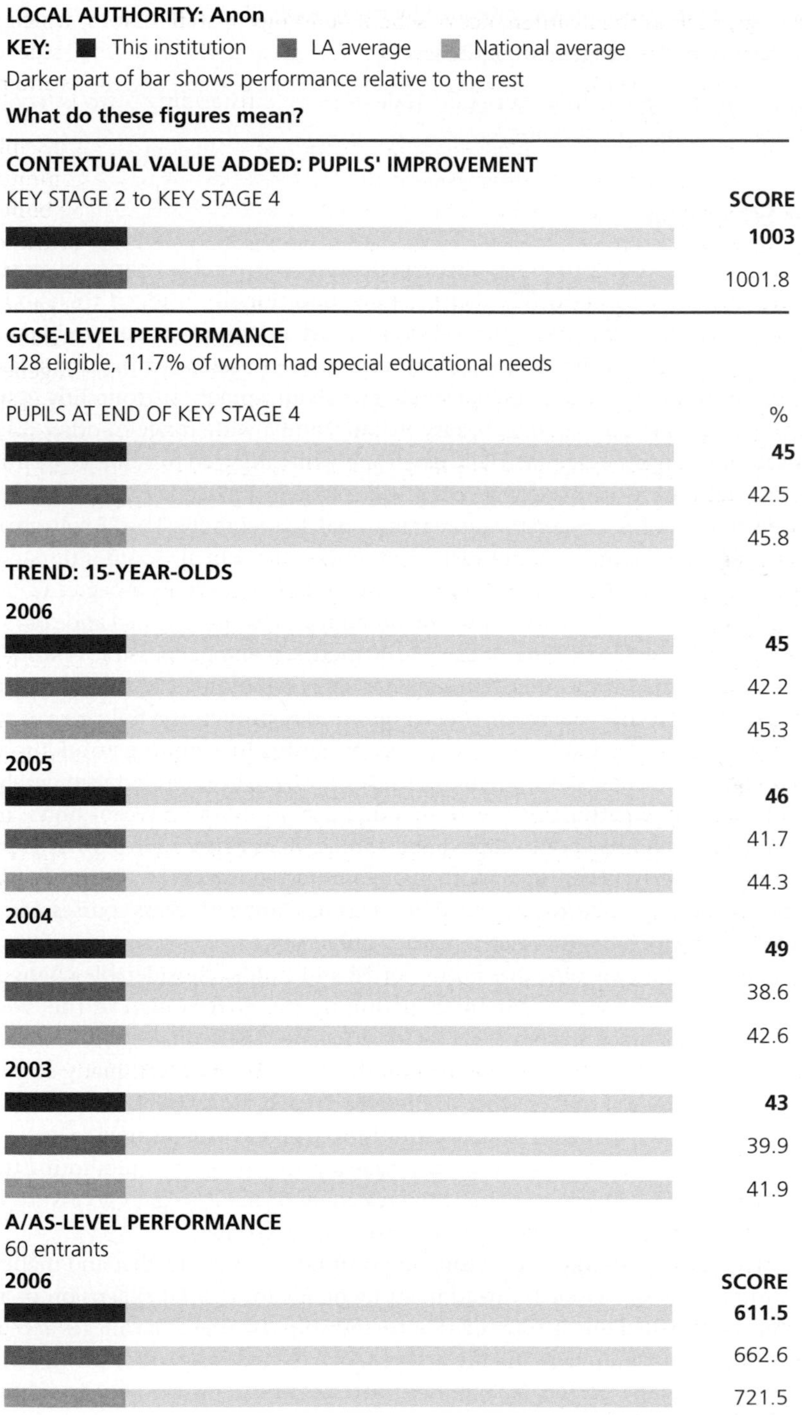

LOCAL AUTHORITY: Anon

KEY: ■ This institution ■ LA average ■ National average
Darker part of bar shows performance relative to the rest

What do these figures mean?

CONTEXTUAL VALUE ADDED: PUPILS' IMPROVEMENT

KEY STAGE 2 to KEY STAGE 4   **SCORE**

1003

1001.8

GCSE-LEVEL PERFORMANCE
128 eligible, 11.7% of whom had special educational needs

PUPILS AT END OF KEY STAGE 4   %

45

42.5

45.8

TREND: 15-YEAR-OLDS

2006

45

42.2

45.3

2005

46

41.7

44.3

2004

49

38.6

42.6

2003

43

39.9

41.9

A/AS-LEVEL PERFORMANCE
60 entrants

2006   **SCORE**

611.5

662.6

721.5

Figure 11.1 Example of school performance

- the care, guidance, and support provided by the school;
- the leadership and management of the school.

The judgements are made on a four-point scale—one is 'outstanding', two is 'good', three 'satisfactory', and four 'inadequate'.

Further Education

The pattern of post-16 education has also experienced considerable change in recent years. In England, further education (FE) colleges have traditionally bridged the gap between school and university. While most have always offered a traditional route to higher education (HE), the strength of the FE colleges has always been their vocational provision. Students could study a range of courses that would give them a practical grounding in business, engineering, sports/leisure, nursing, beauty therapy, and a wide range of other disciplines. These vocational courses were practically based and while they led to valuable qualifications in their own right, were often used by young adults to gain a place at a university in competition with students who selected the more traditional A-level route. The FE college provided an entirely different learning environment, not unlike that which would ultimately be encountered at university, and which importantly could offer students a degree of flexibility not available in schools. Methods of assessment tended to be more varied and courses could usually be studied in full, part-time, or day release modes, making it possible to work towards a university place while at the same time experiencing employment for the first time.

FE colleges also played a vital role in their communities, providing a full range of academic and practical courses for adult learners who were interested in acquiring an additional qualification or developing new skills. Often this study may have been undertaken purely for the pleasure of learning something new, with no other goal in mind. In recent times, however, much of this provision has been adapted and extended and new routes towards part-time qualifications have been established. With many more adult learners wishing to gain a place in higher education, FE colleges responded by creating a range of access courses, the successful completion of which helps to gain a place at university.

While much of the foregoing description of FE still holds, considerable change has recently impacted on the sector. The introduction by the government of the 'vocational A-level' blurred the academic/vocational divide and since these qualifications are designed to develop in students the skills demanded by the modern employer, many schools have taken the decision to add one or more of these to their sixth form portfolio. Schools that could once have been regarded as feeder institutions to FE have hence now to be regarded as competitors. Indeed given that many schools have a vested interest in promoting their own post-16 provision, FE colleges may find it increasingly difficult to gain access to potential students to communicate the benefits of what they have to offer.

At the other end of the scale, the division in portfolios between further and higher education institutions has also eroded. Government demands for a rapid expansion of access to higher education fuelled the development of partnerships between FE colleges and universities. It is now not uncommon to find the first year of a degree programme being delivered in an FE college and many postgraduate professional qualifications are now franchised to FE providers. While the development of some FE/HE partnerships has clearly facilitated this blurring in distinction between the two portfolios, it has also led to the creation of considerable additional competition. In some regions FE colleges now compete directly with HE providers for students.

■ **CASE STUDY**

PARTNERSHIPS WITH THE UNIVERSITY OF PLYMOUTH

In 2004 the University of Plymouth won a major national award for the launch of a new partnership scheme with colleges. Rather than compete with them the University sought ways in
which they might work together to their mutual advantage. Creating a new sub-brand of the
University—the University of Plymouth Colleges (UPC)—Plymouth hoped to raise awareness of
higher education provision in its feeder institutions and to encourage 'non-traditional' students
to participate in study. Its partners, by contrast, gained benefit from the University of Plymouth
brand and access to relevant faculty and other educational resources. The partnership is now
one of the largest in the country involving over 5000 of the University's students undertaking
HE studies in one of 19 partner institutions spread throughout the South West region.

The UPC organization is entirely focused on running the partnership network and provides a
management structure and quality processes that recognize the importance of shared responsibility and open relationships between the partners.

The faculty is organized around eight subject forums: art and design; business and tourism;
education; technology; science, agriculture, and sport; arts and humanities; health and social
work; and social sciences. Each forum links the Partner College and University staff and
students together. It provides the focus for shared programme design and development;
assessment, student support, quality review, and quality enhancement. Some forums have developed online and other resource materials. Each forum has a chair who is seconded to UPC
for 50% of their time. All provision within UPC is subject to the same quality assurance
procedures as internal programmes of the University.

The majority of courses are at foundation degree and HNC/D level, covering a full range of
curriculum areas. However, there are a small number of complete, specialist degrees, mainly
delivered in the larger Colleges. For the great majority of programmes there are planned and
assured progression routes to top-up honours degree provision within the University. In addition, FE provision has been mapped against University entry statements to ensure progression
to the University. This work not only strengthens the ability for students to progress seamlessly
from one institution to another but also provides the opportunity to develop programmes
across the FE/HE boundary.

Through the scheme the university has achieved a set of impressive performance indicators
for widening participation and retention:

- around 60% of students are over 21 and 40% of full-time students over 25;
- nearly 40% of provision is part-time;
- around 25% come from lower socio-economic groups;
- 91% come from state schools (this is above the government benchmark);
- about 30% enter with traditional 'A' level profiles;
- around 70% come from the South West;
- an excellent retention rate of 89%;
- around 78% of HND students and 84% of degree students in UPC colleges re-enrol
  between stage 1 and 2;
- only about 8% withdraw overall—well below the government benchmark of 10%.

This combination of wide social participation and impressive retention is unusual, and has led the National Audit Office to cite the University of Plymouth as an example of good practice in widening participation.

Case compiled from resources at www.plymouth.ac.uk<http://www.plymouth.ac.uk>.

These changes have led to a great deal of marketing complexity, reflected in the almost exponential increase over the past ten years in the number of institutions now making marketing appointments at a senior level. There are, after all, considerable dilemmas facing an institution that must now compete directly with both schools and universities. Marketing resources are now split between an ever-increasing number of target markets and even where sufficient resources are likely to be available it is often difficult to decide on a suitable strategy to adopt. The development of a coherent positioning strategy is particularly problematic.

There have also been changes to the way in which FE is funded, deliberately aimed at encouraging competition between colleges which have traditionally operated within their own geographical boundaries. Funding now depends not only on absolute measures of success, but also on patterns of relative success between competing institutions. Moreover, the funding mechanism itself has altered, placing a greater emphasis on student outcomes. No longer is funding awarded simply for the number of students on a course; the emphasis is now on the achievements of those students at the end of their studies. High drop-out or failure rates can now have a dramatic effect on the level of funding received. There has therefore never been a greater need to instil a market orientation among college administrators and staff. Simply recruiting greater numbers of students is no longer an appropriate goal.

Higher Education

Over the past 30 years, the pattern of higher education in the UK has changed almost beyond all recognition. A plethora of different providers now exist, catering for an equally diverse population of students. Higher Education Institutions (HEIs) have been forced by government policy to forge closer links with industry, research funders, and markets for education overseas. In an attempt to categorize this change, Bargh et al. (1996) draw a distinction between what they perceive as a trend towards massification and a trend towards marketization.

Massification

The growth of the HE student population has been spectacular. This has been due in no small measure to the UK government's target for 50% of 18–30 year olds to participate in some form of higher education by 2010. Total student numbers have risen from a mere 50,000 in 1939 (about 25 per cent of whom were studying medicine or dentistry) to 324,000 at the time of the Robbins report in 1963, to over 2.3 million today (HESA 2008). The ability to experience higher education is no longer the privilege of a select few. What was, certainly until the early 1960s, very much an elite system has now been transformed into a mass system with levels of access that rival those attained in most European countries and North America.

Given the great rise in student numbers, change has been forced on the pattern of institutions providing the education. In the late 1950s there were no more than 24 universities providing a very narrow range of highly specialized courses. After the expansion of the system recommended by Robbins, the number increased to 45, and after the ending of the so-called binary divide between universities and polytechnics in 1992, 93 such institutions then existed. There are 126 today. When one considers that there are also a further 60 HEIs not classified as universities and well over 400 further education colleges, as mentioned previously, which have a stake in higher education, the move to a mass system of provision is all but complete. Nor has change merely been confined to a growth in the number of providers. While the sector comprised only a handful of institutions, all governed by similar academic and professional values, there was little variation in the 'character' of each institution. The arrival of a situation where there are over a hundred different universities has encouraged a greater degree of heterogeneity. One university is no longer much like another, and considerable scope now exists for the development of a unique institutional 'personality'.

In 1963 the average British university had a mere 2750 students. Today the average university has well over 8000 full-time equivalents and approaching 20,000 students in total enrolled. The small and historically intimate nature of most institutions has therefore been lost and the expansion in student numbers has led to the creation of ever-larger sites and even split-site campuses. The task of managing this change has fallen to increasing numbers of professional administrators. New management frameworks have been implemented and this has in turn led to the erosion of what was once almost purely an academic culture, with its own unique set of attitudes, beliefs, and behaviours.

One of the key reasons for the growth in student numbers after Robbins was the creation of a mandatory award system that would subsidize the course fees of HE students and greatly assist students in meeting their costs of living over the duration of their studies. This had the impact not only of encouraging participation, but also of persuading students that distance was no longer a problem and that study could therefore be undertaken at whichever UK institution they desired. The home-based student therefore became the exception rather than the rule, and moving away from home began to be seen as part of the natural process of growing up and gaining one's independence.

The difficulty for HEIs and indeed successive governments after Robbins has been that a greater freedom of student choice, both to enter higher education and to study those subjects that were individually most attractive, has meant that demand for subjects deemed to be of crucial importance to the future health of the economy, such as the sciences or engineering, was often sadly lacking. Faced with additional spaces on these programmes, universities switched their attention in these areas to the attraction of overseas students for the first time. Since the fees were subsidized (at least until the Thatcher government took office), the attainment of a British education was a very attractive option. The experience gained by universities of recruiting overseas students at this time was later to pay dividends since the recruitment of overseas students has recently taken on a whole new significance. Not only are such individuals no longer subsidized by the UK government, the fees charged to overseas students are now set at rates that often greatly surpass those charged to UK or EC nationals. Moreover, at the undergraduate level, the government now controls the overall number of home students that a given university is expected to attract. Under- or over-recruitment is now penalized by the funding framework. Once the quota of home students has been recruited, the only way that the revenue stream from a particular course can then be increased is through the recruitment of overseas students who, since they are full-fee paying, are not included in the institutional quota. Such students therefore constitute an important and extremely profitable target market.

The nature of the academic product has also changed. More than a quarter of all students are now mature students and the number of part-time students has increased sharply, particularly on postgraduate programmes. The Internet has greatly enhanced distance-learning opportunities and the nature of provision has changed to reflect the needs of key new customer groups. There has also been a general blurring of the distinction between academic, vocational, and continuing education as HEIs have attempted to respond (in most cases) to the needs of their various constituencies.

Marketization

In recent years, successive government policy has encouraged the development of a market culture. Institutions are now in a position where they must compete for scarce resources and even consider alternative sources of funding, such as that provided by private enterprise. Moreover, the new market comprising of 126 competing institutions has afforded HE customers an unprecedented level of choice. This has already led to the creation of an unoffocial 'Ivy League' of institutions, a process recently encouraged by the decision of a number of foreign governments to limit the number of campuses to which they are prepared to send students (O'Leary 1996).

At the undergraduate level, the decision by the British government to charge fees to all but the most underprivileged of students put great pressure on institutions to communicate to potential students the benefits of continuing their education and of studying at their particular campus. Only Scottish students studying in Scotland have been spared this expense. Indeed, variable fees have now been introduced in the other countries of the Union, thereby allowing the 'better' institutions to charge more for their provision. Since students must now bear the cost of their studies, at least in the longer term, it is fair to assume that greater consideration will be given to *where* these studies will take place. There are clear internal marketing implications for this policy change since, as students now pay for their education, they are likely to have higher expectations of the quality of service they will receive. Institutional managers and teaching staff need to be especially sensitive to the needs of their fee-paying clients.

In addition, universities and other institutions that provide higher education are now subject to an unprecedented level of external scrutiny; the demands made of them have expanded and expectations have changed. League tables are now published in respect of the quality of both teaching and research; prospective students, or their sponsors, can use this information to allow them to make a more informed choice. The level of research funding provided to each university is now highly dependent on the research rating achieved, and this is set to become more so. There is a very real threat that the traditions of both teaching and research being conducted alongside one another at every UK institution will shortly come to an end, creating new categories of university, some of which will be perceived as being more desirable than others. Senior management will therefore have to ensure that appropriate strategies are put in place now to ensure that their desired positioning is maintained and developed over time. This will only be achievable if both the internal and external marketing activity is focused on this goal and coordinated to ensure that the *whole* institution moves forward in the direction required.

The remainder of this chapter will therefore examine how providers might respond to these challenges, commencing with what for most institutions will be the key marketing issue, namely how a market orientation might be achieved. As will shortly be demonstrated, introducing such a radical change of emphasis is perhaps more difficult in this sector than in any other, given both its history and the traditional freedoms afforded to its academic staff.

Education in the USA

While the preceding discussion focused on the UK, the issues identified above are common to many countries. In the United States, for example, many of the provisions of the UK's Education Act of 1988 have been mirrored in the Bush administration's No Child Left Behind Act of 2001 (NCLB). This is a federal law that aims at improving the performance of primary and secondary schools by increasing standards of accountability and offering parents more flexibility over which schools their children might attend. Just as in the UK the Act requires that assessments in basic skills be given to all children in certain grades, if federal funding is to be forthcoming. NCLB requires school districts to provide a report card on how its schools and the school district are doing. For individual schools, the report card data includes whether the school has been identified for school improvement and how its students performed on state tests compared to other students in the school district and the state. For the district, the report includes the combined test scores of the students at all the district's schools. Although a bipartisan Act the effect of its introduction is hotly debated. Since standards are set locally, there is an argument that individual states might lower their achievement goals and motivate teachers to 'train to the test'. On the flip side it is argued that systematic testing provides a unique insight into which schools are not performing, highlighting where interventions might be necessary to reduce the achievement gap.

In American universities many of the same issues also apply. Competition is certainly a key issue, since while student demand for places at the top 50 US degree-awarding institutions still outstrips supply, the picture elsewhere in the sector is radically different. The vast majority of institutions continue to have to actively solicit student interest. There are currently over 3000 degree-awarding institutions in the USA, each contributing to the production of over 2.5 million new bachelor degrees every year. The sheer number of institutions and the wide range of courses on offer make it essential that HEIs communicate effectively with their target markets and carve out a clear positioning which serves to differentiate their provision from that offered by others, especially those within the same geographic region.

In addition to competition, the USA continues to experience a healthy growth in what has now become a large market for part-time and adult education. Moreover, fees are as much an issue in the USA as in the UK and, faced with strong domestic competition, many HEIs are now just as much concerned with the expansion of overseas recruitment as their UK counterparts.

We may thus conclude that the issues identified above will be of equal concern to educational management in many other countries. While the structure of the educational system will certainly differ, the forces shaping the development of change will be likely to exhibit strong degrees of similarity. Indeed, as we move increasingly towards a global market for education, this level of similarity can only grow in significance.

Changing Perspectives on Marketing in Higher Education

It is against this backdrop that the need for marketing can be assessed. Perhaps marketing's greatest contribution lies in its ability to facilitate the exchange process that takes place between the HEI and each of the customer groups it addresses. It can provide a detailed understanding of the needs of such customers and ensure that the institution addresses these needs in as efficient and comprehensive a manner as possible. In the competitive environment in which most HEIs now operate, enhanced customer satisfaction may be one of the few remaining ways in which institutions can create and sustain a credible source of competitive advantage. Marketing can help deliver this satisfaction, and much more besides. Indeed, in the education context, Kotler and Fox (1985) found that marketing can offer an HEI four major benefits, namely:

- greater success in fulfilling the institution's mission;
- improved satisfaction of the institution's publics;
- improved attraction of marketing resources;
- improved efficiency in marketing activities.

Despite the benefits, however, the HE sector has been slow to embrace the concept and although many institutions have now appointed marketing officers, the actual influence that such professionals can have is often severely limited. In a major study of marketing in further and higher education, Higher Education—The International Student Experience (HEIST) (1995) traces the evolution of the marketing function over 40 years. The authors recognize that although certain behaviours are symptomatic of a particular historical phase, examples of each stage of development are still very much in evidence.

- *Beginnings*. The impact of the Robbins report, as highlighted above, was to completely change the pattern of educational provision. Universities were faced with a need for expansion and the need to explain this to the local communities in which they were based. It became necessary to negotiate with a variety of groups to plan the expansion, such as resident groups, traders, local authorities, etc. In response, many universities appointed administrators whose primary function was to manage the institution's relationship with these publics.

- *Placating the press*. This phase began in the late 1960s in response to developments such as the student revolt and subsequent critique by the press of university management, whom press reports accused of being too soft on the troublemakers who had instigated the problems. For the first time, media professionals were appointed, often ex-journalists themselves, to manage the difficult relationship that ensued with the press. Their primary role was to ensure that potentially damaging publicity was, as far as possible, deflected.

- *Winning hearts and minds*. By the mid-1970s, the press relations function had risen in importance. Senior management began to recognize the importance of a proactive rather than a purely reactive approach. In recognition of this, the press office function in many institutions was renamed 'external relations'. These new departments were empowered to generate favourable publicity for the institution and to coordinate any lobbying activity that might prove necessary. The public image of many universities had been badly damaged by the years of student revolt and a key external relations function was to rebuild the image of higher education. There was, however, also a need to communicate to government and other funders the desirability of maintaining the level of funding attracting to the sector. The mid-1970s were characterized by a period of serious public expenditure constraint.

- *Selling the system*. It was not until the early 1980s that institutions recognized that their relationships with the press and government funders were not the only relationships that should be fostered at a senior level within a university. Changes in government policy had raised the significance of overseas recruitment, soliciting donations from alumni, and selling short courses and conferences, etc. At around this time, the first attempts were therefore witnessed to coordinate this diverse activity into a unified external relations function. Media or marketing professionals began to be recruited to manage all these important aspects of activity, and depending on the nature of the institution some commonality in reporting structures was achieved. This will be returned to below.

• *Marketing institutions*. By the late 1980s, a new trend in the marketing of education had begun to emerge. Universities started to apply marketing, both as a philosophy and a management function, to the way in which their institution was managed. Formal planning and an adherence to an institutional mission became the norm across the sector and newly created marketing departments now helped coordinate both departmental and institutional contact with key customer groups. Moreover, in more enlightened organizations, these marketing departments established a two-way dialogue with academic departments, ensuring that genuine customer input was fed back to those who had the responsibility for the design and creation of new course programmes. Without overriding academic freedom, those mechanisms served to ensure that the programmes offered to the market reflected the needs of those who would ultimately consume them.

To HEIST's original list we might now add a sixth category—*strategic marketing orientation*—since a number of universities are now making efforts to integrate their marketing activities, developing strong and unifying brands and ensuring that an individual's experience of those brands is consistent no matter who they have contact with, or what communication they happen to be exposed to. These institutions place a high degree of emphasis on the development and communication of a distinctive personality.

■ **CASE STUDY**

FURMAN UNIVERSITY

In the late 1990s Furman University developed a new strategic positioning focused on the notion of 'engaged learning'. Students were able to extend their classroom education through activities such as participation in research, international travel, internships in other states, and a variety of service learning projects. The theme of 'engagement' now pervades all the University's communications with campaigns designed to 'engage' students on an emotional level through the web and offline publications. The University abandoned the once-per-year viewbook (prospectus) approach and switched to a pattern of regular communication three times per year. The *engagefurman* magazine allowed the university to reinforce key messages and develop the brand through a conversation with potential students. Importantly, these communications were supported by a microsite (www.engagefurman.com), the content of which was carefully integrated with the offline communication. The goal was to give prospective students a seamless experience of having contact with the University. Additional web traffic was generated by the placement of web extensions in the print version so that students could access other images online or when reading about a student movie could be linked with a Quicktime version. The site offers a virtual tour of the campus with selected video allowing prospective students to learn more about Furman's engaged teaching philosophy. It also allows them to get a sense of campus life as they can access online journals (blogs) (see Figure 11.2) of existing students and view clips video-shot by student guides. One guide, for example, takes students through the library, study rooms, and other hangouts;

Figure 11.2 Furman online journals

Source: © 2008 Furman University. Reproduced with kind permission.

another explores athletics on campus. Shot in an improvisational style, the videos allow students to see the unscripted life.

Case compiled from resources at www.furman.edu<http://www.furman.edu>.

A strategic approach to marketing also allows an organization to be more responsive to the environment in which it operates. In the coming years institutions will have to be ready to face a number of new challenges.

• Competition for traditional and non-traditional students will increase due to a demographic downturn in the number of school leavers in 2009 (Hayes 2007).

• Competition will be particularly intense in the 'practical' rather than the 'liberal' arts (Brint 2002). As Kirp (2003) notes, no one is warring over philosophy majors, the brunt of the competition will tend to focus on the newer and more practically oriented subjects of study.

• Competition will also intensify for the brightest students. In the US where the top schools routinely reject seven out of every eight candidates the smarter schools have replaced admissions officers with enrolment managers. The change reflects more than mere semantics. Good schools recognize that the students they are able to attract drive their reputation in the market and are therefore going to great lengths to facilitate the enrolment of the individuals who will be likely to make the biggest difference. The goal of the admissions process is now one of improving market position.

• At the lower end of the market, students and parents will place more emphasis on value, owing to the rapidly escalating prices of higher education. They will ask what they will get for their money and expect a justification for why fees might vary between institutions.

• As colleges and universities reach out to markets that are non-traditional (i.e. not part of their middle and upper middle class base) they will be having contact for the first time with individuals who do not understand, or who may not place as much value upon, the advantages of a College education (Hayes 2007).

• There will be a dramatic rise in the number of non-traditional students with a consequent rise in the diversity of needs that must be met (Madden 2007). This is in part what Kerr (2001) refers to as a teeming multidiversity.

• The quality of marketing at competing institutions will rise. While the leading universities have always been marketing savvy, the downturn in student numbers will force a growing professionalism across the sector (Bok 2003).

• New technologies will play an increasing role in both the marketing of education and its subsequent delivery (Slaughter and Leslie 1998, Dunn 2000).

• Competition for top faculty will intensify. As Kirp (2003: 5) notes, 'the most sought after faculty regard their primary attachment as not to their school, not to their discipline but to themselves. For those favored few, every spring becomes a season of greed, as competing offers are weighed, not just in terms of salary but also in terms of research support, reduced teaching obligations and the like'. Sadly, in the author's experience, this appears never to happen in the domain of nonprofit marketing.

Achieving a Market Orientation in Higher Education

At the time of writing, comparatively few universities appear to have reached the final of these stages of development and fully embraced marketing at a strategic and philosophical level. There are typically a number of reasons for this.

• *Academic values.* Marketing is still perceived by many as being incompatible with the educational mission and some academics continue to equate marketing with selling, and feel that their institution should be 'above' such practices. Others feel that marketing should not be necessary because they have a strong belief in the desirability of their subject and their right to deliver it as they see fit. Academics, by virtue of their professional status, tend to be more concerned with the future of their discipline and will often focus on the narrow interests thereof. As Jarratt (1985: 33) noted, in many universities there exist 'large and powerful academic departments together with individual academics who sometimes see their academic discipline as more important than the long-term well-being of the university which houses them'. Boxall (1991: 12) concurs:

The activities and priorities of universities have traditionally been determined primarily by the preferences and aspirations of their academic staff, given voice through various faculties and internal committees. Indeed, the very essence of a university has been the self-determining community of academic professionals, whose rights to set their own agenda were enshrined in the unwritten charter of academic freedom.

- *Conflict between management and academic interests.* Difficulties are also encountered because of the split in responsibility for dealings with customers between departments and the institution's central administrative function. In most institutions, responsibility for marketing is split between these two areas, and this can give rise to a degree of tension. Many departments have the desire to be masters of their own destiny and hence want to take responsibility for all marketing activity, while others express reluctance and would be delighted if those working for the university's central administration could deal with the whole process. For their part, university marketers usually want to maintain some control over the activities of individual departments, but are reluctant to have too much 'local' involvement as their role within the university has usually to be more strategic in nature. There is therefore a need to achieve some form of balance in this relationship, although in practice this can be difficult given the antipathy that can exist between academic and administrative staff. 'In almost all HE institutions there is a "them and us" aspect to the manager–academic relationship, which will vary from nothing more sinister than staff club banter . . . to real conflict and tension especially at a time of cuts' (Palfreyman and Warner 1996: 12).

- *The lack of a strategic perspective.* Given the usually high number of subject specialisms that can be found in a particular university, it is often the case that it is only the senior administration of the institution who have the capacity to take a strategic perspective and are uniquely placed to do so (Lockwood and Davies 1985). The problem, however, lies in convincing academic staff of the need for this perspective and the need to implement any strategy that might be suggested as a result of it. Many academics fail to recognize that the desirability of offering new courses in their individual disciplines must be viewed against the capacity of other developments in other subject areas, to offer even greater utility for one or more of the institution's customer groups. Clearly only those developments which are optimal from the perspective of the whole institution should be supported. Very often, however, the power to make such decisions is vested in a university committee structure heavily dominated by academics, each fighting for the welfare of their own specific discipline. 'Universities are commonly not outwardly market oriented—courses are sometimes established and maintained for the status of a department or an institution, rather than where there is clear evidence of an economic level of long-term demand' (Moore 1989: 120).

- *The diversity of marketing activity.* The point has already been made above that responsibility for marketing activity can be shared between individual departments and marketers working for the central administration. Regrettably, however, marketing activity is also conducted by a variety of other players, making coordination difficult. In a typical university these might include:

    - *The development office.* Staff in this department of a university will typically be involved in raising funds from both individual and corporate donors. They also have responsibility for the fostering of links with alumni.

    - *The international office.* The responsibility for overseas recruitment is often devolved to an international officer, who will travel extensively, visiting institutions in other countries and attending educational fairs, etc.

    - *Schools liaison office.* Liaison with feeder institutions remains an important activity in aiding student recruitment. Dedicated staff will tour local schools, giving presentations and offering advice in respect of university course options.

- *Admissions office.* Usually split between undergraduate and postgraduate admissions. Admissions staff are often the first point of contact for students wishing to obtain information about the taught or research degrees currently being offered. The office will also deal with correspondence and applications from individual students. In this sense, it acts as a liaison between the academic department and the individual applicant and will probably also issue the final notice of acceptance or rejection.

- *Press office.* Most universities have dedicated staff whose sole function is to foster good relations with the press. Since their role is almost certainly now a proactive one, such individuals are constantly monitoring the work of academic departments to ascertain whether opportunities exist to promote the teaching, development, or research work being undertaken.

- *Business relations.* Many university missions now address the need for the institution to make a contribution to the economic health of the country and/or region in which the institution is based. This often involves working closely with commercial enterprise to conduct joint research, train staff, or sell the expertise of university academics who might undertake paid/unpaid consultancy. Since successive governments have been keen to provide increasing numbers of undergraduates with business experience, this function may also have the responsibility for arranging and supervising student projects and placements.

- *Research office.* Given the importance of research income (particularly for the established universities), it would now be highly unusual to find a university that did not have a fairly senior member of staff responsible for the administration of research grants and the coordination of bids to the respective funding agencies.

- *The conference office.* The potential to generate a very lucrative revenue stream from offering university facilities, both teaching and residential, to clients seeking a conference facility has long been recognized. The marketing of the site and its facilities will usually be the responsibility of a dedicated team.

While this list is not exhaustive, it does serve to illustrate the great diversity in marketing activity that would normally be undertaken in a typical university. Coordination can therefore be a very significant issue for senior management to address.

- *The influence of research.* The remuneration systems within the majority of universities, and indeed the academic system in general, continues to reward individuals for excellence in research to the near exclusion of all else. While many universities include in their reward structures the criteria of excellence in teaching and/or administration, in reality, the quality of an individual's research output is still of over-riding concern. Given this, the concept of rewarding an individual for the quality of any marketing activity they might have responsibility for is almost laughable! As one colleague put it recently, 'you can't even gain promotion for being an excellent teacher—what chance marketing?'

The incentive for many academics to devote time to marketing is therefore sadly lacking and many staff prefer, understandably, to concentrate on those aspects of their role for which they will gain some reward. Active researchers therefore jealously guard their time and can be reluctant to engage in 'peripheral' activities such as visiting schools, attending education fairs, or interviewing business clients. It is ironic that since administrative workloads in HE often reflect the level of research an individual is able to generate, it can often be the least able members of staff who find their time being allocated to marketing and administration activity.

■ **CASE STUDY**

STARTING THE PROCESS—ACHIEVING CHANGE IN AN 'ESTABLISHED' UNIVERSITY

There are several difficulties that will be encountered in achieving a marketing orientation in an HE setting. Whatever the route undertaken, it is likely to be fraught with difficulty and often subject to outright condemnation by senior members of academic staff. What follows is a description of the process that was initiated by a major, long-established UK university in its bid to become market-oriented. In essence, the senior management of the university recognized the need to focus on the needs of individual customer groups, so that the university could respond more personally to their needs. They also saw the need to design new programmes that would be attractive to the market and to be more aggressive in promoting certain aspects of the institutions work and provision. The following steps were therefore initiated.

1. *Managing the Process.* A marketing committee was established to consider how the process of change might be initiated, involving senior academics and administrators and a marketing facilitator. It was felt important to demonstrate the importance with which this change was viewed and hence both the Vice-Chancellor and Registrar were in attendance.

2. *Marketing Audit.* The marketing committee initiated a university-wide audit of marketing activity. This audit had both strategic and tactical perspectives and was designed to gather data in respect of the external changes that would impact on the university over the next five-to-ten-year period. Data was also gathered in respect of the competition, the needs of each key customer grouping, and the relative success/failure of past marketing activity. The methodology employed consisted of a series of personal interviews with staff, students, alumni, members of the local residential/business communities, and research funders. A questionnaire was also completed by each Head of Department (see Figure 11.3).

3. *SWOT Analysis.* Once the data had been gathered, a comprehensive SWOT analysis was conducted, revealing three major weaknesses that urgently needed to be addressed:

• *The lack of a coordinated marketing intelligence system.* Most departments and administrative functions having contact with university clients maintained their own databases or records of such contact. There was no way in which the data could be shared between all those who might have an interest therein. Moreover, there existed no mechanism within the university to conduct any form of primary marketing research. As a result the institution had almost no understanding of the needs of any of its key customer groups.

• *Habitual under-recruitment in key subject areas.* Much of the university's provision was either unattractive to potential students or poorly marketed. The university was also found to be struggling to recruit overseas students in key subject areas and hence to maintain and build market share in many foreign markets.

• *The lack of a coherent identity.* The university lacked a corporate identity, and communications with customer groups were often visually poor and lacking in a common theme. A university logo was in existence, but its use was uncoordinated and not informed through research. Moreover, university managers (and academics) were all found to have their own views on how the university should position itself in the market and this diversity tended to be reflected in the communications they had with their market.

Departmental Guide to the Process of Auditing Marketing Activities

Introduction

The purpose of this document is to guide you through the process of carrying out a marketing audit for your department. It should be remembered that the central purpose of the audit is to assist you in determining 'where you are now' in marketing terms and what the opportunities may be for future development. Not every question asked will be of relevance for your department but you should distinguish between those that you perceive as having no relevance and those which you are unable to answer due to a lack of information.

The Macro Environment

1. The wider environment

Factor	Details
What political (government) decisions are likely to impact on your department within the next three years?	
What macro-economic factors might impact on your department within the next three years?	
Are there any technological developments, planned, or likely, which will occur over the next three years that could affect your department's activities?	

Customer Segments

2. Please indicate for each programme your department offers, both the total number of enquiries received and the number of students to finally enrol.

Course	1992/3		1993/4		1994/5		1995/6		1996/7	
	Enqs	Enrl	Enqs	Enrl	Enqs	Enrl	Enqs	Enrl	Enqs	Enrl

3. Examining the table above, do any trends emerge? If so, please give details.

Figure 11.3 Departmental marketing audit

4. For each programme your department offers, please indicate the profile of the student body over the past five years.

Programme Title					
	1992/3	1993/4	1994/5	1995/6	1996/7
Number of Male Students					
Number of Female Students					
Number of Full-time Students					
Number of Part-time Students					
Number of Mature Students					
Number of Overseas Students					

5. Examining the table(s) above, are any trends in enrolment evident? Please give details.

6. In the case of each programme, please indicate where your current students first heard of your provision.

Course	Primary Methods of Communication

7. From which regions of the country do you presently recruit for your undergraduate programmes? Do you tend to recruit from certain types of school?

8. For each programme please indicate where you are currently advertising/promoting the programme.

Course	Location of Advertising/Promotional Activity (if any)

9. Comparing your answers to questions 6 and 7, can you identify any promotional activity which would appear to be ineffective? Could this be improved?

10. Comparing your answers to questions 6 and 7, can you identify communication channels that could be enhanced with an additional spend? If so, please specify.

11. Can you identify any changes which might be likely to take place in the markets for your programmes over the next three years? How are these changes being monitored? What actions do you propose to take as a result?

12. For each programme, please indicate the two institutions which you would describe as your closest competitors.

Course	Competitors

13. Do you have copies of the most recent literature produced by these institutions?

☐ Yes   ☐ No

Figure 11.3 (continued)

14. Is this information circulated to course coordinators and admissions tutors?

☐ Yes   ☐ No

15. What unique features can your department offer that the two competitors identified above cannot?

16. What unique features can competitor 1 offer that [your university] cannot? (If necessary please specify this by programme.)

17. What unique features can competitor 2 offer that [your university] cannot? (If necessary please specify this by programme.)

18. How has a knowledge of these features been integrated in the design of marketing communications?

19. If your department has an undergraduate programme (or programmes), how have the numbers of applications compared with those made to other institutions over the past five years?

Programme Title					
Institution	1992/3	1993/4	1994/5	1995/6	1996/7

20. What forms of promotion do each of your key competitors currently undertake?

Competitor 1 (Insert name)	Competitor 2 (Insert name)

Research

21. Over each of the past five years, what is the average amount of research funding that has been attracted per staff member? (i.e. the total research income generated, divided by the number of full-time staff or equivalents.)

	1992/3	1993/4	1994/5	1995/6	1996/7
Research Income per Staff Member					

22. How do the current year's figures compare with the national average?

☐ Well Above
☐ Above
☐ Equivalent
☐ Below
☐ Well Below

Figure 11.3 (continued)

23. If the figures are below, or well below, the national average, what steps will be taken to increase the level of research funding being attracted?

24. Do mechanisms exist within your department to monitor the success of individual applications for funding and to learn from the design/content etc. of those that proved successful? If yes, please give details.

25. Have members of staff from funding bodies been invited to the department to meet members of staff and discuss application procedures over the past three years? If so, please give details.

26. Do opportunities exist to involve the business community in research? Are these opportunities currently being exploited?

Other Customer Groups

27. Are there any aspects of your department activities which you feel could be of value to the local/national business community? If so, please give details.

28. What mechanisms currently exist to promote these features/facilities to the business community?

29. Could the university offer additional assistance in this regard? If so, please give details.

30. Which professional bodies do your staff belong to? Do you know the CPD requirements set out by these professional bodies for their members? Are you an accredited provider for these institutions?

Own Marketing Activity

31. Has your department considered any of the following activities:

Activity	Yes (and currently use)	Yes (and rejected)	No
Attending Educational Fairs (UK)			
Attending Educational Fairs (Overseas)			
Providing Guest Lectures in Schools			
Providing Guest Lectures for Professional Bodies			
Providing Events for School/College Tutors			
Providing Events/Competitions for Schools (not open days)			
Advertising Undergraduate Courses			
Advertising Postgraduate Courses and/ or Research			
Releasing Occasional Press Releases through External Relations			
Links with Overseas Institutions			
Providing Speakers for High Profile Events— e.g. International Conferences			

32. If activities have been considered and rejected, please indicate why this decision was taken.

Figure 11.3 (continued)

33. On what basis are admissions tutors selected within your department? Are these qualities relevant to the target market?

34. What additional expertise would assist you in making your marketing more effective?

35. What market research would typically be undertaken by your department prior to the introduction of a proposed new programme?

36. What market research in respect of any key customer group would normally be undertaken by your department on an annual basis?

SWOT Analysis

This completes the marketing audit process. You should now have access to a variety of marketing intelligence data. This information should now be interpreted in terms of whether it represents a:

Strength
Weakness
Opportunity
Threat

Strengths and weaknesses are factors which relate to the internal aspects of your department's activities. The opportunities and threats relate to the information gathered about the environment external to the university (e.g. competitor activity).

Looking back over the data gathered, please interpret it in terms of whether you consider it to be a strength, weakness, opportunity, or threat. You should also list any other relevant factors which occur to you as you complete this section.

Strengths	Weaknesses
a)	a)
b)	b)
c)	c)
d)	d)
e)	e)

Opportunities	Threats
a)	a)
b)	b)
c)	c)
d)	d)
e)	e)

Figure 11.3 (continued)

4. *Agreement of an Action Plan*. In the light of the audit findings, an action plan was agreed to implement change. Specifically the following steps were taken.

• *Creation of a Marketing Forum.* Heads of Department, admissions tutors, and all those involved in some way with the marketing of the university were invited to attend an occasional meeting of a new marketing forum. The format of the forum was initially flexible, being agreed upon by the participants themselves. Its role developed into a facility for individuals to share their own experiences with marketing, discuss best practice, and analyse individual problems that had been encountered. Membership of the forum was open and meetings were held at lunchtimes to minimize the inconvenience to individual schedules.

• *Appointment of a University Marketing Officer.* It was intended that this person would form an integral part of the external relations team and have input into university marketing at both a strategic and a tactical level. Specifically, she was to be given responsibility for the coordination of the effort to achieve a market orientation and to help shape the future positioning strategy of the university. At a tactical level, she would also be available to advise departments which required individual guidance and assistance.

• *The Creation of a New Permanent External Affairs Committee.* It was decided to add an additional committee to the university's existing governance structure. The new committee would have ultimate responsibility for all university marketing activity (i.e. all those aspects listed above). As such, the new body was designed to provide a mechanism to ensure that all marketing activity was coordinated and appropriate, given the institution's long-term strategic plan. Reporting directly to Senate, with all senior staff in attendance, the committee was also to include representatives of the key customer groups. The president of the Students Union and representatives from local industry and commerce were thus invited to sit as members of the committee. It was further determined that given the diversity of marketing activity undertaken, it was unlikely that time would permit the committee to have anything other than a decision-making role. Three working groups, or sub-committees, were thus also established, the purpose of each was to address one of the three key weaknesses highlighted above, i.e. student recruitment, creation of a marketing intelligence system, and the development and coordination of a corporate image.

• *Provision of Marketing Training.* The university's staff development unit was instructed to provide an ongoing programme of marketing training throughout the academic year. Enrolment was open to all academic and administrative staff and training was structured to allow individuals to study towards a recognized qualification, or merely to deepen their knowledge of a particular aspect of marketing, depending on their individual requirements.

• *Control Mechanisms Implemented.* The university recognized that many departments required marketing communications support, in respect of how to plan and implement the promotion of their individual courses. Since each department had traditionally planned in a vacuum, the university had on one occasion placed four different advertisements in one magazine, each of which painted a slightly different picture of life on its campus. It was thus decided that all promotional activity would have to be cleared centrally by the new marketing officer, who would also offer advice in respect of the appropriateness of the activities planned. She could also ensure that the university gained as much synergy as possible from all its activities and obtained the best possible financial deals from the media. The effectiveness of all the forms of promotion utilized was also to be monitored centrally, so that the advice given to departments could ultimately be informed by experience gained in the market.

The university also developed a set of guidelines designed to govern the use of the university logo and other materials that might be used in communications with customer groups. The aim was to standardize the production of literature so that it was immediately apparent that each brochure was part of a wider institutional 'family' of publications.

The reader will note that the changes implemented in the case represent a 'softly, softly' approach to achieving change and quite a different route to that which might typically be taken in industry. Senior management recognized the need not to overtly push academic staff towards the attainment of a market orientation. They felt that the provision of training, in-house marketing consultancy (by the new marketing officer), and marketing intelligence should demonstrate the practical benefits that marketing could provide. This in turn, it was felt, would help generate a much more positive perspective on what marketing could offer the institution, and thus gradually begin to alter its culture.

Key Educational Publics

Previously in this chapter the term 'customer' has been used to refer to those groups of individuals or organizations served by another organization. In the educational context, however, institutions often have contact with groups or individuals who, while they may not be involved in an exchange process with an educational institution (in a strict sense of the word), still have a vested interest in the work carried out by these bodies and its management. It may therefore be helpful, in attempting to achieve a market orientation, to develop a focus not only on customers, but also more generally on key educational publics. Kotler and Fox (1985: 24) define the term 'public' as 'a distinct group of people and/or organizations that has an actual or potential interest in and/or effect on an institution'.

Educational institutions probably have the most diverse range of publics of any category of nonprofit. When one considers that each of these will be likely to have a unique set of expectations of an institution, the complexity of educational marketing can begin to be appreciated.

School Publics

Looking first at school publics, Davies and Ellison (1991) suggest that the following groups are worthy of consideration.

Internal Publics

Governors

Governors have the capacity to shape the future direction of the school and as such have a need to be informed about ongoing developments. They also need to be informed about changes taking place in the external environment and from time to time lobbied about the desirability of a particular response. Governors may also need marketing support to communicate policy decisions and the underlying rationale for them to other school publics, such as pupils, staff, parents, and increasingly, the wider community.

Staff

As the providers of the educational service, staff are arguably the most important of all the educational publics. It is staff who interact on a daily basis with the key customers of the school: parents and pupils. The attitudes and behaviour of staff can therefore have a profound impact on the performance of a school and its role in a community. Of late, the role of the staff has taken on a particular significance because of the introduction of league tables. Since these tables consist almost entirely of lists of quantitative criteria such as performance in exam results, there is a danger that schools could concentrate too heavily on these aspects of their role. Teaching staff have traditionally been able to take a more holistic view of the development of individual children and taken steps to ensure that social, artistic, physical, and academic concerns are all addressed. Since these aspects are all key components of the academic product, institutions need to ensure that staff are still encouraged to continue to give consideration to these 'softer' aspects of their role.

Regular Visitors and Helpers

School visitors and helpers play a vital role in shaping the image that the school has within a community. If these individuals leave the school with a favourable impression they are likely to impart it to others and hence enhance the overall image and reputation of the institution.

Current Pupils

It is current pupils, however, who have the greatest capacity to shape the nature of the relationship of a school with its community. Their attitude, appearance, and behaviour all communicate something of the quality of the educational experience the school is providing. Current pupils often need to be reminded of this fact and persuaded that it is ultimately in their best interests to ensure that the school is seen in as positive a light as possible.

Current Parents

Parents represent a key public for both primary and secondary schools. In both cases they now have the right to select the institution at which their child will be educated. Schools therefore need to reassure parents that the right decision has been taken and to enable them to do this an ongoing dialogue must be maintained. It has to be recognized that parental expectations of a school have now changed and they expect to have a greater influence over the child's education. Communications with the school must thus be both frequent and informative. The days of the preparation of report cards, which read simply 'could do better', have long since passed.

External Publics

Prospective Parents

The parents of prospective students are a key focus of external marketing activity. For a detailed discussion of the nature of the relationship that should be developed with this target public, see the section below on influencing student buying behaviour.

Prospective Staff

For many schools, the recruitment of appropriately qualified staff is a significant issue. In a competitive market the school will have to ensure that it effectively markets its location, the quality/behaviour of its pupils, and the management culture of the school, alongside the more traditional package of direct benefits that every employer now offers.

Other Educational Institutions

Effective liaison with feeder institutions can play a major role in recruitment activity. Often, designated secondary-school teachers will be given responsibility for developing relationships with key feeder schools in the immediate area. The cultivation of this relationship may involve regular visits to such institutions and meetings with staff, parents, and pupils, in a bid to make the transition from one school to another as seamless as possible.

The Local Community

The local community is a public which is increasing in importance. While schools have always been concerned to be seen to be living in harmony with local residents, the role of community liaison has in the past has been reactive in nature. Since parents often build their perception of particular schools from listening to the local grapevine, influencing this grapevine proactively has now become a priority. The advent of community education has also compelled schools to specifically develop this target group. Many schools now market evening courses designed to meet the needs of local people and draw in valuable income.

Commerce and Industry

With educational funding becoming increasingly restricted, many schools have now regis-tered as charities and are attempting to solicit support from corporate donors in the same way as other charitable organizations. The educational standards set and the overall reputa-tion of a given school will doubtless exert considerable influence over a decision of whether or not support will be granted. Good links with industry and commerce are also important to find work placements for those students who require them. If a school has a bad reputa-tion, employers are likely to be less willing to offer its pupils placements.

The Local Education Authority

While the role of the LEA has declined in significance in recent years, they remain key school publics by virtue of the access that they can provide to discretionary funding. They are also important targets since schools may have the desire to influence funding policies at a local level and will therefore want to develop close links that can be exploited for lobbying purposes, as and when the need arises.

University/College Publics

The list of important publics for those institutions involved in the delivery of FE or HE is even longer. To those identified above we may add research funders, alumni, accredited organizations, and local/national media, although not even this list should be regarded as exhaustive.

Research Funders

Research funders constitute an important public, particularly for universities to address. These fall generally into one of two categories. The first are quasi-governmental organiza-tions that exist to act as a conduit to channel government support into those projects or de-partments deemed most worthy of support. The destination of this form of funding is now highly dependent on the performance of a department (or more accurately a unit of assess-ment) in the Research Assessment Exercise (RAE). Other government funding is available through the research councils and this may be bid for on an ad hoc basis as projects present themselves. The second category of research funders is essentially grant-making trusts which exist to support particular forms of research. The process of applying for funds from such organizations is usually, although not always, competitive. While one would hope that deci-sions taken in respect of research funding would always be objective and based on the qual-ity of past research and/or the application submitted, the impact of a favourable image and an institution's record of gaining publicity for its research should not be underestimated.

Alumni

The careful cultivation of alumni can serve a number of purposes. Good alumni relations can greatly aid student recruitment, particularly in some overseas markets where personal recommendations are of great importance. Alumni can also be a valuable source of publicity for the university, as the achievements of past students are often newsworthy. Moreover, an alumni network can unlock doors that lead to research funding, consultancy, student placements, and even quite sizeable donations of cash support.

Accredited Organizations

With the expansion of higher education a great many institutions now accredit colleges to teach one or more aspects of their provision. Franchise or accreditation arrangements are now common. In the former a college delivers a course programme on a university's behalf, while under the latter arrangement, a university agrees to recognize a college course as meeting a particular standard, and awards an appropriate qualification to participants on completion. In recent years the development of such arrangements has been popular in the UK, but also with educational establishments abroad. Indeed, there has been a phenomenal growth in overseas links, primarily because they can prove extremely lucrative, not only in terms of the revenue generated, but also in terms of the number of future university applicants generated. As a consequence, responsibility for the development of such links tends now to be administered at a most senior level within the majority of HE institutions.

Local/National Media

Given the significance of the output of qualified individuals from colleges and universities to the national economy, it is no surprise that there is considerable media interest in the activities of universities. The activities and successes of individual students are often of great interest, as are the nature of the relationships that a university has with all its other publics. Carefully managed, the publicity this generates can have a very positive impact on the overall image of the institution.

In a short text such as this, it is impossible to examine in great detail the manner in which relationships with all the 'publics' identified above could be developed. The remainder of this chapter will therefore concentrate on the impact that marketing can have on arguably the most important of these—potential students.

Influencing Student Buying Behaviour

Chapman (1986) was among the first to apply the buying behaviour literature to the education sector. He suggested that in selecting a suitable institution at which to study, students (and/or their parents) pass through a number of uniquely definable stages.

Stage 1: Pre-Search Behaviour

Students will give early consideration to their choice of the next educational establishment to attend although, at this stage, little or no effort is made to gather information about the various options available. Students will passively 'register' the existence of information to which they are exposed. This may be general institutional advertising, or it may be casual discussions with family or friends. It is at this stage, however, that attitudes towards different providers will begin to be formed. This is a crucial stage of the process, since these attitudes, be they positive or negative, will help the student in the future to develop her own shortlist of potential institutions at which to study.

The marketing task at this point is to ensure that the institution maintains a relatively high profile within its target markets. Favourable publicity about the activities of students and/or staff, links with feeder institutions, open days, special events, etc. can all help create and reinforce positive attitudes towards an organization. Similarly, the local grapevine can often be persuaded to act in an institution's favour through the careful cultivation of links with the broader community.

Stage 2: Search Behaviour

By the time students actively seek out course information, the evidence suggests that a short-list of potential providers has already been formed. For the student it is then only a matter of comparing between this limited number of choices. They will utilize a variety of sources of information to help them in this task and look for data in respect of a wide range of decision criteria. Since these criteria will vary substantially between the various levels of education, this is a matter that will be returned to in some detail below.

■ CASE STUDY

DE MONTFORT UNIVERSITY

De Montfort University has attempted to attract more early applications from students and meet increasingly competitive performance targets with a new marketing strategy. The institution decided to enhance the coherence of its message by targeting potential students with a mixed strategy campaign. It abandoned traditional broad-based communications in favour of relevant press and radio activity using niche media. It decided to use niche youth-friendly publications and programmes to attract youngsters, including buying space on sixth-formers' homework diaries and placing postcards in colleges. The university also aimed to improve its overall branding stategy by ensuring its message remained consistent across all faculties.

Case compiled from resources at www.dmu.ac.uk<http://www.dmu.ac.uk>.

Stage 3: Application Decision

Having researched the options available, the student will then utilize the decision-making criteria referred to above to identify a small number of institutions to which an application will be made. At this stage the selected institutions will respond by either rejecting the application or making an offer of a place. It is often the case that this offer will be dependent on a specified level of performance in forthcoming examinations.

The marketing task at this point is to ensure that applications are dealt with as promptly and 'personally' as possible. In higher education, while almost all undergraduate applications are dealt with by the Universities and College Admissions Service (UCAS), the time taken to respond by a particular institution can still make a substantial difference. This is particularly true of postgraduate education, where many students are keen to guarantee themselves a place as soon as the decision to study has been taken. In a market where a great similarity in portfolios now exists between institutions, those that are seen to provide a high standard of 'customer care' and that respond quickly to communications will undoubtedly gain an advantage.

Stage 4: Choice Decision

The next stage of the process involves the student in accepting one or more of the offers that has been made. In most cases, this acceptance does not form the basis of a binding contract with the education provider, and hence multiple acceptances are common.

It is absolutely essential that providers realize at this point that they will be competing with only a small number of other institutions. Since many still fail to maintain a dialogue with prospective students from the time at which an offer is issued until the student arrives on campus, there remains a substantial marketing opportunity. Institutions that maintain a dialogue, perhaps by sending copies of information sheets, newsletters, course information, and/or reading lists, have all recognized the importance of such communications in psychologically bonding a student to their institution. The reader will recall the issue of 'tangibility' in service marketing from Chapter 4. High-quality, informative communications that help prepare students for their forthcoming programmes of study can greatly raise the level of tangibility and serve to reduce the inevitable stress that will result from having to choose between the final few institutions.

Stage 5: Matriculation Decision

At the final stage of the process, the student has to decide at which institution she will study and register as a student on the campus. At this stage the marketing task is to welcome new students and ensure that the transition to their new way of life is as smooth as possible. At an undergraduate level, universities have many years of experience of running informative and often highly entertaining 'Freshers Week' programmes to help ensure that students make new friends and settle in before the commencement of their studies.

The needs of mature, overseas, and postgraduate students are likely to be somewhat different. Many may need help to arrange accommodation (often for their whole family), medical care, English language support, religious services, and more specific help to identify all the key university services that they are likely to need during their stay. An increasing number of institutions have come to recognize the needs of these individuals and now operate separate induction programmes that ensure, as far as possible, that these are catered for.

While all the stages of the decision-making process are important and marketing has a clear role to play in each, the key communication issue for most institutions (and certainly the allocation of the largest proportion of the marketing budget) revolves around Stages 1 and 2. Institutions need to ensure that they communicate effectively with students early in their decision-making process. The difficulty for most providers, however, lies in deciding exactly what to say and to whom. The remainder of this section will attempt to shed some light on this issue, by analysing in some detail how decisions in respect of education provision are taken in the cases of primary, secondary, and higher education.

Primary Education

The key decision makers in respect of the appropriate provider of a primary education are now (by virtue of the Education Act) the parents of the individual child. Interestingly parents have been shown to give consideration to this issue at a very early stage in their child's development. Indeed, many will have decided on an appropriate primary school well before their child reaches the age of two years (Bussell 1994). Given this, one may legitimately ask what sources of information a parent might use in reaching their decision. After all, most appear to have been taken before any direct contact with a school has been initiated. Bussell found that the key source of information utilized by parents was the local grapevine, emphasizing once again the importance for schools of maintaining close relationships with their local community. Online research and information hubs such as www.goodschoolsguide.co.uk (or in the United States www.greatschools.net and www.schoolmatters.com) are now playing a critical role.

Only limited academic research has been conducted in this domain, but Petch (1986), in a series of 400 interviews with parents, determined that the following evaluative criteria were used to compare between the various options available.

- *Happiness*. Parents' perceptions of the atmosphere in a particular school are important. Most parents will at some stage visit prospective providers, even if the visit serves only to confirm an earlier decision. Since most visits can be timed to allow classroom activity to be viewed, the happiness of the pupils can be, albeit subjectively, assessed.

- *Location*. Parents have been shown (for obvious reasons) to favour schools that are geographically closer to the family home.

- *Discipline*. The level of discipline imposed on students is a significant factor for parents. Most like to feel that good standards of discipline are rigorously enforced.

- *Facilities*. These can include computing, library, and recreational resources provided.

- *Friends*. The placement of children belonging to friends of the family can be relevant.

- *Siblings*. The school selected for an older brother/sister can influence a decision.

- *Teachers*. The perceived quality of the teaching staff is another criterion.

- *Reputation*. The overall reputation of the school is also considered.

- *Safety*. The perceived safety of the environment created by the school is another factor.

Barnes (1993) provides a useful planning framework that schools may use to consider the nature of the 'product' on offer. As Figure 11.4 makes clear there are both tangible and intangible dimensions to the service provided and schools should consider both the intrinsic and extrinsic components of these.

Secondary Education

By the stage at which decisions have to be taken in respect of secondary education, the child herself now has considerably more say. Studies by Thomas and Dennison (1991) and Alston (1985) both confirm the importance of the child in the decision-making process. Children

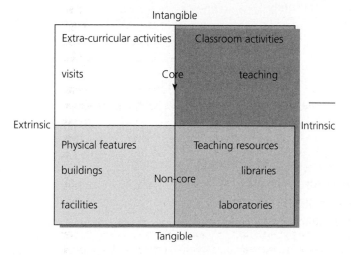

Figure 11.4 The nature of the school product

Source: Barnes, C. (1993) *Practical Marketing for Schools,* Oxford, Blackwell.

appear to be influenced by visits from secondary school teachers and visits to their potential new schools. The most important factors in influencing a child's decision are, however, where friends will study, the facilities offered, and, surprisingly, the existence of a uniform. Children appear not to want to attend a school where the pupils appear scruffy, or where they feel bullying might occur (West and Varlaam 1991).

The impact of written communications should also not be underestimated in communicating with potential pupils. West and Varlaam (1991) found that 70 per cent of children had read the school brochures of potential new schools. This fact has important implications for the style in which such publications are produced, since they should obviously be written in a manner easily accessible by 11/12-year-olds.

The decision in respect of which school to attend appears to be taken before the last year of primary education (Stillman and Maychell 1986), with a surprising amount of agreement between children and their parents over which school should be selected. Indeed, West et al. (1995) found that parents and children agree in 83 per cent of cases. Despite the increasing involvement of the child in the decision, however, the levels of parental input and concern remain high. Over 87 per cent will visit the school their child will ultimately attend and 94 per cent will take the time to read the school brochure. Of the factors that have the most influence on parental choice, discipline, exam results, and happiness are all primary considerations (see for example West et al. 1995; West and Varlaam 1991; or Hammond and Dennison 1995).

Higher Education

Undergraduate Students

Grabowski (1981), in a comprehensive review of the literature, found that the following factors all appeared to have an impact on student choice:

- athletic facilities
- academic reputation
- quality of college faculty
- economic status of family
- availability of financial aid
- conversations with former students
- geographic location
- opinions of high-school teachers and counsellors
- effectiveness of the institution in getting jobs for its graduates
- institution's competition
- interviews
- older brothers and sisters who attended the institution
- parents and family preferences
- physical plant and facilities
- activities of recruiters
- size of establishment
- social activities
- specific academic programmes
- visits to campus.

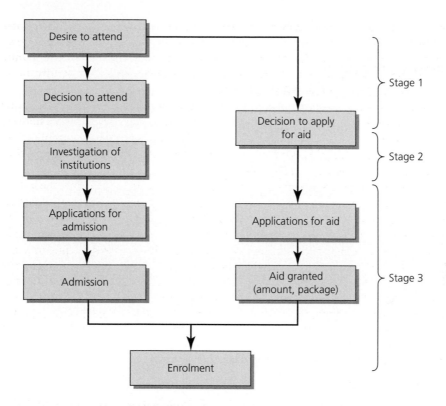

Figure 11.5 The Hansen and Litten model

Source: Hansen, K.H. and Litten, L.H. (1989) 'Mapping The Road to Academe: A Review of Research on Women, Men and the College-Selection Process'. In Perun, P.J. (ed), *The Undergraduate Woman: Issues in Educational Equity,* Lexington, Lexington Books, 73–98.

A key perspective on the HE decision making process is depicted in Figure 11.5. The Hansen and Litten model (1989) portrays the process undertaken by students as being affected by a plethora of situational factors ranging from the characteristics of the student themselves (e.g. race and personality), to environmental factors such as occupational structure and cultural conditions, to college characteristics like financial aid availability and ambience. Their three-stage model suggests that a student initially decides to participate in post-secondary education. During the second stage the student investigates institutions and creates a set of 'possibles'. The process of applying to an HEI and enrolling is the last stage. Within these three stages there exist five distinct processes that a student passes through: having college aspirations, starting the search process, gathering information, sending applications, and enrolling.

While the knowledge that all these factors have the capacity to influence a decision is helpful, it does not leave an HE marketer with a sense of how to prioritize their effort and select appropriate media for communication. The available research suggests that prospectuses (or in the US 'viewbooks') are the most crucial form of marketing communication, but it is important to recognize that they often serve only to confirm decisions that have already been made (Chapman and Johnson 1979).

In respect of other forms of marketing, Chapman and Franklin (1981) and Kealy and Rockel (1987) agree that close liaison with high-school personnel and arranging 'sampler' events such as campus visits are of primary importance in influencing the decision-making process.

■ **CASE STUDY**

UNIVERSITY OF CHICAGO

The University of Chicago was one of the first institutions to recognize the importance of building relationships with potential students early in their academic careers. When Michael Behnke became Vice President and Associate Dean of College Enrollment the University had a history of using its prospectus (viewbook) as the primary marketing tool and this was typically sent to high school students in their penultimate year of study. It was very typical of university marketing materials of the time and focused on providing pictures of the campus or students hard at work.

His new approach was to target younger students around the age of 16, the goal being to contact them before they were targeted by others. He tripled the size of the mailing programme and developed a relational approach that consisted of initial communication followed by regular reminders. More critically he redesigned the viewbook to capture the essence of university life and convey what the overall student experience would be like. The quirky and stylish 'The Life of the Mind' debuted in 1999 and the number of applications rose by 22%. Importantly the number of freshman with SAT scores of 1500 or higher also rose by 65%.

Today the publication can be viewed online and pdfs featuring different aspects of student life downloaded. The focus on student life has been maintained as an image from a recent issue (see Figure 11.6) demonstrates.

Case compiled from resources at www.chicago.edu<http://www.chicago.edu>.

Figure 11.6 'The Life of the Mind'
Source: © 2008 University of Chicago.

The University of Chicago case makes an important point that targeting potential students early is now a key component of university marketing. Although it can help improve competitive position, it plays a wider role in encouraging able students to consider going on into HE (Stupak 2001). By age 16 many children may already be turned off to education and in recognition of this some institutions now offer taster sessions for children at much earlier stages of their high school careers. This can generate a sense of excitement and in some cases even lead to students aspiring to greater success in their studies.

Finally, no discussion of marketing to prospective undergraduates would be complete without some consideration of the role that existing students can play in facilitating the process. They can be key ambassadors for the institution and play an active role as guides during open days and school visits, but they can also get involved more proactively and participate in visits to feeder institutions. As previous examples in this chapter have highlighted, they can also be featured online with blogs posted on the organization's website.

However, such involvement presupposes that students are satisfied with the quality of their experience and thus likely to paint a 'helpful' picture of what life would be like. The notion of students as customers is now far from new, but what is new is an increasing interest on the part of researchers in student satisfaction with a university and the factors that drive it. In particular institutions are recognizing that they need to understand and manage student expectations (Sander et al. 2000) because (as we established earlier) their perceptions of service quality will depend on these expectations (See also Telford and Masson 2005). Positive perceptions of service quality have been linked to increased student participation (Claycomb et al. 2001), increased positive word of mouth, and an enhanced likelihood that further courses will be taken in the future (Marzo-Navarro et al. 2005, Schertzer and Schertzer 2004). A key component of that overall perception is the perception of the quality of lecturing staff (Hill et al. 2003), and Voss et al. (2007: 957) identify that students want 'lecturers to be knowledgeable, enthusiastic, approachable and friendly. They should possess sufficient communication and teaching skills and be able to choose the most suitable teaching method from a variety of teaching tools'. There is a clear role for internal marketing to ensure that, as far as possible, this proves to be the case.

Postgraduate Students

In the largest study of its kind, HEIST (1995) studied the criteria used by postgraduate students to select an institution. They found that the factors listed in Table 11.1 were cited as having the most influence.

Table 11.1 Factors influencing postgraduate student choice

Factor	% of students citing as primary consideration
Course content	32
Location	19
Availability of funding	12
Reputation of institution	10
Only institution offering course	7
Recommendation	4
Other	16

Source: O'Neill, I. (1995) *Taught Postgraduate Education: The Student Experience*, Maidstone, HEIST. Reproduced with kind permission.

At a postgraduate level, the nature of the course content would seem to be altogether more important than at an undergraduate level. Intense promotional activity is therefore likely to be much less effective than an early consideration of customer needs/wants and a course design that reflects these. Interestingly, postgraduate students appear to seriously consider only a very small number of potential providers. In the USA Houston (1979) found that the number of graduate schools considered by a student averages around three, with only two key sources of information in respect of these being utilized, namely prospectuses and peer-related contacts. There is some evidence that this continues to be the case, although online sources of information are now the norm in obtaining details of the courses on offer.

Education Marketing—Planning and Control

Marketing Strategy

It is apparent from the above that the task of marketing an educational institution is more complex than that for almost any other category of nonprofit. A diversity of publics with an equally diverse set of needs and wants make it almost impossible to derive one plan that will adequately serve the needs of the whole institution. It is therefore normal practice to address the marketing strategy that will be followed at an institutional level and to delegate authority for the production of individual tactical plans to specific departments or centres. Each of these can then develop a tactical mix that will be appropriate for the educational publics that they deal with on a daily basis.

Clearly, decisions must be taken at a strategic level in respect of the overall direction in which the institution will be taken, perhaps utilizing Ansoff as a framework (see Ansoff 1968). Market segmentation and positioning/branding are also likely to be centrally decided as they are both likely to have profound implications for the development of subsequent tactical plans. In particular the positioning and branding selected by an education institution will pervade every aspect of the work that it subsequently engages in. Unlike many consumer markets where individual offerings can be separately positioned, in education markets it is rare to be able to escape from the overall 'image' that a particular supplier has in the market. While most students recognize that departments in a university will vary in quality and will try to take a subject rather than an institutional perspective, it would be a brave marketer who would claim that the overall positioning and branding of the university, in terms of perceived quality and status, does not have a considerable impact on student choice. There are a small number of institutions, for example, which tend to be selected as a fallback position by students if they fail to be accepted at one of the Oxbridge universities. Interestingly these institutions are continually selected as second choice, irrespective of the subject being studied. At a postgraduate level this phenomenon is perhaps less in evidence, since students are often motivated to apply by the research ranking achieved by an individual department. Even in these cases, however, students are doubtless mindful of how the institution will be perceived in the minds of potential employers on completion of their studies.

The difficulty for senior managers is that the branding strategy selected needs to be consistent and hence capable of implementation in each of the very diverse markets that the institution serves. Accomplishing this is no easy matter, the temptation being to select a brand based on vague academic values such as excellence in teaching or research. There cannot be many institutions that do not perceive themselves as striving for excellence in both these key areas! A good branding strategy should be unique and summarize neatly the key facets of the

■ **CASE STUDY**

ARCADIA UNIVERSITY

One of the most successful rebranding exercises in the history of education marketing took place in 2001 when Beaver College in the suburbs of Philadelphia transformed itself into Arcadia University. There were numerous reasons for the change. Beaver wanted to sever the connections with its past as a women's college and to be clear to its target audiences that it was a fully fledged university. The name 'Arcadia' was selected as it had its origin as a picturesque region of ancient Greece and had associations with being a peaceful environment for thought and learning.

Of course, there was also a need to eliminate the link between the college's old name and modern slang for a private part of the female anatomy. Indeed in the process of rebranding many unhelpful suggestions in respect of possible alternatives were submitted to the college offices including Gynecollege and the University of the Southern Region. The newly revamped Arcadia was, however, destined to have the last laugh. Applications doubled in the four years following the rebranding and average student SAT scores increased by 60%.

Not all this success can be put down to the change of name, however. The Vice President of Enrollment Management introduced a number of changes that simultaneously aimed at altering the perception of the university. Notable here was the investment in a relational database allowing the college to get away from 'dear student' letters and develop a more personalized approach. A TQM (total quality management) approach was also adopted, designed among other things to make visits to the campus more memorable. The success speaks for itself.

Case compiled from resources at www.arcadia.edu<http://www.arcadia.edu>.

organization, thus allowing some scope for modification in response to the requirements of each individual market.

Branding aside, the Arcadia case raises a second key strategic issue that institutions now have to address, namely that of CRM. Modern relational databases should allow institutions to develop a holistic perspective on how they will manage individual client relationships. It should now be possible to integrate all stakeholders in a database, tracking, for example, individuals when they are first encountered as children, through the time when they become prospective students, through when they matriculate, to when they graduate, and ultimately become donors to the institution (Arnett et al. 2003). As individuals move through a lifetime of interactions the college or university can collect and utilize data about them to implement strategies that enhance and intensify their relationships (Madden 2006). In effect the university becomes a community hub that grows, evolves, and matures through an individual's life (Bingham et al. 2001).

Madden (2007: 292) articulates a useful example of what this might mean in practice:

Among the possible foci of contributing to the life of the stakeholder could be enhancing college preparation of young people; bringing prospective freshman applicants to campus to interact with students and meet with faculty in their area of interest; building a service culture towards the university community as an undergraduate student; offering students who are about to graduate opportunities for service and leadership in the alumni association; offering senior undergraduate students opportunities for interaction with alumni in their prospective career interests; asking new graduates to mentor and help undergraduates in the same field; asking older alumni to connect senior undergraduates with career opportunities in their companies; asking new graduates to volunteer in going on recruiting assignments for the university; offering career counseling for graduates who have been out of school for three to five years; offering continuing education directed at subjects that address current life needs, such as raising children, investing and changing careers; offering alumni travel opportunities; asking alumni to take leadership roles in the alumni association . . .

Marketing Tactics

The responsibility for the development of tactical plans will vary considerably from institution to institution. In schools, it is likely that one plan will be developed centrally with the help of senior teaching staff and administrators. In the case of an FE college a central institutional plan is also likely to exist, although responsibility for marketing individual courses is likely to be devolved to the members of academic staff who have the responsibility for coordinating each programme. In a university, the picture is likely to be more complex, with separate tactical plans being developed by a multitude of different administrative and academic departments. In this environment it is absolutely essential that some mechanism exists to coordinate the actions of each. Greater coordination can lead to a considerable number of benefits, including the placement of joint advertising (leading to overall cost reductions), greater buying power, a sharing of ideas and experience, and the careful planning of support activities. A department within one well-known institution recently advertised its presence in clearing for the first time and was swamped with high numbers of phone calls. No additional administrative staff had been devoted to the task of dealing with enquiries and none of the operators who took the calls were even aware that the advert had been placed. What could have been a very effective promotion was thus sabotaged by a failure to communicate with other key 'marketing' staff.

Control

The issue of control is of particular significance for educational institutions. Given the great diversity in marketing functions throughout the organization it is crucial that effective control mechanisms are put in place to ensure that the institution as a whole moves in the direction that has been envisaged. Where control is lacking, there can be a risk of strategic drift, where decisions are taken on an incremental basis by individual managers or academics with very different perspectives of the global situation. A lack of control can also result in an organization paying little attention to costs, the returns being generated by each marketing activity, and both the efficiency and effectiveness thereof.

Control activity can best be categorized as follows:

1. *Strategic control*. At a strategic level, the emphasis is largely on ensuring that the organization 'gets to where it wants to be'. Senior management will have taken a range of decisions relating to the strategic direction of the institution, segmentation issues, and positioning. They will also have had considerable input to portfolio matters, pricing, and promotion. Strategic control therefore needs to ensure that the decisions taken were implemented in the manner envisaged and that the desired effect in terms of the strategic health of the organization has been realized (i.e. that the marketing activity has been effective). The key strategic control is thus the marketing audit referred to earlier, which should be undertaken on a regular basis.

2. *Efficiency control.* Institutions will also want to ensure that they are making an efficient use of their resources. Marketing activity could well be effective in the sense that it is aiding the achievement of the institutional objectives, but it may be costing the organization more than is necessary. The efficiency of the marketing activity undertaken is thus an important issue on which to focus control. Typically this might be undertaken at a functional level, measuring, for example, the efficiency of various forms of promotional activity, e.g. attendance at overseas fairs, advertising, direct mailshots, etc. Desired levels of efficiency can be compared against actual and remedial action instigated where necessary.

3. *Profitability control.* The profitability of each activity also needs to be controlled. Setting targets for each course, department, faculty, etc. may be one way of achieving this. Alternatively, an institution-wide perspective could be adopted and profitability measured by key customer segment.

4. *Annual plan control.* A key focus of control activity is the annual institutional plan. Marketers need to measure:

- *Sales/market shares.* Actual figures should be compared with the budgeted figures.
- *Sales/expense analysis.* In many institutions this is referred to as the allowable cost per sale. Organizations need to decide in advance just how much they are prepared to spend to secure each sale, and monitor performance against this target.
- *Conversion rates.* Institutions will wish to ensure that a sufficient number of enquiries are actually converted into sales. If the conversion rate appears to be dropping in one department, this may indicate that its portfolio is becoming less attractive, or that its marketing is of poor quality.
- *Drop-out rates.* A key test of the quality of marketing activity in education is the extent to which it allows individuals to self-select the courses that are right for them. Monitoring drop-out rates can hence be a helpful control mechanism in ensuring that a high quality of contact is maintained with each target group. Individuals should have no difficulty in determining in advance which courses are right for them and taking action accordingly.

Despite the length of the above list, however, it is important that a balance be struck between ensuring that adequate control mechanisms exist and allowing individual marketing functions sufficient scope to develop their own creativity. Departments should be encouraged to explore the utility of new marketing techniques and not be afraid to experiment with new ideas, even if this means an occasional 'failure'. The control procedures employed within a particular organization should therefore allow sufficient scope for this to take place without compromising the integrity of the overall institutional position.

■ **SUMMARY**

In this chapter we have examined a number of the key environmental influences for change on education at all levels within the UK. Issues of competition and enhanced student choice are now matters of concern to all education marketers irrespective of where they might happen to work within the sector. Importantly, these changes should not be viewed as taking place only in the UK—in many other countries the same environmental forces are shaping the manner in which educational frameworks are developed and maintained. Against this backdrop, it was argued here that the most important marketing issue for educational institutions to address is the early attainment of a genuine market orientation. This involves organizations in fostering greater degrees of collaboration between internal departments, monitoring the performance and activities of key competitors, and developing a focus on a wide range of institutional publics.

To date, research undertaken into the needs/wants of these publics has been comparatively sparse, although the findings of a number of the more important studies have been reported here. If institutions are to successfully develop course provisions that are attractive to the market they need to have a detailed understanding of the market's needs. Indeed, an understanding of how and when decisions are taken in respect of educational provision is essential if providers are to effectively market their provision to the key organizational publics of potential students and their parents. Only when such knowledge has been gained can organizations hope to develop meaningful strategic and tactical plans that will capture the imagination of their market and ultimately lead to superior marketing performance.

■ DISCUSSION QUESTIONS

1. Research the provisions of the Education Act 1988, or the No Child Left Behind law in the United States. What are the implications of this piece of legislation for the marketing of secondary education?

2. What are likely to be the key institutional barriers to the attainment of a marketing orientation in the education sector? How might these be overcome?

3. How might a competitive focus be accomplished? What categories of data should an educational institution try to capture in respect of its key competitors?

4. To what extent might marketing, at a philosophical level, be likely to conflict with the traditional concept of academic freedom? Are the two necessarily incompatible?

5. For your own institution, or one with which you are familiar, list its key publics. How might relationships with each of these key publics be developed and maintained over time?

6. For your own institution, pick a faculty group or course that you are personally familiar with. Critically evaluate its approach to the digital marketing of its courses. How might this be improved?

7. To what extent do you think the traditional college viewbook (prospectus) still has a role to play in university marketing? Might it be replaced in the coming years? If so, by what?

8. Why is the concept of marketing 'control' of particular relevance to higher education institutions? What difficulties are likely to be encountered in attempting to control the marketing activities undertaken? How could these difficulties be overcome?

■ REFERENCES

Allen, A. and Higgins, T. (1994) Higher Education—The International Student Experience, HEIST, Leeds.

Alston, C. (1985) *The Views of Parents Before Transfer*, Secondary Transfer Project, Bulletin 3 (RS991/85), Inner London Education Authority.

Ansoff, I. (1968) *Corporate Strategy*, London, Penguin Books.

Arnett, D.B., German, S.D. and Hunt, S.D. (2003) 'The Identity Salience Model of Relationship Marketing Success: The Case of Nonprofit Marketing', *Journal of Marketing*, Vol. 67, No. 2, 89–105.

Bargh, C., Scott, P. and Smith, D. (1996) *Governing Universities, Changing the Culture?*, Buckingham, SRHE and Open University Press.

Barnes, C. (1993) *Practical Marketing For Schools*, Oxford, Blackwell.

Bingham, F.G., Quigley, C.J. and Murray, K.B. (2001) 'A Response to Beyond the Mission Statement: Alternative Futures For Today's Universities', *Journal of Marketing for Higher Education*, Vol. 11, No. 4, 19–27.

Bok, D. (2003) *Universities in the Marketplace: The Commercialization of Higher Education*, Princeton, Princeton University Press.

Boxall, M. (1991) 'Positioning the Institution in the Marketplace', in *Universities in the Marketplace*, CUA Corporate Planning Forum, Conference of University Administrators in Association with Touche Ross.

Brint, S. (2002) *The Future of the City of Intellect: The Challenging American University*, Stanford, Stanford University Press.

Bussell, H. (1994) 'Parents and Primary Schools: A Study of Customer Choice', *Proceedings of 1994 Marketing Education Group Conference*, Coleraine.

Chapman, R. (1986) 'Toward a Theory of College Selection: A Model of College Search and Choice Behaviour', in *Advances in Consumer Research*, Vol. 13, ed. R.J. Lutz, and Association for Consumer Research, Provo, UT.

Chapman, R.G. and Franklin, M.S. (1981) 'Measuring the Impact of High School Visits: A Preliminary Investigation', AMA Educators Conference Proceedings, Chicago.

Chapman, D.W. and Johnson, R.H. (1979) 'Influences on Students' College Choice: A Case Study', Ann Arbor, MI, Project CHOICE, School of Education, University of Michigan.

Claycomb, V., Lengnick-Hall, C.A. and Inks, L.W. (2001) 'The Customer As A Productive Resource: A Pilot Study and Strategic Implications', *Journal of Business Strategies*, Vol. 18, No. 1, 193–218.

Davies, B. and Ellison, L. (1991) *Marketing the Secondary School*, Harlow, Longman Industry and Public Services Management.

Dunn, S.L. (2000) 'The Virtualizing of Education', *Futurist*, Vol. 34, No. 2, 34–9.

Grabowski, S.M. (1981) *Marketing in Higher Education*, Washington, AAHE ERIC Higher Education Research Report, No. 5.

Hammond, T. and Dennison, W. (1995) 'School Choice in Less Populated Areas', *Educational Management and Administration*, Vol. 23, No. 2, 104–13.

Hansen, K.H. and Litten, L.H. (1989) 'Mapping The Road To Academe: A Review of Research on Women, Men and the College-Selection Process'. In Perun, P.J. (ed), *The Undergraduate Woman: Issues in Educational Equity*, Lexington, Lexington Books, 73–98.

Hayes, T. (2007) 'Delphi Study of the Future of Marketing of Higher Education', *Journal of Business Research*, Vol. 60, 927–31.

HEIST (1995) *The Role of Marketing in the University and College Sector*, Leeds, HEIST.

Higher Education Statistics Agency (HESA) (2008) 'Higher Education Student Enrolments', http://www.hesa.ac.uk/index.php/content/view/119/161/accessed January 2008.

Hill, Y., Lomas, L. and MacGregor, J. (2003) 'Students' Perceptions of Quality in Higher Education', *Quality Assurance in Education*, Vol. 11, No. 1, 15–20.

Houston, M. (1979) 'Cognitive Structure and Information Search Patterns of Prospective Graduate Business Students', *Advances in Consumer Research*, Vol. VII, 52–7.

Jarratt Committee (1985) *Report of the Steering Committee for Efficiency Studies in Universities*, London, CVCP.

Kealy, M.J. and Rockel, M.L. (1987) 'Student Perceptions of College Quality: The Influence of College Recruitment Policies', *Journal of Higher Education*, Vol. 58, No. 6, 683–1103.

Kerr, C. (2001) *The Uses of the University* (5th edn), Boston, MA., Harvard University Press.

Kirp, D.L. (2003) *Shakespeare, Einstein and the Bottom Line: The Marketing of Higher Education*, Boston, MA., Harvard University Press.

Kotler, P. and Fox, K. (1985) *Strategic Marketing for Educational Institutions*, Englewood Cliffs, NJ, Prentice Hall.

Lockwood, G. and Davies, J. (1985) *Universities, The Management Challenge*, Windsor, NFER Nelson.

Madden, C.S. (2006) 'Building University Community: A Customer Relationship Management Lifecycle Approach', *Symposium for the Marketing of Higher Education*, Chicago, American Marketing Association: 1–2.

Madden, C.S. (2007) 'The Promise of Marketing in Higher Education: Where We Have Been, Where We Are and Where We Are Going', in Sargeant, A. and Wymer, W. (eds) *The Routledge Companion to Nonprofit Marketing*, London, Routledge, 280–96.

Marzo-Navarro, M., Pedraja-Iglesias, M. and Rivera-Torres, M. (2005) 'Measuring Customer Satisfaction in Summer Courses', *Quality Assurance in Education*, Vol. 13, No. 1, 53–65.

Moore, P.G. (1989) 'Marketing Higher Education', *Higher Education Quarterly*, Vol. 43, No. 2, 108–24.

O'Neill, I. (1995) *Taught Postgraduate Education: The Student Experience*, Maidstone, HEIST.

Palfreyman, D. and Warner, D. (eds) (1996) *Higher Education Management: The Key Elements*, London, Society for Research Into Higher Education.

Petch, A. (1986) 'Parental Choice at Entry to Primary School', *Research Papers in Education*, Vol. 1, No. 1, 26–41.

Sander, P., Stevenson, K., King, M. and Coates, D. (2000) 'University Students' Expectations of Teaching', *Studies in Higher Education*, Vol. 25, No. 3, 309–23.

Schertzer, C.B. and Schertzer, S.M.B. (2004) 'Student Satisfaction and Retention: A Conceptual Model', *Journal of Marketing in Higher Education*, Vol. 14, No. 1, 79–91.

Slaughter, S. and Leslie, L. (1998) *Academic Capitalism: Politics, Policies and the Entrepreneurial University*, Baltimore, Johns Hopkins University Press.

Stillman, A. and Maychell, K. (1986) *Choosing Schools: Parents, LEAs and the 1980 Education Act*, Windsor, NFER Nelson.

Stupak, R.J. (2001) 'Perceptions Management: An Active Strategy For Marketing and Delivering Academic Excellence At Liberal Arts Colleges', *Public Administration Quarterly*, Vol. 25, No. 2, 229–46.

Telford, R. and Masson, R. (2005) 'The Congruence of Quality Values in Higher Education', *Quality Assurance in Education*, Vol. 13, No. 2, 107–19.

Thomas, A. and Dennison, W. (1991) 'Parental or Pupil Choice—Who Really Decides in Urban Schools?' *Education Management and Administration*, Vol. 19, No. 4, 243–51.

Voss, R., Gruber, T. and Szmigin, I. (2007) 'Service Quality in Higher Education: The Role of Student Expectations', *Journal of Business Research*, Vol. 60, 949–59.

West, A., David, M., Hailes, J. and Ribbens, J. (1995) 'Parents and the Process of Choosing Secondary Schools: Implications for Schools', *Education Management and Administration*, Vol. 23, No. 1, 28–38.

West, A. and Varlaam, A. (1991) 'Choosing a Secondary School: Parents of Junior School Children', *Educational Research*, Vol. 33, No. 1, 22–30.

12   Healthcare Marketing

OBJECTIVES

By the end of this chapter you should be able to:

1. understand and describe a number of different healthcare systems;
2. understand and describe the changing relationship between healthcare providers and their patients;
3. understand and describe sources of potential value for patients in the healthcare domain;
4. describe and apply the concept of the value chain;
5. identify sources of competitive advantage;
6. conduct a SPACE analysis;
7. conduct a needs/capacity assessment;
8. develop and implement a competitive strategy for a healthcare organization;
9. select an appropriate competitive posture and positioning strategy for a healthcare organization.

Introduction

The relevance of the marketing concept to the delivery of healthcare services has long been recognized, and it was as long ago as 1971 when the first journal article on the subject by Zaltman and Vertinsky appeared in the *Journal Of Marketing*. Since then, a variety of other writers have entered the fray and two key healthcare marketing textbooks by MacStravic (1975) and Kotler and Clarke (1987) were pivotal in gaining greater academic credibility for the subject. More recent contributions by authors such as Hillestad and Berkowitz (2004) and Berkowitz (2006) have moved the topic into the twenty-first century and dedicated journals such as *Health Marketing Quarterly* and *Marketing Health Services* (together with specialist conferences run by organizations such as the American Marketing Association) have heightened our understanding of almost every facet of the health marketing mix.

In a brief overview such as this it will be impossible to do justice to the plethora of material that currently exists. Rather, the approach adopted will be the same as in previous chapters, with a focus being developed on a number of the key marketing issues faced by healthcare marketing organizations. Notable here is the increasingly competitive environment faced by healthcare professionals and an increasing realization that to be successful, institutions must respond appropriately to the needs of their local community and within that the needs of their individual patients.

In this chapter we will therefore build on the coverage of marketing strategy introduced in Chapter 5 and consider the alternatives open to healthcare organizations. In the light of the changing environment, the focus will be on the development of competitive strategy and strategic 'posture' and positioning. While the examples given here will all be drawn from the domain of healthcare, all the models and frameworks that will be introduced are capable of being applied to a wide range of different categories of nonprofit. We will also consider critical issues such as patient satisfaction, the provision of healthcare information, and the key roles played by marketing in both primary healthcare and the marketing of hospital services. We begin however by examining the healthcare marketing context.

Healthcare Systems

It is important to begin this section of the text by defining exactly what we mean by the expression 'healthcare system'. The World Health Organization (WHO) defines health as 'a state of complete physical, mental and social well being and not merely the absence of disease or infirmity' (WHO 1986: 1). The system established by every member of the WHO should hence be capable of responding to a wide range of physical, chemical, infectious, psychological, and social problems. In short, the concept of healthcare is much wider than many people believe. Healthcare, as Edgren (1991) argues, should be viewed as much broader in scope than mere medical care. Healthcare systems thus need not only to give consideration to medical treatment but also to a range of social, cognitive, and emotional factors— societies must not only *be* clinically healthy, they should *feel* healthy too. Marketing thus has a key role to play in managing the expectations of customers and matching these as far as possible to the range of services provided. Marketing can also help in developing the quality of communications with various healthcare communities and in encouraging individuals to adopt healthier lifestyles, thus minimizing the use of resources.

There are a wide variety of different healthcare systems in operation around the world and these may be characterized by the percentage of their financing that is drawn from either public or private funds and whether healthcare delivery is controlled privately or by the government. This idea is illustrated in Figure 12.1.

The United Kingdom's healthcare system is a good example of socialized medicine (Rintala 2007). Medical treatment is largely free at the point of delivery. Since devolution a separate National Health Service (NHS) now operates in each of the countries that comprise the union. They now differ in many respects, but at the core they all provide free physician and hospital services to all permanent residents. The costs of any medication are typically born by the State, although in England a flat fee for each item prescribed is now payable unless the patient is exempt by virtue of factors such as having a low income or a permanent disability. The system is funded entirely from general taxation and the costs are substantial. The NHS is estimated to be the world's third largest employer and the cost of running it is estimated to be around £104 billion in 2007/8 (HM Treasury 2007).

The NHS has been the focus of much political attention in the past two decades with successive governments of both political persuasions attempting to raise the standards of service

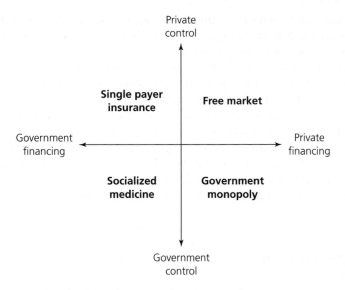

Figure 12.1 International healthcare systems

provided to patients while at the same time looking to cut cost. The key changes introduced are as follows:

• Money now 'follows the patient'. Essentially NHS funds are now allocated to reflect the size of the population local to particular healthcare providers. Adjustments are made to account for different demographic patterns and patterns of need. A facility also exists for family doctors (or in the language of the UK, general practitioners or GPs) to refer patients to a hospital of their choice, which may not necessarily be the local one. Under such circumstances funding will follow the patient to the hospital selected for treatment.

• Regulation of the healthcare market has been achieved through written contracts. Contracts are now drawn up between purchasers and providers which specify in detail the nature of the services to be provided, how many patients will benefit, and at what cost.

• Healthcare providers now have greater management autonomy. Providers are free to compete for service contracts and have the freedom to structure themselves in an appropriate manner in order to facilitate this process. Business units may, for example, be constructed around key competencies.

• Healthcare providers are now subject to medical and other audits to monitor the quality of healthcare provided and thus create greater accountability. The Audit Commission has also been given responsibility for conducting what might be termed 'value for money' audits as part of the new financial framework.

• Increasing use is being made of private healthcare providers to reduce excess demand for NHS treatment. At the time of writing the current target is for 15% of non-essential surgery to be provided by private hospitals (Hewitt 2005).

The changes in the UK have also served to switch the emphasis from cure to prevention, creating the need for the first time for GPs to actively encourage their patients to attend their practice for a range of preventative treatments and healthcare advice. Moreover, GPs are now obliged to see their patients on a regular basis irrespective of whether or not they are sick. This monitoring system has compelled GPs to play a greater role in enhancing the overall health of the nation and for the first time many have had to consider researching the ongoing needs of the individuals comprising their local community. Marketing skills are therefore beginning to be sought for the first time and a number of larger practices now have a dedicated individual responsible for fulfilling such a role. Typically this might involve researching demand, promoting a range of health/wellness clinics, the attraction of new patients, and the general facilitation of healthier lifestyles in the local community.

By contrast the United States has opted for a free market option, with the notable exception of the care provided to vulnerable groups. The very poorest members of American society are looked after by the State through the Medicaid and Medicare systems. The federal government presently pays over 60 per cent of the cost of Medicaid, with the balance being met from the finances of each individual US state. Tough decisions thus have to made at a local level both about the cut-off point at which Medicaid cover will be triggered and the range of services that will be provided. All too often there is a trade-off between the two (Ranade 1994).

The Medicare scheme makes provision for the care of the elderly and disabled, while Medicaid is available to help the poor. In addition the State Children's Health Insurance Program looks after the children of low-income groups and the Veterans Health Administration provides healthcare to military veterans. A separate system—TRICARE—exists to assist currently serving military personnel and their families. It is estimated that around 27% of the US population is covered by one or other of these programmes (DeNavas-Walt et al. 2007) with the balance being expected to make provision for their own care, typically through an insurance scheme offered by an employer. A further 60% of Americans are covered in this way and as the system is a fee-paying one, Americans have traditionally had a much greater choice of where they will receive their medical treatment. In addition, individual doctors are remunerated not by the State but by fees and so these tend to reflect the quality of their individual reputation. Marketing has therefore long played a role in communicating with the healthcare market and the promotion of all forms of medical care is quite commonplace. Of course the US system also has its disadvantages, notably that around 13% of Americans are uninsured and not covered by the programmes listed above. Although universal health care provision is certainly not the norm in the USA it is interesting to note that a small number of states (e.g. Massachusetts) have recently taken steps to provide healthcare coverage for a wider percentage of their population.

In Australia there is a flourishing private healthcare system and a system of Medicare for those who can't afford it. Australian Medicare is funded through a combination of a 1.5% levy on income tax and general government revenue. Interestingly, an additional charge of 1% is levied on higher income earners who choose not to participate in private health insurance. In France the social security system refunds patients for the costs of their care in both private and public facilities. The percentage of the reimbursement varies, but it is typically of the order of 70%. Many individuals choose to cover themselves for these additional costs by taking out supplemental insurance. Both public and private hospitals exist, but most doctors operate in private practice (Roemer 1991).

A plethora of different models therefore exist and the need for marketing, or more precisely, the nature of its application will vary substantially by context. Although the relevance of the marketing concept at a philosophical level is universal, since all societies have the right to expect that their healthcare systems will reflect the clinical needs and wants of their people, the need for its application at a functional level will differ from country to country. In the USA, for example, it is usual to encounter communication campaigns promoting practitioners in all branches of healthcare, whereas only the private institutions in the UK currently find it necessary to maintain such a heightened public profile. In the USA GPs also advertise openly to attract new patients, since they rely on fees to survive. In the UK, however, where historically levels of income have been guaranteed, advertising is all but nonexistent. That said, British GPs are now having to learn new marketing communications skills as individual practices begin to face up to the need to encourage patients to adopt healthier lifestyles and engage with a range of health and wellness initiatives.

The Healthcare Marketing Challenge

Healthcare marketing suffers from a number of complexities. To begin with, the healthcare product is probably the most intangible of all the services previously described. The consumer has no real way of being able to assess the competence of a surgeon, for example, either before or after an operation has been completed. They have simply to put their faith in the skills of the medical profession and take everything on trust. Of course, patients can and do form opinions about the quality of the healthcare product, based on a whole series of surrogates, including their physical surroundings and the bedside manner of their physician. Ironically it is thus possible for a patient to leave a hospital dissatisfied with the service they have received, even if their operation was performed to the very highest of technical standards. Unfortunately the reverse is probably also true and physicians who are among the least competent of their profession can still attain very high levels of customer satisfaction by paying careful attention to other aspects of the service encounter. Putting aside the ethics of the latter approach to healthcare, it seems clear that marketing has much to offer medical professionals in allowing them to manage their 'brand' by supporting excellence achieved in clinical care with good-quality customer service.

Intangibility is, however, only one of the particular difficulties that healthcare marketers need to overcome. France and Grover (1992) list a number of other factors which serve to complicate the marketing task.

Mismatch between Customer Expectations and Actual Delivery
While all service encounters offer a multitude of opportunities for the provider to fall short of the customer's expectations, this is perhaps a particular risk for healthcare providers. While a given individual may have set expectations about the outcome of a particular treatment, his physiology and psychology will in practice mitigate this substantially. No two individuals are alike and they will enter a programme of treatment suffering with various degrees of the ailment, have different demographic characteristics, and different levels of physical strength and recuperative power. All these individual characteristics are quite beyond the control of the physician and yet will still impact substantially on the outcome achieved. Equally, whatever the quality of the medical outcome, the psychology of the patient will determine how this is actually perceived. Moreover, psychology will also determine the emphasis that patients will place on the various components of the overall service. Thus some patients require a greater degree of hand-holding and/or information than others. Practitioners therefore have the difficult task of forming a judgement about the degree of support required and acting accordingly.

The Number of Service Providers

In a healthcare setting, the individual patient will encounter a variety of different categories of personnel. During the course of attending a hospital for a routine operation, for example, patients will have to deal with administrative staff, nurses, anaesthetists, catering staff, hospital porters, a variety of physicians, and their own surgeon. Thus a variety of opportunities exist for the encounter to go awry.

Unpredictable Demand

It is almost impossible to predict with any degree of accuracy the demand for a healthcare service. Newly emerged strains of virus, serious accidents, natural disasters, and even armed conflicts make planning complex. Provision clearly has to be set at a level that will meet all foreseeable demands, but perishability can then become a problem. Under-utilization of a service can cause serious financial problems during a 'lean' period. Marketing can hence have an important role to play in attempting to even out demand as far as is practical.

Derived Demand

One of the major difficulties for healthcare marketers is that it can be difficult to know when to market and to whom. The key decision maker will often not be the patient, but rather their GP, a specialist, or a member of their immediate family. This is an issue for healthcare providers in the USA where considerable choice in respect of an appropriate provider can be exercised.

Of all these difficulties, the inherent intangibility is perhaps the most difficult for healthcare marketers to come to terms with. The increasingly competitive environment is making it essential for those working in this area to clearly differentiate their provision, and intangibility complicates this process. The most obvious route to the achievement of this goal is to position an organization as providing excellence in clinical care but, since the patient has no way of directly evaluating this, the search for an appropriate competitive advantage is problematic. Moreover, many categories of healthcare provider (e.g. hospitals) provide such a wide range of clinical services that to position an institution as being 'a provider of excellent standards of clinical care' would be meaningless. Excellence in which field?

Mapping Consumer Value in Healthcare

Fundamentally, organizations are successful when they create genuine value for customers. Hospitals are no exception and they may generate value from making it easy for patients to access their services, from the range and quality of services available, from their admissions procedures, from the friendliness and trustworthiness of staff, from their billing procedures etc. (Gioia et al. 2000). Indeed, the value created in the healthcare product will be a complex amalgam of patient satisfaction with many different facets of their experience (Hart and Milstein 2003). The task for the healthcare marketer is to identify what these may be and to generate coherent competitive and positioning strategy for the organization, based on this added value.

Over the years there has been a good deal of interest on the part of researchers in where this value might lie. Ware et al. (1978), in a detailed review of the literature, identified four factors in the healthcare setting (i.e. physician interaction, availability of services, continuity/confidence, and efficiency/outcomes of care). In later work Brown and Swartz (1989)

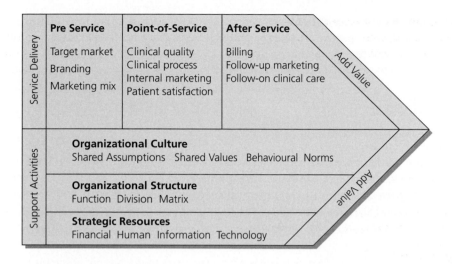

Figure 12.2 The value chain

Source: adapted from Porter, M.E. (1985) *Competitive Advantage: Creating and Sustaining Superior Performance,* New York, Free Press.

identified physician interaction as being the most important of these and concluded that a fifth dimension of convenience/access should be added.

Allied to the factor 'ease of access' is the concept of waiting time which may also warrant consideration, particularly by primary physicians. A number of studies have confirmed that the time spent waiting for a doctor is inversely related to patient satisfaction (see LuAnn and Andersen 1980). When one considers that Maister (1985) found that anxiety can increase the perception of waiting time, this additional factor's relevance to the healthcare setting is readily apparent.

More recently Sage (1991) identified five key factors namely: access, choice, information, redress, and representation. In the context of primary healthcare, Gabbott and Hogg (1994) also established that factors relating to the nature of the individual practice such as the range of services offered and the ease of access to them are important, as are the responsiveness and empathy of the physician. Their work has been confirmed in many more recent studies (e.g Sargeant and Kaehler 1998).

A more structured way of looking at value in this context is to adapt the value chain, a tool originally developed by the Harvard strategist Michael Porter (1980). It is depicted in Figure 12.2.

Pre-Service Value Creation

The top row of activities is likely to be the primary source of patient value and ranges from pre-service to point-of-service to after-service. In respect of the former, patients may derive value from the marketing activities undertaken by the organization. While these may well have attracted the patient in the first place they can also add value by reassuring them and helping to build trust and confidence in the institution. Riley Children's Hospital in Indianapolis, for example, offers a video tour of the hospital through its website so that children know exactly what to expect when they arrive (http://www.rileykids.org/hospital/videotour/01_rileyshospital.html).

The brand too can help add value for patients by conveying information about the quality of the treatment that may be expected and the style of its delivery. The Mayo Clinic provides a good example of this in practice.

■ CASE STUDY

MAYO CLINIC

The Mayo Clinic has arguably one of the strongest brands in medicine in the United States. It is the largest integrated nonprofit group practice anywhere in the world. More than 3300 physicians, scientists, and researchers and 46,000 allied health staff work at Mayo Clinic which has sites in Minnesota, Florida, and Arizona. Collectively, the three locations now treat more than half a million people each year. What unifies this vast organization is a common guiding philosophy that begins with the fundamental value that 'the needs of the patient come first'. Of course one might argue that all healthcare providers strive to do this, but at the Mayo the brand philosophy guides literally every facet of the organization's thinking and operations.

Elements of the Mayo model include:

1. A Team Approach

In the search for an accurate diagnosis and the best treatment options for each patient, Mayo physicians from multiple medical specialties work together in teams. This cooperative science is a hallmark of Mayo Clinic patient care and derives from the insight of the founders of the clinic that medicine is far too complex for any one person to have a comprehensive understanding of. As a collaborative team, medical specialists work together to diagnose each patient and recommend courses of treatment.

2. Physician-Directed Care

Each patient is assigned a personal physician who directs the patient to other medical specialists and discusses care with the patient when all evaluations are complete. Whenever possible, patients returning to Mayo Clinic are scheduled to see the same physician. The Mayo physician also communicates and coordinates with the patient's local, hometown physician.

3. Modern Systems

Mayo Clinic utilizes an electronic, up-to-date, integrated medical record designed so patient medical information, lab test results, and reports are all available when the physician and patient meet. This system, along with many others, and a set of well-defined processes, allows patients to have multiple medical evaluations and tests on the same day or be scheduled for next-day surgery or other procedures.

4. Respect and Compassion

Patients report that the most significant difference between Mayo Clinic and other healthcare centres is that at Mayo Clinic, everyone cares about them. In each step of the patient's care, the medical team listens to the concerns of the patient and family and responds with respect and compassion to best meet the needs of the patient. When the patient meets the physician, the examination is unhurried. Because physicians at Mayo receive a fixed salary, their pay is not based on quantity or number of patients seen. Rather, physicians spend the time they deem necessary to provide quality patient care. Mayo Clinic also respects the patient's time through a simultaneous, efficient evaluation process. In many cases, within a short period, patients can be examined by multiple medical specialists and complete testing and evaluation, followed by next-day surgery. This capability is appreciated by patients who may travel long distances to seek health care at Mayo Clinic.

Case compiled from resources at www.mayoclinic.com<http://www.mayoclinic.com>.

Sharma (2007) argues that 'branding is an experience. It is more than just providing the best-in-class technologies and treatments. Branding aims to convert each patient treated into a brand ambassador for the hospital. Brands are built around experiences, which linger in customers' minds.' The Mayo clinic has taken advantage of this by having past patients share their experiences of the organization with others online (See Figure 12.3). The stories are genuinely uplifting examples of what the clinic has been able to achieve and offer both insight and hope for incoming patients.

Point-of-Service Value Creation

Once admitted, the patient will derive value from other aspects of a hospital's value chain, notably the facilities the organization offers and of course the clinical expertise of the doctor or surgeon. The value added here is derived from the expectations in respect of outcomes

Figure 12.3 Patient stories at the Mayo Clinic

Source: © 2008 TheMayoClinic.com

set up through the organization's marketing (and of course clinical consultations) and the organization's eventual performance. Some hospitals are expanding the experiences they offer to patients by including features that would previously have been the domain of hotels, such as room service meals and comfortable terry bath robes. Others offer private rooms, guest rooms for family members, the elimination of formal visiting hours, and personalized websites where patients can store their personal health profile, risk assessments, and test results.

The SERVQUAL model discussed earlier in this text also has relevance here in guiding managerial thought and investment. Lytle and Mokwa (1992) helpfully adapt it to conceptualize the healthcare 'product'. Their perspective is depicted in Figure 12.4.

1. Core Benefit

The core benefit is the outcome that the patient is seeking from the treatment she receives. This expectation will be shaped by conversations with family or friends, literature that the patient might have read in connection with her illness, and the advice and opinions of her physicians. Patients will clearly evaluate their experience according to the extent to which

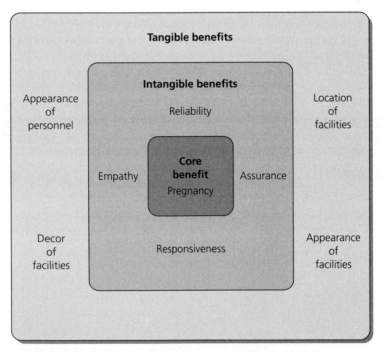

Core benefit	The nucleus of the product offering
Intangible benefits	Physician/patient/staff interactions
Tangible benefits	Physical environmental surroundings

Figure 12.4 Healthcare product bundle of benefits

Source: reprinted with permission from Lytle and Mokwa (1992) *Journal of Healthcare Marketing,* Vol. 12, No. 1.

their expectations of its outcome have been met. Obviously they cannot assess the clinical skills of their physician, but they can assess the difference in how they feel after the healthcare intervention has taken place.

2. Intangible Benefits

The intangible benefits are received from the quality of the interaction which takes place between the patient and the physician and their staff. The four SERVQUAL dimensions of reliability, empathy, assurance, and responsiveness are each key areas for the healthcare provider to address as it is relatively easy for the patient to form an opinion on these. In the case of comparatively minor interventions, where clinical benefits may be difficult to assess, these intangible elements will form the basis of the majority of the overall assessment of service quality.

3. Tangible Benefits

The competence of the medical personnel is difficult for a patient to assess. They have no way of being able to compare their surgeon's level of competence with that of another. They can, however, appraise the appearance of the facilities, the extent to which the latest technology appears to be being utilized, the comfort afforded by the physical surroundings, and the overall appearance of the personnel. These aspects, when combined, will allow the patient to form a perception of the overall competence of their healthcare provider.

After-Service Value Creation

In the final link of the value chain the focus shifts to after-service activities such as follow-up contacts with the patient, support in the local community, education and wellness programmes, and exposure to subsequent marketing that reassures the individual of the quality of their clinical experience. A number of hospital websites now include value-added information on managing long-terms conditions and assistance that may be available locally. Indeed, many hospitals now have rehabilitation care teams who work with patients to develop personalized discharge plans specifying the support that will be needed, where this support may be found, and who to turn to for advice. Some plans also offer guidance on what care will be like after discharge and perhaps templates and checklists that the patient can use to establish their own progress when they leave the institution. All these can clearly be a source of added value.

Support Activities

Underpinning the primary sources of patient value are three classes of support activity, namely the culture of the organization, its structure, and the strategic resources at its disposal.

The culture of the organization is particularly important because it is this that will drive the style of the healthcare delivery. It establishes the shared assumptions that the organization will work from (e.g the Mayo Clinic's perspective that the needs of the patient will always come first). It also establishes a sense of shared values and behavioural norms that will drive how staff will interact with patients. This 'way of doing things' therefore underpins service delivery and the selection of new services that are consistent with the culture of the organization. An example is provided on the next page.

■ **CASE STUDY**

YORK HOSPITAL

York Hospital has a culture which stresses the importance of providing personalized care to patients. Since 1995 this has shaped the delivery of a programme known as PATH (Patient Approach To Healthcare). It originally began with an emphasis on maternity patients but has now been expanded to include other patient groups. Nursing and social service staff are tasked with developing an understanding of the pattern of provision in one of four community categories in surrounding towns and villages. They therefore visit local physicians in these communities and meet with pregnant women in their doctor's offices. Later, when the women are admitted to the hospital they are offered a room in their selected 'community' and are cared for by the staff they met before admission.

If it is likely that their stay in hospital will provoke problems at home such as issues with childcare, PATH will arrange for help to be offered through local volunteers. On discharge patients without their own transport will have this provided and when they arrive home their ongoing care will be provided by the same staff that have cared for them throughout the process. Follow-up calls are also arranged on a regular basis so that individuals can raise any questions or concerns.

Importantly, PATH is not limited to hospital service alone. If it is determined that patients will need additional support in the local community, staff will arrange to make referrals to programmes that they have personal familiarity with. The programme has been highly popular with the hospital achieving 90% 'exceptional' ratings on its patient satisfaction surveys. Both physicians and staff see PATH as a way of organizing and delivering optimal value.

Case compiled from resources at www.yorkhospital.com<http://www.yorkhospital.com>.

Identifying Competitive Advantage

Conducting a value-chain analysis for a healthcare provider can provide valuable insight into the value added by the organization. It is thus the first step in identifying the competitive advantage an organization currently possesses or might possess. In seeking to map competitive advantage it is not enough to understand where the organization adds value; it is also necessary to have a sense of whether these sources of value are genuinely distinctive or shared with other providers in the marketplace. Thus while a hospital might see itself as distinctive because it offers access to cutting-edge treatments, if these are also being trialled by another hospital in the area they are *not* a source of competitive advantage (Crook et al. 2003). An understanding of competitive advantage is absolutely critical as it feeds into the design of positioning, branding, and of course competitive strategy.

An approach for identifying competitive advantages and disadvantages is provided in Figure 12.5. Each component of the value chain is evaluated to determine what strengths and weaknesses it offers the organization. While the value chain can be the primary input to this analysis it is important to recognize that there are other perspectives on competitive advantage that also offer utility. In the context of healthcare the work of Boulding and Christensen (2003) has particular resonance. They suggest that competitive advantage may be based on

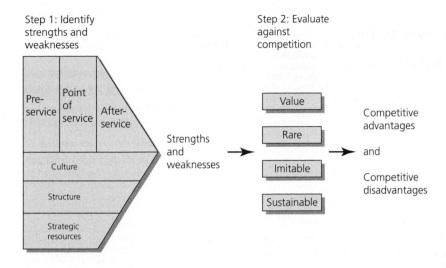

Step 1: Identify strengths and weaknesses

Step 2: Evaluate against competition

Pre-service | Point of service | After-service

Culture

Structure

Strategic resources

Strengths and weaknesses

Value

Rare

Imitable

Sustainable

Competitive advantages

and

Competitive disadvantages

Figure 12.5 Healthcare application of the value chain

possessing rare or abundant resources, special resources/skills, or management/logistical resources. Thus, while the value chain may be a good source of ideas, it will also be useful to complement this when appraising the strengths and weaknesses of an organization by focusing too on resources, competencies, and capabilities.

The resultant strengths are appraised to determine whether they offer value and, if so, to what degree. Some factors will offer a high degree of value to patients, while others will not. The possession of the latest scanner technology may be a highly significant source of value, while providing inpatients with access to wireless internet is less impactful. In this stage of the process the nature of the value is also critical. Is it rare or possessed by many organizations? If the latter it will probably not serve as a source of competitive advantage. Equally, is the source of value imitable? The provision of wireless internet access could be easily copied by competitors, but possessing the leading surgical technology would likely require a substantial capital investment and would therefore deter many competitors from emulating. Finally, the source should be sustainable. If the source is transitory it will not be worthwhile developing a competitive strategy on this basis since valuable resources will ultimately be wasted. As an example a hospital may regard a facility to diagnose and treat leukaemia in children as a major source of competitive advantage, but if this facility is based on one highly skilled medical practitioner and her knowledge alone, the competitive advantage may not be sustainable. She may well decide to take up employment elsewhere and if the hospital has staked a considerable part of its reputation on that provision, it will be severely weakened as a consequence. Guidance on how to interpret this analysis is provided in Figure 12.6.

The same approach should be adopted for weaknesses. An organization will probably have many of these and it will be important to prioritize those that could leave the organization vulnerable. Action can be taken to minimize or offset strategically significant weaknesses. The detail of how to interpet this analysis is provided in Figure 12.7.

The organization is now armed with information about both its competitive advantages and its competitive disadvantages and can proceed to develop its strategy accordingly (Hodgetts et al. 1999).

Is the value of the strength high or low? (High/Low)	Is the strength rare? (Yes/No)	Is the strength easy or difficult to imitate? (Easy/Difficult)	Can the strength be sustained? (Yes/No)	Implication
H	N	E	Y	No competitive advantage. Most competitors have the strength and those that do not can develop it easily. All can sustain it.
H	N	E	N	No competitive advantage. All competitors have the strength which is easy to develop. Strength is not sustainable so it represents only a short-term advantage.
H	N	D	Y	No competitive advantage. All competitors have the strength but it is difficult to develop so care should be taken to maintain this strength.
H	N	D	N	No competitive advantage. Many competitors possess the strength but it is difficult to develop and those who do possess it will not be able to sustain the strength. Only a short-term advantage.
H	Y	E	Y	Not a source of long-term competitive advantage. Because it is valuable and rare, competitors will do what is necessary to develop this easy-to-imitate strength. Short-term advantage. Should not base strategy on this type of strength but should obtain benefits of short-term advantage.
H	Y	E	N	Not source of competitive advantage. The strength is easy to imitate and cannot be sustained. Short-term advantage. Do not base strategy on this type of strength but obtain benefits of short-term advantage.
H	Y	D	Y	Source of long-term competitive advantage. If value is very high it may be worth 'betting the organization' on this strength.
H	Y	D	N	Possible source of short-term competitive advantage but not a strength that can be sustained over the long run.

Figure 12.6 Strategic thinking map of competitive advantages relative to strengths

Source: Swayne, L.E., Duncan, W.J. and Ginter, P.M. (2006) *Strategic Management of Health Care Organizations,* 5th edn, Malden MA, Blackwell Publishing, p173. Reproduced with kind permission.

Is this characteristic of high or low value? (High/Low)	Is this weakness common among competitors? (Yes/No)	Is it easy or difficult to correct this weakness? (Easy/Difficult)	Can competitors sustain their advantage? (Yes/No)	Implications
H	Y	E	Y	No competitive disadvantage in short run. Weakness of our organization but others are also weak. Weakness is easy to correct. If we fail to correct, competitors could achieve an advantage.
H	Y	E	N	No competitive disadvantage. Weakness of our organization but also a weakness of competitors. Easy to correct weakness and competitors are not able to sustain their advantage.
H	Y	D	Y	No short-term competitive disadvantage. Competitors also possess the weakness, but it is a dangerous situation that must be addressed to ensure competitors do not overcome this difficulty and correct it first. Competitors' ability to sustain advantage could become long-term competitive disadvantage.
H	Y	D	N	No competitive disadvantage. Weakness is common and is difficult to correct. Competitors cannot sustain any advantage represented by this weakness.
H	N	E	Y	Short-term competitive disadvantage. Competitors are not weak in this area but the weakness is easy to correct. The organization should move quickly to correct this type of weakness.
H	N	E	N	Not a competitive disadvantage. Competitors are not weak in this area but the weakness is easy to correct. Competitors cannot sustain any advantage provided by our weakness. Should correct even though any advantage will be short term.
H	N	D	Y	Weakness represents a serious competitive disadvantage. The weakness is valuable, most competitors do not have it, it is difficult for us to correct, and competitors can sustain their advantage. Attention is demanded.
H	N	D	N	A serious competitive disadvantage in the short term. Attention directed toward difficulty of overcoming weakness relative to the ability of competitors to retain the advantage.

Figure 12.7 Strategic thinking map of competitive disadvantages relative to weaknesses

Source: Swayne, L.E., Duncan, W.J. and Ginter, P.M. (2006) *Strategic Management of Health Care Organizations,* 5th edn, Malden MA, p173. Reproduced with kind permission.

Strategic Position and Action Evaluation

Combining information about competitive advantage with other critical strategic issues can provide an organization with a strong sense of its market position and the strategy that might naturally flow from this. Strategic Position and Action Evaluation or SPACE is a helpful starting point here since it suggests how appropriate various strategies might be based on four dimensions: service category strength; environmental stability; relative competitive advantage; and the organization's own financial strength.

An example of a SPACE chart is illustrated in Figure 12.8. Listed under each of the four dimensions are factors to which individual numerical values ranging from 0 to 6 can be assigned. The numbers are then added together and divided by the number of factors to give an average. The averages for environmental stability and competitive advantage each have the number 6 subtracted from them to produce a negative number. The average for each dimension is then plotted on the appropriate axis of the SPACE chart and connected to create a four-sided polygon. Figure 12.9 illustrates the factors determining each dimension, although it should be remembered that these need not be carved in stone. Readers are advised to tailor these where necessary to suit their own context. Figure 12.10 summarizes the different SPACE profiles that can result from the analysis.

The value of the SPACE analysis is that it suggests the strategy that might be most appropriate for each profile that might result. This is illustrated in Figure 12.11. Although many of these alternatives will be familiar from Chapter 5 a number are new and are defined on page 394.

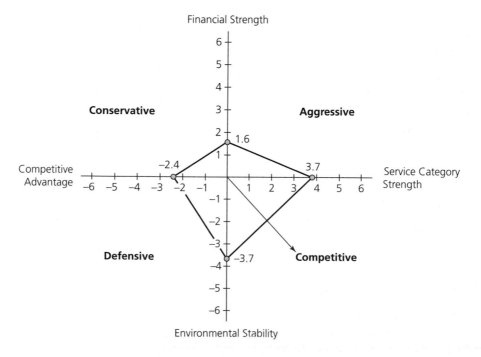

Figure 12.8 Sample SPACE chart

Factors Determining Environmental Stability										
Technological changes	Many	0	1	2	3	4	5	6	Few
Rate of inflation	High	0	1	2	3	4	5	6	Low
Demand variability	Large	0	1	2	3	4	5	6	Small
Price range of competing services	Wide	0	1	2	3	4	5	6	Narrow
Barriers to entry into market	Few	0	1	2	3	4	5	6	Many
Competitive pressure	High	0	1	2	3	4	5	6	Low
Price elasticity of demand	Elastic	0	1	2	3	4	5	6	Inelastic
Pressure from substitute products	High	0	1	2	3	4	5	6	Low
Factors Determining Service Category Strength									
Growth potential	Low	0	1	2	3	4	5	6	High
Profit potential	Low	0	1	2	3	4	5	6	High
Financial stability	Low	0	1	2	3	4	5	6	High
Technological know-how	Simple	0	1	2	3	4	5	6	Complex
Resource utilization	Inefficient	0	1	2	3	4	5	6	Efficient
Capital intensity	Low	0	1	2	3	4	5	6	High
Ease of entry into market	Easy	0	1	2	3	4	5	6	Difficult
Productivity, capacity utilization	Low	0	1	2	3	4	5	6	High
Factors Determining Competitive Advantage									
Market share	Small	0	1	2	3	4	5	6	Large
Product quality	Inferior	0	1	2	3	4	5	6	Superior
Product life cycle	Late	0	1	2	3	4	5	6	Early
Product replacement cycle	Variable	0	1	2	3	4	5	6	Fixed
Customer/patient loyalty	Low	0	1	2	3	4	5	6	High
Competition's capacity utilization	Low	0	1	2	3	4	5	6	High
Technological know-how	Low	0	1	2	3	4	5	6	High
Vertical integration	Low	0	1	2	3	4	5	6	High
Speed of new service introductions	Slow	0	1	2	3	4	5	6	Fast
Factors Determining Financial Strength									
Return on investment	Low	0	1	2	3	4	5	6	High
Leverage	Imbalanced	0	1	2	3	4	5	6	Balanced
Liquidity	Imbalanced	0	1	2	3	4	5	6	Balanced
Capital required/available	High	0	1	2	3	4	5	6	Low
Cash flow	Low	0	1	2	3	4	5	6	High
Ease of exit from market	Difficult	0	1	2	3	4	5	6	Easy
Risk involved in business	Much	0	1	2	3	4	5	6	Little
Inventory turnover	Slow	0	1	2	3	4	5	6	Fast
Economies of scale and experience	Low	0	1	2	3	4	5	6	High

Figure 12.9 SPACE factors

Source: Rowe, A.J., Mason, R.O., Dickel, K.E. and Snyder, N.H. (1994) *Strategic Management: A Methodological Approach,* 4th edn, Reading MA, Addison-Wesley Publishing. Reproduced with kind permission of Dr Alan J. Rowe.

Expansion of Scope Strategies

Related Diversification

This involves entering a market similar to those that the organization is presently involved with. A hospital might therefore decide to provide additional services for the local community it serves.

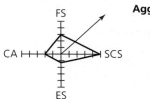

Aggressive Profiles

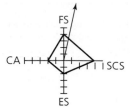

A financially strong organization that has achieved major competitive advantages in a growing and stable service category

An organization whose financial strength is a dominating factor in the service category

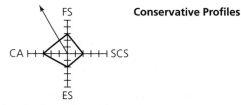

Conservative Profiles

An organization that has achieved financial strength in a stable service category that is not growing; the organization has no major competitive advantages

An organization that suffers from major competitive disadvantages in a service category that is technologically stable but declining in revenue

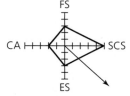

Competitive Profiles

An organization with major competitive advantages but limited financial strength in a high-growth service category

An organization that is competing fairly well in a service category where there is substantial environmental uncertainty

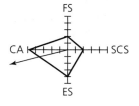

Defensive Profiles

An organization that has a very weak competitive position in a negative-growth, stable but weak service category

A financially troubled organization in a very unstable and weak service category

Figure 12.10 SPACE strategy profiles

Source: Rowe, A.J., Mason, R.O., Dickel, K.E. and Snyder, N.H. (1994) *Strategic Management: A Methodological Approach,* 4th edn, Reading MA, Addison-Wesley Publishing. Reproduced with kind permission of Dr Alan J. Rowe.

Unrelated Diversification

This involves entering new markets that are unrelated to its present operations. A hospital might therefore consider developing a range of medical supplies or its own medical school. Palich et al. (2000) conclude that financial performance tends to increase as organizations

Conservative	Aggressive
• Status quo • Unrelated diversification • Harvesting	• Related diversification • Market development • Product development • Vertical integration
Defensive	Competitive
• Divestiture • Liquidation • Retrenchment	• Penetration • Enhancement • Product development • Market development • Status quo

Figure 12.11 Strategic alternatives for SPACE quadrants

Source: Swayne, L.E., Duncan, W.J. and Ginter, P.M. (2006) *Strategic Management of Health Care Organizations,* 5th edn, Malden MA, p305. Reproduced with kind permission.

move from a single business focus to related diversification, but that it falls when organizations engage in unrelated diversification.

Vertical Integration

This occurs when an organization expands along the channel of distribution. It can be either backward vertical integration (towards suppliers) or forward vertical integration (towards patients). Vertical integration is generally undertaken to reduce costs because it can cut out the 'middlemen' in the production of healthcare. It also gives organizations greater control, particularly in the case of backward integration since they can ensure that appropriate supplies of an appropriate quality are delivered at the appropriate time.

Contraction of Scope Strategies

Divestiture

This involves a decision to sell off a service unit because of a desire to withdraw from a market despite its current viability. In both the UK and the US many institutions have withdrawn from the provision of laundry, catering, and even pharmacy provision, preferring instead to put these services out to tender and enable more of a focus to be developed on clinical care (Jonas et al. 2007).

Liquidation

This also involves a decision to withdraw a programme or service, but in this case the assumption is that the unit is no longer viable and therefore cannot be sold off as a going concern. The assets associated with the service are therefore disposed of instead. In the UK a number of hospitals built in Victorian times are now coming to the end of their useful lives and are being closed down and ultimately replaced by facilities and services more suited to the modern era.

Harvesting

This is an appropriate strategy when a market has entered long-term decline. It involves the organization managing the decline by trying to generate as much surplus cash as possible. It will require planning an orderly exit, probably through a strategy of progressive downsizing.

Retrenchment

This strategy is a response to the declining profitability or surplus generated by a service. Typically this occurs because of an increase in costs, although the market itself would still be regarded as viable. It involves redefining the target market and selectively eliminating costs or assets that are expensive to maintain. In the context of healthcare examples may include a decision to focus more selectively on certain groups of patients, or a specific geographical catchment area. It might also involve a reduction in the range of services provided. It is not uncommon for healthcare providers to initially want to 'round out' a service line, adding procedures for which demand may not be as great and appointing staff to offer them. This adds in significant additional cost that may not be justified if demand begins to fall. Retrenchment by developing a more narrow focus may then be necessary.

Maintenance of Scope Strategy

Enhancement

This occurs where a management team feels that although an organization is moving towards its goals, there remains a need to do certain things better. This normally involves neither expansion nor contraction of scope, but instead requires an improvement in the operations of the nonprofit. Examples may include the introduction of a TQM (total quality management) system to improve the quality of the patient experience, or it may involve the imposition of targets (as in the UK in the early 2000s) to reduce the time patients might have to wait to see a specialist or obtain their treatment.

Status Quo

This is distinct from a strategy of 'do-nothing' which implies inaction. If the strategy is to pursue the status quo, management has taken a conscious decision to maintain the current market share and thus keep the service operating at current levels. The strategy pursued essentially allows the nonprofit to sustain the service into the foreseeable future. A hospital might thus monitor the marketing of competitors and where necessary seek to counter their activity with marketing of its own. Pursuing the status quo with one service area is often the selected option where management attention is focused on the needs of other markets and/or services where the potential for more rapid growth is perceived.

Figure 12.12 provides an example of a SPACE profile and depicts an organization that has a 'conservative' profile, which suggests a number of strategic alternatives the organization might pursue in the future. The analysis indicates that the nonprofit suffers from a major competitive disadvantage in a service category that is technologically stable but declining in revenue. It may therefore pursue a strategy of maintaining the status quo or more likely decide to harvest the service concerned. If it is a service that is difficult to withdraw from, perhaps because it is the only provider in a geographical region, then a strategy of diversification may be more appropriate to develop additional sources of revenue that can ultimately be used to 'prop up' the ailing service.

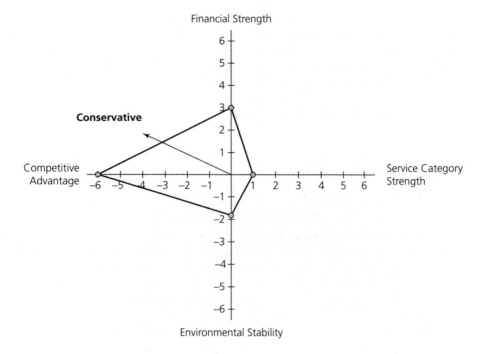

Figure 12.12 Conservative SPACE profile

Programme Evaluation

Of course the utility of the SPACE analysis is based on an assumption that the factors on each of the axes are the factors that are most important for an organization to consider in taking strategic decisions about the services that will be provided. In a free market, market share, service category strength, and competitive advantage are all critical factors. In socialized medicine, it is unlikely that this will be the case, although the recent changes in the UK's National Health Service have explicitly encouraged competition and hence made a SPACE analysis relevant to many UK contexts.

That said, this is a textbook on nonprofit marketing and much nonprofit provision is about providing services where the mechanism of the market fails to adequately meet the needs of society. That need may be niche, in the sense that only a small number of people are affected and it is therefore less attractive for providers to address it; or it may involve aiding vulnerable groups who lack the resources to pay for their own care. There are many such healthcare gaps in the United States where, as we established earlier, a large proportion of the population lacks even basic medical insurance. Under a regime of socialized medicine, the focus is less on the mechanisms of the market, but rather on ensuring that the majority of need can be met locally (for the convenience of patients) and that the pattern of delivery is adequately matched to this need and/or the relevant public policy priorities.

In both these scenarios the basis for the selection of strategy will be different and a needs/capacity assessment may be more appropriate. The idea is illustrated in Figure 12.13. Community need will be a function of the needs of patients or the public in that community, the degree to which other providers have the requisite skills and resources to *better* meet that

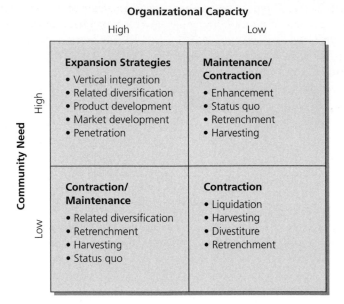

Figure 12.13 Public health and not-for-profit adaptive decisions

Source: Swayne, L.E., Duncan, W.J. and Ginter, P.M. (2006) *Strategic Management of Health Care Organizations,* 5th edn, Malden MA, p309. Reproduced with kind permission.

need, and public/community health objectives. Organizational capacity will be a function of the extent to which the nonprofit has the requisite skills and resources to deliver the service, the fit with its mission and values, and, of course, the extent to which funding may be available to make the service a reality. The appropriateness of various strategies to each mix of factors is also depicted in Figure 12.13.

Strategic Posture

The nature of the strategy an organization may select will also be driven in part by its strategic posture, or the manner in which it typically responds to changes in the market or wider environment. Miles et al. (2003) offer a helpful characterization of commonly adopted strategic postures. These include:

- *Defenders:* Organizations that are highly focused on one (usually stable) market. They focus on a narrow range of products or services and defend these aggressively against the competition. They achieve this either by being lowest cost or by differentiating their offering from that of the competition. They make little effort to seek other market opportunities and react aggressively to counter the marketing activity of competitors seeking to enter the market or expand their market share.

- *Prospectors:* By contrast these are organizations who are always ready to take advantage of new market opportunities. They seek to find ways to exploit new potential and to expand the scope of the organization. They will be among the first to react to changes in health policy and at the vanguard of innovation in employing the latest technologies and approaches.

- *Analysers:* Miles et al. argue that this posture is an amalgam of the defender and prospector approach. Analysers think carefully about how they will balance the need for stability and change within the organization. They are strategically more cautious than prospectors and will typically follow others into a market when they have had the opportunity to learn from their mistakes and discern the optimal approach.

- *Reactors:* The other three postures are proactive in the sense that the organizations play an active role in responding to the challenges in the environment and capitalizing on any opportunities that they discern. Reactors, as the name suggests, tend only to change strategy when forced to do so by environmental pressures. Their approach tends to be piecemeal and lacks a firm overriding vision or strategy to move the organization forward. This may arise because of a failure on the part of management to articulate a clear strategy, or it may occur because of the fundamental inappropriateness of the organization's structure, systems, or procedures. These can all serve to hamper an appropriate response to changing conditions.

The concept of posture is important because it will impact on the selection of appropriate strategy and limit or shape an organization's ability to develop a competitive advantage.

Strategic Positioning

The series of analyses presented in the previous sections should allow an organization to determine where its competitive advantage might lie and a number of strategies that it can adopt as a consequence. In this final section on strategy we examine the critical issue of strategic positioning, defining how the organization will be perceived in relation to its key competitors. Clearly, this will depend to no small degree on the sources of sustainable competitive advantage that can be exploited and projected to the market.

As we established in Chapter 5, Porter (1980) argues that there are two broad approaches to positioning, being either low cost or differentiating the nature of the service provision in some way. Cost leadership requires the aggressive construction of efficient scale facilities, the vigorous pursuit of cost reduction, tight cost and overhead control, and cost minimization in key areas such as R&D, service, sales force, advertising and so on. Much nonprofit healthcare in the United States is positioned on this basis, but in many countries the provision of care for the elderly (where long-term costs can be a highly significant issue) is a market where positioning on the basis of cost can commonly be encountered. It must be remembered that low cost does not equate to poor quality. Organizations positioned on this basis are frequently as concerned about quality as those that seek differentiation. Indeed, a low-cost strategy will only succeed where a good base level of quality is maintained. The value for money provided for customers remains a highly significant issue.

In respect of differentiation providers could aim to position themselves as 'the best in the world at . . .' (Quinn 1992). Hence the key clinical benefit of sending a patient to a particular institution would be clear to all healthcare purchasers. Indeed the portfolio of services could support the identified area of expertise, providing clinical service in related areas and building up appropriate resources accordingly. Where a wide portfolio of existing provision is already in evidence, however, the healthcare marketer may be better advised to seek elements of positioning which can have a direct benefit for the attraction of patients to every clinical service the organization can offer. There are comparatively few ways in which such a 'global' positioning might be accomplished, and a reliance on some aspect of the overall service quality provided has hence become commonplace. If a particular organization can build a reputation in the marketplace for being a provider of a high-quality service, greater numbers of customers will be attracted. From the perspective of the provider, this means a concentration not only on clinical care, but also on the wider range of surrogates discussed earlier which patients use to build up their own perceptions of the quality of their experience (Thomas 2007).

Tactical Healthcare Marketing

The previous sections have focused very deliberately on some of the key strategic issues that healthcare marketers might face. In this concluding section we move on to consider the tactical role marketing might play and examine some of the critical issues in the marketing of both primary healthcare and the marketing of hospital services.

Marketing Primary Healthcare

There are a range of marketing issues that primary healthcare practitioners (such as GPs) now need to address, including those listed below.

Identification of Market Needs

A careful identification of needs within their geographical catchment area is essential for every GP practice. An analysis of current and future healthcare needs will allow a practice to plan its portfolio of services. GP practices, for example in an area with an increasingly elderly population, may need to plan for the inclusion of chiropody or physiotherapy services at some stage in the future. If demand is likely to be high, it may be more cost-effective for these to be provided within the confines of the practice rather than contracting other institutions to provide it. An analysis of need may also yield valuable information in respect of the range of preventative clinics that would best serve the community. Practice nursing staff may run a range of highly specialized clinics dealing with issues such as drug abuse, smoking, alcoholism, obesity, arthritis, asthma, and, perhaps more commonly, motherhood.

Promotion of Healthcare Clinics

Once a decision has been taken about the appropriateness of running a particular clinic, its existence will need to be carefully promoted among the patients of the surgery most likely to benefit. At a superficial level, this might require the staff to produce posters which could be displayed in the waiting room, local libraries, and community centres. More imaginative practices will use database records to promote the clinic specifically to those individuals they perceive would derive the greatest benefit (Walshe and Smith 2006).

Enhancement of Customer Satisfaction

Perhaps the greatest contribution that marketing can make to healthcare lies in its ability to direct resources to those areas most likely to increase overall customer satisfaction. The preceding discussion has already highlighted the dimensions of the service encounter that could offer the greatest utility in this regard and it is a matter for individual practices to determine the factors of most relevance to their own circumstances. An understanding of how patients evaluate the quality of the healthcare they receive can allow those responsible for managing a GP practice to 'value engineer' the service they provide, concentrating resources in those areas most likely to enhance the overall experience of their clients. Similarly, cost savings could be made in those areas where little or no value is currently being perceived (Kelly 2006).

Information/Education

While space here does not permit a detailed analysis of all the factors capable of influencing patient satisfaction, it is worth enlarging for a moment on the provision of healthcare information. Healthcare information has the capacity to influence satisfaction both directly and indirectly, and in an age when consumers are increasingly expected to make their own decisions in respect of treatments and providers, the role of marketing in communicating effectively with customers will become increasingly crucial.

Indeed, the increased availability of good-quality healthcare information has led to many individuals becoming what Berkowitz and Flexner (1980) refer to as 'activist health care consumers', a lifestyle category evidenced by rapidly increasing sales of home diagnostic equipment, greater involvement in decisions, and a general move (at least in the USA) towards increased 'doctor shopping'. This is a relatively new phenomenon since medical information, only a few years ago, used to be the preserve of the medical profession and be disseminated solely through scholarly journals and specialized conferences (Bunn 1993). Patients were ill-informed and could hence exercise little judgement over the suitability of the treatment their physician was recommending. Today, the doctor is no longer even the primary source of medical information (Jenson 1987), with a wide range of communication channels now available for 'consultation', including:

- health magazines;
- medical textbooks;
- libraries;
- the Internet and in particular information sites such as webMD;
- pre-recorded health messages—such as those supplied by a number of food manufacturers;
- television/radio/general interest magazines;
- trusts/foundations—specializing in a particular medical complaint;
- other medical professionals.

One result of this explosion in healthcare information has been a move towards medical terminology finding its way into everyday language (Johnsson 1990) and the facilitation of a healthcare system in which consumers are encouraged to take a greater responsibility for their own health by adopting healthier lifestyles.

Healthcare information can also be viewed as flowing internally between the provider and the patient while they are under the care of that institution. Recent meningitis scares and the emergence of a number of vicious strains of flu virus have placed the onus on GPs to supply up-to-date and timely information to those most at risk. It is no longer sufficient for practice staff to 'fire-fight' problems as they arise. A marketing perspective can help plan communications mechanisms that can easily be activated should the unthinkable occur. Moreover, as the society in which we live continues to age, it is likely that ever greater demands will be placed on the healthcare service. It will therefore be increasingly in GPs' interest to educate patients in the self-diagnosis of a range of minor ailments so that they can select their own treatments and avoid unnecessary consultations.

Motivation of Practice Staff

If the marketing concept is adopted at a philosophical as well as a functional level, GPs will be encouraged to view their own practice staff as customers and treat them accordingly. There have been a number of instances reported of late where GPs have instructed their practice nurses to run a particular category of clinic and then failed to offer any additional support that might prove necessary. Internal marketing could hence have much to offer GPs to help them to consider the requirements of their staff for adequate training and support.

Attraction of Patients

The new healthcare framework rewards GPs, among other things, for the number of patients they are able to attract. While in most regions of the country a general shortage of doctors means there is no shortage of demand, those practices that do face direct competition will need to carefully assess its impact and plan their marketing strategy accordingly. Marketing skills can also be immensely valuable for new practices which are only just beginning to attract patients for the first time. In such cases, patients need to be given sufficient reason to switch from their existing practice and to register with a new GP. Marketing's role in such circumstances is to assist practice managers in overcoming consumer apathy and giving patients enough encouragement to ensure that sufficient numbers make the transition.

Marketing Hospital Services

The quality of hospital marketing varies considerably from country to country. In the USA it has long been recognized that marketing has a significant role to play in the attraction of patients, although there still remain some small pockets of resistance among hospital administrators (McDevitt and Shields 1985). Given that Wrenn (1994) determined that as little as a 10 per cent improvement in a hospital's marketing orientation could be associated with a $25 million increase in total net patient revenues and an 8 per cent increase in occupancy rates, it is no surprise that a change in perception is presently ongoing.

In the USA, over 79 per cent of individuals have a preferred hospital, although the strength of this bond does not appear to be particularly strong. Inguanzo and Harju (1985) found that fewer than 50 per cent of these individuals would characterize their preference as 'strong'. The strongest degrees of loyalty would appear to be exhibited by people living in the east of the country, in cities housing between 50,000 and 5,000,000 people, aged 55 or older, and with household incomes of under $15,000. We may thus conclude that most segments of US society would be willing to change healthcare provider if given a sufficient reason to do so. Factors such as the level of new technology employed, the courtesy of staff, cost, and the recommendation of a primary physician have all been shown to influence switching behaviour. Healthcare marketers within a hospital thus have a key role to play in the development of future hospital business (Thomas and Calhoun 2007).

In the UK, however, the framework within which most hospitals work is rather different. Until recently, hospital income was guaranteed and as a consequence there was no requirement to view healthcare purchasers as customers. As hospitals now face competitive pressures many are starting to recognize the need to market their services and to employ full-time marketers to assist them in this task. In particular, NHS hospital trusts require marketing skills to do the following.

- *Redefine their catchment areas.* Since hospitals are no longer restricted to treating patients within their immediate geographical area, there is a need to redefine the target market, concentrating on those areas which have the densest populations and hence the greatest demand for healthcare resources.

- *Define the competition.* In many regions of the country it may be possible to avoid damaging direct competition with neighbouring hospitals by emphasizing those aspects of the service that complement the other provision available locally. Even in cases where this proves not to be possible it will be necessary to monitor competitor activity and to benchmark hospital performance accordingly.

- *Network.* Despite the prevailing aura of competition it may well be in the interests of some hospitals to cooperate. Where service gaps exist, collaborative agreements could be developed to ensure that adequate coverage of all medical specialisms is provided within one geographical region.

- *Get close to customers.* Given that GPs now have the power to purchase hospital services from wherever they choose, it may be appropriate for a hospital to consider appointing a GP practice coordinator who will tour the local practices explaining the range of services available and the unique advantages of sending patients to their particular institution. Indeed since many NHS Trusts now have such an appointment, a hospital which fails to get close to its customers in this way may find itself at a significant disadvantage.

- *Identify the customers.* Hospitals need to identify those individuals who have the greatest capacity to influence the healthcare decision. In the USA, where patients arguably have greater choice, this is a key issue as the decision-making unit can often be complex. Moreover, the cultivation of customer loyalty becomes extremely important in retaining family business. Phillips (1980) found that the key to sustaining loyalty lies in the careful targeting of female patients. Women account for 70 per cent of all hospital admissions and have been shown to be responsible for over 70 per cent of their family's healthcare decisions—they therefore represent an important target market.

- *Involve customers in new service developments.* While it may be difficult to involve the end users of healthcare services in this way, there is no reason why intermediaries such as GPs should not be actively involved in the design of new hospital services. Having contributed actively to the birth of a new service, GPs are thereafter more likely to use it for the benefit of their patients. The process of service development is also likely to strengthen relationships between GPs and key management/clinical staff within the hospital.

- *Develop employees.* Given the key role of all hospital staff in delivering an appropriate level of service quality, hospital staff should be treated as internal customers of the organization and treated as the administration would have them treat external customers. Good internal communications and customer care training programmes should be initiated and the results monitored to ensure the achievement of the desired outcomes.

- *Conduct internal promotion.* There is still much resistance to marketing, particularly in UK hospitals. In order to win the hearts and minds of clinical staff, marketing staff need to promote their successes. Only when clinical staff understand the benefits that accrue to the hospital in increased patient throughput, job security, and enhancements to service quality, will marketing build a better reputation for itself. Marketing successes should hence be unashamedly promoted throughout the whole organization.

- *Incorporate three areas into institutional development: cost, quality, customer satisfaction.* Careful costing of all activities, together with a detailed analysis of service quality, should allow hospital marketers to engineer the value they deliver to their customers. This in turn should greatly enhance levels of customer satisfaction.

• *Not underestimate the impact of change*. The health services of most developed countries are currently in a state of flux. Ageing populations and a time of economic constraint are forcing governments to take a long hard look at the way in which healthcare is managed and delivered. Healthcare marketers therefore need to monitor their external environment particularly closely to ensure that they stay in touch with both proposed and actual change. Only by responding to environmental challenges ahead of the competition will the long-term stability of any healthcare organization be truly assured. (Source: adapted from Crowther 1995 and Petrochuk and Javalgi 1996.)

■ SUMMARY

In this chapter we have reviewed the healthcare frameworks of both the USA and the UK. In the UK, substantial changes have recently been introduced in the manner in which the NHS is managed, through the creation of quasi-markets in which healthcare purchasers now have a greater right to choose their provider. This structural change has created a need for marketing skills within the sector as institutions begin to respond for the first time to the threat of competition.

Given the rise in this competition, this chapter has deliberately focused on the development of competitive strategy and within that mapped out a process by which institutions can identify appropriate sources of sustainable competitive advantage. The value chain was introduced as a key planning tool and SPACE analysis employed this insight to assist organizations to think through the organizational strategy that might be most appropriate as a consequence. The chapter also examined the concept of strategic positioning and the relationship between this and the sources of value identified earlier. In the current environment, positioning is likely to become *the* key marketing issue for healthcare marketers to address. Indeed this drive towards the attainment of some unique position in the market will undoubtedly compel healthcare institutions to give greater consideration to the needs of their patients and the value for money they are able to offer.

■ DISCUSSION QUESTIONS

1. In your role as the marketing director of a NHS Trust, prepare a briefing document for a newly recruited marketing colleague, explaining the changes that have recently taken place in the healthcare environment and the additional need for marketing that this has created.

2. In what ways might the marketing of a healthcare service differ from the marketing of other nonprofit services described in this text? Why should this be so?

3. What are the key service quality dimensions that should be addressed by hospital marketers in a bid to enhance overall customer satisfaction?

4. As the newly appointed marketing manager of a GP practice, what steps would you take to enhance patient satisfaction with the service provided?

5. Why is the provision of good-quality information becoming an increasingly important issue for healthcare marketers to address?

6. With reference to your own healthcare organization, or one with which you are familiar, describe the issues that would need to be addressed under each of the headings of the 'typical' marketing plan introduced in Chapter 3.

7. For your own organization, or one with which you are familiar, conduct a value chain analysis. What does this tell you about the potential competitive advantage the organization might possess? What additional analysis would you need to conduct to verify that this was the case?

8. Visit the websites of two local primary care physicians (GPs). Compare and contrast the approach taken to the provision of healthcare information online. How might this be improved?

■ REFERENCES

Berkowitz, E.N. (2006) *Essentials of Health Care Marketing*, 2nd edn, Sudbury MA., Jones and Bartlett.

Berkowitz, E.N. and Flexner, W. (1980) 'The Market for Health Services, Is there a Non-Traditional Consumer?' *Journal of Healthcare Marketing*, Vol. 1, No. 1, 25–34.

Boulding, W. and Christensen, M. (2003) 'Sustainable Pioneering Advantage? Profit Implications of Market Entry Order', *Marketing Science*, Vol. 22, No. 3, 371–83.

Brown, S.W. and Swartz, T.A. (1989) 'A Gap Analysis of Professional Service Quality', *Journal of Marketing*, Vol. 53 (April), 92–8.

Bunn, M.D. (1993) 'Consumer Perceptions of Medical Information Sources: An Application of Multidimensional Scaling', *Health Marketing Quarterly*, Vol. 10, No. 3, 83–104.

Crook, T.R., Ketchen D.J. and Snow, C.C. (2003) 'Competitive Edge: A Strategic Management Model', *Cornell Hotel and Restaurant Administration Quarterly*, Vol. 44, No. 3, 44–56.

Crowther, C. (1995) 'NHS Trust Marketing: A Survival Guide', *Journal of Marketing Practice: Applied Marketing Science*, Vol. 1, No. 2, 57–68.

David, F. (1989) *Strategic Management*, 2nd edn, Columbus, OH., Merrill Publishing Company.

De-Navas Walt, C., Proctor, B.D. and Smith, J. (2007) *Income, Poverty, and Health Insurance Coverage in the United States: 2006*. Washington, D.C., US Census Bureau.

Edgren, L. (1991) *Service Management Inm Svensk Halso-Och Sjukvard*, Lund, Sweden, Lund University Press.

France, K.R. and Grover, R. (1992) 'What is the Health Care Product?' *Journal of Health Care Marketing*, Vol. 12, No. 2, 31–8.

Gabbott, M. and Hogg, G. (1994) 'Care or Cure: Making Choices in Healthcare', *Unity in Diversity*, Proceedings of the MEG Conference, University of Ulster.

Gioia, D.M., Schultz, M. and Corley, K.C. (2000) 'Organizational Identity, Image and Adaptive Strategy', *Academy of Management Review*, Vol. 25, No. 1, 63–81.

Hart, S.L. and Milstein, M.B. (2003) 'Creating Sustainable Value', *Academy of Management Executive*, Vol. 17, No. 2, 56–67.

Hewitt, P. (2005) Speech on 13 May. Accessed online on 30 May 2007 at http://news.bbc.co.uk/1/hi/health/4542009.stm.

H.M. Treasury (2007) *Building Britain's Long Term Future: Prosperity and Fairness for Families: Economic and Fiscal Strategy Report and Financial Statement and Budget Report*, London, The Stationery Office.

Hillestad, S.G. and Berkowitz, E.N. (2004) *Health Care Market Strategy*, 3rd edn, Sudbury MA., Jones and Bartlett.

Hodgetts, R.M., Luthans, F. and Slocum, J.W. (1999) 'Redefining Roles and Boundaries: Linking Competencies and Resources', *Organizational Dynamics*, Vol. 28, No. 2, 7–21.

Inguanzo, J.M. and Harju, M. (1985) 'What Makes Consumers Select a Hospital?' *Hospitals*, Vol. 16 (March), 90–4.

Jenson, J. (1987) 'Most Physicians Believe Patients Obtain Health Care Information from Mass Media', *Modern Health Care*, Vol. 17, No. 19, 113–4.

Johnsson, B.C. (1990) 'Focus Group Positioning and Analysis: A Commentary on Adjuncts for Enhancing the Design of Health Care Research', *Health Education Quarterly*, Vol. 7, No. 1, 152–68.

Jonas, S., Goldsteen, R. and Goldsteen, K. (2007) *An Introduction to the US Health Care System*, New York, Springer Publishing Company.

Kelly, D.L. (2006) *Applying Quality Management in Healthcare*, 2nd edn, Chicago, Ill., Health Administration Press.

Kotler, P. and Clarke, R.N. (1987) *Marketing For Health Care Organizations*, New Jersey, Prentice Hall.

LuAnn, A. and Andersen, R. (1980) *Healthcare in the USA*, Beverly Hills, Sage Publications.

Lytle, R.S. and Mokwa, M.P. (1992) 'Evaluating Health Care Quality: The Moderating Role of Outcomes', *Journal of Health Care Marketing*, Vol. 12, No. 1, 4–14.

MacStravic, R.E. (1975) *Marketing Health Care*, Gaithersburg, Aspen Publishers.

MacStravic, S. (2004) 'Make It Personal', *Marketing Health Services*, Vol. 24, No. 3, 21–5.

Maister, D.H. (1985) 'The Psychology of Waiting Lines', in Czepiel, J., Solomon, M.R. and Suprenant, C.F. (eds) *The Service Encounter*, Lexington, Lexington Books.

McDevitt, P.K. and Shields, L.A. (1985) 'Tactical Hospital Marketing: A Survey of the State of the Art', *Journal of Health Care Marketing*, Vol. 5, No. 1, 9–16.

Miles, R.E., Snow, C.C., Meyer, A.D. and Coleman, H.J. Jr (2003) 'Organizational Strategy, Structure and Process', *Academy of Management Review,* Vol. 3, No. 3, 546–62.

Palich, L.E., Cardinal, L.B. and Miller, C.C. (2000) 'Curvilinearity in the Diversification–Performance Linkage: An Examination of Over Three Decades of Research', *Strategic Management Journal*, Vol. 21, No. 2, 155–74.

Petrochuk, M.A. and Javalgi, R.G. (1996) 'Reforming the Health Care System: Implications for Health Care Marketers', *Health Marketing Quarterly*, Vol. 13, No. 3, 71–86.

Phillips, C.R. (1980) 'Single Room Maternity Care for Maximum Cost Efficiency', *Perinatology-Neonataology*, March/April, 21–31.

Porter, M.E. (1980) *Competitive Strategy*, New York, Free Press.

Quinn, J.B. (1992) *Intelligent Enterprise*, New York, Free Press.

Ranade, W. (1994) *A Future for the NHS*, Harlow, Longman.

Rintala, M. (2007) *Creating the National Health Service: Aneurin Bevan and the Medical Lords*, London, Taylor & Francis.

Roemer, M.I. (1991) *National Health Systems of the World. Vol. 1: The Countries*, New York, Oxford University Press.

Rowe, A.J., Mason, R.O., Dickel, K.E. and Snyder, N.H. (1994) *Strategic Management: A Methodological Approach*, 4th edn, Reading MA., Addison-Wesley Publishing.

Sage, G.C. (1991) 'Customers and the NHS', *International Journal of Health Quality Assurance*, Vol. 4, No. 3, 23–34.

Sargeant, A. and Kaehler, J. (1998) 'Factors of Patient Satisfaction with Medical Services: The Case of G.P. Practices in the U.K.', *Health Marketing Quarterly*, Vol. 16, No. 1, 55–77.

Sharma, J. (2007) *Nurture Your Brand*, http://www.expresshealthcaremgmt.com/200704/strategy01.shtml, accessed 10 Jan 2008.

Swayne, L.E., Duncan, W.J. and Ginter, P.M. (2006) *Strategic Management of Health Care Organizations*, 5th edn, Malden MA., Blackwell Publishing.

Thomas, R.K. (2007) *Health Services Marketing: A Practitioner's Guide*, New York, Springer Publishing Company.

Thomas, R.K. and Calhoun, M. (2007) *Marketing Matters: A Guide for Healthcare Executives*, Chicago. Ill., Health Administration Press.

Walshe, K. and Smith, J. (2006) *Healthcare Management*, Milton Keynes, Open University Press.

Ware, J.E., Davies-Avery, A. and Stewart, A.L. (1978) 'The Measurement and Meaning of Patient Satisfaction', *Health and Medical Care Services Review*, Vol. 1 (Jan/Feb), 14–20.

World Health Organization (1986) *Basic Documents*, 36th Edition, Geneva, Switzerland, World Health Organization.

Wrenn, B. (1994) 'Differences in Perceptions of Hospital Marketing Orientation Between Administrators and Marketing Officers', *Hospital and Health Services Administration*, Vol. 39, No. 3, 341–58.

Zaltman, G. and Vertinsky, I. (1971) 'Health Services Marketing: A Proposed Model', *Journal of Marketing*, Vol. 35 (July), 19–27.

13 | Social Entrepreneurship

OBJECTIVES

By the end of this chapter you should be able to:

1. define the terms 'social entrepreneur', 'social entrepreneurship', and 'social enterprise';
2. describe how social enterprises differ from other forms of nonprofit and for-profit organizations;
3. understand the factors that drive success in social enterprises;
4. understand the contribution that marketing can make to the development of social entrepreneurship and social enterprise;
5. describe the limitations of a market-oriented approach to social welfare;
6. explain how nonprofit funders are becoming increasingly entrepreneurial in their approach.

Introduction

The term 'entrepreneur' originated in eighteenth-century France and was originally employed by the Irish economist Richard Cantillon to refer to 'someone who undertakes' in the sense of undertaking a significant task. By the turn of the twentieth century it had morphed to mean someone who created value by reforming or revolutionizing an industry. Today the term is applied more widely to refer to those who identify an opportunity for change and exploit it (Dees et al. 2001). Business entrepreneurs therefore seek out new business opportunities and exploit them for their personal financial gain. In doing so they can frequently change the face of business, just as Stelios Haji-Ioannou did with the creation of the budget airline easyJet. While business entrepreneurs change the face of business, social entrepreneurs act as the change agents for society, seizing opportunities others miss and improving systems, inventing new approaches, and creating solutions to change society for the better. While a business entrepreneur might create entirely new industries, a social entrepreneur comes up with new solutions to social problems and then implements them, often on a large scale (Ashoka 2008).

Social entrepreneurs are thus the founder of an initiative, while the term 'social entrepreneurship' refers to the process of identifying, creating, and manifesting the social value they deliver. The related term 'social enterprise' refers to the organization entrepreneurs create to deliver this value (Mair and Martí 2006). As we shall see later, these social enterprises can be either for-profit or not-for-profit or some amalgam of the two.

In this chapter we examine the nature of social enterprise, how these may differ from other organizational types, and explore the characteristics of effective initiatives. We will also look at the process of social entrepreneurship and offer numerous examples of successful professional practice, focusing in particular on those that demonstrate effective marketing. The chapter will also consider entrepreneurial approaches to nonprofit funding and the drawbacks of a social entrepreneurial approach to the satisfaction of human need. We will begin however by providing a working definition of the social entrepreneurship construct.

What Is Social Entrepreneurship?

Social entrepreneurship is an attempt at the creation new social value through the creation of a new enterprise, such as self-employment, creating a new business or nonprofit, or the expansion of an existing social enterprise by an individual, team of individuals or firm.

There are two important components to this definition. Firstly, it would be a mistake to believe that all social entrepreneurs derive no personal benefit from their work. Many can and do make a healthy profit out of serving societal need. The difference between a social entrepreneur and a business entrepreneur is simply that the social entrepreneur has social goals that sit alongside the need to make a profit. Venkataraman (1997: 133), for example, observes that entrepreneurship is 'particularly productive from a social welfare perspective when, in the process of pursuing selfish ends, entrepreneurs also enhance social wealth by creating new markets, new industries, new technology, new institutional forms, new jobs and net increases in real productivity.'

Thus, profit might be their central motive, but it does not preclude others (Shane et al. 2003). Indeed, many social entrepreneurs derive no personal gain from their activities at all; many have only a social goal. They seek only the value that may be added to society and for the enterprise to offer a significant social contribution (Kanter and Summers 1987). Taylor and Khoo is one such example.

■ **CASE STUDY**

TAYLOR AND KHOO

Taylor and Khoo is a unique fashion and homewares label (founded by Kylie Taylor and Valerie Khoo) that provides employment and opportunity for people in poverty in Cambodia and supports the needs of about 120 orphan children at the Sunrise Angkor Orphanage in Siem Reap (See Figure 13.1). On a visit to the country the two women were deeply moved by the suffering of the poor and the stark and basic needs of the children in the orphanage. In one of the poorest countries in the world, orphanages barely survive. The orphanage stretches its US$5 a day government funding to feed, clothe, and accommodate the children. There is little—if anything—left over. When the children are sick, there's no money for a doctor or medicine. Taylor and Khoo was created to help tackle this and other issues.

Their business model is simple. The Taylor and Khoo range includes exquisite women's clothing in handwoven Khmer silk, men's accessories such as neck ties, as well as silk placements and napkins, cushions, and sumptuous silk bedspreads. Importantly, all these products are supplied by individual seamstresses and workshops that employ disadvantaged groups. Rather than being exploited, these individuals all benefit directly from their labours, being paid a full

Figure 13.1 Orphans at the Sunrise Angkor Orphanage
Source: © Taylor and Khoo.

market rate for what they produce. Neither Kylie nor Valerie receives any income from Taylor and Khoo. All profits from the organization are used to support the orphanage by buying food, medicine, and other basic necessities.

The ultimate aim is for Taylor and Khoo to become a self-sustaining, profit-making venture that will operate without the involvement of the founders and provide a secure source of funding for orphans in poverty for many years to come.

The Taylor and Khoo range is currently available from their store in Skygarden, Pitt Street Mall, Sydney and through special events in Singapore. Some items are also available from their online store at http://www.taylorandkhoo.com/onlinestore.htm. Supporters are also invited to make a donation to help the orphanage at http://www.taylorandkhoo.com/donate.htm.

Kylie and Valerie can be seen talking about their work on YouTube at http://www.youtube.com/watch?v5B40rg1OnO1w.

Case compiled from resources at http://www.taylorandkhoo.com.

	Continuum of Options		
	Purely Philanthropic	**Hybrids**	**Purely Commercial**
General motives, methods and goals	Appeal to goodwill	Mixed motives	Appeal to self-interest
	Mission driven	Balance of mission and market	Market-driven
	Social value creation	Social and economic value	Economic value creation
Key Stakeholders			
Beneficiaries	Pay nothing	Subsidized rates and/or mix of full payers and those who will pay nothing	Pay full market rates
Capital	Donations and grants	Below market capital and/or mix of payers and those who pay nothing	Market rate capital
Workforce	Volunteers	Below market wages and/or mix of volunteers and fully paid staff	Market rate compensation
Suppliers	Make in-kind donations	Special discounts and/or mix of in-kind and full price	Charge market prices

Figure 13.2 The social enterprise spectrum

Source: Dees, J.G., Emerson, J. and Economy P. (2001) *Enterprising Nonprofits: A Toolkit for Social Entrepreneurs*, New York, Wiley, p15. Reproduced with kind permission.

Secondly, social entrepreneurs come in many different guises. They can lead for-profit or nonprofit enterprises. Many social enterprises are constituted as for-profits, while many more are trading arms of nonprofit organizations, thus using for-profit activity to support broader nonprofit activity (Cook et al. 2001). Many large charities, particularly those involved in the relief of poverty, now have fair-trade operations that allow poor communities to work their way out of poverty by being paid a fair sum for the goods they supply. The traditional boundaries between for-profit and nonprofit are therefore changing with organizations of all types now actively seeking to achieve social goals. Such aims are no longer the preserve of the nonprofit as Figure 13.2 makes clear.

Uplifting the lot of the poor or investing in community development are tasks that are now regularly undertaken by businesses, nonprofits, or some hybrid of the two. As Figure 13.2 shows, the key difference in the approach is a switch from aid (where clients pay nothing for the services they receive) to trade, where some payment, or even full market rates, are paid by the prospective clients. Authors such as Pearson (2002) see this switch as significant because the difficulty with aid is that it is frequently not sustainable and can promote dependency. As an example, while shipping agricultural aid to developing countries can alleviate their short-term need, it makes it impossible for local suppliers to sell what little they do produce, which makes them in turn reliant on aid and ultimately incapable of making any contribution to the need in their community. By contrast, expecting individuals to make a payment for what they receive does not stifle local productivity and allows economic value to continue to be created in the local community. If the community itself plays a part in developing the new pattern of trade, with new businesses being created to support it, the impact of the intervention can be even greater.

Payments for the products/services provided by the enterprise may be made at the prevailing market rate, or a hybrid approach to pricing can be adopted. In the ASEMBIS example below, clients who can afford to pay the market rate for the service are expected to do so, while poorer clients pay only what they can afford. While there is a certain social equity in this approach, it also ensures that everyone pays and thus establishes the principle that there is considerable value in the work the organization does. Appropriate eye care is therefore regarded as an issue that should be taken seriously in the communities the organization serves.

■ **CASE STUDY**

ASEMBIS

In November 2001, Costa Rica, a country of nearly four million people, had only 70 ophthamologists. The overwhelming majority of these worked in the capital city of San José. In addition to the shortage of medical professionals, ocular services were not included in the primary scope of services of the Ministry of Health, and most practitioners had private practices, providing expensive care that was inaccessible to even the middle classes. As a result, most low-income families had no access to eye care and many children suffering from blindness or visual impairment were misdiagnosed as learning disabled, severely impacting their personal development.

ASEMBIS was formed to provide a large range of curative, preventative, and optical services. Medical services offered by the organization include ophthamology, optometry, eye surgery, and low-cost lenses, as well as nose, ear, and throat care. Although treatments are provided at low cost, there has been no trade-off in quality. The excellence of ASEMBIS's services is such that middle-class patients are increasingly willing to pay full market rates for its services, thus helping subsidize the balance of the work. Payment is based on a sliding scale so that low-income patients pay according to their resources.

ASEMBIS trains promoters who travel the country to test and detect visual and hearing problems. They also train schoolchildren (vision guardians) as community-wide promoters for vision care through their innovative programme 'Little Windows of Light'. This model enables the first level of diagnosis to happen in schools and communities rather than in clinics, therefore providing a solution on a massive scale. ASEMBIS has served over 600,000 people in Costa Rica at the time of writing.

Case compiled from resources at www.ashoka.org<http://www.ashoka.org>.

The Social Entrepreneurship Process

Mair and Martí (2006: 37) define social entrepreneurship as 'a process involving the innovative use and combination of resources to pursue opportunities to catalyze change and/or address social needs.' From this perspective social entrepreneurs act as change agents by:

1. Adopting a mission to create and sustain social value. For social entrepreneurs, the mission of social improvement is critical and it often takes priority over generating profits. Instead of looking for a short-term 'fix', social entrepreneurs look for ways to create lasting improvements in their field of interest (Waddock and Post 1991).

2. Recognizing and relentlessly pursuing new opportunities to serve their mission. Where other individuals see barriers to achievement of goals, entrepreneurs see opportunities to re-think the problem and develop innovative solutions. Social entrepreneurs have a vision of how they will achieve their goals and they are fundamentally determined to make that vision a reality.

3. Acting boldly and responsively to societal need without limiting themselves to the resources currently in hand. Social entrepreneurs innovate to find more efficient ways of achieving their goals, but they are also very persuasive when it comes to attracting additional resources from others. They typically explore all the financial options open to them, drawing funds from purely philanthropic sources, commercial lenders, and from the trading activities they and their organization are engaged in. They tend not to be bound by norms and traditions which suggest that only certain sources of funding should be exploited.

4. Being accountable to the constituencies served and for the outcomes achieved. Social entrepreneurs take steps to ensure that they are creating value. They seek to provide real social improvements to their beneficiaries and their communities as well as an attractive social and/or financial return to their investors. The work of the Grameen Bank provides a good illustration of how this can be achieved.

■ CASE STUDY

GRAMEEN BANK

The Grameen Bank was set up by Muhammad Yunus in 1976 to provide micro-credit to some of the world's poorest communities. The underlying premise of Grameen is that, in order to emerge from poverty, landless peasants need access to credit, without which they cannot be expected to launch their own enterprises, however small these may be. In defiance of the traditional banking convention where no collateral (in this case, land) meant no credit, the Grameen Bank relied instead on the will of its borrowers to succeed in their undertakings and thus to repay their loans.

The Grameen model works as follows: a bank branch is set up with a branch manager and a number of centre managers to cover an area of around 15 to 22 villages. The manager and their team begin work by visiting the villages to familiarize themselves with the local milieu in which they will be operating and identify the prospective clientele. They also begin work explaining the purpose, functions, and mode of operation of the bank to the local population. Thereafter, groups of five prospective borrowers are formed. In the first stage, only two of these individuals are eligible for, and receive, a loan. Loans are small, but sufficient to finance the micro-enterprises undertaken by borrowers: rice-husking, machine repairing, purchase of rickshaws, buying of milk cows, goats, cloth, pottery. The group is observed for a month to see if the members are conforming to the rules of the bank. Only if the first two borrowers begin to repay the loan over this period, do the other members of the group become eligible themselves for a loan. Because of these restrictions, there is substantial peer pressure for individuals to honour their obligations. In this sense, the collective responsibility of the group serves as the collateral on the loan. The repayment rate on loans is of the order of 95%, impressive by any banking standards.

Case compiled from resources at www.grameen-info.org/<http://www.grameen-info.org/>.

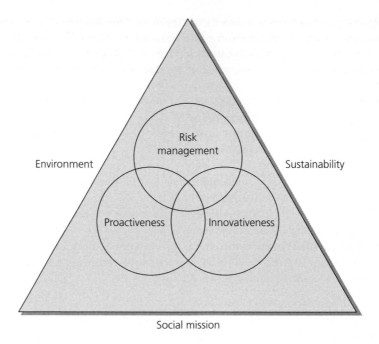

Figure 13.3 Bounded multidimensional model of social entrepreneurship

Source: Weerawardena, J. and Sullivan-Mort, G. (2006) 'Investigating Social Entrepreneurship: A Multidimensional Model', *Journal of World Business*, Vol. 41, 21–35. Reproduced with kind permission of Elsevier.

The Grameen case illustrates a number of the key facets of the social entrepreneurship process. Professor Yunus articulated a clear social mission, namely to break the cycle of poverty and furnish the poor with a means to work themselves out of poverty. To enable this to happen he introduced the social innovation of 'micro-credit', extending very small lines of credit to individuals who lacked traditional collateral. To secure these small loans he was able to leverage one commodity that the poor could offer, namely their own social capital. The group set-up acts to minimize the risk to the bank by using social pressure to ensure that the loans are actually repaid and the model is sustainable because only when payments begin to be collected do other members of the group qualify for loans of their own. The approach thus demonstrates characteristics common to many social initiatives. These are illustrated in Figure 13.3.

Success in Social Ventures

There has been considerable interest on the part of researchers in the factors that drive success in social ventures. Early work focused on the characteristics of the entrepreneurs themselves determining that success was a function of the extent to which the individual possessed outstanding leadership skills (Prabhu 1998, Thompson et al. 2000), passion for the cause (Bornstein 1998), and strong ethical fibre (Drayton 2002). Borins (2000) also argued that a critical skill for social entrepreneurs to possess was the ability to generate the commitment of followers (e.g. volunteers, donors, customers etc.) by effectively articulating the mission and goals of the organization in terms of social values rather than in purely economic terms.

The difficulty with this work on traits is that it doesn't offer much by way of practical help to aspiring social entrepreneurs. It offers them no guidance on what they might learn from others to optimize their own chances of success. As a consequence more recent work has shifted to focus on the characteristics of the entrepreneurship process itself. Sharir and Lerner (2006), for example, identify eight such characteristics as contributing to the success of social ventures.

The Nature of the Entrepreneur's Social Network

It takes considerable effort to bring together the requisite set of skills and resources to make a venture a reality. Funding will need to be identified and sought and considerable amounts of volunteer time may be necessary. As a consequence social entrepreneurs with good-quality and relevant social networks (or with the ability to quickly assemble them) will be likely to experience a higher probability of success (Roure and Keeley 1990).

Total Dedication to the Venture's Success

Sharir and Lerner's analysis suggests that successful entrepreneurs are dedicated to the social goals they want to achieve. The strength of that determination appears to drive the likelihood of success.

The Capital Base at the Establishment Stage

Many social enterprises lack access to market capital to see the business established. As a consequence it is important that the funds available at the outset are sufficient to see the organization through the establishment phase and to the point where revenues from the product/service are sufficient to sustain the venture.

The Acceptance of the Idea in the Public Discourse

As in the for-profit trading environment it will be important that the target audience recognize the value in what the venture is trying to achieve. Otherwise there is a risk that the organization may face opposition from other organizations working in this domain, government, or even the public itself. The Grameen Bank for example piloted the idea in one location before scaling up the enterprise. The value created by the enterprise must fit well within the current cultural and social framework.

The Composition of the Venturing Team, Including the Ratio of Volunteers to Salaried Employees

The technical/managerial skills of the team assembled will also play a part as will the cost of employing relevant expertise. Volunteer labour obviously has the effect of lowering the start-up costs and in many cases this can make the difference between success and failure (Francis and Sandberg 2000).

Forming Long-Term Cooperations in the Public and Nonprofit Sectors

Himmelman (1996) regards cooperation as a process in which individuals in organizations exchange information, coordinate and share resources, risk, and responsibility. It generates a synergy that benefits all parties. Sharir and Lerner identify that the number and quality of cooperative arrangements also impact on the likely success of the venture.

The Ability of the Service to Stand the Market Test

If the venture is able to generate appropriate fees from its customers it will have much less reliance on government and grant income. Government and foundation grants are typically only a short-term solution to funding and thus being able to achieve a sustainable business model early in the ventures operations will be essential for long-term sustainability (Letts et al. 1999).

The Entrepreneur's Previous Managerial Experience

Finally, the extent to which the entrepreneur has a successful track record in management will play a role in determining the success of an enterprise. This is a factor commonly emphasized in the broader entrepreneurship literature (e.g. Shane et al. 2003).

Social Entrepreneurship and Alleviating Poverty

As we noted earlier much social entrepreneurship activity has been directed at the alleviation of poverty. Numerous organizations have struggled with how best to assist the over two-thirds of the world's population that is marginalized from the formal economy. These individuals exist on mere dollars per day and as a consequence are ignored by traditional markets, forcing them to rely on inefficient or sub-standard supplies and frequently individuals who exploit them for their own financial gain. It is a sad reflection on our society that the most disadvantaged people can often end up paying more for the basic necessities of life because they fall victim to thieves and unscrupulous traders. To add to their economic woes the poor are often deprived of even the most basic of necessities including electricity, housing, and healthcare.

The excellent website **http://www.globalrichlist.com/** (see Figure 13.4) brings home to the visitor just how fortunate they are compared with the majority of the world's population. Users

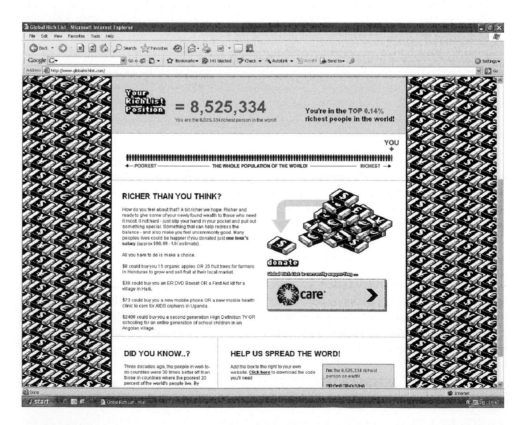

Figure 13.4 Global rich list

Source: globalrichlist.com. Reproduced with kind permission.

can input their own annual income into the site, which responds by generating a rich list position showing how relatively well off they are. The site is highly effective at motivating the user to want to do something about poverty; in this case giving to the charity Care International.

The roots of this poverty are complex and beyond the scope of this text. It is, however, driven in no small measure by the inability of these individuals to participate actively in their domestic economy and thus to use what resources they do have to begin to work themselves out of this condition.

A primary difficulty is that the poor have limited individual purchasing power which makes them unattractive to the conventional market. It has been argued in the past that it would cost far more to conduct business with this group than it would ever be possible to recoup in the prices that might be charged. Channels of distribution would be long and complex and, in cases where credit had to be offered, there would be little prospect of enforcing such loans. The examples of Grameen and ASEMBIS have graphically illustrated how such difficulties can be overcome, leading authors such as Budinich (2005: 7) to argue that the difficulty is illusory. 'In most instances, focusing on the limited purchasing power of individual low-income consumers is simply a reflection of our inability to imagine and develop a product offering and a viable business model for this market segment.' Creative solutions can be found. Budinich (2005) suggests that these solutions might involve the following.

Designing Products and Services That Tap into the Wealth of the Poor

Although they might lack economic resources many of the world's poorest communities boast highly skilled individuals who lack only the opportunity to employ them to their own advantage. In the Taylor and Khoo case, for example, skilled workers are given the opportunity to earn wages that reflect the true market prices for the products they create. Other communities can be rich in social capital with highly developed social and self-help networks. Many social initiatives take advantage of these extended networks, leveraging them to achieve scale that could not be achieved if they were trading with each individual seperately. The Cemex example below illustrates one way in which this can be successfully achieved.

Engineering Value

Succeeding in reaching scale requires not only providing an affordable product, but in re-thinking the value chain, considering every facet through from production to pricing, promotion, and delivery to end consumers. Pricing in the Cemex case is actually slightly above the market norm, but the company engineers enough value to make it worth individuals doing business with it. Indeed, such is the value created, that although customers pay slightly more for their building materials, overall they can save a great deal of time and money.

Leveraging the Power of Communities as Both Consumers and Producers

To maximize the impact of the initiative, interventions should seek to increase the income of small producers and micro-entrepreneurs in the target community. Aside from the obvious benefit to these individuals, this in turn can have the synergistic effect of increasing the demand for goods and services. Notice in the Cemex case how the company has managed to keep its promotional costs low through the use of female promoters. The promoters actively sell the idea into the community and gain 'points' when others sign up that they can use to put towards the cost of their own building materials. In the Grameen Village Phone example (also below), the company is in effect creating a network of female entrepreneurs each of whom will run their own business selling calls to others in their community and doubtless making many calls of their own too. In both these examples the community is being viewed by marketers as both a consumer and a producer.

■ **CASE STUDY**

CEMEX AND PATRIMONIO HOY

Two-thirds of the world's population (four billion people) struggle to survive at the bottom of the economic pyramid, yet they represent a neglected multi-trillion-dollar market that is growing steadily in an otherwise turbulent global economy. The Cemex Corporation of Mexico has recently developed a strategy to tap into this market, enabling 20,000 very poor families to purchase building materials and upgrade their homes without receiving subsidies. Indeed, through its innovative approach Cemex has been able to make a profit on these transactions.

Patrimonio Hoy is a for-profit initiative of Cemex, Mexico's largest multinational corporation. Cemex manufactures cement, a key component of construction in the developing world. During Mexico's economic crisis in 1994, when the value of the peso crashed, Cemex noticed that the revenues from its large-scale customers and middle- and upper-income individuals dropped by 50 per cent, but sales to its low-income, do-it-yourself 'homebuilder' consumers dropped only 10 to 20 per cent. In other words demand from lower-income households was shown to be less susceptible to fluctuations in the national economy. Cemex thus saw an opportunity to offset losses it might incur during economic downturns and allow it to continue growing market share. Low-income 'do-it-yourself' consumers thus became a critical market segment for the firm to address.

In Guadalajara six million residents live in poor-quality accommodation, often with families of ten members sharing only two rooms. Residents typically save to expand their homes and iron lattices typically extend upwards from the roof so that further storeys can be added at a future date. Progress is typically very slow with families often taking over four years to save enough for a one-room extension to ease the overcrowding. Life is tough and the overcrowding merely exacerbates the tensions that accompany a life of poverty. Many young people are 'turfed out' onto the street at an early age where they learn delinquency, theft, and prostitution.

The average low-income homebuilder takes 13 years to finish a small house and this discouraging rate of progress reflects the many obstacles that low-income homebuilders face. Banks and other businesses will not engage with the poor residents of informal settlements where the legal status of their property ownership is doubtful, and where residents cannot document

Figure 13.5 Patrimonio Hoy
Source: Cemex and Patrimonio Hoy.

assets, collateral, references, or regular sources of income. Over time, this neglect has led the poor to become resigned to their fate, feeling that they will not be able to better their position and obtain a better quality of life for their families.

In spite of the despair, many poor communities do put money aside to save for improvements. They have traditionally done so by forming a savings club or tanda. Here groups of individuals (typically around ten) make a small weekly contribution of around 100 pesos. Each week, one member of the tanda is selected by lottery to receive the entire pool until every member has taken the pool once. Cemex found through research that although much of the money being saved in tandas was for the purposes of home improvement, little of the money actually ended up being spent on that purpose. Instead it was spent on living essentials, dealing with emergencies, or assisting family and friends. In many poor communities people acquire status by virtue of their participation in the community, so assisting others confers an advantage and is therefore a critical component of everyday life.

Buying building materials is a major challenge for the poor. A bag of cement can cost over twice the average daily earnings of a family and when one is bought it is often not used wisely. While the poor can be very committed to DIY improvements, their building skills are frequently not the best. Buildings can be structurally unsafe and/or significant quantities of materials can be spoiled or wasted.

In 1999 when Patrimonio Hoy began its operations it was therefore facing a variety of marketing challenges. The key facets of the approach it adopted are detailed below:

1. Cemex developed a strong brand for the programme—Patrimonio Hoy. In translation this means Patrimony Today and conveys a sense that the programme will yield something of value that will pass between the generations. It was designed to overcome the resignation felt by many individuals and to make a promise that change could not only be delivered, but be delivered in a timely fashion.

2. The programme targeted women. Cemex's research told them that women tend to assume the responsibility for maintaining household unity and a family's progress. They would thus be more interested in the topic of housing improvements. Because they were also more connected to the experiences of their children they would also be significantly more motivated to find a solution. The research proved to be correct and women were ultimately found to be highly reliable clients.

3. To develop this custom, the company neglected advertising in favour of personal selling. It recruited informal leaders in the community, 98 per cent of who were women, to serve as 'promoters'. These promoters first form a savings group with neighbours, family, or friends, and then begin enrolling others to form their own savings groups. When they sign up new members, they earn points, which they can exchange for cash or building materials. Promoters are given ID badges and bright blue T-shirts emblazoned with Patrimonio Hoy logos. This makes them easy to identify in the community and deters fraud.

4. Community members and potential promoters are introduced to Patrimonio Hoy in a group session at the local Patrimonio Hoy office rather than being approached as individuals. This helps make their first encounter a sanctioned, communal activity. It also helps prevent new members from being socially isolated when they begin pursuing new habits that aren't a part of the traditional culture. Otherwise, envy, suspicion, and misunderstanding can spread as others notice that Patrimonio Hoy members are beginning to accumulate savings and improve their homes.

5. No paperwork is required to join the initiative. There is no need for proof of identification, assets, or collateral. Members are bound by their honour and reputation in the community.

6. Members are invited to form savings clubs, like tandas, in which each member contributes a minimum of 120 pesos per week. Each Patrimonio Hoy savings group consists of three persons. After members join a savings group, Patrimonio Hoy calls its members 'partners' rather than customers. Group size is significantly smaller than would be the case in a traditional tanda, but as a consequence the bonds between the individuals are typically stronger and there is hence more cohesion. The commitment is also longer term, typically well over a year, and the penalties for missing payments are well publicized so that everyone is clear from the outset how the scheme will operate. Each member of the group is obliged to take a turn at collecting the payments and thus enforcement of the terms.

7. Unlike the tandas, and to ensure that the saved funds are actually used for housing, the scheme delivers raw materials for building such as cement and iron, not cash. After two weeks Cemex makes a first delivery of building materials to each member of the group. Because this occurs before sufficient savings have accumulated to fully pay the bill, Cemex is, in effect, advancing credit. Additional deliveries of materials are made to each member every ten weeks. The structure is seen as fairer than the tanda system of awarding pay-offs by lottery because this gives an advantage to those who receive the pool first.

8. Customer payments cover the cost of cement and other materials but they also include a fee for a package of other services. Cemex does not compete on price and in fact the cost of its cement is typically slightly more than a buyer would pay from an alternative supplier. The fee covers a range of value-added services such as assistance from engineers and architects, a construction school where DIY homebuilders can learn basic skills, a free storage facility for the materials (to prevent spoilage on the street), and a freeze on the costs of materials when an individual enrols so that they are insulated from fluctuations in the economy.

9. When a family finishes a room, they become a 'living testimonial' to the programme and are issued a diploma. They are also presented with a 'celebration' kit containing family-size soft drinks and tacos. The idea is that they will throw a party for their neighbours which helps build social capital and actively promotes the desire to get ahead in life. Traditionally such attitudes had been the source of suspicion and envy and the goal of the parties is to diffuse this tension and encourage others to want to engage with the company.

The Patrimonio Hoy initiative has proved successful in achieving the business goals of Cemex. It allows the company to achieve scale and generate a profit while making a genuine difference to the poor of the country. From the customer's perspective, while the raw materials might be more expensive in terms of cost per unit, the ultimate cost is substantially lower. An average do-it-yourself homebuilder in Mexico takes four years to build a room of 100 square feet. Participants in Patrimonio Hoy can build the same-size room, with better quality, in around 18 months and at two-thirds the cost.

Case compiled from resources at http://www.cemexmexico.com/index.asp and http://www.iccwbo.org/WBA/id7031/index.html.

■ **CASE STUDY**

GRAMEEN TELECOM'S VILLAGE PHONE PROGRAMME

GrameenPhone is a commercial operation providing cellular services in both urban and rural areas of Bangladesh, with approximately 40,000 customers. In rural areas where isolation and poor infrastructure services are often the norm, telecommunications can play an extremely important role in enhancing rural social and economic development. A new programme of GrameenPhone is enabling women to retail cellular phone services in rural areas and thus to offer telephone services to many thousands of additional people. It works by allowing village women access to micro-credit from the Grameen Bank to acquire digital cellular phones and subsequently re-sell phone calls and phone services within their villages. Grameen Telecom estimates that when its programme is complete, 40,000 Village Phone operators will be employed for a combined net income of $24 million per annum.

The programme has a highly significant impact on poverty reduction because:

• It saves villagers who would otherwise have to travel long distances to do business in a city from having to do so. The cost of such a trip ranges from two to eight times the cost of a single phone call, meaning real savings for rural people of between 132 to 490 Taka ($2.70 to $10) for individual calls. There are also obvious savings in terms of time and hardship to the individual associated with the travel. The programme therefore offers significant quality of life benefits that are difficult to measure.

• Villagers also use the phone to discuss family and financial matters, notably 'remittances'. Bangladesh is a labour-exporting country with many rural villagers (predominantly men) working in the Gulf States. Transferring cash from a Gulf State to a rural village in Bangladesh is fraught with risks and the Village Phone acts as a powerful instrument to reduce the risk associated with remittance transfers by providing a source of accurate information about foreign currency exchange rates. The Village Phone thus acts as a medium for allowing household enterprises to take advantage of market information to reduce their expenses and improve their profit.

• Reducing the risk of remittance transfers from overseas workers has important implications for rural households and villages. Remittances tend to be used for daily household expenses such as food, clothing, and healthcare. They are thus an important factor in meeting household subsistence needs and can make up a significant portion of household income. Remittance funds are also spent on capital items including building or improving housing, buying cattle or land, and buying consumer goods such as portable tape/CD players and televisions. Once subsistence needs are met, remittances tend to be used for 'productive investments' or for savings.

• The income that Village Phone operators derive from the Village Phone is about 24 per cent of their household income on average and in some cases can be as high as 40 per cent. By participating in the programme Village Phone operators become socially and economically empowered.

Case compiled from resources at http://www.grameen-info.org/grameen/gtelecom/.

The Contribution of Marketing

It should by now be clear that marketing has much to offer social entrepreneurs in the achievement of their objectives. At a philosophical level traditional models of market orientation will not lend themselves easily to this context. While the creation of profit may be one goal it will not be the only goal of a social enterprise. As has been shown above, social enterprises are at least as concerned with the overall benefit that will accrue to society. Thus the notion of a societal orientation is much more in keeping with what marketing will be expected to deliver in this context. The societal orientation model will also add value by virtue of its focus on a wider range of stakeholders and the recognition that collaboration may be at least as much of an issue as competition in many markets. Indeed, the reader will recall that the existence of networks of collaborators has been shown to be a critical factor in determining the success or failure of an enterprise. Societal orientation can therefore provide a useful model for social entrepreneurs to adopt when thinking through how they will approach marketing in this context.

The full range of marketing tools, models, and frameworks also has resonance in this domain. Many facets of the traditional mix, such as pricing, take on even greater significance in stimulating or meeting marketing demand. This may be as simple as offering products at low cost, thus bringing them within the poor's ability to pay (see the IOWH case below) or it may involve greater creativity, perhaps employing price discrimination and charging different segments of customers different rates according to their ability to pay. Alternatively it could involve enhanced creativity in payment mechanisms, allowing payments to be made over time, offering micro-credit, or packaging the product into single units or multiple bundles which can be sold on in the community itself.

As the cases in this chapter have illustrated, social enterprises do not give away their products, even to the poorest individuals. Aside from the fact that they will want to make a profit on the transaction, charging requires customers to make a conscious allocation of their scarce resource and thus to signal their priorities. By doing so they come to place significant value on the products and services they will receive which is turn acts to reduce unnecessary consumption and reduce waste. Consumers are keen to conserve resources they value.

As social enterprises employ business methods, the full range of planning tools and techniques available to the marketer have equal relevance to this domain. While pricing is a highly significant issue, so too is the engineering of value and ensuring appropriate distribution and promotion take place in the target market. While the promotional mix will be very limited in scope, the application of personal selling, sales promotion, public relations, and advertising will all have relevance.

Of course, not all social enterprises are concerned with the relief of poverty and there are many thousands of such organizations in developed countries such as the USA, UK, and Australia focused on other goals. They may well be tackling poverty in these countries, but equally they can seek to deal with a wide range of other societal issues, such as social inclusion, drug/solvent abuse, crime, and community development. In these countries the marketing employed will likely be a hybrid of nonprofit and for-profit activity, with many of the ideas expressed in this text supplemented with ideas from the marketing mainstream. Indeed, if the enterprise is being initiated by a for-profit organization, the pattern of marketing may have more in common with that of traditional businesses. In this case, however, one would still hope that the philosophy that underpins its application would at the minimum reflect something of the societal orientation alluded to earlier and that as a consequence the needs of the vulnerable were not exploited for personal gain. Providing genuine societal benefit at a profit is a different proposition entirely.

■ **CASE STUDY**

INSTITUTE FOR ONE WORLD HEALTH (IOWH)

The IOWH was formed by Dr Victoria Hale in 2000 and became the world's first nonprofit pharmaceutical company developing drugs to meet the needs of the poor (**www.iowh.org**). Hale found that drug companies would frequently shelve ideas for new drugs because in their judgement they would never be profitable. With the help of these companies and their scientists IOWH would track down compounds that showed promise but which weren't being actively exploited. When one was found, the drug company would grant them development rights through a licensing agreement or donation of a patent. IOWH would then develop the drug using donated funds and voluntary contributions of time and expertise from pharmaceutical scientists.

The drugs would be developed into safe, effective, and affordable medicines and therapies. By partnering and collaborating with industry and researchers, by securing donated intellectual property, and by utilizing the scientific and manufacturing capacity of the developing world, IOWH can deliver affordable, effective, and appropriate new medicines where they are needed most.

Case compiled from resources at www.oneworldhealth.org/<http://www.oneworldhealth .org/>.

Drawbacks of the Social Enterprise Model

In this brief review of social entrepreneurship it is important to realize that the approach is not without its critics. While there can be little doubt that entrepreneurs have made and continue to make a real difference to the societies in which they operate, there can be a downside to the way in which they operate and the model may therefore not be appropriate to every social context. The most pervasive of these criticisms is cited by Eikenberry and Kluver (2004) who note that social enterprises may choose only to enter into (or to continue with) activities that are profitable. That is, after all, a key reason for their existence. Clients who ether can't afford to pay, or who can't afford to pay enough, are neglected. Rosenman et al. (1999) share this view, suggesting that organizations relying on commercial revenue are driven to weed out clients who are difficult to serve. They won't move beyond their marginal cost of production when deciding on price and thus many potential customers will be cut out of the market. Their need will doubtless be no less pressing than anyone else's, but it can become marginalized as society, governments, and donors perceive that the problem has been tackled and move on to other issues.

There is unfortunately some evidence that this is the case. Salamon (1993) notes that the nonprofit sector's increased reliance on commercial revenue has caused a shift from services targeted to the poor to those able to pay. Similarly, Alexander et al. (1999) in a study of market-oriented nonprofits found that the focus in their provision had moved from public goods (such as research, teaching, advocacy, and serving the poor) to meeting individual client needs.

A second key drawback of the approach, it is argued, is that it can impact negatively on what is known as 'social capital'. Social capital is essential to the well-being of society because it aids in the development of trust between the individuals that comprise it. This trust is necessary not only for successful social relations, but it is also essential to the health of an economy because individuals must have a base level of trust in one another if they are to be able to trade. Adler and Kwon (2002: 17) capture the significance of the construct when they define social capital as 'the goodwill engendered by the fabric of social relations that can be mobilized to facilitate action'.

A shift to a social enterprise model has two important impacts on social capital.

1. In the past nonprofits needed to maintain a network of relationships with a variety of different stakeholders to survive (e.g. donors, members, volunteers etc.). This network helped develop social trust around the organization. When nonprofits rely on commercial revenue there is less need to build these networks thereby discouraging social participation (Aspen Institute 2001). The social enterprise model encourages a shift in focus from the creation of relationships to the creation of more opportunities to sell product. This tends to develop so-called 'professional competency' but it can also serve to devalue the work of volunteers as organizations seek to exert greater control over their workforce and create greater uniformity in respect of style and approach (Alexander et al. 1999). In other words something of the voluntary ethos or character of the sector will be lost.

2. The second point is related to the first. Even in cases where an organization might have the desire to continue to build social capital, marketized nonprofits lack the resources to make this a reality. They are deflected away from this by a compulsion to direct resources to other more pressing priorities. Ryan (1999: 135) argues that citizen engagement is endangered when

a nonprofit seeks to become a more competitive provider. In most cases nonprofits are not being funded to strengthen society but to provide social services. As the market pressures them to become more competent at jobs like project management and more attentive to the strategic demands of their industry, how committed can they remain to this civic dimension?

These fears are very real. There is increasing evidence that adopting a social enterprise perspective can have important social ramifications. Backman and Smith (2000), for example, cite the example of an arts organization that eliminated its volunteer programme because it was not considered cost-effective. The authors also cite evidence that nonprofit boards are morphing to place greater value on business skills than they do on links into the community. A new generation of board members have entirely different backgrounds and perspectives to their predecessors and thus push nonprofits towards a more businesslike model. Whether this is always a good thing is a philosophical debate beyond the scope of this text, but there can be little doubt that the traditional values of the sector will be impacted and the clients of nonprofit organizations will find it increasingly difficult to discern much difference in the approach of nonprofit and for-profit alike. Should the nonprofit sector strive to retain a unique identity and resist the imposition of business models and perspectives? While these deliver us ever greater efficiency in 'production' are we on the brink of losing what Lord Dahrendorf refers to as the 'creative chaos' of the voluntary sector? Society will be a much poorer place if this proves to be the case.

Entrepreneurial Philanthropy

Before leaving the topic of entrepreneurship it will be worthwhile looking at how the model is beginning to impact on traditional nonprofit funders and in particular on grant-making trusts and foundations. It was not that long ago, for example, when Bill Drayton, the founder of Ashoka, bemoaned the ability of social entrepreneurs to gain funding from these bodies. 'What a social entrepreneur needs and what a foundation provides is an almost perfect mismatch.' What was driving this critique was a realization that foundations were very traditional in their giving patterns, with firmly established and often inflexible criteria for grants and exhibiting a remarkable degree of risk aversion in their approach. This latter observation has been supported by other sector commentators such as McIlney (1998) who regard it as an anomaly. Foundations are actually ideally placed to take risk by virtue of the fact they are funded from an endowment. They are 'uniquely qualified to initiate thought, experiment with new ventures and dissent from prevailing attitudes' yet they demonstrate scant regard for such behavior (McIlnay 1998: 126). This seems to stem from the 'centrist' orientation of many boards, managers seeking to preserve their individual reputations, and a general desire not to court controversy (Osberg 2006). As a consequence individuals and organizations seeking funding (particularly non-traditional funding) tend to contort their real needs to suit the requirements of the funder.

The CEO of the Edna McConnell Clark Foundations, Michael Bailin, notes:

You come to a foundation with an idea that you hope is worth funding and you hope to get some money. But first you have to be willing to do what the foundation feels is important to do (and) you try to shoehorn their requests into your other activities, because you are a not-for-profit and you need the money. What you end up doing is taking on an activity that doesn't really belong in your portfolio but fits at the periphery and provides some overhead. That can degrade the quality, focus and effectiveness of a not-for-profit's key programs (quoted in Grossman and Currin 2002: 5).

Osberg (2006) sees a new form of foundation giving beginning to emerge led by a new generation of philanthropist who have a more market-oriented perspective on their philanthropy. Schervish et al. (2001), for example, note that individuals who have made their money through exploiting developments in modern technology adopt giving practices that are market conscious and knowledge based. The new approach being adopted by these donors and their foundations is depicted in Figure 13.6 and contrasted with the traditional approach in Table 13.1.

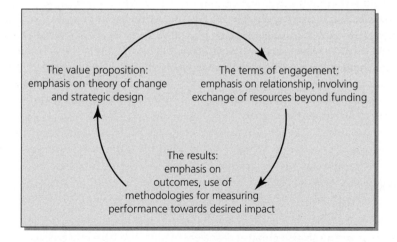

Figure 13.6 Three points of orientation for market-conscious, knowledge-driven philanthropists

Source: Osberg, S. (2006) 'Wayfinding Without A Compass: Philanthropy's Changing Landscape and its Implications for Social Entrepreneurs', in Nicholls, A. (ed.) *Social Entrepreneurship: New Models of Sustainable Social Change,* New York, Oxford University Press, p316. Reproduced with kind permission.

Table 13.1 Traditional vs market-based grant-giving

Traditional patterns of behaviour	Market-based patterns of behaviour
Define the problem	Create value proposition
Invite applications	Seek out partners
Mitigate risk	Tolerate risk
Fund the programme or project	Fund core operations and capacity
Emphasize grant transaction	Emphasize relationship
Vest accountability in grantee	Share accountability
Strive for clarity, consistency	Strive for flexibility, responsiveness

Source: Osberg, S. (2006) 'Wayfinding Without A Compass: Philanthropy's Changing Landscape and its Implications for Social Entrepreneurs', in Nicholls, A. (ed.) *Social Entrepreneurship: New Models of Sustainable Social Change*, New York, Oxford University Press, p 317. Reproduced with kind permission.

The new market-based foundations think through how they want to facilitate change, outlining what role they are prepared to play in tackling a given problem. They look for the added value they could deliver by investing in a particular area of service provision or need. The emphasis is on the desire to bring about a sustainable change in their area of interest. Having defined this value proposition they then seek out partners who will help them in fulfilling this goal. Rather than taking just handing out 'dainty dabs' of money (McIlney 1998) and focusing only on programme costs, they develop close working relationships with these partners, recognizing all their funding needs (i.e. including those for administrative overheads) and working with them to their mutual advantage. Rather than holding the grantee solely accountable for the achievement of the outcomes, they share that accountability as part of the partnership, being prepared to change course should circumstances demand it. Rigidity in respect of how the funds can be applied is replaced with systems that offer greater flexibility and responsiveness. Finally, the methods of evaluation are focused not on how the money has been spent, but rather on the outcomes that have been achieved. As Patty Stonesifer, the president of the Bill and Melinda Gates Foundation, recognizes, it is ' harder in philanthropy to know you did the right thing' (cited in Byrne 2002). Modern foundations, such as the Bill and Melinda Gates Foundation, work closely with the organizations they fund to develop measures appropriate to the context and find optimal programmes to deliver on these goals.

■ **SUMMARY**

In this chapter we have distinguished between the terms 'social entrepreneur', 'social entrepreneurship', and 'social enterprise' and provided definitions of each. We have also explored the nature of social enterprise in some detail and provided many case examples of successful organizations. It was argued that all categories of organization be they for-profit or not-for-profit can engage in this form or enterprise, although a new hybrid category of organization is emerging which regards the pursuit of profit and social goals as being of equal worth.

Much social entrepreneurship activity has been directed at the alleviation of poverty and the example of the Grameen Bank provided a powerful illustration of how an understanding of the way in which poorer communities function can help drive creative solutions to what have historically been regarded as insurmountable difficulties. While the poor may not be able to provide traditional collateral, intangible assets such as reputation in the community can be as, if not more, effective as a means of securing a loan. The wider role of social entrepreneurship in alleviating poverty was explored, as were the characteristics of effective programmes.

The chapter concluded by looking at a number of the drawbacks of the social enterprise model, notably its impact on the generation of social capital and the blurring of the lines it facilitates between nonprofit and for-profit, resulting in a possible loss of identity for 'voluntary' sector organizations. It also examined the role of entrepreneurship in relation to the provision of funding and reported a change emerging in the traditional pattern of foundation funding.

■ DISCUSSION QUESTIONS

1. What is social entrepreneurship? How does it differ from business entrepreneurship?

2. Explain why traditional aid to poorer communities might promote dependency on the organizations providing it. What benefit might there be in the approach adopted by a social entrepreneur?

3. Visit the website **www.aflatoun.org.** Evaluate this initiative against the criteria for success proposed by Sharir and Lerner (2006). In your view, does their model adequately explain the success of the organization? If not, how might you modify it to take account of this case?

4. Conduct a value chain analysis of the Cemex (Patrimonio Hoy) case study. From where does this organization generate value? (Hint: think through not only the components of the value chain but also the linkages between the various elements.)

5. What dangers do you see in the application of social entrepreneurship to tackling societal problems? Can these be overcome and, if so, how?

■ REFERENCES

Adler, P.S. and Kwon, S. (2002) 'Social Capital: Prospects for a New Concept', *Academy of Management Review*, Vol. 27, No. 1, 17–40.

Alexander, J., Nank, R. and Stivers, C. (1999) 'Implications of Welfare Reform: Do Nonprofit Survival Strategies Threaten Civil Society', *Nonprofit and Voluntary Sector Quarterly*, Vol. 28, No. 4, 452–75.

Ashoka (2008) 'What Is A Social Entrepreneur?', http://ashoka.org/social_entrepreneur accessed 21 January 2008.

Aspen Institute (2001) The *Nonprofit Sector and the Market: Opportunities and Challenges*, Publication 01-013, Washington DC., Aspen Institute.

Backman, E.V. and Smith, S.R. (2000) 'Healthy Organizations, Unhealthy Communities?' *Nonprofit Management and Leadership*, Vol. 10, No. 4, 355–73.

Borins, S. (2000) 'Loose Cannons and Rule Breakers, Or Enterprising Leaders? Some Evidence About Innovative Public Managers', *Public Administration Review*, Vol. 60, 498–507.

Bornstein, D. (1998) 'Changing The World On A Shoestring', *Atlantic Monthly*, Vol. 28, No. 1, 34–9.

Budinich, V. (2005) 'A Framework for Developing Market Based Strategies That Benefit Low-Income Communities', Ashoka website, http://ashoka.org/files/FEC_Framework.pdf accessed January 2008.

Byrne, J. (2002) 'The New Face of Philanthropy', *Business Week*, 2 December, p88.

Cook, B., Dodds, C. and Mitchell, W. (2001) *Social Entrepreneurship: False Premises and Dangerous Forebodings*, Centre of Full Employment and Equity, University of Newcastle, Working Paper No 01-24.

Dees, J.G., Emerson, J. and Economy, P. (2001) *Enterprising Nonprofits: A Toolkit for Social Entrepreneurs*, New York, Wiley.

Drayton, W. (2002) 'The Citizen Sector: Becoming As Entrepreneurial and Competitive As Business', *California Management Review*, Vol. 45, No. 4, 120–32.

Eikenberry, A.M. and Kluver, J.D. (2004) 'The Marketization of the Nonprofit Sector: Civil Society At Risk', *Public Administration Review*, Vol. 64, 132–40.

Francis, D.H. and Sandberg, W.R. (2000) 'Friendship Within Entrepreneurial Teams and Its Association With Team and Venture Performance', *Entrepreneurship Theory and Practice*, Vol. 25, No. 2, 5–26.

Grossman, A. and Currin, D. (2002) *EMCF: A New Approach At An Old Foundation*, Harvard Business School Publishing Case Study No. 9-302-090.

Himmelman, A.T. (1996) 'On The Theory and Practice of Transformational Collaboration: From Social Service To Social Justice', in Huxham, C. (ed.) *Creating Collaborative Advantage*, London, Sage.

Kanter, R.M. and Summers, D.V. (1987) 'Doing Well While Doing Good: Dilemmas of Performance Measurement in Non-Profit Organizations and the Need for a Mutiple-Constituency Approach', in Powell, W.H. (ed.) *The Non-Profit Sector: A Research Handbook*, New Haven CN., Yale University Press.

Letts, C.W., Ryan, W.P. and Grossman, A. (1999) *High Performance Non-Profit Organizations That Innovate Naturally*, San Francisco, CA., Jossey-Bass.

Mair, J. and Martí, I. (2006) 'Social Entrepreneurship Research: A Source of Explanation, Prediction and Delight', *Journal of World Business*, Vol. 21, 36–44.

McIlney, D. (1998) *How Foundations Work*, San Francisco, Jossey Bass.

Osberg, S. (2006) 'Wayfinding Without A Compass: Philanthropy's Changing Landscape and Its Implications for Social Entrepreneurs', in Nicholls, A. (ed.) *Social Entrepreneurship: New Models of Sustainable Social Change*, New York, Oxford University Press.

Pearson, N. (2002) Social Entrepreneurship Network Conference—Dinner Address, Carlton Crest, Melbourne, Australia, March, www.partnerships.org.au/library/sen_conf_dinner_address.htm accessed January 2008.

Prabhu, G.H. (1998) 'Social Entrepreneurship Management. Leadership in Management,' www.mcb.co.uk/services/conferenc/sept98/lim/paper_a2.htm accessed January 2008.

Rosenman, M., Scotchmer, K. and Van Benschoten, E. (1999) *Morphing Into The Market: The Danger of Missing Mission*, Washington DC., The Aspen Institute.

Roure, B.R. and Keeley, R.H. (1990) 'Predictors of Success in New Technology Based Ventures', *Journal of Business Venturing*, Vol. 5, 201–20.

Ryan, W.P. (1999) 'The New Landscape for Nonprofits', *Harvard Business Review*, Vol. 77, No. 1, 127–36.

Salamon, L.M. (1993) 'The Marketization of Welfare: Changing Nonprofit and For-Profit Roles in the American Welfare State', *Social Service Review*, Vol. 67, No. 1, 127–36.

Shane, S., Locke, E.A. and Collins, C.J. (2003) 'Entrepreneurial Motivation', *Human Resource Management Review*, Vol. 13, No. 2, 257–79.

Sharir, M. and Lerner, M. (2006) 'Gauging The Success of Social Ventures Initiated By Individual Social Entrepreneurs', *Journal of World Business*, Vol. 41, 6–20.

Schervish, P., O'Herlithy, M. and Havens, J. (2001) 'Agent Animated Wealth and Philanthropy: The Dynamics of Accumulation and Allocation Among High Tech Donors', Presentation to the Association of Fundraising Professionals Annual Conference, April.

Thompson, J., Alvy, G. and Lees, A. (2000) 'Social Entrepreneurship: A New Look At The People and the Potential', *Management Decision*, Vol. 38, No. 5, 328–38.

Venkataraman, S. (1997) 'The Distinctive Domain of Entrepreneurship Research', in Katz, J. and Brockhaus, R. (eds) *Advances in Entrepreneurship: Firm Emergence and Growth*, Vol. 3, Greenwich CT., JAI Press, 119–38.

Waddock, S.A. and Post, J.E. (1991) 'Social Entrepreneurship and Analytic Change', *Public Administration Review*, Vol. 51, No. 5, 393–401.

Weerawardena, J. and Sullivan-Mort, G. (2006) 'Investigating Social Entrepreneurship: A Multi-dimensional Model', *Journal of World Business*, Vol. 41, 21–35.

14 Volunteer Support and Management

OBJECTIVES

By the end of this chapter you should be able to:

1. understand the significance of volunteering to the nonprofit sector;
2. describe current trends in volunteering;
3. identify where volunteers may be recruited from;
4. utilize knowledge of volunteer motivation in a recruitment campaign;
5. develop a volunteer recruitment plan;
6. utilize a range of research findings to develop a volunteer retention strategy.

Introduction

Recent years have seen many changes in the pattern of volunteering across the developed world. Changes in lifestyle, in the numbers of women entering the workforce, and in working patterns have impacted both on the nature of volunteer activity and on the demographic characteristics of typical volunteers. These observations aside, there are few truly global trends in volunteering since the propensity to volunteer and individual volunteer behaviour seem to be a function of the nature of the society in which this takes place. The percentage of adults engaged in volunteering in the UK, for example, has remained pretty static in recent years, while in the USA a downturn has been noted. In the USA 26.2% of the population volunteered during 2006. This compares with 27.4% in 2002.

The reasons for this slight decline are probably a function of the fact that volunteering spiked after September 11 2001 and is now returning to its longer-term norm (Wilhelm 2007). The results will have been disappointing for the Bush administration, however, since the President has expended much effort on getting increasing numbers of people to volunteer and to volunteer for longer. His strategy to achieve this included the establishment of the USA Freedom Corps, which was charged with the task of encouraging Americans to embrace a new 'culture of responsibility' and to commit 4000 hours over their lifetimes to serve their neighbours and country. It should be remembered, however, that the federal government has only been gathering data on volunteering since 2002 so it is probably too early to be drawing any firm conclusions in respect of longer-term trends. Key findings from the Bureau of Labor study are reported in Table 14.1.

Table 14.1 Key findings from the Bureau of Labor statistics on volunteering

	% Men	% Women	% Population	Median annual hours
Age				
16–19	22.5	26.6	24.5	39
20–24	14.4	21.1	17.7	41
25–34	18.2	27.1	22.6	36
35–44	25.6	35.3	30.5	52
45–54	26.6	33.5	30.1	55
55–64	26.0	30.7	28.4	60
65 and over	22.8	24.6	23.8	96
Race				
White	24.2	31.4	27.9	52
Black or African American	15.7	20.2	18.2	60
Asian	16.7	18.5	17.7	36
Hispanic or Latino	10.1	17.2	13.5	48

Source: 2007 Bureau of Labor statistics.

Other key findings from the study included:

- Women continued to volunteer more than men, with 29.3 per cent of females saying they volunteered versus 22.9 per cent of males.

- Married persons volunteer at a higher rate (31.9%) than those who have never been married (19.2%).

- Parents with children under 18 were more likely to assist a nonprofit group than people without children in that age range (33.7% versus 23.2%).

- Individuals with higher levels of educational attainment volunteered at higher rates than did those with less education.

- Churches account for the highest percentage of volunteering (35.6%), followed by youth/education work (26.2%) and social/community service (13.1%).

In England, the most recent government study of volunteering was conducted in 2006 by the Department for Communities and Local Government as part of its citizenship survey. The demographic profile of volunteers for 2005 is reported in Table 14.2.

In this study a distinction is drawn between formal and informal volunteering. Formal volunteering is giving unpaid help through groups, clubs, or organizations to benefit other people or the environment. Informal volunteering is defined as unpaid help as an individual to people who are not relatives. The final column depicts the overall percentage of the population who regularly engaged in at least one form of volunteering during 2005.

More recently in the UK, nfpSynergy (2008) have tracked trends in volunteering from the beginning of the twenty-first century. Their methodology (a telephone survey of 3000 individuals per year) relies on respondents' own perceptions of whether they have volunteered or not. It is interesting to note that substantially lower levels of volunteering are then reported. Their research for the UK in the period 2001–2007 found:

- Levels of volunteering increased from 2001 to 2003 (from 16% to 20%) and have then remained static around the 19% level since then.

Table 14.2 Percentage of people who volunteered at least once a month in the 12 months before interview (England 2005)

		% Informal volunteering	% Formal volunteering	% Volunteering
Gender	Male	32	27	45
	Female	41	31	54
Age	16–19	50	32	63
	20–24	44	26	52
	25–34	37	25	49
	35–49	37	32	51
	50–64	35	30	48
	65–74	37	31	50
	75 and over	29	21	38
Ethnicity	White	37	29	50
	Asian	30	20	39
	Black	41	30	52
	Mixed race	44	34	58
	Chinese/Other	31	20	39

Source: Volunteering England 2005. Reproduced by kind permission of the Stationery Office Ltd.

- As in the USA women are more likely to volunteer than men (21% versus 16%) and there has been little change in this gap over the period.
- In respect of socio-economic groups, ABs remain the most likely to volunteer, although other social groups have begun to catch them up, with CDEs having shown greater increases in volunteering over the period.
- Volunteering has increased among 16–44 year olds and levels have remained flat among 45–54s and 65+s. Notably 55–64 is the only age group among which volunteering has shown an overall decrease. Their data in this respect is reported in Figure 14.1.

It seems clear from the statistics on both sides of the Atlantic that the incidence of volunteering is generally high, although there are obviously very wide fluctuations in reporting depending on how volunteering is defined and whether individuals are left to self-report their activities or prompted with specific definitions of what this may include. Even conservative estimates, however, suggest that one-fifth of the population has volunteered at least once for a nonprofit in the preceding three months. Thus voluntary activity appears to touch the lives of a great many people as they seek to help others in their community. As we shall see, however, these figures belie a number of uncomfortable facts about the nature of volunteering and how organizations treat the individuals who elect to donate their time. Levels of volunteer attrition are high and levels of satisfaction with the work they undertake are relatively low. Nonprofits have a long way to go to meet the needs of these individuals and in particular to improve the way they market themselves to such individuals, both before and after recruitment (Bennett and Barkensjo 2005).

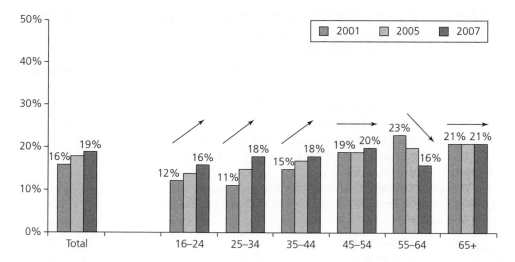

Figure 14.1 Volunteering by age
'Have you given time as a volunteer in the last three months, to a charity or other organization, or in your local community?' Yes—by age.
Base: 3,000 adults 16+, Britain, 2007.

Source: Charity Awareness Monitor, nfpSynergy. Reproduced with kind permission.

Recruiting Volunteers

Identifying the Need

The starting point for many organizations in the recruitment of volunteers lies in determining the tasks that volunteers might legitimately be able to perform. As a consequence organizations commonly begin by asking 'What can volunteers do around here?' This approach is overly simplistic and Jackson (2001) highlights three major weaknesses of adopting this perspective:

- An organization can screen out potential options based on staff's own beliefs about volunteer competence. Sadly, research has consistently shown that staff often undervalue volunteer input and perceive significantly lower levels of competence than is the case (Fisher and Cole 1993).

- An organization can run the risk of inventing work for volunteers to do, so that they have got something to give them, rather than because it genuinely requires such input.

- Volunteers can be used as a vehicle for offloading the most burdensome or mundane tasks the organization must carry out, resulting in poor motivation and a high post-recruitment attrition (or turnover) rate.

Instead the author recommends that the following process be adopted.

- Staff and volunteers should be asked to list the things they do in their job, or in a specific area of their job. It is important that this process be as precise as possible (i.e. answering the phone, filing etc., rather than simply saying 'admin').

- Using this list as a backdrop, staff and volunteers should then be asked to indicate which of their tasks they like doing, which they dislike doing, and which they should be doing. They should also be asked why they hold these views.

- Staff and existing volunteers should then be asked to create a 'wish list' of things that they would ideally like to be able to achieve, and that they wish the nonprofit could achieve if it/they had the time, skills, money etc.

Jackson argues that this data provides fertile ground in which to evaluate the need for volunteers and to ensure, where such new roles are created, that a genuinely meaningful post, with a number of potentially enjoyable tasks, can be developed. The involvement of existing volunteers in this process is key because it furnishes management with a detailed insight into what currently motivates volunteers and what might motivate them in the future. Using this data to define a potentially satisfying role lies at the heart of the concept of internal marketing, as discussed in Chapter 2.

Having identified the nature of the role to be created, a nonprofit will then be in a position to develop a job description. At a minimum such job descriptions typically comprise the following elements.

Title

Organizations should avoid 'volunteer' and use the nature of the role as the basis for providing an appropriate job title.

Overall Purpose

The job description should explain what the purpose of the role will be, how it relates to other roles in the organization, and the contribution that it will make to the achievement of the mission.

Activities and Key Outputs

This section of the job description maps out the tasks that the volunteer will fulfil and the measures of success that will be used to gauge their performance. Some organizations map out a range of suggested activities to achieve the outputs rather than being prescriptive. This allows the volunteer some flexibility and respects the fact that individuals can often bring a substantial amount of personal and subject expertise to their role.

Supervision

It will also be important to specify the individual or individuals to whom the volunteer will report. In some cases this can be a supervisor in the functional part of the organization in which they are working, or it may be a specialized volunteer service coordinator (VSC). While the use of a VSC can assist in certain circumstances because such individuals have a good understanding of the nature of volunteering, it can often be better for volunteers to be supervised directly by the 'line supervisor' in whose department they are working. The reason for this is simply that the volunteer can then feel an integral part of the team rather than an outsider, donating their time.

Benefits

The job description should outline the benefits that will accrue as a result of the individual volunteering their time. In the USA, these benefits can have considerable value, with volunteers being remunerated by vouchers (for use in local stores) or some form of allowance. In the UK, where the legal definition of a volunteer is a little different, direct remuneration is avoided as a contract of employment can thereby be created and conditions such as the national minimum wage would then apply. Formal benefits in the UK are rare and where they are available they are typically tied to the cause. Volunteers to a heritage charity, for example, may qualify for free or reduced entry to the site for themselves and members of their family.

Timeframe and Site

The job description will contain the details of where the volunteer will work, the hours it is expected that they will contribute, and for how long they will continue to work in this capacity. While some volunteer posts involve an open-ended commitment, many organizations are realizing that modern lifestyles no longer permit this level of commitment and that an open-ended need might dissuade volunteers. There may thus be circumstances where a specific timeframe is included in the job description so that both parties know from the outset how long the arrangement will last.

Arrangements for Reimbursement of Out-of-Pocket Expenses

A good job description will also contain a summary of the categories of expenses that will be reimbursed (e.g. travel) and the typical length of time it will take the organization to reimburse the volunteer. This is considered good practice because a clear statement from the outset can prevent any future misunderstandings (Fisher and Cole 1993).

Equal Opportunities Statement

Finally, every job description should contain an equal opportunities statement, which spells out the organization's stance on recruiting individuals with disabilities or from minority groups. It is important to note that this should be more than a simple statement of policy from the trustees of the organization; it should also be backed up with training to staff, to ensure that the reality of volunteer recruitment is grounded in this statement.

These are the basic components of a volunteer job description. From a marketing perspective, it is important to recognize that this document will play a critical role in persuading appropriate individuals to apply (or not!). The best job descriptions therefore move beyond these basics and are written in such a way as to reflect the marketing role many undoubtedly play. At its simplest level, this means that job descriptions should move beyond a simple list of uninspiring tasks. Jackson (2001) argues that job descriptions should explain how the tasks the volunteer must perform fit into the larger picture of what the organization does and in particular how the responsibilities of the post will assist in the achievement of the mission. He also advocates focusing on results rather than tasks, so that where appropriate the volunteer can have some flexibility over how his role is performed. A brief example is provided on the next page.

Of course, the job description is only half of the recruitment equation. It is now common practice to develop a person specification which translates the role that will be performed into a series of skills and abilities that will be necessary to satisfactorily complete that role. Person specifications thus address the likely demographic profile of the volunteer, their skills and abilities, their availability, and any motivational needs they might have. As we shall see later in this chapter, volunteers can be motivated by a variety of perceived needs (e.g. to develop new skills, to acquire new social contacts) and the organization may have a preference, in a particular role, for someone who is motivated by a specific need. This should be specified and used to inform the recruitment process. Person specifications normally distinguish desirable characteristics from essential characteristics. As we shall see later, this distinction can be enormously helpful in performing an initial screen of completed applications.

Sources of Volunteers

All of the leading writers on volunteer management, such as Govekar and Govekar (2007) or Wymer and Starnes (2001a), make the fundamental point that for volunteers to be attracted to an organization they have to be asked. While this might seem a little facile, some

---

OVERALL PURPOSE

To keep fundraising staff up-to-date on internal and external volunteering issues by producing a monthly newsletter, *Volunteering News.*

Key Result

Volunteering News will be a dynamic publication, promoting, networking, and allowing volunteer managers to share successes and learn from each other.

Suggested Activities

Undertake internal marketing of *Volunteering News* to ensure the readership is aware of the networking potential of the publication.

Measures of Success

By (a certain date), a third of the internal news articles will be from volunteer managers other than the editor or volunteer development manager.

By (a certain date) a letters/networking section will be a regular feature.

Source: Jackson 2001: 5–6

---

organizations either shy away from approaching likely volunteer prospects, or fail to utilize the network of contacts that the organization already has. The 1997 National Survey of Volunteering in England showed that 50 per cent of the people who did volunteer did so because they were asked, and similar percentages have been reported in the USA. All staff and existing volunteers may thus have a part to play in identifying appropriate individuals who might be able to assist the organization.

If utilizing this network of contacts is impractical, or existing links have already been exhausted, Wymer and Starnes (2001a) argue that volunteer recruitment can then be achieved either directly or indirectly. Direct recruitment consists of a nonprofit reaching out directly to potential volunteers through activities such as advertising, direct marketing, publicity, events, and public speaking engagements.

Indirect recruitment occurs when other institutions are used as intermediaries to assist in the process of recruitment. Many communities now have volunteer referral centres which act as a focal point for individuals who are interested in giving up their time. These referral centres promote community volunteering and keep a wealth of up-to-date information about the opportunities available (Ellis 1989).

In the search for volunteers it is important that a nonprofit exploit all the opportunities that may exist for indirect recruitment through third parties. The rationale here is simply that scarce resources need not be wasted on an activity that can be better accomplished by another organization. Authors such as Ellis (1994) and Senior Corps (2008) cite the Retired and Senior Volunteer Program (RSVP) in the USA as one such example. It acts as a clearing-house for 'seniors' who are looking for opportunities to volunteer and are unsure of where they might apply and how their skills might be used. In the UK there is a network of volunteer bureaux that provide this function and Councils for Voluntary Service (CVS). There is also Timebank, a national charity that aims to get more people volunteering across the country. Timebank works with a number of partners to achieve this goal, including the BBC and 'Do-It', the

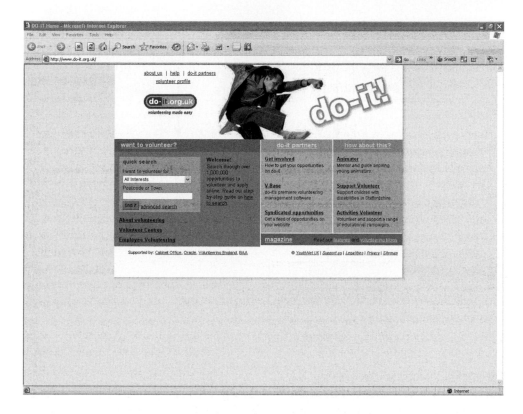

Figure 14.2 Do-It national volunteering database

Source: © 2008 youthnet.org. Reproduced with kind permission.

national volunteering database, found online at www.do-it.org.uk. Do-It offers a postcode-searchable database featuring over 850,000 volunteering opportunities from major charities such as the National Trust and Oxfam and local voluntary and public-sector organizations. This is illustrated in Figure 14.2.

All these intermediaries specialize in fostering volunteering and have missions both to promote volunteering as an activity and to broker links between volunteers and potential beneficiary organizations. Equally, nonprofits can foster indirect recruitment by looking to other organizations with complementary missions whose members might have an interest in volunteering for the cause. Scouting groups, Lions Clubs, and Rotary Clubs might all have a role to play here, and may prove to be fruitful sources of volunteers.

The Communication Process

Having defined the nature of the role and determined the volunteer characteristics that would be desirable to meet these needs, the organization can then turn its attention to recruiting the right individual(s). At this point it needs to decide whether it will attempt to recruit individuals directly, or whether it would be better to operate through intermediary groups or organizations, as outlined above. Irrespective of the approach adopted, the organization must be clear about what it has to offer and the volunteer needs it could meet. It must then translate this into a strong recruitment message, which in the case of direct recruitment would form the

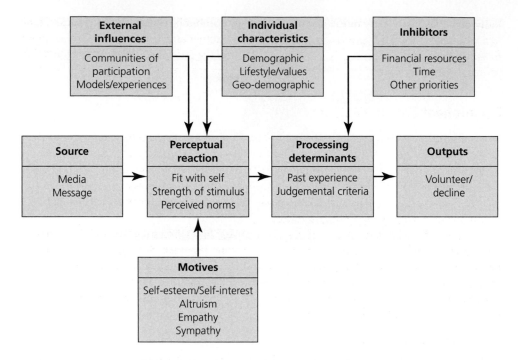

Figure 14.3 The communication process

basis of a campaign, and with indirect recruitment the fundamental nature of the proposition that can be passed on through third parties.

To structure our discussion of the communication process we will employ the model depicted in Figure 14.3. Here the recruitment communication is generated by the nonprofit and directed at individuals most likely to have an interest in supporting the organization. A good way of achieving this is to look at the profile of the existing volunteer base and to attempt to target others who appear to match the characteristics of existing volunteers. Organizations can also look back over the campaigns they have run in the past and refine both the quality of their targeting and the nature of communications they create.

Whatever form the ask might eventually take, there are a variety of variables which the literature suggests will tend to impact on a potential volunteer's perceptual reaction to the message being conveyed. The key variables here are the fit of the charity with a given donor's self-image, the existence of perceived norms of behaviour in their social group, and the strength of the stimulus the nonprofit is able to generate.

If the message survives this initial 'filter' and is perceived as being potentially relevant, a more cognitive decision-making process is entered into. Here, the literature suggests that two key categories of variable will impact on the manner in which the volunteering decision is processed: the individual's past experience with the nonprofit (if any), and the criteria that he might use to evaluate potential organizations for support. If the outcome from this cognitive process is favourable, the model concludes that the individual will elect to offer his support to the organization.

Of course, life isn't this neat! There are a number of personal and interpersonal influences that can either enhance a volunteer's motivation to respond or detract from it. Equally, an individual may be strongly motivated to offer her support but be constrained by a lack of time or pressure from other life priorities. The decision of whether and how to respond to a request to volunteer time is thus highly complex. In the next section we will employ the model shown in Figure 14.3 as a framework to consider the lessons from recent volunteer research.

Recruitment Communications

As the model indicates, there are two key facets to the communication for consideration. The first is the medium that will be employed, the second the nature of the message that will be imparted. Extant research has consistently shown that face-to-face requests to donate time are the most effective at engendering support. Other media lag way behind this in terms of effectiveness. Peer-to-peer 'asks' from staff, recruiters, and particularly other volunteers are thus a powerful way of expanding support.

In respect of the message that should be conveyed, Ellis (1994) suggests that designing an appropriate recruitment communication is a far from easy task. She argues that organizations can frequently sound 'desperate' to recruit the help that they need and that the very act of appearing so desperate may put off some individuals from offering their time.

Rather than conveying desperation, extant research suggests that recruitment messages should be upbeat and convey three distinct categories of information:

1. the importance of the cause;
2. the efficacy of the programme of work the organization undertakes;
3. the benefits that the post would offer the volunteer (e.g. feeling useful/productive, or the social interaction that would be afforded) (Wymer 1999; Okun 1994).

An example of a volunteer recruitment communication is presented in Figure 14.4. Notice how each of these three themes are reflected in the content.

Volunteers needed for nonprofit chapter launch in Philly
On Your Feet Project (OYFP), a national 501(c)(3)-recognized nonprofit organization, is launching a chapter in Philadelphia. OYFP is entirely volunteer-run, and currently has chapters in New York and San Francisco. In these cities, OYFP builds partnerships with other nonprofit organizations and sponsors events on their behalf. These programs generate public awareness for the partner organizations, while also providing a way for young people to learn about the causes that partner organizations support and to get involved in the community. For example, in 2003, OYFP ran 17 events, including art and photography shows, concerts, film screenings, and comedy jams, benefiting nine nonprofit organizations, such as Direct Relief International, HELP USA, and the Urban Justice Center.

I am looking for people who would like to get involved with OYFP Philadelphia in any way, from being a part of the leadership of the organization, to helping to plan events, to just attending events. If you are interested in this exciting opportunity to make a difference in the community while meeting other like-minded individuals, please contact Jessica Merlin at jessica@onyourfeetproject.org. If you know of anyone else who might be interested in getting involved, feel free to forward this message. For further information about the organization, feel free to visit our website at **www.onyourfeetproject.org**.

For more information contact Jessica Merlin at (215) 806-1888 or write to:

On Your Feet Project
Center City
Philadelphia, PA 19103

Figure 14.4 Example volunteer recruitment communication
Source: © 2008 On Your Feet Project.

Perceptual Reaction

As we discussed above, whether the recruitment communication will be perceived as relevant to the potential volunteer will be a function of the fit of the nonprofit with a given individual's self-image, the existence of perceived norms of behaviour in their social group, and the strength of the stimulus the organization is able to generate.

In respect of the first variable—fit with desired self-image—Coliazzi et al. (1984) noted that individuals are more likely to help those who are perceived as being similar to themselves. They will thus tend to filter those messages from nonprofits existing to support disparate segments of society. The extremely wealthy, for example, tend to avoid causes involving the poor, such as homelessness, and are much more likely to support organizations that they, or members of their social class, can benefit from. Similarly, Millet and Orosz (2001) identified that people from ethnic minorities are significantly more likely to filter out messages from nonprofits not serving members of their community.

A factor closely related to the above is the issue of perceived norms. There is considerable evidence that volunteers will be motivated to filter messages on the basis of normative concerns (Morgan et al. 1979). People appear to pay considerable attention to what others contribute within their respective societal group and are thus significantly less likely to volunteer if they do not see others taking similar action. In an interesting study of volunteer behaviour, Fisher and Ackerman (1998) found that perceived norms were key in triggering volunteering behaviour where the voluntary action was perceived to be important to the group's welfare and where the volunteer was motivated by the potential for social recognition.

The strength of the stimulus can also be an issue. Clearly the stronger the stimulus generated by a particular nonprofit, the easier it will be for it to cut through competing messages from other organizations. To achieve this, a number of factors need to be considered. The first is the perceived urgency of the need. In general, high degrees of urgency would appear to engender high degrees of support (see, for example, Newman 1977; Pancer et al. 1979). It would also appear that approaches that build up the degree of personal responsibility are more effective at engendering a response (see Geer and Jermecky 1973). Clear and unambiguous requests for support are similarly more likely to engender compliance than those that are vague or general in nature (Clark and Word 1972).

Processing Determinants

The model suggests that potentially relevant messages will be subjected to a further and perhaps more cognitive decision-making process. Two key factors warrant consideration here: an individual's past experience with an organization, and the decision-making criteria they will apply.

In respect of the former, a variety of authors have argued that once a link is forged with a nonprofit, a given individual will be significantly more likely to help again in the future and to help in a variety of different ways (e.g. Kaehler and Sargeant 1998). A good source of 'new' volunteers can therefore be individuals who have volunteered in the past, or individuals who have been involved in campaigning/lobbying or even donating funds to the organization in the past. Of course this presupposes that the individual's experience will have been a happy one; if they were dissatisfied in some way, they are highly unlikely to wish to renew their association.

In respect of the conscious decision-making criteria that might be applied, there is a clear link here between the individual's motives for support (which we shall discuss below) and whether the individual believes these are likely to be met. Individuals might also evaluate potential recipient organizations on the basis of the extent to which they believe that the organization is doing good work and having the promised impact on the beneficiary group. There is evidence that the perceived efficiency of the organization (i.e. not 'squandering' resources on fundraising and administration) can also have a role to play in deciding whether support will be offered (Glaser 1994).

Motives

Economists have long argued that volunteers take decisions in respect of their support by reference to the degree of utility they will attain (Collard 1978). Under this view, volunteers will select charities to support on the basis of whether they have benefited in the past or believe that they will in the future (Frisch and Gerrard 1981). Individuals could, for example, volunteer for those organizations that will do them political good and/or serve to enhance their career, perhaps through the networking opportunities that will be accorded (Amos 1982). Volunteers may also evaluate potential recipient organizations against the extent to which their support will be visible, or noticeable by others within their social group, thereby enhancing the volunteer's standing (Cnaan and Goldberg-Glen 1991).

Sargeant and Jay (2004) argue that volunteers can also derive utility from:

- the ability to make a difference;
- the ability to enhance their self-worth or self-esteem;
- the ability to obtain experiences that can be useful in paid employment;
- the ability to meet others—it is interesting to note that women appear to derive more social rewards from volunteering than men (Ricks and Pyke 1973);
- the ability to prepare for a volunteer 'career' after retirement;
- the ability to get inside institutions and organizations and ensure that they are doing what they profess to be doing.

Many of these themes are reported in the conclusions of other empirical work. In a study of the motives for volunteering for charity shops, for example, Horne and Broadbridge (1994) found that key motives included the opportunity to meet people and make friends. The researchers also found that this form of volunteering could follow as a consequence of previous retail experience.

A number of psychosocial motives for supporting organizations by volunteering time have also been reported. In particular, individuals are significantly more likely to volunteer if they can empathize with the recipient group (Eisenberg and Miller 1987; Mount and Quirion 1988) or have sympathy with them (Clary and Synder 1991; Schwartz 1977).

Clearly one or more of these motives can be specifically addressed in a recruitment campaign.

Individual Characteristics

In the introduction to this chapter the demographic profile of a typical volunteer was addressed in both the UK and the USA. Organizations can use either this generic profile or (ideally) the profile of their existing volunteer base to ensure that messages are appropriately targeted. As the model suggests, the demographic profile of the recipients of a recruitment message will drive in no small measure the extent to which they perceive it as being relevant.

These general comments aside, Ellis (1994) suggests that the demographic variable 'lifestage' may have a particularly key role to play in volunteering. The author argues that as adults enter a new stage, they look for ways of giving meaning to their lives and enhancing their self-worth. Thus moving from a stage where they have children at home to the empty-nest syndrome can prompt a re-evaluation, as can a move from paid employment into retirement.

A number of psychographic variables have also been highlighted as distinguishing volunteers from non-volunteers, with the topic of individual values receiving undoubtedly the most attention to date (Heidrich 1988; Williams 1987).

Values are beliefs about what is important in life. They:

- are relatively few in number;
- serve as a guide for culturally appropriate behaviour;
- are enduring or difficult to change;
- are not tied to specific situations; and
- are widely accepted by the members of a society (Rokeach 1973).

They are thus broad beliefs that affect individual attitudes to other people, organizations, objects, or circumstances and in the context of volunteering would be likely to drive how a person might respond to a communication message.

One of the most widely cited categorizations of consumer values was developed by Rokeach (1973). It is depicted in Figure 14.5.

A number of authors have employed this categorization to distinguish between volunteers and non-volunteers and concluded that volunteers generally place a higher degree of importance on the pro-social values in this list (see, for example, McClintock and Allison 1989).

Terminal	**Inner harmony**
Comfortable life	(freedom from inner conflict)
(a prosperous life)	**Mature love**
An exciting life	(sexual and spiritual intimacy)
(a stimulating, active life)	**National security**
Sense of accomplishment	(protection from attack)
(lasting contribution)	**Pleasure**
World at peace	(an enjoyable, leisurely life)
(free of war and conflict)	**Salvation**
World of beauty	(saved, eternal life)
(beauty of nature and the arts)	**Self-respect**
Equality	(self-esteem)
(brotherhood, equal opportunity for all)	**Social recognition**
Family security	(respect, admiration)
(taking care of loved ones)	**True friendship**
Freedom	(close companionship)
(independence, free choice)	**Wisdom**
Happiness	(a mature understanding of life)
(contentedness)	

Figure 14.5 Categorization of consumer values

Source: Rokeach (1973). Reproduced by kind permission.

Marketers may thus reflect these values in their recruitment communications, indicating how a given role might aid in the attainment or expression of a particular value.

In a further use of Rokeach's work, Wymer and Samu (2002: 983) studied differences in values between male and female volunteers. They conclude that of the eight values for which there were significant differences between the two groups, female volunteers weighted the values of a 'sense of accomplishment', 'world at peace', and 'mature love' more heavily. The values of 'a world of beauty', 'self-respect', 'social recognition', and 'true friendship' were weighted more heavily by male volunteers.

Their findings suggest that there may be a need to segment volunteer recruitment messages by gender and to appeal to a number of specific individual values in each communication. Of course, it is important to recognize that this research was conducted in the USA and that values are, by definition, culture-specific. The same results may therefore not be observed in Europe or indeed any other country.

External Influences

Individual behaviour can also be shaped by the events that an individual experiences during the course of their life, in particular their early life. In the context of volunteering, it is therefore likely that models and experiences from one's youth will shape future adult behaviour. Thus those who were helped by volunteers themselves or who grew up in a family with a strong tradition of volunteering are significantly more likely to exhibit such behaviours (Smith and Baldwin 1974).

In looking for external influences on behaviour, however, it is also necessary to look beyond the immediate family group. Wider communities of participation may be of relevance. These are defined as networks of formal and informal relationships entered into either by choice or by circumstance (e.g. schools, soup kitchens, soccer groups) that bring an individual into contact with need (Schervish 1993; 1997). Individuals will be predisposed to support causes connected in some way with these communities. Lohmann (1992), for example, found that helping behaviour was frequently related to personal membership of networks, societies, political groups, social movements, or religious, artistic, or scientific communities.

A Gallup survey concluded that above-average levels of volunteering were reported by those who had:

- been active in student government;
- gone door-to-door fundraising;
- previously undertaken volunteer work;
- always wanted to make a change in society;
- belonged to a youth group or similar;
- seen someone they admired (other than a family member) help others;
- been helped by others themselves (Gallup 1992).

Writers such as Wymer (1996) have shown that individuals who have social contact with existing volunteers are significantly more likely to respond positively to a request to volunteer themselves. Data from Independent Sector (2000) confirms this, with 90 per cent of people being asked to serve by their peers accepting the role. Of course it is not just contact with volunteers that can predispose individuals to agreeing to offer their own time. Emotional contact with the cause or issue itself can prompt volunteering behaviour. Wymer and

Starnes (1999) found that a high proportion of hospice volunteers learned about opportunities to help when a friend or loved one had been terminally ill. In such circumstances, the need to volunteer can be a response to the death of someone they cared for.

Barriers

Even where an individual might otherwise be motivated to volunteer their time and respond to a recruitment solicitation, there are a number of barriers that can prevent them from agreeing to participate. The issue of time poverty is particularly critical here. Modern lifestyles are such that many individuals do not believe they have enough spare time to volunteer. Schindler-Rainman (1988: 153) argues that typical volunteers of the future will be 'less willing to commit themselves to open-ended long-term volunteer assignments. Instead what they will seek out are volunteer roles that have a fixed end-date and a measurable outcome, and give evidence of making a real contribution to the problems facing society . . .'.

As a consequence, programmes need to include both short- and long-term places for volunteers, so that persons who cannot commit themselves for long periods will not be lost as a human resource for the programme.

There are also issues of distance and safety (Wymer and Starnes 2001a). Many volunteers otherwise willing to help may not be willing to travel far from their home. They may prefer instead to seek other opportunities to volunteer that do not require them to travel. Equally, in some contexts, individuals may be concerned with their own safety. Working with individuals with mental illness or substance abuse problems, for example, can be perceived as unsafe even if adequate safeguards exist, or where the risk is illusory. Both these issues have the capacity to block willingness to engage with an organization.

The Recruitment Process

The typical volunteer recruitment process is presented in Figure 14.6. Once a recruitment campaign has been conducted and completed application forms received, it will be necessary to subject the applications to an initial screening. This is typically done by comparing the person specification (described earlier) with the personal details supplied by the applicants. In the author's experience few, if any, applicants meet all of the desirable characteristics outlined in the person specification, but the organization should find a few that do meet all of the essential criteria they outlined and exhibit one or more of the desirable characteristics. References from these applicants may then be applied for (criminal record checks included if appropriate) and these can either be considered in advance of an interview, or alongside an interview. Those candidates deemed suitable at interview and who can provide satisfactory references will then be put through an induction/training programme and, if appropriate, placed on probation for a specific period of time after which their appointment can be confirmed.

Induction

Induction is a critical part of the recruitment process as it allows the organization to brief the volunteer on its history, mission, and the nature of the role they will perform. It is important as it serves to explain how the role the volunteer will perform forms part of the organization as a whole. It also provides the volunteer with all the information and initial skills they might need to satisfactorily carry out their role. In the context of palliative care, for example, the National Council for Hospice and Specialist Palliative Care Services (NCHSPCS) (1996)

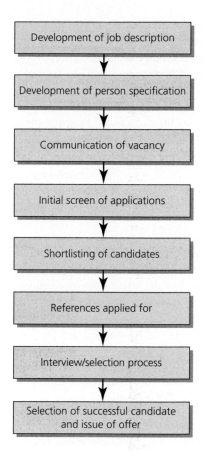

Figure 14.6 Volunteer recruitment process

advocates the provision of an introduction to voluntary service work that ensures that the key principles of palliative care are properly understood, namely:

- focus on quality of life;
- whole-person approach;
- care encompasses both the dying person and those who matter to that person;
- patient autonomy and choice;
- emphasis on open and sensitive communication.

Such training leaves no one in any doubt as to what is expected regarding confidentiality, professionalism, or maintaining the organization's good image and reputation.

However, as Ratje (2003: 17) notes, 'nonprofit organizations often rely on volunteers as a vital component of their interaction with clients and potential donors. Yet selection, training and motivation for volunteers can be poor or non-existent.'

This will undoubtedly lead to poor performance and can give rise to a great deal of dissatisfaction on the part of the volunteer, who might ultimately decide to quit. A lack of formal training can also place the organization in breach of legal requirements since there may, for example, be a requirement for basic health and safety education. From a marketing perspective, the failure to induct the volunteer presents further problems, one of which I have already alluded to above. To quote Ratje (2003: 17) once more: 'imagine a potential donor for a homeless shelter who walks in the door with a checkbook in hand, but then speaks with a volunteer who knows little about the mission, the tax deductability of the donation or just has a bad attitude.' The impact on the organization's brand image and ability to fundraise would obviously be profound, and yet successive studies have found that a lack of training or induction is one of the most cited problem areas by volunteers (Wymer and Starnes 2001b). It would thus appear that the nonprofit sector has much to do to improve these aspects of volunteer management. For a detailed consideration of induction/training issues, the reader is advised to consult a specialist text such as Fisher and Cole (1993) or Doyle (2002).

Retaining Volunteers

Many organizations struggle to retain volunteers. Turnover rates in excess of 100 per cent have been reported by some in the course of a typical year. To calculate the rate of turnover, the following formula is typically used. It was developed by the US Department of Labor for the purposes of measuring staff turnover rates in the private sector, but it is equally applicable to a nonprofit context (Mathis and Jackson 1982).

$$\frac{\text{[Number of volunteer separations during the year]}}{\text{[Total number of volunteers at midyear]}} \times 100$$

There are also more subtle problems created by high turnover rates. High turnover occurs for a reason and a high turnover can suggest that there is something wrong with the role the volunteer is being asked to perform or the circumstances in which it is being conducted. The environment could be over-challenging (or, at the other extreme, very dull) or it may be unfriendly or unsupportive. All these things can come back to haunt an organization as a dissatisfied volunteer will likely tell many of their friends about their poor experience. In short, a high turnover rate can impact negatively on an organization's brand or reputation.

Interestingly, research tells us that volunteers are most likely to quit after three months, six months, and twelve months of volunteering (Fischer and Schaffer 1993). The authors tell us that this occurs because volunteers begin their work in a honeymoon stage of euphoria, but regress to 'post-honeymoon blues' after gaining some experience. After longer periods of time, they are likely to quit because they were not able to accomplish what they had hoped or because the organization doesn't represent the values they thought it did on joining.

We also know that some categories of volunteers are more likely to experience turnover than others. Heidrich (1988) identified that fraternal service organizations, veterans' organizations, and cooperatives had a lower turnover than most groups, while youth-serving organizations had a higher turnover.

Sources of Dissatisfaction

We have already alluded to a number of sources of volunteer dissatisfaction, but it is worth elaborating for a moment on what the literature suggests are the key reasons volunteers quit working for nonprofit organizations. Wymer and Starnes (2001b) provide a helpful summary of the available research and suggest that the following factors are common causes of turnover.

Unreal Expectations

The volunteer may find that the work he has been asked to do does not meet his initial expectations. This could clearly be the fault of either the nonprofit or the individual himself. The individual could have approached the work with an overly optimistic view of what could be accomplished, or the nonprofit could have painted too glowing a picture of the time commitment, type of work, or probable impact on the cause.

Lack of Appreciative Feedback from Clients and Co-Workers

There is evidence that many volunteers feel undervalued by either the nonprofit or its clients.

Lack of Appropriate Training and Supervision

A number of volunteers quit because they feel unsupported by the organization or ill-equipped to perform the duties they have been requested to undertake. Problems can also arise with supervision since, as we noted earlier, organizations must make tough decisions about whether to supervise the volunteer as a volunteer, or whether to have them supervised by the line manager in the service department in which they are working. The balance of evidence is that volunteers prefer the latter, so that they can feel part of a team, but the real lesson from the literature is that 'it depends' and as a consequence the issue must be approached with some sensitivity (Leviton et al. 2006).

Excessive Demands on Time

Some volunteers find that longer hours are required than they had originally envisaged, or that the work they are undertaking encroaches on their home life and eats into the time available for other leisure pursuits.

Lack of Personal Accomplishment

Equally, some volunteers discover that the post is not as personally rewarding as they had originally thought. Perhaps there is less opportunity to learn new skills, or they are simply unable to make the difference they had hoped for (Kaufman et al. 2004).

Burnout/Emotional Exhaustion

Some volunteers find themselves physically and psychologically exhausted by their role. Others find that the role evokes excessive anxiety, which impacts on their home life. Volunteers working in human service environments, particularly those related to substance abuse programmes, the mentally ill, or the critically ill are significantly more likely to quit for this reason (Lafer 1991).

Fear of Liability

Kadlec (1998) identified that up to 10 per cent of volunteers are worried about liability issues. These include concerns about being held responsible for:

gross negligence, poor decisions involving the organization's funds, conflicts of interest to include taking advantage of a financial opportunity at the expense of the nonprofit or any kind of self-dealing without proper disclosure, not ensuring the organization is carrying out its mission as articulated to government agencies, spending donations for purposes other than what they were given for, damages in personal injury cases and not complying with rules and regulations set by federal, state and local governments, such as lobbying restrictions and building codes (Wolf 1990: 52–3).

Such are the scales of these concerns that US Congress has now passed the Volunteer Protection Act to provide some immunity from these issues.

Stigmatization

A number of volunteers will quit because they fear that long-term involvement will leave them stigmatized in their communities if they continue to work for what might be perceived as 'unpopular causes' (Kadlec 1998). Snyder et al. (1999) quote the examples of AIDS charities and those dealing with drug/substance abuse.

Feelings of Second-Class Status with Respect to Full-Time Staff

A common issue raised by dissatisfied volunteers is their relationship with paid staff. Many report being treated as in some sense inferior to paid staff, despite the fact that their time was being volunteered, rather than paid for.

This latter point warrants some elaboration. As Sargeant and Jay (2004) note, the interface between staff and volunteers can be a particular source of conflict. Staff are often critical of the attitude of volunteers, who can appear to be:

- short-term members of the team and therefore not likely to assume responsibility for the long-term repercussions of their activity;
- insufficiently aware of the workings and ethics of the organization and thus likely to make mistakes when representing it;
- unwilling to take direction or guidance.

The attitude of management with regard to volunteers is thus absolutely critical. By setting an example, in the way that they treat volunteers, they can be key to the maintenance of good relations between paid and unpaid staff. The optimum attitude is to treat volunteers entirely straightforwardly and as much as possible like paid professional staff. This should encompass full training, opportunities for development and advancement, and the setting and monitoring of targets, benchmarks, and goals. This 'professionalization' of volunteering is challenging for nonprofits, and carries significant costs, but experienced organizations maintain that it brings results and greatly reduces turnover. 'The steady transformation of the volunteer from well-meaning amateur to trained, professional unpaid staff member is the most significant development in the nonprofit sector' (Drucker 1990).

Retention Strategies

Given the range of issues highlighted above, nonprofits need to give adequate consideration to the issues that might arise in all the volunteer roles they are creating and seek to minimize the opportunity for things to go wrong. As we have just noted, the role of management is key, but so too is the creation of processes that effectively integrate volunteers into the organization and into the systems that are often in place to assist paid staff in dealing with many of these issues.

While the following list is not exhaustive, the volunteer management literature suggests that the following points are worthy of consideration.

1. *Screening.* The process of screening applicants for volunteer posts should be rigorous. Every effort must be taken to filter out individuals who are not physically or psychologically suited to the role that has been created. Individuals can also be screened out who have unrealistic expectations, or whose motivation seems unsuited to the role.

2. *Matching.* Every effort must be taken to match volunteers with particular roles. As we noted earlier, every role should contain some pleasant tasks alongside the boring and mundane. Variety should be created, and this should be matched to the needs of specific individuals wherever possible.

3. *Tenure*. This is a simple point, but surprisingly effective if actioned. Stittleburg (1994) notes that volunteers are significantly less likely to quit a project where a specific end-date has been supplied (i.e. they are significantly more likely to work out their contract). It appears that a fixed-term obligation is more likely to be honoured than an open-ended commitment.

4. *Support*. Throughout this chapter the opportunities to provide greater support to volunteers have been highlighted. The literature suggests that the following points are among the most critical to address.

Communication

Applebaum (1992) tells us that volunteers suffer from difficulty contacting staff, a lack of feedback from case workers, concerns about value of written reports, a misunderstanding of policies or procedures, and not being briefed properly by staff. It is essential that volunteers, irrespective of the hours that they work (which can often be why such problems occur—since they may not be on site when staff briefings take place), are party to the same internal communications as paid staff.

Inclusion in Decision Making

Volunteers should be invited to participate in any staff consultations the organization may undertake—and be invited to offer suggestions for service improvements in the same way as paid staff.

Supervision

Irrespective of the line approach adopted, supervision must be friendly, accessible, and supportive (Applebaum 1992).

Recognition Programmes

Nonprofits may either create a formal recognition system or deal with recognition on a more ad hoc basis as the need arises. Simple communications, such as notes of thanks, a mention in a newsletter or internal paper, or an expression of gratitude to a spouse or employer have all been found to be effective forms of recognition. Other nonprofits have nominated volunteers for external awards, displayed positive client comments on noticeboards, or created a graduated reward programme, such as providing passes to community parks and recreation areas and passing on coupons from local businesses. Also, certificates, pins, and recognition dinners form the backbone of volunteer recognition programmes in the USA.

Performance Award Systems

In the USA some categories of volunteer receive formal rewards based on their results or level of commitment. Volunteer fire-fighters and paramedics, for example, can earn points which can be redeemed either for cash or merchandise from local stores. Ellis (1989: 9) notes that 'such programmes allow people to "bank" credit for volunteering that they do and later "withdraw" their credit for some volunteer work by someone else on their behalf or for local "currency".'

Performance Evaluation or Appraisal

Volunteers should be subjected to the same internal programme of evaluation as paid staff. Most commonly, this may be a periodic appraisal of their performance, and ideally the organization's performance in assisting them to achieve their personal goals. An action plan for the coming period can be agreed upon and appropriate development opportunities actioned.

Watch the Door

Many nonprofits now conduct exit interviews of volunteers when they terminate their support. This can be an excellent way of identifying areas in which the organization might improve the quality of support and opportunities it offers to its volunteer base. While some turnover will be due to unavoidable factors, such as relocation or a change in the individual's lifestyle, there will undoubtedly be some volunteer turnover that proves to be due to one or more of the factors discussed earlier and on which the organization can take action to improve.

Recruiting Board Members

Before leaving the topic of volunteer management it is worth examining briefly the topic of board recruitment. In both the USA and the UK, volunteers are frequently required to comprise the board that will oversee the management of a nonprofit organization and ensure that its resources are appropriately directed towards the 'objects' it was set up to achieve. In the UK such boards have tended to comprise individuals with particular expertise in the cause, perhaps medical practitioners in the case of medical charities and conservationists in the case of wildlife organizations. In the USA, while there may indeed be individuals present with 'subject' expertise, the focus has been equally on individuals who may either make a substantial financial contribution to the cause, or who are acquainted with individuals who could make such a contribution.

In both countries, finding the right people to serve on the board and thus shape the future direction of an organization is a far from easy task, particularly for those organizations that lack a social profile. Nonprofits such as museums and galleries have a big advantage here, as there may be a high degree of prestige associated with becoming a board member of one of these institutions. A board role can be highly visible within a particular community and signal much about the individual(s) who have agreed to undertake this responsibility. Nonprofits without such a profile, or a tangible set of assets that may act as a recruitment mechanism in themselves, have a more difficult task in identifying and recruiting the right individuals.

As a starting point, Widmer (1985) suggests that four incentives apply to participation in nonprofit boards:

1. *material incentives*—tangible rewards in goods, services, or money for oneself or one's group;

2. *social incentives*—intangible rewards following from associating with others—friendship, status, and honours;

3. *development incentives*—learning new skills or assuming civic responsibilities;

4. *ideological incentives*—intangible rewards that come from helping achieve something greater than oneself.

Scanlan (2002) found that people willing to take on leadership roles have:

• an interest in the big picture—the overall welfare and progress of the community;

• a social entrepreneur approach to the community, including a strong desire to solve problems through action and make it a better place (see also Dees and Economy 2001);

• limited ability to take on new commitments of time and energy, especially commitments that are longer term (heading campaigns for organizations with which they are not already associated, committee or board service with organizations with which they have previously been involved, etc.);

• unwillingness to take on vague or not clearly defined tasks that lack timeliness, goals, and specific outcomes;

- responsiveness to peers, colleagues, and close friends when asked by them to do something, especially if the something fits into some or all of the other categories above.

Clearly many of these factors can be reflected in the way that individuals are approached to volunteer in this capacity. It is important to recognize here the critical role that will be played in recruitment by the existing board. Research has shown that 43 per cent of board members first talked of volunteering with an existing board member. This stresses the high reliance of organizations in this context on personal networks and acquaintances. However, in some circumstances it may be appropriate to advertise for board members, particularly when specific expertise is required and where few personal contacts exist.

■ SUMMARY

In this chapter we explored a range of issues in relation to volunteer recruitment and retention. While some readers may feel that many of the issues we have addressed fall in the domain of Human Resource Management (HRM) rather than marketing per se, I would argue that the attraction of appropriately qualified individuals and the matching of these individuals to tasks where they will make a genuine contribution is essentially a marketing task. I would also argue that the excessively high level of turnover faced by many organizations is testimony to a general lack of internal marketing currently taking place within the sector. It seems clear that a great number of volunteers continue not to be regarded either as internal customers or even stakeholders of an organization, and thus many of the tools and techniques of internal marketing may well have a real contribution to make to future development (see also Mitchell and Taylor 2004). A fundamental point, often repeated throughout this chapter, is the need to start the whole process of volunteer recruitment and management with a thorough and clear understanding of what requirements these individuals might have of the organization. Retention can then be greatly enhanced by ensuring that these requirements are met and even extended and developed over time.

■ DISCUSSION QUESTIONS

1. Look again at Figure 14.1. What reasons might there be for the increase in volunteering among the 16–24 and 25–34 age groups? Why might volunteering in the 55–64 category have declined?

2. You have been approached by a local hospice for help in expanding its existing volunteer base from 20–35 carers. Outline a volunteer recruitment plan that could be used for this purpose.

3. As the head of community fundraising for a large national nonprofit, you have been asked to make a presentation to one of your local branches about how it might identify and recruit new volunteer fundraisers. Explain how a knowledge of volunteer motivation can be used to inform a recruitment strategy.

4. Visit the website http://www.junction49.co.uk. Using your understanding of volunteer motivation, how would you evaluate the design and content of this site?

5. As the newly appointed Head of Volunteer Services for a national nonprofit, you have been concerned to discover that your organization currently has a 90 per cent annual attrition rate of volunteers. Develop a presentation to your Board of Trustees explaining why this should be addressed as a matter of urgency.

6. What are the primary reasons for volunteers terminating their support? What steps might an organization utilizing volunteer counsellors to assist young drug addicts take to ensure that its retention rate is as high as possible?

■ REFERENCES

Amos, O.M. (1982) 'Empirical Analysis of Motives Underlying Contributions to Charity', *Atlantic Economic Journal*, Vol. 10, 45–52.

Applebaum, S. (1992) *Recruiting and Retaining Volunteers from Minority Communities: A Case Study*, Ann Arbor, MI, UMI Dissertation Services.

Bennett, R. and Barkensjo, A. (2005) 'Internal Marketing, Negative Experiences and Volunteers' Commitment to Providing High-Quality Services in a UK Helping and Caring Charitable Organisation', *Voluntas: International Journal of Voluntary and Nonprofit Organizations*, Vol. 16, No. 3, 251–74.

Clark, R.D. and Word, L.E. (1972) 'Why Don't Bystanders Help? Because of Ambiguity?' *Journal of Personality and Social Psychology*, Vol. 24, 392–400.

Clary, E.G. and Synder, M. (1991) 'A Functional Analysis of Altruism and Prosocial Behaviour: The Case of Volunteerism', in *Review of Personality and Social Psychology*, London, Sage, 119–48.

Cnaan, R.A. and Goldberg-Glen, R.S. (1991) 'Measuring Motivation to Volunteer in Human Services', *Journal of Applied Behavioural Sciences*, Vol. 27, No. 3, 269–84.

Coliazzi, A., Williams, K.J. and Kayson, W.A. (1984) 'When Will People Help? The Effects of Gender, Urgency and Location on Altruism', *Psychological Reports*, Vol. 55, 139–42.

Collard, D. (1978) *Altruism and Economy*, New York, Oxford University Press.

Dees, J. and Economy, P. (2001) 'Social Entrepreneurship', in Dees, J., Emerson, J. and Economy, P. (eds.) *Enterprising Nonprofits*, New York, John Wiley & Sons, 4.

Doyle, D. (2002) *Volunteers in Hospice and Palliative Care*, Oxford, Oxford University Press.

Drucker, P.F. (1990) *Managing the Non-Profit Organisation: Practices and Principles*, London, Harper Collins.

Eisenberg, N. and Miller, P.A. (1987) 'Empathy, Sympathy and Altruism: Empirical and Conceptual Links', in Eisenberg, N. and Strayer, J. (eds.) *Empathy and Its Development*, New York, Cambridge University Press, 292–316.

Ellis, S.J. (1989) *Volunteer Centers: Gearing up for the 1990s*, Alexandria, VA, United Way of America.

Ellis, S.J. (1994) *The Volunteer Recruitment Book*, Philadelphia, Energize.

Fischer, L.R. and Schaffer, K.B. (1993) *Older Volunteers: A Guide For Research and Practice*, Newbury Park, Sage Publications.

Fisher, J.C. and Cole, K.M. (1993) *Leadership and Management of Volunteer Programs*, San Francisco, Jossey Bass.

Fisher, R.J. and Ackerman, D. (1998) 'The Effects of Recognition and Group Need on Volunteerism: A Social Norm Perspective', *Journal of Consumer Research*, Vol. 25 (Dec), 262–75.

Frisch, M.B. and Gerrard, M. (1981) 'Natural Helping Systems: A Survey of Red Cross Volunteers', *American Journal of Community Psychology*, Vol. 9 (Oct), 567–79.

Gallup (1992) 'Volunteering in the UK', Gallup survey.

Geer, J.H. and Jermecky, L. (1973) 'The Effect of being Responsible for Reducing Others' Pain on Subjects' Response and Arousal', *Journal of Personality and Social Psychology*, Vol. 27, 100–108.

Glaser, J.S. (1994) *The United Way Scandal—An Insiders Account of What Went Wrong and Why*, New York, John Wiley & Sons.

Govekar, P. and Govekar, M. (2007) 'Volunteer Recruiting, Retention and Development' in Sargeant, A. and Wymer, W. (eds) *The Routledge Companion to Nonprofit Marketing*, London, Routledge.

Heidrich, K.W. (1988) *Lifestyles of Volunteers: A Marketing Segmentation Study*, PhD dissertation, University of Illinois at Urbana-Champaign.

Horne, S. and Broadbridge, A. (1994) 'The Charity Shop Volunteer in Scotland: Greatest Asset or Biggest Headache?' *Voluntas*, Vol. 5, No. 2, 205–18.

Independent Sector (2000) *Volunteering, Volunteering Levels and Number of Hours Recorded.* Available online at www.indepsec.org/GrandV/s_keyf.htm.

Jackson, R. (2001) 'How to Recruit and Retain the Right Volunteers', Proceedings, *Recruiting, Retaining and Training Volunteers*, Henry Stewart Conferences, London, October.

Kadlec, D. (1998) 'Pitch In, Get Sued,' *Time*, Vol. 151, No. 24, 79.

Kaehler, J. and Sargeant, A. (1998) 'Returns on Fund-Raising Expenditures in the Voluntary Sector', Working Paper 98/06, University of Exeter.

Kaufman, R., Mirsky, J. and Avgar, A. (2004) 'A Brigade Model for the Management of Service Volunteers: Lessons From The Soviet Union', *International Journal of Nonprofit and Voluntary Sector Marketing*, Vol. 9, No. 1, 57–68.

Lafer, B. (1991) 'The Attrition of Hospice Volunteers', *Omega*, Vol. 23, No. 3, 161–8.

Leviton, L.C., Herrera, C., Pepper, S.K., Fishman, N. and Racine, D.P. (2006) 'Faith in Action: Capacity and Sustainability of Volunteer Organizations', *Evaluation and Program Planning*, Vol. 29, No. 2, 201–7.

Lohmann, R. (1992) 'The Commons: A Multidisciplinary Approach to Nonprofit Organization, Voluntary Action and Philanthropy', *Nonprofit and Voluntary Sector Quarterly*, Vol. 21, 309–24.

Mathis, R.L. and Jackson, J.H. (1982) *Personnel: Contemporary Perspectives and Applications*, 3rd edn, St Paul, West Publishing Company.

McClintock, C.G. and Allison, S.T. (1989) 'Social Value Orientation and Helping Behaviour', *Journal of Applied Psychology*, Vol. 19, No. 4, 353–62.

Millet, R. and Orosz, J. (2001) *Cultures of Caring: Philanthropy in Diverse American Communities*, The Kellogg Foundation.

Mitchell, M.A. and Taylor, S. (2004) 'Internal Marketing: Key To Successful Volunteer Progams', *Nonprofit World*, Vol. 22, No. 1, 25–6.

Morgan, J.N., Dye, R.F. and Hybels, J.H. (1979) *Results From Two National Surveys of Philanthropic Activity*, Michigan, University of Michigan Press.

Mount, J. and Quirion, F. (1988) 'A Study of Donors to a University Campaign', *The Philanthropist*, Vol. 8, No. 1, 56–64.

National Council for Hospice and Specialist Palliative Care Services (1996) *Education In Palliative Care*, London, NCHSPCS.

Newman, C.V. (1977) 'Relation Between Altruism and Dishonest Profiteering From Another's Misfortune', *Journal of Social Psychology*, Vol. 109, 43–8.

nfpSynergy (2008) *Who Volunteers? Volunteering Trends: 2000–2007,* London, nfpSynergy.

Okun, M.A. (1994) 'The Relation Between Motives for Organizational Volunteering and the Frequency of Volunteering by Elders', *Journal of Applied Gerontology*, Vol. 13, No. 2, 115–26.

Pancer, S.M., McCullen, L.M., Kabatoff, R.A., Johnson, K.G. and Pond, C.A. (1979) 'Conflict and Avoidance in the Helping Situation', *Journal of Personality and Social Psychology*, Vol. 37, No. 8, 1406–11.

Ratje, J.M. (2003) 'Well Prepared Volunteers Help the Brand Image', *Marketing News*, 14 April, 17.

Ricks, F.A. and Pyke, S.W. (1973) 'Women in Voluntary Social Organizations', *The Ontario Psychologist*, Vol. 5, No. 2, 48–55.

Rokeach, M. (1973) *The Nature of Human Values*, New York, The Free Press.

Sargeant, A. and Jay, E. (2004) *Fundraising Management*, London, Routledge.

Scanlan, E.A. (2002) 'Strategic Task Forces', *International Journal of Nonprofit and Voluntary Sector Marketing*, Vol. 7, No. 4, 334–42.

Schervish, P.G. (1993) 'Philosophy as Moral Identity of Caritas', in Schervish, P.G., Benz, O., Dulaney, P., Murphy, T.B. and Salett, S. (eds.) *Taking Giving Seriously*, Center on Philanthropy, Indianapolis, Indiana University Press.

Schervish, P.G. (1997) 'Inclination, Obligation and Association: What we Know and What we Need to Learn about Donor Motivation', In Burlingame, D. (ed.) *Critical Issues in Fund Raising*, Hoboken, NJ, John Wiley & Sons.

Schindler-Rainman, E. (1988) 'Administration of Volunteer Programs', In Daniel, T. (ed.) *The Nonprofit Organization Handbook*, 2nd edn, New York, McGraw Hill.

Schwartz, S. (1977) 'Normative Influences on Altruism', In Berkowitz, L. (ed.) *Advances in Experimental Social Psychology*, New York, Academic Press, 221–79.

Senior Corps (2008) 'Part of the Corporation For National Services: RSVP Programs', available online at www.seniorcorps.org, accessed on 28 Jan 2008.

Smith, D.H. and Baldwin, B.R. (1974) 'Parental Socialization, Socio-Economic Status and Volunteer Organization Participation', *Journal of Voluntary Action Research*, Vol. 3, 59–66.

Snyder, M., Omoto, A.M. and Crain, A.L. (1999) 'Punished for their Good Deeds', *The American Behavioural Scientist*, Vol. 42, No. 7, 1175–92.

Stittleburg, P.C. (1994) 'Recruiting and Retaining Volunteers', *NFPA (National Fire Protection Association) Journal*, Vol. 88, No. 2, 20, 109.

Widmer, C. (1985) 'Why Board Members Participate', *Journal of Voluntary Action Research*, Vol. 14, No. 4, 9–23.

Wilhelm, I. (2007) 'Volunteering By Americans Hits Four-Year Low', *Chronicle of Philanthropy*, 22 February, p1.

Williams, R.F. (1987) 'Receptivity to Persons with Mental Retardation: A Study of Volunteer Interest', *American Journal of Mental Retardation*, Vol. 92, No. 3, 299–303.

Wolf, T. (1990) *Managing A Nonprofit Organization*, New York, Simon and Schuster.

Wymer, W.W. (1996) *Formal Volunteering as a Function of Values, Self-Esteem, Empathy and Facilitation*, DBA dissertation, Indiana University.

Wymer, W.W. (1999) 'Understanding Volunteer Markets: The Case of Senior Volunteers', *Journal of Nonprofit and Public Sector Marketing*, Vol. 6, No. (2/3), 1–24.

Wymer, W.W. and Samu, S. (2002) 'Volunteer Service as Symbolic Consumption: Gender and Occupational Differences in Volunteering', *Journal of Marketing Management*, Vol. 18, 971–89.

Wymer, W.W. and Starnes, B.J. (1999) 'Segmenting Sub-Groups of Volunteers for Target Marketing: Differentiating Traditional Hospice Volunteers from other Volunteers', *Journal of Nonprofit and Public Sector Marketing*, Vol. 6, No. (2/3), 25–50.

Wymer, W.W. and Starnes, B.J. (2001a) 'Conceptual Foundations and Practical Guidelines for Recruiting Volunteers to Serve in Local Nonprofit Organizations: Part 1', *Journal of Nonprofit and Public Sector Marketing*, Vol. 9, No. 1, 63–96.

Wymer, W.W. and Starnes, B.J. (2001b) 'Conceptual Foundations and Practical Guidelines for Retaining Volunteers Who Serve in Local Nonprofit Organizations: Part 2', *Journal of Nonprofit and Public Sector Marketing*, Vol. 9, No. 1, 97–118.

15 Public Sector Marketing

OBJECTIVES

By the end of this chapter you should be able to:

1. describe recent changes in the scope and development of the UK public sector;
2. determine appropriate boundaries for the application of a marketing approach;
3. assess the quality of public sector services;
4. understand the relevance of marketing to critical public sector issues such as CCT and public accountability;
5. apply marketing tools and ideas to a variety of public sector contexts.

The Development of the Public Sector in the United Kingdom

Historic Overview

As we noted in the Preface to this book, the term 'public sector' is typically used to refer to a set of institutions that a given society feels is necessary for the basic well-being of its members. The aims of these institutions are determined by the State and their budgets are typically derived from taxation, collected both locally and nationally. These resources are then divided between the institutions on the basis of a politically determined allocation, rather than market mechanisms or even by the likely take-up of services by citizens. It is argued that this approach ensures that a wide variety of needs are addressed by the State, rather than just those of the majority of individuals. In most Western countries the State now provides at least a proportion of key services such as healthcare, education, social services, defence, housing, policing, and transport.

In many countries there is now widespread acceptance that the State should take responsibility for providing a basic minimum of service in relation to each of these areas. There is also general acceptance that it is society itself, and in particular taxpayers, who should shoulder the responsibility for paying for this. This has, however, not always been the case. Looking back over the seventeenth, eighteenth, and even nineteenth centuries, the State was generally regarded as a source of forced tribute, either in the form of taxes or conscription to the armed forces. This was widely despised and state intervention in social life was viewed with great suspicion. It was not until the early part of the twentieth century that individuals began to recognize a wider role for the State in tackling a range of social issues and, equally, began to recognize the legitimacy of the State seeking to fund these initiatives through general taxation.

While there had been a number of interventions by the State in social life throughout the late nineteenth and early twentieth centuries (such as the introduction of the state pension in 1908) it was not until the Second World War that the pace of change accelerated. During the war the government had been compelled to assume considerable responsibility for many facets of everyday life, including the rationing of food, clothing, electricity etc. This created a climate where State involvement in social life was considered more acceptable, a feature of UK society that continued long after the cessation of hostilities.

In 1942 the Beveridge Report (the Report on Social Insurance and Allied Services) marked a landmark shift in government thinking and policy. Beveridge believed that a goal of full employment (or, rather, 95 per cent employment to allow for some mobility in the workforce) was achievable and that this in turn would lead to increasing consumption and a greater standard of living for all UK citizens. To achieve this 'full' employment he sought to tackle what he saw as the primary obstacles to its attainment, namely 'Want, Disease, Ignorance, Squalor and Idleness'. As a consequence he developed a number of policies designed to overcome these difficulties, with the concept of income security at their core. Initially his ideas met with only limited support from the wartime coalition government. It was not until after the 1945 election, which returned a Labour government, that many of his ideas were realized. Beveridge's vision and what ultimately became known as the 'welfare state' was created by a series of Acts of Parliament enacted between 1944 and 1949. These are briefly summarized below.

1944 Education Act

It was decided that greater opportunity would be afforded to all children, irrespective of their background, to realize an appropriate education. It was also decided that this should be funded and shaped by the State. The Act created a situation where an examination known as the '11+' would determine the aptitudes of children and decide whether these were practical, technological, or academic. On the basis of this test children were then streamed to attend secondary modern, technical, and grammar schools according to their needs (or rather what the government defined as their needs). It remained possible for wealthier parents to opt out of this process and send their children to a private school, but for all other parents the choice of school rested on the outcome of the 11+ examination. While to modern ears this may sound rather a draconian policy it should be remembered that the government's intent was to ensure an appropriate education for all members of society.

1945 Family Allowances Act

In a bid to assist families to avoid poverty, it was decided to pay an allowance to the parents of every child from birth until the age of 16. The size of this allowance was to be determined by HM Treasury and applied to all children in a given family except the first-born. It was not until 1977 that the first-born children in a family became eligible for this allowance.

1946 National Health Service Act

Under this Act healthcare was intended to be largely free at the point of delivery, although even in these early days there remained scope for some charges to be made. The Act also required local authorities to take on some responsibility for healthcare delivery and to take care of the disabled or long-term infirm in their area.

1946 National Insurance Act

This Act established a series of benefits that would assist citizens to cope financially with adverse circumstances such as maternity, sickness, retirement, unemployment, and the death of a spouse. Many of the original ideas proposed by Beveridge were brought into existence by this Act although, as the reader will imagine, the additional burden that this placed on taxpayers was immense.

1947 Town and Country Planning Act

The government had recognized the need to achieve a better balance in the geographical spread of the working population. It was felt that the best way of achieving this was to control the nature and location of the housing stock and/or business/industrial enterprise. Accordingly, this Act made it compulsory to apply for those seeking to build new developments or amend existing ones to seek planning permission to do so.

1948 National Assistance Act

This Act was significant in that it marked the end of the Poor Laws that had historically provided the responsibility in law for taking care of the poor and needy in society. It recognized that the State was now taking over that responsibility and would in future provide a specific minimum level of assistance which was deemed to be enough to allow the individual(s) to better their position.

1949 Housing Act

This Act sought to deal with the aftermath of the Second World War and to create housing to replace that which had been damaged or destroyed by the Luftwaffe. It also recognized that the birth rate was rising rapidly in the post-war era and as a consequence the need to build a lot of new housing, swiftly, was one of the most pressing problems facing the government.

The Period 1945–1979

The growth in the welfare state was coupled with a series of nationalizations. Civil aviation, transport, electricity, gas, iron, and steel were all nationalized in the immediate post-war period. The legislation to achieve this, together with the Acts listed above, greatly increased the number of civil servants that were required to manage these additional commitments. This gave rise to an increasing bureaucracy and the need for a systems approach to management to cope with the sheer scale of the State apparatus. While initially welcomed by the public, it was not long before the perception of the civil service became unfavourable; in particular it was seen as being impersonal and mechanistic.

The costs of managing this government bureaucracy over the next 30 years were considerable. In periods of high economic growth and low unemployment the financial burden presented by the welfare state was perhaps less of an issue due to the accompanying rise in income from taxation and falling demand for State benefits. In periods of higher unemployment, however, the demand for State benefits created a heavy burden on the taxpayer and, when coupled with economic events such as the oil crisis of 1972–4, presented the Treasury with a real problem. It had to juggle rising needs on the one hand with the need to cap public spending on the other. It was against this backdrop that Margaret Thatcher was able to come to power in 1979 arguing the case that the State had become unwieldy and as a consequence should be cut back. She was also able to argue successfully that State control should be replaced by individual choice.

The Period 1979–2007

The period 1979–97 saw a succession of Conservative governments. Authors such as Thomson (1992) have argued that the early years in particular were characterized by a fervent desire to roll back the frontiers of the State and that as a consequence there was scarcely any area of the public domain that remained untouched. She argues that the central themes of these governments were efficiency, effectiveness, and economy as manifest by policies of privatization, delegation, competition, enterprise, deregulation, service quality, and the curtailment of trade union powers. This period is of considerable interest to the study of public sector marketing since, as we shall shortly see, many of the changes in policy instituted by these Conservative governments still have resonance in management practices today. Indeed the New Labour government that took office in 1997 has pursued many of these ideas, offering citizens a number of new rights in respect of the quality of services they receive and seeking to enhance user engagement in their planning and delivery.

Recent changes in public sector thinking and management are summarized below.

- *Commercialization*. Successive governments have sought efficiency gains, value for money in public services, and have encouraged or compelled the institution of market mechanisms (such as compulsory competitive tendering) to ensure the best value for taxpayers in the provision of services.
- *User involvement*. Recent governments have also encouraged user control of services, enhanced consultation with users, and/or made provision for formal redress should a poor quality of service be delivered.
- *Evaluation of performance*. To ensure that value for money is provided by government services, there has been a marked increase in formal measures of performance, together with regular inspections and audits.
- *Strategy*. Successive governments have encouraged the development of formal planning procedures, frequently borrowing ideas from the domain of strategic management as developed in the commercial sector.
- *Collaboration*. There has also been a move to foster and improve collaborative working across agencies whether between or within sectors, e.g. working with the voluntary sector or the collaboration of heath and social care.

Recent decades have therefore seen considerable change in the manner in which successive governments have both viewed the public sector and sought to manage it for the wider benefit of society. In this chapter we will seek to explore the relevance of marketing to this domain, and address the critical marketing issues raised by recent changes to management practice in this context.

The Perception of Marketing

Since 1979, both Labour and Conservative governments have made efforts to introduce private sector management ideas, believing that improvements in the quality of service delivery and/or efficiency gains would result. This fascination with commercial management practices has led to an increasing interest in the topic of marketing, yet as Laing and McKee (2001) note, marketing has conventionally been viewed by public service professionals as antipathetic to the delivery of public services. Public services, it is argued, should be provided irrespective of demand and irrespective of the ability on the part of the user to pay the economic cost of providing that service. As a consequence, they argue, marketing is unnecessary.

While this may be a convincing philosophical argument, the policies of successive governments have created quasi-market mechanisms (particularly in relation to healthcare), competitive tendering procedures, greater public accountability, and a rapid growth in outsourcing the provision of government services through the integration of private sector suppliers into the wider public sector. In circumstances where organizations are forced to compete against each other for the right to provide services and where organizations are increasingly compelled to match the needs of service users with provision and to justify their priorities and expenditures in the public arena, the diversity of need for effective marketing practice becomes clear (Walsh 1994; Keaney 1999).

Despite the potential benefits of a marketing approach Buurma (2001) lists a number of objections to marketing typically raised by government officials or departments.

The Government Is a Monopolist Supplier (van der Hart 1991)

In such circumstances it is argued that there is no need for marketing, as there is no competition to beat. Since the customer has no choice there is no longer a need to market the one supplier they can use. Of course this argument is a little naïve since customers can, and frequently do, elect to substitute alternative services or to simply withdraw from the market altogether (as the case study below illustrates).

The Citizen Is More than a Customer

While this is undoubtedly true, this argument does not preclude the use of marketing tools. Indeed, it strengthens the need for effective marketing. Aside from choosing to use a particular government service, citizens may also use their democratic vote to help shape policy and

---

■ CASE STUDY

HULL SCHOOL DINNERS

A children's revolt recently foiled government attempts to introduce healthier menus for school lunches. A pioneering scheme to replace fry-ups and stodgy puddings with pastas and lighter options was rejected by pupils in 2004 and has led to a big fall in the number of children having school meals. The most convincing evidence of the unpopularity of healthy menus was reported in Hull. There the school meals policy was launched by Stephen Twigg, the Schools Minister, in February 2004. The city which suffers from Britain's highest levels of obesity decided to cut back on traditional foods such as hot dogs, fish fingers, and meatballs. Instead a meal plan devised by the council's own caterers was implemented and pupils were offered meals such as macaroni bake, chicken risotto, savoury cheese wedge, turkey curry, salad, and naan bread. But four weeks after the healthy menus were introduced in 79 primary and nursery schools, the number of children on school meals fell by nearly a quarter. At one primary school take-up slumped from 50 per cent to 15 per cent. Even children entitled to free meals, whose parents were deemed too poor to feed them, preferred to go without.

to achieve what they personally regard as the optimum allocation of government expenditure between the available options. Marketing tools can be used to help politicians to convey the desirability of particular options and/or portray the wider benefit that will accrue to society as a consequence of a particular option. Marketing can even be employed to encourage individuals to exercise their democratic rights to vote.

Collective Goods (e.g. Local Government Services such as Recycling Collections) are Free Goods

This argument suggests that marketing is not necessary since there is no exchange between the supplier and the user. Users frequently do not pay the supplier directly for the services they receive. However, this neglects the fact that while the service may be provided free of charge the term 'free goods' merely reflects the compensation side and not the sacrifice that must be made by the user in using those collective goods. Thus, while a local authority may offer a recycling facility to the residents in a certain area, the fact that it is offered free of charge may not be enough in itself to stimulate use of the service. Inculcating a particular pattern of behaviour is often a key facet of achieving government objectives and cost alone may not be a determining factor, as the following case study demonstrates.

■ CASE STUDY

MUNICIPAL RECYCLING

The 1990s have been characterized as the decade of recycling. Goldstein (1997) reports that the national recycling rate in the USA climbed from 9 per cent in 1989 to 28 per cent in 1996, suggesting that civic environmentalism had entered the mainstream of behavioural norms. During this time, the nature of the recycling business also changed markedly, evolving from periodic paper drives by Scouts troops and volunteers into a challenging, complex, and expensive service that now competes with other local programmes for scarce resources (Folz 1999).

The data in Table 15.1 were collected by Folz from municipal recycling coordinators in 265 cities. The table indicates that for these cities recycling participation increased by 36 per cent over the period 1989–96. As one might expect, participation in mandatory programmes in both years was higher than that reported by voluntary programmes. However, the largest improvement in participation occurred in voluntary programmes, which average a 50 per cent increase over the period. The table also indicates that offering a kerbside pick-up led to a much higher level of participation than leaving citizens to make their own way to local recycling centres with their materials.

Folz was able to use the statistical technique of regression to explore the relationship between the participation rates obtained by each city and a range of accompanying policies or factors. His results for both mandatory and compulsory schemes are summarized below.

Mandatory. The most significant factor in increasing participation in mandatory schemes appears to be the timing of the kerbside pick-up. Those cities that collected materials for recycling on the same day as other solid household waste experienced higher levels of participation. His data also revealed that the use of penalties or sanctions for improper recycling behaviour or a failure to recycle were associated with higher participation rates. It is interesting to note that the magnitude of the recycling goal set by the city did not appear to drive behaviour, suggesting that

Table 15.1 Municipal recycling data 1989–1996

Indicator	1989	N	1996	N	Difference	% change
Mean participation rates (all cities)	53.53	149	72.80	139	+19.27	+35.99
Mandatory programmes	76.51	47	80.01	71	+03.50	+04.57
Voluntary programmes	43.02	101	65.27	68	+22.25	+51.22
Kerb-side pick-up	49.83	71	68.78	55	+18.95	+38.03
Drop-off only	26.96	30	50.39	13	+23.49	+87.32

Source: © Blackwell Publishing. Reproduced with kind permission.

customers do not find the municipal targets to be of direct relevance to them when a mandatory recycling scheme is in existence.

Voluntary. In voluntary schemes there appeared to be a link between these municipal targets and participation. The data suggests that the nearer the target year to achieve a particular level of recycling, the more motivated individuals were to recycle. Folz argues that a near-term goal may constitute a more salient appeal to citizen altruism. Of the other factors that were found to drive behaviour, the supply of free recycling bins was a highly significant factor, as was the appointment of neighbourhood 'block leaders' who were responsible for encouraging recycling among the households in their immediate vicinity.

It is interesting to note that across both categories of schemes, those cities that had introduced variable fees, or volume pricing for the collection of solid waste, had significantly higher levels of participation.

The case study illustrates that the simple provision of a service, even a free service, does not in itself ensure that citizens will participate. There is therefore a key role for marketing to play in understanding the real costs (perhaps opportunity costs in this recycling case) of participation in a scheme and the factors that could potentially motivate people to change their behaviour (Kotler and Lee 2007).

The Boundaries of Marketing

While we have argued above that marketing has considerable relevance to the public sector environment, it is important not to overstate the case and to recognize that there may be some aspects of government provision in which it would not be appropriate for marketing concepts or ideas to play a role.

The literature suggests that there are two ways of determining the relevance of marketing to specific public sector contexts. The first of these springs from a fundamental understanding of the nature of the exchange that is taking place. Readers will recall from Chapter 1 that *exchange* lies at the heart of the marketing concept. In the commercial context the nature of this exchange is easy to define, with something of value changing hands between both parties. In its simplest form, this would be the exchange of money for a product or service.

In the public sector context, however, authors such as Koster (1991) have argued that the exchange process is altogether more complex, with income from local and national taxation funding the supply of services that the taxpayer himself may derive no benefit from (e.g. the provision of a sports centre they don't use) or perhaps only indirectly benefit from (e.g. through effective policing preventing crime in their neighbourhood) (Pandya and Dholakia 1992).

Koster (1991) argues that for an exchange to be deemed a marketing exchange a number of criteria must be met. These are summarized below.

- There must be two or more parties involved. These parties must wish to achieve their objectives through an exchange with the other(s).
- The exchange must take place on a voluntary basis and both parties should have the freedom to enter into the exchange or not as they see fit.
- There must be a mutual exchange of value between both parties.
- The objects of this exchange should not be identical, i.e. both parties must exchange a different source of value to the other.
- The nature of the exchange should be characterized as a 'win-win'. To both parties the value received should represent more than the cost of the sacrifice.
- There should be communication between both parties.
- The nature of the relationship between the parties is viewed as legitimate by society and rests on good faith.
- The exchange involves both parties in rights and obligations that are mutual.
- Both parties have a mechanism to hold the other accountable for non-compliance.

Looking down through this list, it is apparent that the provision of many government services could legitimately (according to Koster) be regarded as marketing exchanges. The provision of some forms of healthcare, education, social care, leisure facilities etc. would seem to meet the criteria for a marketing exchange and as a consequence many of the ideas and tools we have elaborated on in previous chapters would be felt to apply.

Applying this framework to the full range of public sector exchanges, it is clear that exchanges such as the imposition of taxation or the internment of prisoners fall outside the domain of marketing.

In seeking to draw this distinction, other authors have preferred to focus on the nature of the services being delivered rather than the nature of the exchange. Authors such as van der Hart (1991), for example, elected to categorize services by the degree to which the user pays for the service and the degree to which the public have contact with the service. The extent to which marketing tools and ideas are of relevance is thus viewed as a function of where a particular service might sit within the matrix depicted in Figure 15.1.

Consider first the top left-hand corner of the matrix. Here we have a group of services that have a high degree of contact with the public, but where the payment for these services is made only indirectly through taxation. In these circumstances, van der Hart argues that marketing concepts are of little relevance since the relationship between the funder and the service is primarily one of good citizenship. Of course, that is not to say that organizations such as the emergency services cannot use specific marketing tools (e.g. to persuade citizens only to call 999—the UK emergency number—in genuine emergencies), but such usage will be rare.

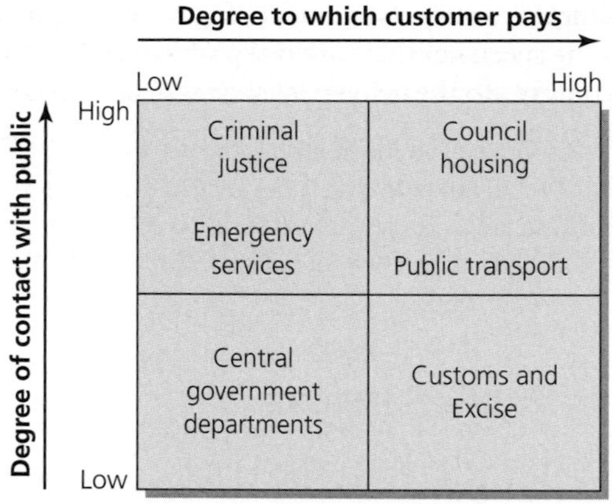

Degree to which customer pays

Figure 15.1 Categorization of public services

Source: van der Hart, H.W.C. (1991) 'Government Organizations
and their Customers in the Netherlands: Strategy, Tactics and
Operations', *European Journal of Marketing,* Vol. 24, No. 7,
31–42. Reproduced with kind permission.

In the top right of the matrix are services that have a high degree of contact with the public and where users are generally expected to pay all, or a percentage of, the costs of providing that service. Here the relationship with users will be characterized by multiple interactions and the income derived from these services is directly related to discrete services to individual users. In such a context the relationship between the service provider and user can legitimately be regarded as one of customer–supplier and the full range of marketing tools and techniques will be of relevance.

In the bottom left quadrant are depicted services that have a low contact with members of the public and where individual users are not typically asked to pay for the service rendered. The majority of the services supplied by central government departments, such as defence, will typically fall into this category. Van der Hart argues that marketing has little or no relevance to this domain.

In the bottom right are services that have a low contact with the public, but where users are expected to pay. An example of an organization in this quadrant might be Customs and Excise or the agency enforcing the payment of the television licence. Here the opportunities to employ marketing concepts and ideas will be limited, except perhaps in respect of the promotion of rules/regulations and the publicizing of particular initiatives.

Laing (2003) prefers to move away from a matrix-style approach in determining the extent to which marketing ideas and tools may be of relevance. Instead he proposes a spectrum of public services where the extent to which marketing may legitimately be applied will be a function of whether a service delivers private (i.e. consumer) or public benefits:

The relevance and applicability of current conceptualizations of marketing within public services can ultimately be viewed as being directly related to the balance between private and social benefit, together with the associated balance between consumer and producer judgement within such services. It is the distinction between the focus of benefit and judgement, rather than whether services are formally delivered in the public or private sectors (the balance of which is dynamic and is largely shaped by ideological considerations), that ultimately determines the extent to which marketing is relevant and the appropriateness of alternative conceptualizations of marketing to public services (Laing 2003: 439).

Clearly there are few difficulties in applying marketing where private benefits predominate, but at the other end of the spectrum there are real problems in applying a set of consumer-focused management concepts to the delivery of such services. Laing concludes:

There is consequently a need for caution in extending the domain of marketing within the public sector to those areas where it is only of tangential relevance in order not to discredit the underlying concepts of marketing in those areas where they offer valid conceptual and practical tools to professionals in meeting the underlying objectives of public sector service provision (Laing 2003: 440).

Characteristics of Public Services

The range of services provided by the public sector is very diverse; from criminal justice and social welfare on the one hand to social housing and public transport on the other. Lane (1995) argues that such services have little in common. Laing (2003), however, believes that there are three defining characteristics. These are detailed below.

1. *Dominance of political objectives*. The provision of public sector services differs because the rationale for their existence and the shape of their provision is not framed in simple economic terms (Graham 1994). The nature of the services is shaped not by an ability to pay on the part of users, but on the basis of what is deemed as being right or good for a particular community. The benefit that accrues from these services is thus better expressed in terms of social profit (Bauer 1966) where, for example, levels of health, education, and housing, benefit not only users, but the community as a whole. Public services are thus targeted to particular groups, not on economic grounds, but on the basis of need and equity (van der Hart 1991).

2. *Primacy of the citizen rather than the consumer*. Public services are targeted at citizens rather than consumers. Walsh (1994: 69) argues that the fundamental relationship between citizen and government 'is not one of simple exchange but one of mutual commitment and (thus) public services are not simply a reciprocation of taxes.'

The notion of citizens having a commitment to the community in which they live and its government is an important one. Schemes and services such as Neighbourhood Watch, recycling, and road safety are only possible with the active participation of citizens, frequently taking actions that are economically sub-optimal for them, but which are taken because of the need to benefit society as a whole. Historically there was a clear understanding of the need for a given individual to support the needs of others. In modern society there is an increasing tendency to define public services in terms of individual benefits (Laing and Hogg 2002), which some authors have argued could potentially be damaging to society as such a consumerist perspective could place increasing and inappropriate demands on public services (Buchanan et al. 1987).

3. *Need to serve multidimensional customers*. Here Laing (2003) argues that public services differ because they are designed to both meet the needs of individuals and the wider society in which they live. In addition to this, the services provided by one component of the public sector may be provided to serve the need of additional stakeholders, such as community groups, interest groups, business/industry, politicians, or even the wider society of the country as a whole. There are clearly parallels here with the voluntary sector as discussed in Chapter 1.

Clearly all these differences must be taken account of in the design of an appropriate approach to the management of public sector marketing.

Quality in Public Services

Recent years have seen an increasing interest on the part of government in the quality of public service provision. Indeed, in the UK a succession of charters have sought to outline the rights that citizens have for a high standard of baseline service in a wide range of public services. These charters are a formal contract between public service providers and their customers or the wider community. The 1980s and 1990s, for example, have seen the introduction of the Citizens Charter, the Job Seekers Charter and the Parents Charter.

Accompanying these charters has been a rise in the measurement of delivered service quality. Frequently this has taken the form of measuring the outputs achieved by each service (e.g. the number of people aided) or the time that it takes for particular actions to occur (e.g. the time spent on a hospital waiting list). More thoughtful public sector suppliers have also sought to measure the user 'experience' employing questionnaires based on the SERVQUAL or other such framework. While such models work well in the context of contact with individuals, they are perhaps less valuable in the context of institutional or organizational relationships. Since, as we noted earlier, many public sector services have institutional stakeholders or clients it is clearly important that the quality of service delivered here is similarly measured and appropriate action taken to enhance quality where weaknesses are identified.

The following case study highlights an innovative approach to the measurement of service quality in this context.

■ CASE STUDY

SOCIAL HOUSING

The Housing Act (1988) marked a change in direction in central government policy towards the provision of social housing within the UK. Whereas previously local authorities had been expected to provide and manage social housing, this was no longer to be the case. Housing associations became the new providers of this housing and local authorities were now mere enablers of its provision. Local authorities were thus required to work in partnership with housing associations to identify need in their area and to facilitate the housing associations in meeting that need. A body known as the Housing Corporation was to oversee the whole process of provision and provide capital finance and ongoing monitoring of performance to ensure value for money. In addition to the funding they might receive from the Housing Corporation, housing associations were also expected to seek private finance to support new social housing provision.

The interaction between these three bodies is depicted in Figure 15.2.

Many of the measures of service quality alluded to in earlier chapters work best in the context of consumer-to-organization relationships. They are less well suited to the dyadic relationships represented in the figure (Rosen and Suprenant 1998). This occurs because these measures are highly focused on one point of view—i.e. the consumers'. Since in the context of Figure 15.2, each organization is in a sense a customer of the other, these forms of service quality measurement tend towards the meaningless.

Working with the South-East Region Housing Corporation to help them understand and improve their relationships in the process of social housing, Williams et al. (1999) employed what they term a service template process (Staughton and Williams 1994) to investigate the

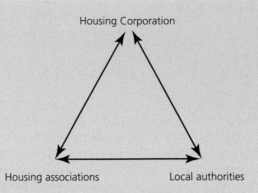

Figure 15.2 Key relationships in the provision of social housing

quality of the relationship between all the three parties alluded to in Figure 15.2. The process they developed is outlined in Figure 15.3.

The process begins with a series of meetings with representatives from each party to discuss each of the relationships under analysis. A separate meeting is held to consider each specific relationship (in this case, two for each institution) and each party to the relationship meets

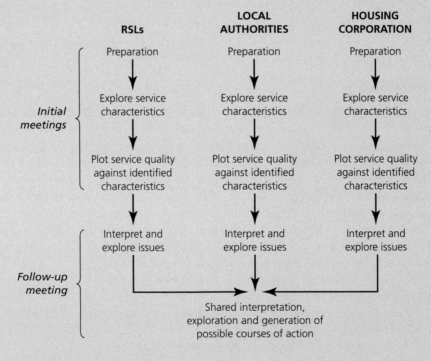

Figure 15.3 Service template process

Source: Williams, C.S., Saunders, M.N.K. and Staughton, R.V.W. (1999) 'Understanding Service Quality in the New Public Sector: An Exploration of Relationships in the Process of Funding Social Housing', *International Journal of Public Sector Management,* Vol. 12, No. 4, 366–79. Reproduced with kind permission.

separately. As a first step, in the preparation phase of the process the service situation and the meanings of any terms outside the participant's normal experience (e.g. customer or service) are clarified.

A brainstorming process of the characteristics of each relationship is then undertaken. The goal here is to develop a list of components that is continually refined until the group of participants as a whole are happy that the relationship has been fully and properly characterized and that a shared understanding of the meaning of the language employed has been fostered.

The next task is to plot the delivered service quality against these characteristics. To facilitate this, positive and negative descriptions of each characteristic are developed, e.g. honest–misleading. Both the expected and delivered service quality is then plotted for each descriptor using a scoring system from 1 to 10 where 10 is regarded as excellent. Finally, each group must consider the importance they place on each aspect of the service by allocating 100 points between each of their dimensions.

An example of the resultant template is reported in Figure 15.4.

The next step of the process is a follow-up meeting to discuss and if necessary refine the template. Each group undertakes this separately. On the conclusion of this refinement each group meets with the other party to the relationship and discusses with them the differences and similarities between their two templates. This is undertaken in the spirit of enquiry rather than in an attempt to justify a particular template or view.

The outcomes from such a process can be reflected upon by both parties to the relationship and, where appropriate, corrective actions taken to improve facets of the service that are presently regarded as underperforming. This will be the case where this has occurred on dimensions of the relationship that are considered important by one or more parties.

Characteristic	Wt.	+ve Extreme	10	9	8	7	6	5	4	3	2	1	–ve Extreme
Deliverability of programme	25	Effective	e	ep	p								Inadequate
Product (House, space, rent)	20	Superior	e		p								Interior
Strategy recognition by RSLs	15	Fulfilled		ep									Ignored
Partnerships–nature	15	Harmonious	e		p								Strained
Management–quality (to tenants)	15	Proactive	e			p							Ineffective
Communication–scope	10	All-embracing		e	p								Lacking
LA input to programme		Minimal		e		p							Intensive
Communication–nature		Open		e	p								Secretive
Strategy: purpose (LA)		Clear	ep	p									Confused
Common purpose		In empathy with	e	p									Disparate

Key: expectations e ep   p perceptions

Figure 15.4 Specimen service template

Source: Williams, C.S., Saunders, M.N.K. and Staughton, R.V.W. (1999) 'Understanding Service Quality in the New Public Sector: An Exploration of Relationships in the Process of Funding Social Housing', *International Journal of Public Sector Management,* Vol. 12, No. 4, 366–79. Reproduced with kind permission.

New Public Sector Management

Many governments in the 1970s and 1980s became committed to reducing the proportion of national income devoted to public expenditure and the range of functions undertaken by government. A neo-liberal agenda challenged the collectivist provision of social welfare by government, arguing that it promoted a culture of dependency with morally damaging impacts upon citizens who demanded ever increasing services and bureaucrats who built ever larger empires to provide them (Humphrey et al. 1993). Competition, or the inculcation of market mechanisms, it was argued, was superior to monopoly situations which were typified by over-supply and excessive costs.

It is against this backdrop that what has become known as New Public Sector Management (NPSM) developed. NPSM is a generic label for a group of policy and administrative solutions characterized by competition, disaggregation, and incentivation. Instead of the State providing the full range of services it had previously identified as desirable for the welfare of society, many services are now put out to private tender and as a consequence pseudo-markets have developed. In effect, state policy-making and direction have been gradually divorced from service delivery.

Under NPSM, 'the state . . . becomes an enabling organization, responsible for ensuring that public services are delivered, rather than producing them directly itself. The delivery functions are entrusted to a variety of other agencies trading for profit or acting as voluntary bodies within a managed market, in which the concept of contract plays a key role' Rowley (1998: 1).

Managers have therefore been transformed from administrators and custodians of resources to accountable managers with greater delegated authority (Parker and Gould 1999). This notion of accountability is significant since managers are increasingly held accountable to the public. The notion of delegated authority is also important because it has afforded managers increasing opportunities to match service provision with the needs of 'customers' in their area. This new-found freedom and flexibility has required public sector managers to learn and practise a range of new marketing skills.

Compulsory Competitive Tendering

A key facet of the new public sector management has been the introduction of contracts for services previously delivered by government. Since 1979, for example, the Ministry of Defence has contracted out support and ancillary services that had traditionally been conducted in house (Uttley 1993). Services such as hospital, catering, domestic services, and laundry were all put out to Compulsory Competitive Tendering (CCT), where a range of private sector organizations, or an existing in-house team, could bid for the right to take over service provision.

Since 1979, successive central government legislation has pushed local government towards placing an ever-greater percentage of its delivery through CCT. In the 1980s local authority sports centres and leisure facilities, catering, street cleaning, and refuse services were all subjected to CCT. More recently CCT has been extended to include white-collar services, but unlike the manual services listed previously, it was determined that white-collar services should be only partially subjected to this process. This measure was designed to take into account the amount of work that could legitimately be 'parcelled up' for tender and to allow for adequate client-side management. It was also deemed necessary to preserve in the

Table 15.2 Percentage of services subjected to CCT

Service	%
Legal services	45
Financial services	35
Personnel services	35
Construction and property services	65
Information technology services	70
Housing management	95

public sector those aspects of infrastructure that provided for core democratic processes (Walsh 1995). At the time of writing, the percentage of each local authority service that may be contracted is shown in Table 15.2.

The introduction of CCT has had a number of marketing implications. First, government departments must ensure that appropriate suppliers are identified and encouraged to bid for the services being tendered. The pseudo-market created by the bidding process must then be managed and the full implications of the approach outlined in each bid explored for the users of the service in question; only then can decisions in respect of the best supplier be taken. Clearly, a range of the skills we have outlined in previous chapters will have a relevance here. There will also be a need for the government department to develop internal marketing ideas and concepts to manage the relationships it develops with each selected supplier. It must not be forgotten that from the public's perspective it will still be the government department that is providing the service. The fact that they have contracted out provision to a third party is, from the public's standpoint, an irrelevance. They are still responsible for the service and the perception of the department by the public will be determined in no small measure by the way in which the contractor fulfils their role. As a consequence internal marketing tools are essential to ensure that the relationship with the supplier works well and that the government department is represented on the ground, by this organization, in the way it would wish.

Accountability

As we noted above, NPSM has provided an impetus to greater accountability on the part of public sector managers (Pendlebury et al. 1994). At the senior management level, Sinclair (1995) has identified five forms of accountability operating.

- *Political*. Senior public sector managers are primarily accountable to government ministers.
- *Public*. Managers are increasingly accountable to the public, lobby groups, community groups, and individuals.
- *Managerial (financial)*. Managers must now show that not only are their processes working as they should, but that the inputs and outputs to their departments are appropriate and represent value for money.

- *Professional.* Many managers are members of a professional association to which they will also be accountable for their actions.

- *Personal.* Managers will also wish to retain fidelity to internalized moral and ethical values. The power of this personal accountability should not be underestimated, as a number of high-profile incidents where senior civil servants have acted as 'whistle blowers' will attest.

The ways in which senior public sector managers are in some sense accountable gives rise to a number of potential tensions. Often the needs of these diverse groups are conflicting, or the accountability in question takes a variety of different and not necessarily complementary forms. Perhaps the most notable of these potential conflicts arises in practice between the needs of ministers on the one hand and the public on the other. As Plowden (1994: 308) notes:

Telling managers that they must pay attention to the views of their customers does not absolve them from responding to politicians. It does not simplify their task. If anything, it complicates it, because they now have to take account both of the modified points of view that filter through the political process and of the direct undiluted force of service users.

Sadly, marketing cannot claim as a discipline to simplify this process, but again, many of the ideas expressed in previous chapters and in particular the notion of a customer orientation and the tools and techniques of marketing research can at least aid managers to develop a clear picture of the needs of both groups. While achieving a balance in terms of the actions taken will still not be easy, it will be facilitated by the use of the best available data.

The Rise of E-Government

E-government refers to the delivery of government information and services online through the Internet or other digital means (West 2004). The nature of Internet delivery allows citizens to access information or engage with services at their own convenience, not just when a government office is open. It is therefore set to revolutionize public sector marketing activity. The Internet also permits two-way interaction allowing public sector managers to easily communicate with, and thus get close to, their customers. It has been argued that this enhanced responsiveness improves the quality of service delivery and in the long run generates greater public confidence in government (Markoff 2000, Raney 2000).

West (2004) argues that there are four general stages of e-government:

1. The billboard stage, where governments simply post information on their website.

2. The partial-service delivery stage, where some aspect of a service is provided online, perhaps an application or screening process.

3. The portal stage, with fully executable and integrated service delivery, and

4. Interactive democracy, with public outreach and accountability-enhancing features.

The author stresses that the categorization does not mean that all government websites go through these stages, merely that e-government has evolved differently in different contexts and countries. Sadly, Chadwick (2001) finds that many government websites in the United States, the United Kingdom, and the European Union are 'predominantly non-interactive and non-deliberative' and little has changed since then. There is therefore a long way to go for modern technology to have the optimum impact on service provision and democracy, but new public sector managers will be increasingly expected to develop skills in this domain.

Conclusions

Throughout this chapter we have examined the marketing implications of a number of changes in government policy and approach. No chapter on public sector marketing would be complete, however, without a brief summary of those facets of marketing that *are* being adopted and *have* met with success.

Buurma (2001) argues that public sector organizations employ four categories of marketing activity:

1. *Marketization.* Marketing is employed to expose services to competitive forces with the policy objectives of bringing down the price level of a given service while matching delivered quality with customer expectations.

2. *Promoting self-interest.* Many government departments employ marketing to secure their future, by seeking support from society for their activities (see, for example, Burton 1999).

3. *Promoting an area of responsibility.* Many public sector marketers have responsibility for promoting specific services. Kriekaard (1994) cites the now common practice of city marketing, where particular places are marketed to both potential tourists and businesses that might be persuaded to relocate to the area.

4. *Marketing to achieve political or social objectives.* Public sector marketers may also employ marketing to achieve specific political or social objectives such as a reduction in drink driving, smoking, obesity, or disease. They may also promote healthy living, exercise, vaccination, and a range of other actions that are deemed socially desirable.

A number of these forms of public sector marketing and their interaction are well illustrated by the following case study.

■ CASE STUDY

ELECTRICITÉ DE FRANCE (EDF)

For a number of years EDF has conducted surveys of its residential customers facing payment difficulties. The aim has been to develop a deeper and fuller understanding of how EDF might work with these customers to avoid them entering into payment difficulties. An analysis of the data conducted by Wodon (2000) suggested four segments of customers who typically faced difficulties.

1. *Default.* These are low-income households who normally succeed in paying their energy bills. Despite their limited financial resources they demonstrate a remarkable capacity to control their budget. This does not mean that they are shielded from disconnection or that they

should not be helped even without the threat of disconnection. Helping these households would lighten the burden of their energy bills. For example, advantageous social tariffs would ease the strain on their lives. In an emergency situation when these households suffer larger than usual payment difficulties, debt forgiveness is welcome.

2. *Extreme poverty*. These households suffer from an accumulation of handicaps. Besides a lack of income they may also lack a decent education or training. They may be poor in health and unemployed (often for a long while). They may have lost hope of finding declared (formal) employment and survive thanks to social security allowances and casual (informal) work. Due to their extreme level of poverty, their inability to pay their energy bills is chronic. To help these households, it is necessary not only to provide short-term access to energy (for example, by providing service limiters instead of disconnecting) but also to invest in their social and human capital so that they may emerge from their state of deprivation in the long run.

3. *Miscalculation*. These are households who, despite medium or high incomes, are unable to pay their bills as a result of a temporary debt problem due to negligence, an accident, or simply miscalculation. Given the temporary nature of the problem, these households are the easiest to assist. A payment plan generally resolves the problem, avoiding the need to modify the base tariff or to write off part of the debt.

4. *Debt overload*. These are households who, despite medium to high incomes, suffer acute difficulties in paying their bills due to the burden of paying interest and capital on a large amount of loans taken out for other goods. Civil bankruptcy, which is similar to reorganization plans used by companies, may prove necessary in order to help these households get back on their feet. Energy distributors would be on equal terms with other creditors which, according to each case, would allow them to find more or less advantageous terms (Wodon 2000: 230).

In employing marketing tools to deal with the sensitive issue of disconnection, EDF recognizes that it is politically unacceptable for it to be seen as disconnecting substantial numbers of customers without first giving them every opportunity to resolve their problems. Failure to deal with this adequately would likely result in increased political interference in the industry on the part of central government, a hostile consumer backlash, and/or a knowledge on the part of managers that they were contributing to France's social problems.

EDF has thus expended much effort in modelling consumer behaviour and attempting to identify those individuals likely to default on payment early in that process. They then take steps to manage the difficulty by offering advice on usage and appropriate adjustments to tariffs. EDF has committed itself to a personalized dialogue with each customer in difficulties, with disconnection viewed only as the last resort.

The introduction of the service limiter described above has also proved important. It has the obvious impact of forcing individuals to make sensible use of their electricity resource and, in effect, to learn to live within their means. Since the use of a limiter could hardly be viewed as a desirable development, the threat of its imposition can also persuade those who do have the ability to pay to do so, and avoid compulsory changes in their consumption.

In addition to the measures that can be taken with individual customers EDF has also attempted to fight poverty in partnership with social welfare agencies. Each local EDF service centre has a 'solidarity officer' who liaises with public and private partners. It also provides finance to local conventions on poverty that allocate financial assistance to households in need.

Of the concepts and tools discussed in this text, the notion of a customer orientation has a clear relevance to public services (see, for example, Rosenthal 1995; Chapman and Cowdell 1998). Kotler and Lee (2007), for example, refer to the benefits that accrue from the development of 'citizen-centered progams' (see Table 15.3). Marketing research techniques have also been used to good effect in assessing need (Severijnen and Braak 1992) and internal marketing can be used to foster and develop relationships with 'external' suppliers now providing government services (Ewing and Caruana 1999).

Of the specific marketing tools that may be adopted Buurma (2001) suggests that the following ideas offer the most relevance to the public sector context.

• Marketing can be employed to develop a clear differentiation of stakeholders and their interests.

Table 15.3 Benefits of citizen-centred programs

Benefit	Example
Increased revenues	When community centers rent out more of their meeting rooms, more people with school-aged children move to rural towns, increasing federal education funding. Seaports get more cruise ships to utilize their ports. Electric utility customers voluntarily pay more to city utilities to help fund renewable energy sources such as wind power.
Increased utilization of services	More companies invite the staff members from the Department of Labor and industries to audit their facilities and train their employees on important safety measures. More people use mass transit. More citizens check out books and tapes from libraries. More residents attend cardiopulmonary resuscitation classes offered at the local fire station.
More purchases of products	More small businesses turn to the US Postal Service for shipping and direct-mail services, and more citizens buy bubble envelopes, pre-inked rubber stamps, scales, holiday cards, and framed Disney stamp artwork.
Better compliance with laws	Citizens are persuaded to dispose of litter properly, not drink and drive, obtain building permits, license pets and use pedestrian crosswalks, and businesses begin to strictly enforce safety regulations at construction sites.
Improved public health and safety	Teenagers postpone having sex, motorists move right for sirens and lights, cell phone users wait until they arrive at their final destination to place the call, mothers breastfeed exclusively for the first six months, and tobacco users call a quit line.
Increased citizen protection of the environment	Homeowners reroute their roof's downspout to a rain garden, compost food waste, fix leaky toilets, install water-efficient showerheads, and abandon their gas blower for a broom and a rake.
Decreased costs for service delivery	More car owners renew their vehicle license online, citizens vote by mail, commuters purchase and print their own bus pass online, and homeowners keep leaves out of storm drains and use the proper containers for garbage, recyclables, and yard waste.
Improved customer satisfaction	Citizens complete their tax forms properly, have their computers and liquids out of their bags before they get to the security line at airports, and show up for appointments at community clinics on time.
Increased citizen support	Citizens vote 'yes' for school bond levies, advocate (even demonstrate) for increased funds for a fire department, and join stream stewardship teams and neighborhood watch programs.

Source: Kotler and Lee (2007). This table is reprinted with permission of Vol. 36, No. 1 of *The Public Manager* © 2007, The Bureaucrat Inc.

- The marketing mix can be employed to match and manage quality levels (see also Foxall 1988).
- Marketing can identify need and demand patterns as the basis for a matching process.
- Market segmentation can be used to bundle and anticipate user/customer needs.
- Relationship marketing can be fostered with particular groups of users/customers.
- The principles of marketing organization and strategic marketing planning also apply in the context of public sector service provision, although the legitimate boundaries of marketing alluded to earlier must be considered here in determining what is truly appropriate.

As we discussed earlier, NPSM has introduced a variety of changes into the way that public sector organizations are managed. In particular, it has revolutionized the approach to service provision and the manner in which service users are now viewed by the organizations that support them. It is clear from the above that marketing can and does have much to offer the public sector, and looks set to play an increasing role in the future.

■ DISCUSSION QUESTIONS

1. To what extent can marketing be applied to all public sector service provision? Are there specific services where marketing would appear to have no relevance? Justify your answer by reference to the frameworks presented in this chapter.

2. What is New Public Sector Management? What role has this played in the development of marketing in the public sector? Why?

3. As a senior manager in a National Health Service hospital, explain to your board how the quality of service your organization provides to both patients and their GPs might be assessed.

4. Look back to the Hull School Dinners case. How might marketing tools have been employed to ensure a higher rate of take-up of the new school dinner menus?

5. Plowden (1994) argues that if managers of public sector services simply pursue the best interests of their own organization in a marketized environment, they do not automatically serve the public welfare or the community's best interests. Where do you stand on this issue? How might you counter this argument?

■ REFERENCES

Bauer, R.A. (1966) (ed) *Social Indicators*, Cambridge, MIT Press.

Buchanan, W.W., Self, D.R. and Ingram, J.J. (1987) 'Non-Profit Services: Adoption or Adaptation of Marketing', *Journal of Professional Services Marketing*, Vol. 2, No. 4, 83–95.

Burton, S. (1999) 'Marketing for Public Organizations: New Ways, New Methods', *Public Management*, Vol. 1, No. 3, 373–85.

Buurma, H. (2001) 'Public Policy Marketing: Marketing Exchange in the Public Sector', *European Journal of Marketing*, Vol. 35, No. (11/12), 1287–1300.

Chadwick, A. and May, C. (2001) 'Interaction Between States and Citizens in the Age of the Internet', Paper presented at the Annual Meeting of the American Political Science Association, 30 August–2 September, San Francisco, CA.

Chapman, D. and Cowdell, T. (1998) *New Public Sector Marketing*, London, Financial Times/Pitman.

Ewing, M.T. and Caruana, A. (1999) 'An Internal Marketing Approach to Public Sector Management: The Marketing and Human Resources Interface', *International Journal of Public Sector Management*, Vol. 12, No. 1, 17–26.

Folz, D.H. (1999) 'Municipal Recycling Performance: A Public Sector Environmental Success Story', *Public Administration Review*, Vol. 59, No. 4, 336–45.

Foxall, G.R. (1988) 'Marketings Domain', *European Journal of Marketing*, Vol. 23, No. 8, 7–22.

Goldstein, N. (1997) 'Biocycle Nationwide Survey: The State of Garbage', *Biocycle*, April, 60–7.

Graham, P. (1994) 'Marketing in the Public Sector: Inappropriate or Merely Difficult?' *Journal of Marketing Management*, Vol. 10, 361–75.

Humphrey, C., Miller, P. and Scapens, R. (1993) 'Accountability and Accountable Management in the UK Public Sector', *Accounting Auditing and Accountability Journal*, Vol. 6, No. 3, 7–29.

Keaney, M. (1999) 'Are Patients Really Consumers?', *International Journal of Social Economics*, Vol. 26, No. 5, 695–706.

Koster, J.M.D. (1991) *Grondslagen van de Marketingwetenschap*, dissertation, Erasmus University, Rotterdam.

Kotler, P. and Lee, N.R. (2007) 'Marketing in the Public Sector', *Public Manager*, Vol. 36, No. 1, 12–17.

Kriekaard, J.A. (1994) *Het Domein Van City Marketing: Een Bijdrage Aan Theorieontwikkeling*, Report No. R 9407/M, Rotterdam Institut voor Bedrijfseconomische Studies, Erasmus University, Rotterdam.

Laing, A. (2003) 'Marketing in the Public Sector: Towards A Typology of Public Services', *Marketing Theory*, Vol. 3, No. 4, 427–45.

Laing, A. and Hogg, G. (2002) 'Political Exhortation, Patient Expectation and Professional Execution: Perspectives on the Consumerization of Health Care', *British Journal of Management*, Vol. 13, No. 2, 173–88.

Laing, A. and McKee, J. (2001) 'Willing Volunteers or Unwilling Conscripts? Professionals and Marketing Service Organizations', *Journal of Marketing Management*, Vol. 17, No. (5–6), 556–76.

Lane, J.E. (1995) *The Public Sector: Concepts, Models and Approaches*, London, Sage.

Markoff, J. (2000) 'A Newer Lonelier Crowd Emerges In Internet Study', *New York Times*, 16 February, A1.

Pandya, A. and Dholakia, A. (1992) 'An Institutional Theory of Exchange in Marketing', *European Journal of Marketing*, Vol. 26, No. 12, 9–41.

Parker, L. and Gould, G. (1999) 'Changing Public Sector Accountability: Critiquing New Directions', *Accounting Forum*, Vol. 23, No. 2, 109–35.

Pendlebury, B., Jones, R. and Karbhari, Y. (1994) 'Developments in the Accountability and Financial Reporting Practices of Executive Agencies', *Financial Accountability and Management*, Vol. 10, No. 1, 33–46.

Plowden, W. (1994) 'Public Interests the Public Services Serve, Efficiency and Other Values', *Australian Journal of Public Administration*, Vol. 53, No. 3, 304–12.

Raney, R. (2000) 'Study Finds Internet of Social Benefit To Users', *New York Times*, 11 May, E7.

Rosen, D.E. and Suprenant, C. (1998) 'Evaluating Relationships: Are Satisfaction and Quality Enough?' *International Journal of Service Industry Management*, Vol. 9, No. 2, 103–25.

Rosenthal, U. (1995) 'Publiek Partnerschap', *Bestuurskunde*, Vol. 4, No. 3, 15–21.

Rowley, J. (1998) 'Quality Measurement in the Public Sector: Some Perspectives From The Service Quality Literature', *Total Quality Management*, Vol. 9, No. (2/3), 321–34.

Severijnen, P.C.A. and Braak, H.J.M. (1992) 'Marktonderzoek Bij Beleidsvoorbereiding En Beleidsbepaling', *Management in Overheidsorganisaties*, 22 Aug, A412–51.

Sinclair, A. (1995) 'The Chameleon of Accountability: Forms and Discourses', *Accounting Organizations and Society*, Vol. 20, No. (2/3), 219–37.

Staughton, R.V.W. and Williams, C.S. (1994) 'Towards a Simple Visual Representation of Fit in Service Organizations: The Contribution of the Service Template', *International Journal of Operations and Production Management*, Vol. 14, No. 5, 76–85.

Thomson, P. (1992) 'Public Sector Management in a Period of Radical Change, 1979–1992', *Public Money and Management*, Summer, 33–41.

Uttley, M. (1993) 'Citizens and Consumers: Marketing and Public Sector Management', *Public Money and Management*, Summer, 9–15.

van der Hart, H.W.C. (1991) 'Government Organizations and their Customers in the Netherlands: Strategy, Tactics and Operations', *European Journal of Marketing*, Vol. 24, No. 7, 31–42.

Walsh, K. (1994) 'Marketing and Public Sector Management', *European Journal of Marketing*, Vol. 28, No. 3, 63–71.

Walsh, K. (1995) 'Competition for White Collar Services in Local Government', *Public Money and Management*, April–June, 11–18.

West, D.M. (2004) 'E-Government and the Transformation of Service Delivery and Citizen Attitudes', *Public Administration Review*, Vol. 64, No. 1, 15–27.

Williams, C.S., Saunders, M.N.K. and Staughton, R.V.W. (1999) 'Understanding Service Quality in the new Public Sector: An Exploration of Relationships in the Process of Funding Social Housing', *International Journal of Public Sector Management*, Vol. 12, No. 4, 366–79.

Wodon, Q.T. (2000) 'Public Utilities and Low Income Customers: A Marketing Approach', *International Journal of Public Sector Management*, Vol. 13, No. 3, 222–40.

■ INDEX